POWER EXCEL
with MrExcel

567 Excel Mysteries Solved

Bill Jelen

Holy Macro! Books
PO Box 82, Uniontown OH 44685

Power Excel with MrExcel

© 2015 by Bill Jelen

Printed in USA by Hess Print Solutions

First Printing: September 2014

Author: Bill Jelen

Cover Design: Shannon Mattiza, 6Ft4 Productions

Interior Illustrations: Bob DAmico, Millennium Design Group

Cover Poster: © 2007 Hatch Show Print in Nashville. Used with Permission.

Cover Photo: Dallas Wallace, Paramount Photo

Published by: Holy Macro! Books, PO Box 82, Uniontown OH 44685

Distributed by Independent Publishers Group, Chicago, IL

ISBN 978-1-61547-038-9

Library of Congress Control Number: 2014915530

TABLE OF CONTENTS

TABLE OF CONTENTS

ABOUT THE AUTHOR

In 1989, Bill Jelen took a job in a finance department to maintain a very expensive reporting tool. When he discovered on day one that this new tool did not work, he began to learn how to use a $299 spreadsheet program in ways no sane person would ever think to use it. To the manager who hired him, he now wants to admit that all the reports that allegedly came out of the $50K 4th GL reporting tool from 1989 through 1994 really were actually produced with Lotus 1-2-3 and, later, Excel.

Thinking he was the smartest spreadsheet guy he knew, Jelen launched MrExcel.com in 1998 and quickly learned that while he knew everything about taking 50,000 rows of mainframe data and turning them into a summary report, there were many people using Excel in many different ways. To all of the people who mailed in questions back in 1998 and 1999, Jelen thanks them for honing his spreadsheet skills. He now admits that he initially knew the answers to none of their questions, but secretly researched the answer before replying to their e-mails.

Today, MrExcel Consulting provides custom VBA solutions to hundreds of clients around the English speaking world. The MrExcel.com Web site continues to provide answers to 30,000 questions a year. In fact, with over 750,000 answers archived, it is likely that the answer to nearly any Excel question has already been posted on the Web site's message board.

Jelen is a regular IMA/IIA speaker circuit. He holds a regular Excel Q&A via his daily Learn Excel from MrExcel podcast. He writes the monthly Excel column for Strategic Finance magazine. There are so many features in Excel, that Jelen has never taught a seminar without learning something new from someone in the audience who reveals some new technique or shortcut. Mostly, though, Jelen learns what Excel annoyances are driving people crazy. The questions in this book are the types of questions Jelen hears over and over.

Jelen is the author of 44 books on Excel. He has produced over 1,800 episodes of the Learn Excel from MrExcel video podcast. He was a regular guest on Call for Help and That Lab with Leo Laporte on TechTV. He is a 10-year Microsoft MVP in Excel. When he isn't writing, you will find him on a kayak.

Jelen lives outside Akron, Ohio with his wife Mary Ellen and two dogs.

DEDICATION

Dedicated to Robert F. Jelen.

ACKNOWLEDGMENTS

This book and its predecessor have been honed by hundreds of people. Through e-mail, podcasts, and seminars, people have added comments, suggestions, and new tips to make the book better.

Shannon Mattiza at 6'4 Media provided a great cover.

New ideas for this book came from: Vincent Adin, James Afflitto, Paul Allen, Andres Alvear, Patrick Amos, Loren Anderson, Rod Apbelbeck, Neil Appleton, Ilia Asafiev, Ed Ascoli, Chris Ayotte, Doug Bailey, David Baker, Brad Barker, Cliff Barnett, Denis Barry, Wolfgang Bartel, Marc Barth, Khader Basha, Tim Bene, Bill Bentley, Joel Berg, Paul van den Berg, A. Besis, Apostolos H. Besis, Matthew Bigelow, Ron Binder, Ram Bista, Ron Black, Jan Boord, Graham Booth, Marilou Borries, Sarah Bourne, Lindsay Boyce, David Braddy, Eddie Bradley, Alan Brady, Tom Bricheri-Colombi, Tom Brichieri-Colombi, Craig Brody, Thor Bronsvig, Lisa Brooks, Alan Brown, Derek Brown, James Brown, Patrick Bruer, Michael Bryson, Shawn Bumgarner, Daniel Burke, Andres Cabello, Travis Carney, Jason Carroll, Price Chadwick, Phil Chamberlain, Mark Chambers, Elden Chandler, Natalie Chapman, Jim Cheap, Ronnie Chio, Jack Chopper, Gopal Chouhan, Richard Clapp, Mike Clark, Todd Cleveland, Nancy Cody, Morne Combrinck, Steve Comer, Dave Connors, Adrien Cooper, Melania Covey, Jordan Crawford, Laura Criste, and David Cuenta.

Also from Dion Daniel, Mark A. Davis, Patrick Delange, Rod Dempsey, Daniel Dion, Tim Dolan, Rob Donaldson, Shannon Duffy, Dawh Duhon, Roy A. Dunn, Diane Durham, Richard E Todd, Adrian Early, Jack Elgin, Micah Emmerson, Bryan Enos, Pablo Esperon, Roger Evangelista, Nora Fazio, Michael Fleet, Mike Fliss, Michael Fockler, Linda Foster, Michael Franchino, Florian Frankl, Bill Fuhrmann, Robert Gabriel, Terry Gamble, Kerry Gao, Mario Garcia, Margarita George, Marc Gershberg, Eric Gibson, Dietmar Gieringer, Mike Gel Girvin, Devin Goldberg, Alex Gordon, Cheri Grady, Mark Grint, Ausdell Hadaway, Markus Hahner, Jeff Hale, Odd Inge Halvorsen, Riham Hammoda, Lorin Hanson, Sue Hartman, Peter Harvest, G. Russell Hauf, Karen Havens, Dermot Hayes, Don Heckerman, Bill Hemlick, Graeme Hemphrey, Rich Herbert, Med venlig Hilsen, Rob Hincks, Andrew Hinton, Steve Hocking, Andy Hoffmann, Mike Howlett, John Hulls, Paul Humphris, Chuck Irby, Bill Jackman, Jerry Jacobson, Neil Jimack, Kasper de Jonge, Rick Johnson, Stefan Johnsson, Al Johnston, Andrew Jones, Jackilyn Jones, Terry Jones in Springfield, Szilvia Juhasz in Southern California, Howard Kaplan, Brad Kennedy, Kambiz Keshvari, Kathe Killian, Paul Kimmel, and Jerry Kohl of Brighton.

More ideas from David Komisar, Ari Kornhauser, Howard Krams, Tanja Kuhn, Ann LaSasso, Jeffrey Latsko, Stacey Lawrence, Rob Leblanc, Johann Manjarrez Ledesma, Paul Leonard, Mark Leskowitz, Laura Lewis, Rene Lie, Bei Lin, Crystal Long, Sérgio Nuno Pedro Lopes, Rick Lubinski, Stuart Luxmore, Patrick C Lynch, Carl MacKinder, Sarker Ashek Mahmud, Roseanne Maish, Romas Malevicius, Micahel Maramzin, Dan Marks, Al Marsella, Joe Marten, Giles Martin, Real Mayer, Dan Mayoh, Sally McBride, Wendy McCann, Bethany McCrea, Bill McDiarmid, Thomas McGough, James McKay, Wyatt McNabb, Sergio Melendez, Isabel Mendoza, David Merkel, Dakshesh Mewada, John Meyer, L. Michael, Henning Mikkelsen, Dan Miller, Mark Miller, Richard Miller, Susan Miller-Wells, Greg Montgomery, Mikal Moore, Terry Moorehouse, Ali Mozaffari, Isabel Mrndoza, Kyle Munson, Lucy Myers, Shawn Nelson, Matthew Netzley, Susan Nicholls, John Nichols, Susan Nichols, Dara Nolan, Bill Northrup, Dolores Oddo, Richard Oldcorn, Jeremy Oosthuizen, and Brent Oswald.

Also from Milind Padhye, Andre Pearson, Michael Pennington, Mario Perez, Dominik Petri, Matthew Pfluger, E. Phillips, Pete Pierron, Stephen Pike, David Plante, Bill Polen, Dave Poling, Sergiy Polovy, Nadar Ponnuturai, Brenton Prior, John Pyskaty, Blaine Raddon, Bob Ragland, Jerry Ransom, Fabien Raynaud, Sandra Renker, Greg Richmond, Russell Richter, Gary Ritter, Bill Robertson, Jamie Rogers, Chris Rohde, Julie Rohmann, Margaret De La Rosa, Vlad De Rosa, Jim S. Rose, Dave Rosenberger, David Rosenthal, Chuck Ross, Hamilton Rozario, Fabian Ruales, Peter Rutter, Marty Ryerson, Tom Saladin , Abdul Salam, Dion Sanchez, Ricardo Santiago, Jack Santos, Lorna A. Saunders, Steve Scaysbrook, Julie Scheels, Lori Schleuter, Randal L. Schwartz, Diane Seals, Robert D Seals, Mark Secord, Ashokan Selliah, Denison Seminar, Bryony Seume, Ewan Shannon, Uma Sharma, Wayne Shelton, Ute Simon, Brett Simpson, Manfred Simrodt, Loh Seok Siong, Don Smith, Chris Sours, Mark Spratt, Daan Sprunken, Harold Starr, Shlomo Stern, Clay Sullivan, Kevin Sullivan, Keith Sumrall, Seiichi Suzuki, Bill Swearer, Mike Syracuse at the Globetrotters, Brian Taylor, James Tays, David Teague, Martin Thelfer, Sarah Thomas, Denise Thomson, Bob Tiller, Mark Tittley, Richard Todd, Michael Tucker, Mr. Andrew Tucker, Breck Tuttle, Bob Umlas, Vaibhav Vaidya, Claude Van Horn, Geoff Vautier, Dinesh Vijaywargiay, Thomas Vogel, J. B. Voss, Wiebe van der Waals, Grant Wang, Tim Wang, Kim Wasmundt, Pam Waymack, Rebecca Weing, Susan Wells, John Wendell, Douglas A. Wesney, Justin White, Neville White, Gary Whiteford, Scott Whyte, Mack Wilk, Shaun Wilkinson, Bill Wood, Chris Wright, Dick Yalmokas, Pat Yong, Kathy Zdarstek, and Deb Zurawski. Many others made a suggestion during a seminar, but all I can remember is something like "Derek in Row 6 in Springfield", "Dan in Philly", "that nice lady on the right side in Kent, Ohio", and others. If you own an Excel Master pin and I didn't list your name, please e-mail me so I can correct the omission.

At Microsoft, the Excel, PowerPivot, Power Map, Power Query, Power View and Excel Web App teams keeps adding new features to Excel. At the IMA, Kathy Williams and Christopher Dowsett keep my Strategic Finance articles in shape

My sister Barb Jelen likely packed and shipped the book if you ordered it directly from MrExcel.com.

My family were incredibly accommodating. Thanks to Mary Ellen, Josh & Zeke.

I am a comic book superhero.

At least, I play one at work. As the mighty man of macro, I have the coolest job in town: playing MrExcel, the smartest guy in the world of spreadsheets.

Well, yes, that is a lot of hype. I am not really MrExcel. In fact, there are so many different ways to do the same thing in Excel that I am frequently shown up by one of my own students. Of course, I then appropriate that tip and use it as my own!

I have incorporated some of these discoveries in a pretty cool 3.5-hour seminar titled Power Excel Tips. This is amazing stuff—like pivot tables, filters, and automatic subtotals. I love to be in front of a room full of accountants who use Excel 40+ hours a week and get oohs and ahhs within the first few minutes. I have to tell you, if you can make a room full of CPAs ooh and ahh, you know that you've got some good karma going. At that point, I know it will be a laugh-filled session and a great morning.

One of these classes, which I was presenting at the Greater Akron Chamber, provided the Genesis moment for this book. One of the questions from the audience was about something fairly basic. As I went through the explanation, the room was silent as everyone sat in rapt attention. People were interested in this basic tip because it was something that affected their lives every day. It didn't involve anything cool. It was just basic Excel stuff. But it was basic Excel stuff that a room full of pretty bright people had never figured out.

Think about how most of us learned Excel. We started a new job where they wanted us to use Excel. They showed us the basics of moving around a spreadsheet and sent us on our way. We were lucky to get 5 minutes of training on the world's most complex piece of software!

Here is the surprising part of this deal. With only 5 minutes of training, you can use Excel 40 hours a week and be productive. Isn't that cool? A tiny bit of training, and you can do 80% of what you need to do in Excel.

The problem, though, is that there are lots of cool things you never learned about. Microsoft and Lotus were locked in a bitter battle for market share in the mid-1990s. In an effort to slay one another, each succeeding version of Excel or Lotus 1-2-3 offered incredibly powerful new features. This stuff is still lurking in there, but you would never know to even look for it. My experience tells me that the average Exceller is still doing things the slow way. If you learn a just couple of these new tips, you could save 2 hours per week.

This book talks about 567 of the most common and irritating problems in Excel. You will find each of these 567 items (which you have been stumbling over ever since your "5 minutes of training") followed by the solution or solutions you need to solve that problem. A lot of these topics stem from questions sent my way in seminars I've taught. They may not be the coolest tips in the whole world, but if you master even half of these concepts, you will be smarter than 95% of the other Excellers in the world and will certainly save yourself several hours per week.

Most of the 567 topics in this book presents a problem and its solution. There are plenty of books that go through all of Excel's menus in a serial fashion. (I've written a few). The trouble with those books is that you have no clue what to look up when you are having a problem. No one at my dinner table has ever used the word concatenation, so why would anyone ever think of looking up that word when they want to join a first name in column A with the last name in column B? (see page 392)

Despite its size, this book is a quick read. You can probably skim all 567 topics in a couple of hours to get a basic idea of what is in here. When you face a similar situation, you can find the appropriate topic, apply it to your own problem, and you should be all set.

This book takes a different approach than others I have tried to use. I am MrExcel, but I am hopelessly clueless with PhotoShop. Wow! This is an intimidating program. I own a ton of books on PhotoShop. There must be a bazillion toolbars in there. Most books I pick up tell me to press the XYZ button on the ABC toolbar. I can't even begin to figure out where that toolbar is. I hate those books. So, my philosophy here is to explain the heck out of things. If you find a topic in this book in which I tell you to do something without explaining how to do it, please send me an e-mail to yell at me for not being clear.

How to Use This Book

Each topic starts with a problem and then provides a strategy for solving the problem. Some topics may offer additional details, alternate strategies, results, gotchas, and other elements, as appropriate to the topic. Each chapter wraps up with a summary and a list of any Excel commands or functions used in the chapter. The screenshots are from Excel 2010 or Excel 2013.

Starting with Excel 2007, Microsoft has organized the ribbon into a series of tabs: the Home tab, the Insert tab, the Page Layout tab, and so on. Within each tab, Microsoft has organized icons into various groups. On the Home tab, for example, there are groups for Clipboard, Font, Alignment, Number, Styles, Cells, and Editing. In this book, if I want you to choose the Delete icon from the Cells group on the Home tab of the ribbon, I say, "Choose Home, Delete." The other option is to say "Choose Home, Cells, Delete," but you never actually choose Cells; it is merely a label, so I generally do not mention the group when I write about a command.

Gotcha: When you are working on a chart, Excel adds three new tabs under the Chart Tools heading, as shown in Figure 1. (These tabs do not appear when you are not working with charts.) You might see Excel Help referring to the "Chart Tools | Design tab". I won't don't do this. There can only be only one Design, Layout, or Format tab available at any given time. If the topic is talking about charts, I am going to assume that you are actually working on a chart, and I will refer to the Layout tab instead of the Chart Tools | Layout tab.

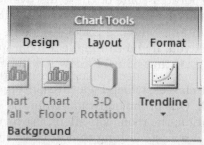

Figure 1 *This book refers to the Design, Layout, and Format tabs.*

Gotcha: Some of the icons on the ribbon tabs have two parts: the main icon and a dropdown. You can see the dividing line between the two parts only when you hover the mouse over the icon. When you need to click the icon itself, this book uses the name of the icon. For example, when you need to select the Paste icon from the Home tab, the text says to choose Home, Paste. When you need to select something from a dropdown under an icon, the text specifies dropdown; for example, when you need to select Paste Values from the Paste dropdown, this book tells you to choose Home, Paste dropdown, Paste Values.

In addition to the tabs across the ribbon, many dialog boxes contain a number of tabs. For example, if you click the Print Titles icon on the Page Layout tab, Excel displays the Page Setup dialog, which has four tabs as shown in Figure 2. If I want you to choose the Header/Footer tab of the dialog, I might write, "Select Page Layout, Print Titles, Header/Footer, Custom Header." Or, I might say, "From the Page Layout tab of the ribbon, select Print Titles. In the Page Setup dialog, choose the Header/Footer tab and then click Custom Header."

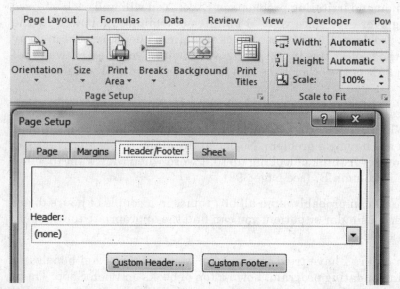

Figure 2 *Select Page Layout, Print Titles, Header/Footer, Custom Header.*

Gotcha: In newer dialog boxes, Excel has abandoned tabs across the top and used a left navigation instead. This is particularly true in the Formatting dialog, in the Excel Options dialog, and in the Trust Center dialog. For such dialogs, I sometimes write to "choose Fill from the left navigation of the Format Data Series dialog," but I also sometimes write "Choose Layout, Format Selection, Fill, No Fill." In this case, Layout is the ribbon tab, Format Selection is the icon, Fill is the name of the category along the left navigation panel, and No Fill is the option to choose.

This book uses the term press to refer to keyboard keys (for example, "press Enter," "press F2"). It uses the term click to refer to buttons and other items you click onscreen (for example, "click OK," "click the Paste icon"). It uses the term select or choose to refer to selections from the ribbon and option buttons and check boxes within dialogs (for example, "select the Home tab," "select the No Fill option").

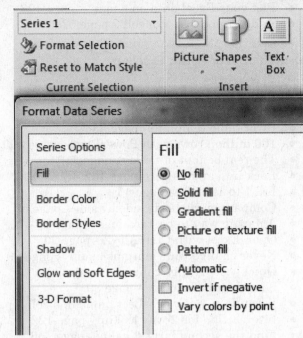

Figure 3 *In this dialog, the tabs move from the top to the left.*

Additional Resources

The files used in the production of this book are available for download at www.mrexcel.com/powerexcelfiles.html. Most topics in the book are covered on the free MrExcel podcast. Visit www.mrexcel.com for details on how to get the podcasts for free.

Quick Start - If You are New to Excel

If you consider yourself new to Excel and don't know where to start, here are some great topics for you.
- Get finished worksheets from Office.com - page 25
- See headings as you scroll - page 32
- Zoom with the mouse - page 36
- Mix formatting within a cell - page 43
- Use the Fill Handle to enter months - page 44
- Fit a report to one page wide - page 58
- Add a watermark - page 58
- Excel can read to you - page 66
- Entering formulas - page 77
- Why dollar signs in formulas? - page 82
- Total without formulas - page 90
- Join two text columns - page 93
- Discover new functions - page 114
- Excel as a calculator - page 118
- Loan payments - page 131
- Calculate a % of total - page 145
- Making decisions with IF - page 158
- Match records with VLOOKUP - page 171
- Dice in Excel - page 197
- How to avoid blank columns - page 248
- Add hundreds of subtotals at once - page 263
- Clean data with Flash Fill - page 307
- Summarize a data set in 6 clicks - page 310
- Show checkmarks in Excel - page 462
- Tame your hyperlinks - page 491
- Circle a cell - page 507

- Plot your Excel data on a map - page 406
- Add a dropdown to a cell - page 523

Quick Start - For Power Excellers

If you think you know Excel really well, I bet you will find some gems in these topics:
- Filter by selection - page 257
- Pivot table template - page 333
- 100 million rows with PowerPivot - page 390
- The real benefit of tables - page 210
- Back into an answer - page 132
- Fill 1 to 100,000 - page 45
- Compare worksheets side by side - page 53
- Amazing way to paste values - page 37
- Open Excel with Ctrl+Alt+X - page 26
- Never change your margins again - page 29
- Quickly rearrange columns - page 39
- See all named ranges - page 89
- Formula to put worksheet name in a cell - page 106
- Intersection for 2-way lookup - page 122
- Find the second largest value - page 156
- Replace IF with Boolean logic - page 160
- Trace formulas - page 211
- See key cells from many worksheets in one place - page 214
- Analyze every date between 2 cells - page 231
- Track negative time - page 237
- Total just the filtered rows - page 259
- Copy just the subtotals - page 267
- Sort the subtotals - page 268
- Show Yes/No in a pivot table - page 326
- AutoFilter a pivot table - page 345
- Generate reports for every customer without a macro - page 348
- Compare two lists faster - page 378
- Clean data with Power Query - page 385
- No more VLOOKUPs with PowerPivot - page 391
- Asymmetric pivot tables for past actuals and future plan - page 400
- Add new data to a chart - page 418
- Easy combo charts - page 434
- Sort left-to-right - page 475
- Pop-up pictures - page 499
- Paste a live picture of cells - page 500

Quick Start - What's New

Here are a few amazing newer features in Excel:
- Keep favorites in the Recent Documents List - page 20
- Create an online survey - page 71
- Embed your spreadsheet in a web page - page 72
- Sort red cells to the top - page 253
- Remove duplicates - page 293
- Import data with Power Query - page 385
- Hundreds of tiny charts in seconds - page 452
- Help your manager visualize numbers - page 456
- Use Document Themes - page 488
- Draw business diagrams - page 513
- Get SmartArt content from cells - page 520

PART 1

THE EXCEL ENVIRONMENT

WHAT IS OFFICE 365? DO I HAVE TO WORK IN A BROWSER?

Problem: My company says they are switching to Office 365. Does that mean I have to edit all of my workbooks online?

Strategy: No. When you get Office 365, you get the full version of Excel 2013. It streams to your computer. You are not stuck working in a browser. You can keep saving your workbooks locally on your own computer or company network. Optionally, if you have to work on a file at home, you can securely save it to your OneDrive account and then open the file from home.

The PR people at Microsoft tell this story: Back in the 1930's, people were afraid of banks, so they kept their money under the mattress. If there was a house fire, their savings were lost. Microsoft says that people keeping their files on the local hard drive is a similar situation: if there is a catastrophe, you local hard drive and the backup media are all going to be lost. I am not quite sure I buy the analogy just yet. After all, the FDIC insures my money in the bank. I don't see an FDIC for data yet.

What's In It For Me: You can get new features sooner. For the last decade, Microsoft would release a version of Office every 3 years. All of the teams: Excel, Word, PowerPoint all had to coordinate and release on the same day. It is inefficient. The Excel team might dream up a new feature, code it, and then you have to wait 3 years to get it. With Office 365, you always get the latest bits. There is discussion that Excel 2015 will be the last large release of Excel. After that, it will all me incremental updates.

As one tiny part of Office 365, you do get to use online versions of Word, Excel, and PowerPoint. These are versions of Excel running in a browser. They work great in an emergency (you are visiting grandma and she doesn't have Excel). In fact, the Excel Web App does a few things better than regular Excel. You can create online surveys. You can have 20 co-workers all working in the same spreadsheet at the same time. Read more about these features later.

WHY DO I HAVE TO SIGN IN TO EXCEL 2013?

Problem: What is the deal with signing in to Office? Any why do they want my Facebook info in Excel?

Strategy: Even if you are not using Office 365 to subscribe to Office, Excel will ask you to store your Office account information in the File, Account pane. This is not some attempt to harvest e-mails so they can spam you about the next MrExcel Power Excel seminar. There are actually good things that happen when you sign in on all of your computers:
- Recent files that you save to OneDrive will appear in the recent list of all of your computers. If you were working on a file at work and save it to the cloud, it will be available when you get home. No more forgetting the USB drive at the office.
- Ribbon customizations are carried through to all of your computers.
- You have a picture of yourself in the Excel window, in case you forget who you are.

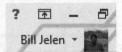

Figure 4 *You are signed in to Office.*

Saving your Flickr & Facebook information allows you to Insert, Online Pictures and easily add photos that you've uploaded to the file sharing sites.

WHY FACEBOOK, LINKEDIN AND TWITTER?

Problem: Why would I connect Excel 2013 to Twitter?

Strategy: You can tweet your workbooks for public use. Follow these steps:
1. Go to File, Accounts and enter credentials for Facebook, Twitter, and/or LinkedIn.
2. Save the workbook to OneDrive.
3. In Excel 2013, go to File, Share, Post to Social Networks.
4. Chose if people can edit or not.
5. Add a message.
6. Click Post.
7. Close the workbook so others can access it.

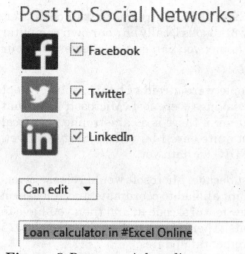

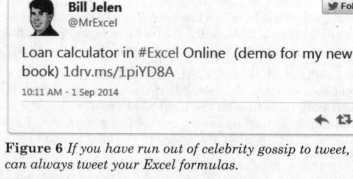

Figure 6 *If you have run out of celebrity gossip to tweet, you can always tweet your Excel formulas.*

When someone follows the 1drv link, they can view, edit, or download your workbook.

Gotcha: Your Facebook friends will think you are a geek.

Figure 5 *Post to social media.*

Tip: If you are new to Twitter, follow @MrExcel for daily Excel tips. I also accept all LinkedIn invites.

HOW CAN I USE EXCEL ON DUAL MONITORS?

Problem: Why is it so hard to use Excel on two monitors?

Strategy: This problem is fixed in Excel 2013. Every Excel workbook gets its own window, complete with a ribbon and formula bar. Open two workbooks, drag on to the other monitor and you will have 36 linear inches of Excel.

In Excel 2010, you have to do one of these hacks:
- Open Excel on the left monitor. Use the "Restore Down" icon in the top right to make the window not be full screen. Drag the right edge of the application window across to the other screen. Use View, Arrange All, Tiled and drag windows to the right side. Downside: the ribbon and formula bar is always on the left monitor.
- Force Excel 2010 to open a second instance of Excel. You can hold down the Shift key while opening Excel to create a second instance of Excel. Downside: you can not copy formulas from one instance to the other.

FIND ICONS ON THE RIBBON

Problem: The new ribbon user interface might be great for people new to Excel, but I knew the old Excel perfectly well. Why did Microsoft put pivot tables on the Insert tab instead of the Data tab

Strategy: The transition does not take that long (in cosmic time), if you follow a few basic rules.

Here are some simple guidelines:
- The Home tab contains the most frequently used commands. If you want to find something, start looking on the Home tab. The Excel 2003 Edit menu, Format menu, and Formatting toolbar is here.

- The most-used commands on the Excel 2003 Insert menu are not on the Insert tab in Excel 2013! Instead, commands to insert cells, rows, columns, and worksheets are on an Insert dropdown on the Home tab. Commands to insert a function or a name are on the Formulas tab. Insert Comment is on the Review tab.
- The Pivot Tables command has been moved from the Data menu to the left side of the Insert tab.
- Most Excel 2003 File menu commands are on the Excel 2013 File tab. This tab is called the Back-stage view and is discussed in detail later. A few File commands are elsewhere. For example, Save Workspace is on the View tab. Page Setup and Print Area are on the Page Layout tab.
- Everything on the old Window menu and most things from the old View menu are now on the View tab.
- Help is now the question mark icon at the top right of the window. Everything else that used to be on the Help menu is now under File, Help. Except Clippy. Clippy has retired.
- The old Tools menu has been split among many tabs. You will find these commands spread among the Review, Formulas, Home, Data, View, and File tabs.

Microsoft does not provide a classic mode, but third party companies do. Check out the Classic Excel Menu from AddInTools.com or Toolbar Toggle. With both of these add-ins, you can work in the Excel 2003 menu, and then switch over to the ribbon menu when you need to access new features.

1

SERIOUSLY, I REALLY CAN'T FIND THIS

Problem: I've looked everywhere, and I can not find certain commands.

Strategy: I will show you some strategies for finding icons, but first, here are the ones that through me for a loop:
- Help is now the question mark at the top right of Excel.
- Save Workspace is now on the right side of the View tab.
- Protect Sheet is now on the Review tab.
- Move or Copy Sheet is in the Format dropdown on Home.
- Insert Rows, Insert Columns is in the Insert dropdown on Home.
- The "X" to close Excel is missing from Excel 2013. It is at the bottom of the Excel 2010 File tab. In either case, you should add the Exit to the Quick Access Toolbar or use Alt+F+X.

Alternate Strategy: You can find any command in the Customize dialog box. Hover over the command to see a tooltip explaining where to find the command in Excel. Follow these steps to locate a command.

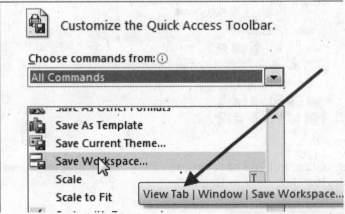

Figure 7 *Hover over a command to find the tab and group name.*

1. The top-left corner of Excel contains a tiny strip with icons for Save, Undo, and Redo. Right-click that strip and choose Customize Quick Access Toolbar.
2. The top left dropdown starts with Popular Commands. Open that dropdown and choose All Commands. You now have an alphabetical list of 2000+ commands.
3. Scroll through the list. When you find your command, hover. A tooltip appears showing you the ribbon tab, the group, then the command.

Gotcha: Sometimes, the tooltip will indicates that your command is in the dreaded Commands Not In The Ribbon category. You will have to add these commands to the Quick Access Toolbar or to the Ribbon in 2010.

WHERE ARE MY MACROS?

Problem: Did Microsoft abandon the macro facility? Where are the buttons to record a new macro, run a macro, and so on? How do I get to the Visual Basic Editor?

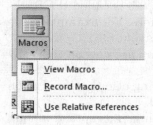

Strategy: Most of the macro icons are hidden. Three macro options appear on the extreme right end of the View tab. You use the Macros dropdown to view macros, record a macro, or use relative references while recording a macro.

To access the rest of the macro functionality, you need to enable a hidden Developer ribbon tab. Choose File, Options, Customize Ribbon. Add a checkmark next to Developer. The Developer tab offers macro commands, buttons from the former Forms toolbar and Control Toolbox, and XML settings.

Figure 8 *A subset of macro commands are available on the View tab.*

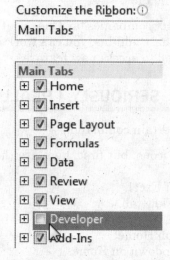

Figure 9 *Microsoft disable the Developer tab by default.*

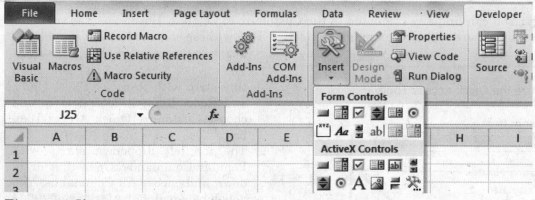

Figure 10 *If you use macros, enable the Developer tab.*

Additional Details: When you are recording a macro, instead of seeing the Stop Recording icon floating above the Excel window, you now see it in the Status Bar, next to Ready.

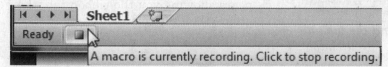

Figure 11 *Once you've recorded a macro, the Stop and Record buttons will appear next to Ready.*

The same area of the status bar includes a Record Macro button when you are not recording a macro. However, because there is not a Relative References button, you cannot effectively record macros without using either the View tab or the Developer tab of the ribbon.

WHAT HAPPENED TO TOOLS, OPTIONS?

Problem: Where is the Excel 2003 Options command?

Strategy: Microsoft now provides an Excel Options dialog. You access it with File, Options.

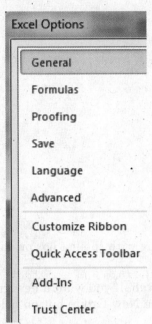

The new Excel Options dialog has 9 categories instead of the previous 13 tabs. It incorporates most settings that used to be in the Options dialog, plus Tools, AutoCorrect, Tools, Macro, Security, Tools, Add-Ins, and many options from the old Help menu.

In what seems like a confusing move, Excel took a few options from the old General tab, combined them with some new options, and moved them to the General category in the Excel Options dialog.

The Advanced category in Excel offers 10 different sections. You will find that many of the former tabs from the Excel 2003 Options dialog have moved to the Advanced category. Instead of flipping from tab to tab to tab in Excel 2003, you can scroll through the long list of Advanced options in Excel.

The final four categories in the Excel Options dialog do not correspond to the Excel 2003 Options dialog:
- Customize Ribbon: For adding groups to the ribbon
- Quick Access Toolbar: For adding icons to the Quick Access toolbar
- Add-Ins: For managing add-ins (similar to Tools, Add-Ins in 2003)
- Trust Center: For managing security and much more

Figure 12 *Now 10 categories instead of 13 tabs.*

The following table maps the Excel 2003 Options dialog tabs to the Excel 2010 Excel Options dialog categories:

Excel 2003 Tab	Excel 2010/2013 Category
View	Advanced (Groups 4 - 6)
Calculation	Formulas & Advanced (Group 6)
Edit	Advanced (Groups 1 and 2)
General	General and Advanced (Group 9)
Transition	Advanced (Group 10)
Custom Lists	Advanced (Group 11) or Popular in Excel 2007
Charts	Advanced (Group 4)
Color	Save
International	Advanced (Group 1)
Save	Save
Error Checking	Proofing
Spelling	Proofing
Security	Removed from the dialog; select File, Save As, click the Tools button, and choose the General category

CUSTOMIZING THE RIBBON

Problem: I want to customize the ribbon.

Strategy: Ribbon customizations in Excel 2010/2013 are weak compared with the customization capabilities in Excel 2003. However, they are better than the inability to customize in Excel 2007.

You might feel like the Pivot Table command belongs on the Data tab rather than on the Insert tab. You can add a new group to the Data tab to hold the pivot table icons.

First, look at the ribbon and decide where you want the new group to appear. Perhaps a good location would be between the Sort & Filter group and the Data Tools group.

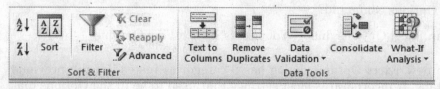

Figure 13 *Decide where you want the new group to appear.*

Right-click anywhere on the ribbon and choose Customize the Ribbon.

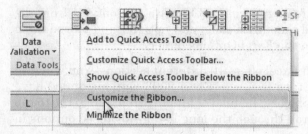

Figure 14 *Right-click the ribbon to access this menu.*

The Customize dialog contains two large list boxes. You will first be working with the list box on the right side of the screen.

Expand the plus sign next to the Data entry to see the groups on the Data tab. If you want a new group to appear after the Sort & Filter group, click Sort & Filter, and then click the New Group button below the list box.

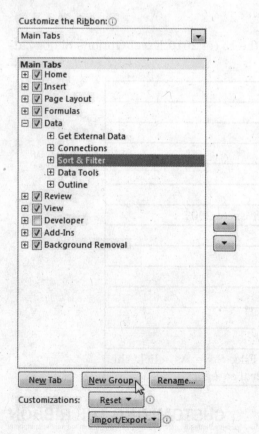

Figure 15 *Choose where the new group should go.*

Excel adds a new group with the name of New Group (Custom). Click the Rename button below the list box.

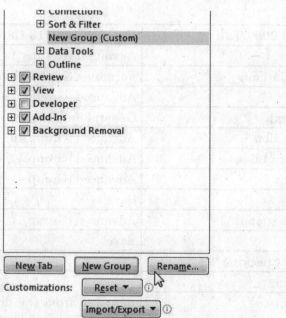

Figure 16 *Choose to rename the group*

Type a new name in the Rename dialog. Also, choose an icon. This icon will appear only when the Excel window gets small enough to force the group into a dropdown, as shown later in Figure 21.

Figure 17 *Type a new name and choose an icon to represent the group.*

Note: The 180 icons available are a far cry from the 4096 icons available in Excel 2003. As I pointed out at the beginning of this chapter, toolbar customization took a giant step backward after Excel 2003.

After renaming the new group in the list box on the right side, it is time to turn your attention to the list box on the left side. It starts out showing Popular Commands. Use the dropdown above the left list box to change from Popular Commands to All Commands.

Scroll down to the commands starting with Pivot. You will see a confusing array of commands. Click the first PivotTable icon, and click the Add button in the center of the screen. Click the second PivotChart icon, and then click the Add button. Click PivotTable and PivotChart Wizard, and then click the Add button.

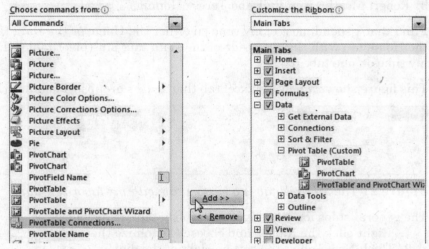

Figure 18 *Choose icons to add to the new group.*

It is sometimes difficult to figure out which icons you want. There are two icons that say PivotTable. The first icon is simply an icon. The second icon is an icon with a rightward-facing triangle on the right side of the list box. That triangle indicates that the second icon is actually a dropdown that leads to more choices. That second PivotTable dropdown icon is the icon at the bottom half of the Insert tab's Pivot Table group. It opens to enable you to choose between PivotTable and PivotChart. You might prefer to use that icon instead.

Two PivotChart icons are available. Hover over each icon to see that the first one is the PivotChart icon available on the PivotTable Tools Options tab. You will also see that the second icon is the one on the Insert tab. The first PivotChart icon will be grayed out unless you are in a pivot table. The second PivotChart icon is the one that is used to create a new pivot chart from a data set.

This figure shows the resulting group on the Data tab.

Figure 19 *The custom group is added to the ribbon.*

If you are wondering why you had to choose an icon back in Figure 17, it is for people who have the Excel window resized to a narrower width. If you make your Excel window narrower, the custom group will eventually get squished down to a single dropdown. Your icon will appear on that dropdown, as shown here.

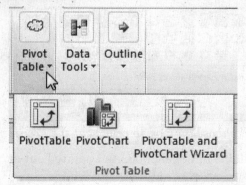

Figure 20 *The icon from Figure 17 shows with a smaller window size.*

Note back in Figure 13 that the Sort icon appears as a large icon with a caption and that the AZ and ZA icons appear as small icons without a caption. How can you specify that the pivot table icon should be large and the pivot chart and wizard icons should be small? You can't. At least not with the Excel interface.

If you want to start writing some XML and VBA, you can gain control over the size and images used in the ribbon. For an excellent book on this daunting task, look for RibbonX: Customizing the Office 2007 Ribbon by Robert Martin, Ken Puls and Teresa Hennig.

I find that I spend most of my time on either the Home or the Data tab. If I could combine the left side of the Home tab with the right side of the Data tab, plus pivot tables, I would probably be able to spend all my time on one tab.

This figure shows a new MrExcel tab that reuses groups from other ribbon tabs to build a new tab.

Figure 21 *The MrExcel tab is a custom tab with my favorite groups.*

The general steps for creating a new ribbon tab are as follows:
1. Right-click the Ribbon and choose Customize the Ribbon.
2. Click New Tab at the bottom right of the dialog.
3. Click Rename and give the tab a name.
4. Use the Up and Down buttons at the right side of the dialog to move the new tab into the proper location.
5. From the left dropdown, choose Main Tabs.
6. In the left dropdown, expand an existing tab and find an existing group that you want to add to your new tab. Click that group and click Add.
7. Repeat step 6 to add additional groups.
8. You can reuse a custom group that you created previously. In the left dropdown, choose Custom Tabs and Groups. You can move the Pivot Table (Custom) tab created earlier in this chapter onto your new ribbon tab.
9. Click OK to finish customizing the ribbon tab.

GO WIDE

Problem: My ribbon looks different than my co-workers.

Strategy: Invest in a wide-screen monitor. The Excel experience dramatically improves at a 1440x900 or 1920x1080 resolution.

When you reduce the size of the Excel window, Excel automatically starts consolidating ribbon options into smaller icons and then groups. The next four figures show details of the Home tab of the ribbon at different sizes.

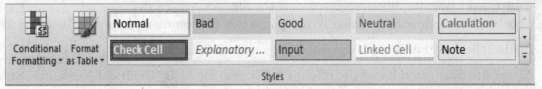

Figure 22 *At 1920 wide, five columns of the gallery are shown*

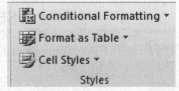

Figure 23 *At a smaller screen, the cell styles gallery is a dropdown.*

Figure 24 *Eventually, the entire Styles group becomes a dropdown..*

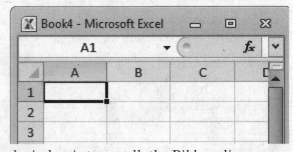

Figure 25 *If the Excel window is too small, the Ribbon disappears.*

If you are the go-to person for solving Excel problems and you are helping a co-worker over the phone without using GoToMeeting, there will be some frustration as you tell them to look for the Bad, Good, Neutral tiles and they can only see a Styles dropdown.

MINIMIZE THE RIBBON TO MAKE EXCEL FEEL A BIT MORE LIKE EXCEL 2003

Problem: The ribbon is taking up a lot of real estate at the top of my screen. It distracts me. I spend 99% of my Excel time in the grid, so I don't need to see the ribbon all the time.

Strategy: You can minimize the ribbon, reducing it to a simple line of Home, Insert, Page Layout, Formulas, and so on, as shown here.

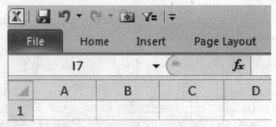

Figure 26 *See four more rows of worksheet by minimizing the Ribbon.*

To minimize the ribbon, you can either press Ctrl+F1 or right-click anywhere on the ribbon and then choose Minimize the Ribbon.

Additional Details: When you either click a ribbon tab with the mouse or use an Excel shortcut key, the ribbon will temporarily reappear. When you select the command from the ribbon, it will minimize again.

Double-click any ribbon tab to permanently exit minimized mode.

Alternate Strategy: Excel also offers a full screen mode. If you choose View, Full Screen, Excel will hide the ribbon, the ribbon tabs, and the Quick Access toolbar. You can press the Esc key to exit this mode.

USE A WHEEL MOUSE TO SCROLL THROUGH THE RIBBON TABS

If you point your mouse at the ribbon and scroll the wheel, you will quickly move from Home to Insert to Page Layout and so on.

WHY DO THE CHARTING RIBBON TABS KEEP DISAPPEARING?

Occasionally, new tabs will appear on the right side of the ribbon. These tabs appear when the current selection includes SmartArt graphics, charts, drawings, pictures, pivot tables, pivot charts, worksheet headers, tables, ink, or when you are in the legacy Print Preview mode.

These new tabs will stay visible as long as the object stays selected. If you click outside of your pivot table or chart, the tabs will disappear. If you are looking at an object and cannot find the tools necessary to edit the object, click the object to bring the tools back.

USE DIALOG LAUNCHERS TO ACCESS THE EXCEL 2003 DIALOG

Problem: I just want to go back to using the Excel 2003 dialogs.

Strategy: Many groups in the ribbon contain a tiny icons called dialog launchers. You can click an icon to return to the old-style dialogs. This figure shows an example of a dialog launcher.

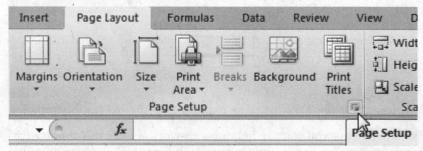

Figure 27 *Take me back to the old dialog.*

Additional Details: It is difficult to describe the dialog launcher icon. If you enlarge the icon, you can see that it looks like the top-left corner of a square with an arrow pointing down and to the right. I am sure there is some artistic rationale why these pixels mean "take me back to the old dialog that I know and love," but I can't figure it out.

ICON, DROPDOWNS, AND HYBRIDS

Problem: The ribbon introduces several new types of controls that you've never used in Excel 2003.

In this figure, the Table and Picture icon will invoke a command. The Shapes and Screenshot icons are dropdowns that lead to a flyout menu.

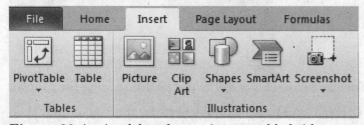

Figure 28 *A mix of dropdowns, icons, and hybrids.*

However, the PivotTable icon is actually two icons. The top half will start a pivot table. The bottom half leads to a flyout. You can't really tell which icons are a hybrid of icon and dropdown until you hover over the icon with your mouse.

Figure 29 *When you hover, a horizontal line divides the icon.*

The other new type of control in the ribbon is a gallery with three arrows at the right side. The first and second arrows in the gallery will scroll through choices one row at a time.

If you click the bottom arrow, the gallery will fly open to reveal all of the choices.

Figure 30 *Galleries have three arrows on the right edge.*

Additional Details: Several icons have an upper (icon) half and a lower (dropdown) half:
- The Paste icon on the Home tab
- The Insert icon on the Home tab
- The Delete icon on the Home tab
- The Pivot Table icon on the Insert tab
- The AutoSum icon on the Formulas tab
- The Macros icon on the View tab

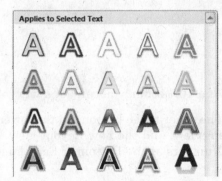

Figure 31 *Use bottom arrow to open the gallery.*

ALL COMMANDS START AT THE TOP (EXCEPT FOR 2 CONTROLS AT THE BOTTOM)

Problem: Microsoft is trying to get away from floating toolbars. In Excel 2003, I could float toolbars right near my work area. The task pane would often appear at the right side of the screen. Microsoft sold the ribbon as easier to use because we always know to start any command at the top of the screen. So, what are those icons in the lower-right corner for?

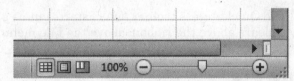

Figure 32 *Control view and zoom in lower right.*

Strategy: The icons in the lower-right corner of the screen control the zoom and switch between Normal view, Page Break Preview, and the new Page Layout view.

The zoom slider gives you one-click access to change the zoom from 10% up to 400%. This is easier to use than the old Zoom dropdown on the Standard toolbar. You just click the + icon at the right to increase the zoom in 10% increments. You click the, icon at the left to decrease the zoom in 10% increments, or you can simply drag the zoom slider to any spot along the continuum. To access the legacy Zoom dialog, click on the digits in the zoom percentage.

As in past versions of Excel, the quickest way to zoom in Excel is to use the wheel mouse. You hold down the Ctrl key while you scroll the wheel on your mouse forward to zoom in or backward to zoom out.

At a 400% zoom, you can get an ultra-close look at the detail of Excel's High-Low-Close stock chart to see that they really don't draw the left-facing Open symbol.

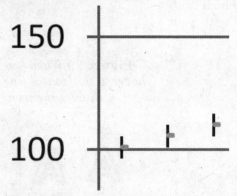

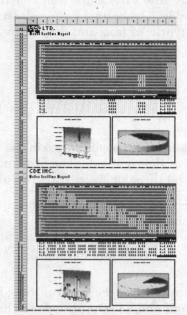

Figure 33 *At 400% zoom, you can see tiny details in charts.*

Figure 34 *At 10% zoom, view hundreds of pages at once.*

At a 10% zoom, you can get a view of your whole document - more than 21,000 cells.

The other three buttons in the lower-right corner of the screen switch between Normal view, Page Break Preview, and the new Layout view. You can read about the cool new Layout view in "How to Print Page Numbers at the Bottom of Each Page" on page 57.

MAKE YOUR MOST-USED ICONS ALWAYS VISIBLE

Problem: With the ribbon, I can only see one-seventh of the icons at any one time. I find that I spend a lot of time on the Data tab, but I annoyingly have to keep switching back to the Home tab. Does Microsoft really think this is better?

Strategy: Microsoft provided the Quick Access toolbar to address this problem. You can add your favorite icons to the Quick Access toolbar and then, because the Quick Access toolbar is always visible, you can invoke your most-used icons without having to switch ribbon tabs so frequently.

The Quick Access toolbar (QAT) starts out as a small bar with the icons Save, Undo, and Redo. It initially appears above the ribbon, above the File menu, as shown here.

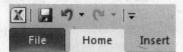

Figure 35 *The QAT starts with three icons.*

If you right-click the Quick Access toolbar, you can choose to move it below the ribbon. This gets your most used icons closer to the grid and provides room for a few more icons.

A dropdown at the end of the QAT offers several popular commands that you can add to the toolbar.

If you have Excel 2010, add Open Recent File to your QAT. This shortcut icon was dropped in Excel 2013, although the Open icon comes close.

For twenty years, Ctrl+P would print your document. Starting in Excel 2010, Ctrl+P takes you to the Print panel in the Backstage view. You then have to click the Printer icon to actually print. Again, this is one more mouse click than previous versions. Add the new Quick Print icon to the QAT if the extra step annoys you.

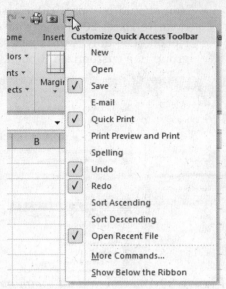

Figure 36 *Add these popular commands to the QAT.*

When you find yourself using a ribbon icon frequently, you can right-click the icon and choose Add to Quick Access Toolbar, as shown below. This is the easiest way to customize the Quick Access toolbar.

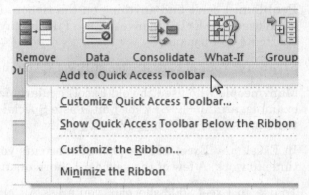

Figure 37 *Right-click a command and add to QAT*

Gotcha: Some of the icons look similar to one another when moved to the Quick Access toolbar. For example, Goal Seek, Go To Special and Scenario Manager use a green crystal ball icon. Unless you are a fortune teller, hover over each icon to see its ToolTip and tell which is which.

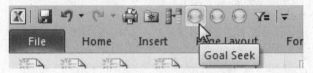

Figure 38 *The green crystal ball is used for too many commands.*

Additional Details: You can right-click the Quick Access toolbar and choose Customize Quick Access Toolbar to reach the full-featured dialog shown in Figure 39. The dialog offers a dropdown of categories on the left. Below this dropdown is a list of icons from the category. Here's how you use this dialog:

- You can select an icon on the left and click the Add button to add the icon to the Quick Access toolbar.
- You can select an icon on the right and click the Up or Down buttons to re-sequence the icons on the Quick Access toolbar.
- You can click the Reset button near the bottom to undo all your customizations and restore the Quick Access toolbar to the initial three buttons.
- You can use the top-right dropdown to say that certain icons should be assigned to the current workbook. Most Quick Access toolbar icons apply to every workbook. However, you can have 10 icons for every workbook and then add 3 additional icons for each specific workbook. The 10 global icons appear first, followed by the 3 local icons.
- You can organize your icons into logical groups and then add a separator between groups. To do this, you click the <Separator> item at the top of the left list and then click Add to add a vertical line between icons.

- You should pay particular attention to the category Commands Not in the Ribbon. If one of your favorite Excel 2003 or earlier commands is in this category, Microsoft completely left it out of the ribbon. The only way to access the command is by adding it to the Quick Access toolbar or a new group in a customized Ribbon.

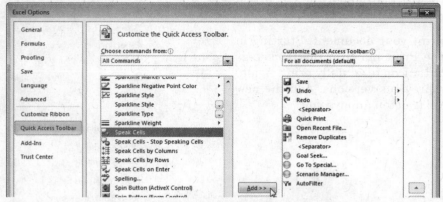

Figure 39 *You can find all commands here.*

THE EXCEL 2003 ALT KEYSTROKES STILL WORK (IF YOU TYPE THEM SLOWLY ENOUGH)

Problem: I can't find anything on the ribbon. I used to use a lot of keyboard shortcuts. For example, I often used Alt+E+I+J to invoke Edit, Fill, Justify. Microsoft completely eliminated the Edit menu, so what shortcuts do I use now?

Strategy: Your old keystrokes still work; you just have to invoke them a bit more slowly than usual.

Many people who used the old Excel regularly memorized a few Alt keyboard shortcuts. My favorites, for example, are Alt+E+S+V for Edit, Paste Special, Values, Alt+O+C+A for Format, Column, AutoFit Selection, and Alt+E+I+J for Edit, Fill, Justify.

In Excel, any Excel 2003 keyboard shortcuts you memorized between the Edit and Window menus continue to work. A few of the keyboard shortcuts from the File menu still work, but others do not.

To use an Excel 2003 shortcut, you press Alt and the first letter rapidly. If you press Alt and E, V, I, O, T, D, or W, Excel will display a ToolTip above the ribbon that says Office 2003 Access Key. At this point, you can continue typing the rest of the Excel 2003 menu shortcut. In this figure, the ToolTip shows that Alt+E+I has been typed, which is two-thirds of the shortcut to reach Edit, Fill, Justify.

> **Office access key: ALT, E, I,**
>
> Continue typing the menu key sequence from an earlier version of Office or press ESC to cancel.

Figure 40 *Old Alt shortcuts still work.*

When you type the final bit of the shortcut, Excel closes the ToolTip and performs the command.

Gotcha: Excel doesn't provide any feedback about what command you are typing. In Excel 2003, you could look at the Data menu to learn what to do after typing Alt+D, but Excel doesn't offer this feature.

Gotcha: It takes Excel a fraction of a second to display the ToolTip. I find that I have to pause briefly after typing Alt plus the first keystroke. For example, if I rapidly type Alt+O+C+A to invoke Format, Column, AutoFit Selection, about half the time, Excel thinks that I typed Format, AutoFormat. It seems that while Excel is busy displaying the ToolTip, the fact that I typed C doesn't make it into the keyboard buffer. Microsoft actually had this fixed during the Excel 2010 beta, but they broke it again in the Excel 2010 final version. If you slow down slightly, the Excel 2003 menu keys will work more reliably. (It's ironic that we have to work more slowly in Excel 2010/2013, isn't it?)

Gotcha: The old keyboard shortcut Alt+H to open Help does not work anymore. Microsoft decided that Alt+H would open the Home tab in all its products, so people who used to use the menu shortcuts for Help are sunk. (Although… there wasn't that much helpful on the old Help menu. I can't imagine anyone memorizing Alt+HA to open the Help, About dialog.) The F1 keystroke still invokes help.

Gotcha: Only some of the keystrokes from the old File menu continue to work. Alt+F opens the File menu, where you are supposed to use the new shortcut keys. The big three continue to work: Alt+F+O is File, Open, Alt+F+N is File, New. Alt+F+C is File, Close. However, beyond that, you will find differences. In Excel 2003, using Alt+F+W would save a workspace. In Excel 2010/2013, the same keystrokes take you to the Print menu. Go figure.

Additional Details: In addition to the Alt key shortcuts, the Ctrl key combinations from previous versions of Excel still work: Ctrl+B is Bold, Ctrl+I is Italic, Ctrl+U is Underline, Ctrl+C is Copy, Ctrl+X is Cut, Ctrl+V is Paste, Ctrl+5 is Strikethrough.

In addition, any keystrokes that you use while working in the grid continue to work. Ctrl+Down Arrow moves to the last row in the current region. Ctrl+* selects the current region, the End+Right Arrow moves to the last column in a contiguous range.

The Function keys continue to work as well. F2 edits the current cell. F4 repeats the last command or adds dollar signs to the last reference when you're entering a formula. F11 continues to create a chart in one click, and the new Alt+F1 will create the same chart as an embedded object.

USE NEW KEYBOARD SHORTCUTS TO ACCESS THE RIBBON

Problem: I never learned the Excel 2003 menu shortcuts. I would like to be able to use the keyboard to access some of the most-used Excel commands.

Strategy: The keyboard shortcuts for Excel allow you to access almost everything on the ribbon and Quick Access toolbar. While the Quick Access toolbar shortcuts are subject to change, the ribbon shortcuts are predictable and worth learning.

You can use the Alt key to access the ribbon tabs. Excel labels each tab of the ribbon with a different letter. In the figure below, you can see that the letters F, H, N, P, M, and A will allow you to access different tabs of the ribbon. The Quick Access toolbar shortcuts are numbers 1 through 9, and then they start using two digits from 09 down to 01. You can type Alt plus one of these letters to switch to a particular ribbon tab.

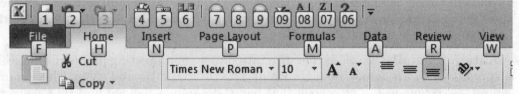

Figure 41 *Press the Alt key to display these tooltips.*

After pressing Alt+H, Excel draws in new shortcut keys to access all of the commands on the Home tab. In Figure 42, you can see that C is Copy, F+P is Format Painter, and F+O is the dialog launcher for the Clipboard group.

Figure 42 *FS stands for Font Size. Why FK for Decrease Font Size?*

Some of these keyboard shortcuts are somewhat obvious; for example, FS stands for Font Size and FF stands for Font Face. AL is Align Left. Other keyboard shortcuts make sense in a historical context; for example, Ctrl+V has meant Paste for 25 years, so it seems natural to use V for Paste. Some of the shortcuts don't seem to have any rhyme or reason; I have no idea why H is used for fill color

In some cases, a keyboard shortcut leads to a new flyout menu or gallery. Some items in that menu will have shortcut keys. Others might require using the arrow keys to select them.

A few commands in Excel 2003 were difficult to reach with the keyboard shortcuts. In Excel, you should be able to reach every command by using the keyboard.

Gotcha: Although it makes sense to memorize keyboard shortcuts for the ribbon, it does not make sense to do so for the Quick Access toolbar. Every computer's Quick Access toolbar will be different, and your Quick Access toolbar will be different if you customize. Although you can invoke Quick Access toolbar commands with the keyboard, it's probably not worth your time and effort to memorize them.

WHY DO I HAVE ONLY 65,536 ROWS?

Problem: Hey! Microsoft said that the grid in Excel was massively large—1.1 million rows by 16,384 columns. I opened my favorite Excel file, and I have only 65,536 rows. What's going on?

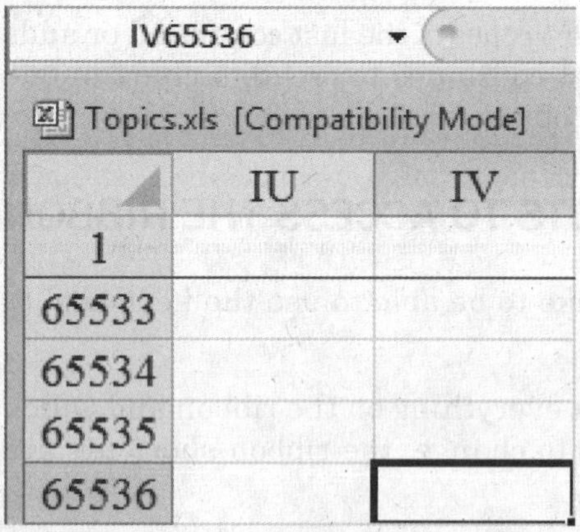

Figure 43 *This workbook only has 65,536 rows.*

Strategy: Files created in Excel 2003 and stored with an .xls extension are opened in Compatibility mode. In this mode, you can only access the original grid size.

If you will not be using this file in Excel 2003 anymore, you should convert it to the new file format. Open the File menu and choose Convert. Excel will update the file, save the file, close the file, and reopen the file. You will have access to the entire grid.

Additional Details: Excel's larger grid introduces an interesting problem. In Excel 2003, you might have a spreadsheet with named ranges such as TAX15, ROI2016, and so on. These names are now actual cell addresses! If you open a workbook that had these names defined and then convert to a new file format, Excel will change the named range to _ROI2016 (with an underscore). While most of your formulas will update, any functions that use the INDIRECT function or VBA code might need to be manually updated.

WHICH FILE FORMAT SHOULD I USE?

Problem: I've been using .xls files for years. What are these new .xlsx, .xlsm, .xlsb, xlam, and .ods file types? Which should I use?

Save as type:	Excel Macro-Enabled Workbook (*.xlsm)
Authors:	Excel Workbook (*.xlsx)
	Excel Macro-Enabled Workbook (*.xlsm)
	Excel Binary Workbook (*.xlsb)
	Excel 97-2003 Workbook (*.xls)
	XML Data (*.xml)
	Single File Web Page (*.mht;*.mhtml)

Figure 44 *XLSX is the ugly step-sister that won't allow macros.*

Strategy: Excel 2003 used XLS, a proprietary binary format. The old .xls binary file format could not handle data beyond row 65,536. So, the new .xlsb file format is a proprietary binary file format that can handle the 17 billion cells in Excel.

The new .xlsm file format is an amazing file format. The entire spreadsheet is saved as a series of text-based XML files, and then that collection of files is zipped into a single file in order to save disk space. You can actually take a look at the insides of an .xlsm file. In Windows Explorer, if you rename the file and add a .zip extension, you can then open the file using any zip utility. This is a fairly exciting advancement because it means people will be able to use third-party tools to generate Excel files without having Excel on their computers. However, the .XLSM file takes a bit longer to open than .XLSB. My preference is .XLSM, but if you have particularly large files to open, then .XLSB might save you some time.

You can tell that security issues have taken a grip on the people at Microsoft. They've introduced a new file format that guarantees that there will be no macros inside. The .xlsx file format uses the same zipped file structure as .xlsm but deletes any macros in the file. As someone who uses macros all the time, I think this is a silly file format. I guess if you plan on doing everything manually in Excel and if you never have any plans to learn how to dramatically increase your efficiency with Excel, then you could adopt the .XLSX file format. Actually, if you fit into this category, you could use Google Docs!

.xlam is another new file format. Developers can deliver Excel add-ins in this file format.

.ODS is a relatively new (2007) file format used across many different spreadsheet programs. Originally developed by Sun Microsystems, there is now a committee who oversees this format. It still isn't quite perfect, as Microsoft points out that you can not robustly store track changes information in this format. If there are pockets of people in your company who are using spreadsheet programs other than Excel, this might be a good format for you.

In case you are working in an office where many people still use legacy versions of Excel, you can always use the Save As command to save an Excel file as an Excel 97-2003 file format. Excel actually supports saving to 27 different file formats, including CSV, DIF, SLK, and other specialized formats.

Additional Details: You will probably choose one file type and stick with it. I've been using .xlsm files without issue for seven years. If you decide on one format, you can tell Excel to always use that file format. To do so, you select File, Options, and in the left pane of the Excel Options dialog, you choose the Save category. From the top dropdown, you select your favorite file format, as shown here.

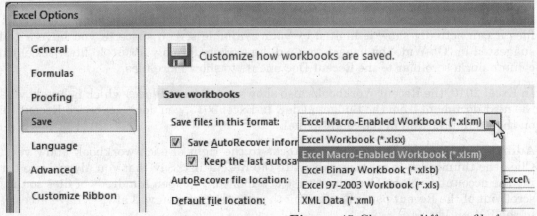

Figure 45 *Choose a different file format*

WHY DOES THE FILE MENU COVER THE ENTIRE SCREEN?

Problem: I opened the File menu, and it covers my worksheet.

Strategy: This is the new Backstage View in Excel 2010. The theory is that all of the commands on the File menu are things you do once your document is done. Since you no longer need the feedback of seeing the command in the worksheet, Microsoft can fill the screen with three panels of information. Those extra panels provide a better experience for printing and recent files.

When you open the File menu, Excel fills 100% of your screen with a three-panel Backstage view. The left portion of the screen works like a left navigation bar. The middle portion of the screen contains a variety of commands related to the choice from the left navigation bar, and the right portion of the screen provides a view of the additional settings related to the command.

The left navigation bar of the Backstage view contains six commands and six categories.

When you invoke a command, the Backstage View closes and the command is performed. When you open a category, two additional panels will appear offering more choices.

The commands are at the top and bottom of the left navigation bar: Save, Save As, Open, and Close are at the top. Options and Exit are at the bottom.

The middle entries of Info, Recent, New, Print, Save & Send, and Help all lead to a two-panel display will more commands.

HOW DO I CLOSE THE FILE MENU?

Problem: When I try to close the Excel File Menu, my document closes.

Strategy: Click another ribbon tab or press Esc to close the backstage view and return to the worksheet. There are three separate places in the File menu that offer an "X" that you would think would close the File menu. Unfortunately, all three of those "X" icons are for closing the workbook.

INCREASE THE NUMBER OF WORKBOOKS IN THE RECENT FILES LIST

Problem: I routinely open the same 20 workbooks. How can I use the Recent Files list to make my life easier?

Strategy: You can show up to 50 recent workbooks. Go to File, Options, Advanced, Scroll down to Display and choose Show The Number of Recent Workbooks.

Display	
Show this number of Recent Workbooks:	35 ⟳ ⓘ
☑ Quickly access this number of Recent Workbooks:	9 ⟳
Show this number of unpinned Recent Folders:	15 ⟳

Figure 46

Gotcha: Although you can specify for the Recent Documents list to show up to 50 files, the number of files it can actually show is limited by your available screen space. If you have a 1440x900 monitor, as suggested in "Go Wide" on page 4, you will have room for only about 36 files. Excel will not add a second column nor a scrollbar to the Recent Documents to show more files.

In Excel 2010, the Recent Workbooks also shows you Recent Places which is handy when you have to open the next document from the Budget folder. In Excel 2013, you don't get to see Recent Places until you click on the Computer icon in the center panel.

Additional Details: The grey thumbtacks to the right of each workbook allow you to create favorites. Click the thumbtack to pin a workbook to the Recent list. Say that you always use three workbooks during the accounting close. Over the course of a month, you open hundreds of files so those three documents scroll out of the Recent pane. By pinning them to the list, you will always have access to those documents in the Recent list.

Additional Details: The Recent Documents list in Excel 2010 works better than the Recently Used File List in Excel 2003. The old list worked fine for files opened through File, Open, but it failed to note files that were opened by double-clicking in Windows Explorer. Now, the Recent Documents list will note files that are opened through Windows Explorer or even files opened through a macro.

Excel's File menu might or might not show you Recent Workbooks. If you don't have another workbook open, clicking File will get you to the Recent pane. If another workbook is open, you will see the Info pane instead. By using the second checkbox in the image above, you can always see 9 recent documents in the File menu.

Using the option in the figure above allows you to use Alt+F+3 to open the third most recent document.

Gotcha: If you are snooping around in files that you should not be looking at, the Recent Documents list can be problematic. The operation of the list changed since Excel 2003. It used to be that you could delete file 5 from the list by changing the setting to 4 files and then back to 9 files. This would clear items 5 through 9 from the list. An "improvement" in Excel 2007 is that if you change the setting from 50 to 5 and then back to 50, Excel will immediately return to showing the last 50 items in the list. If you are trying to hide your trail, you have to set the setting back to 0 files. This is the only way to delete the file list from the cache.

CHANGE ALL PRINT SETTINGS IN EXCEL

Problem: Print settings appear in many different places in Excel. I am never sure if I should go to Page Setup, the Print dialog, or the Options button in the Print dialog.

Strategy: Excel 2010's File menu introduces the new Print panel. Get there by using Ctrl+P or File, Print. This panel leverages all of the goodness of the new three-panel Backstage View.

As shown below, the new Print panel offers settings from the Print dialog, Printer Options dialog, Page Setup dialog, and the Print Preview.

Additional Details: There are a few tricks to the new Print pane. Look below the Print Preview on the right side of the screen. Little icons there give you all of the functionality that you might have used in the legacy print preview. The far right icon is Zoom. The icon to the left of zoom will draw the margins and column width markers in so you can adjust them in the preview. Move to the next page using the page control on the bottom left side of the Print Preview.

Gotcha: If you don't have a wide screen monitor, and if your document is in landscape mode, you may not like the print preview in this panel. Go back to the old Print Preview as discussed in the previous topic.

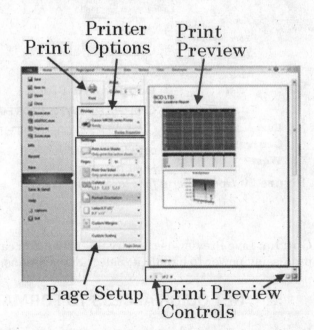

Figure 47 *Most of the print settings in one place.*

Additional Details: The Settings section of the Print panel offers a new type of control. Normally, you might have a dropdown called Orientation. You would open the dropdown to see Portrait and Landscape and to see that one of those items is selected. The Office team created a new control for this panel that shows you the current selected item. When you open the dropdown, you see additional choices.

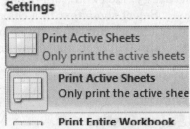

Figure 48 *The dropdown name shows you what is selected.*

I JUST WANT THE OLD PRINT PREVIEW BACK

Problem: I don't like change. I don't have time to learn about the backstage view. I don't like anything new. Just give me the old Print Preview command.

Strategy: Customize the Quick Access Toolbar as shown back near Figure 39. Choose All Commands from the left dropdown. Scroll down until you find Print Preview Full Screen. Add this to the Quick Access Toolbar or to a Ribbon group.

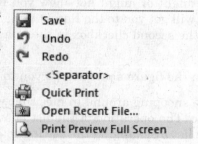

Microsoft left the Print Preview Full Screen in Excel for people who write macros and need the macro to pause while someone deals with the print preview settings. Using the icon above will allow you to use the old familiar Print Preview.

Figure 49 *This is the old Print Preview.*

USE LIVE PREVIEW

Problem: I often need to figure out which font to use and want to preview the different styles on a chart or SmartArt graphic.

Strategy: The Live Preview feature in Excel makes choosing from a gallery very easy. You just select a range in Excel and then open the Font dropdown. When you hover over a font name in the list, Excel will show you the selection in that font.

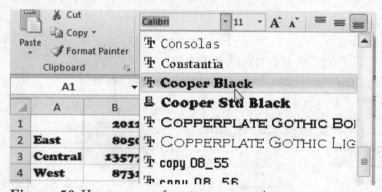

Figure 50 *Hover over a font to see a preview.*

Note that the change is not permanent in the worksheet. You can continue hovering over new fonts, and Excel will show you a preview of the font.

When you find a font that looks good, you can click the font name to select it. Excel will then apply the font to the selected range.

Additional Details: Many galleries besides the Font dropdown offer Live Preview. It is likely that even more galleries will inherit this feature in future versions of Excel.

Gotcha: Live Preview is memory intensive. You can turn off the feature if your computer doesn't have the processing power to handle it. Select File, Options, General, Enable Live Preview.

GET QUICK ACCESS TO FORMATTING OPTIONS USING THE MINI TOOLBAR

Problem: Why do I have to always go to the top of the window to reach formatting commands? I loved having floating toolbars in Excel 2003. Why did Microsoft get rid of them?

Strategy: Excel now offers one floating toolbar, but it is elusive. Here's how you use it:
1. Select some text in a chart. Look very closely above and to the right of the selection. Excel draws in a nearly invisible Mini toolbar. (It may not even appear in the printed version of this book.) Look for the Bold icon above the final "a" in Data in this figure.

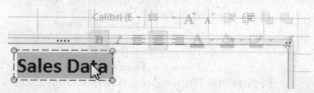

Figure 51 *The Mini toolbar starts out nearly invisible.*

2. Move the mouse toward the Mini toolbar. The Mini toolbar will become more visible and will be available for use.

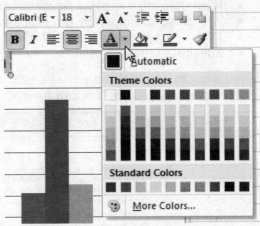

Figure 52 *Move the mouse toward the toolbar, and it will solidify.*

1

Gotcha: If you generally select text by dragging the mouse from right to left, you will never see the mini toolbar. I used Excel for months without ever causing it to appear.

Additional Details: If you move the mouse toward the Mini toolbar and then away, the Mini toolbar will solidify and then disappear. You can keep making it appear and disappear, but if you eventually get a certain number of pixels away from the toolbar, Excel will hide the toolbar until you re-select the data.

Additional Details: The Mini toolbar will appear often in Word. In order for it to appear in an Excel cell, you have to select only a portion of the characters in the cell. In this case, you will see an abbreviated version of the Mini toolbar.

You can also cause the Mini toolbar to appear if you select cells and right-click.

WHAT IS PROTECTED MODE?

Problem: Any time that I download a file from our file sharing site, it opens in Protected mode.

Strategy: I am sure that you regularly get files from other people in your company. They arrive via Outlook or you download them from an Internet site. I always worry that those people aren't smart enough to avoid getting viruses or that they actually hate me and would maliciously slip something bad into the workbook_open macro to cause problems with my computer.

In Excel 2003, if you opened a file with a macro, it stopped right away and made you choose whether to enable or disable macros. Have you ever thought about this question? How the heck should I know whether I should enable the macros when I haven't even had a chance to look around the worksheet (or examine the macro code, if you are comfortable with that)?

When you answered Enable Macros in Excel 2003, you were really taking a risk.

Now, any file that comes from a potentially dangerous location is open in the new Protected mode in Excel 2010. Here is the cool thing about Protected mode: You can look at the workbook. You can scroll through it or go to other worksheets. You can look at the macros. When you are convinced that the file is safe, you click a button and the workbook is available in regular mode.

This is brilliant. You get to actually look at the workbook, and while doing so it cannot harm your computer. You get to make an educated decision as to whether the workbook may prove harmful.

And, you know what? A lot of the time, you won't even have to leave Protected mode. You can look at the worksheet, see what you need to see, and close the workbook.

If you need to edit the workbook, use the button shown in here.

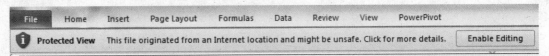

Figure 53 *When you are convinced that the workbook is safe, enable editing.*

Additional Details: The following is a list of files that will open in Protected Mode. Any file that did not originate on your computer can open in protected mode.

- Files that you download from the Internet
- Files in your temporary Internet folder
- Files that you open from Outlook
- Files that fail validation

If you want to adjust those settings, click the words in the information bar in Figure 53, and then choose Protected View Settings. You can turn off Protected mode for any of the situations shown here.

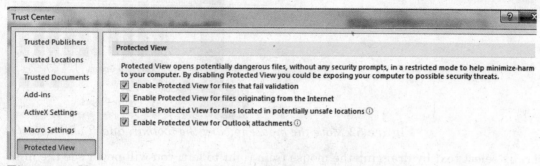

Figure 54 *You can tweak which files open in Protected Mode.*

USE A TRUSTED LOCATION TO PREVENT EXCEL'S CONSTANT WARNINGS

Problem: Excel is more security-conscious than in the past. In fact, many features that I rely on are now disabled, such as links to external files, external queries, and macros.

Strategy: Microsoft will ease up if you store your files in a trusted location. Follow these steps:

1. Store all your files with macros and data for links in a folder on your hard drive. Make sure no viruses are in the folder. Delete any dragons, centaurs, and grues from the folder. Make sure you don't store your kid's delete-all-files-on-the-hard-drive science project in that folder.
2. Select File, Options. In the left pane of the Excel Options dialog, choose Trust Center. Click the Trust Center Settings button. In the left pane, choose Trusted Locations.
3. Near the bottom, click the Add New Location button.
4. In the Microsoft Office Trusted Location dialog, click the Browse button. Browse to the correct folder and click OK.

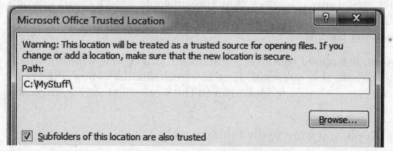

Figure 55 *Open anything from this folder without warnings.*

5. If you want the subfolders of the location to be trusted as well, select the Subfolders of This Location Are Also Trusted check box.
6. Click OK to add the trusted location. Click OK to close the Trust Center. Click OK to close the Excel Options dialog.

Results: You will now be able to open files with links and external data queries without a hassle, if they are in a trusted location.

Additional Details: Microsoft is now counting on *you*. Please, don't randomly right-click on attachments in spam e-mails and choose to save them in the trusted location.

MY MANAGER WANTS ME TO CREATE A NEW EXPENSE REPORT FROM SCRATCH

Problem: My manager wants me to design a new expense report completely from scratch. It seems intimidating to create this report from scratch.

Strategy: There are hundreds of free prebuilt documents available to registered owners of Excel, so "starting from scratch" isn't as frightening as it might seem. When you select File, New and then select a category from the list at the left, Excel will show you all the available documents. To use a document, you click the thumbnail and choose Download.

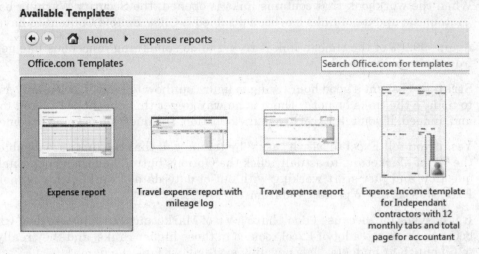

Figure 56 *Get free templates from the New File dialog.*

Additional Details: The variety of documents available is amazing. For instance, choose More Categories from the left, and you can access identification cards, games, fantasy football trackers, scorecards, and tournament brackets. Before you design a new form, see if Excel has such a form already available.

Gotcha: This feature is available only to people who own legitimate copies of Excel. If you are using a pirated version, you cannot access the templates.

OPEN A COPY OF A WORKBOOK

Problem: I have a workbook called invoice.xlsm. I want to keep the original file unchanged and save each new version as a new workbook. However, I tend to forget to use Save As, so I often overwrite this workbook.

Strategy: When using the Open command, you can specify that you want to open the file as a copy. Here's how you take advantage of this option:

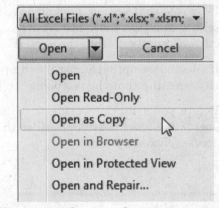

1. Instead of clicking the Open button to open a file, click the dropdown arrow next to the Open button. Choose Open as Copy. The file that opens will be named Copy (1) of invoice. xlsm.
2. Select File, Save As to save the file with a new name. Note that even if you forget to use Save As, at least you will not overwrite the original invoice.xls.

Figure 57 *Open as Copy to prevent saving over the original.*

EXCEL'S OBSESSION WITH SECURITY HAS HAMPERED LINKED WORKBOOKS

Problem: It used to be easy to set up a link between one workbook and another workbook. When you sent the file to someone else, they had to answer the Update Links message. Starting with Excel 2007, you now get a security warning that the recipient can easily ignore. This means they may not get the current values.

Strategy: Links were used as an important technique by many people. 99.9% of the people used links for good things. It is possible for someone to do bad things with a link. Hence, Microsoft stopped updating links. You will have to do some retraining of the people who receive your workbooks.

When the workbook that contains links is opened, the Security Warning bar above the worksheet says, "Automatic update of links has been disabled.". Click Enable Content to have the links update.

Again, 99.9% of the time, a link is trying to do something innocuous like getting last year's budget total from a closed workbook.

Strategy: I spent a good hour trying to figure out how to have Excel simply ask the question, "Do you want to update the links or not?" There is no way to get this question. I talked to the folks on the Excel team and, indeed, if you tell Excel to ask the question, the question is going to come in the form described above.

Yes, if you tell Excel to ask, it "asks" by telling you that the links are disabled. You have to convince Joe, the VP of Marketing, to actually click the Options button and then click Enable. Joe can easily *ignore* the question and just start working with out-of-date data. Frankly, this is more dangerous than whatever Excel was trying to protect you from.

It is easy for me, because I don't have a VP of Marketing that I have to deal with. I feel bad for you, though, because there are a lot of Excel rookies in those higher ranks, and they really want an excuse to not have to fill out their budgets. This new link system just fans the flames.

Here are your options (aside from staying with Excel 2003). If you choose File, Options, Trust Center, Trust Center Settings, External Content, you have the three choices shown here.

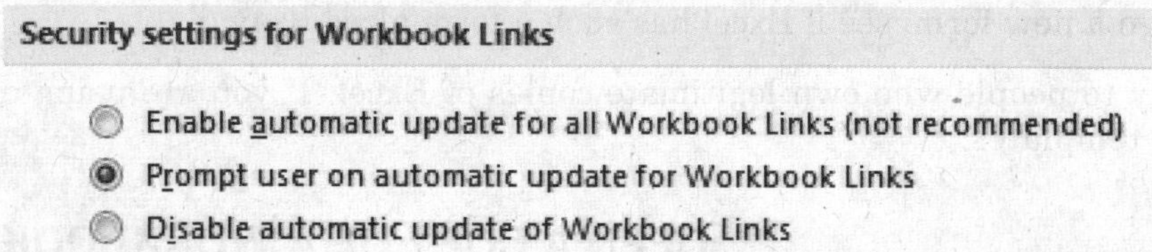

Security settings for Workbook Links

- ◯ Enable <u>a</u>utomatic update for all Workbook Links (not recommended)
- ◉ <u>P</u>rompt user on automatic update for Workbook Links
- ◯ <u>D</u>isable automatic update of Workbook Links

Figure 58 *Link choices starting in Excel 2007.*

If I wrote that screen, I would have made the middle option be: "Completely freak out Joe in Marketing by telling him that there is a security risk in his workbook and offer to help protect him by not giving him the current numbers from the server."

If you choose option 1, Excel will update the links without asking. If you choose option 2, you get the security warning that the recipient can ignore. If you choose option 3, the links won't update.

Before you send the workbook to Joe, you might as well visit the Trust Center and make the decision for Joe. If Joe has network access to the linked files, choose the unrecommended option 1. If Joe doesn't have access, choose option 3.

OPEN EXCEL WITH CTRL+ALT+X

Problem: I love keyboard shortcuts in Excel. Why isn't there a keyboard shortcut to open Excel?

Strategy: You can assign a keyboard shortcut to Excel.

Go to your Start menu and find the icon for Excel. Right-click the icon and choose Properties. In the properties dialog, there is a Shortcut Key box. Click in the box and type Ctrl+Alt+X. Click OK.

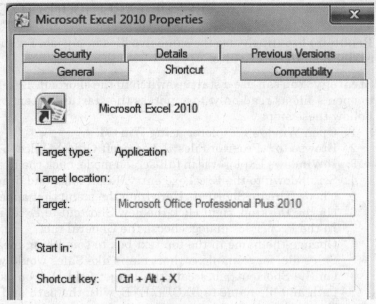

Figure 59 *Assign a shortcut key to the program.*

You can now launch Excel with Ctrl+Alt+X. You might wish to add other shortcuts, such as Ctrl+Alt+N for Notepad, and so on.

HAVE EXCEL ALWAYS OPEN CERTAIN WORKBOOK(S)

Problem: I always use Excel to work on a particular workbook. Every time that I open Excel, I want this workbook to open automatically

Strategy: You can place the file you want to always open (or a shortcut to the file) in the XLStart folder, which is generally found in the %AppData%\Microsoft\Excel\ folder. Anything in this folder will automatically start when Excel starts.

Alternate Strategy: You can specify one folder to act as an additional XLStart folder. Follow these steps:
1. Move the Excel workbook or workbooks to a new folder. Excel will try to open every file in this folder, so make sure you do not have other files in it.
2. Open Excel. Select File, Options.
3. Click Advanced in the left pane of the Excel Options dialog.
4. Scroll down to the General section. Enter the path to the folder from step 1 in the At Startup, Open All Files In text box, as shown here.

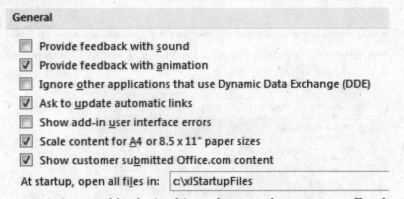

Figure 60 *Any workbooks in this path open when you open Excel.*

Alternate Strategy: Another strategy is to use a command-line switch, as discussed in "Set Up Excel Icons to Open a Specific File on Startup."

SET UP EXCEL ICONS TO OPEN A SPECIFIC FILE ON STARTUP

Problem: I routinely use the same five files in my job. I want a series of five icons on my Desktop so I can easily open these five files.

Strategy: You can use a startup switch in the shortcut. Excel offers startup switches to open a specific file, to open a file as read-only, to suppress the startup screen, or to specify an alternate default file location. Follow these steps.

1. Open Windows Explorer using Win+M.
2. Browse to %ProgramFiles%\Microsoft Office\Office15\
3. If Windows Explorer is in full-screen mode, click the Restore Down button so you can see the desktop.
4. Scroll down to the Excel.exe entry. Right-click and drag it to the Desktop.
5. Choose Create Shortcuts Here from the menu that appears when you release the right mouse button.
6. On the Desktop, right-click the new Shortcut to Excel icon and choose Properties.
7. In the Properties dialog, choose the General tab.
8. Change the name in the top text box to something meaningful. If this icon will be used to open the Sales file, for example, a short name like Sales would work.
9. On the Shortcut tab, locate the Target field. As you can see below, this field contains the complete path and file name to EXCEL.EXE, with the path and file name enclosed in quotation marks. (The Target field is not big enough to display the entire path, so you must click in the field and press the End key in order to see the end of the entry.)

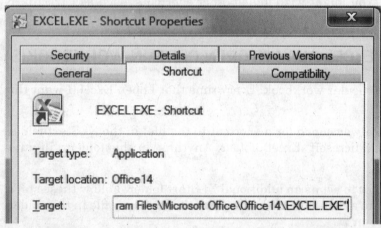

Figure 61 *Use the End key to move to the end of the field.*

10. After the final quote in the Target field, type a space and the path and file name.

You can now click that icon to open the particular Excel file.

USE A MACRO TO CUSTOMIZE STARTUP

Problem: Every time I open a workbook, I would like to put the file in Data Form mode or invoke another Excel menu as the file opens.

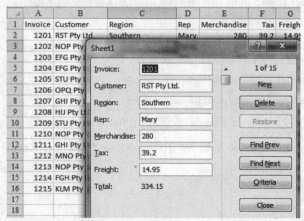

Figure 62 *The data form is increasingly difficult to find in Excel.*

Strategy: Startup switches can only do so many things. You will have to use a Workbook_Open macro in order to force Excel into Data Form mode. Follow these steps:

1. In Excel, type Alt+T followed by M and S.
2. Choose Disable All Macros with Notification. Click OK.
3. Open your workbook.
4. Press Alt+F11 to open the VBA Editor. **Gotcha:** The Microsoft Natural Multimedia keyboard does not support the use of Alt+function keys. You might have to type Alt+T followed by M and D.
5. Press Ctrl+R to show the Project Explorer in the upper-left corner. You should see something that looks like VBAProject (Your BookName) in the Project Explorer.

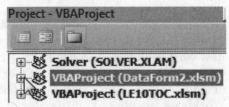

Figure 63 *Click the + to expand the project.*

6. If there is a + to the left of this entry, press the + to expand it. You will see a folder underneath, called Microsoft Excel Objects. If there is a + to the left of this entry, press the + to expand it, also. You will now see one entry for each worksheet, plus an entry called ThisWorkbook.
7. Right-click ThisWorkbook and choose View Code from the context menu.
8. Copy these three lines of code to the large white code window:

```
Private Sub Workbook_Open()
    ActiveSheet.ShowDataForm
End Sub
```

9. Press Alt+Q to return to Excel.
10. Select File, Save As, Excel Macro-Enabled Workbook.
11. Close the file.
12. Open the file. The information bar tells you that macros have been disabled.
13. Select Options, Enable This Content. The data form will open.

Alternate Strategy: To prevent Excel from automatically disabling macros, you can save the file in a trusted location. See "Use a Trusted Location to Prevent Excel's Constant Warnings" earlier in this section.

Gotcha: The data form used to be an option on the Excel 2003 Data menu. It is hidden in Excel today. To invoke this command, you can either press Alt+D+O or add the command to your Quick Access toolbar.

Additional Details: The simple Workbook_Open macro invokes a Menu command. It is possible to build highly complex macros that would control literally anything. For a primer on macros, consult *VBA and Macros for Microsoft Excel 2013* from Que Publishing.

CONTROL SETTINGS FOR EVERY NEW WORKBOOK AND WORKSHEET

Problem: Every time I start a new workbook or insert a new worksheet, I always make the same customizations, such as setting print scaling to fit to one page wide, setting certain margins, adding a "Page 1 of n" footer to the worksheet, making the heading row bold, and so forth. How can I have these settings applied to every new workbook or worksheet?

Strategy: Two files control the defaults for new workbooks and inserted worksheets. You can easily customize a blank workbook to contain your favorite settings and then save the file as book.xltx and sheet.xltx. Then, any time you either click Ctrl+N for a new workbook or insert a worksheet, the new book or sheet will inherit the settings from these files. Follow these steps to create book.xltx:

1. In Excel, open a new blank workbook with Ctrl+N.
2. Customize the workbook as you like. Feel free to make adjustments to any of the following:
- Page layout settings
- The print area
- Cell styles
- Formatting commands on the Home tab
- Data, Validation settings
- The number and type of sheets in the workbook
- The window view options from the View tab

3. Decide where you want to save the file. This can be either in the XLStart folder (generally C:\Program Files\Microsoft Office\Office*nn*\XLStart) or in the alternate startup folder. (See "Have Excel Always Open Certain Workbooks".)
4. Select File, Save As, Other Formats.
5. In the Save As dialog, open the Save as Type dropdown and choose Excel Template (*.xltx).
6. Browse to the XLStart folder you specified in step 3.
7. Save the file as book.xltx.

Results: All subsequent new workbooks created with Ctrl+N will inherit the settings from the book.xltx file.

Gotcha: Excel 1 through Excel 2003 had a "New" icon on the Standard toolbar and a "New..." icon on the File menu. While these icons sound similar, they are very different. The regular "New" icon will create a new workbook based on book.xltx. The "New..." icon leads to a panel where you can select a template from Office Online. This trick will not work with the File, New command in Excel 2010. You have to use Ctrl+N or add the old "New" icon to the QAT or ribbon. The problem is worse in Excel 2013, where the Blank Workbook tile offered on the Start Screen is equivalent to "New..." and will not load Book.xltx.

Additional Details: You should also set up a workbook with one worksheet and save this workbook as sheet.xltx. All inserted worksheets will inherit the settings from this file.

Additional Details: If you regularly create macros, save the files with the .xltm extension instead.

AUTOMATICALLY MOVE THE CELL POINTER IN A DIRECTION AFTER ENTERING A NUMBER

Problem: If I type a number and then press a direction arrow key, Excel will enter the number and move the cell pointer in the direction of the arrow key. However, if I am using the numeric keypad, it is much more convenient to use the Enter key on the numeric keypad than to use the arrow keys. By default, Excel will move the cell pointer down one cell when I press Enter. Is there a way to have Excel automatically move the cell pointer to the next cell to the right after each entry?

Strategy: You can select File, Options. On the Advanced tab of the Excel Options dialog, you select the first setting, "After Pressing Enter, Move Selection Direction," and choose Right from its dropdown.

Results: The cursor will automatically move one cell to the right every time you press the Enter key.

Additional Details: Override this setting by pressing Ctrl+Enter. The cell pointer will stay in the current cell.

RETURN TO THE FIRST COLUMN AFTER TYPING THE LAST COLUMN

Problem: I learned in "Automatically Move the Cell Pointer in a Direction After Entering a Number" how to set up the cell pointer to move right after I press Enter. This works great. I just typed figures for Q1, Q2, Q3, and Q4 (see below). So I can quickly enter all four quarters, is there any way to make Excel jump to cell B3 after I type in cell E2?

◢	A	B	C	D	E	F
1	Region	Q1	Q2	Q3	Q4	
2	City of London	1322	587	896	1121	
3	Barking and Dagenham					
4	Barnet					
5	Bexley					
6	Brent					
7	Bromley					

Figure 64 *Can Excel jump to the first column in the next row?*

Strategy: Yes! Here's what you do:
1. Set up Excel to move right as described in the previous topic.
2. Select the range before you start typing the data. For example, in the figure above, you might select B3:E99. Although you have selected a rectangular range, B3 is the active cell.
3. Type 123 and press Enter. Excel will move to B4.

4. Repeat this to fill in the numbers for Q2, Q3, and Q4. When you press Enter in cell E3, Excel will move to B4.

	A	B	C	D	E
1	Region	Q1	Q2	Q3	Q4
2	City of London	1322	587	896	1121
3	Barking and Dagenham	123	234	345	456
4	Barnet				
5	Bexley				

Figure 65 *Excel will jump to B4 from E3*

Alternate Strategy: There is another way to handle this situation, although it's not as straightforward as the method just described. Whereas the method just described requires you to use Right as the Move Selection Direction, this strategy requires that setting to be set to Down:

1. Select File, Options, Advanced. Open the dropdown for After Pressing Enter, Move Selection Direction, and choose Down. Click OK.
2. Select cell B5. Type a value and press Tab. Excel will jump to C5.
3. Type a value for Q2 and press Tab. Excel will jump to D5.
4. Type a value for Q3 and press Tab. Excel will jump to E5.
5. Type a value for Q4 and press Enter. Excel will jump back to cell B6!

I have no idea how Excel knows how to do this. Apparently, Microsoft programmed in a bit of logic to remember the first column you tabbed out of. When you switch from Tab to Enter, Excel will jump down one row and back to that column. Amazing. If you make a mistake in a previous cell, use Shift+Tab to move backwards through the list.

ENTER DATA IN A CIRCLE (OR ANY PATTERN)

Problem: I need to fill out a form in which the data fields jump all over the place. I start in cell H1, then jump to H5, then E4, then B2, and so on. This figure shows the sequence of fields I have to fill out.

	A	B	C	D	E	F	G
1							1
2	4						
3				3			
4							2
5		5	6	7	8		
6		9	10	11	12		
7						13	
8		14					

Figure 66 *You want to enter data in this sequence.*

Strategy: You can use the method described in "Return to the First Column After Typing the Last Column" to solve this problem. The solution relies on the fact that Excel can remember the sequence in which you select cells. Follow these steps:

1. For now, ignore cell 1. Click in cell 2.
2. Hold down the Ctrl key and click cell 3.
3. Keep holding down the Ctrl key while you select cell 4, 5, 6, and so on, in order. (Yes, it absolutely matters that you select the cells in the correct order.)
4. After you select the last cell, keep holding down the Ctrl key and select cell 1.
5. Click the mouse in the Name box (the area to the left of the formula bar that shows an address like H1) and type MyData. Press Enter. Nothing will happen. The Name box will return to saying H1.

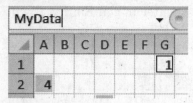

Figure 67 *Name the selected range.*

   6. Save the file.

When you need to fill in the cells, select the Name box dropdown and choose MyData. Cell 1 will be selected. Type a value and press Enter. Excel will jump to cell 2. Keep typing values and pressing Enter, and Excel will jump to the fields in the correct order.

Additional Details: This technique works because Excel defines the named range as a specific sequence of cells. Use Formulas, Name Manager, Edit. You will see that the name is defined in the same sequence as you selected the cells: "=Sheet1!$G$4,Sheet1!$D$3,Sheet1!$A$2,Sheet1!$B$5,Sheet1!$C$5,Sheet1!$D$5,Sheet1!$E$5,Sheet1!$B$6,Sheet1!$C$6,Sheet1!$D$6,Sheet1!$E$6,Sheet1!$F$7,Sheet1!$B$8,Sheet1!$G$1".

HOW TO SEE HEADINGS AS YOU SCROLL AROUND A REPORT

Problem: I have a spreadsheet that has headings at the top. I want to scroll through the data and always see the headings.

	A	B	C	D	E
1	**Sales Report - 2012**				
2					
3	**Rep**	**Customer**	**Product**	**Qty**	**Revenue**
4	Joe	RST Company	GHI	624	55536
5	Mary	EFG Pty Ltd	GHI	605	53845
6	Dan	TUV Company	DEF	733	65237
7	Dan	CDE GMbH	XYZ	634	56426
8	Bob	BCD Corporation	ABC	795	70755

Figure 68 *You want to see row 3 headings even if you scroll to row 800.*

Strategy: Select one cell in the data. Press Ctrl+T and click OK. Your data will be formatted. When you scroll the headings out of view, the headings will replace column letters A, B, C.

	Rep ▾	Customer ▾	Product ▾	Qty ▾	Revenue ▾
99	Bob	EFG, Inc.	ABC	594	52866
100	Mary	UVW, Inc.	ABC	640	56960
101	Joe	XYZ S.A.	XYZ	417	37113
102	Bob	RST Company	ABC	674	59986

Figure 69 *Tables will keep the headings in view.*

This strategy uses the table concept introduced in Excel 2007. It automatically adds Filter dropdowns and formats the table. It also precludes the use of some features like the View Manager. For a more flexible strategy, use Freeze Panes as discussed next.

Alternate Strategy: You can use the Freeze Panes command on the View tab. In order to make the Freeze Panes command work, you must place the cell pointer in the correct location before using the command.

In the spreadsheet shown in Figure 68 it would be really handy to have row 3 always visible while you scroll. Here's how you make that happen:

   1. Use the arrow at the bottom of the vertical scrollbar to move row 3 to the top of the window.

   2. Place the cell pointer in cell A4. You're going to use the Freeze Panes command, which will freeze all visible rows above the cell pointer and all visible columns to the left of the cell pointer. If you place the cell pointer on the heading for column A, you will not freeze any columns, only the rows.

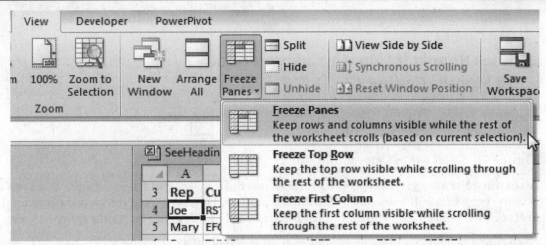

Figure 70 *Cells above and left of the active cell is frozen.*

3. With the cell pointer in cell A4, select View , Freeze Panes , Freeze Panes. A solid horizontal line will be drawn between rows 3 and 4. As you scroll down, you will always be able to see the heading rows.

Additional Details: To turn off this feature, go to the View tab and select Freeze Panes, Unfreeze Panes. The Unfreeze Panes menu item is visible only after you have frozen the panes.

See Also: "How to See Both Headings and Row Labels as You Scroll Around a Report," "How to Print Titles at the Top of Each Page"

HOW TO SEE HEADINGS AND ROW LABELS AS YOU SCROLL AROUND A REPORT

Problem: I have a wide spreadsheet. There are headings at the top of the spreadsheet, and there are several columns of labels at the left side of the spreadsheet. I also have monthly sales figures that extend far to the right. I need to be able to scroll through the sales figures while always seeing both the headings at the top and the labels at the left of the spreadsheet.

	A	B	C	D	E	F	G
1	**OurCo LLC**						
2	**Sales Report by Month, Customer and Region**						
3	**12 Months Ending 12/31/2012**						
4							
5	Country	Region	District	Sales Rep	Customer	Product	Jan
6	USA	West	No. California	Joe	RST Company	GHI	37
7	Australia	Australia	Australia	Mary	EFG Pty Ltd	GHI	40
8	USA	Central	Chicago	Dan	TUV Company	DEF	86
9	Germany	Germany	Germany	Dan	CDE GMbH	XYZ	73
10	USA	Central	Minneapolis	Bob	BCD Corporation	ABC	65

Figure 71 *See columns A:F as you scroll right.*

Strategy: Use the Freeze Panes command on the View tab. You must place the cell pointer in the correct location before using the command.

In the spreadsheet shown above, you might want A1:F5 visible all the time. Then, you could scroll through the monthly figures and always be able to see the customer information in the left columns and the month name information in row 5. Here's how you make it happen:

1. Select cell G6. This is the first non-frozen cell.
2. Select View, Freeze Panes, Freeze Panes. You will see a solid line between columns F and G and between rows 5 and 6.

Results: As you scroll, you can always see the headings.

	A	B	C	D	E	F	S	T
1	OurCo LLC							
2	Sales Report by Month, Customer and							
3	12 Months Ending 12/31/2012							
4								
5	Country	Region	District	Sales Rep	Customer	Product	Oct	Nov
102	USA	Central	Cleveland	Mary	UVW, Inc.	ABC	23	34
103	France	France	France	Joe	XYZ S.A.	XYZ	70	65

Figure 72 *Scroll out to October and you can still see A:F.*

Alternate Strategy: Some people prefer to use Split instead of Freeze Panes. I am not a fan of Split since it is too easy to scroll from one quadrant to another. However, several viewers provided reasons why they prefer Split. Search YouTube for "Learn Excel 1101" for a demo on using split.

Note that the Split handles were removed after Excel 2010.

WHY IS THE SCROLLBAR SLIDER SUDDENLY TINY?

Problem: I have a worksheet with two or three screens of data. I can easily grab the vertical scrollbar and move to the top or bottom of the data set. Something happened, and now the huge scrollbar slider has become really tiny. Further, if I move it just one pixel, instead of jumping to the next screen of data, Excel will move to row 4500.

	A	B	C	D	E	
30	29	Data	Data	Data	Data	Da
31	30	Data	Data	Data	Data	Da
32	31	Data	Data	Data	Data	Da
33	32	Data	Data	Data	Data	Da
34	33	Data	Data	Data	Data	Da
35	34	Data	Data	Data	Data	Da
36	35	Data	Data	Data	Data	Da
37	36	Data	Data	Data	Data	Da
38	37	Data	Data	Data	Data	Da
39	38	Data	Data	Data	Data	Da
40	39	Data	Data	Data	Data	Da
41	40	Data	Data	Data	Data	Da

Row: 30

Normal / Small

Figure 73 *Normally, the slider will take you to the last row with data.*

Strategy: Someone pressed End+Down Arrow key to move to row 1048576.

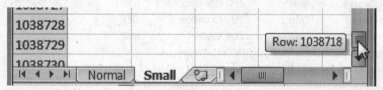

1038728	
1038729	
1038730	

Row: 1038718

Normal / **Small**

Figure 74 *Accidentally activate a cell at the bottom. The slider is tiny.*

You can often restore the size of the slider by moving it completely to the top of the spreadsheet. If this does not work, then there is one rogue cell way below your data that has become activated. Perhaps someone pressed the Spacebar or applied text formatting or something. Follow these steps:

1. Note the last row that you believe to contain data.
2. Press the End key and then press the Home key. Excel will jump to the intersection of the last active row and the last active column. This row is usually way beyond the row that you believe to be the last row.
3. Delete all rows from the bottom of your data set to the rogue last row.
4. Save the workbook. The scrollbar slider will return to full size.

Saving the workbook is the key. Even after you delete the extra rows, Excel will not restore the size of the scrollbar.

JUMP TO THE EDGE OF THE DATA

Problem: I have thousands of rows of data. I want to quickly move to the edge of the data using my mouse.

Strategy: To jump to the bottom of the data, double-click the bottom edge of the active cell.

	A	B
1	Jan	Feb
2	6834	8529
3	6607	7355
4	8776	5203
5	5201	8637
6	8553	2943

Figure 75 *Double-click the bottom of the active cell.*

Result: Excel will navigate down until the cell before a blank cell.

Additional Details: Double-click the right edge of the active cell to move to the right edge of the data.

Alternate Strategy: For keyboard fans, using Ctrl+Down Arrow or pressing End followed by the Down Arrow will do the same thing.

JUMP TO NEXT CORNER OF SELECTION

Problem: I have a large column of numbers stored as text. I like to use the error correction dropdown that appears next to the first cell in the selection in order to convert the text to numbers. However, if I choose the first cell, then select the range with Ctrl+Shift+Down Arrow, I can no longer see the error dropdown.

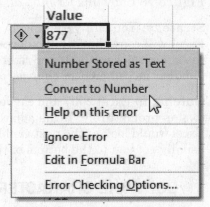

Figure 76 *If you select more than a screen of data, you can not see this icon at the top of the range.*

Strategy: Pressing Ctrl+Period will keep your selection, but move the active cell to the next corner of the selection. This is a great way to see the top of your selection, including the error icon.

If you have a single-column range selected, a single Ctrl+Period will get you to the top. If you have a rectangular range selected, pressing Ctrl+Period will move in a clockwise sequence to the next corner.

If the active cell is currently in the bottom-right, it might require you to press Ctrl+Period twice.

Additional Details: If you press Ctrl+Period to return to the top, then press it again to return to the bottom, the error icon remains in view. This suggests that the intention was to show the error icon even in the original case, but a bug is preventing it.

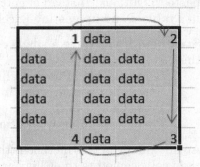

Figure 77 *The active cell moves clockwise to the next corner.*

ZOOM WITH THE WHEEL MOUSE

Problem: I have to constantly zoom in and out on my worksheet. The zoom slider is a hassle.

Strategy: Hold down the Ctrl key while rolling the mouse wheel. Roll away from you to zoom in. Roll towards you to zoom out.

Additional Details: Most people use the scroll wheel to scroll up and down. Did you know that you can also use the mouse to scroll side to side? Click and hold the mouse wheel then move the mouse left or right to scroll sideways. This only works when you have a horizontal scrollbar available.

COPY A FORMULA TO ALL DATA ROWS

Problem: I have a worksheet with thousands of rows of data. I often enter a formula in a new column and need to copy it down to all of the rows. I try to do this by dragging the fill handle. But as I try to drag, Excel starts accelerating faster and faster. Before I know it, I've overshot the last row by thousands of rows. I start dragging back up. Again, Excel starts accelerating. Soon, the cell pointer is moving somewhere close to the speed of sound, and I find that I've overshoot the last row in the other direction. I end up going down and up, down and up. I call this frustrating process the "fill handle dance." Is there a way to stop the madness?

E2		f_x	=MAX(D2-C2,0)	
	A	B	C	D	E
1	Salesrep	Date	Quota	Sales	Over Quota
2	Joe	1/1/2014	800	666	0
3	Dan	1/1/2014	800	1290	
4	Mary	1/1/2014	800	896	

> Double-Click the Fill Handle!

Figure 78 *Copy this formula all the way down.*

Strategy: You can very quickly copy a formula down to all the rows by double-clicking the fill handle. Excel will copy the formula down until it encounters a blank row in the adjacent data. The fill handle is the square dot in the lower-right corner of the cell pointer box. When you hover your mouse over the fill handle, the cell pointer changes to a plus.

Gotcha: In Excel 2007 and earlier, a single blank cell in the adjacent column would cause the copy action to stop prematurely. If the adjacent column is particularly sparse, you could hide that column and then Excel would look at the next visible column to the left. This algorithm was improved in Excel 2010 and will usually get you to the bottom of the data.

COPY THE CHARACTERS FROM A CELL INSTEAD OF COPYING AN ENTIRE CELL

Problem: I need to copy from Excel to Outlook. Microsoft applies weird formatting to the values when I paste to Outlook. Instead of getting just the text, it almost seems like Outlook is wrapping the cell value in a table. I end up pasting Excel data to Notepad, then copying from Notepad.

Strategy: If you have a single cell to copy and want to grab just the characters from the cell, you follow these steps:
1. Select the cell. Put the cell in Edit mode by pressing F2.
2. Select all the characters in the cell by pressing Ctrl+A.
3. Press Ctrl+C to copy.
4. Paste to another application. Excel will not try to place the text in a table.

An advantage of this method is that characters copied to the Clipboard will remain on the Clipboard longer than cells copied to the Clipboard. If you copy a cell, the Clipboard is cleared when you press Esc or save the file. If you copy characters to the Clipboard, they will stay on the Clipboard after these events.

Alternate Strategy: If you have several cells to copy, you can just copy and paste the cells. After you paste to Outlook, a Paste Options icon will appear. You can open the icon and choose Keep Text Only to convert the table to text.

After converting the pasted cells to text, you will have plain text that appears as if you simply typed the values

A FASTER WAY TO PASTE SPECIAL

Problem: What's up with the paste command? What do all of those icons mean?

Strategy: The new Paste Options menu could be one of the biggest time savers in your hour-to-hour use of Excel.

Microsoft took a look at data to see which command is the most frequently undone command. It turns out that it was Paste. Yes, Paste seems simple enough, but there are myriad Paste Special options, and many people were confused about which elements of the copied cells would get pasted.

Even if you are an absolute pro at using Paste Special, you are going to love the new Paste Options menu because it will let you perform tasks that you perform several times an hour with far fewer keystrokes.

Do a normal copy and paste. As in Excel 2003, a little Clipboard appears on screen. This Clipboard has been in Excel for a while, but because I had to grab the mouse to open the dropdown, I never used that menu.

In Excel 2010, the little Clipboard icon also indicates that you can open the dropdown by pressing the Ctrl key one more time.

When you press Ctrl again, you see a series of icons that let you change the type of paste that you just performed. For example, you could click the first icon in the third row to paste as values.

Furthermore, if you hover over that icon, you will learn that pressing V is the shortcut key for pasting values.

So, if you are a keyboard person, you might find yourself doing the following:

- Ctrl+C to copy
- Ctrl+V to paste
- Ctrl to open the Paste Options dialog
- V to change the paste to values

Figure 79 *Press Ctrl after doing a paste to open this menu.*

For keyboard-centric people, this is a pretty fast way to convert formulas to values.

If you prefer to use the mouse, try this amazing trick: hold down the shift key while you drag the border of a selection. When you release the mouse, choose Copy Here as Values Only from the menu that appears.

Additional Details: If you usually paste by using the right-click menu, you will see that the right-click menu includes icons for Paste, Paste Values, Paste Formulas, Transpose, Paste Formats, and Create Links.

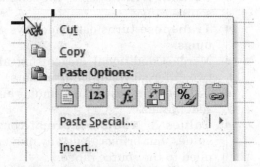

Figure 80 *The right-click menu offers 6 options.*

When you hover over one of those icons, the rest of the context menu disappears so that you can see the effect of the paste in Live Preview.

If you hover over Paste Special in the right-click menu, the menu will disappear and you have access to all 15 icons.

If you regularly use the Paste icon in the Home tab, the dropdown at the bottom of the tab now leads to a menu with the 15 icons. There are still some options in Paste Special that are not available in the icons. You can access those commands by using the Paste Special menu item at the bottom of this figure.

Many times each day, I convert formulas to values by using Ctrl+C, Alt+E+S+V, Enter.

Sometimes, I need to copy values and formats to a new place. In the new place, I have to do Alt+E+S+V, Enter, Alt+E+S+T+Enter.

As mentioned previously, you can use Ctrl+C, Ctrl+V, Ctrl, V to change formulas to value. To paste values and formats, you now use the new Ctrl+V, Ctrl, E to paste values and number formatting.

There might be an even faster way. This key is the right-click key. Use Ctrl+C, Right-Click Key, V to paste as values. If you need to paste values and formats, the Right-Click, E keys will do it.

Figure 81 *The paste dropdown in Excel 2010 offers the icons.*

The one complaint that I have heard about the Paste Options menu is that it is tough to figure out what the icons mean. Photocopy Figure 82 and hang it up by your desk.

The following list describes each of the 15 items in the Paste Options menu:

- **Paste** is a regular paste. You get formulas, borders, and formats.
- **Formulas** pastes the formulas. It will not change formatting.
- **Formulas & Formatting** will paste the formulas and any numeric formatting. Borders, comments, and fills are not pasted.
- **Keep Source Formatting** is similar to a regular paste.
- **No Borders** pastes everything except for the borders.
- **Column Widths** copies the column widths from the source range.
- **Transpose** turns data sideways. Rows become columns.
- Merge Conditional Formatting allows you to mix two different conditional formats.
- **Values** eliminates the formulas and paste their current values.
- **Values & Number Format** converts formulas to values, but brings along any numeric formatting applied to the source range.
- **Values & Formatting** converts formulas to values, but brings along the cell formatting, too.

Icon	Key & Action
	P - Paste
	F - Formulas
	O - Formulas & Formatting
	K - Keep Source Formatting
	B - No Borders
	W - Column Widths
	T - Transpose
	G - Merge Conditional Format
	V - Values
	A - Values & Number Format
	E - Values & Formatting
	R - Formatting
	N - Paste Link
	U - Static Picture
	I - Linked Picture

Figure 82 *Keys in Paste Options menu.*

- **Formatting** pastes only the formats.
- **Paste Link** will create formulas in the pasted range that point back to the source range.
- **Static Picture** pastes a picture of the copied range. This picture might include cells, SmartArt, charts, and so on. When the original range changes, this picture does not change.
- **Linked Picture** pastes a live picture of the copied range. When something changes in the original range, the picture reflects that change. This used to be called the Camera Tool in Excel 2003.

QUICKLY TURN A RANGE ON ITS SIDE

Problem; I have a column that contains 20 department names going down a column. I need to build a worksheet with those names going across row 1.

◢	A
1	Department
2	Accounting
3	Finance
4	Marketing
5	Sales - East
6	Sales - Central
7	Sales - West

Strategy: Copy the data. Select a new blank cell. Do a Paste Transpose. Here's how:

1. Highlight the department names in column A.
2. Ctrl+C to copy the cells to the Clipboard.
3. Move the cell pointer to a blank area of the worksheet. Your paste region can not start in the same cell as your copy region.
4. Open the Paste dropdown. Click the Transpose icon.

Figure 83 *Turn this data sideways.*

Figure 84 *Use this icon to turn the pasted data sideways.*

Gotcha: The columns you paste to will not automatically resize to fit the data. To fix this problem, you can select the appropriate range (in this case, C1:Z1) and then choose Home, Format, AutoFit Column Width.

Additional Details: You can use Transpose to convert a horizontal row of numbers into a column. In addition, you can use it to turn a rectangular range on its side.

QUICKLY REARRANGE ROWS OR COLUMNS

Problem: I want to move row 5 to appear after row 7. I don't want to sort. I don't want to insert a new row, copy, paste, delete the old row. What is the fastest way?

Strategy: This topic will cover some little-known shortcut keys.
- Shift+Spacebar selects the entire row.
- Ctrl+Spacebar selects the entire column.
- Shift+Drag Border will insert the selected range in a new spot.
- Ctrl+Plus Sign will insert cells above or to the left
- Ctrl+Minus sign will delete the selection.

Here is an example. Say that you want to move row 4 after row 7 and that you want to move Bobby after Peter.

1. Select the whole row using Shift+Spacebar.
2. Hold down the shift key. Drag the lower border of the selection and drop it below row 7.
3. Select a cell in D. Select the whole column using Ctrl+Spacebar.
4. Shift+Drag the right border of the selection after column F.

◢	A	B	C	D	E	F
1	Jan	Marcia	Cindy	Bobby	Greg	Peter
2	2	2	2	2	2	2
3	3	3	3	3	3	3
4	4	4	4	4	4	4
5	5	5	5	5	5	5
6	6	6	6	6	6	6
7	7	7	7	7	7	7
8	8	8	8	8	8	8
9	9	9	9	9	9	9

Figure 85 *You want to rearrange this data.*

◢	A	B	C	D	E	F
1	Jan	Marcia	Cindy	Greg	Peter	Bobby
2	2	2	2	2	2	2
3	3	3	3	3	3	3
4	5	5	5	5	5	5
5	6	6	6	6	6	6
6	7	7	7	7	7	7
7	4	4	4	4	4	4
8	8	8	8	8	8	8
9	9	9	9	9	9	9

Figure 86 *Shift-drag the selection to move it.*

If you wanted to delete column B, select one cell in B, Ctrl+Spacebar to select the whole column, then Ctrl+Minus to delete.

COPY CELLS FROM ONE WORKSHEET TO MANY OTHER WORKSHEETS

Problem: I have 12 monthly worksheets in a workbook. I've made changes to January and now need to copy those changes to the other 11 worksheets. Is there an easy way?

Strategy: After you've successfully made changes to January, you can follow these steps:
1. Select the January worksheet. Hold down the Shift key and select the December worksheet. Alternatively, right-click the January sheet tab and choose Select All Sheets. Excel will select all 12 worksheets and make the January worksheet the active sheet. **Note:** If your changes are in a middle sheet, such as April, then the process is different. First, click the April worksheet. Next, Shift+click the December sheet, and then Ctrl+click the January, February, and March sheets.
2. Select the cells you want to copy. If the cells are not adjacent to one another, select the first range and then hold down Ctrl while selecting the remaining ranges.
3. Select Home, Fill, Across Worksheets.

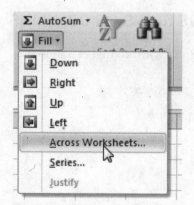

Figure 87 *The Fill icon is in the Editing group.*

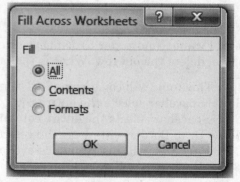

Figure 88 *You can also use this to copy formatting to other sheets.*

4. From the Fill Across Worksheets dialog select whether to copy values, formats, or both.
5. Right-click any sheet tab and select Ungroup.

Gotcha: If you fail to ungroup, any changes you make to the active worksheet will be made to all worksheets.

Additional Details: Home, Fill, Across Worksheets is fairly difficult to use. You have to be able to group sheets and then make the sheet with the changes to copy the active (top) sheet. The steps listed here are designed to help select all sheets. If you need to copy from March to only June, September, and December, however, you might do this:
1. Select March to make it the active sheet.
2. Hold down Ctrl and select June to add it to the group.
3. Hold down Ctrl and select September to add it to the group.
4. Hold down Ctrl and select December to add it to the group.
5. Select Home, Fill, Across Worksheets.

QUICKLY COPY WORKSHEETS

Problem: I've created the perfect report for January. I've formatted the column widths. I've changed the Page Setup. I have custom views. I need to make copies of the report for February through December in the current workbook.

Strategy: You need the Move or Copy command. Normally, you would right-click the January worksheet tab, choose Move or Copy, choose New Book, Create a Copy, OK. However, there is a faster way.

While holding down the Ctrl key, drag the January worksheet tab and drop it to the right of the January tab.

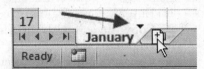

Figure 89 *Ctrl+Drag the tab to make a copy.*

Watch the black triangle pointer. The worksheet copy will be added where the indicator appears.

Gotcha: The name for the new worksheet will be January (2). Double-click the worksheet name and type a new name.

Additional Details: If you have two workbooks opened and use View, Arrange, Vertical, you can Ctrl+Drag a worksheet from one workbook to another.

FIND TEXT NUMBERS

Problem: I suspect that there are cells in my data that contain text numbers instead of numbers. I know that numbers entered as text cause a variety of problems. For example, although a formula such as =E3+E4 will include the text number in E3, most functions, such as SUM or AVERAGE, will ignore the text cells. Text versions of a number will sort to a different place than numeric versions. If I use a MATCH or VLOOKUP function, a text version of 3446 will not match a numeric version of 3446. How can I find text entries that need to be converted to numbers?

Strategy: In versions before Excel 2002, there was no easy way to visually locate these cells. In versions of Excel from Excel 2002 through Excel 2010, these text cells, as well as a variety of other potential errors, are noted by a dark green triangle in the upper-left corner of the cell. As shown below, cells C6, E2, E3, E6, and E7 have triangles in their upper-left corners because they are text entries that look like numbers.

	A	B	C	D	E
1	Invoice	Rep	Customer	Product	Sales
2	1041	Chaz	1183	ABC	216
3	1047	Amy	5719	XYZ	345
4	1061	Amy	4056	DEF	349
5	1070	Amy	9484	XYZ	111
6	1086	Amy	3446	DEF	150
7	1089	Deb	2506	DEF	127
8	1101	Ben	7142	ABC	345

Figure 90 *Some cells contain text that looks like numbers.*

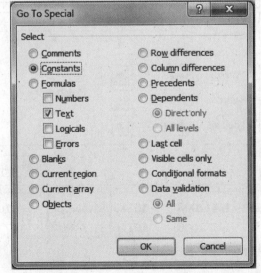

Figure 91 *Choose Constants. Deselect Numbers.*

Instead of looking for those little triangles, here's an easier way to locate all the text entries so you can convert them to numbers:

1. Select the entire range of data by selecting one cell and then pressing Ctrl+*.
2. Select Home, Find & Select, Go To Special. Excel will display the Go To Special dialog.
3. Select Constants. Deselect the options Numbers, Logicals, and Errors, leaving only Text selected.

Results: All the text entries will be highlighted.

Additional Details: There are a number of ways to convert these cells from text to numbers. The easiest way is to get all the text cells in one contiguous range. If you can sort the data by column E descending, all the text entries will sort to the top of the list.

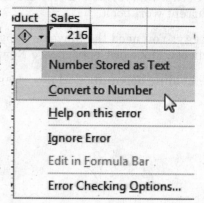

In Excel 2002 and newer versions, you can convert a contiguous range of text numbers. To do so, you use the Error (exclamation point) dropdown and select Convert to Number. This method works only if the top-left cell in your selection contains a number stored as text.

For earlier versions of Excel, you can use the following trick:

1. Enter a zero in a blank cell.
2. Copy the cell with the zero by using Ctrl+C.
3. Highlight the text cells.
4. Choose Edit, Paste Special. In the Paste Special dialog that appears, select Values and Add and then click OK.

Adding a zero to the text cells will cause them to be converted to real numbers.

Figure 92 *Open the error dropdown to convert text to numbers.*

Alternate Strategy: The fastest way to convert a column of numbers to text is to select the column and type Alt+DEF (that is, Alt+D followed by E then F). This little command uses the default Text to Columns settings which will convert your text to numbers.

WHY CAN'T EXCEL FIND A NUMBER?

Problem: The Excel Find and Replace dialog drives me crazy. I always have to go to the Options button to specify that it should look in Values. In the figure below, the mouse pointer is showing the value that Excel says is not there is actually there. Why can't Excel find a number?

	A	B	C	D	E
1	Date	Invoice	Amount	Tax	
2	1/2/2008	10101	$1,569.20	94.15	

Find and Replace

Find	Replace

Find what: 1364.80   ▼   No Format Set

Within: Sheet ▼   ☐ Match case

Search: By Rows ▼   ☐ Match entire cell contents

Look in: Values ▼

               Find All   Find Next

| 16 | 1/4/2008 | 10115 | $1,364.80 | 81.89 | |
| 17 | 1/7/2008 | 10116 | $1,784.2? | 107.06 | |

Microsoft Excel   ✕

Microsoft Excel cannot find the data you're searching for.

OK

Figure 93 *Psst, Excel! Try looking under the mouse pointer.*

Strategy: You've pointed out a lot of the problems with Find and Replace. Let's take a quick review to uncover some of the problems. First, when you select Home, Find & Select, Find, Excel presents the simplified version of the Find and Replace dialog without the important settings shown at the bottom of the figure above.

There are important settings hiding behind the Options button. These settings will often cause a Find to fail. Say that you have a calculation for sales tax in column D. Cell D3 shows 70.81 as the result of a formula. By default, Excel is searching the formulas instead of the values. If you tried Find without changing Formulas to Values, it will not find $70.81.

Searching the text of the formulas is a bit annoying. How often do you say to yourself, "Wow, I wonder in which cell I used the SQRTPI function?" But even more annoying are the other settings, such as Match Case and Match Entire Cell Contents. These settings can be useful, but if you happened to change them at 8:04 a.m. today and haven't closed Excel since then, even though you've opened and closed 40 other workbooks and are working on something completely different, Excel will remember that previous setting. You will often get stung by a strange setting left behind earlier in the day, or even a setting changed when a macro tried to use the Find command with Match Entire Cell Contents turned on.

So why can't Excel see the 1354.80 value in Figure 93? Excel is displaying cell C16 with a currency symbol and a comma, and in order to find the cell, you have to search for $1,354.80! Because Excel's forte is numbers, it's rather disappointing that Excel works like this. But when you understand it, you can work around it.

Additional Details: People often ask how they can search through all sheets in a workbook. You do this by changing the Within dropdown from Sheet to Workbook.

Additional Details: Amazingly, Excel can find cells that are displaying as number signs (#) instead of numbers. Say that you have a column where 5% of the numbers are showing as #####.

Now, any sane person would make the column wider or turn on Shrink to Fit, but Excel allows you to perform the following rather crazy set of steps:

1. Select the range of numbers. Press Ctrl+F to display the Find dialog.
2. Type ### in the Find What dialog.
3. If the dialog is not showing the options, click the Options button.
4. Ensure that Look In is set to Values and that Match Entire Cell Contents is not checked.
5. Instead of clicking Find, click Find All. Excel adds a new section to the dialog, with a list of all the cells that contain ###.
6. While the focus is still on the dialog, click Ctrl+A. This will select all the cells in the bottom of the Find All dialog.

You can now format just the selected cells. For example, you could choose fewer decimals or a smaller font size, or you could choose to display the numbers in thousands.

Gotcha: In Step 6, you are supposed to press Ctrl+A to select all of the found cells. Be careful that the focus is on the dialog box before pressing Ctrl+A. For example, if you change the font size, the focus would switch to the worksheet, even though the dialog is still displayed. Pressing Ctrl+A at this point would select all cells in the worksheet instead of just the matching cells. To reestablish focus on the dialog box, you need to click the title bar of the Find and Replace dialog.

MIX FORMATTING IN A SINGLE CELL

Problem: I'd like to use strikethrough on the text in part of a cell. Is this possible?

Strategy: You can apply different formatting to certain characters in a cell.

You select the cell and then press F2 or double-click the cell. Select characters with the mouse or by using the arrow keys in combination with the Shift key. You can then apply formatting. Many icons on the Home tab of the ribbon are enabled. Any formatting shortcut keys, such as Ctrl+5 for strikethrough, will work. If you need to apply superscript or subscript, you use the Format Cells dialog by pressing Ctrl+1 or click the dialog launcher in the bottom-right corner of the Font group.

C	D	E
Select part of a cell	Gotcha: Watch out for red...	See Notes[1]
~~July 8, 2012~~ July 28, 2012	Read The Cay and summarize	H_2O

Figure 94 *Format a subset of characters in a cell.*

Gotcha: In addition to the character formatting, you can apply other formatting to the entire cell. For example, in C5, you can safely apply italic or underline to the cell without removing the bold from the first word. However, if you apply bold to the entire cell, Excel will not remember that you started with just the first word bold. You can not use the Bold icon on the entire cell to toggle back to the formatting shown in the figure.

Gotcha: If you later use the Justify command, the internal formatting will be lost.

ENTER A SERIES OF MONTHS, DAYS, OR MORE BY USING THE FILL HANDLE

Problem: I need to create a new worksheet. My first task is to enter the 12 month names across row 1. Is there a faster way than typing them all?

Strategy: You type the first value and drag that cell's fill handle to the right or down. Follow these steps:
1. Type January in cell B1. If you now press the Enter key, Excel will normally move the cell pointer to B2. You can press Enter and then press the Up Arrow key to move back to B1, or you can simply press Ctrl+Enter to accept the cell value and stay in the current cell.
2. The square dot in the lower right corner of the cell is the fill handle. Click it and drag right or down. As you drag, a ToolTip will show you the value that will be entered in each cell.

	A	B	C	D
1		January		
2				March
3				

Figure 95 *As you drag, a ToolTip shows values to be filled.*
3. When you release the mouse button, Excel will fill the series with month names.

Additional Details: Excel can extend many other built-in series in addition to month names:
- Jan will extend to Feb, Mar, and so on.
- MON will extend to TUE, WED, and so on.
- Q1 will extend to Q2, Q3, Q4, Q1. (Also Qtr 1 or Quarter 1)
- Room 10 will extend to Room 11, Room 12, and so on.
- 1st period will extend to 2nd period, 3rd period, and so on.
- Today's date (press Ctrl+;) will extend to tomorrow's date.
- For quarters and years, use 1Q 2015 or 1Q-15 or 1Q.15.

Gotcha: Excel can extend many built-in series, but can it count 1, 2, 3, and so on? If you enter 1 in cell B1 and drag the fill handle down, what do you think you will get? 1, 2, 3. What will you actually get? 1, 1, 1.

Many people tell me to enter 1 in B1, 2 in B2, select B1:B2 and drag the fill handle. While this works, there is a faster way: You can enter 1 in B1 and then hold down the Ctrl key while you drag the fill handle. Excel will fill with 1, 2, 3. Alternatively, select the 1 and the blank cell next to the 1. Drag down. Excel will fill 1, 2, 3.

The Ctrl key can be used to copy instead of fill. Select a date or text. To copy without incrementing, drag the fill handle while holding down Ctrl.

Additional Details: If you forget to hold down Ctrl, you can open the Auto Fill Options dropdown that appears at the end of the range. You can select Fill Series to change the 1, 1, 1, 1 to 1, 2, 3, 4.

Gotcha: The Fill Options icon can be difficult to dismiss. This is particularly annoying if it is covering up data. The Esc key will not make it go away. One fast way to dismiss the icon is to resize a column on the worksheet.

If you need to fill odd numbers, you can enter 1 in B1 and 3 in B2. Select B1:B2 and drag the fill handle.

There are other fill possibilities as well. One cool option is Fill Weekdays. You enter a starting date in a cell, place the cell pointer in that cell, right-click, and drag the fill handle down several cells. A ToolTip will indicate that you are filling the series with daily dates. When you release the mouse button, you will have several options. Choose Fill Weekdays to fill in only Monday through Friday dates.

To fill the 15th and last of each month, select both dates, right-click the fill handle and drag. When you release the mouse, choose Fill Months.

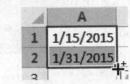

Figure 97 *Select both dates.*

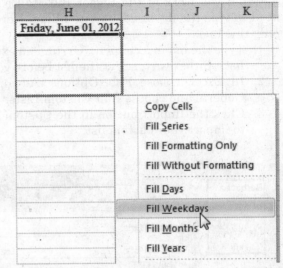

Figure 96 *Right-click and drag the fill handle to access these options..*

2	1/31/2015
3	2/15/2015
4	2/28/2015
5	3/15/2015
6	3/31/2015
7	4/15/2015

Fill Days
Fill Weekdays
Fill Months
Fill Years

Figure 98 *Right-drag, fill months.*

Additional Details: The fill handle is a shortcut to default settings you can also get by selecting Home, Fill, Series. You can enter a value in a cell, select that cell, and choose Home, Fill, Series to display a dialog where you can specify any type of series.

Say that you want to fill the numbers from 1 to 1,000,000. Try this:
1. Enter the number 1 in a cell and select that cell.
2. Right-click the fill handle. Drag down one cell. Drag back up. Release the mouse button.
3. Choose Series... from the bottom of the flyout menu. (Be careful, you want "Series..." from the bottom, not "Fill Series" from the top.
4. In the Fill Series dialog, choose Columns. Enter a Stop Value of 1,000,000. Click OK.

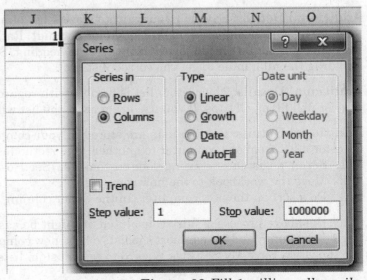

Figure 99 *Fill 1 million cells easily.*

HAVE THE FILL HANDLE FILL YOUR LIST OF PART NUMBERS

Problem: Sure, the fill handle is good for filling months, days, and sequential numbers. But what about the really annoying lists I have to type all the time at work? I have to type lists of product lines, company regions, sales rep names, and so on.

Strategy: No matter what job you do, you probably have some annoying list of items that you have to type over and over. If your list contains from two to 96 items, you can add your list of items to the Custom Lists dialog. You can then fill items from the defined custom lists by using the fill handle.

Say that you work at the Bigger Burrito Co., and you constantly need to type the flavors of burrito filling. Here's how you can simplify this task.

1. Type the list in a column. (Or, find an existing range with the list.) Either way, select the list before going to step 2.
2. In Excel, choose File, Options, Advanced. Scroll down to General and choose Edit Custom Lists.
3. Click the Import button in the Custom Lists dialog in order to import your custom list.

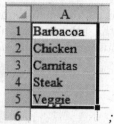

Figure 100 *Type this list for the last time.*

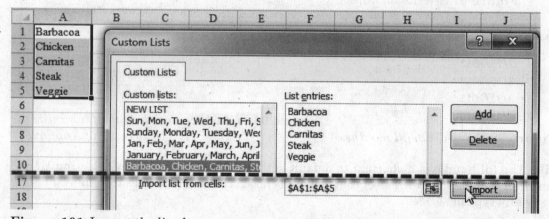

Figure 101 *Import the list from a range.*

Note that if you later change the flavors in this list, you can edit the list in this dialog. Make sure to click the Add button to commit the changes..

After you add the custom list, you can type any item from the list in a cell and then drag the fill handle. Excel will fill in the remaining items from the list. If you go too far, the list will repeat.

Additional Details: Say that you want to store a list of names, and the first name in the list is a really long name, such as John Jacob Jingleheimer Schmidt. Rather than having to type this name to start the list, you could make the first item in the list the heading. So, perhaps you could type Class1 or MktgDept and drag the fill handle to get the correct list.

Additional Details: The custom list is flexible with regards to case. If you type the first item in all caps, the list will fill as all caps. If you use lower case, the list will fill as lower case.

Additional Details: Custom lists are stored in your computer's registry. It is therefore very difficult to transfer a list from one computer to another. One method is as follows:

1. Set up a custom sort using your custom list. (See How to Sort a Report into a Custom Sequence)
2. Move the workbook to the new computer.
3. Do a sort on the new computer. In the Order column, select Custom Lists. Click Add.

Since the above process is fairy convoluted, it might be easier to copy the lists into a blank workbook on the old computer, and then import the lists on the new computer. If you have Excel 2003 installed, you can use the Office Save My Settings Wizard to save custom lists.

TEACH EXCEL TO FILL A, B, C

Problem: The fill handle can fill weekdays, months, quarters, and now numbers. Why can't it fill A, B, C?

Strategy: Create a list of the alphabet. Save that list as a custom list as described above. Here is a fast way to create the alphabet.
1. Select a range that is one column wide and 26 rows tall.
2. Type =CHAR(ROW(A65)). Press Ctrl+Enter.
3. Ctrl+C to copy. Paste, Values using your favorite method or Context+V in Excel 2010.

Character number 65 is a capital letter A. Using ROW(A65) will return the number 65 in the first cell, 66 in the next cell, and so on. This handy formula will create the letters from A to Z.

Import the range as a custom list as described in the previous topic.

USE EXCEL AS A WORD PROCESSOR

1

Problem: I need to type some notes at the bottom of a report. How can I make the words fill each line as if I had typed them in Word?

	A	B	C	D	E	F	G	H	I	J	K
70	This prospectus includes forward-looking statements.										
71	All statements other than statements of historical facts contained in this prospect										
72	including statements regarding our future financial position, business strategy an										
73	and objectives of management for future operations, are forward-looking stateme										
74	The words "believe", "may", "will", "estimate", "continue", "anticipate", "intend"										
75	events and financial trends that we believe may affect our financial condition, res										
76	financial needs.										

Figure 102 *This paragraph needs to fit in A:G.*

Strategy: You can use Fill, Justify. Follow these steps:
1. To have the words fill columns A through G, select a range such as A70:G85. Include enough extra blank rows in the selection to handle the text after word wrapping.
2. Select Home, Fill dropdown, Justify. (The Fill dropdown now appears in the Editing group of the Home tab. It often appears as a blue down-arrow icon.)

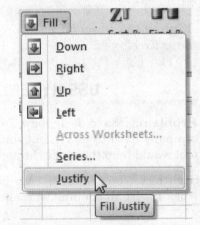

Figure 103 *Select Fill Justify.*

Results: Excel will rearrange the text to fill each row.

Gotcha: If you have a few words in bold in one cell, this formatting will be lost. **Gotcha:** If you later change the widths of columns A:G, you will have to use the Justify command again to force the data to fit. **Gotcha:** Do not use this method if any of your cells contain more than 255 characters. Excel will silently truncate those cells to 255 characters without any notice!

Alternate Strategy: You can also use a text box to solve this problem. You simply click the Text box icon on the Insert tab, draw a text box to fill columns A through G, and paste your text into the text box. You can then format the text box to hide its border: Select the text box and on the Drawing Tools Format tab, select Shape Outline, None.

Additional Details: Starting in Excel 2007, you can give a text box multiple columns. To do so, you select the text box. On the Drawing Tools Format tab, you click the dialog launcher icon in the bottom-right corner of the Shape Styles group to display the Format Shape dialog. In the left pane, you choose Text Box. Then you click on Columns and specify two columns, with separation between them of 0.1".

This prospectus includes forward-looking statements. All statements other than statements of historical facts contained in this prospectus, including statements regarding our future financial position, business strategy and plans and objectives of management for future operations, are	looking statements. We have based these forward-looking statements largely on our current expectations and projections about future events and financial trends that we believe may affect our financial condition, results of operations, business strategy, short term and long term business

Figure 104 *Textboxes now support multiple columns.*

ADD EXCEL TO WORD

Problem: My co-worker is working on a report in Word. I need to add a table and chart to Word. I hate Word.

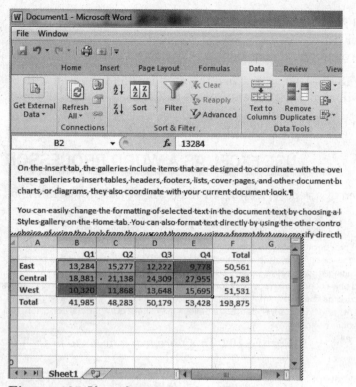

Figure 105 *If you have to work in Word, it is better to have Excel.*

Strategy: You can use the full power of Excel in Word. While you are typing the document, you can put all of the Excel ribbon tabs in the Word ribbon. Follow these steps:

1. Place the insertion point where the table should start.
2. Select Insert, Object. Word will display the Object dialog box.
3. Choose Microsoft Excel Worksheet. Click OK. You now have Excel ribbon tabs at the top of Word!
4. Build your worksheet in the frame. You can use the resize handles in the corner of the frame to make the worksheet as wide and tall as necessary.
5. Consider using View, Show, and uncheck Gridlines. This will hide the gridlines when the worksheet is embedded in Word.
6. Click outside the spreadsheet frame. The worksheet appears in Word.

Additional Details: It seems bizarre, but if you need to put a Word paragraph in Excel, you can use the same trick in Excel. Choose Insert, Object, Microsoft Word.

USE HYPERLINKS TO CREATE AN OPENING MENU FOR A WORKBOOK

Problem: I have designed a budget workbook that has various worksheets. Managers throughout the company need to use it, but some of the managers are not entirely comfortable with Excel. A navigation tool would help them get through the worksheet.

Strategy: You can make your first worksheet a menu with hyperlinks. Here's how:

1. Insert an opening worksheet called Menu. Add an entry for each section of the workbook.

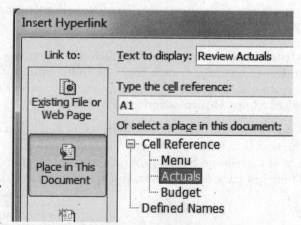

Figure 106 *Column B will become clickable hyperlinks.*

Figure 107 *Choose the proper worksheet.*

2. Select cell B4 and then select Insert, Hyperlink or press Ctrl+K.
3. In the Insert Hyperlink dialog, choose Place In This Document from the left icons.
4. Select the correct worksheet. Verify the cell address of A1.
5. Optionally, click the ScreenTip button and provide friendly text that will appear when someone hovers over the link.

Gotcha: If you don't provide ScreenTip text, Excel will display a distracting ToolTip.

Results: The cell becomes a clickable hyperlink. Clicking on the link will take the manager to the Actuals worksheet.

Additional Details: Be sure to provide a hyperlink on the Actuals worksheet to take the manager back to the menu

Additional Details: It is tricky to select a hyperlinked cell. One method: Click on the hyperlink and hold the mouse button for two seconds. When the hand icon changes to a plus icon, let go of the mouse button. To edit an existing hyperlink, you use the Insert, Hyperlink command again or right-click the cell and choose Edit Hyperlink.

See Also: "Remove Hyperlinks Automatically Inserted by Excel" on page 491.

ARRANGE WINDOWS TO SEE TWO OR MORE OPEN WORKBOOKS

Problem: I have two workbooks open. One workbook contains a list of airport codes and their respective cities. In the other workbook, I am building a list of recommended packing items for students going on a seven-city tour. Currently, I am shifting back and forth between the workbooks, using Ctrl+Tab every time I forget an airport code. It would be cool if I could see both workbooks at once.

Strategy: Select View, Arrange All. The Arrange Windows dialog will appear, giving you four Arrange options. Select Vertical and click OK to see the two workbooks side by side.

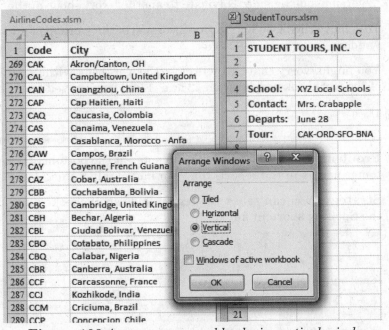

Figure 108 *Arrange open workbooks in vertical windows.*

Results: You will see both windows, side by side. One window is the active window (look for the non-greyed out X icon in top right). Any data entry will occur in the active cell of that workbook.

You can resize the window widths by hovering your mouse at the right edge of the left workbook. The cell pointer changes to a two-headed horizontal arrow. Click and drag the edge of the left window until you have the proper width.

Repeat for the left edge of the right workbook.

To go back to full screen mode, click the Maximize icon at the top of both workbooks.

Gotcha: If you have additional workbooks open, they will also appear side by side. The side-by-side display works fine for 2 or 3 workbooks but would not work for 20 open workbooks because each workbook would be too narrow to see

Additional Details: Starting in Excel 2003, a new command makes it possible to scroll two open workbooks simultaneously. You use the View Side by Side icon on the View tab of the ribbon.

Gotcha: If you are comparing two workbooks that are supposed to be similar, it is likely that someone added some rows to one workbook or the other. When you initially turn on View Side by Side, the workbooks will be synchronized so that when you see row 150 in the first workbook, you will see row 150 in the second workbook. However, if someone inserted 10 rows in the original workbook, you might need row 150 of the original workbook to line up with row 140 of the second workbook. Follow these steps to correct the problem:

1. In the View tab of the ribbon, turn off Synchronous Scrolling by clicking the second icon.
2. Press the Down Arrow key until row 140 is at the top of the left window. In the right window, press the Down Arrow key until row 150 is at the top of that window.
3. Choose the Synchronous Scrolling icon again to force the workbooks to scroll together. Now, when you move down in either workbook, both workbooks will scroll together.

COMPARE TWO WORKSHEETS SIDE BY SIDE

Problem: I need to compare two worksheets from the same workbook side by side.

Strategy: This is possible! Chose View, New Window.

You will notice that there is now a :2 in the title bar after your file name. You've just created a second "camera" that can focus on a different area of your workbook. The second view can either be another worksheet or a different area of the current worksheet.

Do Window, Arrange, Vertical as described in the previous topic. You will now see the :1 version and the :2 version side by side. Navigate to another worksheet in the :2 version.

To remove the :2, switch to the :2 version of the workbook and click the Close Window (X) icon to close that window.

You might worry that this will close the workbook without saving. Instead, it will close the second window of the workbook and both the :2 and :1 will be removed from the title bar. The workbook will remain open.

SPELL CHECK A REGION

Problem: I want to spell check the notes at the bottom of a report, but I don't want to spell check the customer names in the report. How can I accomplish this?

Strategy: You can select the region to be spell checked and then choose Review, Spelling. (Or press F7, the Spelling shortcut key).

Figure 109 *Select cells before invoking the Spelling command..*

Results: Excel will spell check just the selected cells.

Gotcha: If you indicate to spell check a single cell, Excel will expand your selection to the entire worksheet. To get around this problem, you can select the desired cell and any one adjacent cell. When you have two or more cells selected, Excel will check only the selection.

STOP EXCEL FROM AUTOCORRECTING CERTAIN WORDS

Problem: Every time I type the name of my WYA Division, Excel changes "WYA" to "WAY,". It is impossible to type WYA without entering it as a formula: ="W"&"Y"&"A".

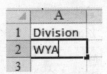

Figure 110 *WYA until...*

Figure 111 *...you type a space or press Enter.*

Strategy: To help correct common mis-typings, Excel has a large list of words that are automatically replaced as you type. This is a good feature, unless you routinely have to type one of the words that Excel thinks is wrong. Luckily, you can edit this list rather than turning it off. Here's how:

1. Select File, Options, Proofing, AutoCorrect Options or Alt+T+A.
2. On the AutoCorrect dialog, go to the AutoCorrect tab.
3. Scroll down the Replace Text as You Type section until you find the entry for replacing WYA with WAY. Select that line and click Delete.

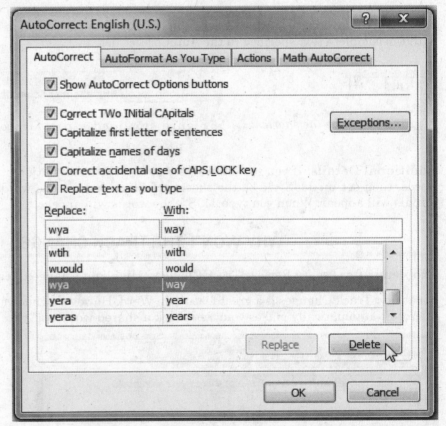

Figure 112 *Delete any replacements that cause problems.*

USE AUTOCORRECT TO ENABLE A SHORTCUT

Problem: I work for John Jacob Jingleheimer Schmidt. It is frustrating to type this name continuously. How can I save time?

Strategy: You can set up an AutoCorrect entry to replace JJJS with John Jacob Jingleheimer Schmidt. Here's how:

1. Select File, Options, Proofing, AutoCorrect Options or Alt+T+A.
2. On the AutoCorrect dialog, go to the Auto-Correct tab.
3. In the Replace section, type JJJS. In the With section, type the complete name. Click Add.

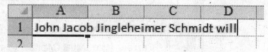

Figure 113 *Add your own shortcut as an AutoCorrect option.*

Results: When you type JJJS in a cell, and then type a space or press Enter, Excel will replace your text with the complete text specified in the AutoCorrect list.

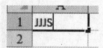

Figure 114 *Type the shortcut...*   **Figure 115** *...and a space to invoke the correction.*

Additional Details: If you sometimes need to use the abbreviation and sometimes need to spell out the words, then set up JJJS> to be the shortcut for spelling out the words. Then, when you type JJJS, the initials will appear. When you type JJJS>, the words will appear.

WHY WON'T THE TRACK CHANGES FEATURE WORK IN EXCEL?

Problem: After I select Review, Track Changes, Highlight Changes, I cannot insert cells. What's going on?

Strategy: Track Changes is a great feature in Word. However, when you turn on Track Changes in Excel, Microsoft automatically makes your workbook a shared workbook.

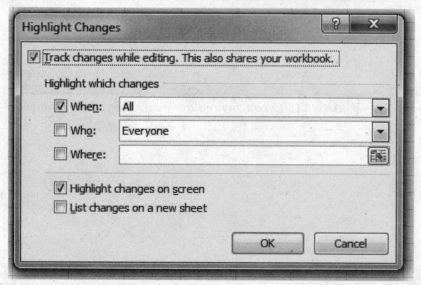

Figure 116 *Tracking changes shares the workbook.*

The shared workbook function in Excel has so many limitations that it is nearly impossible to use. When you share a workbook, you cannot do any of the following tasks:

- Insert blocks of cells
- Create an Excel Table
- Delete worksheets
- Merge or unmerge cells
- Sort or Filter by Formatting
- Change conditional formatting or data validation
- Create or change charts or PivotCharts
- Insert drawing objects, hyperlinks, or scenarios
- Assign, change, or remove passwords, protect or unprotect sheets
- Create, change, or view scenarios
- Use automatic subtotals
- Group or outline data
- Create or change pivot tables, including using slicers
- Create or modify sparklines
- Record, edit, or assign macros
- Enter CSE or array formulas
- Use data tables
- Work with XML data
- Use a data form

It is possible that a novice Excel user might never use these features. It is even possible that before you bought this book, you never used them. However, sharing a workbook makes it virtually unusable for an intermediate Excel user. There is no strategy to get around this. Unless your changes will involve only radically simple worksheet changes, you should avoid the Track Changes and Share Workbooks options.

Alternate Strategy: Visit Litera.com for a third-party application that can compare an original and current version of a workbook and show all changes, including changes to graphic elements such as charts.

SIMULTANEOUSLY COLLABORATE ON A WORKBOOK WITH EXCEL WEB APP

Problem: We have five co-workers who need to edit the same workbook. When someone (Marcia…) leaves it open, the rest of us are forced into Read-Only mode.

Strategy: The Excel Web App has solved this problem. This is one of those things that the Excel Web App does better than regular Excel.

From Excel 2013, us File, Save As, OneDrive. Once the file is on OneDrive, use File, Share, Get a Sharing Link. Next to the Edit Link, click Create Link. Excel will generate a URL that will be impossible to remember. Copy that URL and send it to your co-workers.

With Excel 2010, Use File, Save & Send, Save to Web and save the file to OneDrive. Then, from Office.com, find the file in your recent documents. Open the workbook. Use Share, Share With People, and choose the editing link.

When people follow the link, they will choose to Edit in Excel Online. Multiple people can have the document open and edit difference cells at the same time. A status bar in the top right shows who is in the document. A color-coded box shows the cell that each person is editing.

Gotcha: Filtering is the one odd thing. If I filter the worksheet to only my records, it gets filtered for everyone. Here at MrExcel, we had to agree on a "no filtering" rule. The Excel team wants to fix this, but it is hard… functions like AGGREGATE will return different answers based on hidden rows.

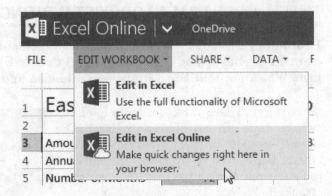

Figure 117 *Choose to Edit online.*

TRANSLATE WITH EXCEL

Problem: I have a client whose German subsidiary sent me an Excel file. The headings are in German. I need to figure out what each column means.

Figure 118 *A rough translation will appear.*

Strategy: Excel added a translation interface to the Review tab of the ribbon. Although the translations are not perfect, they can give you a general idea of the meaning of a passage or paragraph. Here's how it works:

1. Select a cell that contains text you want to translate.
2. Select Review, Translate. The Research task pane appears along the right side of the window.
3. In the From dropdown, choose German.
4. In the To dropdown, choose English. In a few moments, a rough translation will appear in the Research pane.

Additional Details: The Research pane offers a link to Translation Options. The Translation Options dialog allows you to prevent translation between certain languages. If you have a rogue employee who is addicted to ordering Italian shoes on company time, perhaps you would want to turn off the Italian to English language pair. The dialog also allows you to choose the translation service to use for any given language. Many language pairs offer only Microsoft Translator. Some language pairs offer a choice between Microsoft Translator and WorldLingo.

Additional Details: If you need to translate an Excel function for someone in your Switzerland headquarters, Excel MVP Mourad Louha runs an Excel Formula Translator at http://en.excel-translator.de/. You can learn that SVERWEIS, BUSCARV, PHAKU, PROCV, FINN.RAD are all different ways to say VLOOKUP.

I AM A LOBBYIST WRITING POLICY PAPERS FOR THE WHITE HOUSE

Problem: I was so embarrassed when some computer guru discovered that I left my name in the Document Properties dialog. The press traced that press release from the White House back to my lobbying firm. Who knew that Excel stored secret hidden information?

Strategy: There are dozens of places where data can get hidden in Excel. The new Document Inspector can find 90% of them. Before you try to pass your work off as someone else's work, try to cover your tracks.

To look for hidden data in your workbook, run the Document Inspector. Use File, Info, Check for Issues, Inspect Document.

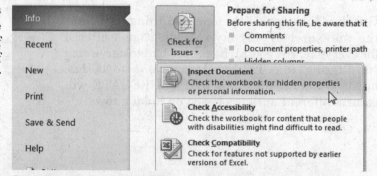

Figure 119 *Inspect the document.*

Excel will look for all the situations shown here.

Gotcha: The Document Inspector finds a lot of hidden data, but not all hidden data. For example, if you hid data by formatting with a white font, or if you used the ;;; custom number format, it will not detect either of these. Further, some personal information might be stored in the Manage Names dialog. The Document Inspector will not discover this information. The figure below shows a cell with white font and another cell formatted with ;;;. As you can see, the Document Inspector reports neither of these.

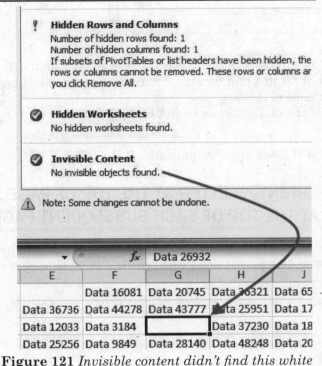

Figure 121 *Invisible content didn't find this white font.*

Figure 120 *Excel helps people cover their tracks.*

Additional Details: The new ExcelAnalyzer software can detect all hidden elements, even the common tricks like ;;; formatting and white font. For more details, see http://www.mrexcel.com/excela-nalyzer.html.

HOW TO PRINT TITLES AT THE TOP OF EACH PAGE

Problem: I have a report that has 90 rows of data. I want to have the title rows print at the top of each printed page.

	A	B	C	D	E
1	**XYZ Corporation**				
2	**Sales by Rep & Day**				
3	**January 2012**				
4					
5	Sales Rep	Date	Quota	Sales	Over Quota
6	Joe	1/2/2012	800	666	0
7	Dan	1/2/2012	800	1290	490
8	Mary	1/2/2012	800	896	96
9	Joe	1/3/2016	800	559	0

Figure 122 *Repeat titles at the top of each printed page.*

Strategy: Printing options are controlled on the fourth tab of the legacy Page Setup dialog box. In this case, you want rows 1 through 5 to print at the top of each page. Follow these steps:

1. Select Print Titles. The Sheet tab of the Page Setup dialog will be displayed.
2. Click the mouse in the Rows to Repeat at Top box.

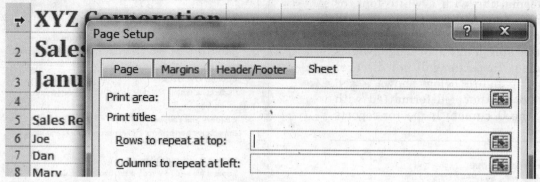

Figure 123 *Select Rows to Repeat at Top*

3. Look behind the dialog box. If you can see the row numbers that you want to repeat, click on the first row and drag down to the last row. Excel should fill in $1:$5 for you. Alternatively, you could type this text or use the RefEdit button at the right edge of the box.
4. There is a Print Preview button at the bottom of the dialog. Check page 2 of the Print Preview to see if the rows are appearing correctly.

See Also: "How to Print Page Numbers at the Bottom of Each Page" on page 57.

PRINT A LETTER AT THE TOP OF PAGE 1
AND REPEAT HEADINGS AT THE TOP OF EACH SUBSEQUENT PAGE

Problem: I am sending out a worksheet that contains a letter followed by a lengthy report. I would like the headings to appear at the top of each page after the first page. I don't want the headings to appear at the top of the letter on the first page.

	A	B	C	D	E	F	G	H	I	J	K	L	M	N	O
1	**Welcome to the 2014-2015 Budget Process**														
2															
3	Dear Manager,														
4															
5	This Excel workbook contains all of the worksheets that you need to complete in order														
6	to produce your forecast for our next fiscal year. The data below shows your actual sales														
7	by SKU for your region. You should build a sales forecast for the next year and then														
8	break the data out by month.														
9															
10	Your forecast should be sent to your regional VP for review no later than noon on														
11	March 12. Thank you for your attention to the forecast process.														
12															
13				Sincerely,											
14															
15				Joe Smith											
16				Director of Operations Analysis											
17				(330) 555-1212											
18															
19	SKU	Prior Sales	Planned Sales	Apr	May	Jun	Jul	Aug	Sep	Oct	Nov	Dec	Jan	Feb	Mar
20	S-001	562													
21	S-002	142													
22	S-003	451													

Figure 124 *You want row 19 to appear at the top of page 2 & beyond.*

Strategy: Follow the steps in the previous topic. Specify $19:$19 as the Rows To Repeat At Top. If you specify that a row in the middle of the print range should be repeated at the top of the pages, it will not begin repeating until the next page.

Results: The headings do not print at the top of page 1, but they do print at the top of pages 2 and beyond.

HOW TO PRINT PAGE NUMBERS AT THE BOTTOM OF EACH PAGE

Problem: I am printing a lengthy report, and I want the pages to be numbered.

Strategy: Headers and footers are controlled in the Page Setup dialog or in the new Page Layout view. This topic will show you the new Page Layout view.

1. Ensure that your document is in Page Layout mode by clicking the middle of the three icons next to the zoom slider in the lower-right corner of the document window. Excel will show your worksheet in virtual pages.

Figure 125 *Page layout mode offers visible headers and footers.*

2. Scroll to the bottom of the first virtual page. Look for the area in the bottom center of the page with the words "Click to add footer." Hover over this area, and a box will appear illustrating the position for three footer areas. Click in the center footer area. A new ribbon tab, Header & Footer Tools, will appear.

Figure 126 *This ribbon tab only appears from Page Layout view.*

3. From the Footer dropdown, select Page 1 of ?. Excel will add a footer such as Page 1 of 10 at the bottom of each page.

4. Click outside the header or footer area to close the Header & Footer Tools tab.

Alternate Strategy: You can also build headers and footers the same way as you did in Excel 2003: If you display the Page Layout tab of the ribbon, a small icon (called a dialog launcher) appears in the lower-right corner of the Page Setup group (see Figure 27 on page 12). You click this icon to display the Page Setup dialog, and then you click the Header/Footer tab and make the appropriate settings.

Additional Details: You can also customize left, center, and right headers as you do the footers.

You can specify different footers for the first page and different footers for odd vs. even pages. You control these settings in the Options area of the Header & Footer Tools Design tab of the ribbon.

Gotcha: Sometimes the footer text will crash into the data from the report. If you have adjusted the lower margin to 0.5 inch, you should adjust the footer margin to 0.25 inch to prevent this condition. Use Page Layout, Margins, Custom Margins to adjust.

Gotcha: Say that you want Sheet1 to be numbered 1 through 10, then Sheet2 to be numbered 11 through 15. Set up each footer to have a page number. When you print, change Print Active Sheets to Print Entire Workbook. If you only want to print a subset of worksheets, put those worksheets in Group Mode before printing. If you print each sheet separately, the numbers will restart on each worksheet.

HOW TO MAKE A WIDE REPORT FIT
TO ONE PAGE WIDE BY MANY PAGES TALL

Problem: After I create a wide report, it prints four pages wide. How do I make it print one page wide?

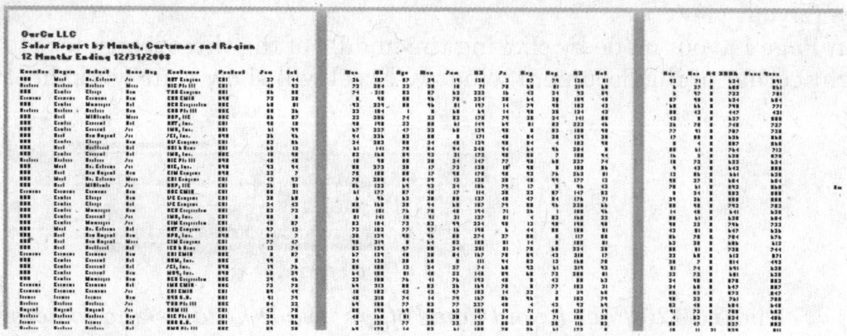

Figure 127 *Taping four pages together leads to copier jams.*

Strategy: Ultimately, you will set the Scale to Fit settings to print to one page wide by any number of pages tall. Before you can do that, you should follow these steps:

1. Eliminate extra columns from the print range. Because this worksheet has some lookup tables beyond column X that you do not want to print, highlight columns A through X and select Page Layout, Print Area, Set Print Area.
2. Set long headings on two lines rather than one. For example, Sales Rep in cell D5 could be on two lines to save width in the column. In cell C5, type Sales, press Alt+Enter, and type Rep. Do the same thing for Prior Year in X5.
3. Make the columns narrower. Select the data in A5:X130 and then select Home, Format, AutoFit Column Width. **Gotcha:** The AutoFit command does not deal well with cells in which Alt+Enter was used, as in step 2. You therefore have to manually adjust the column width of columns D and X.
4. Change the orientation to Landscape by selecting Page Layout, Orientation, Landscape.
5. Adjust the margins by selecting Page Layout, Margins, Custom Margins. On the Margins tab of the Page Setup dialog, set the top, left, and right margins at 0.25 inch. Adjust the bottom to 0.5 inch and the footer margin to 0.25 inch. Alternatively, use Print Preview and click the Show Margins icon in the lower right. You can now drag the margins to a new location.
6. On the Page Layout tab, open the Width dropdown in the Scale to Fit group. Choose 1 page. (This is much easier than using the Page Setup dialog, as discussed in the following alternate strategy.)

Results: The report will fit on one page wide and three pages tall.

Alternate Strategy: You can use the Page Layout dialog to indicate that the report should fit to one page wide by <blank> pages tall. On the Page Layout tab of the ribbon, click the dialog launcher in the lower-right corner of the Page Setup group. Choose the Page tab of the Page Setup dialog. Choose Fit To. Leave the first spin button at 1 Page(s) Wide. Using your mouse, highlight the 1 in the spin button for Tall. After the 1 is highlighted, press Delete to leave this entry completely blank. Before Excel 2007, you followed this rather convoluted process to create a setting equivalent to step 6 above.

See Also: "How to Fit a Multiline Heading into One Cell" on page 247.

ADD A PRINTABLE WATERMARK

Problem: I would like to add a "Draft" watermark on each page of my printed worksheet.

Strategy: The center header is the gateway to adding a semitransparent watermark image that will print behind your document.

To effectively use this trick, you need to create a graphic that has a fair amount of white space at the top of the picture. The figure below shows a DRAFT stamp at the bottom of some white space. You can create this graphic in Photoshop or any photo-editing tool. I actually created this in Excel as WordArt. On the Page Layout tab, uncheck view Gridlines to create the white space. I then used the free Greenshot utility to capture a region of the screen.

Figure 128 *Add whitespace above..*

Follow these steps to create the watermark:

1. Select the Page Layout view icon in the bottom-right corner of the Excel window.
2. Click in the Center Header zone at the top of the worksheet. Excel displays the Header & Footer Tools Design tab.
3. Click the Picture icon on the Header & Footer Tools tab. Browse for and select your picture. Excel inserts &[Picture] in the header.

If your graphic is too large or small, use the Format Picture icon. You can adjust the size, but not the location. If you need more or less white space, you will have to go back to Photoshop to change the graphic.

This figure shows the resulting graphic drawn in behind your numbers.

ShipDate	Customer	Quantity	Revenue	COGS
1/1/2004	VWX GMBH	1000	22810	10220
1/2/2004	MNO COR	100	2257	984
1/2/2004	MNO COR	500	10245	4235
1/3/2004	HIJ GMBH	500	11240	5110
1/4/2004	HIJ GMBH	400	9204	4088
1/4/2004	FGH, CO	800	18552	7872
1/4/2004	RST PTY L	400	9152	4088
1/5/2004	CDE INC.	400	6860	3388
1/7/2004	RST S.A.	400	8456	3388
1/7/2004	LMN LTD.	1000	21730	9840
1/7/2004	RST PTY L	600	13806	6132
1/9/2004	RST S.A.	800	16416	6776
1/9/2004	XYZ GMBH	900	21015	9198
1/10/2004	HIJ GMBH	900	21465	9198
1/10/2004	RST INC.	900	21438	9198
1/12/2004	HIJ GMBH	400	9144	4088
1/12/2004	CDE INC.	300	6267	2541
1/14/2004	OPQ, INC.	100	1740	847
1/14/2004	OPQ, INC.	100	2401	1022
1/14/2004	RST INC.	1000	19110	8470
1/15/2004	MNO COR	500	9345	4235
1/16/2004	WXY, CO	600	11628	5082
1/16/2004	RST INC.	900	21888	9198
1/17/2004	LMN INC.	300	5961	2952
1/19/2004	MNO COR	100	2042	984

Figure 129 *The header appears behind your document.*

PRINT MULTIPLE RANGES

Problem: I want to print five sections of my worksheet, but the print areas are not next to each other.

Strategy: Choose the first range to print and use Page Layout, Print Area, Set Print Area.

Choose the next range to print. This time, a new menu item is available. Choose Page Layout, Print Area, Add to Print Area.

You can continue adding additional ranges to the print area.

Gotcha: Unfortunately, Excel will add a page break between each section of the print area.

Figure 130 *Add non-adjacent print ranges.*

ADD A PAGE BREAK AT EACH CHANGE IN CUSTOMER

Problem: My data is sorted by customer in column A. I want to put each customer on a different page.

Strategy: The easiest way to do this is to add a subtotal by using the Data, Subtotals command. In the Subtotal dialog, you can choose to have a page break between groups. For more about subtotals, see "Add Subtotals to a Data set" on page 263.

However, let's assume that you cannot use the automatic Subtotals feature for some reason. It helps to understand page breaks.

Excel page breaks can either be automatic or manual. If you access Print Preview and then close Print Preview, Excel will draw in the automatic page breaks.

In this particular report, it turns out that with these margins and print size, Excel would normally offer an automatic page break after row 46. After you do a Print Preview, Excel draws in a dashed line after row 46 to indicate that this is an automatic page break.

	A	B	C	D	E	F
1	Customer	Region	Date	Quantity	Product	Revenue
43	Exxon	West	3-Apr-12	100	XYZ	2178
44	Exxon	East	8-Apr-12	500	DEF	12095
45	Exxon	East	22-Apr-12	300	ABC	5439
46	Exxon	Central	9-May-12	500	ABC	8785
47	Exxon	Central	10-May-12	500	XYZ	11000
48	Exxon	Central	20-May-12	100	XYZ	2149
49	Exxon	East	22-May-12	100	DEF	2319

Figure 131 *The dashed line is an automatic page break.*

You can add a manual page break to any row. You position the cell pointer in column A on the first row for a new customer and then select Page Layout, Breaks, Insert Page Break. Excel will draw in a dotted line above the cell pointer to indicate that there is a page break after row 8.

	A	B	C	D	E	F
1	Customer	Region	Date	Quantity	Product	Revenue
7	Ainsworth	East	23-Feb-12	1000	XYZ	20940
8	Ainsworth	East	1-Mar-12	400	XYZ	8620
9	Air Canada	West	30-Mar-12	300	ABC	5859
10	Air Canada	Central	18-Apr-12	200	XYZ	4948

Figure 132 *Slightly longer dashes indicate a manual page break.*

Here is a zoomed-in view of the different dashes used for each break. I am not sure the difference will even show up in the book or e-book.

Automatic:

Manual:

Because you've added a manual page break after row 8, Excel will automatically calculate that it can fit rows 9 through 54 on page 2. The location for the next automatic page break is now shown at row 55 instead of row 47.

Automatic page breaks will move around. Say that you change the margins for the page, using Page Layout, Margins. Excel will now calculate that the end of the second page is at another row.

Unlike automatic page breaks, manual page break will never move.

To add the rest of the page breaks, you move the cell pointer to the next cell in column A that has a new customer and select Page Layout, Breaks, Insert Page Break. Because you have 50 of these to insert, you might want to use the keyboard shortcut: Alt+I+B or Alt+P+B+I.

Additional Details: Selecting each new customer is tedious. Microsoft provides a shortcut for finding the next cell in the current column that is different from the active cell. However, it is difficult to use this shortcut. You will have to decide if it is worth the hassle. You start with the cell pointer on a customer. Then you press Ctrl+Shift+Down Arrow to select all the cells below the current cell. You press the F5 key and then click the Special button. Finally, you select Column Differences and click OK. The cell pointer will move to the first row that contains a new customer. You can then use the Breaks, Insert Page Break command. You can repeat this whole series of events by holding down the Alt key while you type EGSM. Release the Alt key and press Enter. Hold down the Alt key while you type IB. If you have hundreds of page breaks to add, mastering this keystroke might be worth the time.

Additional Details: These steps might be easier than the above. Insert a new column A. The formula in A3 is =IF(B3=B2,1,True). Copy this formula down to all rows. Select column A. Press F5, then click Special. In the Go To Special dialog, choose Formulas. Uncheck Numbers, Text, and Errors, leaving only Logicals selected. Click OK. Do Alt+I+B to insert a break at the first customer. Press Enter to move to the next customer. Press F4 to repeat the last command (insert break). Continue pressing Enter, F4, Enter, F4 until you reach the bottom. You can then delete column A.

Additional Details: To remove a manual page break, you should put the cell pointer in the first cell under the manual page break. When the cell pointer is in this location, the Breaks dropdown offers a Remove Page Break option.

To remove all page breaks, you select all cells by using the box to the left of column A. The Breaks dropdown will now offer the option Reset All Page Breaks.

Gotcha: To insert a row page break, you must either select the entire row or have the cell pointer in column A. If you select Insert Page Break while in cell C9, Excel will insert a horizontal page break above row 9 and also a vertical page break to the left of column C. This is rarely what you want.

SAVE MY WORKSHEET AS A PDF FILE

Problem: I want to send my worksheet to a high-level manager, but I don't want him screwing around with the formulas. Can I send it as a PDF file?

Excel will let you save your workbooks as PDF files. In Excel 2013, use File, Export, Create PDF/XPS. In Excel 2010, use File, Save & Send, Create PDF/XPS Document, Create PDF/XPS Document. (That's not a typo, you have to click two different icons that say the same thing.)

Think of Saving as PDF as if you are printing the workbook to a PDF file. In the Publish as PDF or XPS dialog, you can click the Options button to control if you want the selection, active sheets, or entire workbook sent to the PDF file.

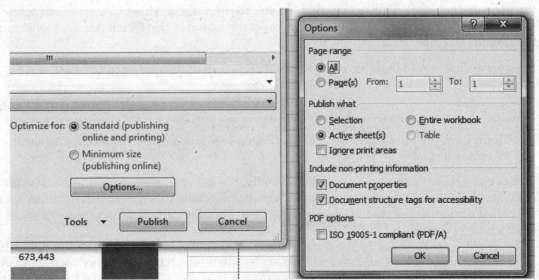

Figure 133 *Print your workbooks to PDF.*

Let's face it. People send you PDF files when they don't want you screwing around with their data. But, let's be truthful here: You need to screw around with that data.

If you have ever tried to select data from a PDF file, copy it, and paste it to Excel, you know that there are three basic kinds of PDF files:

- Files that paste amazingly well to Excel
- Files that paste a table into a single column
- Files where the text and numbers have been converted to an image so that you can't copy and paste to Excel

You would think that a PDF file created by Microsoft Excel would automatically create a file that would round-trip beautifully to Excel. Unfortunately, they use the second type of file that will not paste nicely back into Excel. This isn't as evil as converting everything to images, but it is almost as bad.

Ironically, if you copy the PDF file, paste to Word, then copy from Word and paste to Excel, the results are better. (How many times have you ever heard *me* suggest that you open Word?) If you have Word 2013, you can natively open the PDF in Word, then copy to Excel.

If you have to regularly take data from PDF files to Excel or Word, I highly recommend a product called Able2Extract from InvestInTech. You can get a free 30-day trial to try it out. The standard version handles either of the first two types of PDF files. The deluxe version can also handle PDF files where everything has been converted to an image. For more details, see www.mrexcel.com/tip107.shtml.

SEND AN EXCEL FILE AS AN ATTACHMENT

Problem: I need to send my currently open Excel workbook as an attachment to an Outlook e-mail message.

Strategy: You can select File, Save and Send, Send Using E-Mail, Send As Attachment.

Excel will open something that looks a lot like the Outlook Send Mail dialog. Fill out the addressee list and the subject line and click Send.

Gotcha: Although this looks like Outlook, it is actually an Excel version of the dialog. While this dialog is displayed, you cannot access other Outlook e-mails. This can be a problem. What if you receive a file from someone not in your address book, edit the file, and then need to send it back? You will find that you need to access the original e-mail to get the sender's e-mail address, but you cannot switch to another e-mail message until you've sent this one.

The solution is to click the Save icon in the Outlook Quick Access Toolbar. Then click the Close Window (X) icon in the upper-right corner of the window. The unfinished e-mail will be saved from Excel to the Outlook inbox, and you will be returned to Excel. You can now safely switch back to the original Outlook e-mail to get the address.

Additional Details: In previous versions of Excel, you had the option to send the current worksheet in the body of an e-mail. This option enabled you to send a worksheet to a recipient who did not have Excel. That original command is still in Excel, you can customize the Quick Access toolbar and find the icon in the Commands Not in the Ribbon section.

A better option would be to save the worksheet as a PDF file and send the PDF file.

SAVE EXCEL DATA AS A TEXT FILE

Problem: I am working with an Excel file. I need to produce a file for another application to read, but that application can read only .txt files.

Strategy: You have a couple options. Typically, the other application will either want the columns to be separated by a fixed number of spaces or separated by commas. Files with columns separated by commas are called comma-separated values, or CSV, files. CSV files are easier to create than space-separated files. Here's how you create a CSV file:

1. Select File, Save As. In the Save as Type dropdown, choose CSV (Comma delimited) (*.csv).
2. Click the Save button. Excel will generally warn you that you are saving the file in a format that will leave out incompatible features. This means that you should re-save the file as an Excel file later in

order to keep the compatible features. Important: Only the current worksheet is saved in the CSV file. If you have multiple worksheets in the workbook, save each worksheet separately.

3. After saving the file as CSV, use Save As to save the file as an Excel file.

Results: The figure below shows the created file as it appears when edited with Notepad. Pay particular attention to the "Molson, Inc" entry. Because cell D5 already contained a comma, Excel was smart enough to surround Molson, Inc with quotation marks.

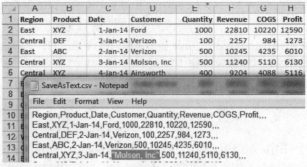

Figure 134 *Excel adds quotes around a cell that contains a comma.*

Gotcha: The dates in column C are written to the file in the same format as they were shown on the worksheet. Most programs will not understand a date such as 1-Jan-04. Check the documentation of the program that will import the information, and if you need to, format column C to appear as mm/dd/yyyy before exporting to CSV.

Alternate Strategy: Another option is to create a file in which each field is supposed to take a fixed number of characters. You might need to use this method to produce a file which is to be imported by another application. In this case, the other application will usually give you a file specification for you to follow. It might indicate the following:

Field Name	Start	Length	Decimals
Region	1	12	
Product	13	10	
Date	23	10	
Customer	33	20	
Quantity	53	8	0
Revenue	61	10	2
COGS	71	10	2
Profit	81	10	2

In this case, you follow these steps:

1. Go through the columns in the worksheet, resetting the column widths. If the other program expects the Region field to be 12 characters wide, for example, select column A and then choose Home, Format, Column Width and set the Column Width text box to 12.
2. Format the dates as specified by the other system. Make sure the Revenue, Cost, and Profit columns show two decimal places. The other system probably will not want field headings, so delete row 1.
3. Select File, Save As. In the Save as Type dropdown, select Formatted Text (Space Delimited).

Gotcha: Excel changes the file name so that it has a .prn extension. Even if you try to change the extension to .txt here, Excel will still save the file with the extension .prn. It is best to leave it as .prn and then rename it in Windows Explorer.

4. When Excel warns you that you will lose features if you have multiple sheets, click Yes.

The figure below shows the resulting file, viewed in Notepad.

```
SaveAsText.prn - Notepad
File  Edit  Format  View  Help
East      XYZ       01/01/14Ford               1000   22810.00   10220.00   12590.00
Central   DEF       01/02/14Verizon             100    2257.00     984.00    1273.00
East      ABC       01/02/14Verizon             500   10245.00    4235.00    6010.00
Central   XYZ       01/03/14Molson, Inc         500   11240.00    5110.00    6130.00
Central   XYZ       01/04/14Ainsworth           400    9204.00    4088.00    5116.00
East      DEF       01/04/14Gildan Activewear   800   18552.00    7872.00   10680.00
```

Figure 135 *Data is neatly aligned in columns..*

USE A LASER PRINTER TO HAVE EXCEL CALCULATE FASTER

Problem: How can I speed up my Excel calculations?

Strategy: Believe it or not, Excel uses your print driver to draw the screen. Having an HP LaserJet as your default printer can enable Excel operations to finish in one-fourth the time it takes if you have a cheap inkjet driver as the default. If response time is critical, you can download and install the printer driver for an HP LaserJet and set it as your default printer during calculations. You don't need to actually have an HP LaserJet—you just need the driver.

Gotcha: If you don't actually have an HP LaserJet printer hooked to your computer, you will have to refrain from using the Quick Print icon and instead print using File, Print and choosing a non-default printer.

CLOSE ALL OPEN WORKBOOKS

Problem: I have 22 Excel Workbooks open. I want to keep Excel open but close all the workbooks. Excel no longer has a Close All icon on the ribbon, and selecting File, Close 22 times can get monotonous.

Strategy: You can add a Close All button to your Quick Access toolbar. Follow these steps:
1. Right-click the Quick Access toolbar and choose Customize Quick Access Toolbar.
2. In the left dropdown, choose Commands Not in the Ribbon.
3. Find the Close All item in the left list. Select Close All. Click the Add button to add the icon to the Quick Access toolbar. Click OK to close the Excel Options dialog.

Results: The Close All icon will be available on the Quick Access toolbar. When you click this icon, Excel will still individually ask you about any unsaved documents. However, it is a faster way of closing all open workbooks than manually closing each one.

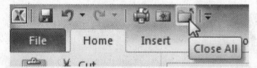

Figure 136 *Close All, but keep Excel open.*

Gotcha: The Close and Close All icons look the same in the Quick Access toolbar. If you want to have both Close and Close All, add them to the Excel ribbon so that the label will appear for each icon.

Additional Details: If your workbooks are unsaved, Excel will ask you if you want to save each one. Here is a cool trick: hold down the shift key while clicking Don't Save. Excel will repeat that answer for all of the remaining workbooks.

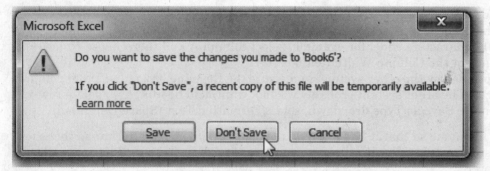

Figure 137 *Shift while clicking to apply the answer to all workbooks.*

I JUST CLOSED AN UNSAVED WORKBOOK

Problem: I had 20 budget files open and I used the previous trick to close all workbooks. I used shift-click on Don't Save to close all without saving. But then I realized that I also had another file opened that I needed to save.

Strategy: If you are in Excel 2010 or later, you might be able to recover that file. You have to meet all of these criteria:
- You have to be using Excel 2010

- The file has to be old enough to have been AutoSaved
- The file must never have been saved (i.e. it is still called Book7 or something like that.

When you realize that you closed Excel and did not save the workbook, follow these steps:
1. Open Excel.
2. Open the File menu and go to the Recent Documents.
3. At the bottom of the right panel, use the Open Recent Documents icon.

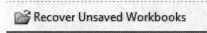

Figure 138 *Find this at the bottom of Recent Places.*

Gotcha: The Recover Unsaved Workbooks feature only handles the workbooks that had never been saved.

As a test, I just closed the workbook from the next topic without saving. When I look at the unsaved documents, I have four books from the last week. None of them are the workbook from 2:10 PM on May 25.

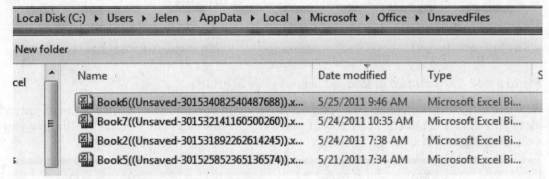

Figure 139 *Microsoft saved four workbooks that I didn't think were important.*

Here's why: the workbook had been saved previously with a real file name. It will not appear in this list. But, you still have hope!

Instead, you should open the last saved version of that workbook. Then, go to File, Info, Manage Versions. The unsaved version of that file could be available there.

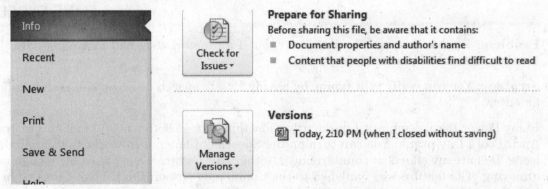

Figure 140 *This is good...the unsaved version is still available.*

You should click on the unsaved version to open it in read-only mode. The message bar will tell you that it is a temporary version.

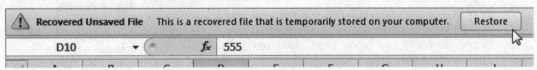

Figure 141 *Examine the workbook to make sure it is better than the last saved version.*

If this workbook is the one you want to keep, click Restore. After you confirm, the workbook will overwrite the saved version.

ROLL BACK TO AN AUTOSAVED VERSION

Problem: I need to roll back to an AutoSaved version. I screwed up something that I can not fix with the 64 levels of Undo.

Strategy: Go to the Excel File menu and choose the Info pane. If any autosaved versions are available, they will be listed under versions.

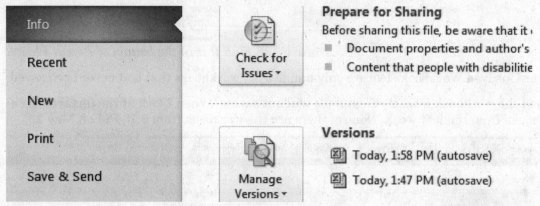

Figure 142 *The last two autosaved versions are available.*

Additional Details: When you open an AutoSaved version, it will open as read only. The info pane will alert you that it is not the most recent version. The message bar in Excel will allow you to make that version the current version.

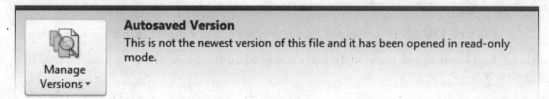

HAVE EXCEL TALK TO YOU

Problem: I have many numbers to enter, but I am notoriously bad at keying data. How can I get my numbers into Excel accurately?

Strategy: You can verify your typing by having Excel's speech utility speak each number as you complete an entry.

In my Power Excel seminars, I frequently show this trick as both a useful tool for proofreading and a great April Fool's Day prank: You can turn on the Speech option on a co-worker's computer and then hide the icons. Despite my efforts at popularizing it, either this feature wasn't used by enough people or it was too annoying. The feature was banished to the Commands Not on the Ribbon category in the Quick Access toolbar customization dialog. To use the Text to Speech option, you have to add the icons to the Quick Access toolbar. To do so, follow these steps:

1. Right-click the ribbon and choose Customize the Quick Access Toolbar. In the left dropdown, choose Commands Not in the Ribbon.
2. Scroll down to the icons that start with S. Locate and click on Speak Cells.
3. Click the Add>> button five times to move the Speak Cells icons to the QAT.

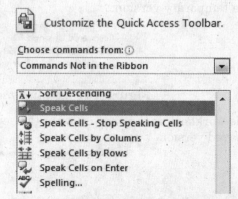

You can now select a range of cells and click the Speak Cells icon. Excel will read you the cells, so you can focus on the original paper from which you're keying the data.

Figure 143 *Add these icons to the QAT.*

Gotcha: If you accidentally select a million cells and ask Excel to speak the cells, you can click the Stop Speaking Cells icon to stop Excel from reading the cells. (I've worked for a couple managers who should have had this button on their forehead.)

Additional Details: You can choose whether Excel should read a rectangular range column by column or row by row by using the Speak Cells by Columns or Speak Cells by Rows icons.

The Speak on Enter icon is a fun icon. Imagine that your co-worker heads out to lunch on April Fool's Day. You could add the Speak on Enter icon to the Quick Access toolbar, turn on this feature, and then remove the icon from the Quick Access toolbar. Your co-worker returns from lunch, starts typing, and is perplexed to find that the computer starts repeating everything he types, reminiscent of the computer on *Star Trek*.

Gotcha: Be careful if you have kids in middle school. I showed some this feature, and they very quickly demonstrated that Excel knows how to say all words, including bad ones!

Additional Details: Visit Control Panel, Speech to make Excel talk faster.

ENTER SPECIAL SYMBOLS

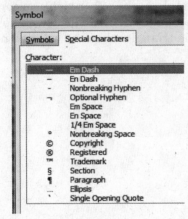

Figure 144 *Look at both tabs.*

Problem: I work in the music business, and I routinely have to enter copyright symbols. How can I do so easily?

Strategy: You can enter (c) followed by a space as a shortcut for the © symbol. You can use (r) for the registered trademark symbol, ®. For other special symbols, you can use Insert, Symbol to display the Symbol dialog.

You simply select any symbol from the Symbol dialog and choose Insert to type the symbol in the cell.

WHAT DO ALL THE TRIANGLES MEAN?

Problem: In "Find Text Entries," you described the green triangles. What are the red triangles and purple triangles that sometimes appear in my worksheets?

Strategy: Each color of triangle serves a different purpose.

The red triangles in the top-right corners of cells are comment indicators. Where you see one of these, someone used Review, New Comment to add a bit of explanatory text to a cell. If you hover over a red indicator, Excel will display the comment, as shown below. If the red indicators are bothering you, use File, Options, Advanced, Display, For Cells with Comment, Show No Comments or Indicators. For more information, see "Leave Helpful Notes with Cell Comments" on page 493.

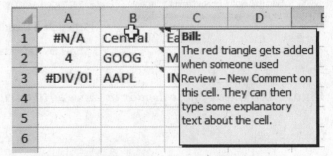

Figure 145 *Red triangles are cell comments.*

The green triangle appears in the top left of a cell. This indicator appears whenever Excel thinks you might have made an error. This figure shows the complete list of errors. You can control which errors are flagged by selecting File, Options, Formulas, Error Checking.

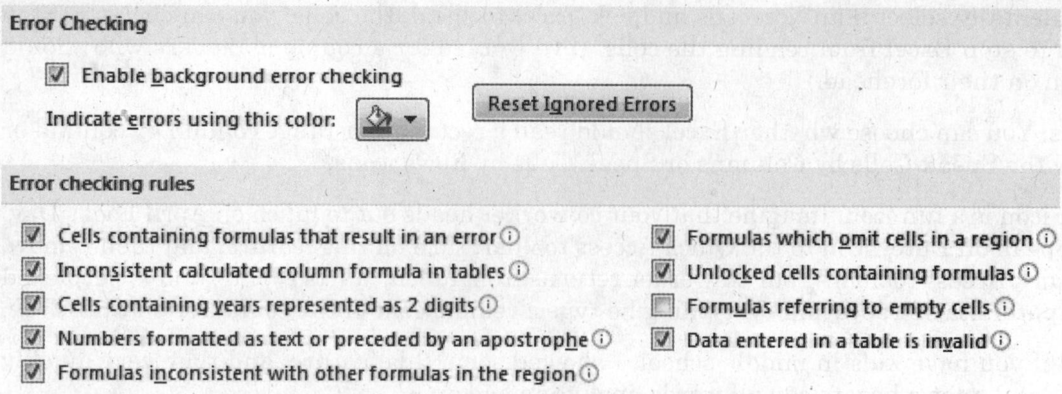

Error Checking

☑ Enable background error checking

Indicate errors using this color: [🎨 ▼]   [Reset Ignored Errors]

Error checking rules

☑ Cells containing formulas that result in an error ⓘ   ☑ Formulas which omit cells in a region ⓘ

☑ Inconsistent calculated column formula in tables ⓘ   ☑ Unlocked cells containing formulas ⓘ

☑ Cells containing years represented as 2 digits ⓘ   ☐ Formulas referring to empty cells ⓘ

☑ Numbers formatted as text or preceded by an apostrophe ⓘ   ☑ Data entered in a table is invalid ⓘ

☑ Formulas inconsistent with other formulas in the region ⓘ

Figure 146 *You can choose which errors Excel should mark.*

Additional Details: Errors are usually flagged with green triangles, but as you can see above, you can change the color used to flag errors. The indicator will always appear in the top left of the cell; you cannot change its position.

Back in Excel 2007, financial symbols would often have a purple triangle in the lower-right corner of the cell. If you open that icon, Excel would offer to insert a stock price in an adjacent cell. The downside to this was that many text values such as TRUE or COST would get a purple triangle when the cell had nothing to do with a stock symbol.

If you still want this functionality in Excel 2010, follow these steps:
1. Type Alt+T+A to display the AutoCorrect dialog.
2. Choose the Actions tab.
3. Choose Enable Additional Actions In the Right-Click Menu.
4. Click OK.

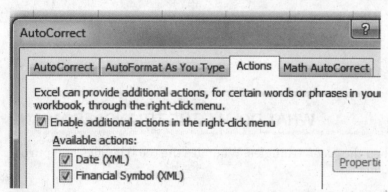

Figure 147 *You have to turn the old SmartTags on.*

When you choose a cell with a financial symbol, right-click the cell. From the bottom of the dropdown, choose Additional Cell Actions.

The actions available for a date now include checking your calendar in Outlook.

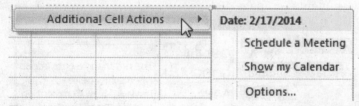

Figure 148 *Check your calendar in Office 2010 by right-clicking a date.*

WHY DOES EXCEL INSERT CELL ADDRESSES WHEN I EDIT IN A REFEDIT BOX?

Problem: There are a few maddening dialog boxes in Excel. Say that you define a name and later need to edit that name. Click somewhere in the RefEdit box. When you press the left or right arrow key to move to another part of the cell, Excel starts inserting cell references.

Here is an example:

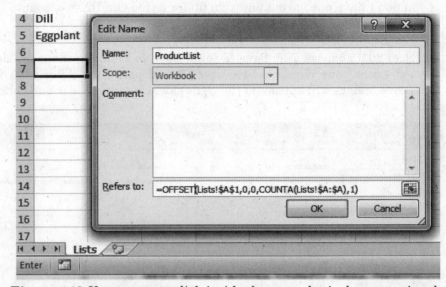

Figure 149 *You meant to click inside the parenthesis, but you missed.*

When you press the right arrow key to move the flashing insertion point after the address, Excel starts inserting cell references. The only action between the figure above and the one below is pressing the right arrow.

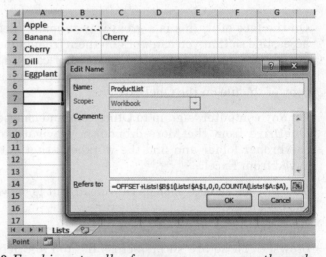

Figure 150 *Excel inserts cell references as you arrow through.*

This is maddening! The solution is very simple, though. Before you touch the arrow keys in a RefEdit box, press F2. You will see the status indicator in the lower left corner of Excel change from Enter or Point to Edit. Once you are in Edit mode, you can use arrow keys.

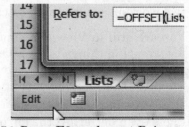

Figure 151 *Press F2 to change Point to Edit. Problem solved.*

EDIT YOUR EXCEL WORKBOOKS ON THE WEB

Problem: I am visiting my aunt today. I got a call from work and I have to change the assumptions in one of my Excel workbooks. My aunt doesn't have Excel.

Strategy: You can edit your Excel workbooks using the Excel Web App.

If you don't have one, go out and sign up for a free OneDrive account

In Excel 2013, the Save As dialog offers your OneDrive as a place to save.

In Excel 2010, choose File, Save & Send, Save to Web. On the right side of the Backstage view, you will have to enter your Windows Live user ID and password. After you've signed in to Windows Live, your OneDrive folders will appear on the right side. Choose a folder and click the Save As icon on the right side of the screen.

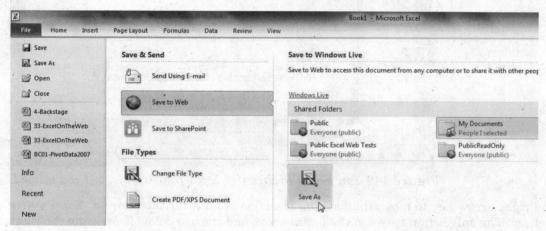

Figure 152 *Save to your OneDrive account.*

On the face of it, this is a great way to make files accessible so that you can work on them from home or on your next business trip. Instead of carrying flash drives back and forth, you can simply keep a copy of the file on the OneDrive.

On any computer, sign in to Office.com and choose OneDrive from the More dropdown. Navigate to the proper folder and find the workbook that you saved from Excel.

You will see choices such as Download, but for now choose View.

The results are shown in the figure here. This is a browser! Those are slicers across the top and left side. That is a pivot table and a chart. At the bottom left of the screen, you will see that there are two worksheet tabs that you can access.

You are still in View Only mode, but you can do a few amazing things in View Only mode. Try selecting new items from the slicers. In a few seconds, the pivot table and pivot chart update!

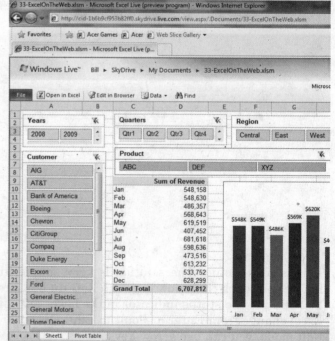

Figure 153 *A workbook rendered in a browser.*

It gets even better. At the top of the screen, choose Edit in Browser.

A ribbon appears above the worksheet with File, Home, Insert, Data, Review, and View.

In edit mode, I typed new labels in J2:J5, some numbers in K2:K4, and a PMT formula in K5. I then formatted cell K5 using formatting commands on the Home tab.

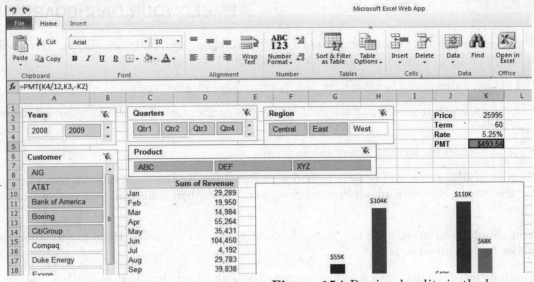

Figure 154 *Do simple edits in the browser.*

All the while, this feels remarkably like Excel. I tried entering the formula using the mouse and tried entering the formula using the arrow keys to point to the other cells.

Some limitations apply as to what you can do in the browser, but there are an amazing number of things that you can do in the browser. A new version of the Excel Web App is released every four months, so the limitations are getting fewer.

You cannot enter a new array formula, but the browser will calculate array formulas that were entered previously. You can adjust row height and column widths. If you have data that is larger than will fit in a cell, you can merge cells so that the entire value will appear.

This is a fairly miraculous browser experience.

If you make changes in the browser, they are automatically saved. When you get back to work, you can open the OneDrive version from your Recent Files list. It all works amazingly well.

CREATE AN ONLINE SURVEY IN EXCEL

Problem: I need to survey a bunch of people and get the results in Excel.

Strategy: The Excel Web App makes this simple. Go to OneDrive.Live.com. Open a new blank workbook. On the Insert tab, choose Survey, New Survey.

A new box pops up. Enter a survey title and subtitle. Build new questions. The survey supports a number of answer types, including Yes/No, Multiple Choice, text.

When you are done, click the Share Survey button. Then Create Link. Then Shorten Link. To try this survey, go to http://1drv.ms/1toyhth.

Get a link to your survey "Power Excel with MrExcel Survey"

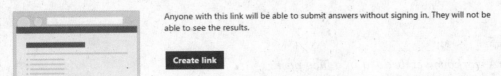

Figure 155 *Create an easy online survey.*

Share the link, and wait for the answers to roll in to your Excel Online spreadsheet:

Figure 156 *Each recipients results get loaded into your online workbook.*

EMBED YOUR DASHBOARD IN A BLOG POST

Problem: I've built an amazing Excel application. It has charts. It has slicers. The whole world would love this app. I need to be able to update this daily, but yet share it.

Strategy: Files saved to OneDrive can be embedded in a web page.

Create an account at Office.com. Add a new folder there to hold the application. Share that folder with everyone.

Save the Excel file to that folder on the OneDrive.

Sign in to Office.com and browse to find your Excel file. To the right of your Excel file is a More dropdown. Choose More, Share, Embed. You will be given the Embed code that you can put in a blog post or a web page.

You should plan on editing the embed code to allow interactivity. Here are all the changes that you can make to the embed code:

To allow interactivity, find &AllowInteractivity=False and change it to &AllowInteractivity=True.

If you want the people reading your blog to type new values in the worksheet, use: &AllowInteractivity=True&AllowTyping=True.

If you want to display a specific region of the worksheet, you can add a named range to the workbook before you save it. Then, add this to the embed code: &Item=MyNamedRange. If the range name includes special characters, you will have to use URL encoding. P&LRange would become P%26LRange. If in doubt, don't use punctuation in your range name!

If you want a specific cell to start as the active cell, use &ActiveCell='Sheet1'!A5.

You can change the size of the frame. The frame always starts at 402 pixels wide by 346 pixels tall, which will cause scrollbars in a large worksheet. Edit the embed code width="600" height="800" frameborder="0" scrolling="yes".

Here is a simple Excel app that I pasted in my blog during the Learn Excel podcast episode 1378.

Excel worksheet in a web page. I will attempt to embed an Excel range here during the episode.

Pricing Bidding War		
List Price	1500	
COGS	279	
Current Proposal Price	750	
Discount %	50.0%	
Gross Profit	471	
GP%	62.8%	
Give 'em another:	10%	discount from list
New Discount	60.0%	
New Proposal Price	600	
New Gross Profit	321	
New GP%	53.5%	
Profit Dropped by:	31.8%	

Figure 157 *A workbook embedded in a blog post.*

To see a demo of embedding, search the Internet for Learn Excel 1378.

SORT, FILTER, CHART YOUR HTML TABLES

If you maintain a website, you probably have some HTML tables filled with data. Wouldn't it be cool to provide a way for your website visitors to sort, filter, and chart that table? The Excel Interactive View is a tiny bit of code that you paste into your web page.

When the visitor to your website clicks the Excel Interactive View button, they will be able to sort, filter, and chart the data.

To see this amazing tool in action, visit: http://www.mrexcel.com/exceleverywhere.html.

To learn how to add the button to your own web page, visit http://www.excelmashup.com/

PRINT ALL EXCEL KEYBOARD SHORTCUTS

Problem: Is there a complete list of keyboard shortcuts?

Strategy: There are many lists floating around the Internet, but the easiest source is right in Excel help.

Click the blue question mark at the top right corner of Excel. Search Excel help for "Keyboard Shortcuts". The resulting article lists all of the keyboard shortcuts. Use the Print icon at the top to print them.

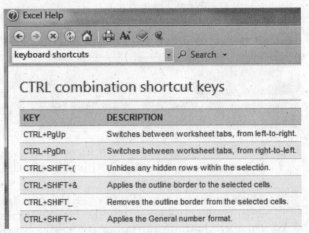

Figure 158 *This Excel help article lists all Excel keyboard shortcuts.*

Or, copy and paste to Excel. After adjusting column widths, you will have a worksheet of the shortcuts.

	A	B
23	CTRL+'	Copies a formula from the cell above the active cell into the cell or the Formula Bar.
24	CTRL+1	Displays the Format Cells dialog box.
25	CTRL+2	Applies or removes bold formatting.
26	CTRL+3	Applies or removes italic formatting.
27	CTRL+4	Applies or removes underlining.
28	CTRL+5	Applies or removes strikethrough.
29	CTRL+6	Alternates between hiding and displaying objects.
30	CTRL+8	Displays or hides the outline symbols.
31	CTRL+9	Hides the selected rows.
32	CTRL+0	Hides the selected columns.

Figure 159 *KeyboardShortcuts.xlsm is in download files for this book.*

GET FREE EXCEL HELP

Problem: I have a question which is not answered in this book.

Strategy: A large community of Excel fans are available at the MrExcel.com message board. Collectively, they answer over 30,000 questions each year. Follow these steps:

1. Browse to www.MrExcel.com
2. In the left navigation bar, choose Message Board
3. In the top right corner, click the link to Register. Registration is free. The site used to allow anonymous postings, but it became too confusing when two people named "anonymous" started participating in a conversation.
4. As you register, a question asks you to confirm that you are 13 or older. Please choose this appropriately, or you will not be able to post.

5. Click the appropriate forum. Most Excel questions, including macro programming questions, should go in the Excel Questions forum.

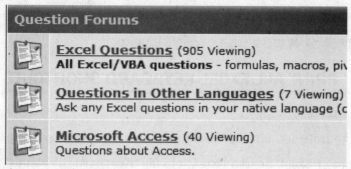

Figure 160 *Choose Excel Questions.*

6. Click the New Thread.

Figure 161 *Start a new question thread.*

7. Use a meaningful subject. "Pivot Table Calculated Fields" is a good subject. "Help" or "Please Help" is not a good subject.

8. Type your question. Read over the question to make sure that someone who has not been dealing with your spreadsheet for the last hour can get a good sense of the meaning.

9. Click the Submit button at the bottom of the form.

Within a minute, your question will appear in the forum. Other readers will check out the question. Usually within 15 minutes, someone will either post a clarifying question or a suggestion on how to proceed. If someone asks a question, provide the best answer that you can.

Usually, within a few iterations of questions, you will have your answer. Sometimes, if the question is particularly interesting, a discussion will break out over the best way to solve the problem.

Additional Details: Over 750,000 answers are archived and searchable. Before posting your question, spend a few minutes searching to see if the problem has already been solved.

PART 2

CALCULATING WITH EXCEL

START A FORMULA WITH = OR +

Problem: Every Excel formula has to start with an equals sign. There is no equals sign on the numeric keypad. It's a pain to type the equals sign.

Strategy: In order to make the transition from Lotus 1-2-3 to Excel less painful, Microsoft allows you to start a formula with the + sign. Because there is a huge plus key on the numeric keypad of most desktop computers, it is often easier to start the formula with plus than with equals, especially if you're entering the rest of your formula using arrow keys. You simply type the plus sign and your formula.

	D	E	F	G	H	I
	SUM			X ✔ fx	+H2/F2	
1	Customer	Quantity	Revenue	COGS	Profit	GP%
2	Ford	1000	22810	10220	12590	+H2/F2
3	Verizon	100	2257	984	1273	
4	Verizon	500	10245	4235	6010	

Figure 162 *Start a Formula with = or +*

Gotcha: After you press the Enter key, Excel will edit the formula to add an equals sign before the initial plus. This will cause people to ask why you are using =+2+2 instead of just =2+2.

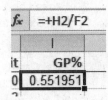

fx	=+H2/F2
	I
it	GP%
0	0.551951

Figure 163 *Excel accepts the formula, but adds an equals sign.*

THREE METHODS OF ENTERING FORMULAS

Problem: I'd like to enter formulas faster. What are the three ways of entering simple formulas?

Strategy: There are three ways of entering formulas. Learning the arrow key method will dramatically improve your efficiency with Excel. This topic will compare all three methods.

Say that you want to calculate total cost in E3 as the case quantity in B3 multiplied by the unit cost in C3.

	A	B	C	D	E
1					
2	Item	Case Pack	Unit Cost	Unit Price	Total Cost
3	ABC	6	6.06	11.95	
4	DEF	6	6.18	13.45	
5	GHI	24	8.35	17.65	

Figure 164 *Calculate unit cost times case pack.*

One way to make this calculation is to simply type the formula:

1. Put the cell pointer in E3 and type =b3*c3 and then press Enter.

	A	B	C	D	E
1					
2	Item	Case Pack	Unit Cost	Unit Price	Total Cost
3	ABC	6	6.06	11.95	=b3*c3
4	DEF	6	6.18	13.45	

Figure 165 *Typing takes only seven keystrokes.*

2. The formula will calculate. You will see the original formula in the formula bar above E1. The worksheet will show the result of the calculation.

E3	▼		f_x	=B3*C3		

	A	B	C	D	E	F
1						
2	Item	Case Pack	Unit Cost	Unit Price	Total Cost	Tot Pri
3	ABC	6	6.06	11.95	36.36	
4	DEF	6	6.18	13.45		

Figure 166 *After pressing Enter, Excel calculates the formula.*

This method is great for short functions that require only a few keystrokes. However, this method gets complicated when you are dealing with complex formulas.

Alternate Strategy: Another way to enter calculations is to use the arrow keys. Anyone who was using spreadsheets in the days of Lotus 1-2-3 often used this method. When you have mastered this method, it is very fast and very intuitive. Here's how it works:

1. Move the cell pointer to E3 and type an equals sign to let Excel know that you are about to enter a formula.
2. Press the Left Arrow key. As shown in Figure 167, a dotted border surrounds the cell to the left of E3. Excel starts to build the formula =D3.

	A	B	C	D	E	F
2	Item	Case Pack	Unit Cost	Unit Price	Total Cost	T P
3	ABC	6	6.06	11.95	=D3	
4	DEF	6	6.18	13.45		

Figure 167 *Type equals, press left arrow.*

3. Press the Left Arrow key two more times. Your provisional formula is now =B3.

SUM	▼	●	✕ ✓ f_x	=B3	

	A	B	C	D	E
2	Item	Case Pack	Unit Cost	Unit Price	Total Cost
3	ABC	6	6.06	11.95	=B3
4	DEF	6	6.18	13.45	

Figure 168 *Press left arrow two more times.*

4. Press * on either the keyboard or the numeric keypad. The dotted border will disappear from B3 and be replaced by a solid-colored border. Pressing any operator key, such as +, -, *, or /, tells Excel that you are moving on to the next part of the formula.

	A	B	C	D	E	
2	Item	Case Pack	Unit Cost	Unit Price	Total Cost	
3	ABC	6	6.06	11.95	=B3*	
4	DEF	6	6.18	13.45		

Figure 169 *Typing an operator returns focus to E3.*

5. Press the Left Arrow key two times. The dotted border reappears. You now have a provisional formula of =B3*C3.

	A	B	C	D	E
		Case			Total
2	Item	Pack	Unit Cost	Unit Price	Cost
3	ABC	6	6.06	11.95	=B3*C3

Figure 170 *Left arrow twice.*

6. Press Enter. The formula will calculate. You will see the original formula in the formula bar above E1. The worksheet will show the result of the calculation.

Additional Details: With this method, you never have to type cell references. You merely point to them using the arrow keys. If you are building formulas that are based on cells near the formula cell, you can enter them very quickly using this method.

Although I used several paragraphs and five screen shots to show this method, it required only eight key-strokes, many of which were repeats of the same keystroke. Further, because you are allowed to start a formula with a plus sign instead of an equals sign, you can enter the entire formula using the keys on and around the numeric keypad on a desktop computer (that is, +←←←*←←Enter).

Alternate Strategy: Another way to enter calculations in Excel is to use the mouse. Normally, people use the keyboard to type the equals sign, math operators, and enter and the mouse to click on cell references. Moving your hand from the mouse to the keyboard takes a lot of time and dramatically slows the entry of formulas. Adding a few icons to your Quick Access toolbar can dramatically speed formula entry. Follow these steps.

1. Using steps from "Make Your Most-Used Icons Always Visible" on page 20, add icons for equals, plus, minus, multiply, divide, exponents, left parenthesis, and right parenthesis to the Quick Access Toolbar. These icons are found in the "Commands Not in the Ribbon" category.
2. Right-click the Quick Access Toolbar and choose Show Quick Access Toolbar Below the Ribbon.

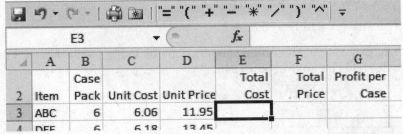

Figure 171 *Add these icons to the QAT.*

3. Start in cell E3. Click the equals sign icon.
4. Click on cell B3 with the mouse.
5. Click on the * sign in the QAT
6. Click on cell C3 with the mouse.
7. Click the checkmark icon to the left of the formula bar to accept your formula.

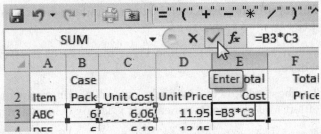

Figure 172 *Complete the formula with the checkmark.*

8. The formula will calculate. You will see the original formula in the formula bar above E1. The worksheet will show the result of the calculation.

There are three basic methods for entering formulas in Excel. Using the easiest method for the situation can radically improve your efficiency.

WHY DOES EXCEL 2013 LOOK LIKE A SLOT MACHINE?

When you type a number in Excel 2013, you will see all of the dependent cells in the visible window animate with the new result dropping in to the cell as if it were a slot machine.

This is one of those beginner features introduced in Excel 2013 to show new Excellers that when you type a value in one cell, Excel is going to the trouble of updating all of these other cells. It seems silly, doesn't it?

However, there is an expert use for this feature. Subconsciously, your mind will start to notice the cells that are not animating that should be. Perhaps one of those new Excellers added with a calculator instead of the AutoSum and hard-coded an answer. You can actually spot these when you notice the total is not animating.

USE PARENTHESES TO CONTROL THE ORDER OF CALCULATIONS

Problem: In what order does Excel perform calculations? For example, is 2+3*4 equal to 20 or 14?

Strategy: In Excel, if you do not use parentheses, the default order of calculations is as follows:
1. Unary minus operation
2. Exponents
3. Multiply and divide, left to right
4. Add and subtract, left to right

Thus, with the formula =5+4*-5^3/6, Excel will do the following:
1. Figure unary minus on -5.
2. Raise -5 to the third power (-5*-5*-5 = -125).
3. Do division and multiplication from left to right (4*-125 is -500. Then -500/6 is -83.3).
4. Add 5 (-83.3 + 5 is -78.3).

The answer will be -78.3.

You can control the order of operations by using parentheses. For example, the formula =(5+4)*-(5^(1/2)) will yield the answer -20.1246.

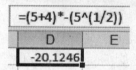

Figure 173 *Use parentheses to override the order of operations.*

Additional Details: In math class, you may remember that nested parentheses use regular parentheses, then square brackets, and then curly braces. In math class, you might have written:
{ (5+4)*[-5*(3/6)]}+3

Forget all that. In Excel, you use regular parentheses throughout.
((5+4)*(-5*(3/6)))+3

When you get the formula error message, it is often because you've missed a closing parenthesis somewhere.

The best trick is to watch the color of the last parenthesis. If it is black, then you have a balanced number of left and right parentheses. If it is any color, then you are missing a parenthesis.

Gotcha: As you enter or edit a formula, when you type a closing parenthesis, Excel bolds the corresponding opening parenthesis. However, this bolded condition lasts for only a moment and disappears before you can figure out what is going on.

LONG FORMULAS IN THE FORMULA BAR

Problem: In legacy versions of Excel a long formula would spill out of the formula bar, covering part of the grid. This is particularly annoying in row 1 because the formula covers the value from the formula.

Strategy: You can expand or collapse the formula bar. If you choose to expand the formula bar (with Ctrl+Shift+U), the grid actually shifts downward so that you can see the formula bar and the cell in the grid.

Here the formula bar is collapsed. You see only the first line of the formula.

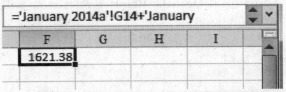

Figure 174 *Only one part of the formula appears.*

If you press Ctrl+Shift+U or click the down arrow icon at the right edge of the formula bar, Excel will shift the grid down and show more lines of the formula.

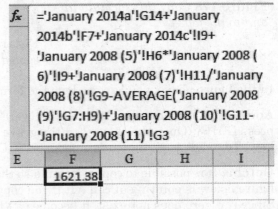

Figure 175 *Excel lowers the grid.*

Gotcha: With a particularly long formula, the formula might not fit in the expanded formula bar. Grab the bar at the bottom edge of the formula bar to make the formula bar even taller.

COPY A FORMULA THAT CONTAINS RELATIVE REFERENCES

Problem: I have 5,000 rows of data. After entering a formula to calculate gross profit percent for the first row, how do I copy the formula down to other rows?

G2			f_x	=IF(E2>0,1-F2/E2,"NA")		
	A	B	C	D	E	F	G
1	Region	Product	Date	Quantity	Unit Price	Unit Cost	GP%
2	East	XYZ	1/1/04	10000	22.81	10.22	55.2%
3	Central	DEF	1/2/04	1000	22.57	9.84	
4	East	ABC	1/2/04	5000	20.49	8.47	

Figure 176 *Copy a formula down to all rows.*

Strategy: All of the cell references in the figure above are known as relative references. The amazing thing about Excel is that when you copy a formula, all of the relative cell references are automatically adjusted. If you copy a formula from row 2 down to row 3, as shown below, then every relative reference pointing at row 2 will change to point to row 3.

=IF(E3>0,1-F3/E3,"NA")			
D	E	F	G
ntity	Unit Price	Unit Cost	GP%
0000	22.81	10.22	55.2%
1000	22.57	9.84	56.4%
5000	20.49	8.47	58.7%

Figure 177 *E2 changes to E3. F2 changes to F3.*

So, the solution to the problem is simply to copy the formula down to all the other rows. A shortcut for doing this is to select the cell and then double-click the fill handle to copy the formula down to all rows with values in the adjacent column. The fill handle is the square dot in the lower right corner of the selection rectangle.

Additional Details: Relative references will move in all four directions. In the figure below, if you copy the formula in cell E5 to D4, the referenced cell will change from D3 to C2 (up one cell, and one cell to the left).

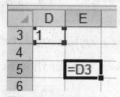

Figure 178 *Copy this formula up and to the left.*

▲	B	C	D	E	F
1					
2					
3			1		
4			=C2	=D2	=E2
5			=C3	=D3	=E3
6			=C4	=D4	=E4

Figure 179 *The original D3 reference changes as the formula is copied.*

In the figure above, you can see how the formula copied to nine other cells will change.

Additional Details: The figures above were shot in Show Formulas mode. To enter Show Formulas mode, press Ctrl+`. (On a U.S. keyboard the grave accent is on the same key as the tilde, ~, just below the Esc key.) To toggle back to regular mode, press Ctrl+` again.

Gotcha: It is possible to copy a formula so that it will point to a cell that does not exist. The formula in the figure below is pointing at cell A1. If you copy that formula up one row, it would need to point to row zero. Since row zero does not exist, it becomes a #REF! error.

▲	A	B	C
1	2		
2			
3			
4			=A1
5			

Figure 180 *This formula already points to the top row.*

▲	A	B	C
1	2		
2			
3		=#REF!	
4			=A1

Figure 181 *Copying the formula up will point to an invalid cell.*

The reference to A1 would have to point to the cell one row above and one column to the left of A1. That cell does not exist, so Excel will return a #REF error.

COPY A FORMULA WHILE KEEPING ONE REFERENCE FIXED

Problem: I have 5,000 rows of data. Each row contains a quantity and the unit price. The sales tax rate for all orders is shown in cell C1. After I enter a formula to calculate the total with sales tax in the first row, how do I copy the formula down to other rows?

`=ROUND((D4*E4)*C1,2)`

▲	C	D	E	F
1	106.5%			
2				
3	Date	Qty	Unit Price	Total
4	1/2/14	4	22.81	97.17
5	1/3/14	10	22.57	
6	1/3/14	8	20.49	
7	1/4/14	8	22.48	

Figure 182 *This formula works in row 4...*

If I copy the formula in F4 to F5, I get an invalid result of zero.

Look at the formula in the formula bar. As I copy the formula, the references to D4 and E4 changed as expected. However, the reference to C1 moved to C2. I need to find a way to copy this formula and always have the formula reference C1.

Note: This may be the most important technique in the entire book. I once had a manager who entered every formula in every data set by hand. I didn't have the heart to tell him there was an easier way

Strategy: You need to indicate to Excel that the reference to C1 in the formula is absolute. You do this by inserting a dollar sign before the C and before the 1 in the formula. For example, you would change the formula in F4 to =ROUND((D4*E4)*$C$1,2).

As you copy this formula down to other rows in your data set, the portion that refers to $C$1 will continue to point at $C$1, as shown below..

=ROUND((D5*E5)*C2,2)

	C	D	E	F
1	106.5%			
2				
3	Date	Qty	Unit Price	Total
4	1/2/14	4	22.81	97.17
5	1/3/14	10	22.57	0.00
6	1/3/14	8	20.49	######

Figure 183 *...but the formula fails in other rows.*

	C	D	E	F	G	H
1	106.5%					
2						
3	Date	Qty	Unit Price	Total		
4	1/2/14	4	22.81	97.17		
5	1/3/14	10	22.57	240.37		
6	1/3/14	8	20.49	174.57		
7	1/4/14	8	22.48	=ROUND((D7*E7)*$C$1,2)		
8	1/5/14	8	23.01	196.05		

Figure 184 *The dollar signs keep C1 pointing to C1,*

Additional Details: See "Create a Multiplication Table" below to learn the effect of using just one dollar sign in a reference instead of two. Read "Simplify the Entry of Dollar Signs in Formulas" on page 85 to learn a cool shortcut for entering the dollar signs automatically.

CREATE A MULTIPLICATION TABLE

Problem: I want to create a multiplication table to help my kids in school. I want to be able to enter a single formula in cell B2 that I can copy to the entire table.

	A	B	C	D	E	F	G	H	I	J	K	L	M
1		1	2	3	4	5	6	7	8	9	10	11	12
2	1												
3	2												
4	3												
5	4												
6	5												
7	6												
8	7												
9	8												
10	9												
11	10												
12	11												
13	12												

Figure 185 *Need a formula to point to row 1 and column 1.*

Strategy: In "Copy a Formula While Keeping One Reference Fixed," you learned how to use an absolute reference, such as $C$1, so that Excel would not change from column C or row 1 as it copied the formula. To create a multiplication table, you need to use a mixed reference. A mixed reference, such as $A2, will lock the formula to column A while allowing the row to change. A mixed reference, such as B$1, will lock the row to row 1 while allowing the column to change.

The formula you need for the multiplication table is a formula that will multiply whatever is in row 1 above the cell by whatever is in column A to the left of the cell.

To have a reference that always points to row 1, you use something in the format of B$1. To have a reference that points to column A, you use a reference in the format of $A2.

1. Enter the formula =$A2*B$1 in B2.

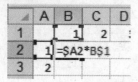

Figure 186 *Multiply column A by row 1.*

2. Copy the formula in B2 to the entire range.

Result: Excel will always properly multiply column A by row 1.

M13						*fx*	=$A13*M$1					
	A	B	C	D	E	F	G	H	I	J	K	L	M
1		1	2	3	4	5	6	7	8	9	10	11	12
2	1	1	2	3	4	5	6	7	8	9	10	11	12
3	2	2	4	6	8	10	12	14	16	18	20	22	24
4	3	3	6	9	12	15	18	21	24	27	30	33	36
5	4	4	8	12	16	20	24	28	32	36	40	44	48
6	5	5	10	15	20	25	30	35	40	45	50	55	60
7	6	6	12	18	24	30	36	42	48	54	60	66	72
8	7	7	14	21	28	35	42	49	56	63	70	77	84
9	8	8	16	24	32	40	48	56	64	72	80	88	96
10	9	9	18	27	36	45	54	63	72	81	90	99	108
11	10	10	20	30	40	50	60	70	80	90	100	110	120
12	11	11	22	33	44	55	66	77	88	99	110	121	132
13	12	12	24	36	48	60	72	84	96	108	120	132	144

Figure 187 *=$A13*M$1 creates the multiplication table.*

CALCULATE A SALES COMMISSION

Problem: The VP of sales in my company has dreamt up the most convoluted sales plan in the history of the world. Rather than just paying the reps a straight commission, this plan involves paying a base rate and a 2% bonus based on the product sold, and a monthly profit sharing bonus. For the spreadsheet below, I need to create a formula that can be copied to all rows and all months.

	A	B	C	D	E	F	G	H	I	J
1	**Base Rate**	2%		**Bonus Factor:**	102%	100%	104%			
3						SALES		COMMISSION		
5	**Rep**	**Product**	**Prod Rate**	**Customer**	**Jan**	**Feb**	**Mar**	**Jan**	**Feb**	**Mar**
6	Jones	ABC	5%	General Motors	15205	9039	13768			
7	Jones	DEF	8%	Molson, Inc.	18716	7023	9876			
8	Doe	DEF	8%	Verizon	11560	12456	15853			

Figure 188 *Perhaps the VP of sales designed the commission plan to test your knowledge of Excel!*

Strategy: This formula will contain all four reference types: relative, mixed, the other mixed, and absolute. While entering the first formula in H6, you want to base the commission calculation on the January sales in E6. As you copy the formula from January to February, you want the E6 reference to be able to change to F6. As you copy the formula down to other rows, you want the E6 to change to E7, E8, and so on. Thus, the E6 portion of the formula needs to be a relative reference and will have no dollar signs.

You multiply the sales by the base rate in B1. As you copy the formula to other months and rows, it always needs to point to B1. Thus, you need to use dollar signs before the B and before the 1: $B$1.

To incorporate the product bonus, you need to multiply sales by the product rate in column C. All the months in row 6 have to refer to C6. All the months in row 7 have to refer to C7. Thus, you need a mixed reference where column C is locked; use the address of $C6.

Finally, to address the monthly profit sharing bonus, the entire commission calculation is multiplied by the bonus factor shown in row 1. The January commission calculation uses the factor in E1. The February factor is in F1. The March factor is in G1. In this case, you need to allow the formula to point to different columns but always to row 1. This requires a mixed reference of E$1.

Now that you have the 4 components of the formula, enter this formula in E6: =E6*($B$1+$C6)*E$1.

	A	B	C	D	E	F	G	H	I	J
1	Base Rate	2%		Bonus Factor:	102%	100%	104%			
3						SALES		COMMISSION		
5	Rep	Product	Prod Rate	Customer	Jan	Feb	Mar	Jan	Feb	Mar
6	Jones	ABC	5%	General Motors	15205	9039	13768	=E6*($B$1+$C6)*E$1		
7	Jones	DEF	8%	Molson, Inc.	18716	7023	9876			
8	Doe	DEF	8%	Verizon	11560	12456	15853			

Figure 189 *The formula contains one of each type of reference.*

J7   *fx* =G7*($B$1+$C7)*G$1

	A	B	C	D	E	F	G	H	I	J
1	Base Rate	2%		Bonus Factor:	102%	100%	104%			
3						SALES		COMMISSION		
5	Rep	Product	Prod Rate	Customer	Jan	Feb	Mar	Jan	Feb	Mar
6	Jones	ABC	5%	General Motors	15205	9039	13768	1086	632.7	1002
7	Jones	DEF	8%	Molson, Inc.	18716	7023	9876	1909	702.3	1027

Figure 190 *Copy the formula, the $ signs keep it calculating correctly.*

The concept of relative, absolute, and mixed references is one of the most important concepts in Excel. Being able to use the right reference will allow you to create a single formula that can be copied everywhere.

SIMPLIFY THE ENTRY OF DOLLAR SIGNS IN FORMULAS

Problem: It is a pain to type the dollar signs in complex formulas such as the formula in the previous topic. How can I make this job easier?

Press the F4 key as you are entering a formula to toggle a reference through the four possible reference types. Here's an example of how to use it:

1. Start to type the formula =E6*(B1.

Figure 191 *Type B1.*

2. Immediately after you type B1, press the F4 key. Excel will insert both dollar signs in the B1 reference.

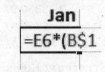

Figure 192 *Press F4*

3. Press the F4 key again. Excel changes the reference from an absolute reference to a mixed reference, with the row portion of the reference locked.

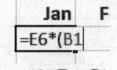

Figure 193 *Row only..*

4. Press the F4 key again. Excel changes the reference to a mixed reference, with the column portion of the reference locked.

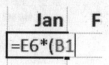

Figure 194 *Column.*

5. Press the F4 key once more. Excel changes the reference back to a
relative reference with no dollar signs.

=E6*(B1

Figure 195 *Relative.*

Here are the steps for entering the complex formula =E6*($B$1+$C6)*E$1:
1. Type =E6*(B1.
2. Press the F4 key once.
3. Type +C6.
4. Press the F4 key three times.
5. Type)*E1.
6. Press the F4 key twice to change E1 to a reference with the row locked.
7. Press Ctrl+Enter to accept the formula without moving the cell pointer to the next cell.
8. Use the mouse to grab the fill handle (the square dot in the lower-right corner of the cell) and drag it
to the right by two cells. Excel will copy the formula from January to the other two months.
9. Double-click the fill handle. Excel will copy the three cells down to all the rows that contain data.

Additional Details: You might find mixed references confusing. As you work on building the first formula, you might know that you need to point to C7. Enter C7 in the formula and then use F4 to toggle
between the various reference types. Say to yourself, "Okay, there is a dollar sign before the C that will
lock the column and let the row change. Is that what I need?" As long as you say this to yourself without
your lips moving, your office mates won't think any less of you.

Additional Details: If you did not add the dollar signs as you typed the formula, you can still use the F4
trick later. Here's how:
1. Use the mouse to highlight the proper reference in the formula bar.
2. Press the F4 key to toggle the highlighted reference through the four reference styles.

You can use the F4 key to easily add dollar signs to a reference in order to toggle it from relative to absolute
to mixed to the other mixed.

LEARN R1C1 REFERENCING TO UNDERSTAND FORMULA COPYING

Problem: All of a sudden, the column letters along the top of my spreadsheet have been replaced by numbers. None of the formulas I enter will work. What's wrong?

=R[-1]C+RC[-1]-RC[-2]

▲	1	2	3	4	5
1	Loan	8,000		Term	24
2	Rate	5%		Pmt	$350.97
3					
4	#	Pmt Amt	Interest	Balance	
5				8,000	
6	1	$350.97	33.33333	$7,682.36	
7	2	$350.97	32.00984	$7,363.40	
8	3	$350.97	30.68084	$7.043.11	

Figure 196 *Why is column B now column 2?*

Strategy: Relax. There are two ways of naming cells, and in this case, someone has turned on the R1C1
style of addressing. To return to the normal A1 style of cell addressing, select File, Options, Formulas.
Uncheck the R1C1 Reference Style check box.

But wait. While you are here, you can learn something fascinating about spreadsheets. In the topic "Copy
a Formula That Contains Relative References," I say that it's miraculous that Excel can automatically

change a formula as you copy it. If you take a couple of minutes to learn about this other method of cell addressing, you will understand that it may not be so amazing after all.

When Dan Bricklin and Bob Frankston invented VisiCalc, they used the A1 style of cell naming. When Mitch Kapor started selling Lotus 1-2-3, he used the same style. When Microsoft came out with its first spreadsheet product, Microsoft Multiplan, it used a very different method of cell addressing, known as R1C1. In the Microsoft system, the rows are numbered just as in the A1 system. However, the columns are also numbered. Each cell is given a name, such as "R4C8," which stands for the cell at row 4, column 8. This is the cell that you and I know as H4.

In the R1C1 style, the formulas are interesting. Look at the A1-style formula shown in cell D6.

	A	B	C	D
4	#	Pmt Amt	Interest	Balance
5				8,000
6	1	$350.97	33.33333	=D5+C6-B6
7	2	$350.97	32.00984	$7,363.40

Figure 197 *Consider the formula in D6.*

The formula in the formula bar says =D5+C6-B6. But think about this formula in plain language. What it really means is "Take the cell just above me, add the interest in the cell just to the left of me, and subtract the payment in the cell two cells to the left of me." Formulas in R1C1 style are rather like this plain language description. If you want to enter a formula in D6 that points to the cell just above, for example, you use =R[-1]C. The number in square brackets after the R indicates to how many rows ahead or back you are referring. In this case, row 5 is one row above row 6, so you put a -1 in the square brackets. There is no number after the C portion of the address, which means you are referring to the same column as the cell that contains the formula.

To refer to a cell that is two cells to the left of the cell with the formula, you use =RC[-2].

The formula can be restated in R1C1 style as follows: =R[-1]C+RC[-1]-RC[-2].

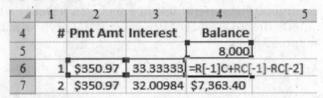

	1	2	3	4	5
4	#	Pmt Amt	Interest	Balance	
5				8,000	
6	1	$350.97	33.33333	=R[-1]C+RC[-1]-RC[-2]	
7	2	$350.97	32.00984	$7,363.40	

Figure 198 *When you get the hang of them, R1C1 formulas are intuitive..*

All relative references in R1C1 style have a number in square brackets—either after the R or after the C or both.

It is very interesting to see how this style handles absolute addresses. Say that you have a formula that points to $E$2. This reference in R1C1 language would be =R2C5. Notice that when there are no square brackets, the formula is saying to always point to row 2 and column 5.

It is also possible to have mixed references. RC1 means this row, but always column A.

Additional Details: Now that you understand the basics of R1C1-style formulas, you can appreciate how Excel can automatically change a formula as you copy it. Remember that Microsoft invented this method for its Multiplan product. Lotus 1-2-3 was the dominant spreadsheet in the late 1980s and early 1990s. Microsoft was battling for market share. Everyone using spreadsheets was familiar with the A1 style. No one would want to learn the R1C1 style in order to switch to Microsoft. So, in its Excel product, Microsoft developed an elaborate system to actually store the formulas in R1C1 style but to translate the R1C1 formulas to A1 style to make it easier for all the Lotus fans to understand.

By default, Microsoft starts with A1-style addressing. However, remember that you are just one check mark away from switching to R1C1-style addressing.

To really see R1C1 in its glory, examine the amortization table example in Formula View mode. (Press Ctrl+` to toggle into Formula View mode.) Below is Formula View mode in A1 style. As you can see, every formula in column D is different.

▲	A	B	C	D
4		# Pmt Amt	Interest	Balance
5				=B1
6	1	=$E$2	=D5*$B$2/12	=D5+C6-B6
7	=1+A6	=$E$2	=D6*$B$2/12	=D6+C7-B7
8	=1+A7	=$E$2	=D7*$B$2/12	=D7+C8-B8

Figure 199 *Miracle that Excel changes every formula from row to row?*

Below shows the Formula View mode in R1C1 style.

▲	1	2	3	4
4		# Pmt Amt	Interest	Balance
5				=R[-4]C[-2]
6	1	=R2C5	=R[-1]C[1]*R2C2/12	=R[-1]C+RC[-1]-RC[-2]
7	=1+R[-1]C	=R2C5	=R[-1]C[1]*R2C2/12	=R[-1]C+RC[-1]-RC[-2]
8	=1+R[-1]C	=R2C5	=R[-1]C[1]*R2C2/12	=R[-1]C+RC[-1]-RC[-2]

Figure 200 *In R1C1 style, every formula is identical to the one above it.*

In A1 style, it seems *amazing* that Excel can change a reference from D10 to D11 when the formula is copied down. However, look closely at the formulas in each row of rows 7 and higher in the R1C1 style shown in this figure. Each formula in a column is identical to the formula located just above it!

While VisiCalc and Lotus 1-2-3 made the formula replication seem amazing because of their A1 reference style, if the Multiplan invention of R1C1 style had taken hold, it would not seem amazing at all because, in fact, every formula is exactly identical as you copy it down through the rows. Microsoft actually had a better system. Just as Beta was superior to VHS but fell by the wayside due to market share, Microsoft's superior R1C1 style lost its battle, and Microsoft chose A1 style as the default in Excel.

If you ever plan on writing VBA macros in Excel, it is important that you understand the R1C1 style of formulas. For general use in Excel, you never really need to totally understand the R1C1 style, but it is interesting to see how Microsoft's R1C1 style is actually better than A1 when you're copying formulas in a spreadsheet.

CREATE EASIER-TO-UNDERSTAND
FORMULAS WITH NAMED RANGES

Problem: How can I create easier-to-understand formulas?

=B3-B4

▲	A	B
1	**Budget**	
2		**FY 2014**
3	Gross Revenue	$92,500
4	COGS	$33,940
5		
6	Gross Profit	$58,560
7		
8	Rent	$15,400
9	Utilities	$1,800
10	G&A	$3,100
11	Expenses	$20,300
12		
13	Operating Income	$38,260

Figure 201 *This formula is not very intuitive.*

Strategy: It would be easier to understand the results if each component of every formula were named for what it represented and not just for the cell it came from. You can therefore use named ranges to make formulas easier to understand:

1. Select cell B3. In the Name box (the area to the left of the formula bar), type Revenue and press Enter.
2. Select cell B4. Click in the Name box, type COGS, and press Enter.

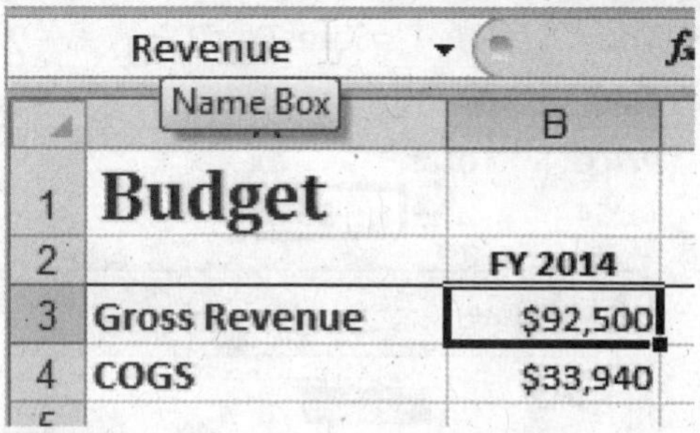

Figure 202 *Type a name in the Name Box and press Enter.*

3. Clear the formula in B6. Reenter the formula and use the mouse to select the cells. Type =. Using the mouse, touch B3. Type -. Using the mouse, touch B4. Excel will enter the formula as =Revenue-COGS. This is easier to understand than a typical formula.

Gotcha: You need a lot of foresight to use this technique. In order to have this work automatically, you are supposed to be smart enough to create the range names before you enter the formula.

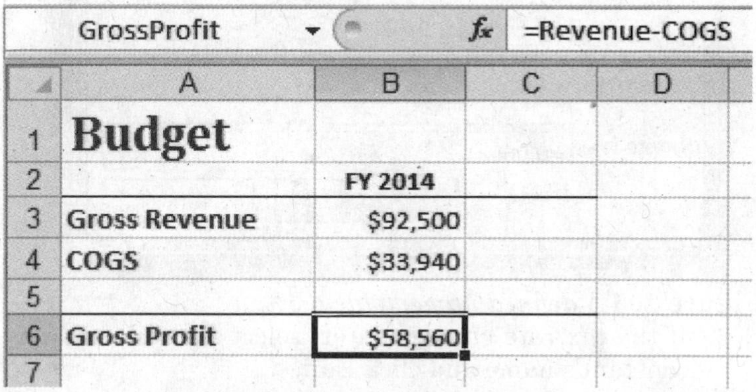

Figure 203 *This formula is easier to understand.*

However, most people create a formula first and then decide to make the worksheet easier to understand. To assign range names after creating formulas, follow these steps:

1. Select Formulas, Define Name dropdown, Apply Names. **Gotcha:** Don't click on the words Define Name; click on the dropdown icon to the right of Define Name.
2. Select all the names you want to apply and click OK.

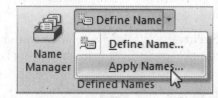

Figure 204 *Apply Names is hidden in the Define Name dropdown.*

Results: A formula like =B6-B11 will be updated to =GrossProfit-Expenses.

Additional Details: One advantage of named ranges: they are always treated as an absolute reference. You don't need to add dollar signs to have the formula always point to that cell.

SEE ALL NAMED RANGES AT 39% ZOOM

Set your zoom to 39% or less. Excel outlines and labels each named range.

USE NAMED CONSTANTS TO STORE NUMBERS

Problem: I've seen how to assign a name to a cell. Is it also possible to assign a name to a constant? That could be useful for a number, such as a local sales tax rate, that changes periodically.

Strategy: Yes, you can assign names to constants. To do so, you follow these steps:

1. Select Formula, Define Name.
2. In the New Name dialog, type a name such as SalesTax in the Name text box. In the Refers To box, type 0.065 and then click OK.
3. In this workbook, you can now use a formula such as =SalesTax*D2.

Figure 205 *A defined name holds 6.5%.*

4. If the tax rate changes later, select Formulas, Name Manager. In the Name Manager, select the constant's name and click Edit.

TOTAL WITHOUT USING A FORMULA

Problem: My manager called on the telephone, asking for the total sales of a particular product. I need to quickly find a total. Is there a faster way than entering a formula?

Strategy: While you're on the phone with your manager, you can highlight the numbers in question. The QuickSum indicator in the status bar will show the total of the highlighted cells.

	A	B
1	Item	Total
2	ABC	91
3	ABC	31
4	ABC	72
5	DEF	21
6	DEF	36
7	DEF	22
8	GHI	65
9	GHI	91
10	GHI	115
11		

Sheet

Sum: 79

Figure 206 *Select numeric cells, and the total appears in the status bar.*

Additional Details: The status bar can simultaneously show a count, a numeric count, a sum, and so on. Right-click the status bar and choose the statistics you would like to show.

Gotcha: The Average, Numerical Count, and Sum parts of the status bar will ignore text entries within the selection. Below, Sum and Numerical Count only factor in B2:B3.

⊿	A	B	C	D	E	F	G
1	Item	**Total**					
2	ABC	91					
3	ABC	31					
4	ABC	72					

⏮ ◀ ▶ ⏭ | Sheet1 / Sheet1 (2) / Sheet1 (3) / **AutoSum** /

Ready | Average: 61 Count: 3 Numerical Count: 2 Sum: 122

Figure 207 *Count, Numerical Count, and Sum will ignore text cells.*

If one of the highlighted cells is an error such as #N/A, the Sum and Average statistics will not appear in the status bar.

⊿	A	B	C	D
9	GHI	91		
10	GHI	115		
11		#N/A		
12				

⏮ ◀ ▶ ⏭ | Sheet1 / Sheet1 (2) ◀

Count: 3 Numerical Count: 2

Figure 208 *An error cell will cause the Sum statistic to disappear.*

Sometimes, when you are trying to find a lone #N/A within a column, it is fastest to start at the top of the column, hold down the Shift key, and start pressing PgDn. As soon as the Sum statistic disappears, you know that you have recently paged past the first #N/A error. (With 1 million rows, it might be faster to use Home, Find & Select, Go To Special, Errors.)

ADD OR MULTIPLY TWO COLUMNS WITHOUT USING FORMULAS

Problem: I've prepared a summary of sales by rep for the month. Due to an accounting glitch, someone gave me a similar file with additional sales made on the last day of the month. I need to add the new sales to the old sales. There is no need to keep the original two columns of partial month's sales.

⊿	A	B	C	D	E	F	G	H
1	XYZ Co - Commission Statement for June							
2								
3	Sales Rep	Sales	Comm %	Commission	Base	Salary		New Sales
4	George Wa	13,125	5%	656.25	1000	1,656.25		609
5	John Adam	11,706	5%	585.30	1000	1,585.30		983
6	Thomas Jef	14,513	5%	725.65	1000	1,725.65		205
7	James Mad	6,857	4%	274.28	1000	1,274.28		536
8	James Mon	6,247	4%	249.88	1000	1,249.88		355
9	John Quinc	10,646	5%	532.30	1000	1,532.30		269

Figure 209 *Add column H to column B.*

Strategy: You can copy the new values in column H and use Home, Paste dropdown, Paste Special, Add to add the values to column B. Follow these steps:

1. Select H4:H22. Type Ctrl+C to copy the cells to the Clipboard.
2. Move the cell pointer to B4. Select Home, Paste dropdown, Paste Special. (Don't select the large Paste icon; instead, choose the dropdown below the icon.)
3. In the Paste Special dialog box, choose the Add option in the Operation section. Optionally, also choose Values in the Paste section in order to preserve the formatting in column B. Click OK.

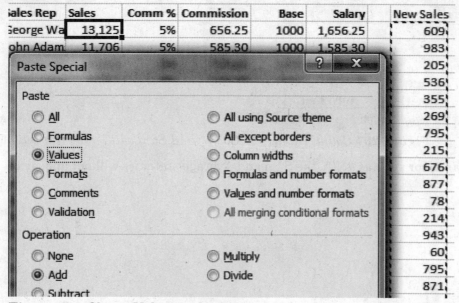

Sales Rep	Sales	Comm %	Commission	Base	Salary	New Sales
George Wa	13,125	5%	656.25	1000	1,656.25	609
John Adam	11,706	5%	585.30	1000	1,585.30	983
						205
						536
						355
						269
						795
						215
						676
						877
						78
						214
						943
						60
						795
						871

Figure 210 *Choose Values and Add.*

Results: The new sales values from column H are added to the values in column B. You can safely delete column H.

Rep	Sales	Co
ge Wa	13,734	
Adam	12,689	
las Jef	14,718	
s Mac	7,393	

Figure 211 *Excel adds the range on the Clipboard to column B.*

Gotcha: If column B is properly formatted and the temporary data in H is not formatted, the default Paste All option will cause the formats in column B to be lost if you choose only Add and not Values.

Additional Details: The technique described here for selecting Add in the Paste Special dialog has an interesting effect if you add cells to a range that contains a formula. Amazingly, Excel handles it correctly. For example cell D4 contains a formula.

f_x	=B4*C4	
	D	**E**
n %	**Commission**	**Ba**
5%	686.70	100
5%	634.45	100

Figure 212 *Before pasting, this cell contains a formula.*

If you select Add in the Paste Special dialog to add a value to this formula, Excel changes the formula to add the value.

f_x	=(B4*C4)+609	
	D	**E**
	Commission	**Base**
	1295.7	1000	2

Figure 213 *After Paste Special Add, Excel modifies the formula.*

Additional Details: You can use the Operation section of Paste Special to handle other situations. In this figure, you might want to increase the contract rates by 2%. Type 102% in a blank cell. Copy that cell. Select the range of contract rates and use Paste Special, Values, Multiply.

1	**Contract**	**Rate**		102%
2	K3504	7.3746		
3	K3350	10.5876		
4	K10761	7.6296		
5	K7205	5.5896		
6	K8213	8.058		

Figure 214 *Multiply this range by the 102% on the clipboard.*

This method was also used in Learn Excel Podcast episode 1348. Someone had received a dataset where a column of numbers needed to be divided by 100. For whatever reason, the creator of the data had put 123 instead of 1.23. The solution was to put 0.01 in a cell, copy the cell, then Paste Special Multiply.

TYPE 123 TO ENTER 1.23

Excel can automatically insert s decimal point like the old adding machines. Go to File, Options, Advanced.

☑ Automatically insert a **decimal** point

Places: 2 ▲▼

Figure 215 *When you type 123, Excel will enter 1.23*

JOIN TWO TEXT COLUMNS

Problem: I have data with first names in column A and last names in column B. I want to merge these two columns into one column.

◢	A	B
1	FIRST	LAST
2	NORAH	JONES
3	PAUL	MCCARTNEY
4	BILL	JELEN

Figure 216 *You want to join A2 and B2 into a single cell.*

Strategy: You can use the ampersand (&) as a concatenation operator in a formula in column C. You change the formulas in column C to values before deleting columns A and B. These are the steps:

1. In cell C2, enter the formula =A2&B2.

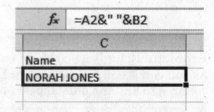

Figure 217 Use & to join text.

2. To insert a space between the first name and the last name, join cell A2, a space in quotes, and cell B2, using the formula =A2&" "&B2.
3. Copy the formula down to all the cells in the range.

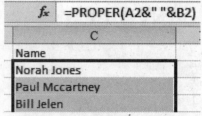

Figure 218 *Join A2, a space, and B2.*

Additional Details: To convert NORAH JONES to Norah Jones, you use the PROPER function. =PROPER(A2&" "&B2) will convert the names to proper case. This will work for all your names except names with interior capitals, such as Paul McCartney or Dave VanHorn. After using the PROPER function, you will have to manually fix any names that have interior capital letters. (Some people suggest entering the last name as Mc Cartney, with a space to prevent this problem.) Note: If you like PROPER, consider UPPER and LOWER to convert text to upper or lower case.

fx	=PROPER(A2&" "&B2)
	C
Name	
Norah Jones	
Paul Mccartney	
Bill Jelen	

Figure 219 *There are also UPPER and LOWER functions.*

Gotcha: If you delete columns A and B while column C still contains formulas, all the formulas will change to #REF! errors. This tells you that you have a formula that points to cells(s) that are no longer there. You can immediately press Ctrl+Z (or Alt+Backspace) to undo the deletion.

`=PROPER(#REF!&" "&#REF!)`

	A
1	Name
2	#REF!
3	#REF!
4	#REF!
5	#REF!

Figure 220 *Delete A:B, the live formulas in C will change to #REF! errors.*

To work around this situation, you first convert all the formulas in column C to values. Follow these steps:

1. Select the data in column C.
2. Press Ctrl+C to copy the data to the Clipboard.
3. Without changing the selection, select Home, Paste dropdown, Paste Values.
4. You can now delete columns A and B.

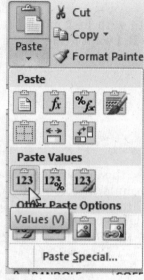

Figure 221 *Convert formulas to values.*

JOIN TEXT WITH A DATE OR CURRENCY

Problem: I just learned about concatenation, and I'm trying to join text with currency and with a date. As you can see in cell B13, when I attempt to join both date and currency with text, the currency loses the dollar sign and the date appears as a strange number. What am I doing wrong?

B13			f_x	="Please remit "&E11&" before "&F1+F3		
	A	B	C	D	E	F	G
1	**INVOICE**				Date:	6/18/2014	
3					Net:	30	
5		Quantity	Item	Unit Price	Total		
6		62	S64	64.08	$3,972.96		
7		76	S69	39.91	3,033.16		
8		83	S85	45.72	3,794.76		
9		27	S39	41.66	1,124.82		
10		57	S52	53.5	3,049.50		
11				TOTAL	$14,975.20		
13		Please remit 14975.2 before 41838					
14							

Figure 222 *The formula in B13 fails miserably.*

Strategy: Excel internally stores dates as numbers and relies on the number format to display the number as a date. In the formula, you can use the TEXT function to convert a date or a number into text with a particular numeric format. For example, the formula =TEXT(F1+F3,"mm/dd/yyyy") would produce the text 07/18/2014. Thanks to the variety of custom number formats, you could also use =TEXT(F1+F3,"dddd, mmmm d, yyyy") to create the text Friday, July 18, 2014.

Additional Details: If you are not sure of the actual custom number format codes, you can query them from any existing cell. Here's an example:
1. Select cell E11.
2. Press Ctrl+1 to display the Format Cells dialog.
3. Click the Number tab and then select the Custom category. Excel will show the actual code used to generate the format in that cell.
4. Highlight those characters, press Ctrl+C to copy to the Clipboard, and paste into the TEXT function.
5. Change the formula in B13 to

```
="Please  remit "&TEXT(E11,"$#,##0.00")&
" before "&TEXT(F1+F3,"dddd, mmmm d, yyyy")
```

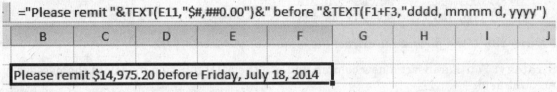

Figure 223 *Use the TEXT function to format dates and currency.*

Additional Details: Excel stores dates as the number of days elapsed since January 1, 1900 (on a PC), or since January 1, 1904 (on a Mac). The 41838 shown in cell B13 of Figure 222 corresponds to July 18, 2014. While this is a fascinating bit of information (if you are Cliff Claven), I've never had a manager call and ask, "Hey, how many days after January 1, 1900, is that receivable due?" This method makes it easy for Excel to calculate differences between two dates.

SORT ON ONE PORTION OF AN ACCOUNT ID

Problem: My company assigns an account ID to every customer. One portion of the account ID contains useful information, such as a parent company code. The first three digits of the account are used to identify an office. How can I sort on the basis of a portion of the account ID?

	A	B	C	D	E	F
1	Account	Product	Jan	Feb	Mar	Q1
2	4010	XYZ	37	82	12	131
3	4021	ABC	89	20	69	178
4	4030	XYZ	73	90	62	225

Figure 224 *Bad design, part of column A indicates an office.*

Strategy: You can insert a new column and use the LEFT function to isolate the necessary digits from the Account field. Here's how:
1. In the blank column, such as G, enter a heading such as Key.
2. In cell G2, enter the formula =LEFT(A2,3). This indicates that the new field should contain just the three leftmost characters in the Account field. Note that Excel also offers the RIGHT function to isolate the rightmost characters.

G2					f_x	=LEFT(A2,3)	
	A	B	C	D	E	F	G	H
1	Account	Product	Jan	Feb	Mar	Q1	Office	
2	4010	XYZ	37	82	12	131	401	
3	4021	ABC	89	20	69	178	402	
4	4030	XYZ	73	90	62	225	403	
5	4030	ABC	55	26	23	104	403	

Figure 225 *Get the first three characters.*

3. Double-click the fill handle in cell G2 to copy the formula down to all the rows in your data set. (The fill handle is the black square dot in the lower-right corner of the cell pointer.)

Results: A certain portion of the Account field is now available in a new column. You can now use data tools, such as Sort, Filter, or Subtotal, to isolate certain offices.

When you need to isolate a portion of the characters in another column, you can do so by creating a temporary column.

HOW TO ISOLATE THE CENTER PORTION OF AN ACCOUNT ID

Problem: My company assigns an account ID in the format SSS-XX-YYYY. I need to isolate the XX portion of the account ID in order to subtotal or sort the data.

⊿	A	B	C	D	E	F
1	Account	Product	Jan	Feb	Mar	Q1
2	105-60-6255	XYZ	77	43	58	178
3	109-50-6681	GHI	0	93	69	162
4	109-50-7003	ABC	80	66	70	216
5	110-70-3415	DEF	50	23	48	121

Figure 226 *Use a formula to extract the middle of the account ID.*

Strategy: You can insert a new column and use the MID function to isolate the necessary digits from the Account field.

The MID function takes three arguments: (1) a cell that contains a text value, (2) the character number where you want the result to start, and (3) the length of the result.

In a well-formed account number, such as 123-45-6789, you can predict that the start of the second segment will always be in the fifth character position and the length of the second segment is always two characters. Therefore, you can follow these steps:

1. In a blank column, such as column G, enter a heading such as Key.
2. In cell G2, enter the formula =MID(A2,5,2).
3. Copy the formula down to all rows.

G2	▼	*fx*	=MID(A2,5,2)

⊿	A	B	C	D	E	F	G
1	Account	Product	Jan	Feb	Mar	Q1	Key
2	105-60-6255	XYZ	77	43	58	178	60
3	109-50-6681	GHI	0	93	69	162	50
4	109-50-7003	ABC	80	66	70	216	50

Figure 227 *Get the middle text, starting at position 5, for a length of 2.*

Additional Details: In order to capture the final four digits of the account number, you could either use =MID(A2,8,4) or =RIGHT(A2,4).

Results: You can now sort by the new column and add subtotals based on the Account field.

HOW TO ISOLATE EVERYTHING BEFORE A DASH IN A COLUMN BY USING FUNCTIONS

Problem: A vendor has given me an Excel worksheet. One field has a manufacturer code, a dash, and a part number. I need to isolate the manufacturer code in a new column, but the manufacturer codes are not always the same length.

⊿	A	B	C	D	E
1	Item		Jan	Feb	Mar	Q1
2	KO-4679855		93	94	85	272
3	CISCO-85590		99	69	76	244
4	MSFT-4904		59	76	76	211
5	KO-8594635		80	55	70	215

Figure 228 *Get the left text, up to the dash.*

Strategy: You can use the FIND function to locate the character position of the dash. You can use that result minus one in the LEFT function.

The FIND function requires two arguments. The first is the text that you are trying to locate. Use a dash in quotation marks. The second argument is the cell that contains the text to search. Here's how the process works:

1. Enter =FIND("-",A2) in cell F2.

2. Copy this formula down to all the other cells. The 3 in cell F2 indicates that the dash is located in the third character position of cell A2. The 6 in cell F3 indicates that the dash is in the sixth position of cell A3.

3. To isolate the manufacturer code, you need a number that is one less than the number in column F, so in cell G2, enter the formula =LEFT(A2,F2-1).

=FIND("-",A2)

	A	B	C	D	E	F
1	Item	Jan	Feb	Mar	Q1	Find
2	KO-4679855	93	94	85	272	3
3	CISCO-85590	99	69	76	244	6
4	MSFT-4904	59	76	76	211	5

Figure 229 *The 3 says the dash is the 3rd character in A2.*

4. Double-click the fill handle to copy this formula down to all cells.

=LEFT(A2,F2-1)

	A	B	C	D	E	F	G
1	Item	Jan	Feb	Mar	Q1	Find	Manufacturer
2	KO-4679855	93	94	85	272	3	KO
3	CISCO-85590	99	69	76	244	6	CISCO
4	MSFT-4904	59	76	76	211	5	MSFT
5	KO-9694625	80	66	70	216	3	KO

Figure 230 *The FIND provides an end point for the LEFT function.*

Instead use a single formula in F2: =LEFT(A2,FIND("-",A2)-1)

HOW TO USE FUNCTIONS TO ISOLATE EVERYTHING AFTER A DASH

Problem: I need to isolate everything after the dash from Figure 230 above.

Strategy: You can use the MID function to extract a portion of text from the middle of the text. The MID function requires three arguments: =MID(*Cell with Text, Character Number to Start, Number of Characters*). You can use the FIND function to locate the dash in the item number and start at one character to the right. Rather than use the LEN function to figure out the length, ask for a really large number for the number of characters. MID will only return characters to the end of the cell.

The FIND function requires two arguments. The first argument is the text that you are trying to locate. In this case, you are trying to locate a dash, so you should include the dash in quotation marks. The second argument is the location of the cell that contains the text to search. Here's how the process works:

1. Enter =FIND("-",A2) in cell F2 and copy it down as in the previous topic.
2. To isolate the part number, you need to start one character to the right of the dash, so start your formula with =MID(A2,F2+1,
3. Next you need the number of characters. While you could use LEN(A2)-F2, it is not necessary. Use a large number such as 20 for the number of characters. This should be large enough to handle the largest possible part number. Close the formula with a).
4. Copy the formula =MID(A2,F2+1,20) down to all rows.

| G2 | | | | fx | =MID(A2,F2+1,20) | | |

	A	B	C	D	E	F	G	H
1	Item	Jan	Feb	Mar	Q1	Find	Item	
2	KO-4679855	93	94	85	272	3	4679855	
3	CISCO-85590	99	69	76	244	6	85590	
4	MSFT-4904	59	76	76	211	5	4904	
5	KO-9694625	80	66	70	216	3	9694625	

Figure 231 *MID with Find*

To combine the two formulas into a single formula, use =MID(A2,FIND("-",A2)+1,20).

HOW TO USE FUNCTIONS TO ISOLATE EVERYTHING AFTER THE SECOND DASH IN A COLUMN

Problem: A vendor gave me a file that contains a three-segment part number. Each segment is separated by a dash, and the length of each segment could be any number of characters. How do I find the second or third segment?

⊿	A	B	C	D	E
1	Item	Jan	Feb	Mar	Q1
2	KO-4679855-A34	93	94	85	272
3	CISCO-85590-B7	99	69	76	244
4	KO-9694625-B951	36	96	94	226

Figure 232 *Isolate the second or third segment.*

Strategy: There is an optional third argument in the FIND function that tells Excel to start looking after a certain character position in the text. In this case, to find the second dash, you want Excel to start looking after the location of the first dash. Here's what you do:

1. As in the prior examples, use =FIND("-",A2) in cell F2 to locate the first dash.
2. Enter =FIND("-",A2,F2+1) in cell G2. The F2+1 parameter tells Excel that you want to find a dash starting at the fourth character position of cell A2.

G2				fx	=FIND("-",A2,F2+1)		

⊿	A	B	C	D	E	F	G	H
1	Item	Jan	Feb	Mar	Q1	Dash 1	Dash 2	Item 1
2	KO-4679855-A34	93	94	85	272	3	11	
3	CISCO-85590-B7	99	69	76	244	6	12	
4	KO-9694625-B951	36	96	94	226	3	11	
5	KO-3664228-A52	80	66	70	216	3	11	
6								

Figure 233 *The 3rd argument is where FIND should start looking.*

3. Enter =LEFT(A2,F2-1) in H2. This formula locates the first segment of the part number.
4. Enter =MID(A2,F2+1,G2-F2-1) in I2. This formula locates the middle segment of the part number.
5. To get the right segment of the part number, use the RIGHT function. (Just like the LEFT function, the RIGHT function requires a cell and the number of characters from the right side of the item number.) To find the number of characters, use =LEN(A2)-G2. So enter the formula =RIGHT(A2,LEN(A2)-G2) in J2.

J2				fx	=RIGHT(A2,LEN(A2)-G2)	

⊿	A	F	G	H	I	J
1	Item	Dash 1	Dash 2	Item 1	Item 2	Item 3
2	KO-4679855-A34	3	11	KO	4679855	A34
3	CISCO-85590-B7	6	12	CISCO	85590	B7
4	KO-9694625-B951	3	11	KO	9694625	B951
5	KO-3664228-A52	3	11	KO	3664228	A52

Figure 234 *Use RIGHT to find the third segment.*

Gotcha: With all these formulas, you are trusting that the vendor always included two dashes in the item number. If there is an item number that does not have a second dash, the second FIND function will return a #VALUE! error, leading to errors in the calculation for the second and third items. Before converting formulas to values and deleting the original part number, you need to sort the data in descending order by column F and then sort in descending order by column G. Any #VALUE! errors will sort to the top of the data set so you can easily locate and correct them.

⊿	A	F	G	H	I	J
1	Item	Dash 1	Dash 2	Item 1	Item 2	Item 3
2	KO-4679855	3	#VALUE!	KO	#VALUE!	#VALUE!
3	CISCO-85590-B7	6	12	CISCO	85590	B7

Figure 235 *The formulas create an error if there is only one dash.*

Result: By using combinations of FIND, LEN, MID, LEFT, and RIGHT, you can parse nearly any data imaginable.

HOW TO SEPARATE A PART NUMBER INTO THREE COLUMNS

Problem: A vendor gave me a file that contains three-segment item numbers. The segments are separated by dashes. The FIND function makes my head hurt, but I need to break the part number into three columns. What do I do?

	A	B	C	D	E
1	Item	Jan	Feb	Mar	Q1
2	KO-4679855-A34	93	94	85	272
3	CISCO-85590-B7	99	69	76	244
4	MSFT-4904-B636	59	76	76	211
5	KO-9694625-B95	80	66	70	216

Figure 236 *Split the item number at each dash.*

Strategy: You can use the Text to Columns command on the Data tab to parse the item number. Follow these steps:

1. Copy the item number to the right side of your data in column F. The Text to Columns command will fill several columns to the right of the original column. Make sure you have plenty of blank columns.
2. Select the entire range of data in column F. Place the cell pointer in cell F2. Press Ctrl+Shift+Down Arrow.
3. Select Data, Text to Columns. The Convert Text to Columns Wizard will work on either data that is delimited or on data that has a fixed width to each segment.
4. Because the data in this example is delimited by a dash, in step 1 of the wizard, leave the radio button on the Delimited setting.
5. Click Next.

> Convert Text to Columns Wizard - Step 1 of 3
>
> The Text Wizard has determined that your data is Delimited.
>
> If this is correct, choose Next, or choose the data type that best describes your data.
>
> Original data type
>
> Choose the file type that best describes your data:
>
> ⦿ Delimited   - Characters such as commas or tabs separate each field.
> ◯ Fixed width   - Fields are aligned in columns with spaces between each field.
>
> Preview of selected data:
>
> 2 KO-4679855-A34
> 3 CISCO-85590-B7

Figure 237 *The dashes are known as delimiters.*

6. By default, step 2 of the wizard assumes that the data is delimited by a tab, so uncheck the Tab check box. Other standard choices are commas, spaces, and semicolons. Since dash is not in the list, you should choose the Other check box. In the Other text box, enter a dash. The Data Preview window will show the data in three columns.
7. Click Next.

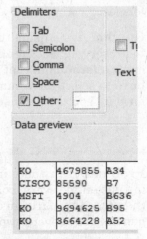

Figure 238 *Specify a dash in the Other box.*

8. Click Next. In step 3 of the wizard, if desired, specify the data type of the columns. Unless you have dates, the General type is okay. Note that if you want to preserve any leading zeros in the second

segment of the item number, you should choose the heading of that field and change it from General to Text.

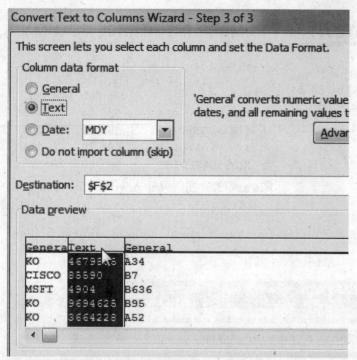

Figure 239 *Use Text only when you have to preserve leading zeros.*

9. Click Finish.

Results: The original column F has been overwritten with the first portion of the result. Columns G and H contain the second and third segments of the item number.

F	G	H
Item		
KO	4679855	A34
CISCO	85590	B7
MSFT	4904	B636
KO	9694625	B95

Figure 240 *You've parsed column A into three new columns.*

Gotcha: The General format will aggressively attempt to convert anything that is remotely similar to a date to a date. For example, a part number of 5-5055 will be imported as May 1, 5055. A fraction such as 1/4 will be imported as January 4 of the current year. If your data includes dashes or slashes, use the Text format.

Gotcha: Avoid using the Text option in step 3 of the wizard unless it is absolutely necessary. In addition to preserving leading zeros, the Text option will change the format of that column to text. When you try to enter a formula in that column, you will get the formula instead of the answer. To solve this problem, you have to select the column, press Ctrl+1 to format cells, and select Number. Then you select any numeric format. You then have to go back and reenter the formulas in order to have them calculate.

EXCEL IS RANDOMLY PARSING PASTED DATA

Problem: Every once in a while, I paste data from a text file to Excel, and Excel will spontaneously parse my data into several columns. I copied the names from the e-mail on the left, but when I pasted to Excel, the names appeared in one, two, or three columns. However, this may not happen tomorrow. It might happen only once every two weeks.

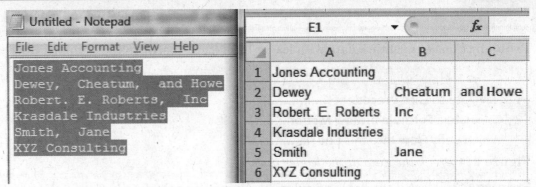

Figure 241 *Excel parsed this data when I pasted.*

Strategy: At some point during this Excel session, you used Data, Text to Columns and specified that the data was delimited by a comma. Whatever settings are left in the Step 2 dialog of the Convert Text to Columns Wizard will be applied to external data pasted to Excel for the rest of the Excel session.

To prevent this from happening, you could close Excel when you're done working with the Convert Text to Columns Wizard. Or you could redisplay the Convert Text to Columns Wizard, go to the Step 2 dialog, and turn off the comma and tab settings. Either method will work.

On the other hand, you might want Excel to have this behavior. Perhaps you need to paste 100 documents to Excel and convert text to columns on each one. In this case, you can convert text to columns manually on the first pasted data, and the rest of the pastes will automatically be parsed using the same delimiter.

I LOSE LEADING ZEROES FROM CSV FILES

Problem: When I open a CSV file in Excel, I am losing the leading zeroes. I need those leading zeroes. I would like to choose Text in step 3 of the Import Text to Columns Wizard, but I never get to see that wizard when I open a CSV file.

Strategy: Excel will walk you through the Text to Columns wizard when you open a .txt file. However, if you open a .csv file, Excel will automatically open the file without allowing you to choose field types. If you find that you are losing leading zeroes when you open a .csv file, simply rename the file from .csv to .txt in Windows Explorer before you open the file.

OPEN CSV FILE WITH DATES IN D/M/Y FORMAT

Problem: Our European subsidiary send me a CSV file. One of the columns is in DD/MM/YYYY format, but my international settings are expecting the dates in MM/DD/YYYY format.

Strategy: You could change your international settings in the Control Panel. However, an easier solution is to rename the .CSV file to a .TXT file and then open the .TXT file in Excel.

As discussed above, you do not see the Text Import Wizard when you open CSV files. When you change the extension, you will get to go through the wizard. In step 3, choose the column and select Date: D/M/Y.

Additional Details: After the import, the dates will be displayed according to your international settings. In the figure below, 17/01/2014 is displayed as 01/17/2014 per the U.S. date format.

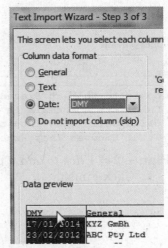

Figure 242 *Choose DMY in Step 3.*

Figure 243

PARSE DATA WITH LEADER LINES

Problem: Someone sent me data with leader lines (........) between the columns. How can I parse the data?

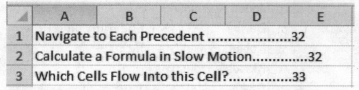

▲	A	B	C	D	E
1	Navigate to Each Precedent 32				
2	Calculate a Formula in Slow Motion..............32				
3	Which Cells Flow Into this Cell?................33				

Figure 244 *Break the data at the leader lines.*

Strategy: First, see if the data is fixed width by changing the font to Courier New or Courier. These fonts are fixed width fonts. If the second field lines up in Courier font, then you know that you can use the Fixed Width version of Text to Columns.

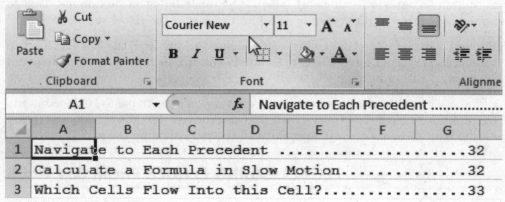

Figure 245 *In Courier New font, this data lines up.*

Follow these steps:

1. Select the data in column A. Use Data, Text to Columns.
2. In Step 1, choose Fixed Width. Click Next.
3. In step 2, click in the data preview area where the second field begins.

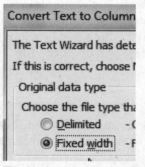

Figure 246 *Choose Fixed Width in step 1.*

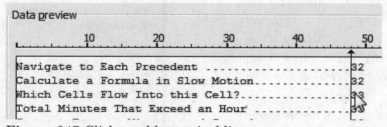

Figure 247 *Click to add a vertical line.*

4. Click Finish.

The resulting data will still have the leader lines in column A. Use Home, Find & Select, Replace. In the Find What box, type two periods. Leave the Replace With box blank. Click Replace All. Click OK. Click Replace All again. Click OK. Finally, replace a single period with nothing. Click Replace All.

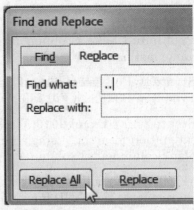

Figure 248 *Use Find and Replace to get rid of leader lines.*

Alternate Strategy: If there are no periods other than the leader lines, you could do a delimited Text to Columns. In Step 1, choose Delimited. In Step 2, choose Other and enter a period as the other delimiter. The important difference is to choose Treat Consecutive Delimiters as One. Click Finish.

Gotcha: This method will fail if any entries in the first field contain a period. After completing the text to columns, go to the presumably blank third column, select a cell, and press Ctrl+Down Arrow. If you run into any data, fix that row manually. If you end up at row 1048576, then you know the column is blank as expected.

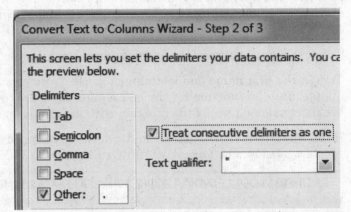

Figure 249 *Treat adjacent periods as one.*

PARSE MULTI-LINE CELLS

Problem: Someone used the Alt+Enter trick discussed later in this book to build address information with three lines in single cells. I need to break this data into columns.

Strategy: The Alt+Enter keystroke creates a character code 10. I've used many tricks to solve this, including =SUBSTITUTE(A1,CHAR(10),",") to change the line feeds to commas. But, the solution is much simpler than this.

Select the data. Use Data, Text to Columns. In Step 1, choose Delimited. In Step 2, choose Other. Click in the Other box and press Ctrl+J. Magically, the data preview will show each line of the cell going to a new column. Apparently, Ctrl+J inserts a character 10 in the Other box.

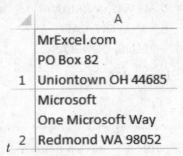

Figure 250 *They used Alt+Enter to enter multi-line data in one cell.*

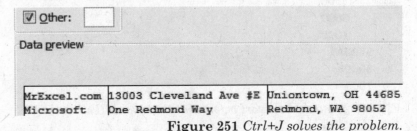

Figure 251 *Ctrl+J solves the problem.*

CHANGE SMITH, JANE TO JANE SMITH

Problem: I have a column of names in last name, first name style. How can I convert the data to first name last name?

Strategy For Excel 2013: Flash Fill comes to the rescue! Type a heading in B1. Type Jane Smith in B2. Type E in B3. Flash Fill will preview the rest of the column. Press Enter. You are done.

Strategy for Excel 2010: While you could do this in many steps, using Text to Columns and then a concatenation formula, a single large formula would also solve the problem. To begin, you need to insert a blank column after column A to hold the calculation.

=FIND(",",A2) will locate the comma within the value in column A. In Smith, Jane, the comma is the sixth character, so the FIND function would return a 6.

The first name starts two characters after the result of the FIND function. It extends to the end of the text. You can use the MID function to isolate the first name. The MID function requires some text, a starting location, and a length. If you ask for more characters than are in the text, then Excel will return from the starting position to the end of the text. For example, if you ask for 50 characters, Excel will handle any first name that has 50 characters or less. Therefore, you use =MID(A2,FIND(",",A2)+2,50).

The last name is always the leftmost characters, so you can use =LEFT(A2,FIND(",",A2)-1).

To join the first name and last name together, you concatenate the function for the first name, a space in quotes, and the function for the last name. You need to be sure to leave the = sign off the LEFT function because you don't prefix the function with an equals sign when it occurs in the middle of the formula.

If you want the text in uppercase and lowercase, you need to wrap the entire function in the PROPER function. As shown below, the formula is =PROPER(MID(A2,FIND(",",A2)+2,50)&" "&LEFT(A2,FIND(",",A2)-1)).

=PROPER(MID(A2,FIND(",",A2)+2,50)&" "&LEFT(A2,FIND(",",A2)-1))

	A	B	C
1	NAME	NAME	ADDRESS
2	SMITH, JANE	Jane Smith	625 Johnson Road
3	ATKINS, ERIN	Erin Atkins	995 Hill Circle
4	VAUGHN, WILLIAM	William Vaughn	226 Franklin Circle
5	LEWIS, MARIAN	Marian Lewis	647 Sycamore Circl
6	MELTON, CARL	Carl Melton	1394 Ash Circle
7	ELLIS, DOUGLAS	Douglas Ellis	552 College Blvd.

Figure 252 *The formula in column B achieves the result..*

CONVERT NUMBERS TO TEXT

Problem: I have a field that can contain numbers and text. I need the numeric entries to sort with the text entries. However, Excel always sorts the numeric entries to the top of the list, followed by the text entries.

	A
1	Style
2	5500
3	6000
4	7000
5	5500A
6	6000B
7	7000A

Figure 253 *Numbers sort before text that looks like numbers.*

Strategy: This is a rare case in which you need to convert numeric entries to text entries.

If you were building this spreadsheet from scratch, you could select column A, select Home, Format, Format Cells, and then format the column as text. This would allow all future entries to automatically be converted to text. However, converting cells to have a text format does *not* retroactively convert numbers to text.

Another option would be to edit each cell that contains a number. To do this, you select the cell, press F2 to edit the cell, press Home to move to the beginning of the cell, and type an apostrophe. Then you press Enter to move to the next cell. This could get very tedious with more than a few cells to change.

The good news is that there is an easier method for converting all the entries in a column to text:

1. Select all the data in a column. Select Data, Text to Columns. In step 1 of the Convert Text to Columns Wizard, indicate that your data is fixed width.
2. In step 2 of the wizard, if you have any vertical lines drawn in the Data Preview section, double-click to remove them.
3. In step 3 of the wizard, choose Text as the column data format.
4. Click Finish. The column will be converted to text.

Alternate Strategy: You could also insert a temporary column with the formula =TEXT(A2,"@").

FILL A CELL WITH REPEATING CHARACTERS

Problem: I need to fill a cell with asterisks before the number. If the cell gets wider, I want more asterisks to appear.

Strategy: Use a custom number format.

Select the cells and press Ctrl+1 (Ctrl and one). Select the Number tab. Choose Number or Currency or whatever style you want for your numbers. Then, in the Category list, choose Custom. You will now be able to edit the custom number format code.

To fill a cell with a character, you enter an asterisk and then that character.

For example, to precede a number with asterisks, you would use **0.00. To precede the number with plus signs, use *+0.00. You can have a number and then fill to the right with a character. Use 0*. to fill with periods.

B	C	D
Display		**Number Format**
************3975.64		**0.00
++++++++++++8929.35		*+0.00
XXXXXXXXXXXX 7154		*X0
3114.49....................		0.00*.
************3490.57		
************542.32		

Figure 254 Custom number formats fill the cell.

Additional Details: Lotus 1-2-3 used to support using * in a cell to fill the cell with asterisks. Excel will still support this, but you have to go to File, Options, Advanced, Transition, and choose Transition Navigation Keys. It seems very unlikely that everyone in your department will want to use these settings, so this method is not as reliable as using the custom number format.

CLEAN HASN'T KEPT UP WITH THE TIMES

Problem: The Excel function CLEAN is supposed to get rid of non-printable characters. It doesn't seem to get them all. And sometimes I would rather replace the non-printable character with a space.

Strategy: CLEAN and TRIM were written a long time ago. The CLEAN function was written in the days when the only characters were 0 through 127. It is designed to remove characters 0 through 31 from data, but it does not touch the new nonprintable characters such as 129, 141, 143, 144, and 157.

The TRIM function removes leading spaces, trailing spaces, and repeated internal spaces. However, it was designed before the advent of the web. TRIM works fine with character 32, but ignores the common character 160 that many web pages use.

You will have better results if you identify the code of the offending character and use =SUBSTITUTE.

	A	B	C	D	E	F
1	Bill Jelen	BillJelen	=CLEAN(A1)			
2	Mike Girvin	Mike Girvin	=SUBSTITUTE(A2,CHAR(10)," ")			
3	Bill Jelen	160	=CODE(MID(A3,5,1))			
4		Bill Jelen	=TRIM(A3)			
5		Bill Jelen	=TRIM(SUBSTITUTE(A3,CHAR(160)," "))			

Figure 255 *Examples of SUBSTITUTE.*

In B1 above, CLEAN does successfully remove the Alt+Enter, but it would look better if there were a space instead. The formula shown in C2 solves the problem by replacing CHAR(10) with a space.

In C4, TRIM is not getting rid of the extra interior spaces. The formula shown in C3 uses CODE to identify that those spaces are character 160 instead of regular spaces. The formula shown in C5 uses SUBSTITUTE to replace the CHAR(160) with a regular space.

ADD THE WORKSHEET NAME AS A TITLE

Problem: I have 12 worksheets, labeled January through December. Is there a formula that will put a worksheet name in a cell?

Strategy: You can parse the sheet name from the CELL function.

The CELL function can return a variety of information about the top-left cell in a reference. =CELL("Col",A1) will tell you that A1 is in column 1. For this particular problem, =CELL("FileName",A1) will return the path, filename, and worksheet name of a saved workbook, as shown in cell A1 below.

A1			*fx*	=CELL("FileName",A1)			
	A	B	C	D	E	F	G
1	C:\Users\Jelen\Desktop\LE10\DownloadFiles\[InfoFunctions.xlsm]January						
2	C:\Users\Jelen\Desktop\LE10\DownloadFiles\						
3	January						

Figure 256 *CELL returns the path, filename and worksheet name.*

To isolate the sheet name, you look for the right square bracket by using the FIND function. Then you use that location plus 1 as the start position for the MID function.

=MID(CELL("FileName",A1),FIND("]",CELL("FileName",A1)+1,25)

returns the worksheet name. Note that the final 25 argument is any number large enough to handle the longest sheet name you've used.

Additional Details: If you need to insert just the worksheet path in a cell, you can use =INFO("Directory") instead of trying to parse it from the CELL function.

Gotcha: The INFO function used to be able to return several bits of information about memory available, total memory, and so on. These results have not been correct since Windows XP. Today, Excel will return #N/A if you use the INFO function to return available memory.

USE AUTOSUM TO QUICKLY ENTER A TOTAL FORMULA

Problem: I have numeric data in Excel. I need to total the rows quickly.

	A	B	C	D	E	F
1	Item	Q1	Q2	Q3	Q4	Total
2	ABC	91	92	22	83	
3	DEF	31	41	17	33	
4	GHI	72	63	82	64	
5	JKL	21	98	4	90	
6	MNO	36	81	52	35	
7	PQR	22	90	87	75	
8	STU	65	85	72	34	
9	VWX	91	40	41	6	
10	Total					

Figure 257 *Add total formulas.*

Strategy: You can use the AutoSum button on the Home tab or Formulas tab. The AutoSum button is a Greek letter sigma.

Figure 258 *A Greek letter sigma is the math symbol for sum.*

Here's how you use AutoSum to add a total formula:

1. Place the cell pointer in cell B10. Click the AutoSum button. Excel analyzes your data and predicts that you want to total the range of numbers above the cell pointer. Excel proposes the provisional formula =SUM(B2:B9).
2. Review the range in the proposed formula, if needed. If the range is correct, press Enter to accept the formula. Excel displays the total.
3. With the mouse, drag the fill handle (the square dot in the lower-right corner of the cell pointer) to the right to include cells C10 through F10 and then release the mouse button. The formula will be copied to all five columns.

Additional Details: You can use Alt+= instead of clicking the AutoSum button.

	A	B	C	D	E	F	G
1	Item	Q1	Q2	Q3	Q4	Total	
2	ABC	91	92	22	83		
3	DEF	31	41	17	33		
4	GHI	72	63	82	64		
5	JKL	21	98	4	90		
6	MNO	36	81	52	35		
7	PQR	22	90	87	75		
8	STU	65	85	72	34		
9	VWX	91	40	41	6		
10	Total	=SUM(B2:B9)					
11		SUM(**number1**, [number2], ...)					
12							

Figure 259 *Excel proposes a formula.*

Gotcha: Blank cells in the sum range will cause AutoSum to exclude cells above the blank cell.

AUTOSUM DOESN'T ALWAYS PREDICT MY DATA CORRECTLY

Problem: When I use the AutoSum button, Excel sometimes predicts the wrong range of data to total. Below, AutoSum worked fine in F2 and F3, but in cell F4, Excel thought I wanted to total the rows above F4. How do I enter the correct range?

Strategy: After you press the AutoSum button, the provisional range address is highlighted in the provisional formula. Using your mouse, you highlight the correct range.

	A	B	C	D	E	F	G
1	Item	Q1	Q2	Q3	Q4	Total	
2	ABC	91	92	22	83	288	
3	DEF	31	41	17	33	122	
4	GHI	72	63	82	64	=SUM(B4:E4)	

Figure 260 *Excel chose the column instead of the row*

AutoSum will work correctly in F2 and F3. It will predict that you want to sum the data in that row. However, in cell F4, Excel has a choice: either sum the two cells in that column or the four cells in the row. Excel always chooses to sum the two cells above in this situation.

After you press the AutoSum button, note that F2:F3 is highlighted in the formula. This allows you to enter the correct range. There are three methods:

- With the mouse, highlight B4:E4 and press Enter.
- With the keyboard, type B4:E4.
- Using the arrow keys, press the Left Arrow key to move to E4. While holding down the Shift key, press the Left Arrow key three times to highlight B4:E4.

AutoSum can also fail when one number in your range contains a SUM formula. The provisional formula will offer to sum a formula extending up to but not including the previous SUM formula.

Alternate Strategy: You can choose to enter all the totals at one time by using the AutoSum button. This is faster than the methods just described and will eliminate the problem described. Follow these steps:

1. Highlight the entire range that needs a SUM formula.
2. Press the AutoSum button. Excel makes a prediction and fills in the total formulas automatically. Excel does not show the provisional formula, so check one formula to see that it is correct.

	A	B	C	D	E	F
1	Item	Q1	Q2	Q3	Q4	Total
2	ABC	91	92	22	83	
3	DEF	31	41	17	33	
4	GHI	72	63	82	64	
5	JKL	21	98	4	90	
6	MNO	36	81	52	35	
7	PQR	22	90	87	75	
8	STU	65	85	72	34	
9	VWX	91	40	41	6	
10	Total	429	590	377	420	
11						

Figure 261 *Select the entire range*

`=SUM(B2:E2)`

	A	B	C	D	E	F
1	Item	Q1	Q2	Q3	Q4	Total
2	ABC	91	92	22	83	288
3	DEF	31	41	17	33	122
4	GHI	72	63	82	64	281
5	JKL	21	98	4	90	213
6	MNO	36	81	52	35	204
7	PQR	22	90	87	75	274
8	STU	65	85	72	34	256
9	VWX	91	40	41	6	178
10	Total	429	590	377	420	1816
11						

Figure 262 *Provisional formulas are not displayed.*

Gotcha: Headings that contain dates or numeric years can really cause problems for AutoSum. Excel will usually get fooled into including the heading in the sum. Be extra cautious when using AutoSum in these situations. Here, Excel incorrectly included the headings in row 1.

There is an amazing workaround. You can select the cells to be totaled plus one extra row and one extra column.

When you click the AutoSum button, Excel correctly adds SUM formulas in the total row and total column.

`=SUM(B1:B9)`

	A	B	C	D	E
1	Item	2014	2015	2016	2017
2	ABC	1	1	1	1
3	DEF	1	1	1	1
4	GHI	1	1	1	1
5	JKL	1	1	1	1
6	MNO	1	1	1	1
7	PQR	1	1	1	1
8	STU	1	1	1	1
9	VWX	1	1	1	1
10	Total	2022	2023	2024	2025
11					

Figure 263 *The numeric year headings are mistakenly included.*

	A	B	C	D	E	F
1	Item	Q1	Q2	Q3	Q4	Total
2	ABC	91	92	22	83	
3	DEF	31	41	17	33	
4	GHI	72	63	82	64	
5	JKL	21	98	4	90	
6	MNO	36	81	52	35	
7	PQR	22	90	87	75	
8	STU	65	85	72	34	
9	VWX	91	40	41	6	
10	Total					
11						

Figure 264 *Select an extra row and an extra column*

`=SUM(B2:B9)`

	A	B	C	D	E	F
1	Item	Q1	Q2	Q3	Q4	Total
2	ABC	91	92	22	83	288
3	DEF	31	41	17	33	122
4	GHI	72	63	82	64	281
5	JKL	21	98	4	90	213
6	MNO	36	81	52	35	204
7	PQR	22	90	87	75	274
8	STU	65	85	72	34	256
9	VWX	91	40	41	6	178
10	Total	429	590	377	420	1816
11						

Figure 265 *Add totals in one click.*

Another AutoSum oddity is shown here. The cell-pointer is directly below a SUM function. There are additional SUM functions in the range that would normally be included in the AutoSum. In that case, AutoSum will only include the other SUM functions.

	A	B	C	D
1	A1	11		
2	A2	12		
3	Total A	23	=SUM(A1:A2)	
4	B8	13		
5	B9	14		
6	Total B	27	=SUM(A4:A5)	
7	C5	15		
8	C6	16		
9	C7	17		
10	C8	18		
11	Total C	66	=SUM(A7:A10)	
12	Grand Total	=SUM(B11,B6,B3)		

Figure 266 *AutoSum only sums the SUM formulas.*

USE THE AUTOSUM BUTTON TO ENTER AVERAGES, MIN, MAX, AND COUNT

Problem: I often enter totals formulas, but in this case, I need to enter an average formula. How can I do it quickly?

	A	B	C	D
1	XYZ Science Lab			
2	Station 123 Temperature Readings			
3				
4	Time	Reading		
5	1:00 AM	86.2		
6	1:05 AM	86.22		
7	1:10 AM	86.21		
8	1:15 AM	86.26		
9	1:20 AM	86.24		
10	1:25 AM	86.31		
11	1:30 AM	86.33		
12	1:35 AM	86.33		
13	1:40 AM	86.43		
14	1:45 AM	86.61		
15	1:50 AM	86.88		
16	1:55 AM	87.18		
17	Average			
18				

Figure 267 *Average the readings.*

Strategy: You use the dropdown arrow located next to the AutoSum button. Instead of selecting Sum, you select the Average option.

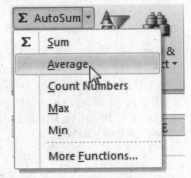

Figure 268 *The AutoSum dropdown offers additional functions.*

DITTO THE FORMULA ABOVE

Problem: I routinely have to sum and average the same range. The sum is easy enough with the Auto-Sum. But when I try to do the average, the formula above is in the way.

=SUM(B5:B10)

	A	B	C	D
1	XYZ Science Lab			
2	Station 123 Temperature Readings			
3				
4	Time	Reading		
5	1:00 AM	86.2		
6	1:05 AM	86.22		
7	1:10 AM	86.21		
8	1:15 AM	86.26		
9	1:20 AM	86.24		
10	1:25 AM	86.31		
11	Total	517.44		
12	Average			
13				

Figure 269 *Add a total and an average.*

Strategy: Go to cell B12. Hold Ctrl while you press the key with the ditto mark. (Remember the ditto mark from elementary school? It was a double quotation mark: ".) Technically, you are pressing Ctrl+Apostrophe, but think of it as Ctrl+Ditto.

Excel will make an exact copy of the formula above and show you the provisional formula. Why is this better than a copy and paste? A copied formula would change the B5:B10 range to be B6:B11. A dittoed range will keep the reference to B5:B10.

10	1:25 AM	86.31
11	Total	517.44
12	Average	=SUM(B5:B10)
13		

Figure 270 *Ctrl+Ditto copies the formula without changing the reference.*

From the point in the figure above, you can press F2, Home, Right Arrow, AVERAGE, Delete, Delete, Delete, Enter.

THE COUNT OPTION OF THE AUTOSUM DROPDOWN DOESN'T APPEAR TO WORK

Problem: I am using the Count option from the AutoSum dropdown on the toolbar, but it does not appear to provide consistent results. Cells B11 and C11 both contain counts of the cells in rows 2 through 10 of each column. One function indicates that there are nine entries; the other function indicates that there are only two. Clearly, both columns have nine entries. What is the problem?

Strategy: The COUNT function will count only numeric entries. If you need to count all entries, you have to use the COUNTA function. One solution is to edit the formula in B2 by adding an A after the T in COUNT. The other method is to enter the formula correctly in the first place. Here's what you do:

=COUNT(B2:B10)

	A	B	C
1		Purchase Order	Amount
2		A12345	878.31
3		05J123	566.41
4		WMJ987	165.91
5		9878	115.97
6		KJHK98	788.5
7		87-9878	890.7
8		34H8987	665.17
9		87888	161.94
10		H12354	681.09
11	Count:	2	9

Figure 271 *Why does Excel think the count is two?*

1. Put the cell pointer in B11. Select AutoSum dropdown, More Functions. There are hundreds of functions available, and it can be difficult to remember
where a function is; for example, you don't know if
COUNTA is in the Math & Trig section or somewhere
else.

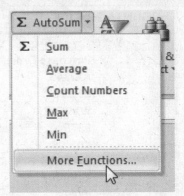

Figure 272 *The AutoSum dropdown can
lead to more functions.*

2. In the Search for a Function box, type the words "count text" then click Go. Excel will propose possible functions. You can click on each function to see a one-line description of what the function does.

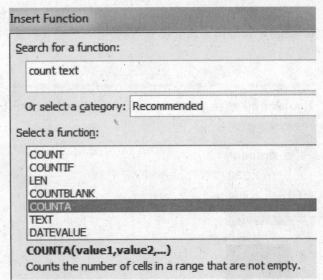

Figure 273 *Excel proposes functions related to your search.*

3. Click on COUNTA and then click OK. Excel will analyze your data and predict the range that you
want to use. However, Excel is not good at predicting data when the range contains numeric and
alphanumeric entries. The Function Arguments dialog box appears. In this particular case, Excel
assumes that you only want to use COUNTA on the range B9:B10.

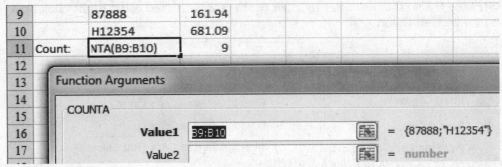

Figure 274 *Excel guessed the range incorrectly.*

4. If you can see the data on the worksheet, use the mouse and highlight the correct range. If the range
is behind the dialog, click the Reference icon at the right edge of the text box. Then highlight the correct range. Alternatively, you can drag the dialog box until your range is completely visible.

5. Click OK in the Function Arguments dialog to accept the formula.

Results: The COUNTA function returns the desired value.

`=COUNTA(B2:B10)`

	A	B	C
1		Purchase Order	Amount
2		A12345	878.31
3		05J123	566.41
4		WMJ987	165.91
5		9878	115.97
6		KJHK98	788.5
7		87-9878	890.7
8		34H8987	665.17
9		87888	161.94
10		H12354	681.09
11	Count:	9	9

Figure 275 *COUNTA returns the expected result.*

Additional Details: COUNTA will not count blank cells. You use COUNTBLANK to return the number of empty cells in a range.

TOTAL THE RED CELLS

Problem: I've marked several cells in red. I need to total the red cells.

	A
1	**Amount**
2	530
3	394
4	473
5	816
6	304
7	689
8	483
9	810
10	285

Figure 276 *Total the red cells.*

Strategy: Use the new filter by color to show only the red cells. Right-click on a red cell and choose Filter, Filter by Cell Color.

Figure 277 *Choose to filter by cell color.*

Only the red cells will be shown. After applying the filter, go to the first visible blank cell below the data and press the AutoSum button or Alt+Equals. When applied to a filtered dataset, the AutoSum button switches from the SUM function to the SUBTOTAL function. This function will sum only the visible cells, providing a sum of the red cells.

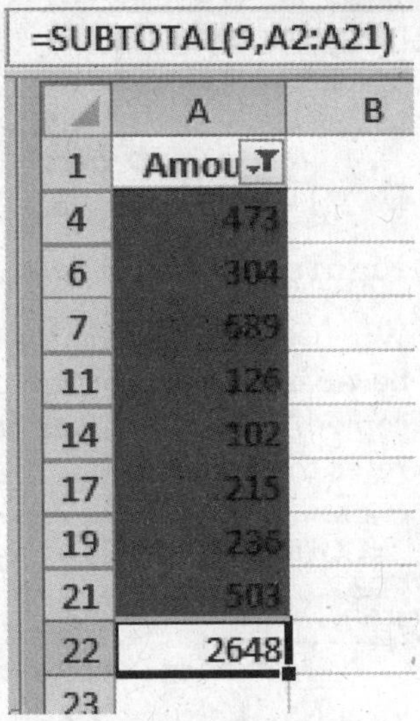

=SUBTOTAL(9,A2:A21)

	A	B
1	Amou ⊤	
4	473	
6	304	
7	589	
11	126	
14	102	
17	215	
19	236	
21	503	
22	2648	
23		

Figure 278 *AutoSum uses SUBTOTAL now.*

Additional Details: This feature will work even if the red has been applied by conditional formatting.

Gotcha: When you clear the filter to show all cells, the formula will include the non-red cells. If you need a formula to add the red cells while displaying the other cells, you would have to use a User Defined Function in the Excel VBA language.

AUTOMATICALLY NUMBER A LIST OF EMPLOYEES

Problem: I work in human resources, and I have a list of employees, separated by department. I have a numeric sequence in column A and the employees' names in column B. Every time the company hires or fires an employee, I have to manually renumber all the employees. How can I make this job easier?

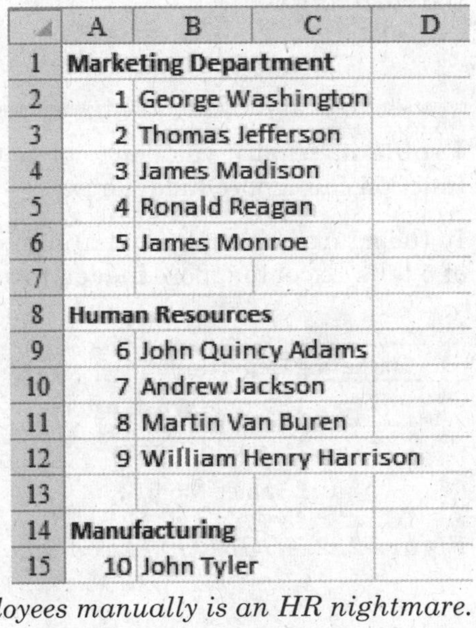

	A	B	C	D
1	**Marketing Department**			
2	1	George Washington		
3	2	Thomas Jefferson		
4	3	James Madison		
5	4	Ronald Reagan		
6	5	James Monroe		
7				
8	**Human Resources**			
9	6	John Quincy Adams		
10	7	Andrew Jackson		
11	8	Martin Van Buren		
12	9	William Henry Harrison		
13				
14	**Manufacturing**			
15	10	John Tyler		

Figure 279 *Numbering the employees manually is an HR nightmare.*

Strategy: You can replace the numbers in column A with a formula that will count the entries in column B. The formula should count from the current row all the way up to row 1.

The COUNT function will not work because it only counts numeric entries. You need to use the COUNTA function and keep in mind the following points:
- The range that should be counted should extend from B1 to the current row.
- The notation to always use B1 is B$1.

Here's what you do:
1. Enter the formula =COUNTA(B$1:B2) in cell A2.

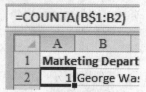

Figure 280 *Count from B1 to the current row.*

When you copy this formula down a row, the range that is counted will extend from B1 to B3. This is because the B2 portion of the formula is a relative reference that is allowed to change as the formula is copied. The dollar sign in the B$1 reference tells Excel that when you copy the formula, it should always refer to row 1.

Figure 281 *The range now extends from B1 to B3.*

The range now extends from B1 to B3.
2. Copy the formula down to all the names in your list. They will be numbered just as when you typed in the names in manually.

Results: When an employee leaves the company, you can simply delete the row, and all of the later rows will be renumbered. When you hire a new person, you can insert a blank row, enter the new hire's name, and then copy any formula from another cell in A to the new row.

While this is a specific example, the concept of using a range as an argument where only one portion of the range contains an absolute reference is a common solution to keeping a running total of all cells above the current row.

AUTOMATICALLY NUMBER THE VISIBLE ROWS

Problem: What if you don't delete the past employees, but you hide the rows? The newer AGGREGATE function can ignore hidden rows.

In the figure below, the first argument of 3 tells Excel to use the COUNTA function. The second argument of 5 tells Excel to ignore hidden rows.

	A	B	C	D	E
1	Marketing Department				
2	1	George Washington	=AGGREGATE(3,5,B$1:B2)		
5	2	Ronald Reagan	=AGGREGATE(3,5,B$1:B5)		
6	3	James Monroe	=AGGREGATE(3,5,B$1:B6)		

Figure 282 *AGGREGATE can ignore errors, other subtotals, or hidden rows.*

DISCOVER NEW FUNCTIONS USING THE FX BUTTON

Problem: There are hundreds of functions available in Excel. I know that I want to find a function to calculate a car payment, but I have no clue which function might do this.

Strategy: To find a function, you can click the Insert Function (fx) button. This button is always available to the left of the formula bar, and it appears 12 additional times in Excel, mostly on the Formulas tab. This figure shows three instances of the fx button. You can click this button to bring up the Insert Function dialog.

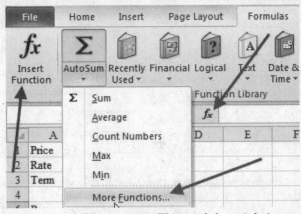

Figure 283 *Three of the 13 fx icons.*

By default, the Insert Function dialog lists the most recently used functions. All of Excel's functions are categorized into these categories: Financial, Date & Time, Math & Trig, Statistical, Lookup & Reference, Database, Text, Logical, Information, Cube, and Engineering. It can be difficult to correctly guess the category. SUM is a Math & Trig function, yet AVERAGE is a Statistical function. Rather than browse each category, you can type a few words in the search box and click Go. Excel will show you the relevant functions to choose from.

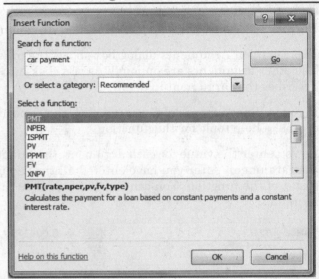

Figure 284 *Search for a function.*

GET HELP ON ANY FUNCTION WHILE ENTERING A FORMULA

Problem: There are hundreds of functions available in Excel. Sometimes I remember that I need to use a particular function, but I cannot remember the sequence of the arguments in the function.

Strategy: In Excel 2002 and later, if you type the equal sign followed by the function and the opening parenthesis, a ToolTip will appear reminding you of the order of the arguments. Any arguments in square brackets are optional. The argument in bold is the argument you need to type next.

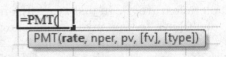

Figure 285 *The ToolTip lists the arguments.*

Alternate Strategy: If you need more help than the ToolTip's abbreviations (for example, pmt, pv) provide, you can use the Function Arguments dialog. To do so, you type the equals sign followed by the function name and the opening parenthesis, and then press Ctrl+A to display the Function Arguments dialog box.

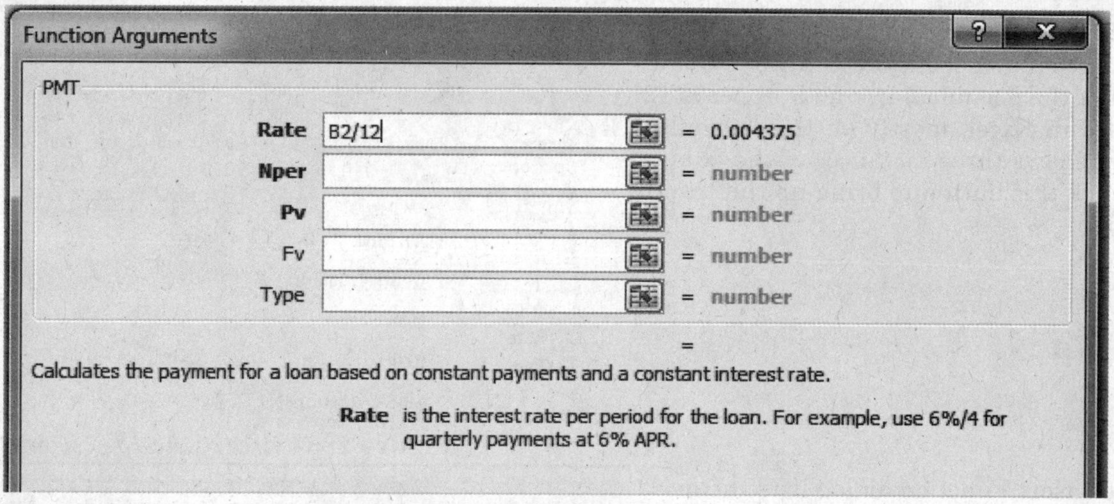

Figure 286 *Notice the help for the current argument at the bottom.*

The Function Arguments dialog box shows the order of the arguments. Arguments in bold are required. The other arguments are optional. As you click into each text box in the dialog box, the text at the bottom describes that argument in detail.

If you still need more help, you can click the hyperlink at the bottom of the dialog box, which leads to the complete help topic for this function.

As you enter the value for each argument, the Function Arguments dialog box will calculate the results of that argument. After you have entered all the required arguments, the Function Wizard will display the result of the function. You can consider whether this result is a reasonable number before accepting the formula.

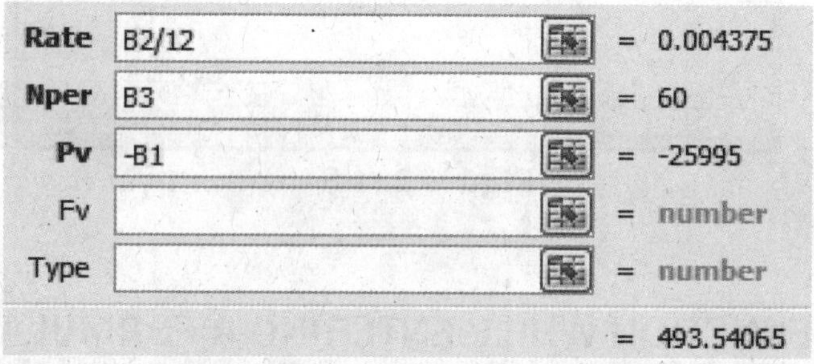

Figure 287 *The solution appears at bottom right.*

YES, FORMULA AUTOCOMPLETE IS COOL, IF YOU CAN STOP ENTERING THE OPENING PARENTHESES

Problem: At an Excel launch event, the Microsoft rep showed off the amazing new Formula AutoComplete feature. I can just type =RA in a cell, and Excel will show me all the functions that start with RA. I don't have to type my functions anymore, but why do I get an error every time I try to do this?

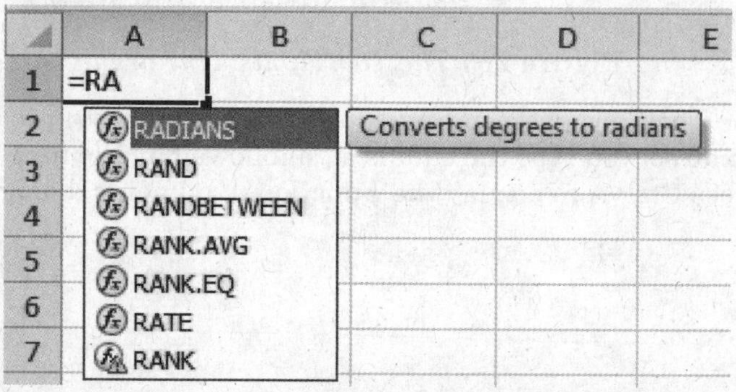

Figure 288 *Yes, Formula AutoComplete is cool.*

Strategy: Watch the parentheses! AutoComplete types the opening parenthesis, but not the closing parenthesis.

Here is how you're supposed to use AutoComplete:

1. Type =RA. Excel displays a list of five functions.
2. Use the down arrow to move to RANDBETWEEN. Excel will show a ToolTip to indicate that the function will return a random number between the numbers you specify.
3. Press the Tab key to accept the function and move to the arguments. I was used to using the Tab key here because I've been using AutoComplete in VBA for a while. However, many people try to press Enter here, which leads to a #NAME? error. After you press the Tab key, Excel fills in the function name and the opening parenthesis.

	A	B	C
1	=RANDBETWEEN(		
2	RANDBETWEEN(**bottom**, top)		
3			

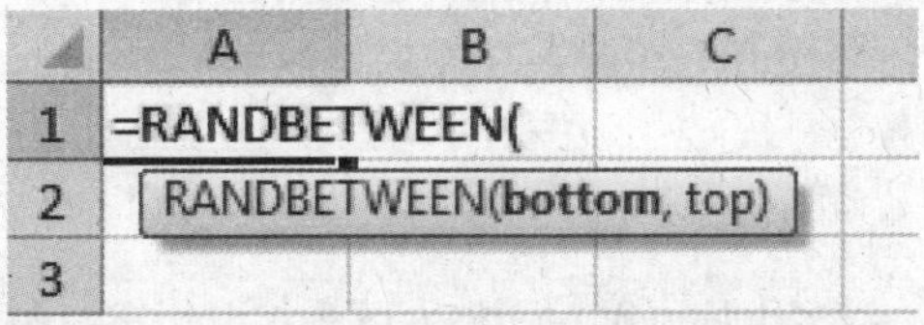

Figure 289 *Press Tab to finish typing the selected function name.*

Gotcha: I will sound ungrateful, but Microsoft types the opening parenthesis for you. I cannot seem to break the habit of typing the opening parenthesis myself. Going back to the days of typing @SUM(, or even typing =SUM(, my fingers automatically type the opening parenthesis. I cannot type =RANDBETWEEN(without typing an opening parenthesis. Here, let me try a few more: =VLOOKUP(=AVERAGE(=TRIM(=MID(=ROMAN(. My brain is simply hard-wired to type that opening parenthesis. I don't even consciously think about typing the parenthesis. It simply just gets typed.

So, as you can guess, every time I use AutoComplete, I get an error saying that I've typed too many parentheses.

I don't have a good solution for this, other than trying to retrain yourself not to type the opening parenthesis.

USE F9 IN THE FORMULA BAR TO TEST A FORMULA

Problem: I have a complex formula that does not appear to be providing the correct result. The formula has multiple terms, and I am not sure which part is not working correctly.

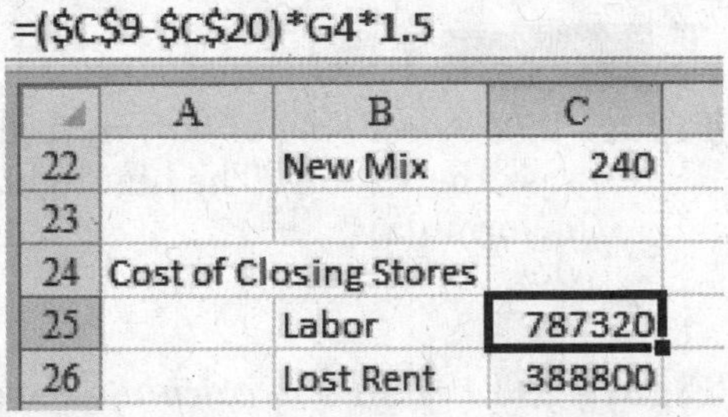

=($C$9-$C$20)*G4*1.5

	A	B	C
22		New Mix	240
23			
24	Cost of Closing Stores		
25		Labor	787320
26		Lost Rent	388800

Figure 290 *Troubleshoot this formula.*

Strategy: You can use F9 to test a formula. Here's how:

1. Select cell C25 and press F2 to put the cell in Edit mode. In this mode, each cell reference in the formula is color coded. The $C$9 text in the formula is blue, and the outline around C9 is blue.

	A	B	C	D	E	F	G
1	Section 1: Historical Trends (Per Month)						
2							
3		Store Type	Size	Rent	Sales	Profit	Labor
4		Regular	1200	2400	12456	6228	6480
5		BigBox	2600	5200	34500	17250	8640
6							
7	Section 2: Number of Stores						
8							
9		Regular	81	30.6%			0.3057
10		BigBox	184				
11							
12	Section 3: Analysis of Profitability of Current Store Mix						
13			Sales	Net Profit	NP%		
14		Total Chain	8.8E+07	4951536	5.6%		
15		Regular	1.2E+07	-2577744	-21.3%		
16		Big Box	7.6E+07	7529280	9.9%		
17							
18	Section 4: Profit Projections with a New Mix of Stores						
19				Sales	Profit	NP%	
20		Regular	0	0	0		
21		BigBox	240	99360000	9820800		
22		New Mix	240	99360000	9820800	10%	
23							
24	Cost of Closing Stores						
25		Labor	=($C$9-$C$20)*G4*1.5				
26		Lost Rent	388800				

Figure 291 *In Edit mode, the formula references are color coded.*

2. To selectively calculate just a portion of the formula, use the mouse to highlight a portion of the formula.

=($C$9-$C$20)*G4*1.5

Figure 292 *Select part of the formula.*

3. Press the F9 key. The highlighted portion of the formula will be replaced with the current result of the formula.

=(81)*G4*1.5

Figure 293 *Press F9 to calculate the highlighted portion.*

4. Press the Esc key to return to the original formula.

Additional Details: If you press F9 without selecting anything, it will calculate the entire formula and replace it in the result.

Figure 294 *Press F9 to calculate the entire formula.*

QUICK CALCULATOR

Problem: I need to find a quick answer to a mathematical problem, and I don't have a calculator. Can Excel help?

Strategy: You can use Excel as a simple calculator. Follow these steps:

1. Go to a blank cell.
2. Type an equals sign.
3. Enter a calculation.

Figure 295 *Type = and a calculation in a blank cell.*

4. Press the F9 key. Excel will display the result.

Figure 296 *The result..*

5. Press the Esc key to clear the cell.

You can start a formula with equals, plus, or minus signs. You could also have typed +14215469*5.

WHEN ENTERING A FORMULA, YOU GET THE FORMULA INSTEAD OF THE RESULT

Problem: When entering a formula, Excel shows me the formula in the cell instead of the result.

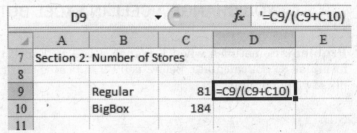

Figure 297 *Excel displays the formula.*

Strategy: There are three possible problems in this case.

Possibility 1: You may have forgotten to start the formula with an equals sign.

Figure 298 *You forgot to start the formula with an equals sign.*

Follow these steps to correct the formula:
1. Select the cell and press F2 to edit the cell.
2. Press the Home key to go to the beginning of the formula.
3. If there see a hidden apostrophe, delete it using the Delete key.
4. Type the = sign.
5. Press Enter. Excel shows the result.

Possibility 2: The cell might have been assigned the numeric format @, which is the code for a text cell. The maddening part of this problem is that this format can get set even without you knowing it. A column can inherit a text format if you import a text file and use the text setting for the import. Here's how you fix this **problem:**
1. Select the problematic cell. Look in the Number group in the Home tab of the ribbon.
2. Confirm that the cell has a Text format assigned.

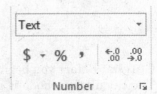

Figure 299 *Text formats will show the formula and not the results.*
Figure 300

3. Change the cell to any format other than Text.
4. This does not fix the formula! Edit the cell using the F2 key and then press Enter.

Possibility 3: The third possibility, which is the least likely, is that you are in Show Formulas mode, as shown here. In this mode, all the cells that have formulas show their formulas.

81	=C9/(C9+C10)			
184				

	Sales		Net Profit	NP%
	=+C15+C16	=+D15+D16		=+D14/C14
	=(C9*E4)*12	=(C9*H4)*12		=+D15/C15
	=(C10*E5)*12	=(C10*H5)*12		=+D16/C16

Figure 301 *See all formulas.*

To fix this problem, you press Ctrl+` to toggle in and out of Show Formulas mode. (On U.S. keyboards, this character is below the Esc key, on the same key as the tilde.)

When a cell shows a formula rather than a result, there are three possible reasons: (1) You forgot to start the formula with an equals (=) sign, (2) the cell is not formatted for numeric data, or (3) the worksheet is in Show Formula mode.

YOU CHANGE A CELL IN EXCEL BUT THE FORMULAS DO NOT CALCULATE

Problem: Sometimes when I change a cell in Excel, the formulas do not calculate. Below, cell C2 indicates that two plus two is not four.

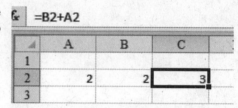

	A	B	C
1			
2	2	2	3
3			

Figure 302 *Excel isn't calculating.*

Strategy: In this case, someone has put the worksheet in Manual calculation mode. You can try pressing F9 to calculate.

There are several variants of recalculating:
- Pressing F9 will recalculate all cells that have changed since the last calculation, plus all formulas that depend on those cells in all open workbooks.
- For quicker calculation, use Shift+F9. This will limit the calculation to the current worksheet.
- For thorough calculation, use Ctrl+Alt+F9. This will calculate all formulas in all open workbooks, whether Excel thinks they have changed or not.
- Pressing Ctrl+Shift+Alt+F9 rebuilds the list of dependent formulas and then does a thorough calculation.

Additional Details: You can change the Calculation Options. Select Formulas, Calculation Options to see the various calculation options.

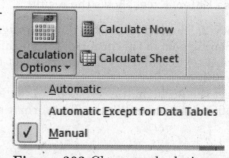

Figure 303 *Change calculation settings.*

Gotcha: Before you begin using manual calculation mode, you need to understand a dangerous situation. The calculation mode is global for all workbooks that are currently open. Say that you open WorkbookA and it is in manual calculation mode. You then open Workbook2 through Workbook9, change a few cells and save them. All the while, WorkbookA remained open in the background. This will change the calculation mode on Workbook2 through Workbook9 to manual. While it is easy to see in Figure 302 that something is wrong, it is not easy to notice that manual calculation mode is on in most workbooks. You can see how manual calculation mode can insidiously spread through your workbooks like a virus.

Gotcha: Before you go back to Automatic calculation mode, ask the person who created the worksheet why it is in Manual calculation mode. Sometimes you will find a spreadsheet with tens of thousands of calculations that takes 30–45 seconds to calculate. It is very frustrating when the system pauses for 45 seconds after every single data entry. If you have a lot of data entry to do, a standard strategy is to use Manual calculation mode because in this mode, you can make several changes and then press F9 to calculate.

If you frequently use Manual calculation mode, right-click on both Automatic and Manual in the Calculations Options dropdown and choose Add to Quick Access Toolbar.

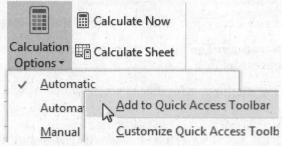

Figure 304 *Add both Automatic and Manual to the QAT*

The result: you will have two checkboxes on the QAT that always show you if you are in Manual or Automatic calculation mode.

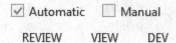

Figure 305 *See at a glance if you are in Manual calculation mode.*

CALCULATE ONE RANGE

Problem: I have a workbook that takes 3 minutes to calculate. I changed to manual calculation mode so I can enter data without waiting for a recalculation after each data entry. I just changed 10 cells and I only want to recalculate the 10 rows that rely on those cells. I don't want to wait 3 minutes when there are only 10 cells that need recalculated.

Strategy: You can press F2 and Enter on each cell that has to be calculated. This will force a single cell to calculate. For 10 cells, try this trick:
1. Select the cells that should be calculated. This must include more than one cell, or Excel will calculate the entire worksheet.
2. Ctrl+H to display the Find and Replace dialog.
3. Type an equals sign in the Find What box.
4. Type an equals sign in the Replace With box.
5. Click the Options >> button. Make sure that Look In is set to Formulas and that Match Entire Cell Contents is not checked.
6. Click Replace All.

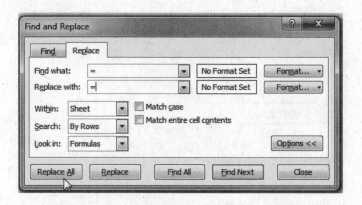

Figure 306 *Replace an equals with an equals.*

Result: Only the selected range will be calculated.

Additional Details: After you have done the six steps above, you can quickly recalculate the selected range by using Ctrl+H, Alt+A. This will re-open the Find and Replace dialog, then do a Replace All with the previous settings.

Tip: If calculation bottlenecks are causing problems, you need to check out the amazing Fast Excel V3 utility from Charles Williams. Details are at http://tinyurl.com/fastexcel.

WHY USE THE INTERSECTION OPERATOR?

Problem: What is the purpose of the intersection operator?

Strategy: The intersection is the most obscure of the operators. Let's run through some examples of other operators first.

The simplest reference is when you point to a single cell.

◢	A	B	C	D	E	F	G	H	I
1		Jan	Feb	Mar	Apr	May	Jun	Jul	Aug
2	ProdA	1	2	3	5	8	13	21	34
3	ProdB	2	3	5	8	13	21	34	55
4	ProdC	3	4	7	11	18	29	47	76
5	ProdD	4	5	9	14	23	37	60	97
6	ProdE	5	6	11	17	28	45	73	118
7	ProdF	6	7	13	20	33	53	86	139
8	ProdG	7	8	15	23	38	61	99	160
9									
10	=SUM(B3)								
11	57								
12	141								

Figure 307 *Pointing to a single cell.*

If you sum two cells and separate those cells with a comma, then Excel will add up the two individual cells. Below, the formula is adding B3 and I3.

◢	A	B	C	D	E	F	G	H	I
1		Jan	Feb	Mar	Apr	May	Jun	Jul	Aug
2	ProdA	1	2	3	5	8	13	21	34
3	ProdB	2	3	5	8	13	21	34	55
4	ProdC	3	4	7	11	18	29	47	76
5	ProdD	4	5	9	14	23	37	60	97
6	ProdE	5	6	11	17	28	45	73	118
7	ProdF	6	7	13	20	33	53	86	139
8	ProdG	7	8	15	23	38	61	99	160
9									
10	2								
11	=SUM(B3,I3)								
12	141								

Figure 308 *Adding two cells.*

When you list two cells and separate those cells with a colon, Excel will add up everything between and including the two cells.

◢	A	B	C	D	E	F	G	H	I
1		Jan	Feb	Mar	Apr	May	Jun	Jul	Aug
2	ProdA	1	2	3	5	8	13	21	34
3	ProdB	2	3	5	8	13	21	34	55
4	ProdC	3	4	7	11	18	29	47	76
5	ProdD	4	5	9	14	23	37	60	97
6	ProdE	5	6	11	17	28	45	73	118
7	ProdF	6	7	13	20	33	53	86	139
8	ProdG	7	8	15	23	38	61	99	160
9									
10	2								
11	57								
12	=SUM(B3:I3)								
13									

Figure 309 *Specifying a range with a colon.*

Everyone using Excel has undoubtedly seen the references as shown above.

There is a different type of reference called an intersection. In this case, you would separate two ranges by a space instead of a comma. =SUM(C2:C8 B3:I3) would give you all of the cells in common between the two ranges.

To see a useful example, it would help to add many range names to the worksheet. Follow these steps:
1. Select A1:I8.
2. From the Formulas tab, select Create From Selection.

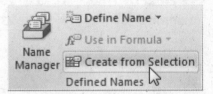

Figure 310 *This creates many names using labels in the range.*

3. Leave Top Row and Left Column checked. Click OK.

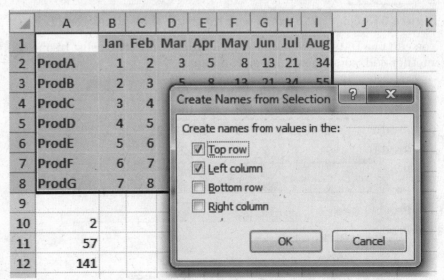

Figure 311 *Base the names on the left column and top row.*

This will create 15 new range names. The name of Mar now refers to D2:D8. The name of ProdG now refers to B8:I8. This itself is a cool trick.

| Mar | | | | f_x | =+C2+B2 | |

◢	A	B	C	D	E	F	G	H	I
1		Jan	Feb	Mar	Apr	May	Jun	Jul	Aug
2	ProdA	1	2	3	5	8	13	21	34
3	ProdB	2	3	5	8	13	21	34	55
4	ProdC	3	4	7	11	18	29	47	76
5	ProdD	4	5	9	14	23	37	60	97
6	ProdE	5	6	11	17	28	45	73	118
7	ProdF	6	7	13	20	33	53	86	139
8	ProdG	7	8	15	23	38	61	99	160

Figure 312 *Each column and each row get a name.*

Going back to the intersection operator, a formula of =SUM(Apr ProdC) will return the intersection of the two ranges. This provides an interesting way to do a two-way loookup.

| COUNTA | | | | X ✔ f_x | =SUM(Apr ProdC) | | | | | |

◢	A	B	C	D	E	F	G	H	I	J
1		Jan	Feb	Mar	Apr	May	Jun	Jul	Aug	
2	ProdA	1	2	3	5	8	13	21	34	
3	ProdB	2	3	5	8	13	21	34	55	
4	ProdC	3	4	7	11	18	29	47	76	
5	ProdD	4	5	9	14	23	37	60	97	
6	ProdE	5	6	11	17	28	45	73	118	
7	ProdF	6	7	13	20	33	53	86	139	
8	ProdG	7	8	15	23	38	61	99	160	
9										
10	2									
11	57									
12	141									
13	=SUM(Apr ProdC)									

Figure 313 *Only cell E4 is in both ranges. The result will be 11.*

You can use Data Validation to add a dropdown to two cells. In one cell, someone could select a product. In another cell, someone could select a month.

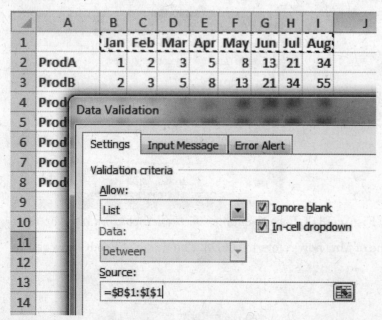

Figure 314 *Add a dropdown for months.*

The INDIRECT(J10) function tells Excel to go to J10 and the name of a range will be found in that cell. In the figure below, the formula in J12 is getting the intersection of ProdF and Apr, which returns the value of 20.

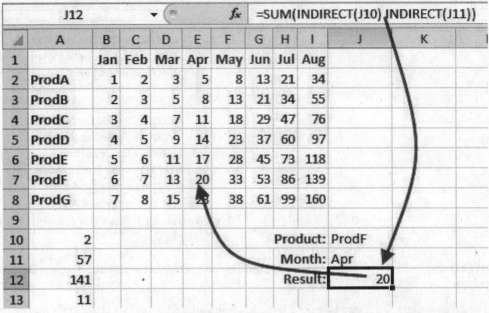

Figure 315 *Intersection of two ranges provides a two-way lookup.*

UNDERSTAND IMPLICIT INTERSECTION

Notice that the formulas in the previous two figures were outside of the range B:I. Those formulas would not work in that area due to a feature called "Implicit Intersection". Here is how it works.

The named range ProdF runs from B7:I7. If you enter a formula anywhere in columns B through I and that formula references ProdF, you will only get the value from that column of ProdF. In the image below, a formula of =ProdF in D10 returns the 13 from cell D7.

D10					▼	:	×	✓	*fx*	=ProdF

◢	A	B	C	D	E	F	G	H	I	J
6	ProdE	5	6	11	17	28	45	73	118	
7	ProdF	6	7	13	20	33	53	86	139	
8	ProdG	7	8	15	23	38	61	99	160	
9										
10				13	=ProdF					

Figure 316 *This formula returns the cell from ProdF that intersects with the formula.*

This clearly is not intuitive. In my Power Excel seminars, I occasionally find people who are taking advantage of the formula, but few are doing it knowingly. In a similar fashion, a formula of =Apr anywhere in rows 2:8 will return only the April sales from that row.

This feels like the old Natural Language Formulas in Excel 2003, but it is a different feature.

FIND THE LONGEST WIN STREAK

Problem: I have some baseball data with a column showing W or L for wins and losses. I want to calculate the longest winning streak.

	A	B	C	D
1	Date	Opponent	Loc	Result
3	4/1/2011	White Sox at Indians	H	L
4	4/2/2011	White Sox at Indians	H	L
5	4/3/2011	White Sox at Indians	H	W
6	4/5/2011	Red Sox at Indians	H	W
7	4/6/2011	Red Sox at Indians	H	W
8	4/7/2011	Red Sox at Indians	H	W
9	4/8/2011	Indians at Mariners	A	W
10	4/9/2011	Indians at Mariners	A	W
11	4/10/2011	Indians at Mariners	A	W
12	4/11/2011	Indians at Angels	A	W
13	4/12/2011	Indians at Angels	A	L

Figure 317 *Find the longest winning streak.*

Strategy: Add a column that will calculate the current winning streak. Then, look for the MAX of that column.

This formula is a classic type of formula that looks at a cell in the current row, makes a decision, and then adds to the value calculated in the previous row. This works great in all cases except in row 2. If you try to add the number 1 to a heading of "Win Streak" in cell E1, you will get a #VALUE error.

The figure above shows one solution: adding a blank row 2 and setting the row height to be very small. A second solution is to have a different formula in E2 than all of the other cells. Both of these solutions make it tough to sort the data (perhaps you want to find the longest Home winning streak so you want to sort by column C.)

A third solution exists. Put the number 0 in the heading for E1. Then, use Ctrl+1 (Ctrl+One) to get to the Format Cells dialog. On the Number tab, choose Custom in the Category list. Type a custom number format of "Winning Streak" including the quotes. This custom number format will allow a zero to be stored in E1, but will force Excel to show the words "Winning Streak" instead.

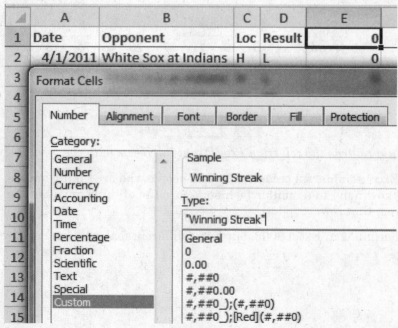

Figure 318 *Store a zero, but display a heading.*

The formula for E2 needs to see if D2 contains a W or an L. If there is a loss, then the winning streak starts over at zero. If there is a win, then add 1 game to the previous winning streak. When you have a conditional calculation like this, use the IF function. The IF function allows one of two calculations depending on the result of a logical test. In this case, the logical test is D2="W". If that is true, the formula should be 1+E1. Otherwise, the formula should be 0. The formula is =IF(D2="W",1+E1,0).

When you copy that formula down to all rows, it will calculate a winning streak.

	E2			fx	=IF(D2="W",1+E1,0)

◢	A	B	C	D	E
1	Date	Opponent	Loc	Result	Winning Streak
2	4/1/2011	White Sox at Indians	H	L	0
3	4/2/2011	White Sox at Indians	H	L	0
4	4/3/2011	White Sox at Indians	H	W	1
5	4/5/2011	Red Sox at Indians	H	W	2
6	4/6/2011	Red Sox at Indians	H	W	3

Figure 319 *Calculate a winning streak.*

To find the longest winning streak of the season, use =MAX(E:E).

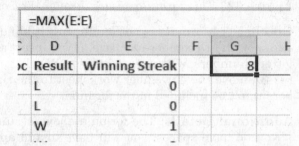

	=MAX(E:E)			
C	D	E	F	G
c	Result	Winning Streak		8
	L	0		
	L	0		
	W	1		

Figure 320 *Find the longest winning streak.*

Additional Details: To find the win/loss record, you can use a formula of =COUNTIF(D:D,"W")&"-"&COUNTIF(D:D,"L").

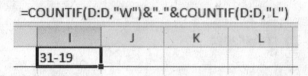

=COUNTIF(D:D,"W")&"-"&COUNTIF(D:D,"L")			
I	J	K	L
31-19			

Figure 321 *Count the number of W and L values.*

ADD B5 ON ALL WORKSHEETS

Problem: I have a workbook with 12 monthly sales reports. Each worksheet has identical rows and columns that show sales by week and region. The worksheets are named January, February, ..., December. I want to have a Total worksheet that sums cell E5 on all the other worksheets.

◢	A	B	C	D	E	F	G
1	Sales Report						
2	January						
3							
4		Week 1	Week 2	Week 3	Week 4	Week 5	Total
5	East	1025	2049	1553	2702	4481	11810
6	Central	1684	2719	3442	4929	2439	15213
7	West	2523	2829	4246	2156	3309	15063
8	Total	5232	7597	9241	9787	10229	42086
9							

|◄ ◄ ► ►|| Total | January | February | March | April | May |◄|

Figure 322 *Add cell B5 from each of the monthly worksheets.*

Strategy: You will use a 3D reference to spear through all of the worksheets. In the simplest form, a 3D reference lists the first worksheet, a colon, the second worksheet, an exclamation point, and then the cell address. =SUM(January:December!B5).

=SUM(January:December!B5)

◢	A	B	C	D
1	Sales Report			
2	Total			
3				
4		Week 1	Week 2	Week 3
5	East	34042	34874	34104
6	Central	37077	30464	39111
7	West	39625	40436	34147
8	Total	110744	105774	107362
9				

|◄ ◄ ► ►| **Total** / January / February / March

Figure 323 *This formula spears through 12 worksheets.*

Gotcha: The formula is not intelligent. It blindly adds up all of the worksheets that are located between January and December inclusive. If you insert a new worksheet in the middle of this workbook to list your lottery numbers, whatever value is in B5 will get added to the formula shown above. If you would for some reason move the November worksheet to the right of the December worksheet, then the November numbers won't be included in the formula.

Additional Details: The formula above assumes that you do not have spaces in the worksheet name. If you do have spaces, you will have to add apostrophes around the worksheet names: =SUM('January 2014:December 2014!B5).

=SUM('January 2014:December 2014'!B5)

◢	A	B	C	D	E
1	Sales Report				
2	Total 2014				
3					
4		Week 1	Week 2	Week 3	Week 4
5	East	34042	34874	34104	35315
6	Central	37077	30464	39111	31891
7	West	39625	40436	34147	34587
8	Total	110744	105774	107362	101793
9					

|◄ ◄ ► ►| **Total 2014** / January 2014 / February 2014

Figure 324 *Add apostrophes or you will set up an intersection.*

The workbook shown below is fairly amazing. In this workbook, there are already four quarterly worksheets that add up the months from that quarter. You want the Total worksheet to add Q1+Q2+Q3+Q4. In an amazing twist, you can use a wildcard while typing your 3D reference. The wildcard has to be inside apostrophes, even if your worksheet names do not include spaces. Type =SUM('Q*!B5). When you accept the formula, Excel will rewrite the formula as =SUM('Q1'!B5,'Q2'!B5,'Q3'!B5,'Q4'!B5).

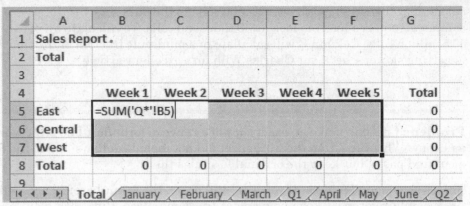

Figure 325 *Use a wildcard in the 3D reference.*

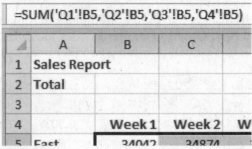

Figure 326 *Amazingly, Excel rewrites the formula for you.*

CONSIDER FORMULA SPEED

Problem: My workbook is calculating really slowly. Are there ways to speed it up?

Strategy: Add more memory to your computer. Get a faster computer. Go to Excel 2010 with 64-bit with multiple CPU cores. Starting in Excel 2007, Excel will split the calculation chain and send a portion to each processor.

Problem: There is no budget for a faster machine.

Strategy: Read Charles Williams white paper on Formula Speed. This document has amazing ideas on how to be mindful of formula speed when building Excel formulas. The document is at http://msdn.micro-soft.com/en-us/library/aa730921.aspx. Charles also sells the Fast Excel V3 utility which will analyze your workbook for bottlenecks. For details: http://tinyurl.com/fastexcel.

One concept in the article is moving a slow-calculating part of a formula out to a helper cell. If you have 1000 formulas that all divide by the same COUNTIF, you could move the COUNTIF to another cell and then have the 1000 formulas point to that one cell.

Another example is creating running totals. There are two choices here; use a formula of "add the cell above me to the cell to the left of me", also represented in R1C1 by =R[-1]C+RC[-1]. The other formula is the ultra-cool =SUM(E$2:E2). This formula's single dollar sign ensure that the range expands. Both provide the same answer.

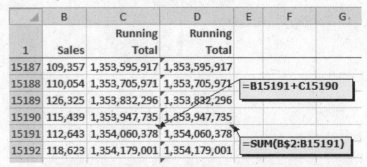

Figure 327 *Both formulas provide the same answer.*

Personally, I would always use the formula shown in Column D, because it is clever. In Charles' article, he points out that Excel only has to look at two cells to calculate cell C15191. It has to look at 15,190 cells to calculate cell D15191. With over 15,000 cells in the data set, this difference is dramatic. To calculate all of column C requires Excel to look at 30 thousand cells. To calculate all of column D requires Excel to look at 115 million cells. Column C will calculate in a miniscule fraction of the time of column D. If your worksheet is getting slower, check out Charles William's excellent article.

EXACT FORMULA COPY

Problem: I need to make an exact copy of a range of formulas. I do NOT want the cell references to change as I copy. Whoever set up the worksheet did not include dollar signs in the formulas. It is like I want to do a cut and paste, but keep the original formulas there.

This is a common problem. If you copy and paste, the formula references will change. If you cut and paste, the formula references keep pointing at the same place. But, with a cut and paste, the original formulas are no longer there.

Strategy: Use Find and Replace to replace the leading equals sign with a word. This changes the formulas to text. Copy the text to the new location, then use Find and Replace to change the word back to an equals sign. You will now have two identical sets of formulae.

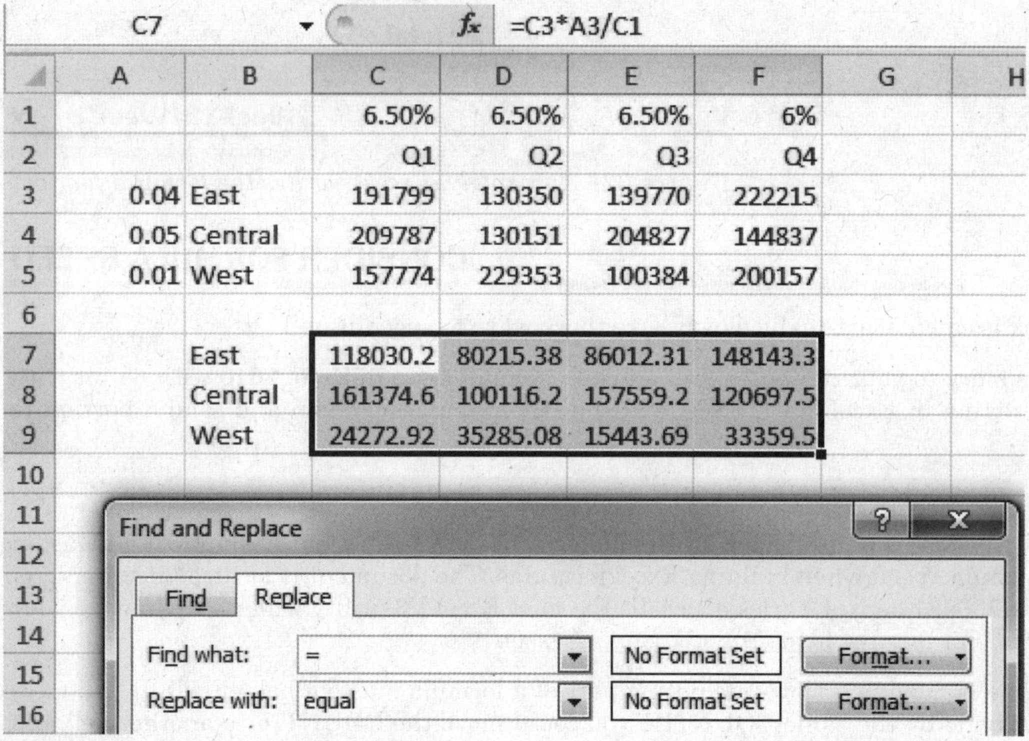

	C7			f_x	=C3*A3/C1		
	A	B	C	D	E	F	G	H
1			6.50%	6.50%	6.50%	6%		
2			Q1	Q2	Q3	Q4		
3	0.04	East	191799	130350	139770	222215		
4	0.05	Central	209787	130151	204827	144837		
5	0.01	West	157774	229353	100384	200157		
6								
7		East	118030.2	80215.38	86012.31	148143.3		
8		Central	161374.6	100116.2	157559.2	120697.5		
9		West	24272.92	35285.08	15443.69	33359.5		
10								

Find and Replace [? X]

Find | Replace

Find what: | =
Replace with: | equal

No Format Set　Format...
No Format Set　Format...

Figure 328 *Replace = with any word.*

After doing that replace, you have text versions of the formulas. Copy the text to a new place.

Use Find and Replace on both the original and copied range to change the word back to an equals sign.

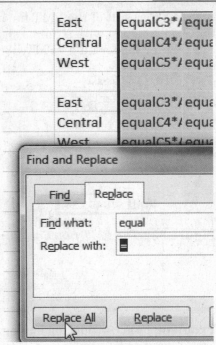

East	equalC3*/equa
Central	equalC4*/equa
West	equalC5*/equa
East	equalC3*/equa
Central	equalC4*/equa
West	equalC5*/equa

Find and Replace

Find | Replace

Find what: equal

Replace with: =

Replace All   Replace

Figure 329 *Change the text back to formulas.*

2

C11			f_x	=C3*A3/C1	
	A	B	C	D	E
6					
7		East	118030.2	80215.38	86012.3
8		Central	161374.6	100116.2	157559.
9		West	24272.92	35285.08	15443.6
10					
11		East	118030.2	80215.38	86012.3
12		Central	161374.6	100116.2	157559.
13		West	24272.92	35285.08	15443.6
14					
15					

Figure 330 *You have an exact copy of the original formulas.*

CALCULATE A LOAN PAYMENT

Problem: I am considering buying a car. I want to calculate the loan payment.

	A	B
1	Price	25995
2	Term	60
3	Rate	5.25%

Figure 331 *Set up the price, term, and interest rate..*

Strategy: To calculate your car loan payment, you can use the PMT function. Follow these steps:
1. Enter price, term in months, and annual percentage rate in cells A1:B3. The PMT function has three required arguments: the interest rate, the number of payments in the loan, and the original loan amount.

Gotcha: The interest rate must be entered as a percentage. If you are planning on monthly payments (which is normal), you have to divide the annual percentage rate by 12.

Gotcha: In financial terms, the bank is loaning you $25,995—a positive amount coming to you. Thus, the payments that you make to the bank are really a negative amount—money leaving your wallet. For this reason, the result of the PMT function will be negative. However, you can precede the third argument of the PMT function with a minus sign in order to return a positive payment amount.

2. Enter the formula =PMT(B3/12,B2,-B1) in cell B5.

=PMT(B3/12,B2,-B1)

	A	B
1	Price	25995
2	Term	60
3	Rate	5.25%
4		
5	Pmt	$493.54
6		

Figure 332 *The PMT function calculates the monthly payment.*

CALCULATE MANY SCENARIOS FOR LOAN PAYMENTS

Problem: I am considering buying a car. I used "Calculate a Loan Payment" to calculate a loan payment. Now I want to do some what-if scenarios in order to see various options of increasing or decreasing the term or price. How can Excel help me with this?

Strategy: You follow the same setup described in "Calculate a Loan Payment." Then you copy cells B1:B5 and plug in different numbers for the price and/or term.

	A	B	C	D	E	F	G	H
1	Price	25995	25995	25995	25995	24995	23995	15995
2	Term	60	66	72	48	60	60	60
3	Rate	5.25%	5.35%	5.45%	5.13%	5.25%	5.25%	5.25%
4								
5	Pmt	$493.54	$455.52	$424.10	$600.12	$474.55	$455.57	$303.68

Figure 333 *Copy so that you can play what-if analyses.*

This is an area where Excel shines. After you have entered the formulas for one loan model, you can easily copy and create many more loan models.

BACK INTO AN ANSWER USING GOAL SEEK

Problem: I've determined that I want to obtain a 60-month loan for a car. The interest rate is 5.25%. I want to find out what loan amount would result in a $425 monthly payment. Currently, the payment for a $25,995 car is too high at $493 as shown previously in Figure 332.

Strategy: Although you could use the PV function to calculate the price of the car, it is easier to use the Goal Seek command:

1. Select Data, What-if Analysis, Goal Seek. This will bring up the Goal Seek dialog.
2. Indicate that you want to set cell B5 to $425 by changing cell B1.

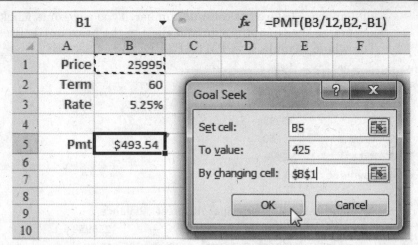

Figure 334 *Back into an answer.*

In a simple case like this one, Goal Seek will almost always succeed. Excel considers different input values until it finds your solution. Within a second, it will report back that it found the correct input cell value.

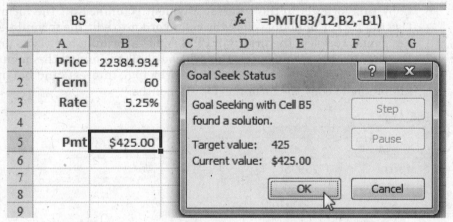

Figure 335 *Excel finds the price to yield the desired payment.*

3. To accept the solution, click OK. To revert to the original value, click Cancel.

Results: Thanks to Goal Seek, you find that you can afford to borrow $22,384.93.

Additional Details: The formulas are still live after you use Goal Seek. You can continue to change terms, rates, and prices to calculate new payments.

Gotcha: When there is not a linear relationship between the two cells, Goal Seek may fail to find a solution.

CREATE AN AMORTIZATION TABLE

Problem: I know it is easy to figure out a monthly payment using PMT. I would like to see my loan balance after each month's payment. How can I build an amortization table?

Strategy: You can use PPMT and IPMT to build this amortization table. Here's how:
1. In a blank section of the worksheet, add the column headings Payment, Date, Principal, Interest, and Balance.
2. Ensure that the formula for Balance in the first row points to the price in B1.
3. In the next row of the table, enter the number 1 for Payment. Ctrl+drag the fill handle to fill in the proper number of payments.
4. Enter the first payment date for the Date. Right-click+drag the fill handle to the last row. When you release the mouse button, choose Fill Months.
5. Enter the PPMT function, using the proper absolute references, so that you can copy the function to column D to be used for IPMT. The syntax is =PPMT(rate, per, nper, pv, [fv], [type]). The only difference from the PMT function is the addition of the period number as the second argument. In C8, type =PPMT(. The rate is B3/12, but after clicking on B3, press the F4 key to add the dollar signs. Type /12 and a comma. Click on the first payment number. Press the F4 key three times so that a dollar

sign appears before the column number. Type a comma. Click on the Term in B2 and press F4. Type a comma. Type a minus sign and click on the price in B1. Press F4 and type the closing parenthesis. The whole formula is =PPMT($B$3/12,$A8,$B$2,-$B$1).

`=PPMT($B$3/12,$A8,$B$2,-$B$1)`

	A	B	C	D	E
1	Price	25995			
2	Term	60			
3	Rate	5.25%			
4	Payment	$493.54			
5					
6	Payment	Date	Principal	Interest	Balance
7					25995
8	1	7/1/2014	$379.81	$113.73	$25,615.19
9	2	8/1/2014	$381.47	$112.07	$25,233.71
10	3	9/1/2014	$383.14	$110.40	$24,850.57

Figure 336 *Calculate the principal payment.*

6. Copy this formula to the Interest Payment column. Edit the formula and change PPMT to IPMT. Use the F2 key or double click the cell in order to edit the formula. Alternatively, select the cell. Use the mouse to select the first P in PPMT in the formula bar. Type an I to change to IPMT.
7. For the Balance formula, use the previous balance minus this month's principal payment.
8. Select the three cells that contain the principal, interest, and balance calculations. Double-click the fill handle to copy the formulas for all months.

`=E66-C67`

	A	B	C	D	E
1	Price	25995			
2	Term	60			
3	Rate	5.25%			
4	Payment	$493.54			
5					
6	Payment	Date	Principal	Interest	Balance
64	57	3/1/2019	$485.00	$8.54	$1,467.76
65	58	4/1/2019	$487.12	$6.42	$980.64
66	59	5/1/2019	$489.25	$4.29	$491.39
67	60	6/1/2019	$491.39	$2.15	($0.00)

Figure 337 *The ending balance should be within a penny of zero.*

Additional Details: To test that the table is correct, scroll to the last row. You should see that the balance reaches zero with the last payment.

Alternate Strategy: Anytime that you have to enter the numbers 1 to nn for a formula, there is a cool alternative. Instead of putting the formulas in the worksheet, use ROW(A1) where the 1 needs to go. When you copy the formula down, it will change to ROW(A2) which will return a 2, and so on.

`=PPMT($B$3/12,ROW(A1),$B$2,-$B$1)`

	A	B	C	D	E
6		Date	Principal	Interest	Balance
7					25995
8		7/1/2014	$379.81	$113.73	$25,615.19
9		8/1/2014	$381.47	$112.07	$25,233.71
10		9/1/2014	$383.14	$110.40	$24,850.57

Figure 338 *Replace the 1, 2, 3 with ROW(A1).*

DO 40 WHAT-IF ANALYSES QUICKLY

Problem: I want to buy a car, and I want to compare eight price points and four loan terms to calculate the monthly payment amount.

Strategy: You can solve this problem by using a data table. You set up the worksheet as follows:

1. Build the model shown in A1:B4 below. Cell B4 will become the top left corner cell of your what-if table.
2. In cells B5:B5, enter the four possible terms you would like to compare. In cells C4:L4, enter the possible loan amounts.
3. Select the rectangular range B5:L9. The upper-left corner of this range contains the formula to calculate your monthly payment.

	B4				f_x	=PMT(B3/12,B2,-B1)					
	A	B	C	D	E	F	G	H	I	J	K	L
1	Price	25995										
2	Term	60										
3	Interest	5.25%										
4	Payment	$493.54	25995	25495	24995	24495	23995	23495	22995	22495	21995	21495
5		48										
6		60										

Figure 339 *Loan terms along the side, loan amounts across the top.*

4. Select Data, What-If Analysis, Data Table. Excel will ask you to specify a row input cell. In other words, Excel will take each cell in the top row of the table and substitute it for the row input cell. Because these cells contain prices, choose cell B1 as the row input cell.
5. Next, Excel wants to know where the cells in the first column of your data table should be used. Because B5:B8 contains loan terms, specify cell B3 as the Column Input Cell. Click OK.

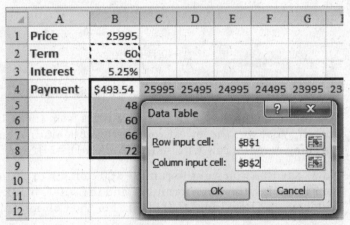

Figure 340 *Each cell in the top row gets plugged into B1.*

Excel will enter an array formula for you, based on the original formula in the top-left cell of the table. It will show you the monthly prices for many combinations of terms and price points.

	A	B	C	D	E	F	G	H	I	J	K	L
1	Price	25995										
2	Term	60										
3	Interest	5.25%										
4	Payment	$493.54	25995	25495	24995	24495	23995	23495	22995	22495	21995	21495
5		48	602	590	578	567	555	544	532	521	509	497
6		60	494	484	475	465	456	446	437	427	418	408
7		66	454	446	437	428	419	411	402	393	384	376
8		72	422	414	405	397	389	381	373	365	357	349

Figure 341 *The formula is replicated for each cell.*

If you are looking for a monthly payment of $425, you will have to either negotiate down to a price of $21,995 with a 60-month loan, $23,995 with a 66-month loan, or choose a 72-month loan.

The formulas in the table are live. You can reenter new values in the first column and row of the table in order to zoom in on possible scenarios.

Additional Details: You can also change the formula in B4, and the table will update.

RANDOM WALK DOWN WALL STREET

The previous example is the classic use of the Data Table function. However, while judging the ModelOff World Financial Championships in New York in 2012, I met professor Simon Benninga and he demonstrated a very different use for data tables.

First, build a column that represents 100 coin flips. If the RAND() is > .5 then you win a penny, otherwise you lose a penny. Add a graph. Every time you press F9, Excel runs the 100 coin flips again and the graph updates.

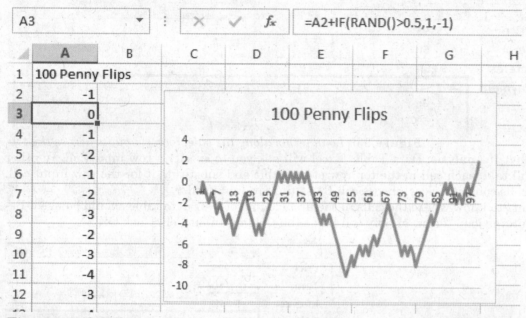

Figure 342 *Simulating 100 coin flips using RAND().*

You might be interested in some statistics from these 100 coin flips. What was the highest you were ever ahead? What was the lowest you were ever behind? Where did you finish after 100 coin flips. Set up formulas going across a row with =MAX(A2:A101), =MIN(A2:A101), and =A101.

Now - say that you want to run the 100 coin flip experiment 1000 times. Select the blank cell to the left of your formulas, the three formulas, and then 1000 blank rows below. Select Data, What-If, Data Table. You will leave the Row Input Cell blank. For the Column Input Cell, choose any blank cell outside of the table.

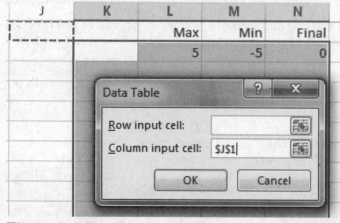

Figure 343 *Run the what-if table based on a blank cell.*

This is a seemingly bizarre request. You are telling Excel to take the 1000 blank cells in K2:K1001, plug them in to the blank J1 cell, and record the results of the Max, Min, and Final. Since those cells are the results of formulas containing =RAND() or =RANDBETWEEN(), each row in the resulting data table represents the results of 100 coin flips. In all, you've effectively modeled 100,000 coin flips.

	L	M	N
	Max	Min	Final
	12	-1	2
	11	-6	-4
	9	-5	2
	8	-4	6

Figure 344 *Each row shows the statistics after 100 coin flips.*

This technique works because your model is based on one of the random functions.

WHAT-IF FOR 3 OR MORE VARIABLES

Problem: The previous trick is cool, but what if I have three or more variables to change?

Strategy: If you have 3 variables to change, make many copies of the worksheet in the above example and change the third variable in each copy of the table.

If you have 3 or more variables, you can reluctantly use Excel's Scenario Manager as described in this topic. If your manager has $99 in the budget, you can instead buy the MrExcel.com Monte Carlo Manager to handle multiple variable scenarios easily.

Excel's Scenario Manager is found in the What-If dropdown of the Data ribbon tab. The tool will let you specify any number of input variables and any number of output variables. For each scenario, you have to type the input variables into a dialog box. The Scenario Manager will then produce a report of all the scenarios.

1. This step is optional, but the output report will be more meaningful if you name all of the input cells and all of the output cells.
2. Select Data, What-If Analysis, Scenario Manager.
3. Click the Add... button in the Scenario Manager dialog.
4. Type a name for the scenario using the current values. Specify the input cells by clicking the first cell and Ctrl+clicking the other input cells. Click OK.

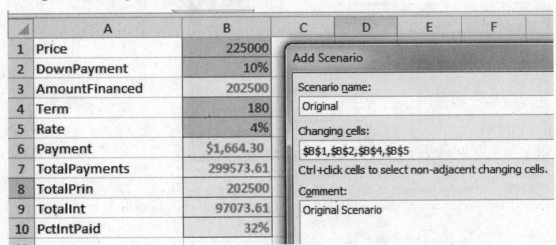

Figure 345 *Specify the input cells.*

5. Excel will show you the current input values. These are probably correct for the first scenario.

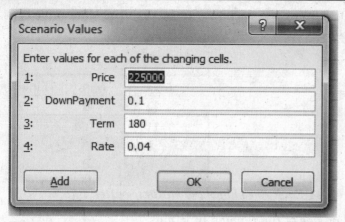

Figure 346 *Verify the values for the original scenario.*

6. Click Add. You will go back to the Add Scenario dialog.
7. Enter a new scenario name and description. Click OK. You will go to the Scenario Values dialog.
8. Enter new input variables for this scenario.
9. Repeat steps 6 to 8 for each additional scenario. When you are done entering scenarios, click OK instead of Add in the Scenario Values dialog.
10. In the Scenario Manager dialog, choose any scenario and click Show to show that scenario in the worksheet.

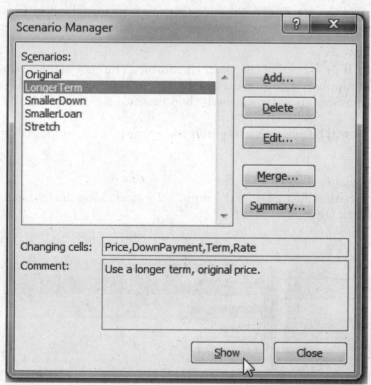

Figure 347 *Choose a scenario and click Show.*

11. To see a comparison of all scenarios, click Summary.
12. In the Scenario Summary dialog, specify the output cells to include in the report.

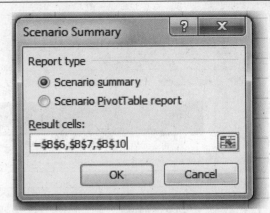

Figure 348 *Specify output cells.*

13. A new worksheet is inserted. It will contain a column for each scenario. Input cells appear in grey. Output cells appear below.

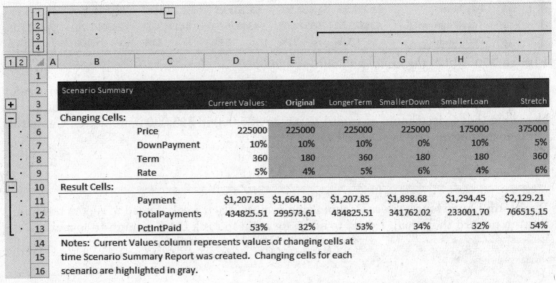

Figure 349 *The summary report compares the scenarios.*

Additional Details: Group and Outline symbols appear around the report. Clicking the minus symbol above column C will hide the notes in rows 14:16 and produces a cleaner report. Clicking the plus symbol to the left of row 3 will reveal the description that you entered for each scenario. Minus symbols next to row 5 or 10 hide the input or output section of the report. The minus symbol above the final column hides all of the scenarios, leaving only the current values.

	A	C	D	E	F	G	H	I
			Current Values:	Original	LongerTerm	SmallerDown	SmallerLoan	Stretch
				Original Scenario	Use a longer term, original price.	Get a 0% Down Loan	Go for a smaller property	Largest House
6	Price		225000	225000	225000	225000	175000	375000
7	DownPayment		10%	10%	10%	0%	10%	5%
8	Term		360	180	360	180	180	360
9	Rate		5%	4%	5%	6%	4%	6%
11	Payment		$1,207.85	$1,664.30	$1,207.85	$1,898.68	$1,294.45	$2,129.21
12	TotalPayments		434825.51	299573.61	434825.51	341762.02	233001.70	766515.15
13	PctIntPaid		53%	32%	53%	34%	32%	54%

Figure 350 *Adjust the group and outline symbols.*

The scenario manager is relatively difficult to use because you must build each scenario by typing the values into a dialog. I wrote the MrExcel Monte Carlo Analysis add-in to allow you to specify the scenarios by saying that Price should go from 175,000 to 325,000 in $25,000 increments. Using this method, you can build dozens or hundreds of scenarios very quickly.

RANK SCORES

Problem: I have four writers working on a project. Each week, I need to report how many pages they have written toward their goal. I want to add a formula to rank them in high-to-low order.

	Pages
Tessa	145.6
Josh	248.0
Ashley	86.6
Lee	96.6

Figure 351 *Rank the scores.*

Strategy: If you are not concerned about ties, you can use the RANK or RANK.EQ function. This function requires two arguments; the cell to be ranked and the range in which to rank the cell. In plain language, you are asking the function to assign a rank to the value in C2 among all values in C2:C5.

=RANK.EQ(C2,C$2:C$5)

	A	B	C
1	Rank		Pages
2	2	Tessa	145.6
3	1	Josh	248.0
4	4	Ashley	86.6
5	3	Lee	96.6

Figure 352 *Assign a rank.*

Note that the C$2:C$5 range in the second parameter uses dollar signs so the formula can be copied down but the range of scores remains the same.

The RANK and RANK.EQ functions are identical. RANK will work in any version of Excel. RANK.EQ will only work in Excel 2010 or newer. RANK was renamed to RANK.EQ in Excel 2010 to differentiate it from RANK.AVG. For a comparison of these functions, see the next topic.

Additional Details: There is an optional third argument. If you don't specify the third argument, the values are ranked in high-to-low order. Sometimes you might need to rank in a low-to-high fashion. Golf is one such instance. In such cases, use a 1 for the third argument of the RANK or RANK.EQ function.

See Also: "Rank a List Without Ties," "Sorting with a Formula"

RANK A LIST WITHOUT TIES

Problem: How are ties handled when ranking?

Strategy: Excel 2010 introduced new ways to handle ties when ranking. In this figure, products B & D are tied with sales of 87. The old RANK and RANK.EQ functions assign both of those products a rank of 2 and no product is ranked as 3.

Statisticians argue that products B & D should each receive a rank of 2.5, since the average of ranks 2 & 3 is 2.5. The new Excel 2010 function RANK. AVG will handle ties in this fashion.

=RANK($B2,$B$2:$B$8)+COUNTIF(B$2:B2,B2)-1

	A	B	C	D	E	F	G
1	Prod.	Sales	Rank	Rank(,,1)	Rank.EQ	Rank.Avg	Custom
2	A	89	1	7	1	1	1
3	D	87	2	5	2	2.5	2
4	B	87	2	5	2	2.5	3
5	G	81	4	4	4	4	4
6	F	75	5	3	5	5	5
7	C	73	6	2	6	6	6
8	E	70	7	1	7	7	7

Figure 353 *Various ways to rank values.*

Excel tricksters who use RANK to sort with a formula as described in the next topic want to make sure that every rank is used exactly once. They will use the formula shown in column G. This formula uses the original RANK function and then adds 1 if the ranked value is appearing a second time in the list.

=RANK($B2,$B$2:$B$8)+COUNTIF(B$2:B2,B2)-1

SORTING WITH A FORMULA

Problem: In "Rank Scores," I learned how to use the RANK function to find the relative rank order of four writers. Now I want to use a formula to produce a sorted list of the writers in high-to-low sequence.

Strategy: In cells A8:A11, you enter the ranks 1 through 4. Then you use the VLOOKUP function to return the name in column B and the pages in column C.

=VLOOKUP($A8,$A$2:$C$5,2,FALSE)

	A	B	C	D
1	Rank		Pages	
2	2	Tessa	145.6	
3	1	Josh	248.0	
4	4	Ashley	86.6	
5	3	Lee	96.6	
6				
7	PRODUCTIVITY REPORT			
8	1	Josh	248.0	
9	2	Tessa	145.6	
10	3	Lee	96.6	
11	4	Ashley	86.6	

Figure 354 *The table in rows 8:11 sorts the original data.*

1. Set up a new table with numbers 1 through 4.
2. The formula in B8:B11 is =VLOOKUP($A8,$A$2:$C$5,2,FALSE).
3. The formula in C8:C11 is =VLOOKUP($A8,$A$2:$C$5,3,FALSE).

After using a RANK function to assign rank values to a list, you can use a second table with the numbers 1 through n and a series of VLOOKUP formulas in order to return a sorted list of the data.

ROUND NUMBERS

Problem: My formula is producing results with many decimal places. I need to round to the nearest cent or nearest dollar or even to the nearest hundred dollars.

Strategy: Use the versatile ROUND function. The function requires a number to be rounded then a precision value. If you use =ROUND(B2,2) you will round numbers to the nearest penny. If you use =ROUND(B2,0) you will round to the nearest dollar. The precision argument can be negative to indicate that you want to round to the left of the decimal point. If you use =ROUND(B2,-2) you will round to the nearest hundred dollars.

C2		f_x =ROUND(B2,2)		
	A	B	C	D	E
	Cost	Calc	Round 2	Round 0	Round -2
1	Cost	Calc	Round 2	Round 0	Round -2
2	217.9808	335.355	335.36	335	300
3	217.9801	335.354	335.35	335	300
4	111.475	171.5	171.5	172	200
5	97.5	150	150	150	200
6	97.4935	149.99	149.99	150	100
7	116.02	178.4923	178.49	178	200

Figure 355 *Round to the nearest penny, dollar, or hundred.*

ROUND can use any number as the precision argument. Although the figure above shows 2, 0, and -2, you could carry this logic forward. To round to the nearest million, use a precision of -6. To round to the nearest thousandth, use a precision of 3.

Additional Details: If you always want to round up or round down, use ROUNDUP or ROUNDDOWN functions. They work just like ROUND, requiring the number to round and the precision. Note that ROUNDUP will round away from zero. This makes sense for positive numbers, the ROUNDUP(1.01,0) will be 2. For negative numbers, the ROUNDUP(-1.01,0) will be -2. This is tricky, since -2 is actually lower than -1.01. If you want -1.01 to round to -1, then use =CEILING(1.01,1).

ROUND TO THE NEAREST $0.05 WITH MROUND

Problem: I know I can use the ROUND function to round to the nearest dollar or penny. How do I round to the nearest nickel or quarter?

Strategy: You can use the MROUND function. This function will round a number to the nearest multiple of the second argument. To round to the nearest nickel, use =MROUND(B2,0.05). To round to the nearest quarter, you use =MROUND(B2,0.25).

=MROUND(B2,0.05)			
	A	B	C	D
	Cost	Calc	Nickel	Quarter
1	Cost	Calc	Nickel	Quarter
2	217.9808	335.355	335.35	335.25
3	217.9801	335.354	335.35	335.25
4	111.475	171.5	171.5	171.5
5	97.5	150	150	150
6	97.4935	149.99	150	150

Figure 356 *Round to the nearest 0.05.*

Gotcha: Both arguments in the MROUND function must have the same sign. This can be difficult when you have a mixture of positive and negative values. The SIGN function will return either a 1 or -1, based on the sign of a number. If there is a possibility that the first argument might be negative, you can multiply the second argument by SIGN of the first argument. =MROUND(B2,0.05*SIGN(B2))

ROUND PRICES TO THE NEXT HIGHEST $5

Problem: I handle pricing for a company, and I have a spreadsheet that shows my cost per SKU. My manager tells me to take the current manufacturing cost for each item, multiply by 2, add $3, and then round up to the next highest multiple of 5.

=B2*2+3

	A	B	C
1	SKU	Cost	Calc
2	A254	17.98075	38.9615
3	A357	10.98	24.96
4	D267	15.99	34.98
5	E359	7.91	18.82

Figure 357 *38.9615 doesn't make a nice price.*

Strategy: After doing the math to get a preliminary price, you can use the CEILING function. This function takes one number and the number to round up to. For example, =CEILING(421,5) will result in 425. Note that with CEILING, the answer is always higher than the original number.

Additional Details: Excel also has a FLOOR function. With the FLOOR function, the number would be rounded down to the nearest multiple of 5.

=CEILING(C2,5)

	A	B	C	D
1	SKU	Cost	Calc	Price
2	A254	17.98075	38.9615	40
3	A357	10.98	24.96	25
4	D267	15.99	34.98	35

Figure 358 *Use CEILING to round up to a multiple.*

ROUND 0.5 TOWARDS EVEN PER ASTM-E29

Problem: Excel always rounds 0.5 up to the next integer. The latest best practice in rounding says to round 0.5 towards the even number.

Back in school, you probably learned to round 0.5 up to the next highest number. In a large data set, this rule is leading to the data set being slightly skewed higher. The guidance published by the ASTM in their rule E29 says that numbers ending in 0.5 should round towards the even number. Theoretically, half the time the number rounds up and half the time the number rounds down, cancelling out the skew.

Strategy: Use =IF(MOD(A2,1)=0.5,MROUND(A2,2),ROUND(A2,0)) instead of ROUND(A2,2).

=IF(MOD(A2,1)=0.5,MROUND(A2,2),ROUND(A2,0))

	A	B	C	D	E
1	Random	Round	E29 Round		
2	23.5	24	24		
3	24.5	25	24		

Figure 359 *Round .5 towards the even number.*

SEPARATE THE INTEGER FROM THE DECIMALS

Problem: I have a column of values that include digits before and after the decimal point. I don't want to round anything, I just want the whole number. Or, I just want the decimal. How can I easily break those apart?

Strategy: Use the INT function to return the integer portion of the number.

=INT(A2)

	A	B	C
1	Value	Integer	Decimal
2	356.2101394	356	0.2101394
3	367.2522423	367	0.2522423
4	9.849509737	9	0.8495097
5	425.266767	425	0.266767
6	403.6333511	403	0.6333511
7	478.6050053	478	0.6050053

Figure 360 *Use INT to chop the decimals off your numbers.*

To lose the integer and keep only the decimals, I use =A2-INT(A2). Another solution is to use MOD(A2,1). The MOD function is equivalent to the math concept of modulo. Divide A2 by 1 and return the remainder.

Gotcha: the INT function for negative numbers may not act like you expect. The INT of -9.1 is -10, since this is the integer just less than -9.1. If your values might contain negative numbers, then consider using the TRUNC function to truncate the decimals. For positive numbers, INT and TRUNC are identical. The only difference is for negative numbers. TRUNC(-9.1) will be -9.

WHY IS THIS PRICE SHOWING $27.85000001 CENTS?

Problem: I have a worksheet in which I expect the cells to show dollars and cents. For some reason, a price in the formula bar is showing a few millionths of a cent.

f_x	=(43.1-43.2)+1
C	D
Price	0.89999999999999990

Figure 361 *Not quite 0.90.*

Strategy: These stray values can happen due to something called floating-point arithmetic. Whereas you think in 10s, computers actually calculate with 2s, 4s, 8s, and 16s. Excel has to convert your prices to 16s, do the math, and then present it to you in tenths. A simple number like 0.1 in a base-10 system is actually a repeating number in binary.

Sometimes seemingly bizarre rounding errors creep in. There is one quick solution, but you have to be careful when using it:

1. Format your prices to have two decimal places. Use either the Format Cells dialog or the Decrease Decimal icon.

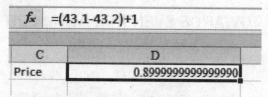

f_x	=(43.1-43.2)+1
C	D	E
Price	0.90	

Figure 362 *Still not 0.90.*

Things now look OK, but if you ever test to see if this value is really 0.90, it will return FALSE.

f_x	=D1=0.9
C	D	E	F
Price	0.90		
		FALSE	

Figure 363 *The formatting is showing 0.90, but the cell really isn't 0.90.*

2. Select File, Options, Advanced. In the Calculation Settings For This Workbook section, select Set Precision as Displayed. Using this setting, Excel will truncate all values to only the number of decimal places shown.

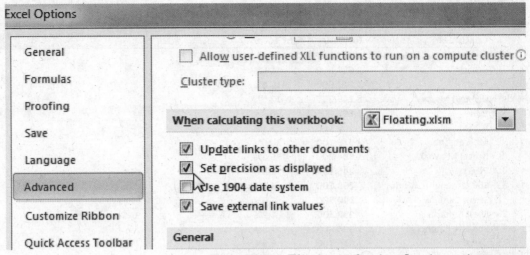

Figure 364 *Eliminate the tiny floating point errors.*

Gotcha: There is neither an Undo command nor any other way to regain those last numbers. However, Excel will warn you that your data will permanently lose accuracy.

Figure 365 *This warning displays while in the Options dialog.*

CALCULATE A PERCENTAGE OF TOTAL

Problem: I have a spreadsheet with sales by customer and a total at the bottom. I want to express each customer as a percentage of the total.

Strategy: Divide each row's sales by the total cell. Follow these steps:

1. Select a cell next to the first revenue cell.
2. Type an equals sign. Press the Left Arrow key.
3. Type the forward slash (/) sign. Press the Left Arrow key. Press Ctrl+Down Arrow key. Your cell pointer should now be on the total cell.
4. Press the F4 key. The formula bar should now show B2/$B$17.
5. Press Ctrl+Enter to enter the formula and stay in the current cell. Format the calculation as a percentage by using the % icon on the Home tab.
6. To use the format 9.2% (that is, one decimal place) instead of 9%, choose the Increase Decimal icon.
7. In cell C2, double-click the fill handle to copy the formula down to the other rows.
8. Add the heading % of Total in cell C1.

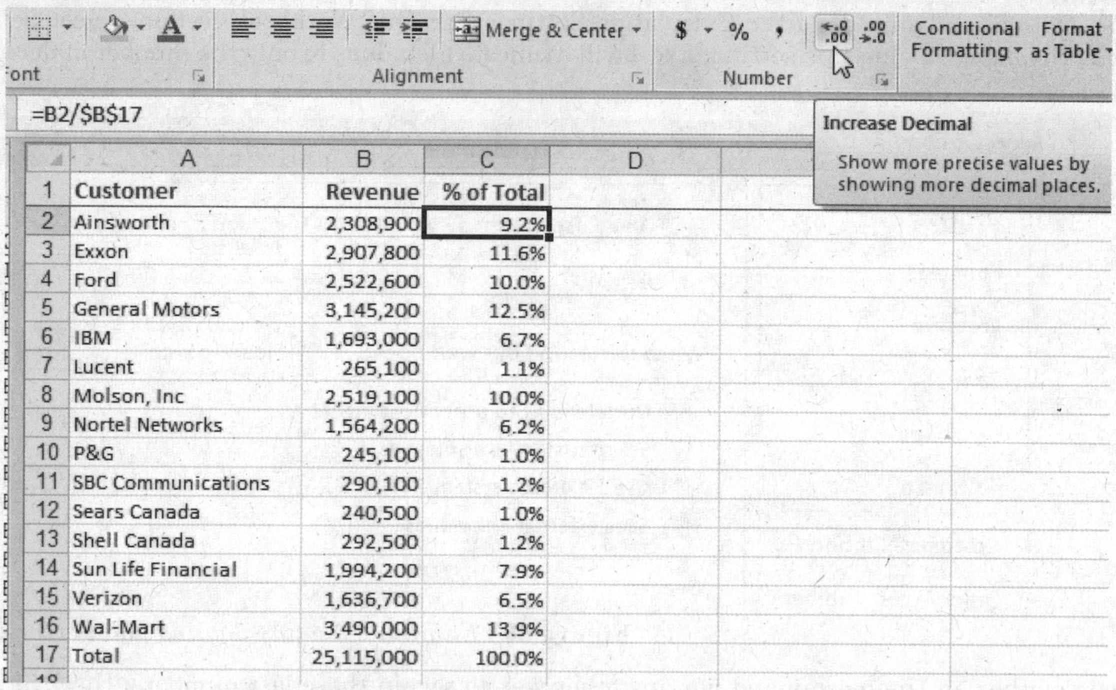

Figure 366 *Show a percentage of total.*

Additional Details: The key element of this procedure is pressing the F4 key to add dollar signs to the reference for the total row. As you copy the formula from C2 to C16, the formula is always going to compare the revenue in the current row to the total revenue in row 17.

Creating a percentage of total is a common task in Excel. Being able to quickly enter an initial formula that can be copied to all cells is a good technique to have in your skill set.

CALCULATE A RUNNING PERCENTAGE OF TOTAL

Problem: I have a report of revenue by customer, sorted in descending order. Management consultants often argue that it's important to concentrate the best team on the 20% of the customers who provide 80% of the company's revenue. How can I calculate a cumulative running percentage of the total so I can determine which 20% of customers to focus on?

Strategy: I hate solutions that require two different formulas, but the intuitive solution to this problem is one of them. You will need one formula for cell C2 and a different formula for cells C3 and below. Here's what you do:

1. In cell C2, enter the formula =B2/$B$18. Format the result as a percentage with one decimal place.
2. Copy C2 to just the next cell, either by dragging the fill handle down one cell or using Ctrl+C and then Ctrl+V.
3. Press F2 to edit cell C3.
4. Type a plus sign and touch cell C2. Press Ctrl+Enter.
5. Double-click the fill handle in C3 to copy this formula down to all the other cells. Note that you do not want this formula to be added to your total row. As shown below, the data set was purposely set up with the total row and the data separated by a blank row in order to prevent this formula from copying to the total row.

=B3/$B$18+C2

	A	B	C	D
1	Customer	Revenue	Running % Tot	
2	Wal-Mart	3,490,000	13.9%	=B2/$B$18
3	General Motors	3,145,200	26.4%	=B3/$B$18+C2
4	Exxon	2,907,800	38.0%	
5	Ford	2,522,600	48.0%	
6	Molson, Inc	2,519,100	58.1%	
7	Ainsworth	2,308,900	67.3%	
8	Sun Life Financial	1,994,200	75.2%	
9	IBM	1,693,000	81.9%	
10	Verizon	1,636,700	88.5%	
11	Nortel Networks	1,564,200	94.7%	
12	Shell Canada	292,500	95.9%	
13	SBC Communications	290,100	97.0%	
14	Lucent	265,100	98.1%	
15	P&G	245,100	99.0%	
16	Sears Canada	240,500	100.0%	
17				
18	Total	25,115,000		

Figure 367 *Add this row's percentage of the total to the previous row.*

Alternate Strategy: If you absolutely want to produce this total with a single formula, you could use the formula =SUM(B2:B$2)/B$18 in C2 and copy it down. This works because the range B2:B$2 is an interesting reference: It says to add up everything from the current row to the top row. This formula seems a bit less intuitive. For large data sets, it will take much longer to calculate than the first method. (See Consider Formula Speed for details.)

USE THE ^ SIGN FOR EXPONENTS

Problem: I have a room that is 10 feet x 10 feet x 10 feet. How do I find the volume of the cube?

Strategy: The formula for volume is width x length x height. In this case, it is 10 x 10 x 10, or 10^3. In Excel, the caret symbol (also known as "the little hat," or "the symbol when you press Shift 6") is used to indicate exponents. Here's how you use it to find the volume of your room:
1. In cell B2, enter 10.
2. In cell B3, enter the formula =B2^3.

The result will be 1,000 cubic feet of volume in the room.

=B2^3

	A	B	C
1			
2		10	1000
3			

Figure 368 *The caret raises a number to a power.*

RAISE A NUMBER TO A FRACTION TO FIND THE SQUARE OR THIRD ROOT

Problem: Excel offers a SQRT function to find the square root of a number. What do I do if I need to figure out the third root or the fourth root of a number?

Strategy: You can raise a number to a fraction to find a root. To find the square root of a number, you can raise the number to the 1/2 power. To find the cube root of a number, you can raise the number to the 1/3 power. To find the eighth root of a number, you can raise the number to the 1/8 power.

Let's look at several examples.

If you need to find the square root, you can use the SQRT function.

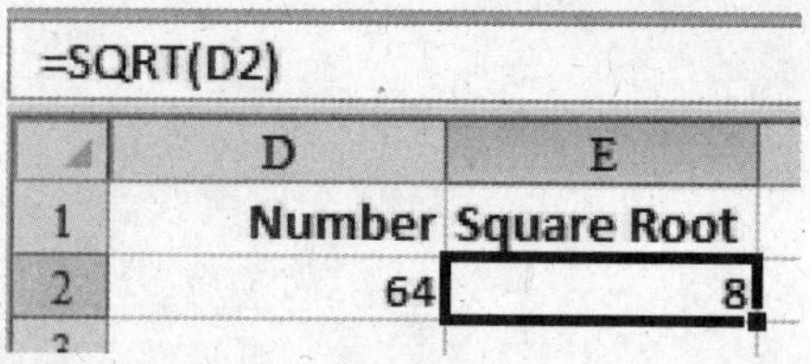

	D	E
1	**Number**	**Square Root**
2	64	8

`=SQRT(D2)`

Figure 369 *SQRT is a built-in function for square roots.*

To calculate a square root, you can raise a number to the one-half (1/2) power. Since (1/2) is a rational number, you could alternatively use =D2^0.5.

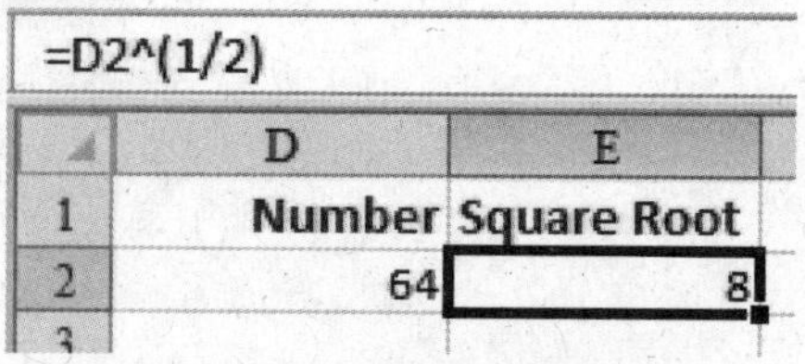

	D	E
1	**Number**	**Square Root**
2	64	8

`=D2^(1/2)`

Figure 370 *Raising to a fraction takes the root.*

To find the cube root of a number, you can raise the number to the one-third (1/3) power.

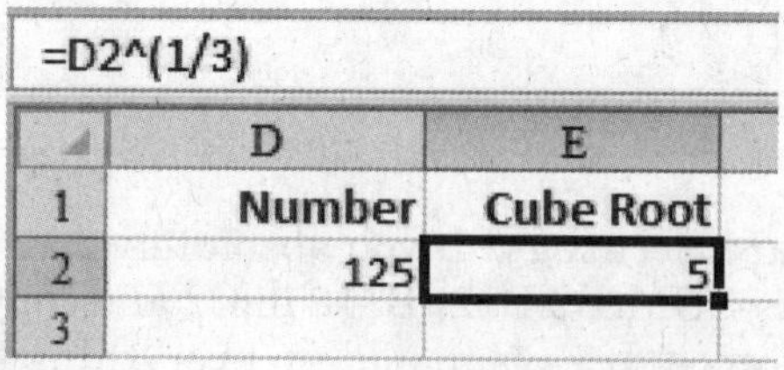

	D	E
1	**Number**	**Cube Root**
2	125	5

`=D2^(1/3)`

Figure 371 *For cube roots, raise to the 1/3 power.*

To find the fourth root of a number, you raise the number to either the one-fourth (1/4) or 0.25 power.

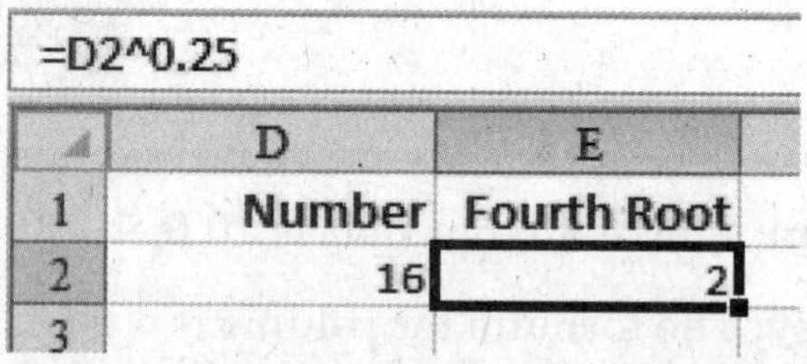

	D	E
1	**Number**	**Fourth Root**
2	16	2

`=D2^0.25`

Figure 372 *Raise to the 1/4 power.*

You can find any root in the same way: To find the nth root, you simply raise the number to the 1/n power. For example, to find the 17th root of a number, you raise it to the one-seventeenth (1/17) power.

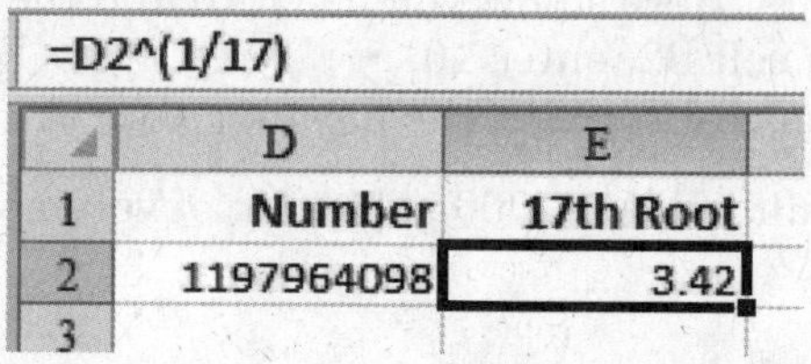

	D	E
1	**Number**	**17th Root**
2	1197964098	3.42

`=D2^(1/17)`

Figure 373 *Find the nth root by raising to 1/n.*

Although Excel only offers a function for a square root, you can use the technique of raising to a fractional power in order to determine any root of a number.

CALCULATE A GROWTH RATE

Problem: I work for a quickly growing company. In the first year, we had $970,000 in sales. In the fifth year, we had $6,175,000 in sales. I need to determine our compounded annual growth rate.

Strategy: Sales in the fifth year are 6,175/970 higher than in the first year. The formula for growth is (Year5/Year1) - 100% or 537%.

=(B6/B2)-1

◢	A	B	C
1		Revenue	Growth
2	Year 1	970,000	
3	Year 2	2,250,000	
4	Year 3	4,580,000	
5	Year 4	5,850,000	
6	Year 5	6,175,000	537%

Figure 374 *Five-year growth rate.*

However, a compounded growth rate is a number, x, that will calculate like this:

Year1 * (100% + x) * (100% + x) * (100% + x) * (100% + x) = Year5

This is the same as: Year1 * (100% + x)^4 = Year5

So, in order to calculate x, you have to be able to find the fourth root of (Year5/Year1). The formula to find the fourth root is to raise the number to the 1/4 power. Thus, the formula to calculate the compounded growth rate is: (Year5/Year1)^(1/4)-100% = x.

To prove that this formula is working, multiply year 1 by 1.5884235 four times. The answer should be very close to Year 5.

=(B6/B2)^(1/4)-100%

◢	A	B	C	D
1		Revenue	Growth	Compounded Growth
2	Year 1	970,000		
3	Year 2	2,250,000		
4	Year 3	4,580,000		
5	Year 4	5,850,000		
6	Year 5	6,175,000	537%	58.84235%

Figure 375 *Compounded growth rate.*

=B2*1.5884235*1.5884235*1.5884235*1.5884235

◢	A	B	C	D
1		Revenue	Growth	Compounded Growth
2	Year 1	970,000		
3	Year 2	2,250,000		
4	Year 3	4,580,000		
5	Year 4	5,850,000		
6	Year 5	6,175,000	537%	58.84235%
7				
8	Check:	6,175,000		

Figure 376 *Prove that the 58.84% growth rate is accurate.*

FIND THE AREA OF A CIRCLE

Problem: I need to order pizza for my department's staff meeting. The pizza place has two deals. I can buy three medium (12") pizzas for $18 or two large (16") pizzas for $20. Which is the better deal?

Strategy: You will have to figure out the area of a 12" pizza vs. the area of a 16" pizza. The formula for the area of a circle is pi * r² (where r is the radius). The radius of a pizza is one-half the diameter. If you enter the diameter of the pizza in B2, the radius is =B2/2.

Pi is a Greek letter that represents 3.141592654. Excel offers the PI function to return this number. It is a lot easier to remember =PI() than the many digits in 3.141592654.

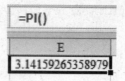

E
3.14159265358979

Figure 377 *=PI() returns the value of pi to 15-digit precision.*

Here's how you determine which is the better pizza deal:

1. Set up a worksheet. In cell B2, enter the diameter of the pizza.
2. In cell C2, calculate the radius as =B2/2.
3. In cell D2, calculate the area of the pizza in square inches, using =PI()*C2^2.

=PI()*C2^2

	A	B	C	D
1	Pizza Size	Diameter	Radius	Area
2	Medium	12	6	113.0973355
3	Large	16	8	201.0619298

Figure 378 *Area is pi times radius squared.*

4. In column E, enter the quantity of pizzas.
5. Calculate the total square inches in column F by using =E2*D2.
6. Enter the cost for the special in column G. In column H, calculate the dollars per square inch of pizza, using =G2/F2.

=G2/F2

	A	B	C	D	E	F	G	H
1	Pizza Size	Diameter	Radius	Area	Quantity	Total Square Inches	Cost	Cost/ Sq Inch
2	Medium	12	6	113.0973	3	339.29	$18.00	$0.0531
3	Large	16	8	201.0619	2	402.12	$20.00	$0.0497

Figure 379 *Cost per square inch.*

Results: From a purely mathematical point of view, the special with two large pizzas is a slightly better deal, pricing the pizza at 4.97 cents per square inch.

Additional Details: My eight-grade math teacher, Mr. Nick Irwin, would like me to mention, for the sake of completeness, that the circumference of the pizza is pi times the diameter. That would be =PI()*B2.

FIGURE OUT LOTTERY PROBABILITY

Problem: The Super Lotto jackpot is $8 million this week. Should I play?

Strategy: It depends on how many numbers are in the game. You need to figure out the number of possible combinations in the game.

You can use the COMBIN function as follows to figure out the number of possible combinations for games in which you choose 6 of 40, 44, 48, and so on numbers:

1. Set up a spreadsheet with the number of balls in the lotto game (40, 44, 48, and so on) in cell A2.
2. In cell B2, identify how many numbers you need to select correctly.
3. Enter the formula =COMBIN(A2,B2) in cell C2.

=COMBIN(A2,B2)

	A	B	C
1	Range 1 to	# to Win	Combinations
2	40	6	3,838,380
3	44	6	7,059,052
4	48	6	12,271,512
5	54	6	25,827,165

Figure 380 *Combinations of choosing 6 numbers.*

If your state lottery game requires you to select 6 numbers out of 40, then the odds against you winning are 3.83 million to 1. For a $1 bet and an $8 million payout, the odds are in your favor.

For a game with 44 numbers, the odds are 7 million to 1. This payoff is only slightly in your favor.

For games with 48 or 54 numbers, the payout is not worth the long odds of the game.

Additional Details: COMBIN figures combinations. Here, the sequence in which the balls are drawn is not relevant. If you had a game in which you had to match both the numbers and the order in which they were drawn, you would want to use the PERMUT function to find the number of permutations of drawing 6 numbers in sequence out of 40.

Additional Details: Since the first edition of this book, two multi-state lotteries have become popular in the United States. These require the player to match five numbers from one pool of numbers and then one number from a separate pool of numbers. This means you have to win two drawings to win the jackpot. Multiply the combinations from the first drawing with the combinations from the second drawing. Here are the calculations for Mega Millions and PowerBall lotteries.

	A	B	C	D	E	F
1	MegaMillions: Match 5 numbers from 1-75, then 1 number from 1-15					
3	Range 1 to	# to Win	Combinations	Bonus 1 to	Combinations	
4	75	5	17,259,390	15	258,890,850	
5						
6						
7	PowerBall: Match 5 numbers from 1-59, and 1 from 1-35					
9	Range 1 to	# to Win	Combinations	Redball 1 to	Combinations	
10	59	5	5,006,386	35	175,223,510	
11						

Figure 381 *The odds are much higher for these lotteries.*

It only makes statistical sense to play the $1 Mega Millions when the jackpot is above $259 million. Because the PowerBall costs $2 to play, it only makes sense when the jackpot is above $350 million. As you can see, lotteries are a tax on people who can't use Excel.

HELP YOUR KIDS WITH THEIR MATH

Problem: My kids have math homework, and I want to check their answers. They are doing least common multiples, greatest common denominators, Roman numerals, and factorials.

Strategy: You can easily solve problems involving least common multiples, greatest common denominators, roman numerals, and factorials using Excel.

Least Common Multiples: When you have to add fractions that have different denominators, one of the first steps is to find the least common multiple of the two denominators. The math homework asks your kids to add 3/26 + 3/4. You want to figure out the least common multiple of 26 and 4, so enter 26 in one cell and 4 in another cell. The formula to find the least common multiple is =LCM(A2:B2). The answer is 52. You can now have your kids change 3/26 to 6/52 and 3/4 to 39/52. Expressing the problem as 39/52 + 6/52 makes it easy to see that the answer is 45/52.

Greatest Common Denominators: This time, the problem is 2/9 + 2/4. The LCM of 9 and 4 is 36 as shown in row 3 above. You can change 2/9 to 8/36 and 2/4 to 18/36. The problem then becomes 8/36 + 18/36. The answer is 26/36. However, can the fraction 26/36 be further reduced? You need to find the greatest common denominator of 26 and 36. To do so, you use the GCD function =GCD(A6:B6). Because the answer is greater than 1, your 26/36 answer can be reduced by dividing both the numerator and denominator by 2; 26/36 is the same as 13/18.

`=LCM(A2:B2)`

▲	A	B	C	D	E
1	First	Second	LCM		
2	26	4	52	=LCM(A2:B2)	
3	9	4	36	=LCM(A3:B3)	
4					
5	First	Second	GCD		
6	26	36	2	=GCD(A6:B6)	
7					
8		Year	Roman		
9		1960	MCMLX	=ROMAN(B9)	
10		1965	MCMLXV	=ROMAN(B10)	
11		1991	MCMXCI	=ROMAN(B11)	
12		1994	MCMXCIV	=ROMAN(B12)	
13		2001	MMI	=ROMAN(B13)	
14		2014	MMXIV	=ROMAN(B14)	

Figure 382 *Middle school math.*

Roman Numerals: Your kids are supposed to use Roman numerals. To do this, you can use the ROMAN function as shown in rows 9:14.

The ROMAN function will work with numbers from 1 to 3,999. If you omit an optional second argument, you will get classic Roman numerals, as shown above.

Calculating Roman numerals is fairly obscure. Other than middle school students and Latin teachers, who has to do this? The NFL commissioner needs to calculate future Super Bowl numbers. The people who do movie credits need to figure out the information to use in the copyright line. Excel wasn't invented when Foreigner IV was released and I somehow doubt that that Holy See fires up Excel when naming the next pope.

If you remember the basics of Roman Numerals, I is 1, V is 5. To show 7, you would use VII. But, to show 4, you would use IV. Since the I occurs before the V, it represents 1 subtracted from 5. Modern convention says that you can represent 4 with IV and 9 with IX, but you can not use IL for 49. The optional second argument of the ROMAN function allows you to break the rules more and more.

`=ROMAN($A$2,B1)`

▲	A	B	C	D	E	F
1		0	1	2	3	4
2	1999	MCMXCIX	MLMVLIV	MXMIX	MVMIV	MIM
3						
4	Table of Roman Numerals					
5	1	I				
6	5	V				
7	10	X				
8	50	L				
9	100	C				
10	500	D				
11	1000	M				
12						

Figure 383 *Excel offers more concise Roman numerals.*

Starting in Excel 2013, you can convert Roman numerals back to regular numbers using the =ARABIC() function. This isn't a function that Microsoft wanted to add to Excel. But, since they are trying to remain compliant with the Open Document Spreadsheet standard, it was added to Excel 2013.

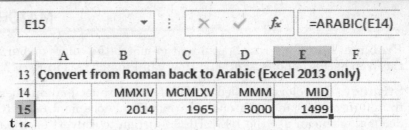

E15			f_x	=ARABIC(E14)	

	A	B	C	D	E	F
13	Convert from Roman back to Arabic (Excel 2013 only)					
14		MMXIV	MCMLXV	MMM	MID	
15		2014	1965	3000	1499	
16						

Figure 384 *Convert from Roman back to Arabic.*

Factorials: The last obscure function you need to help with the math homework is the factorial function, FACT. A factorial is a number multiplied by every integer between itself and 1. To write 5 factorial, you use the number followed by an exclamation point. So, for example, 5! is 5 x 4 x 3 x 2 x 1, or 120. Use =FACT(5) to calculate 5!.

=FACT(B2)

	B	C
1	Number	Fact
2	5	120
3	7	5040
4	8	40320
5	10	3628800
6		

Figure 385 *The factorial of 5 is 5 x 4 x 3 x 2 x 1, or 120.*

CONVERT UNITS

Problem: I need to convert units of measure. I can never remember that there are .453 kilograms in a pound or 2.54 centimeters in an inch.

Strategy: You can use the CONVERT function to convert a certain number of one unit to another unit. The CONVERT function works with units of weight, distance, time, pressure, force, energy, power, magnetism, temperature, and liquid measure.

The syntax for this function is =CONVERT(number, from unit, to unit). It's important that you use the correct abbreviations (for example, lbm for pounds mass), so look in Excel help if you need to.

This figure shows a sampling of the conversions possible with this function.

=CONVERT(A2,B2,C2)

	A	B	C	D	E
1	Number	From	To	Results	Comment
2	100	lbm	kg	45.35924	Pounds to kilograms
3	1	Nmi	mi	1.150779	Nautical miles to miles
4	1	in	ang	2.54E+08	Inches to angstroms
5	1	yr	sec	31557600	Seconds in a year
6	1	T	ga	10000	Teslas to Gauss
7	68	F	C	20	Fahrenheit to Celsius
8	1	tbs	tsp	3	Tablespoon to teaspoon
9	100	cl	oz	33.81402	Centiliters to ounces
10	1	in	cm	2.54	Inches to centimeters
11					

Figure 386 *CONVERT handles many conversion factors.*

MATCH WEB COLORS WITH HEX2DEC

Problem: I need my Excel document to match the colors on our website. I can tell from the HTML that the Web background is #FF9007. How can I match this in Excel?

Strategy: The colors specified in HTML are hexadecimal numbers. This numbering system has 16 digits, from 0 through 9 and A through F. Your Excel document uses RGB (Red, Green, Blue) values, which are decimal. You can use the HEX2DEC function to convert each pair of hex digits to decimal. Here's what you do:

1. In three cells, enter each pair of digits from the color code. Enter an apostrophe before 07 to keep the leading zero.
2. Enter a formula of =HEX2DEC(B2). Excel will convert the FF to 255. This is the red value for the color in Excel.
3. Copy the function to the other two cells. The second value is the green value. The third value is the Blue value.
4. Select the area to be formatted.
5. Choose Home, Paint Bucket dropdown and choose More Colors. On the Custom tab of the Colors dialog, choose 255 for Red, 144 for Green, 7 for Blue. Click OK.

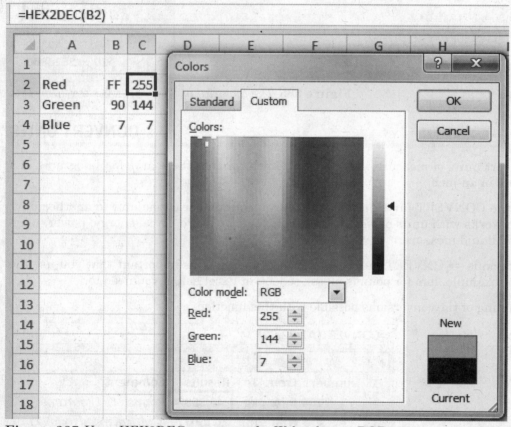

Figure 387 *Use =HEX2DEC to convert the Web colors to RGB.*

Additional Details: To convert RGB values to hexadecimal, you use DEC2HEX.

Historically, Excel offered functions to convert between Binary, Octal, Decimal, and Hexadecimal. Excel 2013 introduces two new flexible functions that handle all numbering systems from Binary (Base 2) to Base 36. To convert from a number in Base 16 to Decimal, use =DECIMAL("B2",16). To convert from decimal 144 to Hexadecimal, use =BASE(144,16).

WILL XOR FIND PEOPLE WHO CHOSE A SINGLE VALUE?

Problem: I need to make sure every attendee to the company dinner chose exactly one entree. The new Exclusive OR (XOR) function introduced in Excel 2013 should make this easy, right?

	A	B	C	D	E	F	G	H
					fx	=XOR(B2,C2,D2,E2)		
1	Name	Steak	Chicken	Fish	Veggie	XOR?		
2	Andy	TRUE	FALSE	FALSE	FALSE	TRUE	=XOR(B2,C2,D2,E2)	
3	Bob	FALSE	FALSE	TRUE	FALSE	TRUE	=XOR(B3,C3,D3,E3)	
4	Carole	FALSE	TRUE	FALSE	FALSE	TRUE	=XOR(B4,C4,D4,E4)	
5	Dale	FALSE	FALSE	FALSE	FALSE	FALSE	=XOR(B5,C5,D5,E5)	
6	Eddie	TRUE	TRUE	FALSE	FALSE	FALSE	=XOR(B6,C6,D6,E6)	
7	Flo	FALSE	TRUE	TRUE	TRUE	TRUE	=XOR(B7,C7,D7,E7)	

Figure 388 *Flo ordered three items, but XOR incorrectly returns TRUE.*

Strategy: It is a horrible story, but the short answer is No.

There is a brilliant team in Redmond who decides what goes into the next Excel. They add functions that are well thought out.

Somewhere else, there is a committee called the Open Document Spreadsheet standards board. These people added 50 functions to the ODS standard. When I look through the list, many of the things were already possible with other Excel functions. However, Microsoft seemed to feel compelled to add those 50 functions to Excel 2013 so they could continue to open ODS documents. XOR is one of those functions.

Like you, I was sort of jazzed that Excel 2013 offered XOR, but as I started to use it, it did not work like I thought that it should. I even filed a bug with Microsoft that XOR(True,True,True) was returning True.

After all, XOR should mean Exclusive Or, which means they only chose one item. Not three items. Not five items. One item.

But, this XOR function is programmed to operate just like the 7486 Chip Set. And that chip set looks at the first pair of values, decides if they are XOR, and then takes that result on to compare with the next value. The chip would evaluate Flo's dinner choices like this:
- Steak=False, Chicken = True. Only 1 is selected, so XOR is True
- Result from Steak|Chicken is True, Fish is True, so XOR is False
- Result from Steak | Chicken | Fish is False, Veggie is True, so XOR is True. Argh.

I quickly got into a argument that based on the English language meaning of "Exclusive Or", their logic was wrong. The Electrical Engineers in the argument quickly explained that there are millions of 7486 chip sets in use and therefore, their need to have XOR match the chip results beats out our need to make sure Flo didn't order three meals. They've come to accept that XOR does not stand for eXclusive OR, but actually stands for "a compleX function to count if an Odd number of inputs are tRue".

So, although the function says "XOR", it really is a bizarre function to measure if there are an odd number of True values. I have no idea when you will need that.

To truly do what all non-EE's understand to be XOR, you could use =COUNTIF(B7:I7,True)=1. Heck, this is even shorter and easier to type than specifying each input cell in XOR. This provides more evidence that the 50 new functions from the ODS board weren't all necessary or well thought-out.

FIND THE SECOND LARGEST VALUE

Problem: I can find the largest and smallest numbers using MAX and MIN. I am trying to identify the largest and smallest three numbers. How can I find the second largest number?

Strategy: Use the LARGE or SMALL functions. These functions take a range of values, then a k value. If you use a k value of 1, the LARGE function is exactly like a MAX: =LARGE(B2:B100,1). The real value in LARGE is the ability to ask for the second largest value using =LARGE(B2:B100,2).

In the figure below, you can see the LARGE and SMALL for an entire set of 10 data points. Note that 66 is reported as both the 5th and 6th largest value due to two 66 entries in the original data set.

=LARGE($A$2:$A$11,C11)

	A	B	C	D	E
1	Original		k	LARGE	SMALL
2	52		1	95	47
3	71		2	84	52
4	58		3	71	54
5	84		4	69	58
6	66		5	66	66
7	69		6	66	66
8	95		7	58	69
9	54		8	54	71
10	47		9	52	84
11	66		10	47	95

Figure 389 *Use LARGE and SMALL to return the kth largest value.*

FORMAT EVERY OTHER ROW IN GREEN

Problem: Got any cool uses for MOD? Got any old-school methods for applying the greenbar format that was in the Excel 2003 AutoFormat dropdown?

Strategy: This topic is about an out-of-the-box method for using MOD to apply a format. If the only goal was to apply alternate-row shading, you could use any of these methods:
- Alt+O+A and choose the Excel 2003 format.
- Ctrl+T, choose Banded Rows and any format.
- Leave row 2 unformatted. Fill row 3 with green. Select row 2 & row 3. Use the fill handle to drag to the bottom of the data set. Open the Paste Options menu and choose Fill Formatting Only.

However, this topic is going to use math to do the formatting.

Consider the ROW function. =ROW(A2) will return 2 because A2 is in the second row of the worksheet. Here is a big range of ROW functions.

=ROW(B4)

	A	B	C	D	E
1	1	1	1	1	1
2	2	2	2	2	2
3	3	3	3	3	3
4	4	4	4	4	4
5	5	5	5	5	5
6	6	6	6	6	6

Figure 390 *The ROW function tells you the row number.*

Now, imagine taking all of those row numbers and dividing by 2. Throw away any integer result, but keep the remainder. This is a strange thought. All of the even number rows will not have a remainder at all. For the odd number rows, say that you take seven divided by 2. You get 3 with a remainder of 1. Throw out the 3 and keep only the remainder. The MOD function will give you only the remainder. =MOD(ROW(A7),2) will return a 1 because 7 divided by 2 has a remainder of 1. The next figure shows the MOD formula for several rows. Notice that you get stripes of 0's and 1's.

=MOD(ROW(E6),2)				
	A	B	C	D	E
1	1	1	1	1	1
2	0	0	0	0	0
3	1	1	1	1	1
4	0	0	0	0	0
5	1	1	1	1	1
6	0	0	0	0	0
7	1	1	1	1	1

Figure 391 *MOD of the ROW, 2 will return stripes.*

So, how do you use this formula to add a green stripe in every other row? You do it with old-school conditional formatting. Follow these steps.

1. Select your range of data. Perhaps it is A2:G900.
2. Make a note of which cell is the active cell. This is the cell address that is shown in the Name box, to the left of the formula bar. You will need this cell address in step 4.
3. Select Home, Conditional Formatting, New Rule.
4. There are six types of rules listed in the top of the New Formatting Rule dialog. Choose the last type, called Use A Formula To Determine Which Rows To Format. When you choose this type, a formula bar appears in the bottom of the dialog. It is called Format Values Where This Formula is True.
5. Click in that formula box. Type a formula similar to this formula, but use the cell address from step 2 instead of A2. =MOD(ROW(A2),2)=1.
6. Click the Format... button.
7. On the Fill tab, choose a fill color. Click OK.

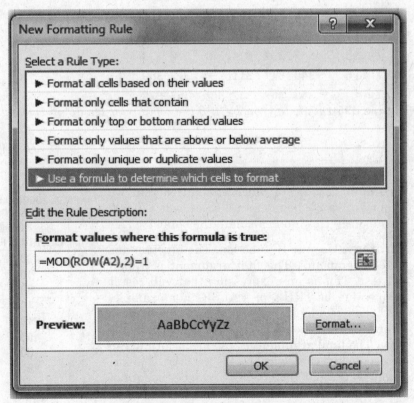

Figure 392 *Your dialog should look like this one.*

8. Click OK to apply the rule.

The range will be filled with an every-other row format.

◢	A	B	C	D	E	F	G
1		Jan	Feb	Mar	Apr	May	Jun
2	Line 1	379	351	379	335	345	329
3	Line 2	390	309	374	356	339	377
4	Line 3	345	333	338	399	364	330
5	Line 4	336	346	363	343	395	399
6	Line 5	347	331	394	382	320	323
7	Line 6	340	311	311	394	322	359
8	Line 7	318	362	332	386	362	328

Figure 393 *Greenbar format.*

The cool part is that if you delete a row or insert a row, the MOD(ROW(),2) formulas will recalculate and the shading will redraw. In the figure below, Line 3a is now green and Line 4 is white.

4	Line 3	345	333	338	399	364	330
5	Line 3a	100	100	100	100	100	100
6	Line 4	336	346	363	343	395	399

Figure 394 *The formatting recalcs after inserting rows.*

Additional Details: With a little math reasoning, you can change the format pattern. What if you wanted the even rows to be formatted? Change the formula to =MOD(ROW(A2),2)=0. If you wanted two rows of green followed by two rows of white, use =MOD(ROW(A2),4)>1.

◢	A	B	C	D	E	F	G
1		Jan	Feb	Mar	Apr	May	Jun
2	Line 1	379	351	379	335	345	329
3	Line 2	390	309	374	356	339	377
4	Line 3	345	333	338	399	364	330
5	Line 3a	100	100	100	100	100	100
6	Line 4	336	346	363	343	395	399
7	Line 5	347	331	394	382	320	323
8	Line 6	340	311	311	394	322	359
9	Line 7	318	362	332	386	362	328

Figure 395 *Divide the row by 4. If the remainder isn't 0 or 1, use green.*

USE IF TO CALCULATE A BONUS

Problem: My VP of Sales announced that we are paying a 2% bonus for all sales over $20,000 this month. How do I calculate the bonus?

Strategy: Use the IF function. The function has three arguments. The first argument is a logical test. This is any expression that will result in a value of TRUE or FALSE. For example, F2>20000 is a logical test. The next argument is a formula that should be used if the logical test is true. The final argument is a value or formula to be used when the logical test is not true. The formula =IF(F2>20000,0.02*F2,0) can be thought of in these words, "If the revenue in F2 is greater than 20,000 then 2% of F2, otherwise 0."

=IF(F2>20000,0.02*F2,0)

◢	E	F	G	H	I	J
1	Quantity	Revenue	COGS	Profit	GP%	Bonus
2	1000	22810	12340	10470	45.9%	456.20
3	100	2257	1038	1219	54.0%	0.00
4	800	18552	9962	8590	46.3%	0.00
5	400	9152	4530	4622	50.5%	0.00
6	400	8456	4558	3898	46.1%	0.00
7	1000	21730	9909	11821	54.4%	434.60
8	800	16416	8503	7913	48.2%	0.00
9	900	21438	10290	11148	52.0%	428.76
10	300	6267	2902	3365	53.7%	0.00

Figure 396 *An IF function calculates the bonus.*

Additional Details: The formula will not pay a bonus for someone who sold exactly $20,000. If such a sale should get a bonus, then use =IF(F2>=20000,0.02*F2,0).

IF WITH TWO CONDITIONS

Problem: The CFO decided we should only pay the 2% bonus if a second condition is met. The GP% must be 50% or higher in addition to the sale being over $20,000.

Strategy: There are three common solutions to this **problem:** nesting IF statements, using AND, using boolean formulas. All three will be discussed here.

The most common solution is nesting one IF statement inside of another. The formula would be: =IF(F2>20000,IF(I2>0.5,0.02*F2,0),0). This first checks if the revenue is over $20,000. The second argument holds a formula to use when the logical test is true. In this case, the second argument is another IF statement that checks to see if the GP% is over 50%.

=IF(F2>20000,IF(I2>0.5,0.02*F2,0),0)

	F	G	H	I	J
1	Revenue	COGS	Profit	GP%	Bonus
2	22810	12340	10470	45.9%	0
3	2257	1038	1219	54.0%	0
4	18552	9962	8590	46.3%	0
5	9152	4530	4622	50.5%	0
6	8456	4558	3898	46.1%	0
7	21730	9909	11821	54.4%	434.6
8	16416	8503	7913	48.2%	0
9	21438	10290	11148	52.0%	428.76
10	6267	2902	3365	53.7%	0

Figure 397 *Using a second IF statement as the second argument.*

Gotcha: Don't forget to type the ,0) at the end of the formula. This will provide the third argument and closing parentheses for the first IF statement.

Imagine if you had to test for five conditions. The above approach becomes unwieldy, as the formula is =IF(Test1,IF(Test2,IF(Test3,IF(Test4,IF(Test5, Formula If True,0),0),0),0),0). Using AND will simplify the calculation.

The AND function will hold up to 255 logical tests. Separate each test with a comma. The AND function will return TRUE if all of its arguments are TRUE. If any argument is false, then AND will return FALSE.

Use the AND() function as the logical test inside the IF statement. =IF(AND(F2>20000,I2>0.5),0.02*F2,0).

=IF(AND(F2>20000,I2>0.5),0.02*F2,0)

	F	G	H	I	J
1	Revenue	COGS	Profit	GP%	Bonus
2	22810	12340	10470	45.9%	0
3	2257	1038	1219	54.0%	0
4	18552	9962	8590	46.3%	0
5	9152	4530	4622	50.5%	0
6	8456	4558	3898	46.1%	0
7	21730	9909	11821	54.4%	434.6
8	16416	8503	7913	48.2%	0
9	21438	10290	11148	52.0%	428.76
10	6267	2902	3365	53.7%	0

Figure 398 *Using AND simplifies the IF statement.*

If you see the power of AND, then you will appreciate the OR and NOT functions. The OR function takes up to 255 logical tests. If any one of the tests is TRUE, then OR will return TRUE.

The NOT function will reverse a TRUE to FALSE and a FALSE to TRUE. Students of logic design might remember that when you algebraically simplify a complex boolean expression, using NOT(OR()) might be the simplest way to create a test.

I've done my Power Excel seminars for thousands of people who use Excel 40 hours a week. 70% of those people suggest using multiple IF statements. 29.9% of those people suggest using AND. Only one person has ever suggested the following clever method.

This formula starts out calculating a 2% bonus for everyone: =F2*0.02. But then the formula continues with two additional terms. =F2*0.02*(F2>20000)*(I2>.5). Those additional terms must be in parentheses. Excel treats (F2>20000) as a logical test and will evaluate that expression to either TRUE or FALSE. As Excel is calculating the formula, one intermediate step will be =22810*0.02*TRUE*FALSE.

When Excel has to use TRUE or FALSE in an calculation, the TRUE is treated as a one. The FALSE is treated as a zero. Since any number times zero is zero, the logical tests at the end of the formula will wipe out the bonus if any one of the conditions is not true. =22810*0.02*1*0 becomes 0. In row 7, =21730*0.02*1*1 becomes $434.60 and a bonus is paid.

=F2*0.02*(F2>20000)*(I2>0.5)				
	F	G	H	I	J
1	Revenue	COGS	Profit	GP%	Bonus
2	22810	12340	10470	45.9%	0
3	2257	1038	1219	54.0%	0
4	18552	9962	8590	46.3%	0
5	9152	4530	4622	50.5%	0
6	8456	4558	3898	46.1%	0
7	21730	9909	11821	54.4%	434.6
8	16416	8503	7913	48.2%	0
9	21438	10290	11148	52.0%	428.76
10	6267	2902	3365	53.7%	0

Figure 399 *Multiplying by a logical test is equivalent to AND.*

Additional Details: Excel treats TRUE as a 1 when you use an operator such as +-*/^ on the TRUE value. This does not happen when Excel is calculating functions. If you enter =SUM(A1:E1) and cells in that range contain a TRUE, the TRUE is ignored.

Gotcha: Don't use this last method when you have an OR condition. Traditionally, AND is equivalent to multiplication and OR is equivalent to addition. While the multiplication concept works fine in Excel, the addition will end up paying a double-bonus: =F2*0.02*((Test1)+(Test2)) might end up with =F2*0.02*2 which is not what you want.

See Also: Learn to Use Boolean Logic Facts to Simplify Logic

TIERED COMMISSION PLAN WITH IF

Problem: I am calculating a commission based on a sliding scale. The rate is based on the size of the sale, using the table shown here.

Strategy: You can solve this with several IF statements or with the unusual form of the VLOOKUP function.

To use the IF function, it is important that you start looking for the largest category first. Say that a cell contains a sale of $21,000. Checking for F2>20000 would return a TRUE, but checking for F2>1000 would be TRUE as well. You need to start checking for the largest value. If the sale is not larger than that value, then move on to checking for smaller values.

Commission Table	
Sale Amount	Rate
>20000	2.00%
>15000	1.25%
>10000	1.00%
>7500	0.25%
>1000	0.10%

Figure 400 *Sales above $15K and less than $20K are paid at 1.25%.*

In the formula below, the IF function is finding the correct rate. The result of the IF function is multiplied by the revenue in F2. This prevents you from having to enter *F2 five different times in the formula.

| | fx | =IF(F2>20000,0.02,IF(F2>15000,0.0125,IF(F2> 10000,0.01,IF(F2>7500,0.0025,IF(F2>1000,0.001, 0)))))*F2 |

F	G	H	I	J	K	L
Revenue	COGS	Profit	GP%	Bonus		
22810	12340	10470	45.9%	456.20		
2257	1038	1219	54.0%	2.26		
18552	9962	8590	46.3%	231.90		

Figure 401 *Five IF statements nested together.*

The formula is =IF(F2>20000,0.02,IF(F2>15000,0.0125,IF(F2>10000,0.01,IF(F2>7500,0.0025,IF(F2>1000,0.001,0)))))*F2.

As the commission plan becomes more complex, you would have to keep adding more IF statements. The current limit is 32 IF statements nested together. As recently as Excel 2003, the limit was 7 IF statements. It does not take long before this method becomes unwieldy.

You'll be learning more about VLOOKUP after about 15 more topics. Most VLOOKUP formulas in this book end with a FALSE to indicate a close match. Here is one case where a VLOOKUP that omits the FALSE can save the day.

To use a VLOOKUP, you have to reverse the order so that the largest lookup value appears at the end of the table. Add a beginning row with zero to handle the sales smaller than $1000. (Actually, depending on how you handle negative values, the negative values might need to be first.)

Sale Amt	Rate
0	0.00%
1000	0.10%
7500	0.25%
10000	1.00%
15000	1.25%
20000	2.00%

Figure 402 *Lookup table where the values go from smallest to largest.*

In the table above, a sale of $5000 is not found in the table. Using a typical VLOOKUP with FALSE at the end would result in an #N/A error. When you leave off the FALSE, Excel will look for the value that is just smaller than 5000. In this case, it will return the 0.10% since 1000 is the level just smaller than $5000.

=VLOOKUP(F2,$L$4:$M$9,2)*F2

H	I	J	K	L	M
Profit	GP%	Bonus			
10470	45.9%	456.20			
1219	54.0%	2.26		Sale Amt	Rate
8590	46.3%	231.90		0	0.00%
4622	50.5%	22.88		1000	0.10%
3898	46.1%	21.14		7500	0.25%
11821	54.4%	434.60		10000	1.00%
7913	48.2%	205.20		15000	1.25%
11148	52.0%	428.76		20000	2.00%

Figure 403 *Leave off FALSE. Lookup finds the just-smaller value.*

Additional Details: You might some day have a situation where you need Excel to find the value in the table that is just larger. You can not do this with VLOOKUP, but you can do it with MATCH. The last argument in MATCH can be 0 for exact match, 1 for the value just lower or -1 for the value just higher. Combine MATCH with INDEX to replicate a range-lookup where you want the just-higher value.

DISPLAY UP/DOWN ARROWS

Problem: I have a series of closing stock prices. If the price for the day goes up, I want to display an up symbol. If the price goes down, display a down symbol.

Strategy: Use an IF statement in combination with a Webdings or Wingdings font.

Most computers have at least four font faces composed of symbols. To easily browse the symbols, enter =CHAR(ROW()) in cells A1:A256. Change the font for column A to Webdings or one of the three Wingdings fonts. As you browse through the symbols and see one that you would like, click on the symbol. Below is a possible arrow to use. You can see that this is in the Wingdings 3 font. From the row number, you know it is character code 199. From the formula bar, you can see that it is the C with a cedilla mark below.

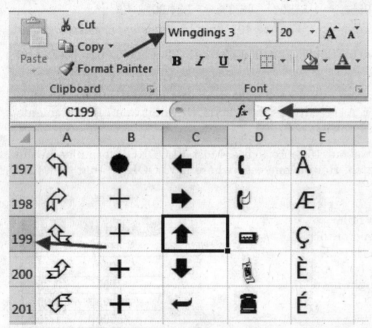

Figure 404 *Character 199 is a possibility.*

If you are reading this and you have a Portuguese keyboard, you probably have a key with the cedilla C. However, you will have to fly to France to find an E with a grave accent. You could try to master the art of holding down Alt while typing 0199 on the numeric keypad, or you could use CHAR(199).

Personally, for me, all of those are too much hassle and I won't use the arrows shown above. Instead, I found the symbols that correspond to letters on my keyboard, so that I can easily type them in the formula.

	A	B	D
1	Font	Letter	Displays As
2	Webdings	6	▼
3	Webdings	5	▲
4	Wingdings 3	p	▲
5	Wingdings 3	q	▼
6	Wingdings 3	r	△
7	Wingdings 3	s	▽

Figure 405 *These six symbols are all typeable on a U.S. keyboard.*

The strategy is to write an IF statement that produces a 5 for positive and a 6 for negative. Then, format those cells to use the Webdings font.

Use a formula such as =IF(B2>B3,5,6) to use the Webdings symbols. If you prefer the filled triangles from Wingdings 3, use =IF(B2>B3,"p","q"). Initially, you will get a column of 5 and 6.

`=IF(B2>B3,5,6)`

	A	B	C
1	Date	Adj Close	
2	31-May-11	12,569.79	5
3	27-May-11	12,441.58	5
4	26-May-11	12,402.76	5
5	25-May-11	12,394.66	5
6	24-May-11	12,356.21	6
7	23-May-11	12,381.26	6

Figure 406 *The formula produces 5's and 6's.*

Select column C and change the font to Webdings. Use Left alignment.

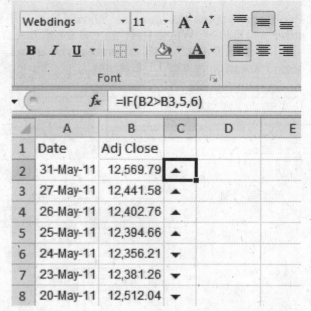

Figure 407 *Convert the column to Wingdings.*

Gotcha: If you ever need to edit the formula in C, it will appear in Webdings font and be unreadable in the cell. Use the Formula bar to see the real formula.

If you want to display the arrows in green and red, change the font color of column C to green. Then use Home, Conditional Formatting, Highlight Cells Rules, Equal to, 5. Open the Format dropdown and choose Custom Format. On the Font tab, choose a bright red.

If you have Excel 2010, you can use the new Up, Flat, Down icon set. See Icon Sets in Part IV of this book.

Alternate Strategy: You can avoid the IF statement and use a custom number format. Use a formula of =SIGN(B2-B3) in column C. This will return a negative one for days that the price went down, positive one for days when the price went up, and a zero for days where the price is unchanged.

Change the custom number format to [green]\r;[red]\s;. Change the font to Wingdings 3.

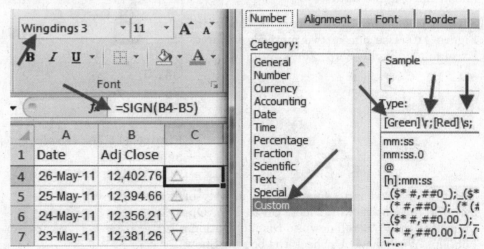

Figure 408 *Forcing Excel to show r for positive and s for negative.*

The custom number format is using three zones. The first zone is showing a lower case r in green for any positive number. The second zone is showing a lower case s in red for any negative number. The third zone is indicated by the final semi-colon and is blank, indicating no symbol for zero values. When you convert column C to Wingdings 3, you get the arrows shown.

STOP SHOWING ZEROES IN CELL LINKS

Problem: I have the data set shown below. I need live formulas that replicate this data set on another worksheet. When I set up the formulas, I get zeroes where the blank cells are located. I can use =IF(ISBLANK(A1),"",A1) to suppress the zeroes, but then if I try to do any math on A1 in the worksheet copy, I am getting #VALUE errors.

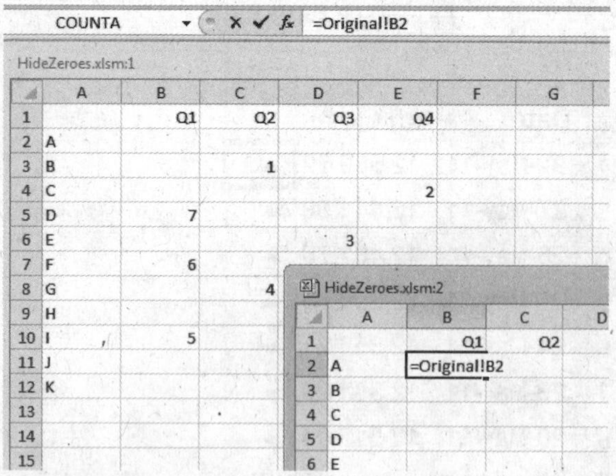

Figure 409 *Set up a link to replicate a table on another worksheet.*

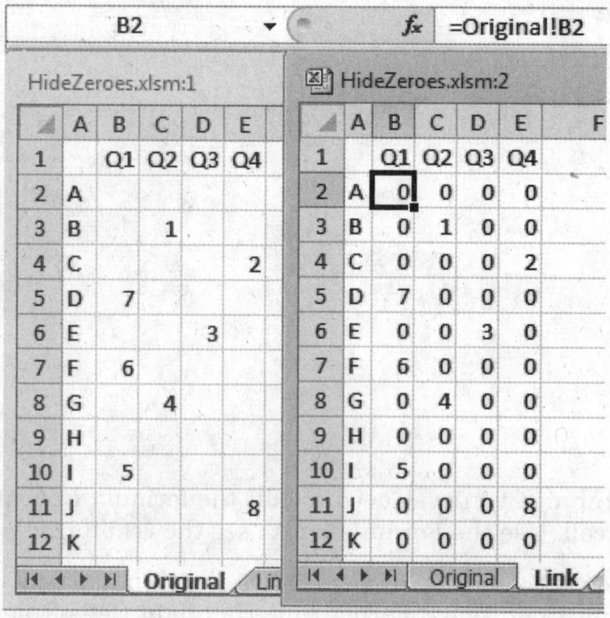

Figure 410 *The result is showing zeroes instead of blank cells.*

If you change the formula to display nothing, the zeroes go away, but there is another problem. A formula such as =C2+B2 will display a #VALUE! error while it would have worked fine in the original data.

Strategy: Go back to the formula shown in Figure 410. Use one of two methods to force Excel to not display zero values.

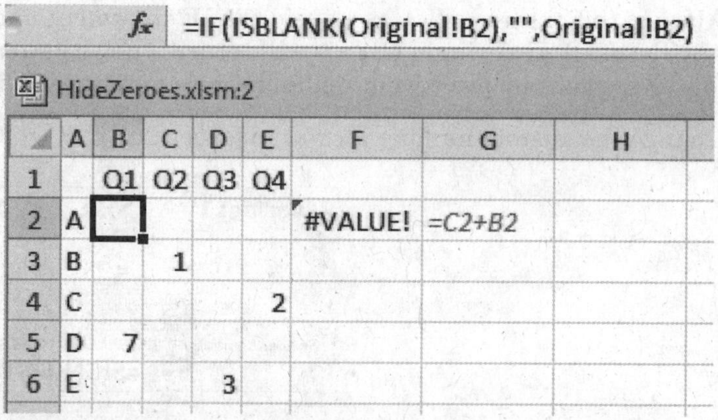

Figure 411 *The IF solves one problem, but creates another.*

The first method is to suppress the display of zero for the entire worksheet. Go to File, Options, Advanced. Scroll down to Display Options For This Worksheet. Uncheck the box for Show a Zero In Cells That Have a Zero Value.

Gotcha: this setting affects the entire worksheet. What if you want zeroes to appear in another range on this worksheet?

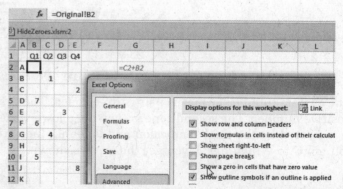

Figure 412 *Zeroes don't appear. The formula in F2 works as expected.*

In that case, you can use a custom number format to suppress zeroes in a particular range. Select B2:E11. Press Ctrl+1 (Ctrl+One). On the Number tab, choose Custom from the listbox on the left. Type a custom number format of 0;-0;. This code will display positive numbers and negative numbers, but suppress zero values.

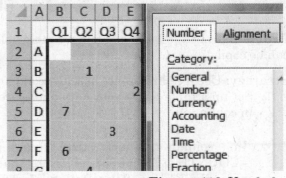

Figure 413 *Use 0;-0;.*

COUNT RECORDS THAT MATCH A CRITERION

Problem: I have a large data set. I want to count the number of records that meet a certain criterion.

	A	B	C	D	E	F
1		Male				
2		Female				
3						
4	Name	Gender	DOB	Age	Dept	Salary
5	Allen	M	10/20/1945	54	Accounting	69000
6	Allison	F	5/20/1979	32	Manufacturing	22000
7	Amber	F	2/19/1970	41	Marketing	36000
8	Andrea	F	4/24/1977	34	Manufacturing	19000
9	Barb	F	11/21/1956	65	Accounting	79000
10	Betty	F	6/25/1983	27	Manufacturing	15000

Figure 414 *Count males and females.*

Strategy: You use the COUNTIF function, which requires two arguments: a range of cells that you want to test and a criteria. To count the records where the gender is M, you use =COUNTIF(B5:B60,"M").

=COUNTIF(B5:B60,"M")

	A	B	C
1		Male	27
2		Female	29
3			
4	Name	Gender	DOB
5	Allen	M	10/20/1945
6	Allison	F	5/20/1979
7	Amber	F	2/19/1970
8	Andrea	F	4/24/1977

Figure 415 *COUNTIF function looks through a range, counting matches.*

Note that the second argument, "M", tells Excel to count records that are equal to M. Because this function is not case-sensitive, the function will count cells with values of M or m.

If you want to count the records where the age is a specific number, you can write the formula either with or without quotes around the number:
```
=COUNTIF(D5:D60,32)
=COUNTIF(D5:D60,"32")
```

You can also establish a criterion to look for items that are below or above a certain number:
```
=COUNTIF(D5:D60,"<21")
```

A criterion can include a wildcard character. To find any text that contains XYZ, you use the following formula:
```
=COUNTIF(A2:A999,"*XYZ*")
```

BUILD A TABLE THAT WILL COUNT BY CRITERIA

Problem: I need to build a summary table using COUNTIF functions. How can I enter one formula that can be copied?

Strategy: Use a cell reference as the second argument in the COUNTIF function. Here's how:

1. Set up a table below your data and place all the possible values for a column, such as department, in column A.

2. In column B of the first row, enter =COUNTIF($E$7:$E$62,A1). Note that you should press the F4 key after selecting E7:E62 to make the first range absolute. This will allow you to copy the formula to other rows.

3. Copy the formula down for the other departments.

=COUNTIF($E$7:$E$62,A1)				
A	**B**	**C**	**D**	**E**
1 Accounting	12			
2 Manufacturing	31			
3 Marketing	9			
4 Sales	4			
5				
6 Name	Gender	DOB	Age	Dept
7 Allen	M	10/20/1945	54	Accounting
8 Allison	F	5/20/1979	32	Manufacturing

Figure 416 Count of records by department.

SUM RECORDS THAT MATCH A CRITERION

Problem: That COUNTIF function is cool. Is there a way to sum all records that match a criterion?

Strategy: There is a SUMIF function that works similar to COUNTIF. In this case, you would look at all values in E8:E63 to see if they are equal to "Accounting". If they are, you want to add up the corresponding value from F8:F63.

=SUMIF($E$8:$E$63,A2,$F$8:$F$63)					
A	**B**	**C**	**D**	**E**	**F**
1	Count	Total Salary			
2 Accounting	12	776,000			
3 Manufacturing	31	884,000			
4 Marketing	9	346,000			
5 Sales	4	208,000			
6					
7 Name	Gender	DOB	Age	Dept	Salary
8 Allen	M	10/20/1945	54	Accounting	69000
9 Allison	F	5/20/1979	32	Manufacturing	22000
10 Amber	F	3/19/1970	41	Marketing	35000

Figure 417 Sum values from F if E is the right department.

The one difference from COUNTIF is that the SUMIF function usually requires you to specify the sum range as the third argument. (I say usually, because you might sometimes want to add up all salaries over $60000. In that case, the first and third arguments would both be F8:F63, so you can omit the third argument).

Additional Details: Starting in Excel 2007, Microsoft added an AVERAGEIF function. This seems fairly redundant to me, since you could easily do =C2/B2 in the current example rather than doing an AVERAGEIF formula.

CAN THE RESULTS OF A FORMULA BE USED IN SUMIF?

Problem: Can the results of a formula be used as the criteria? I would like to add all numbers that are above average.

Strategy: The second parameter of the SUMIF/COUNTIF can be a calculation, but you must concatenate a comparison operator in quotes with the formula. Consider this formula:

=SUMIF($F$6:$F$61,">"&AVERAGE($F$6:$F$61),$F$6:$F$61)

The criteria is ">"&AVERAGE(F6:F61). Excel first calculates the average, then joins the operator with the result. In the second step of evaluating the formula, Excel has changed the formula to ">39535.71".

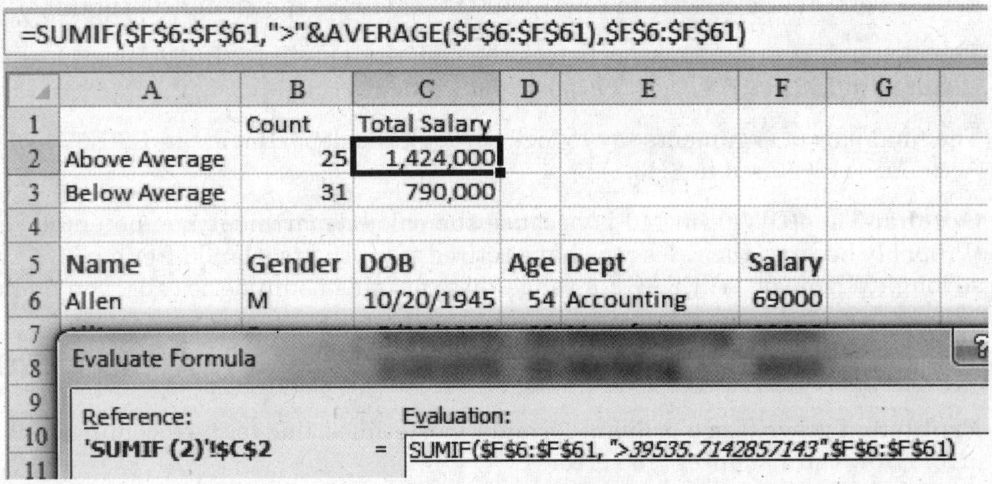

=SUMIF($F$6:$F$61,">"&AVERAGE($F$6:$F$61),$F$6:$F$61)

	A	B	C	D	E	F	G
1		Count	Total Salary				
2	Above Average	25	1,424,000				
3	Below Average	31	790,000				
4							
5	Name	Gender	DOB	Age	Dept	Salary	
6	Allen	M	10/20/1945	54	Accounting	69000	

Evaluate Formula

Reference:
'SUMIF (2)'!$C$2

Evaluation:
= SUMIF($F$6:$F$61, ">39535.7142857143",$F$6:$F$61)

Figure 418 *The criterion is built from a formula.*

CALCULATE BASED ON MULTIPLE CONDITIONS

Problem: COUNTIF and SUMIF have been around since Excel 97. Whenever someone learns how to use these functions, they inevitably come up with a situation where they need to count or sum or based on more than one condition.

Strategy: Before Excel 2007, you had to use the SUMPRODUCT function or a complicated array formula. Starting in Excel 2007, you can use SUMIFS, COUNTIFS, or AVERAGEIFS.

Get it? SUMIFS is the plural version of SUMIF. It can handle up to 127 different criteria.

Gotcha: Although SUMIF and SUMIFS sound the same, Microsoft had to reverse the order of the arguments to make SUMIFS work. In particular, the Sum_Range argument which was third in SUMIF has been moved to the first argument in SUMIFS.

To set up a SUMIFS or AVERAGEIFS, use these arguments:
- Sum_Range: The range of numbers to add is specified first.
- Criteria_Range1: A range of values to check.
- Criteria1: The value to look for in Criteria_Range1
- You can then repeat pairs of Criteria_Range and Criteria for each additional condition.

Say that you want to calculate average salary by department and age range. This requires three sets of criteria. The department has to match. Since you want to report on ages by decade, you need to look for ages >=30 and <40.

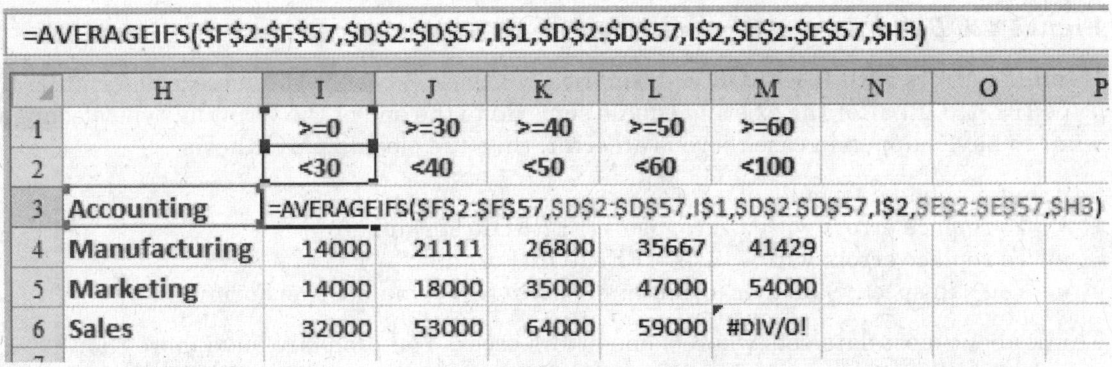

=AVERAGEIFS($F$2:$F$57,$D$2:$D$57,I$1,$D$2:$D$57,I$2,$E$2:$E$57,$H3)

	H	I	J	K	L	M	N	O	P
1		>=0	>=30	>=40	>=50	>=60			
2		<30	<40	<50	<60	<100			
3	Accounting	=AVERAGEIFS($F$2:$F$57,$D$2:$D$57,I$1,$D$2:$D$57,I$2,$E$2:$E$57,$H3)							
4	Manufacturing	14000	21111	26800	35667	41429			
5	Marketing	14000	18000	35000	47000	54000			
6	Sales	32000	53000	64000	59000	#DIV/0!			

Figure 419 *Averaging based on three conditions.*

Note: The data being averaged is similar to the data in the previous several topics. I am not showing columns A:F in the above figure because it would be too small. See Figure 414 for the columns in the data set. The headings are in row 1 and the data is in rows 2 through 57.

The first argument is the range with the values that you want to average. This is F2:F57.

The next pairs of arguments specify that Excel should look through D2:D57 for ages that are greater than zero. Note the single dollar sign before the 1 in I$1. This lets you copy the formula. This argument will always point to the criteria in row 1, but the reference can change to column J, K, L, and M.

The next pair of arguments say to look through the ages in D2:D57 for ages less than 30. Again, the criteria is stored in I$2.

The final pair of arguments say to look through the departments in E2:E57 looking for records that match Accounting as stored in $H3.

Gotcha: The #DIV/0! in M6 is because the sales department has no employees above 59 years of age. (Probably because the sales reps have retired to a private island after earning those huge commissions for so long.) When you AVERAGE a range that contains no numeric cells, you end up dividing by zero.

AVOID ERRORS USING IFERROR

Problem: I've written a brilliant formula. Sometimes, due to the incoming data, the formula generates an error. How can I suppress the errors?

Strategy: Starting in Excel 2007, Excel offers the amazing IFERROR function. Don't confuse this with the =ISERROR(), =ISERR(), =ISNA() functions. This new IFERROR function is very cool.

Before Excel 2007, to head off errors, you would have to test for any of the conditions that would cause an error. This might mean taking the very long formula from Figure 419 and making it insanely long:

=IF(COUNTIFS($D$2:$D$57,I$1,$D$2:$D$57,I$2,$E$2:$E$57,$H3)=0,"--",AVERAGEIFS($F$2:$F$57,$D$2:$D$57,I$1,$D$2:$D$57,I$2,$E$2:$E$57,$H3))

There are 20 cells in Figure 419, and 19 of them are working just fine. Yet, this formula will force Excel to do a complete SUMIFS before it can figure out if it should put -- or go on to calculate the AVERAGEIFS. This a huge amount of complexity just to zap one #DIV/0! error.

=IF(COUNTIFS($D$2:$D$57,I$1,$D$2:$D$57,
$H3)=0,"--",AVERAGEIFS($F$2:$F$57,$D$2:$D$57,I$1,$D$2:
$D$57,I$2,$E$2:$E$57,$H3))

	H	I	J	K	L	M
1		>=0	>=30	>=40	>=50	>=60
2		<30	<40	<50	<60	<100
3	Accounting	27000	46000	49000	67833	82333
4	Manufacturing	14000	21111	26800	35667	41429
5	Marketing	14000	18000	35000	47000	54000
6	Sales	32000	53000	64000	59000	--

Figure 420 *Before Excel 2007, error handling was slow and complex.*

Handling errors with IFERROR is dramatically easier. Say that you have any formula. Edit the formula. Type IFERROR(after the existing equals sign. Go to the end of the formula, type a comma, then what you want to have happen in case there is an error, then the closing parenthesis.

Say that you had a formula of =Formula.
- To replace errors with a zero, use =IFERROR(Formula,0)
- To replace errors with --, use =IFERROR(Formula,"--")
- You can specify another formula: =IFERROR(Formula,OtherFormula).

Think about most data sets where some errors occur. You probably have more than 95% of the cells that calculate without an error and less than 5% that generate errors. The IFERROR function is smart enough to try the first calculation and only move on to the second argument when it gets an error. This will be a drastic time savings when you don't have to use =IF(ISNA(VLOOKUP()),"--",VLOOKUP()) anymore.

`=IFERROR(AVERAGEIFS($F$2:$F57,$D$2:$D$57,I$1,$D$2:$D$57,I$2,$E$2:$E$57,$H3),"-")`

⬛	H	I	J	K	L	M	N	O	P
1		>=0	>=30	>=40	>=50	>=60			
2		<30	<40	<50	<60	<100			
3	Accounting	27000	46000	49000	67833	82333			
4	Manufacturing	14000	21111	26800	35667	41429			
5	Marketing	14000	18000	35000	47000	54000			
6	Sales	32000	53000	64000	59000	-			

Figure 421 *IFERROR simplifies error checking.*

Additional Information: Excel 2013 adds the =IFNA() function. Say that you want to catch any VLOOK-UP functions that return #N/A, but you want to allow any underlying DIV/0 errors to show through. The IFNA in Excel 2013 will only convert #N/A to the alternate value.

MULTIPLE CONDITIONS USING SUMPRODUCT

Problem: Before Excel introduced SUMIFS in Excel 2007, you would have to use the SUMPRODUCT function to solve problems that can be solved by SUMIFS.

Strategy: Once you get the hang of it, SUMPRODUCT is cool.

Say that you want to calculate the sales of Green XL EasyXL shirts. This figure uses 37 formulas to calculate the $6800.

`=D4*F4*G4*H4`

⬛	A	B	C	D	E	F	G	H	I	J
1	Amount of Red, XL, EasyXL?							37 Formulas in this box		
2										
3	Color	Size	Style	Amount		(Color ="Green")	(Size ="XL")	(Style= "EasyXL")		Product
4	Red	L	MrXL	100		FALSE	FALSE	FALSE		0
5	Blue	L	EasyXL	200		FALSE	FALSE	TRUE		0
6	Green	L	MrXL	300		TRUE	FALSE	FALSE		0
7	Red	L	EasyXL	500		FALSE	FALSE	TRUE		0
8	Blue	XL	MrXL	800		FALSE	TRUE	FALSE		0
9	Green	XL	EasyXL	1300		TRUE	TRUE	TRUE		1300
10	Red	XL	MrXL	2100		FALSE	TRUE	FALSE		0
11	Blue	XL	EasyXL	3400		FALSE	TRUE	TRUE		0
12	Green	XL	EasyXL	5500		TRUE	TRUE	TRUE		5500
13									Sum:	6800
14										
15	Formulas:									
16		F4	=A4="Green"							
17		G4	=B4="XL"							
18		H4	=C4="EasyXL"							
19		J4	=D4*F4*G4*H4							
20		J13	=SUM(J4:J12)							

Figure 422 *9 rows, 3 conditions, 37 formulas.*

The SUMPRODUCT function replaces those 37 formulas with a single formula. Here is the basic structure:

`=SUMPRODUCT((Criteria1)*(Criteria2)*(Criteria3),(Numbers))`

I am guessing that SUMPRODUCT was added to Excel to do matrix multiplication. Multiply one rectangular range by another rectangular range and sum the products.

Before Excel 2007 came along, Excel tricksters started using SUMPRODUCT to do SUMIFS before SUMIFS was invented.

In essence, you are telling Excel to multiply four arrays of values.

- The first array is (A4:A12="Green"). This evaluates to the array of TRUE/FALSE values shown in F4:F12.
- The next array is (B4:B12="XL"). Notice that you always put these logical tests in parentheses in order to force Excel to evaluate them first. This array results in the values shown in G4:G12.
- The next array is (C4:C12="EasyXL"). It evaluates to the values in H4:H12.
- The last array is the numbers in D4:D12.

Flip back to Figure 399 to read what happens when you multiply a number by TRUE or FALSE. A number times TRUE is the number. A number times FALSE is 0.

When you understand that TRUE is like 1 and FALSE is like 0, you can see that the only amounts which make it through to column J are those where each of the conditions is TRUE.

800	0	1	0	0
1300	1	1	1	=D9*F9*G9*H9
2100	0	1	0	0
3400	0	1	1	0
5500	1	1	1	5500
			Sum:	6800

Figure 423 *Any FALSE becomes a 0, making the product for that row 0.*

Additional Details: Calculations in the grid are handled a bit differently than calculations that use functions. 10*TRUE*TRUE in the grid comes out as 10. However, =SUMPRODUCT(10,TRUE,TRUE) will not work. The SUMPRODUCT program refuses to convert the TRUE values to 1's on the fly. I don't know if this is a bug, or if it is simply a matter of the original intention of SUMPRODUCT was to multiply matrices of numbers.

So, according to the syntax in Excel Help, one might think that this formula would work:
=SUMPRODUCT(A4:A12="Green",B4:B12="XL",C4:C12="EasyXL",D4:D12)

It does not. There are workarounds, and several really smart people disagree on which workaround is the best. We all agree that you have to do some mathematical operation on the logical arrays to coerce them to change from TRUE/FALSE to 1/0. Several people do this in a two-step process. They use a unary minus to change the TRUE to -1 and the FALSE to 0. They then have to use a secondary unary minus to convert the -1 back to 1. Their formula might look like this:
=SUMPRODUCT(--(A4:A12="Green"),--(B4:B12="XL"),--(C4:C12="EasyXL"),D4:D12)

There are downsides to this formula. Excel has to touch each logical formula twice using this method, once for each unary minus. Also, for a brief time, Excel 2007 was letting the AutoCorrect change the minus minus to an em-dash. Brilliant in Word, not at all useful in an Excel formula.

When I do a SUMPRODUCT, I don't use the double unary minus. Instead, I multiply all of the logical arrays together. This calculation is like doing a calculation in the grid, so it automatically converts TRUE/FALSE to 1/0.
=SUMPRODUCT((A4:A12="Green")*(B4:B12="XL")*(C4:C12="EasyXL")*(D4:D12))

The detractors of this method say that Excel Help indicate that the arrays should be separated by commas, not by parentheses. They say that using this method you are doing all of the work in Excel and you are not letting SUMPRODUCT do any multiplying. By having Excel do the work, the only thing left to do is to SUM the results of the products done by Excel. I don't buy this argument. The fact is that *something* has to do the multiplication, and I don't care if it is the Excel calculation engine or the SUMPRODUCT function. If I am reducing SUMPRODUCT to a SUM function, so be it.

If you really want to let SUMPRODUCT do some multiplying, then use a hybrid of the two approaches:
=SUMPRODUCT((A4:A12="Green")*(B4:B12="XL")*(C4:C12="EasyXL"),D4:D12)

`=SUMPRODUCT((A4:A12="Green")*(B4:B12="XL")*(C4:C12="EasyXL"),D4:D12)`

	A	B	C	D	E	F	G	H	I	J
1	Amount of Red, XL, EasyXL?					6800				
2										
3	Color	Size	Style	Amount						
4	Red	L	MrXL	100						
5	Blu	L	EasyXL	200						

Figure 424 *One of three ways to do a SUMPRODUCT.*

Gotcha: While SUMPRODUCT is powerful, the built-in SUMIFS will calculate sometimes 1000 times faster than SUMPRODUCT. If everyone using your worksheet is using Excel 2007 or newer, use SUMIFS instead.

Gotcha: Up through Excel 2007, there was an obscure add-in called the Conditional Sum Wizard. This add-in would not use SUMPRODUCT or SUMIFS. It would build a formula such as {=SUM(IF(A4:A12=" Green",IF(B4:B12="XL",IF(C4:C12="EasyXL",D4:D12,0),0),0))}. Anytime you see the curly braces around the formula, it is a super-secret type of formula that Microsoft calls an array formula. If you attempt to edit this formula, you have to finish the formula by holding down Ctrl+Shift while pressing Enter.

USE VLOOKUP TO JOIN TWO TABLES

2

Problem: My I.T. department gave me a data set with Item Number, Date, and Quantity sold. They didn't put an item description in there. If I call back and ask them to re-do the file, it will take 3 weeks. Can I quickly fill in the item descriptions?

	A	B	C	D
1	Item	Date	Qty	Description
2	W25-6	8/15/2014	878	
3	CR 50-4	8/15/2014	213	
4	CR 50-4	8/16/2014	744	
5	BR26-3	8/17/2014	169	
6	CR50-6	8/17/2014	822	
7	ER46-14	8/17/2014	740	

Figure 425 *You need item description here.*

I have a second table that maps item number to item description.

Strategy: Use VLOOKUP. This is the single most important function in Excel. VLOOK-UP will save you time and time again.

SKU	Description
BG33-3	14K Gold Bangle Bracele
CR50-3	14K Gold Cross with Ony
RG75-3	14K Gold RAY OF LIGH
RG78-25	14K Gold Ballerina Ring
W25-6	18K Italian Gold Women'
BR26-3	18K Italian Gold Men's B

Figure 426 *You have a table with the item descriptions..*

In this situation, VLOOKUP requires four arguments:
- The value to look up. In this case, it is cell A2.
- A table with the lookup value in column 1 of the table. You always want to enter the table with dollar signs throughout the reference. That way, you can copy the VLOOKUP formula to other rows. In this case, the table is in $L$3:$M$30.
- A column number in the table to return. Unlike Lotus 1-2-3, Excel will allow you to return the key column in the table, so the SKU column above would be column #1. The Description column is column 2.
- The fourth argument in VLOOKUP is always FALSE. If you don't put a FALSE as the fourth argument, Excel will give you results that almost match. This is NEVER what you want when you are solving these types of problems.

The formula for D2 is =VLOOKUP(A2,$L$3:$M$30,2,FALSE).

=VLOOKUP(A2,$L$3:$M$30,2,FALSE)

	A	D	E	L	M	
1	Item	Description				
2	W25-6	=VLOOKUP(A2,$L$3:$M$30,2,FALSE)		SKU	Description	
3	CR 50-4	14K Gold Onyx Cross		BG33-3	14K Gold Bangl
4	CR 50-4	14K Gold Onyx Cross		CR50-3	14K Gold Cross
5	BR26-3	18K Italian Gold Men's Bracelet		RG75-3	14K Gold RAY (
6	CR50-6	14K Gold Onyx Cross with White Cubic Zirconia Stones		RG78-25	14K Gold Baller
7	ER46-14	14K Gold Fish Hoop Earrings		W25-6	18K Italian Gold
8	RG78-25	14K Gold Ballerina Ring w/ Blue & White CZs (Women's Rings, CZ Rings)		BR26-3	18K Italian Gold
9	BR15-3	14K Gold Onyx Men's Bracelet		BR15-3	14K Gold Onyx
10	Cross50-5	14K Gold Onyx Cross with White Cubic Zirconia Stones		BG33-8	14K Gold Bangl
11	CR50-2	14K Gold Onyx Cross		BG33-17	14K Gold Bangl
12	BR26-3	18K Italian Gold Men's Bracelet		CR 50-4	14K Gold Onyx
13	ER41-4	14K Gold Swiss Cut Earrings		CR50-2	14K Gold Onyx
14	RG75-3	14K Gold RAY OF LIGHT Onyx Men's Ring (Men's Rings)		CR50-1	14K Gold Onyx
15	RG75-3	14K Gold RAY OF LIGHT Onyx Men's Ring (Men's Rings)		Cross50-5	14K Gold Onyx
16	CR 50-4	14K Gold Onyx Cross		CR50-6	14K Gold Onyx
17	BR26-3	18K Italian Gold Men's Bracelet		ER41-4	14K Gold Swiss
18	CR 50-4	14K Gold Onyx Cross		ER46-14	14K Gold Fish H
19	RG75-3	14K Gold RAY OF LIGHT Onyx Men's Ring (Men's Rings)		ER46-7	14K Gold Hollov
20	CR50-6	14K Gold Onyx Cross with White Cubic Zirconia Stones		ER46-22	14K Gold Hoop
21	RG75-3	14K Gold RAY OF LIGHT Onyx Men's Ring (Men's Rings)		ER46-28	14K Gold Earrin
22	Cross50-5	14K Gold Onyx Cross with White Cubic Zirconia Stones		ER46-29	14K Gold Hoop
23	CR 50-4	14K Gold Onyx Cross		ER 46-33	14K Gold Hollov
24	BG33-17	14K Gold Bangle Bracelet with Star Design		ER49-20	14K Gold Hoop/
25	RG78-25	14K Gold Ballerina Ring w/ Blue & White CZs (Women's Rings, CZ Rings)		ER49-21	14K Gold Hoop/
26	RG75-3	14K Gold RAY OF LIGHT Onyx Men's Ring (Men's Rings)		ER49-22	14K Gold Tube/
27	CR50-6	14K Gold Onyx Cross with White Cubic Zirconia Stones		ER80-63	14K Gold Ruby
28	CR50-6	14K Gold Onyx Cross with White Cubic Zirconia Stones		ER89-47	14K Gold Two-T
29	ER46-28	14K Gold Earrings		P411A	14K Gold Lion F
30	BR26-3	18K Italian Gold Men's Bracelet		P330	14K Gold Eagle
31	ER41-4	14K Gold Swiss Cut Earrings			

Figure 427 *If you can enter the VLOOKUP with your eyes closed, I will give you a spot on my team when Excel becomes a sport in the Olympics.*

Additional Details: I used to be a manager of financial analysis. On the job posting form when I was hiring financial analysts, I would list a single requirement: "Can do VLOOKUPs in your sleep". It really is the single most important Excel skill.

Additional Details: To me, the world breaks down into two kinds of people, those who can do VLOOK-UPs, and everyone else.

EVERY VLOOKUP ENDS IN FALSE

Problem: My VLOOKUPs aren't working. It is returning other values from the table.

Strategy: You have to end your VLOOKUPs with FALSE as the fourth argument. If you don't put FALSE at the end of your VLOOKUP, then you are using a completely different function. There are people who leave the FALSE off the VLOOKUP. If you don't specify FALSE, then you are letting Excel assume that you want TRUE as the range_lookup argument. You are asking for trouble. You will hate VLOOKUP when you e-mail an incorrect document to the entire department. Don't ever write a VLOOKUP that does not end in FALSE.

The only exceptions:
- Some people put a zero instead of FALSE. That's fine. It saves you 4 characters of typing, but it still runs the FALSE version of VLOOKUP.
- Commission accountants have permission to use the approximate version of VLOOKUP, but only 1% of the time. They must specifically be trying to eliminate a bunch of nested IF statements as shown all the way back in Figure 403.
- Scientists. I get it. They do range lookups all the time. If you are a scientist reading this book, send it back to me and I will send you Gerry Verschuuren's Excel for Scientists book.
- Very clever Excel tricksters will utilize a loop hole in the range_lookup version of VLOOKUP to return the last non-blank value in a row or column.

Everyone else should be using the ,FALSE version of VLOOKUP every time.

LOOKUP TABLE DOES NOT HAVE TO BE SORTED

Problem: I think the lookup table has to be sorted.

Strategy: I don't care what your professor said, if you are using the ,FALSE version of VLOOKUP, the lookup table does not have to be sorted.

Since 99.9826% of VLOOKUPs have FALSE at the end, the table does not have to be sorted in 5759 out of every 5760 cases.

Sure, when you don't have FALSE or 0 at the end of your lookup table, then the table has to be sorted.

People who have to sort the lookup table

	Population	VLOOKUPs per Year	Total
Scientists because they are doing range lookups	350000	87	30,450,000
Excel authors and trainers, answering why TRUE?	24	8	192
Commission Accountants, once a month	175000	12	2,100,000
Total Sorted VLOOKUPs			**32,550,192**

Figure 428 *There are specific situations where you sort the lookup table.*

However, most of the time, the lookup table does not have to be sorted.

People who don't have to sort the lookup table

	Population	VLOOKUPs per Year	Total
Everyone Else	749474976	250	187,368,744,000
Commission Accountants, most of the time	175000	238	41,650,000
Excel authors and trainers, rest of the time	24	242	5,808
Scientists, half the time	350000	87	30,450,000
Total Non-Sorted VLOOKUPs			**187,440,849,808**

Figure 429 *Most people don't have to sort the lookup table.*

In case you are more of a visual person instead of a number person, here is the pie chart:

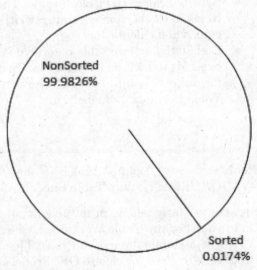

NonSorted
99.9826%

Sorted
0.0174%

Figure 430 *Most accountants will go their entire lives and never use the version of VLOOKUP that requires the table to be sorted.*

2

BEWARE OF #N/A FROM VLOOKUP

Problem: A few of my VLOOKUPs are giving me the #N/A error.

```
=VLOOKUP(A67,$L$3:$M$30,2,FALSE)
```

	A	D
1	**Item**	**Description**
66	BG33-8	14K Gold Bangle Bracelet with Star Design
67	BG33-9	#N/A
68	CR50-6	14K Gold Onyx Cross with White Cubic Zirconia Stones
69	ER46-22	14K Gold Hoop Earrings

Figure 431 *BG33-9 is a new item and isn't in the lookup table.*

Strategy: This is common when you are doing VLOOKUP. It tells you that the lookup value is not found in the first column of the table. When you encounter an #N/A error, add that item to the table (see the next topic).

Additional Details: To isolate the #N/A errors, sort your data descending (using the ZA icon). All of the #N/A errors will sort to the top.

Additional Details: If you don't want to update the lookup table with new values, but prefer to have alternate text entered, use IFERROR:

=IFERROR(VLOOKUP(),"Item Not Found").

Gotcha: If you leave the #N/A errors in the data set and try to add up that column, the SUM will be #N/A. One single #N/A causes all downline formulas to calculate as #N/A.

ADD NEW ITEMS TO THE MIDDLE OF YOUR LOOKUP TABLE

Problem: I have to add BG33-9 to my lookup table. When I enter it in row 31, the #N/A error does not go away.

Strategy: You would have to rewrite the VLOOKUP to point to $L$3:$M$30. Instead, you could use any of these clever strategies:
- Insert new cells anywhere in the middle of your lookup table. For example choose L7:M7 and do Alt+I+E followed by Enter. This will Insert Cells and shift the remaining items down.
- Specify L:M as the lookup table. This uses the whole column as the lookup table. Now, you can add items to the bottom without rewriting the formula. Excel is smart enough to only use the non-blank cells when calculating.
- Ctrl+T the lookup table before you add new values. When you type new values in row 31, the table expands to include the new row. In one of those scary bits of Excel magic, they actually rewrite your formulas to point to the extra row in the VLOOKUP formula. This happens even if you are not using Table Formula Nomenclature.

CONSIDER NAMING THE LOOKUP TABLE

Problem: My lookup table is on another worksheet. The VLOOKUP is really confusing =VLOOKUP(A2,'Lookup Table Sheet'!$A$2:$B$30,2,FALSE).

Strategy: Many people in my live seminars say that they use a range name to name the lookup table. Go to your Lookup Table Worksheet. Select cells A2:B30. Click in the Name Box to the left of the formula bar. Type a simple name like ProdTable and press Enter. Remember - the name can not contain a space. ProdTable or Prod_Table are OK. Prod Table is not.

Future VLOOKUPs can be entered as: =VLOOKUP(A2,ProdTable,2,FALSE). This is simpler to enter.

REMOVE LEADING AND TRAILING SPACES

Problem: None of my VLOOKUP formulas are working. I can clearly see that there is a match in the lookup table, but Excel cannot see it.

=VLOOKUP(A2,$L$3:$M$30,2,FALSE)

	A	D E	L	M
1	Item	Description	SKU	Description
2	BG33-8	#N/A	BG33-3	14K Gold Ban
3	Cross50-5	#N/A	BG33-8	14K Gold Ban
4	RG78-25	#N/A	CR50-3	14K Gold Cros
5	BG33-8	#N/A		

Figure 432 *None of the VLOOKUP functions work.*

Strategy: A common problem is that either the item in column A or Column L has trailing spaces. This can happen if you downloaded the data from another system.

To fix this problem, you select cell A2 and press the F2 key to put the cell in Edit mode. A flashing insertion cursor will appear at the end of the cell. Check to see if the insertion cursor appears immediately after the last character or a few spaces away.

Edit cell L2 to see if there are trailing spaces. You will likely find that either column has trailing spaces. Below, you can see that there are a couple trailing spaces after the Item in column A. These trailing spaces cause the VLOOKUP to not classify the cells as a match. Although you can tell that "BG33-8 " is the same as "BG33-9", Excel cannot.

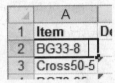

	A	
1	Item	D
2	BG33-8	
3	Cross50-5	

Figure 433 *Column A has trailing spaces.*

You can use the TRIM function to remove leading and trailing spaces from a value. If there are spaces between words, it will change consecutive spaces to a single space. For example, =TRIM(" Bill Jelen ") would change the cell contents to "Bill Jelen".

Additional Details: If the trailing spaces appear in your lookup value, use TRIM around that one value. Change =VLOOKUP(A2,$L$3:$M$30,2,FALSE) to =VLOOKUP(TRIM(A2),$L$3:$M$30,2,FALSE).

If the trailing spaces appear in the lookup table, then you can actually TRIM the entire table with one bizarre modification. Change the formula above to =VLOOKUP(A2,TRIM($L$3:$M$30),2,FALSE). But, don't press Enter after making the edit. Instead, hold down Ctrl and Shift and then press Enter.

Gotcha: That formula where you TRIM the entire lookup table is going to be insanely slow. It is fine for impressing your friends who use Excel, but in real life, it would be better to add a temporary column to TRIM each individual cell in column L. Then, copy that column and paste as values over column L.

Alternate Strategy: The other common problem of VLOOKUPs failing is numbers stored as text being used to look up a table with numeric values. Select column A and do Alt+DEF. Repeat with column L. Alt+DEF does a text to columns and converts text numbers to real numbers.

YOUR LOOKUP TABLE CAN GO ACROSS

Problem: Someone built this lookup table going across the worksheet. How can I use VLOOKUP?

	F	G	H	I	J	K	L	M	N	O	P	Q
1	**Bonus Rates**											
2	Jan	Feb	Mar	Apr	May	Jun	Jul	Aug	Sep	Oct	Nov	Dec
3	1.5%	2.4%	3.0%	1.2%	1.9%	1.0%	2.1%	2.4%	2.2%	1.6%	2.5%	2.8%

Figure 434 *The table is going the wrong way.*

Strategy: The "V" in VLOOKUP stands for Vertical Lookup. Excel also offers an HLOOK-UP for horizontal lookup tables. If you are in a bizarre mood, you could actually use HLOOKUP: =HLOOKUP(B3,$F$2:$Q$3,2,FALSE).

Alternate Strategy: You will most likely do what I and every other person using Excel does: Copy F2:Q3. Select cell F5. Do Paste, Transpose. This turns the lookup table back so it is vertical. Then you can do a VLOOKUP.

COPY A VLOOKUP ACROSS MANY COLUMNS

Problem: I've entered a VLOOKUP for January. I need to copy the formula across eleven additional columns.

Strategy: There are a few things you can do to make this process simpler:
- Press F4 three times when entering the lookup value. This will change A2 to $A2. The single dollar sign ensures the lookup will always reach back to column A for the lookup value.
- Press F4 once when entering the lookup table. This will change the lookup table to have four dollar signs, $P$4:$AB$227. Alternatively, name the lookup table first, then you won't have to use dollar signs. See "Consider Naming the Lookup Table"

The big problem is the third argument. I find that I end up editing each copied formula to change to 2 to a 3, then a 4, then a 5, and so on.

I have two solutions for this.
- Enter a temporary row with the numbers 2 through 13 stretching across the row. This row could be above the table you are trying to build. Then, instead of specifying 2 as the column to return, you can point to B1 and press F4 twice to change it to B$1.

=VLOOKUP($A4,$P$4:$AB$227,C$1,FALSE)

◢	A	B	C	D	E	F	G	H	I	J	K	L	M
1		2	3	4	5	6	7	8	9	10	11	12	13
2													
3	Acct	Jan	Feb	Mar	Apr	May	Jun	Jul	Aug	Sep	Oct	Nov	Dec
4	A308	6	1	9	2	9	1	5	4	4	4	7	3

Figure 435 *Use a temporary column with the column numbers.*

- The other solution is to replace the ,2, with ,COLUMN(B1),. The COLUMN function returns the column number of the given cell. Since B1 is in the second column, it will return a 2. I like to say that this is the world's geekiest way of writing the number 2. However, the advantage is that when you copy this formula to the right, the reference inside the COLUMN function will automatically change to C1, which is in column 3. Using this method allows you to enter one formula without having the temporary values in row 1.

=VLOOKUP($A3,$P$3:$AB$226,COLUMN(C1),FALSE)

◢	A	B	C	D	E	F	G	H	I	J
1										
2	Acct	Jan	Feb	Mar	Apr	May	Jun	Jul	Aug	Se
3	A308	6	1	9	2	9	1	5	4	
4	A219									

Figure 436 *Use COLUMN(C1) to write a 3.*

Additional Details: The second method will slow your VLOOKUPs down, as Excel has to calculate the COLUMN function in every row of your lookup table.

Alternate Strategy: You can speed up the VLOOKUPs if you add one column of MATCH functions and then use 12 columns of the incredibly speedy INDEX function. Before you can do this, though, you need to learn about these two incredibly arcane functions.

INDEX SOUNDS LIKE AN INANE FUNCTION

Problem: I was reading Excel Help for fun the other day and I read about a function called INDEX. Who in their right mind would ever use =INDEX(B4:G22,2,4) to point to cell F6?

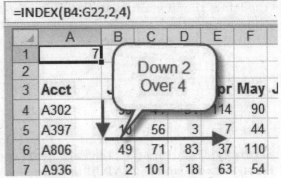

Figure 437 *The INDEX function seems useless.*

Strategy: You will never use INDEX without using MATCH as either the second or third argument. Come back to INDEX after you see what MATCH does.

YOU ALREADY KNOW MATCH, REALLY!

Problem: The author of this book is jamming two functions that I have NEVER heard of on the same page. He is starting to hack me off.

Strategy: Really, if you know and love VLOOKUP, you already know MATCH. Let me compare and contrast:

- The first argument is a lookup value just like VLOOKUP.
- The lookup table is a single column, not a rectangular range.
- You don't have to specify a column number, so leave off the third argument.
- The last argument could be FALSE just like VLOOKUP, although most people use zero instead of FALSE.

Figure 438 *MATCH is a VLOOKUP in disguise.*

So far, so good. It is just like a VLOOKUP.

The one difference that seems confusing... MATCH does not return a value from the table. MATCH tells you which row in the table contains the MATCH. I remember reading about this in Excel help and wondering when I would ever have a manager call me up and ask, "Hey Bill, what ROW is that in?" Here is the trick: You will ALWAYS be entering your MATCH inside of an INDEX function. So, back to INDEX.

INDEX SOUNDS LIKE AN INANE FUNCTION - II

Strategy: The trick is to use INDEX to return a value. Use MATCH as the second and/or third argument to calculate which row or column to return on the fly.

The next four topics show how you can use MATCH with INDEX to solve some common problems.

Problem: The lookup table is maintained by another department. They built it with the price to the left of the item number. Can I specify -1 as the third term of the VLOOKUP to indicate that I want a value to the left of the key field?

G	H	I	J	K
Price	**SKU**	**Description**		
37.95	BG33-3	14K Gold Bangle Bracelet with \		
27.95	CR50-3	14K Gold Cross with Onyx		
54.95	RG75-3	14K Gold RAY OF LIGHT Onyx		
39.95	RG78-25	14K Gold Ballerina Ring w/ Blue		
45.95	W25-6	18K Italian Gold Women's Watc		
28.95	BR26-3	18K Italian Gold Men's Bracelet		

Figure 439 *Lookup a value to the left of SKU.*

Strategy: Unfortunately, the Excel team doesn't offer the ability to VLOOKUP to the left of the key field. However, you can use MATCH to figure out which price to use.

Before you see how to solve this with MATCH and INDEX, the obvious solution would be to copy column G over to column J and then do a VLOOKUP. You are suspending reality here and assuming that you can't move the price. Perhaps the data is coming in from a web query and is refreshed every five minutes?

The SKU's are in H2:H29. They are not sorted, nor do they have to be. Each SKU occurs only once.

Look at the formula in C6. It is =MATCH(A6,$H$2:$H$29,0) which tells Excel to find CR-50 in the range of H2:H29. The final 0 indicates that you are looking for an exact match.

`=MATCH(A6,$H$2:$H$29,0)`

	A	B	C		G	H	I
1	**Item**	**Qty**	**Where**		**Price**	**SKU**	**Descri**
2	ER46-22	30	18		37.95	BG33-3	14K Go
3	ER41-4	18	15		27.95	CR50-3	14K Go
4	BR15-3	18	7		54.95	RG75-3	14K Go
5	CR50-1	12	12		39.95	RG78-25	14K Go
6	CR50-3	18	2		45.95	W25-6	18K Ital
7					28.95	BR26-3	18K Ital

Figure 440 *MATCH locates CR50-3 in the lookup table.*

Look at the answer from the MATCH function. It says CR50-3 is in row 2, but you can see that CR50-3 is actually in H3 which is row 3 of the spreadsheet. This is an important distinction. MATCH returns the relative position of the item within the lookup range. The answer of 2 says that CR50-3 is in the second cell of H2:H29.

Now that you know the position of the item within the lookup table, you can use the INDEX function to return the price.

You will specify the range of prices as the first argument of the INDEX function. The second argument specifies the row within the lookup table. When you have a single-column lookup table, you do not have to specify the column in the third argument. MATCH assumes you want column 1.

The prices are in G2:G29. Use:

=INDEX(G2:G29,

MATCH(A6,$H$2:$H$29,0)).

`=INDEX($G$2:$G$29,MATCH(A6,$H$2:$H$29,0))`

	A	B	C	D	E	F	G	H
1	**Item**	**Qty**	**Where**	**Total**			**Price**	**SKU**
2	ER46-22	30	51.95	$1,558.50			37.95	BG33-3
3	ER41-4	18	44.95	$809.10			27.95	CR50-3
4	BR15-3	18	53.95	$971.10			54.95	RG75-3
5	CR50-1	12	55.95	$671.40			39.95	RG78-2!
6	CR50-3	18	27.95	$503.10			45.95	W25-6
7	Total	96		$4,513.20			28.95	BR26-3
8							53.95	BR15-3

Figure 441 *Essentially a VLOOKUP Left.*

FAST MULTI-COLUMN VLOOKUP

Problem: I have to do twelve columns of VLOOKUP. The lookup table is large. The data set is even larger. It is taking forever to calculate.

VLOOKUP is an expensive function. It takes a lot of time to find the exact match in the lookup table. Worse, consider one row of your table. Excel might have to search through a 200-row table to locate the SKU when looking up the January value. When Excel goes to look up the February value, it must begin the search all over again. Yes, just a nanosecond earlier, Excel found A308 for January, but this is a new cell for February and Excel starts all over.

From a time perspective, MATCH and VLOOKUP take about as much time to calculate. INDEX takes a fraction of time. Excel can head directly to a particular row and grab the value.

Strategy: Add a soon-to-be-hidden column called Where and put a MATCH formula there to figure out where the product is located. Once you know where the product, use 12 columns of INDEX to return the columns from the lookup table.

This figure shows the Where column. This column takes about as long to calculate as the January VLOOKUP would take.

Now that you have the MATCH running the Where column, you can build an incredibly simple INDEX function. It is interesting to consider the placement of dollar signs in this formula.

=MATCH(A3,$Q$3:$Q$226,0)

	A	B	C	D	E
1					
2	Acct	Where	Jan	Feb	Mar
3	A308	208			
4	A219	119			
5	A249	149			
6	A154	54			
7	A128	28			
8	A229	129			

Figure 442 *Product A308 is found in the 208th row of the lookup table.*

1. In cell C3, enter =INDEX(R$3:R$226,$B3). You are using $ before 3 and 226 to make sure that the lookup table is always pointing from row 3 to row 226. However, you are not using dollar signs before column R. R3:R226 contains the January values. When you copy this formula to the right one cell, the lookup table shifts to the February column and points to S$3:S$226. The second argument of INDEX uses a single dollar sign before column B. This way, as you copy the formula, it is always pointing back to column B to get the row number of this product in the lookup table.
2. Copy C3 to D3:N3.
3. Select C3:N3.
4. Copy it down to all rows by double-clicking the fill handle in the lower right corner of N3.
5. Hide column B.

=INDEX(U$3:U$226,$B5)

	A	B	C	D	E	F	G	H	I	J
1										
2	Acct	Where	Jan	Feb	Mar	Apr	May	Jun	Jul	Au
3	A308	208	6	1	9	2	9	1	5	
4	A219	119	0	0	5	0	2	8	8	
5	A249	149	1	7	1	3	2	9	6	
6	A154	54	2	5	8	0	3	3	5	
7	A128	28	4	1	8	6	2	5	7	
8	A229	129	5	5	4	7	8	1	5	
9	A111	11	0	7	1	1	5	8	2	
10	A225	125	7	6	4	3	4	7	6	

Figure 443 *This table is 10 times faster than all VLOOKUPs.*

The MATCH with INDEX solution shown here solves the whole problem of editing the third argument of the VLOOKUP for each column. Two simple formulas create the entire table. Plus, it runs much faster that using 12 columns of VLOOKUP.

I've met people who tell me that they have quit using VLOOKUP and rely entirely on MATCH and INDEX.

SPEED UP YOUR VLOOKUP

Problem: I have to do thousands of VLOOKUPs and they are taking almost a minute every time that I recalculate the worksheet.

Strategy: Although it is counter-intuitive, two VLOOKUPs with the True argument will run over 100 times faster than the typical VLOOKUP. This is one time the lookup table will have to be sorted.

Gotcha: The reason you don't use the True version of VLOOKUP is that it returns the wrong answer when the key field is not found. In the figure below, item 102 is missing from the lookup table. Instead of returning #N/A, the True version of VLOOKUP returns the answer from the next-lower item number. This is useless and dangerous!

f_x	=VLOOKUP(D3,$G$2:$H$5,2,TRUE)					
D	**E**	**F**	**G**	**H**	**I**	
Item	Price		Item	Price		
101	1		101	1		
102	1		103	2		
103	2		104	4		
			105	8		

Figure 444 *The True version of VLOOKUP returns the wrong answer.*

The foremost expert on Formula Speed is Charles Williams, creator of the FastExcelV3 utility. While most people would give up on the True version of VLOOKUP after seeing the above error, Charles realized that the True version of VLOOKUP is hundred times faster than the False version of VLOOKUP.

So, Charles thought up the idea of doing an extra VLOOKUP(A2,Table,**1**,True) before the real VLOOKUP. When you do a VLOOKUP to return the 1st item in the lookup table, you would normally get back the same value that you are looking up. In other words, =VLOOKUP(101,G2:H5,1,True) better return 101. If it returns something other than 101, then you know that the item is not found.

In the figure below, a formula in column C does a VLOOKUP to return column 1 from the lookup table. A formula in column D checks to see if B2=C2. If the result in D is True, then you know it is safe to do a VLOOKUP in column E. Otherwise, you should report that the value is Not Found.

✕ ✓	f_x	=VLOOKUP(B2,$G$2:$H$5,1,TRUE)						
B	**C**	**D**	**E**	**F**	**G**	**H**	**I**	
Item	Item	Equal?	Answer		Item	Price		
101	101	TRUE	1		101	1		
102	101	FALSE	Not Found		103	2		
103	103	TRUE	2		104	4		
					105	8		

C2: =VLOOKUP(B2,$G$2:$H$5,1,TRUE)

D2: =B2=C2

E2: =IF(D2,VLOOKUP(B2,$G$2:$H$5,2,0),"Not Found")

Figure 445 *Using a VLOOKUP in C2 to find if the result in E2 is correct or not.*

You don't have to do this in three columns as shown above. You can do a single formula with two VLOOK-UPs: =IF(D2=VLOOKUP(D2,$G$2:$H$5,1,TRUE),VLOOKUP(D2, $G$2:$H$5,2,TRUE),"N/A").

If you see my live seminar, I probably showed how to use FastExcelV3 to time these formulas. I routinely take a 40-second recalc time and have it go to 0.2 seconds by using this formula. It is worth the hassle if you have a spreadsheet that is taking forever to calculate.

Note: This page contains just 1 of hundreds of amazing tricks from Charles Williams. Check out FastExcelV3 at http://tinyurl.com/fastexcel.

RETURN THE NEXT LARGER VALUE IN A LOOKUP

Problem: I am using a lookup table to calculate a late-payment penalty. As soon as a customer is 1 day late, they are charged the penalty for the first month. When they reach 31 days late, they pay for two months. After 60 days late, they are billed for half months.

Strategy: Earlier in "Nest IF Statements", there was an example using the approximate version of VLOOKUP. This rare version would look for a match. When one is not found, it would return the row just smaller than the lookup value. In this case, you need the VLOOKUP to go the opposite way. VLOOKUP can not do that, but MATCH can.

Make sure that your penalty lookup table is sorted from high to low. (Hmmm, back in Figure 428, I should add rows for Credit Card Company Analysts and IRS Agents.)

	J	K
2	**Days Late**	**Penalty**
3	165	8.250%
4	150	7.500%
5	135	6.750%
6	120	6.000%
7	105	5.250%
8	90	4.500%
9	75	3.750%
10	60	3.000%
11	30	1.500%
12	0	0.000%

Figure 446 *Another rarity: the lookup table sorted descending.*

You will see this calculation take shape after many intermediate steps. In real life, you could do all of these steps in a single formula.

Calculate a Penalty Row in F2 with =MATCH(E2,$J$3:$J$12,-1).

=MATCH(E2,$J$3:$J$12,-1)

	C	D	E	F
1	**Due Date**	**Date Paid**	**Days Late**	**Penalty Row**
2	2/4/2014	2/6/2014	2	9
3	3/12/2014	5/19/2014	68	7
4	4/16/2014	6/9/2014	54	8
5	1/15/2014	2/14/2014	30	9
6	2/22/2014	3/2/2014	8	9

Figure 447 *Find the row with the appropriate penalty.*

Take a look at the results of that formula. In row 5, the payment is 30 days late. There is an exact match in Figure 446 for 30 days late, so the formula returns the exact match. However, in rows 2 through 4, there is no exact match. Because the third argument of MATCH is -1, Excel is returning the result from the next higher row in the table. The 68 days late in F3 is matched to the 75 day penalty in row 7 of the table.

=INDEX($K$3:$K$12,F2)

	E	F	G	H
1	**Days Late**	**Penalty Row**	**Penalty %**	**Penalty $**
2	2	9	1.50%	64.55
3	68	7	3.75%	40.84
4	54	8	3.00%	128.31
5	30	9	1.50%	50.70

Figure 448 *Use INDEX to return the Penalty % from the table.*

This is a third example of something that you can do with MATCH and INDEX that you can not do with a regular VLOOKUP.

TWO-WAY LOOKUP

Problem: I need to do a lookup where I find the product ID down the left side and the month from the top row. I need to return the intersection of that row and column.

Strategy: You can use a MATCH to find the row, a second MATCH to find the column, and then an INDEX to return the correct value.

In this example, the person using the spreadsheet uses the Validation dropdowns in J2 and J3 to select a product and month.

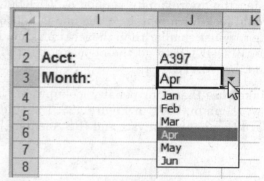

Figure 449 *Select a product and month.*

The lookup table has products in column A and months in row 1.

	A	B	C	D	E	F	G
1	Acct	Jan	Feb	Mar	Apr	May	Jun
2	A302	99	41	31	114	90	1
3	A397	10	56	3	7	44	50
4	A806	49	71	83	37	110	14

Figure 450 *Find product A397 and Apr.*

Your first formula will use MATCH to find the row within the table. Use =MATCH(J2,$A$2:$A$20,0). This is the same type of MATCH described in the previous three topics. The answer of 2 indicates that A397 is found in the second row of the lookup table.

The second formula will use MATCH to find the column within B1:G1. This means that MATCH can go both ways and essentially do an HLOOKUP. Use =MATCH(J3,B1:G1,0). The result of 4 indicates that Apr is in the fourth column of the lookup table.

Finally, use the INDEX function to return the value from row specified by the MATCH in J5 and from the column specified in J6. Use this formula: =INDEX(B2:G20,J5,J6).

=MATCH(J3,B1:G1,0)

	I	J	K	L	M
1					
2	Acct:	A397			
3	Month:	Apr			
4					
5	Which Row?	2	=MATCH(J2,$A$2:$A$20,0)		
6	Which Column?	4	=MATCH(J3,B1:G1,0)		
7	Result?	7	=INDEX(B2:G20,J5,J6)		

Figure 451 *The MATCH in J6 is like an HLOOKUP.*

COMBINE FORMULAS INTO A MEGA-FORMULA

Problem: When I need to build a complex calculation, I sometimes need to build several intermediate formulas to help figure out the problem. When these formulas are all working, can I combine the logic from the intermediate formulas into a single formula?

Strategy: Using temporary sub-formulas is a great way to figure out a somewhat complex formula. There is a relatively easy way to get all of these formulas back into a single formula.

Consider the previous example, a formula in J7 =INDEX(B2:G20,J5,J6) references two other cells J5 and J6. Each of those cells contain a formula.

Strategy: You can select characters in the formula bar and copy them to the Clipboard with Ctrl+C. When you copy an entire cell, you introduce many complexities, including the problem that you cannot paste this cell into the middle of a formula or into the Replace dialog. Instead, by copying characters from the formula bar, you have regular text on the Clipboard and can either paste into another formula or in the Replace dialog. Here's what you do:

1. Select cell J5. In the formula bar, click the mouse after the equal sign and drag to the end of the formula. Press Ctrl+C to copy these characters to the Clipboard. Exit Edit mode by pressing the Esc key.
2. Select cell J7. In the formula bar, highlight the reference to J5
3. Press Ctrl+V to paste the formula from J5 to replace the reference to J5.
4. Select cell J6. Press F2, Ctrl+Shift+Home, Shift+Right Arrow, Ctrl+C, Esc. These keyboard short-cuts edit the cell, then select everything but the equals sign.
5. Select cell J7. Select the reference to J6
6. Press Ctrl+V to paste the formula from J6 to replace the reference to J6.

The result is a single formula that replaces the three formulas.

=INDEX(B2:G20,MATCH(J2,$A$2:$A$20,0),MATCH(J3,B1:G1,0))

◢	I	J	K	L	M	N
1						
2	**Acct:**	A397				
3	**Month:**	Apr				
4	**Result?**	7				

Figure 452 *This is an intimidating formula once it is all combined.*

Result: Your coworkers will be amazed at your ability to create massive formulas.

Alternate Strategy: Instead of following the steps just outlined, you can use the Replace dialog to combine the intermediate formulas into mega-formulas. Follow these steps:

1. Select cell J5. In the formula bar, use the mouse to select everything from immediately after the equals sign to the end of the formula. Press Ctrl+C to copy those characters to the Clipboard. Press the Esc key to exit the formula bar.
2. Select cells J7:J8. **Gotcha:** Make sure this selection contains two cells, even if you are only working on a single formula! If you select two or more cells, the Replace All command will work only within the selection. If you select only one cell, the Replace All command will extend to all 17 billion cells in the worksheet.
3. Select Home, Find & Select, Replace or Ctrl+H.
4. In the Find What box, type J5.
5. Tab to the Replace With box. Press Ctrl+V. Excel will copy the characters from the J5 formula into the dialog.
6. Click the Options button.
7. Make sure the Look In dropdown is set to Formulas. Make sure that Match Entire Cell Contents is unchecked. (If you start a new Excel session, both of these settings will be correct. However, the dialog remembers the settings from the last find and replace you did earlier in the current session, so it is always worth your time to click the Options button to make sure these settings are correct.)
8. Click Replace All. Excel will remove the reference to J5 from the selected cells and replace it with the characters from J5.
9. Repeat step 1 for cell J6.
10. Repeat steps 2–8.

Depending on how many times the intermediate formulas are referenced in the final formula, using Find and Replace might be faster than using the copy and paste method.

Gotcha: Be careful that your target formulas don't contain references that contain some other form of B2 and C2, such as B20 or C210909. If your formulas do contain such references, when you replace B2, Excel will blindly put the B2 formula where the characters B2 appear in B20.

COMBINE TWO LISTS USING VLOOKUP

Problem: I have a list of month-to-date sales by customer. My co-worker just sent me a list of sales for yesterday. I need to combine and merge these lists.

	A	B	C	D	E
1	XYZ Co				
2	Month to Date Sales				
3	Through 06/17/2014			Sales for 6/18/2014	
4					
5	Customer	Revenue MTD		Customer	Revenue
6	Exxon	68,200		Air Canada	1551
7	Lucent	62,744		Compaq	1963
8	Ainsworth	60,461		Compton Petroleı	1568
9	P&G	60,299		Ford	2629
10	HP	55,251		Gildan Activewea	2116
11	General Motors	54,569		IBM	1377
12	Chevron	54,048		Lucent	3137
13	Bell Canada	51,240		Molson, Inc	2273
14	Shell Canada	47,521		Nortel Networks	2355
15	Nortel Networks	47,104		Sun Life Financial	1028
16	Kroger	46,717		Wal-Mart	1327
17	Molson, Inc	45,460			
18	Gildan Activewear	42,316			
19	Compaq	39,250			
20	Verizon	35,367			
21	Compton Petroleum	31,369			
22	Air Canada	31,021			
23	IBM	27,533			
24	Wal-Mart	26,535			
25	Sun Life Financial	20,550			
26					

Figure 453 *Combine these lists.*

This is a 3-step process:

- Do a MATCH or a VLOOKUP(,,1,) on the second list to find new customers. Add the new customers to the original list with previous sales of 0.
- Now that the first list contains a superset of customers in either list, do a VLOOKUP on the first list to get the sales from the second list.
- Add previous sales to new sales and convert to values. You can now delete the new list.

When you want to figure out if a customer in column D is already in column A, most people will do =VLOOKUP(D6,A6:A25,1,False). This will either show the customer name or #N/A. In this case, you are interested in the #N/A records.

However, now that you've read about MATCH, you can just as easily use MATCH to find which customers are in the other list. Use =MATCH(D6,$A$6:$A$25,0). In the figure below, all of the customers in column D have a match except Ford.

Any customers with #N/A are new customers and need to be added to the list of customers in column A. If you get a few #N/A values, sort by column F to bring the new customers together. Copy just the customer name and paste to the bottom of the list in column A. Enter $0 as the sales in column B for the new customers.

fx =MATCH(D6,$A$6:$A$25,0)

	D	E	F
5	Customer	Revenue	There?
6	Air Canada	1551	17
7	Compaq	1963	14
8	Compton Petroleı	1568	16
9	Ford	2629	#N/A
10	Gildan Activewea	2116	13
11	IBM	1377	18
12	Lucent	3137	2
13	Molson, Inc	2273	12
14	Nortel Networks	2355	10
15	Sun Life Financial	1028	20
16	Wal-Mart	1327	19

Figure 454 *Ford is missing from the 1st list.*

In the current example, only Ford is new, so you can copy Ford from D9 and paste to A26. Enter zero in B26. In real life, though, you will have a several customers who are new. Copy and paste below the first customer in A. Add zero to all the corresponding cells in B.

You've now completed the first of three steps. The next step is to add the real VLOOKUP to the first list.

=VLOOKUP(A6,$E$6:$F$16,2,FALSE) would return a mix of revenue values and #N/A errors. When an existing customer had no revenue on June 18, the result of the VLOOKUP will be #N/A. You can use the new IFERROR function to replace those #N/A values with zeroes.

Insert two new columns before column D. Label these temporary columns Addl Rev and New Total.

The formula in the new C6 is =IFERROR(VLOOKUP(A6,$F$6:$G$16,2,FALSE),0). Copy that formula down to row 26.

=IFERROR(VLOOKUP(A6,$F$6:$G$16,2,FALSE),0)

	A	B	C
5	Customer	Revenue MTD	Addl Rev.
6	Exxon	68,200	0
7	Lucent	62,744	3,137
8	Ainsworth	60,461	0
9	P&G	60,299	0

Figure 455 *Do a VLOOKUP to get sales from June 18 in the first list.*

If you want to check your work, use AutoSum to add a total at the bottom of column C and the bottom of column G. Both totals should match.

That completes step two of three steps. The final step is to combine revenue from column B and column C.

In D6 enter a formula of =B6+C6. Copy this formula down.

	A	B	C	D
1	XYZ Co			
2	Month to Date Sales			
3	Through 06/17/2014			
4				
5	Customer	Revenue MTD	Addl Rev.	New Total
6	Exxon	68,200	0	68,200
7	Lucent	62,744	3,137	65,881
8	Ainsworth	60,461	0	60,461
9	P&G	60,299	0	60,299

Figure 456 *Add the old and new revenue.*

Copy D6:D26. Select B6 and Paste Values.

Gotcha: Don't worry that column D is showing a higher value than it should. Column D is still adding the current day's revenue to the new total in B. You will be deleting column D very soon. If you don't want column D to ever show a wrong value, you could copy D and paste values on top of itself first.

Change the date in A3 to indicate that the report has data through 6/18.

Delete the temporary columns C through H.

It looks like the original data was sorted by descending revenue. Choose cell B6 and click the ZA button on the Data tab of the ribbon.

This process of comparing and combining two lists using VLOOKUP is a staple of data analysis. There is a faster and easier way to do this. See "Use a Pivot Table to Compare Two Lists" on page 378.

WATCH FOR DUPLICATES WHEN USING VLOOKUP

Problem: I used the VLOOKUP function to get sales from a second list into an original list, and then I received the next day's sales in a file. When I use the MATCH function to find new customers, there is one new customer: Sun Life Fincl.

This is not really a new customer at all. Someone in the order entry department created a new customer instead of using the existing customer named Sun Life Financial. As a quick fix, you copy cell D9 and paste it in cell D6. This seems like a fine solution and resolves the #N/A error in F6

However, when I enter the VLOOKUP formula in column C to get the current day's sales, there are two rows that match Sun Life Financial..

Sales for 6/19/2014		
Customer	**Revenue**	**There?**
Sun Life Fincl.	3541	#N/A
Molson, Inc	2944	12
Bell Canada	2834	8
Sun Life Financial	2815	20
Lucent	2528	2
Chevron	2362	7
Wal-Mart	2183	19

Figure 457 *Is this really a new customer?*

Strategy: It's important that you understand how VLOOKUP handles duplicates in the lookup list. The VLOOKUP function is not capable of handling the situation described here. When two rows match a VLOOKUP, the function will return the sales from the first row in the list. You will get the $3541, but you will not get the $2815.

=IFERROR(VLOOKUP(A25,$F$6:$G$12,2,FALSE),0)

	A	B	C
25	Sun Life Financial	21,578	3,541
26	Ford	2,629	0

Figure 458 *VLOOKUP returns the first match that it finds.*

If you are not absolutely sure that the customers in the lookup table are unique, you should not use VLOOKUP. You could use a SUMIF function instead. See "Sum Records That Match a Criterion" on page 166 for details.

RETURN THE LAST ENTRY

Problem: Someone has logged some data. For each group, data starts in row 5 and continues down for some number of rows. There are a different number of data points in each column. I need to get the last entry in each column.

	A	B	C	D	E	F	G	H
2	Final Entry:							
3								
4	Group		A	B	C	D	E	F	G
5		7194	1774	1544	1107	1558	1035	1104
6		10219	2822	3343	2922	3112	2430	3089
7		3102	4125	4556		2994	3894	4426
8		5469		5884		6146	5852	6415
9		1778		7858		7513	7199	
10		11809		7415			9022	
11		4397					10784	
12							12112	
13								
14								

Figure 459 *Return the final number in the column.*

Strategy: There are multiple solutions to this problem. You could combine the unwieldy OFFSET with COUNT, but this topic will show you how to solve the problem using the approximate match version of VLOOKUP.

Flip back to Figure 402 and Figure 403 where you used the approximate match version of VLOOKUP to find a commission rate. The table had entries like 1000, 5000, 10000, and 20000. When someone had a sale of $12,345, the VLOOKUP would find the commission rate for the $10,000 level, because $10,000 was just less than the $12,345 that you were looking up.

You can take advantage of a loophole in Excel. Say that you are looking up a number that is larger than any value in the table. When that happens, Excel will return the last non-blank entry in the table. Since the scientists, commission accountants, and IRS agents who regularly use the approximate VLOOKUP always sort their data ascending, returning the last non-blank entry in the table works for them.

In this case, the data is not sorted nor should it be sorted. However, if you ask VLOOKUP to look for a really large number, it will automatically return the last non-blank entry in the column!

Some will suggest that you should use 9.99999999999999E+307 as the lookup value. This is the largest number possible in Excel. However, rather than type all of those characters, you can simply use a number that is larger than anyone would expect. For example, if you work for a company that has $1 Million in revenue per year, there is no way that the sales for one day would ever exceed $100K. You could safely search for 99999.

In the formula below, I held down the 9 key for a second and ended up searching for 9.9 million. It doesn't matter exactly what you are searching for, just so long as it is larger than any possible number in the list. Use =VLOOKUP(9999999,B5:B20,1,TRUE).

=VLOOKUP(9999999,B5:B20,1,TRUE)

▲	A	B	C	D	E	F	G	H
1								
2	Final Entry:	4397	4125	7415	2922	7513	12112	4426
3								
4	Group	A	B	C	D	E	F	G
5		7194	1774	1544	1107	1558	1035	1104
6		10219	2822	3343	2922	3112	2430	3089
7		3102	4125	4556		2994	3894	4426
8		5469		5884		6146	5852	ZZZ
9		1778		7858		7513		
10		11809		7415		#N/A	9022	
11		4397					10784	
12							12112	

Figure 460 *This VLOOKUP returns the last numeric value.*

This is a really cool use of the rare version of VLOOKUP. As you can see in column G, the formula doesn't get confused by blank cells. It will only return numeric values, so the errant ZZZ entry in H8 is ignored. The #N/A error in F10 is ignored.

If the entries in the column are text, then you would search for some text which will occur alphabetically after any text that you might expect. For example, search for "ZZZZZZ".

`=VLOOKUP("ZZZZZ",B5:B20,1,TRUE)`

▲	A	B	C	D	E	F	G	H	I
1									
2	Final Entry:	TIL	BCS	AHO	TAS	RAF	HKV	BAR	
3									
4	Group	A	B	C	D	E	F	G	
5		NHU	WRS	MTA	SWM	LTF	ACN	123	
6		WEN	LWE	IWO	TAS	HNV	BDF	123	
7		KTL	BCS	PAJ		KHV	UKV	123	
8		CVM		JSF		XGI	HLK	BAR	
9		HFB		JJV		RAF	YOH	234	
10		MIG		AHO			TNI		
11		TIL					AMQ		
12							HKV		
13									

Figure 461 *Search for ZZZZZZ to return the last text entry.*

Column H above illustrates a problem with this method. If the values can contain text or a number, the VLOOKUP will not work.

What if the data is turned sideways and you need to get the last value from each row? Use HLOOKUP instead of VLOOKUP.

`=HLOOKUP(9999999,D2:P2,1,TRUE)`

▲	A	B	C	D	E	F	G	H
1	Final							
2	4397		A	7194	1778	11809	4397	
3	1774		B	1774				
4	7415		C	1544	7858	7415		
5	1107		D	1107				
6	7513		E	1558	7513			
7	12112		F	1035	7199	9022	12112	
8	1104		G	1104				
9								

Figure 462 *Get the last entry from each row.*

Additional Details: You do not have to put the ,TRUE at the end of any of these formulas. If you leave off the fourth argument, Excel assumes that you mean TRUE. However, since 99.9% of the VLOOKUPs in the world use FALSE at the end, I put the TRUE out there to help remind me that something unusual is happening with this formula.

RETURN THE LAST MATCHING VALUE

Problem: VLOOKUP returns the first match that it finds. I need to get the last match in the data. In this figure, I want to lookup A and find the 12 from row 5, since that is the latest data for A.

	A	B
1	A	15
2	C	10
3	B	7
4	B	5
5	A	12
6	C	15
7	C	10
8		
9		

Figure 463 *Find the last match for each letter.*

Strategy: Use =LOOKUP(2,1/($A$1:$A$7=D2),$B$1:$B$7).

=LOOKUP(2,1/($A$1:$A$7=D2),$B$1:$B$7)

	A	B	C	D	E	F	G
1	A	15		Last Match?			
2	C	10		A	12		
3	B	7		B	5		
4	B	5		C	10		
5	A	12					
6	C	15					
7	C	10					
8							
9							

Figure 464 *No one at your office will have a clue what you are doing.*

First, LOOKUP is an ancient function that Excel includes for backwards compatibility with Quattro Pro. It is a bizarre little function that takes a lookup value, a lookup vector, and a results vector. It always uses the Approximate Match version that you would get when using TRUE at the end of your VLOOKUP. Like the approximate match, LOOKUP expects the table to be sorted, but since you are using this formula to trick Excel, the table does not have to be sorted.

People end up using LOOKUP instead of VLOOKUP because LOOKUP works with arrays that VLOOKUP won't work with. Both this topic and the next topic show of the array-handling ability of LOOKUP.

This formula came from the MrExcel Message Board, originally posted to a MrExcel MVP named Fairwinds.

Let me explain the formula step by step, starting with A1:A7=D2. This comparison will produce a series of TRUE/FALSE values. In the figure above, you would end up with {TRUE; FALSE; FALSE; FALSE; TRUE; FALSE; FALSE}.

Next, the formula divides that array into the number 1. Flip back to Figure 399 to see that Excel treats TRUE like 1 and FALSE like 0. Of course, 1/1 is 1. But 1/0 is a DIV/0 error. After doing the division, you have a series of values that are either 1 or #DIV/0!: {1; #DIV/0!; #DIV/0!; #DIV/0!; 1; #DIV/0!; #DIV/0!}.

Figure 465 *From the Evaluate Formula dialog, after the fourth step.*

If you flip back to Figure 460, you can see that the approximate VLOOKUP is ignoring text entries and error values. Calculating same thing works here.

Also, in the last topic, there was a question if you should look for 9.99999999999999E+307 or simply 99999999. As you learned in the last topic, you just have to search for a number that is larger than any expected value. The logical test is either going to return 1 or #DIV/0!. There is no way that you will ever get anything larger than a 1 at this point of the formula. So, you can simply search for a 2.

When LOOKUP is searching for a 2 in {1; #DIV/0!; #DIV/0!; #DIV/0!; 1; #DIV/0!; #DIV/0!}, it can not find the 2. It thus uses the last numeric entry. In this case, it is the 1 that was calculated from cell A5. LOOK-UP will return the fifth entry from the results vector. Since the results vector is B1:B7, Excel will return the 12 from cell B5.

Additional Details: The community of Excel aficionados at the MrExcel.com Message Board create some of the wildest formulas that I've ever seen. I took a collection of these formulas and put them in my book, Excel Gurus Gone Wild.

SUM ALL OF THE LOOKUPS

Problem: Are there any other arcane tricks with the old LOOKUP function that you can use to close out this string of topics on lookup?

Strategy: I am glad that you asked!

Say that you want to figure out the total bonus payments for the month so that you can accrue money to pay the bonus. You aren't ready to pay the bonus yet, so you don't have to do all the lookups. You just want one formula that does all of the lookups and totals the values.

Using SUM(VLOOKUP()) will not work, even if you use Ctrl+Shift+Enter to make it an array formula.

However, using SUM(LOOKUP()) with Ctrl+Shift+Enter will correctly do all the individual lookups and sum them.

Gotcha: As mentioned in the last topic, the LOOKUP command only does the approximate-match type of lookup, so this trick is likely only useful to the SCAIA (aka Scientists, Commission Accountants, and IRS Agents for those of you who have not been paying careful attention.)

Type the formula =SUM(LOOKUP(C2:C26,E2:E6,F2:F6)) but do not press Enter.

	A	B	C	D	E	F	G	H
	=SUM(LOOKUP(C2:C26,E2:E6,F2:F6))							
1	Invoice	Rep	Amount		Sale	Bonus		
2	1001	Carole	12835		0	0		
3	1002	Andy	19634		5000	5		
4	1003	Carole	898		10000	12		
5	1004	Hector	7747		20000	50		
6	1005	Andy	6239		25000	100		
7	1006	Gary	19867					
8	1007	Andy	27537		Total			
9	1008	Dale	679		Bonus			
10	1009	Flo	24240		=SUM(LOOKUP(C2:C26,E2:E6,F2:F6))			
11	1010	Kevin	25314					
12	1011	Larry	12375					
13	1012	Dale	27502					
14	1013	Flo	7822					

Figure 466 *One formula does many lookups.*

Instead, hold down Ctrl+Shift. While holding Ctrl and Shift, then press Enter. In the formula bar, Excel will add curly braces around the formula. The result is correct.

A	B	C	D	E	F
{=SUM(LOOKUP(C2:C26,E2:E6,F2:F6))}					
1006	Gary	19867			
1007	Andy	27537		Total	
1008	Dale	679		Bonus	
1009	Flo	24240		652	
1010	Kevin	25314			

Figure 467 *LOOKUP can return an array. VLOOKUP can not.*

EMBED A SMALL LOOKUP TABLE IN FORMULA

Problem: I have a small 5-row lookup table hidden out in column AA:AB. The sales reps who use the spreadsheet might inadvertently delete a row in their data, deleting the lookup table. Can I put the lookup table somewhere that they won't destroy it?

Strategy: One solution is to move the lookup table to a new worksheet and hide the worksheet. However, if the lookup table is small, you can embed it right in the VLOOKUP formula. Follow these steps:

1. Select the cell with the VLOOKUP formula.
2. Press F2 to put the cell in edit mode
3. Select the characters that represent the lookup table.

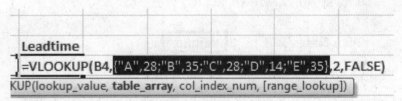

	A	B	C	D	E	F
1	Sales Forecast					
2						
3	Customer	Product	Leadtime			
4	ABC	C	=VLOOKUP(B4,$AA$3:$AB$7,2,FALSE)			
5	XYZ	D	VLOOKUP(lookup_value, **table_array**, col_index_num,			
6	ZZZ	C	28			

Figure 468 *Select the table array portion of the formula.*

4. Press F9. This calculates the selected portion of the formula. In this case, it puts {"A",28;"B",35;"C", 28;"D",14;"E",35} into the formula.

Leadtime
=VLOOKUP(B4,{"A",28;"B",35;"C",28;"D",14;"E",35},2,FALSE)
KUP(lookup_value, **table_array**, col_index_num, [range_lookup])

Figure 469 *Press F9. Excel inserts the array into the formula.*

5. Enter the formula. Copy it down to the other rows. You can now safely delete the lookup table.

It helps to understand Excel's array syntax. The curly braces indicate that this is an array. Each comma means you should move to a new column. Each semicolon means that you should move to a new row.

Gotcha: It is difficult to later edit the table. You can try to puzzle it out by staring at the commas and semi-colons in the formula bar. Or, you can copy the array and put it back in the worksheet. You have to follow these steps:

1. Select the array from the formula, including the curly braces.
2. Ctrl+C to copy the characters from the clipboard.
3. Select a five-row by 2 column blank section of the spreadsheet.
4. Type an equals sign. Press Ctrl+V. Press Ctrl+Shift+Enter. Excel will put the array back into the worksheet as an array formula. This looks OK, but you can not edit individual cells in the range.

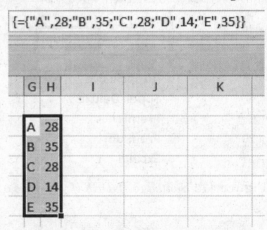

{={"A",28;"B",35;"C",28;"D",14;"E",35}}

	G	H	I	J	K
	A	28			
	B	35			
	C	28			
	D	14			
	E	35			

Figure 470 *The table is back, but it is not editable, yet.*

5. With the entire range selected, do a Copy and then Paste Values. You can now edit individual cells in the table.

I DON'T WANT TO USE A LOOKUP TABLE TO CHOOSE ONE OF FIVE CHOICES

Problem: I have to choose among five choices. I don't want to nest a bunch of IF functions, and I really don't want to add a lookup table off to the side of my worksheet. Is there a function that will allow me to specify the possible values in the function?

Strategy: In this situation, you can use the CHOOSE function.

The first argument of the CHOOSE function is a number from 1 to 254. You then specify the values for each possible number, entered as separate arguments. For example, =CHOOSE(2,"Red","Green","Blue") would return Green.

It is a bit frustrating that you must specify each choice as a separate argument. I always want to specify a single range such as Z1:Z30 as the list of arguments but this will not work. However, if you already have the list of arguments somewhere, you don't need to use CHOOSE; you can easily use VLOOKUP or INDEX in such a case.

Here, a CHOOSE function returns the description of the plan number chosen in cell B5.

=CHOOSE(B5,"All-inclusive","Super-Deluxe","Premier","Premium","Excella")

▲	A	B	C	D	E	F	G
1	Name:	Jane Smith					
2	Address:	123 South Main					
3	City St Zip:	Anytown, MA 01234					
4							
5	Plan Code:	3	Premier				
6							

Figure 471 *Choose is great for short lists.*

Gotcha: CHOOSE works only if your plan codes are 1, 2, 3, and so on. If you have plan codes of A, B, C, and so on, you should probably use a lookup table in an out-of-the way location. Or you could use =CODE(B5)-64 to convert the A to a 1 and so on.

Additional Details: If you have a list of plan names somewhere, you might be tempted to enter =CHOOSE(B5,B7,B8,B9,B10,B11). Instead, it is easier to use =INDEX(B7:B11,B5). The INDEX function will return the B5th item from the list in B7:B11.

=INDEX(B7:B11,B5)

▲	A	B	C
1	Name:	Jane Smith	
2	Address:	123 South Main	
3	City St Zip:	Anytown, MA 01234	
4			
5	Plan Code:	4	Premium
6			
7		All-inclusive	
8		Super-Deluxe	
9		Premier	
10		Premium	
11		Excella	

Figure 472 *Switch to INDEX if you have a list in a range.*

LOOKUP TWO VALUES

Problem: I have to lookup two values. I need to match both a company code and a cost center.

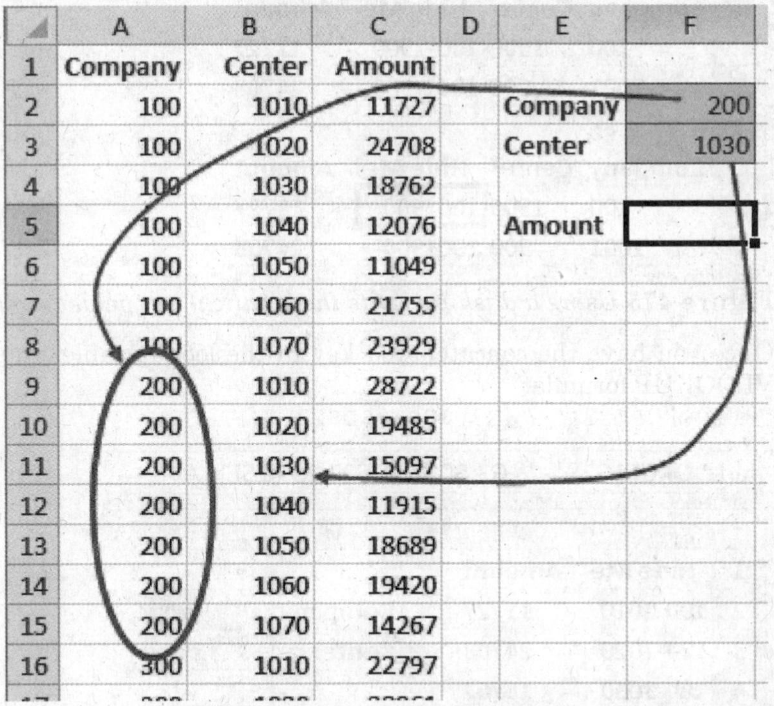

◢	A	B	C	D	E	F
1	Company	Center	Amount			
2	100	1010	11727		Company	200
3	100	1020	24708		Center	1030
4	100	1030	18762			
5	100	1040	12076		Amount	
6	100	1050	11049			
7	100	1060	21755			
8	100	1070	23929			
9	200	1010	28722			
10	200	1020	19485			
11	200	1030	15097			
12	200	1040	11915			
13	200	1050	18689			
14	200	1060	19420			
15	200	1070	14267			
16	300	1010	22797			

Figure 473 *Match both the Company and Center.*

Strategy: There are three solutions to this **problem:** (a) Concatenated key, (b) OFFSET, or (c) SUMIFS. The concatenated key will only work if you are allowed to add a new column to the left of column C. The SUMIFS will only work if the value to be returned is numeric. The OFFSET will only work if all of the company codes are sorted together as shown above.

With a concatenated key, you will insert a new column before the Amounts in column C. You want to join column A, a unique separator, and column B. For example, =A2&"-"&B2 would produce a key of 100-1010.

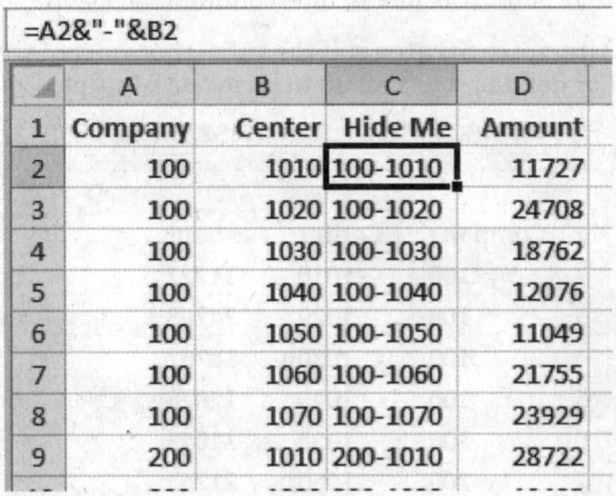

`=A2&"-"&B2`

◢	A	B	C	D
1	Company	Center	Hide Me	Amount
2	100	1010	100-1010	11727
3	100	1020	100-1020	24708
4	100	1030	100-1030	18762
5	100	1040	100-1040	12076
6	100	1050	100-1050	11049
7	100	1060	100-1060	21755
8	100	1070	100-1070	23929
9	200	1010	200-1010	28722

Figure 474 *Build a concatenated key in your data.*

The separator text is optional. In real life, you might have two company/center combinations that would look the same once joined. Using a dash in between will prevent this ambiguity.

`=A6&B6`

	A	B	C	D
1	Company	Center	Hide Me	Amount
2	100	1900	100-1900	11727
3	1001	900	1001-900	24708
4				
5	Company	Center	Hide Me	Amount
6	100	1900	1001900	11727
7	1001	900	1001900	24708

Figure 475 *Using a dash prevents the identical key fields in red.*

Once you have the concatenated key in the lookup table, you can join the key fields on-the-fly in your VLOOKUP formula:

`=VLOOKUP(G2&"-"&G3,$C$2:$D$22,2,FALSE)`

`=VLOOKUP(G2&"-"&G3,$C$2:$D$22,2,FALSE)`

	C	D	E	F	G
1	Hide Me	Amount			
2	100-1010	11727		Company	200
3	100-1020	24708		Center	1030
4	100-1030	18762			
5	100-1040	12076		Amount	15097
6	100-1050	11049			
7	100-1060	21755			
8	100-1070	23929			

Figure 476 *Join the two key fields as the first argument of VLOOKUP.*

As mentioned earlier in this topic, this method only works if you are able to add the concatenated key to your data. It is fine to hide column C so no one see it, but you have to have the field there.

Alternate Strategy: If the value that you are trying to return is numeric, you can use DSUM or SUMIFS. For details, see "Calculate Based on Multiple Conditions" on page 167.

`=SUMIFS($C$2:$C$22,$A$2:$A$22,F2,$B$2:$B$22,F3)`

	A	B	C	D	E	F
1	Company	Center	Amount			
2	100	1010	11727		Company	200
3	100	1020	24708		Center	1030
4	100	1030	18762			
5	100	1040	12076		Amount	15097
6	100	1050	11049			
7	100	1060	21755			

Figure 477 *The new SUMIFS would solve the problem.*

Alternate Strategy: Use the OFFSET function. Purists will argue that OFFSET is a volatile function and therefore slows down your calculation times. However, OFFSET will often solve problems where you need to reference a range that is moving or resizing.

OFFSET is used to point to a range. The location and size of the range is calculated as the formula is being calculated.

OFFSET allows five arguments. At least one of the four final arguments should be a formula that is calculated on the fly. When OFFSET is set up to return a range of cells, you will find yourself using OFFSET inside of another function such as SUM, or in this case, inside of VLOOKUP.

The syntax is =OFFSET(Reference,Rows Down from There, Columns Right from There, Rows Tall, Columns Tall). For example, you could start with a reference of B1, move down N rows, move right 0 rows, make the range be 7 rows tall and 2 columns wide.

In the next figure, a MATCH function in F5 figures out where the lookup table for this company begins. The COUNTIF in F6 figures out how tall the lookup table should be. Both of these numbers will feed into an OFFSET function that is shown for illustration in F7. The actual formula is found in F9, where the OFFSET is used to describe the lookup table in the VLOOKUP formula.

=VLOOKUP(F3,OFFSET($B$1,F5,0,F6,2),2,FALSE)

	A	B	C	D	E	F	G	H
1	Company	Center	Amount					
2	100	1010	11727		Company	200		
3	100	1020	24708		Center	1030		
4	100	1030	18762					
5	100	1040	12076		Where start?	8	=MATCH(F2,A2:A22,0)	
6	100	1050	11049		How Tall?	7	=COUNTIF(A:A,F2)	
7	100	1060	21755		Offset:	OFFSET($B$1,8,0,7,2)		
8	100	1070	23929					
9	200	1010	28722		Lookup:	15097		
10	200	1020	19485					
11	200	1030	15097		OFFSET(Starting Point,			
12	200	1040	11915		Rows Down, Columns Right,			
13	200	1050	18689		Height, Width)			
14	200	1060	19420					
15	200	1070	14267					
16	300	1010	22797					

Figure 478 *OFFSET is slow, but versatile.*

ADD COMMENTS TO A FORMULA

Problem: I spent a great deal of time perfecting the formula shown below. I would like to leave myself notes about it so I can figure it out again six months from now.

=RANK(B4,$B$4:$B$13)+COUNTIF(B$3:B3,B4)

	A	B	C	D	E	F
1	Widget Production				Widget Producti	
2						
3	Name	Total	Rank		Rank	Name
4	Ashley	80	6		1	Carl
5	Bill	80	7		2	Dora
6	Carl	92	1		3	Jerry
7	Dora	90	2		4	Harry

Figure 479 *Will you remember why you added the COUNTIF?*

Strategy: An old Lotus 1-2-3 function—the N function—is still available in Excel. It turns out that N of a number is the number and N of any text is zero. Thus, you can add several N functions to a formula without changing the result, provided that they contain text.

If you have figured out some obscure formula, you can leave yourself notes about it right in the formula.

```
=RANK(B4,$B$4:$B$13)+N("The first part of the formula
returns a rank, but ties are given the same value")+
COUNTIF(B$3:B3,B4)+N("The CountIf finds any cells in the
rows above this row that match this row. For each row that
matches, 1 is added to the rank. This ensures that the
second occurence of a tie is given a one-higher ranking.")+
N("For more details, see the MrExcel book")
```

N(value)	B	C	D	E	F	G	H
1	Widget Production			Widget Production			
2							
3	Name	Total	Rank		Rank	Name	Total
4	Ashley	80	see th		1	Carl	92

Figure 480 *Add your comment as text in the N() function.*

CREATE RANDOM NUMBERS

Problem: I want to create a range of random numbers or letters.

Strategy: You use the RANDBETWEEN function. This function will return a random integer between lower and upper limits. Here are some examples:

- =RANDBETWEEN(1,100) for random integers between 1 and 100.
- =RANDBETWEEN(100,500)/100 for random prices between $1.00 and $5.00
- =RANDBETWEEN(-20,20)/100 for random growth from 80% to 120%/
- For random capital letters, use: =CHAR(RANDBETWEEN(65,90)).
- For a random item from a list stored in B7:I7, use =INDEX($B$7:$I$7,RANDBETWEEN(1,8)).

=RANDBETWEEN(-20,20)/100

	A	B	C	D	E	F	G	H	I
1	1-100	28	77	12	9	70	81		
2	$1-$5	4	1.89	3.73	3.28	2.54	1.96		
3	±20%	-15%	-6%	20%	-3%	10%	-9%		
4	Letters	Z	P	V	M	V	L		
5	From a List	Bat	Cat	Cat	Fish	Dog	Fish		
6									
7	List of Values	Ant	Bat	Cat	Dog	Eel	Fish	Game	Hat

Figure 481 *Generate random values.*

Additional Details: The last bullet point shows off an interesting and undocumented feature of INDEX. Normally, you would specify =INDEX(range,row,column). This would mean that you would have to specify =INDEX(B7:I7,1,RANDBETWEEN(1,8)). However, when you range is exactly one row tall, Excel will use the second argument as a column number instead of a row number.

Alternate Strategy: Excel also offers the RAND function, which will return a decimal between 0 and 0.9999999. Instead of using the formula =RANDBETWEEN(1,10), you could use =INT(RAND()*10)+1.

Additional Details: Every time you press F9 or enter a new value in the worksheet, the random numbers will change. You might want to change the formulas to values to freeze the random numbers. To do this, you select the range of random numbers, press Home, Copy, and then select Home, Paste dropdown, Paste Values to convert formulas to numbers.

Gotcha: These are actually pseudo-random numbers. If you are performing complex modeling involving millions of numbers, patterns may emerge.

RANDOMLY SEQUENCE A LIST

Problem: The students in my class must present an oral book report. Rather than have them go alphabetically, I want to randomly sequence them. How can Excel help me do that?

Strategy: Put the students in column A. Add a =RAND() formula in column B. Sort by column B. Each time that you sort, the students will be in a different sequence.

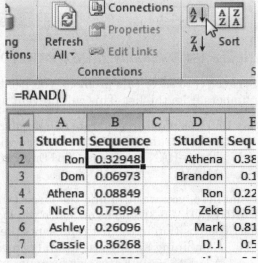

Figure 482 *Sort by the RAND() column.*

Gotcha: The data is sorted, and then column B is recalculated. It will appear that the new figures in column B are not in any order. This is because the sort was based on the previous values in column B.

PLAY DICE GAMES WITH EXCEL

Problem: My Monopoly set is missing the dice. How can I create a spreadsheet that will simulate randomly rolling two dice?

Strategy: You can use the RANDBETWEEN function and clever spreadsheet formatting to simulate two or more dice. Follow these steps:
1. Select cell B2. Select Home, Format, Row Height. Set the row height to 41.
2. In cell B2, enter the formula =RANDBETWEEN(1,6).
3. With cell B2 selected, click the Center and Middle Align buttons on the Home tab of the ribbon.
4. In the Font group of the Home tab, choose the Bold icon. Select 24 point from the font size dropdown.
5. Choose Thick Box Border from the Border dropdown.
6. Copy cell B2 and paste it to cell D2. As shown below, you will have the two dice required for Monopoly.
7. Copy B2 to make additional dice if necessary.

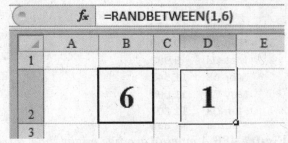

Figure 483 *Create dice with Excel.*

Results: You will have one die in cell B2 and another in cell D2. Every time you press the F9 key, you will have a new roll of the dice.

GENERATE RANDOM WITHOUT REPEATS

Problem: I want Excel to generate numbers for the lottery. Once a number is chosen, I don't want that number to appear again. Using RANDBETWEEN, it is possible to get duplicates.

`=RANDBETWEEN(1,56)`

	A	B	C	D	E
1	42	49	39	42	10
2					

Figure 484 *Eventually, RANDBETWEEN returns duplicates.*

Strategy: to solve this problem, you need to sort the 56 numbers into a sequence and choose the top five numbers from the list. This will prevent any duplicates from showing up.

Say that you want to generate five numbers from 1 to 56. Follow these steps:

1. Select a range that is one column wide by 56 rows tall.
2. Type =RAND(). Press Ctrl+Enter to enter that formula in all of the cells. In my example, I used A1:A56.

From here, you want to find the largest values using =LARGE(A1:A56,1) then =LARGE(A1:A56,2), then LARGE(A1:A56,3), and so on. Once you locate the largest value, use MATCH to find that value within the list. The position in the list represents the lotto number.

3. Combining all of those formulas together, you get =MATCH(LARGE($A$1:$A$56,COLUMN(A1)),$A$1:$A$56,0). Enter this formula in C2:G2.
4. For the extra ball, use a regular old =RANDBETWEEN(1,46).

`=MATCH(LARGE($A$1:$A$56,COLUMN(A1)),$A$1:$A$56,0)`

	A	B	C	D	E	F	G	H	I	J
1	0.754509		Mega Millions Chooser (Random, No Repeats)							
2	0.758215		36	54	38	18	22	11		
3	0.091466									

Figure 485 *You won't get any repeats in C2:G2.*

Additional Details: For PowerBall, enter numbers in A1:A59. Change the 56 in the formula above to a 59. Change the formula in H2 to get numbers from 1 to 39.

CALCULATE A MOVING AVERAGE

Problem: I have 36 months of sales data. In order to create a prediction of sales, I want to calculate a three-month moving average. Later, I will create a trendline from the moving average.

	A	B
1		Sales
2	Jan-08	10,123
3	Feb-08	10,558
4	Mar-08	9,982
5	Apr-08	11,547
6	May-08	11,090
7	Jun-08	11,607
8	Jul-08	11,988

Figure 486 *A moving average might show a trend in this data.*

Strategy: You need two months of history before you can begin calculating a three-month moving average. When you have that, follow these steps:

1. In cell C4, enter the formula =AVERAGE(B2:B4). Note that when you enter this formula, Excel will be concerned because the formula will ignore similar data in cell B5. In this case, you are smarter than Excel, so you can use the Caution (exclamation point) dropdown to tell Excel to ignore the error.
2. Double-click the fill handle in C4 to copy the formula down to the rest of your data set.

Results: Moving averages are good if the underlying data has spikes in the sales. It is difficult for an automatic system to predict spikes. A moving average smooths these spikes out of the system. A forecast based on the moving average line may be more accurate than a forecast based on the original data.

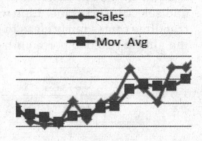

Figure 487 *The three month moving average shows a forecastable trend.*

CALCULATE A TRENDLINE FORECAST

Problem: I have monthly historical sales data. I want to predict future sales by month.

Strategy: You can use the least-squares method to fit the sales data to a trendline. Excel offers a function called LINEST that will calculate the formula for the trendline.

	A	B	C
1	Mo#		Sales
2	1	Mar-08	10,221
3	2	Apr-08	10,696
4	3	May-08	10,873
5	4	Jun-08	11,415
6	5	Jul-08	11,562

Figure 488 *Forecast future data.*

You might remember from math class that a trendline is represented by this formula: $y = mx + b$

In this example, y is the revenue for the month, m is the slope of the line, x is the month number, and b is the y-intercept. If you were to look at the data, you might guess that the prediction for a given month is $10,000 + Month number x $400. In this case, the value for b would be 10,000, and the value for m would be 400. This is just my wild guess; Excel can calculate the number exactly.

LINEST is a very special function. Instead of returning one number, it actually returns two (or more) numbers as the result. If you select a single cell and enter =LINEST(C2:C35), it will return a single number, which is of no help. Entering the formula the wrong way returns a single answer of 204.8133. The first time you do this, you might wonder how the number 204.81 could describe a line.

It turns out that Excel really wants to return two numbers from the function. Here's the trick:

1. Select two cells that are side by side.
2. Type the function in the first cell. After you type the closing parenthesis, press Ctrl+Shift+Enter. Excel returns both the slope and the y-intercept.

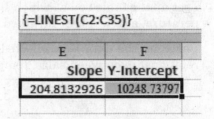

Figure 489 *The results appear in 2 cells.*

3. Add a Prediction column. In column D, enter a formula to calculate the predicted sales trendline. The formula is the intercept in F2 plus the slope in E2 times this row's month number.

f_x =$F$2+$E$2*A2

	A	B	C	D	E	F
1	Mo#		Sales	Prediction	Slope	Y-Intercept
2	1	Mar-08	10,221	10,454	204.8132926	10248.73797
3	2	Apr-08	10,696	10,658		
4	3	May-08	10,873	10,863		

Figure 490 *Use the results of the LINEST to predict sales.*

You will now be able to graph columns B:D to show how well the prediction matches the historical actuals.

Additional Details: When the data along one axis of your data contains dates, it is best to delete the heading in the upper-left corner of your data set before creating the chart. You clear cell B1, select B1:D47, and select Insert, Line, Line with Markers. As shown below, the resulting chart shows that the predicted trendline comes fairly close to the actuals. You can also see that the formula predicts that you will be selling almost $20,000 per month one year from now.

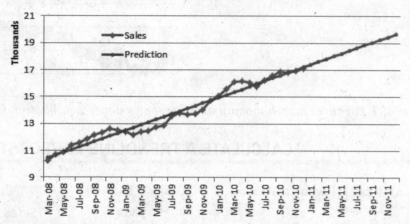

Figure 491 *Plot actuals vs. forecast to see if the sales match a trend.*

Gotcha: When you select two cells for the LINEST function, they must be side by side. If you try to select two cells that are one above the other, you will just get two copies of the slope.

Alternate Strategy: A different method is to use the INDEX function to pluck a specific answer from the array.

=INDEX(LINEST(C2:C35),1,1) will return the first element from the array. This is the slope.

=INDEX(LINEST(C2:C35),1,2) will return the second element from the array. This is the y-intercept.

See Also: "Add a Trendline to a Chart" on page 430.

BUILD A MODEL TO PREDICT SALES BASED ON MULTIPLE REGRESSION

Problem: I run a Gelato stand. After 10 days of sales, I discovered that each day, I would either make a lot of money or nearly go broke. As I analyzed sales, I began to feel that temperature and rain might be two important determining factors in how much money I make. On rainy or cool days, fewer people buy gelato.

I set up the table below, which shows each day's sales, temperature, and whether it rained.

Based on the data I've collected, how can I determine the relationship between sales, temperature, and rainfall?

	A	B	C
1	Sally's Gelato Stand		
2			
3	Temperature	Rain	Sales
4	64	1	$28
5	95	0	$270
6	74	1	$48
7	84	1	$68
8	94	1	$88
9	75	0	$150
10	56	0	$36
11	85	0	$210
12	65	0	$90
13	55	1	$10
14			

Figure 492 *Sales swing wildly from day to day.*

Strategy: You need to do a multiple regression. After a multiple regression, you will have a formula that predicts sales like this:

```
Y = m1x1 + m2x2 + b
Sales = Temperature x M1 + Rain x M2 + b
```

The LINEST function can return the values M1, M2, and b that best describe your sales model. Here's what you do:

1. LINEST is going to return three values, so select a range of three cells that are side by side. The first argument is the range of known sales figures. The second argument is the range of temperatures and rainfall.
2. Press Ctrl+Shift+Enter to calculate the array formula.

`{=LINEST(C4:C13,A4:B13)}`

◢	A	B	C	D	E	F	G	H
1	Sally's Gelato Stand							
2								
3	Temp	Rain	Sales			Rain	Temp	Y Intercept
4	64	1	$28			-98.8	4	-149.6
5	95	0	$270					
6	74	1	$48					
7	84	1	$68					

Figure 493 *Enter one formula in three cells.*

3. Enter a prediction formula in column D to see how well the regression calculation describes sales. The results are so-so. The prediction in D6 is right on the mark. The predictions in D11 and D12 are off by $20 each—an error of 10%.

`=$H$4+($G$4*A4)+($F$4*B4)`

◢	A	B	C	D	E	F	G	H
1	Sally's Gelato Stand							
2								
3	Temp	Rain	Sales	FC		Rain	Temp	Y Intercept
4	64	1	$28	$8		-98.8	4	-149.6
5	95	0	$270	$230				
6	74	1	$48	$48				
7	84	1	$68	$88				
8	94	1	$88	$128				
9	75	0	$150	$150				
10	56	0	$36	$74				
11	85	0	$210	$190				
12	65	0	$90	$110				
13	55	1	$10	-$28				

Figure 494 *Use LINEST to produce a forecast.*

4. To get the additional statistics that LINEST can return to show how well the results match reality, add a fourth argument: TRUE. Be sure to enter the function in a five-row range.

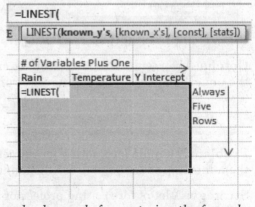

Figure 495 *Choose five rows and several columns before entering the formula.*

5. Press Ctrl+Shift+Enter. You will get the results shown here.

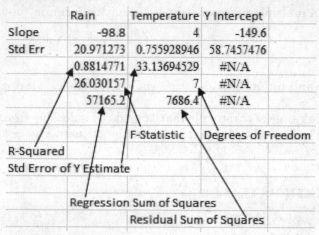

	Rain	Temperature	Y Intercept
Slope	-98.8	4	-149.6
Std Err	20.971273	0.755928946	58.7457476
	0.8814771	33.13694529	#N/A
	26.030157	7	#N/A
	57165.2	7686.4	#N/A

F-Statistic   Degrees of Freedom

R-Squared
Std Error of Y Estimate

Regression Sum of Squares
Residual Sum of Squares

Figure 496 *Excel performs the regression and provides statistics.*

I only somewhat paid attention in statistics class, but I know that a key statistical indicator is the R-squared value. It ranges from 0 to 1, where 1 is a perfect match, and 0 is a horrible match. The 0.88 value here confirms that the prediction model is pretty good but not perfect.

Additional Details: Regression models try to force actual results into a straight-line formula. The fact is that life may not fit in a straight-line formula. Because I created the spreadsheet used here, I know that the actual data in the gelato model uses the formula (Temperature - 50) x $2 if raining and (Temperature - 50) x $6 if not raining. In this example, Sally was correct that ice cream sales are dependent on rain and temperature, but even a powerful regression engine could not predict the absolutely correct formula.

Alternate Strategy: The Analysis ToolPak still offers tools to do Regression, as well as testing correlation, exponential smoothing, create histograms, generate random numbers, create samples, and more. You have to enable the add-in first. Type Alt+T followed by I. Add a checkmark next to Analysis ToolPak and click OK.

You will now have a Data Analysis icon on the right side of the Data ribbon tab. Click the icon and Excel offers a list of tools. Although some of these tools offer older dialog boxes that really need updating, they can often produce far more detailed results. The Regression tool creates charts of the residuals, Anova analysis, and tables of statistics about the regression.

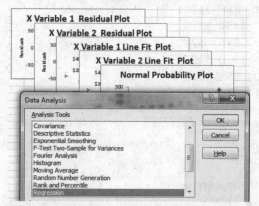

Figure 497 *The Analysis ToolPak offers a variety of statistical tools.*

Gotcha: The results from the ToolPak are not live formulas! They are a one-time snapshot. If you change the underlying data, you will have to run the analysis tool again.

MEASURE THE ACCURACY OF A SALES FORECAST

Problem: I handle forecasting for my company. I collect forecasts from the sales reps and attempt to turn them into a production plan for the manufacturing plant. Can Excel help me with this chore?

Strategy: A lot of forecasting professionals measure forecast error as (Forecast-Actual)/Forecast.

=(C2-D2)/C2

	A	B	C	D	E
1	Product	Customer	Forecast	Actual	FC Err %
2	DEF	Wal-Mart	300	270	10%
3	XYZ	Molson, Inc	100	130	-30%
4	XYZ	Ainsworth	400	0	100%
5	ABC	Ainsworth	0	400	#DIV/0!
6	ABC	General Motors	100	100	0%
7	DEF	Wal-Mart	800	800	0%

Figure 498 *Most agree that (F-A)/F is the measure of error.*

However, there are two kinds of problems in forecasting. If you forecast 400 units and the order does not show up, then the manufacturing plant has 400 sets of material on hand and nowhere to send them. Inventory goes up. This is bad. On the other side, if you forecast 0 units and an order for 400 shows up, the plant has to scramble and start buying material on the gray market. This means the product cost could double and your profits go away. This is also bad.

You need a formula for forecast accuracy that treats both of these situations as equally bad. You take the absolute value of (Forecast-Actual) and divide by the larger of the forecasts or actuals. To calculate forecast accuracy using my formula, you follow these steps:

1. Whether the forecast was high or low, the error is always a positive number, so calculate the absolute error on a product-by-product basis. Use the ABS function to returns the absolute value of a number.

=ABS(C2-D2)

C	D	F
Forecast	Actual	Error
300	270	30
100	130	30
400	0	400

Figure 499 *Figure out the absolute size of the error.*

2. Calculate the divisor (which is what I call the "Size of the opportunity to mess up"). Missing a 1,000-unit sale is much worse than missing a 2-unit sale. For column G, use the MAX function to find what is larger: forecast or actuals.

=MAX(C2:D2)

C	D	F	G
Forecast	Actual	Error	Divisor
300	270	30	300
100	130	30	130
400	0	400	400

Figure 500 *Size of opportunity for negative consequences.*

3. Calculate the error percentage by dividing F2/G2.

	fx	=F2/G2				

C	D	E	F	G	H
Forecast	Actual	FC Err %	Error	Divisor	Error %
300	270	10%	30	300	10%
100	130	-30%	30	130	23%
400	0	100%	400	400	100%
0	400	#DIV/0!	400	400	100%
100	100	0%	0	100	0%
800	800	0%	0	800	0%
500	1000	-100%	500	1000	50%
900	922	-2%	22	922	2%
800	850	-6%	50	850	6%
400	450	-13%	50	450	11%
4300	4922	-14%	1482	5352	28%

Figure 501 *Calculate error percentage.*

As shown above, the traditional forecast error calculation is in E. The forecast error calculation you just did is in H. Sometimes these two calculations are the same. Overall, though, because my calculation takes into account the negative effect of an unforecasted order showing up, my error percentage will be higher (and, I feel, more meaningful).

This started out as a topic on using ABS and MAX functions but turned into a sermon on the best way to calculate forecast accuracy. Note that I am currently the only person I know who calculates accuracy this way. When I bounce it off the pros at forecasting conventions, they reject this method. So, if you are doing forecasting, use this method at your own risk.

SWITCHING COLUMNS INTO ROWS USING A FORMULA

Problem: Every day, I receive a file with information going down the rows. I need to use formulas to pull this information into a horizontal table. It is not practical for me to use Paste Special, Transpose every day. Below, you can see that the first formula in B2 points to A4. If I drag this formula to the right, there is no way that it will pull values from A5, A6, A7, and so on.

	B2			fx	=A4	

	A	B	C	D
1				
2		Apples		
3				
4	Apples			
5	Banana			
6	Cherry			
7	Dill			
8	Eggplant			
9	Fish			
10	Graham Crackers			
11				

Figure 502 *Dragging the fill handle will fail here.*

Strategy: You can use the INDEX function to return the nth item from the A4:A10 range. It would be cool if there were a function that could return the numbers 1, 2, 3, and so on as you copy across.

The formula =COLUMN(A1) will return a 1 to indicate that cell A1 is in the first column. While this is not entirely amazing, the beautiful thing about this function is that as you copy to the right, =COLUMN(A1) will change to =COLUMN(B1) and return a 2. Any time you need to fill in the numbers 1, 2, 3 as you go across a row, you can use the =COLUMN(A1) in the first cell. As you copy, Excel will take care of the rest.

Therefore, if you use the formula =INDEX($A$4:$A$10,COLUMN(A1)) in cell B2, you can easily copy it across the columns.

Gotcha: You need to use A1 as the reference for the COLUMN function no matter where you are entering the formula. In this example, the first formula is in column B. That is irrelevant. Even if the formula starts in column XFA, you will still point to A1 in order to return the number 1.

=INDEX($A$4:$A$10,COLUMN(A1))

◢	A	B	C	D
1				
2		Apples	Banana	Cherry
3				
4	Apples			
5	Banana			
6	Cherry			

Figure 503 *Copy B2 across to transpose with a formula.*

Alternate Strategy: It is slightly harder to use, but the TRANSPOSE function will perform the same task as COLUMN. The trick is that a single function has to be entered in many cells at once. Follow these steps:

1. Count the number of cells in A4:A10. In this case, it is seven cells.
2. Select seven horizontal cells. In this case, select B2:H2.
3. Type =TRANSPOSE(A4:A10). Unlike INDEX, dollar signs are not necessary in this formula. Do not press Enter.
4. Because this function will return many answers, you have to hold down Ctrl+Shift while you press Enter. Excel will add curly braces around the function, and the seven values will appear across your selection.

{=TRANSPOSE(A4:A10)}

◢	A	B	C	D	E
1					
2		Apples	Banana	Cherry	Dill	E|
3					
4	Apples				
5	Banana				

Figure 504 *A single TRANSPOSE function fills in these cells.*

The advantage of using TRANSPOSE over using Paste Special, Transpose is that the TRANSPOSE function is a live formula. If cells in column A change, they will change in row 2.

Additional Details: The example in this topic is a trivial example of merely copying the cells. In real life, you might need to do calculations instead of copying the data. You can use calculations with either the INDEX or TRANSPOSE functions. For example, the formula shown above squares the number and adds 1.

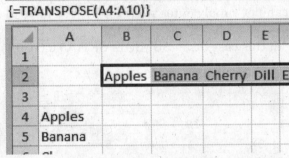

{=TRANSPOSE(A4:A10)^2+1}

◢	A	B	C	D	E	F	G	H
1								
2		26	10	197	101	145	26	257
3								
4	5							
5	3							
6	14							
7	10							
8	12							
9	5							
10	16							

Figure 505 *Do calculations while transposing.*

SUM A RANGE THAT IS C5 ROWS TALL

Problem: I need to add up a range that starts in cell A5 and is C5 rows tall. A formula in C5 is calculating a number and I need to include that many cells in the SUM.

Strategy: Use the versatile OFFSET function. OFFSET will let you:
- Start from a specific cell or range of cells,
- Move a certain number of rows from the starting position,
- Move a certain number of columns from the starting position.

The first three arguments get you to a top left corner cell for the dynamic range. Note that if the starting cell is J10, you can point to J15 with a second argument of 5 or point to J5 with a second argument of -5. In a similar fashion, a third argument of 1 will point to K10. A third argument of -1 will point to I10.

Those first three arguments get you to a starting cell. In this current question, you don't need any of that information, because you know that you are always starting from A5. Your formula will start with OFFSET(A5,0,0,...

OFFSET allows you to specify two more optional arguments.
- The fourth argument describes the height of the dynamic range.
- The fifth argument describes the width of the dynamic range.

You can use OFFSET(A5,0,0,C5,1) to return a range that is 1 column wide, and a variable number of rows tall.

Gotcha: In most cases, OFFSET will point to a range that is more than one cell tall. In these cases, you can not simply enter =OFFSET(). You have to use the OFFSET as an argument in another function.

In this case, use =SUM(OFFSET(A5,0,0,C5,1)). Change the 5 in C5 to a 3, and the formula sums A5:A7.

=SUM(OFFSET(A5,0,0,C5,1))

	A	B	C
4	29		
5	1		5
6	2		
7	4		31
8	8		
9	16		
10	32		
11	64		

Figure 506 *This formula sums A5:A9.*

=SUM(OFFSET(A5,0,0,C5,1))

	A	B	C
4	29		
5	1		3
6	2		
7	4		7
8	8		
9	16		
10	32		
11	64		

Figure 507 *Change C5 to a 3, and the sum range resizes.*

OFFSET can be used to point to one cell above the current cell. Why would you go to that hassle when a simple formula does the same thing?

=A4

	A	B	C	D	E	F
1	Task	Previous Task		Task	Previous Task	
2	Step 1			Step 1		
3	Step 2	Step 1		Step 2	Step 1	
4	Step 3	Step 2		Step 3	Step 2	
5	Step 4	Step 3		Step 4	Step 3	
6	Step 5	Step 4		Step 5	Step 4	

Figure 508 *Who needs OFFSET when =A4 works?*

What happens when you delete row 4? The simple formula in column B changes to a #REF! error. The OFFSET formula in column E continues to work.

=OFFSET(E4,-1,-1)

	A	B	C	D	E	F
1	Task	Previous Task		Task	Previous Task	
2	Step 1			Step 1		
3	Step 2	Step 1		Step 2	Step 1	
4	Step 4	#REF!		Step 4	Step 2	
5	Step 5	Step 4		Step 5	Step 4	

Figure 509 *If rows might be deleted, OFFSET saves the day.*

Additional Details: The starting range can be more than one cell. In the example that follows, the starting range is A4:A11. The third argument of the OFFSET function uses MONTH(A1) to move five columns to the right. This formula will total the column corresponding to the date in cell A1.

=SUM(OFFSET(A4:A11,0,MONTH(A1)))

	A	B	C	D	E	F	G	H
1	5/31/2014							
2	508							
3		Jan	Feb	Mar	Apr	May	Jun	Jul /
4	N.E.	47	52	57	63	69	76	84
5	M.A.	32	35	39	43	47	52	57
6	S.E.	50	55	61	67	74	81	89
7	M.W.	25	28	31	34	37	41	45
8	S.C.	50	55	61	67	74	81	89
9	G.P.	49	54	59	65	72	79	87
10	P.N.	49	54	59	65	72	79	87
11	SoC.	43	47	52	57	63	69	76
12								
13								

Figure 510 *Use OFFSET to move a range n columns to the right.*

Gotcha: OFFSET is a volatile function. This means that with every calculation of the worksheet, the OFFSET is recalculated, even if none of the cells in the table changed. Those cells could stay the same for a whole month, yet OFFSET will recalculate every time that you change a cell anywhere in this worksheet. Many OFFSET functions can cause your worksheet to slow down. In many cases, you can use INDEX instead.

Back in the VLOOKUP topics, you read how to use =INDEX(B4:M11,row,column) to return one cell from a range. If you leave out the row argument blank, Excel will return all of the rows. The formula of =SUM(INDEX(B4:M11,,MONTH(A1))) will return an equivalent result.

=SUM(INDEX(B4:M11,,MONTH(A1)))

	A	B	C	D	E	F
1	5/31/2014					
2	508					
3		Jan	Feb	Mar	Apr	Ma'
4	N.E.	47	52	57	63	6
5	M.A.	32	35	39	43	4

WHATEVER HAPPENED TO THE @@ FUNCTION?

Problem: Back in Lotus 1-2-3, there was an @@ function. If you used @@(A3), Lotus would go to A3. A3 was supposed to contain a valid cell reference. Say that A3 contained the text C5. The @@ function would then return the value from cell C5.

Strategy: In Excel, this is called the INDIRECT function. Here are a few examples of how it works.

In the simplest case, consider a formula of =INDIRECT(F2). Excel will go to F2 and use the cell address found there. In the following figure, the answer in F4 first looks to F2 then to C1.

=INDIRECT(F2)

	A	B	C	D	E	F
1	1	9	17	25		
2	2	10	18	26		C1
3	3	11	19	27		
4	4	12	20	28		17
5	5	13	21	29		
6	6	14	22	30		
7	7	15	23	31		
8	8	16	24	32		

Figure 511 *F2 says to look at cell C1.*

The cell reference in the INDIRECT can be calculated on the fly. In this example, the VLOOKUP points to a different worksheet based on the quarter number in column B. INDIRECT uses concatenation to build something that looks like a worksheet reference.

=VLOOKUP(A2,INDIRECT("Q"&B2&"!A1:B99"),2,FALSE)

	A	B	C	D	E
1	Center	Quarter	Result		
2	1060	2	200		
3	1060	1	100		
4	1060	3	300		
5	1030	4	400		
6	1040	4	400		
7	1060	2	200		

Sheet1 **Report** Q1 Q2 Q3 Q4

Figure 512 *Q2!A1:B99 is calculated on the fly inside of the INDIRECT.*

Additional Details: If you have used range names, the value inside of INDIRECT can point to a range name. This creates some interesting lookup possibilities. For an example, see "Why Use the Intersection Operator?" on page 122.

TABLES ARE LIKE A DATABASE IN EXCEL

Problem: Excel isn't like Access. I am an Access person and Excel annoys me.

Strategy: If you have database-like data in Excel, define the data as a table.

Many spreadsheets in Excel contain a two-dimensional table of data. You have headings in the first row, and each row of the worksheet represents a different record in a table.

Because a common task in Excel is dealing with tables, Excel 2010 has added several features for dealing with tables. One of the best benefits of the table functionality is that charts and pivot tables based on a table will automatically grow with the table.

To turn on the features, select a single cell in the dataset and press Ctrl+T. Excel will assume your table extends to either the edge of the spreadsheet or to a blank row and blank column. The Create Table dialog will ask you to confirm the range for the table and that the first row contains headers.

Figure 513 *Excel guesses the current region as the address for the table.*

When you apply a table, you will notice the following features:
- Excel applies a default table formatting. You can change to another style using the Table Styles gallery on the Table Tools Design tab.
- Excel turns on the Filter dropdowns on each heading. You can use these dropdowns to sort by a column or to filter a column.
- If you are in the table and scroll so the headings are not visible, the headings will replace column letters A, B, C and so on. New in Excel 2010, the Filter dropdowns will remain available after the first row scrolls out of view.
- You can add totals to the bottom of the dataset by using the Total Row check box in the Table Tools Design tab.

The following features are not immediately visible, but will work:
- Any new data typed in the blank row below the table will be made part of the table. This means that any charts, pivot tables, or formulas that refer to the table will automatically apply to the new data.
- A resize handle in the bottom-right corner of the table allows you to drag to manually extend the table to include additional columns.
- You can use the Table Style Options check boxes to turn on alternate formatting for the first column, last column, header row, total row, or to apply alternating shading to rows or columns.
- Any formulas that point to columns in the table will be written in a new table nomenclature. Enter a formula once and Excel will copy it to all rows of the table.

Gotcha: the filter dropdowns cover up some of the headings. You will find that you end up left-aligning headings so that you can read the headings. You can turn off the filter dropdowns by using Data, Filter.

Gotcha: sometimes you turn on the table functionality to quickly apply a format to the table. It is okay to use Ctrl+T to create and format a table and then immediately use Table Tools, Convert to Range to turn the table back into a normal range. The table formatting remains!

Additional Details: For more information on table, check out the book Excel Tables by Zack Barresse and Kevin Jones.

DEALING WITH TABLE FORMULAS

Problem: Once I define something as a table, the formulas are strange.

Strategy: You are seeing the new structured referencing in a table. Here is how it works.

Suppose you want to add a Profit % column to a table. Follow these steps:
1. Enter a heading of GP% in cell H1.
2. Format cell H2 as a percentage. Do this before you enter the formula.
3. In cell H2, type an equals sign. Click the Profit in G2. Type a divide sign. Click the Revenue in F2. You will already notice something different: Excel is building a formula of =[@Profit]/[@Revenue].

E	F	G	H	I	J
Quantity ▼	Revenue ▼	Profit ▼	GP% ▼		
1000	22810	12590	=[@Profit]/[@Revenue]		
100	2257	1273			
500	10245	6010			

Figure 514 *The table formula syntax is like the natural language syntax.*

4. Press the Enter key to complete the formula. Excel automatically copies the formula down to all the rows in your dataset!

The automatic copying of the formula is a great feature. However, there will be a few times when you do not want this to happen. If so, find the AutoCorrect dropdown and open it. You will have choices to turn of the calculated column or to turn off the feature permanently.

G	H	I	J	K	L	M
ofit ▼	GP% ▼					
12590	55%					
1273	56%					
6010	59%	↰ Undo Calculated Column				
6130	55%					
5116	56%	▪ Stop Automatically Creating Calculated Columns				
10680	58%	⚡ Control AutoCorrect Options...				
5064	55%					
3472	51%					
5068	60%					
11890	55%					

Figure 515 *Override automatic formula copying.*

RENAME YOUR TABLES

Problem: Is a formula such as =SUM(Table1[Revenue]) supposed to be meaningful?

Strategy: When you create a table by pressing Ctrl+T, Excel gives the table a generic name, such as Table1, Table2, and so on. If you rename the table, the formulas will start to make more sense. Here's what you do:
1. Convert a range to a table by selecting one cell in the range and pressing Ctrl+T and clicking OK.
2. Click in the Table Name field in the Properties group in the Design ribbon and type a new name for the table. A name such as tSalesData might be more meaningful than Table1.

Results: Excel will rewrite any formulas that point to the table to use the new table name. For example, it will change the =SUM(Table1[Revenue]) you asked about to =SUM(SalesData[Revenue]).

CHARTS , VLOOKUP & PIVOTS EXPAND WITH THE TABLE

Problem: I always have to add new data to the bottom of my data. Then, I have to redefine the charts, pivot tables, and lookup tables that are based on this data.

Strategy: Using tables simplifies this process. Even if you have existing charts, VLOOKUP, and pivot tables, you can benefit from changing the data set to a table.

Below, a chart is based on a table that contains 4 weeks and 3 months.

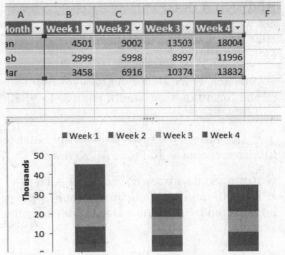

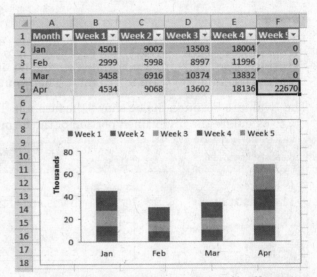

Figure 516 *This chart is based on a table.*

If you enter new data next to the table, the rows and columns will be added to the table and automatically added to the chart.

Gotcha: Tables were designed during the Excel 2007 development cycle. While one team was designing tables, the charting team was busy completely rewriting the chart engine. Time was running short, and the chart team opted not to support table syntax in the SERIES formula.

Additional Details: Pivot tables will expand with the table, but you have to click the Refresh button on the PivotTable Tools Options ribbon tab to refresh the cache. This is still far easier than redefining the data range like you would have to do for non-table pivots.

Figure 517 *The chart automatically grows because it is based on the table.*

BEFORE DELETING A CELL, FIND OUT IF OTHER CELLS RELY ON IT

Problem: I am about to delete a section of a worksheet that I believe is no longer being used. However, I know that if I delete the cell, and some other far-off range relies on the cell, the far-off range will change to the dreaded #REF! error. How can I determine if any other range refers to this cell?

Strategy: You can select the cell that you are considering for deletion and then select Formulas, Trace Dependents. (*Dependents* are other cells that rely on the current cell for calculation.)

Blue arrows will draw from the active cell out to any dependents. Below, , you can see that cell F4 is used to calculate H4.

	A	B	C	D	E	F	G	H
1		Section 1: Historical Trends (Per Month)						
2								
3		Store Type	Size	Rent	Sales	Profit	Labor	Net
4		Regular	1200	2400	12456	6228	6480	-2652
5		BigBox	2600	5200	34500	17250	8640	3410
6								

Figure 518 *Blue arrows point to dependent cells on this worksheet.*

If a dependent is on another worksheet, Excel will draw a black arrow to the other worksheet icon. Double-click the line that leads to the other worksheet icon. Excel will show you a list of the off-sheet dependents.

Additional Details: If you re-click Trace Dependents, Excel will draw second-level dependents. Below, you can see that F4 is used to calculate H4, and H4 is used to calculate D15 and E20.

If you click Trace Dependents several times, you will see all of the formulas that would change to #REF! if you delete cell C4.

You also have a big mess on your spreadsheet! To get rid of all arrows, choose Remove All Arrows.

Gotcha: Some advanced functions such as =INDIRECT("F" & D4/600) might be pointing to your target cell and will not be detected by the Trace Dependents command.

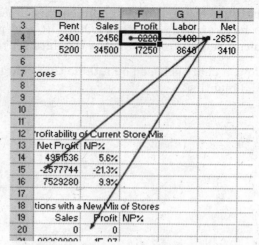

Figure 519 *Second-level dependents.*

CALCULATE A FORMULA IN SLOW MOTION

Problem: I am trying to trace how a formula is calculating. What should I do?

Strategy: Use the Evaluate Formula command on the Formulas ribbon tab. You select the cell that contains the formula you want to examine. Then you select Formulas, Evaluate Formula.

The Evaluate Formula dialog shows the formula. The first item to be calculated is underlined. Click Evaluate to calculate the underlined portion of the formula.

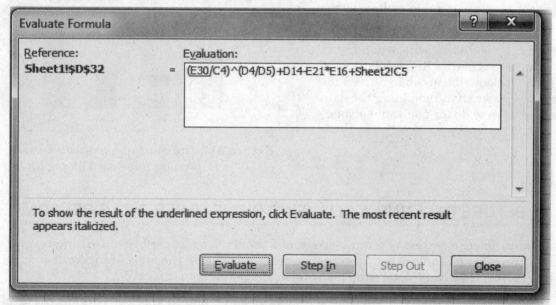

Figure 520 *The underlined term will be evaluated next.*

With each click of Evaluate, Excel will calculate the underlined portion and show the results in italics. It will underline the next step in the calculation.

Additional Details: Any time the next term to be calculated is a cell reference, you can click the Step In button to evaluate the formula in that cell. You click Step Out to close the most recent detail level and go back one level.

WHICH CELLS FLOW INTO THIS CELL?

Problem: I have a large formula, and I would like to visually see how the cell is calculated.

Strategy: One way to handle this is to select the cell and then press F2 to edit the cell. All the references in the formula will light up with different colors. If the precedent cell is in the visible portion of the window, the cell will be surrounded by a box of the same color as the formula.

Alternate Strategy: If you need a more permanent view of the calculations than pressing F2 provides, you can use the Formula Auditing menu to draw blue arrows from all the precedent cells. To do so, you select cell D32 and then select Formulas, Trace Precedents. Excel will draw blue arrows from all the cells that are referenced in the D32 formula. As shown near the bottom left of this figure, the arrow from the other worksheet icon indicates that at least one reference is on another worksheet. Double-click the arrow to see a list of those off-sheet precedents.

If you click Trace Precedents enough times, Excel will trace the precedents of all the arrowed cells. After a few iterations of the command, you will see that nearly all the cells factor in to the calculation.

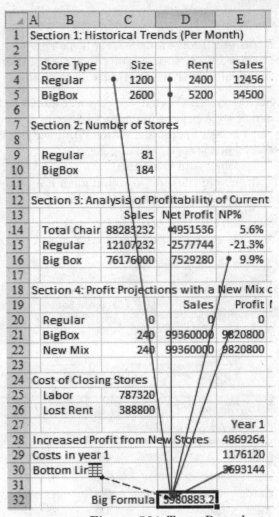

Figure 521 *Trace Precedents.*

COLOR ALL PRECEDENTS OR DEPENDENTS

Problem: The auditing arrows are confusing. Can I simply color the precedent or dependent cells?

Strategy: Use Go To Special. Follow these steps.
1. Select one cell in your worksheet.
2. Choose Home, Find & Select, Go To Special
3. In Go To Special choose Precedents.
4. You now have a choice. Do you want only the direct precedents or all precedents.

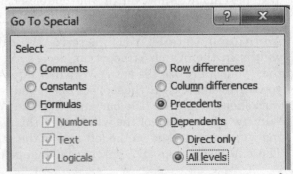

Figure 522 *Choose Direct Only or All Levels.*

5. Click OK. Excel selects all of the cells that are precedents or dependents.
6. Open the paint bucket menu on the Home tab and choose a color. You now have a permanent indicator of the precedents or dependents.

Gotcha: This method will not mark the off-sheet precedents or off-sheet dependents.

MONITOR DISTANT CELLS

Problem: I have a massively large spreadsheet. I'm working on calculations in the top of the spreadsheet but need to monitor results in several other worksheets. It is a pain to travel back and forth to monitor those cells. Is there another way to do this?

Strategy: The Watch Window was added to Excel without much fanfare in 2002. This window is a favorite tool of VBA programmers, and Microsoft added it to the regular Excel interface. Here's how you use it:

1. Select Formulas, Watch Window. The Watch Window, a floating dialog box that you can move around your screen, will appear.
2. Click Add Watch.
3. Using the Add Watch dialog, navigate to and touch the cell that you want to watch. Alternatively, you can first navigate to the cell, click Add Watch, and click Add.

For each cell that you add to the Add Watch dialog, you can always see the formula and the result of that formula in the Watch Window. You can add cells from other sheets and even from other workbooks.

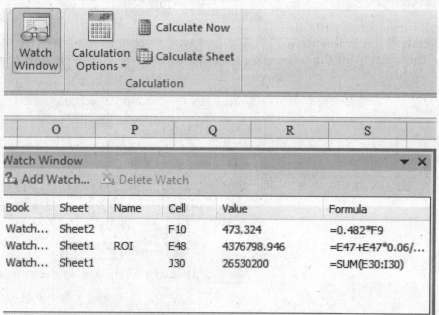

Figure 523 *Watch various cells.*

Additional Details: The cells listed in the Watch Window act as bookmarks! You can double-click a cell and jump to the cell, even if it is on another worksheet.

Gotcha: If you change the numeric format of a number, it does not automatically appear in the Watch Window. However, if you double-click the Value in the Watch Window, it will update.

Additional Details: You can resize the column widths in the Watch Window, as necessary. Further, you can resize the entire Watch Window, and you can even dock it to the top, bottom, or side of the worksheet. Grab the title bar and drag the Watch Window off the edge of the window. In this figure, the window is docked on the left side of the screen. There is easily room for 3 dozen cells to appear.

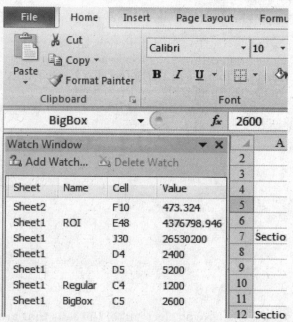

Figure 524 *Dock the watch window.*

USE REAL DATES

Problem: I hate Excel dates. I try to do a calculation and I get a number like 42342. Or I try to calculate the number of days between an invoice and a payment and I get an answer like January 15, 1900.

Strategy: It will take five minutes to understand how Excel stores dates. Open a blank worksheet. Type a number in the range of 40000 to 42000 in cell A1. Select that cell. Hold down the Ctrl key while you drag the fill handle down for several cells. At the bottom of the list, enter a 1. Over in column C, enter =A1 and copy it down. You should have two identical columns of numbers.

	A	B	C
	=A1		
1	41687		41687
2	41688		41688
3	41689		41689
4	41690		41690
5	41691		41691
6	41692		41692
7	41693		41693
8	41694		41694
9	41695		41695
10	41696		41696
11	1		1

Figure 525 *Two sets of numbers.*

Select column C. On the Home tab, open the General dropdown and choose Long Date. Column C will change to show dates in the modern era, plus January 1, 1900.

	A	B	C	D
1	41687		Monday, February 17, 2014	
2	41688		Tuesday, February 18, 2014	
3	41689		Wednesday, February 19, 2014	
4	41690		Thursday, February 20, 2014	
5	41691		Friday, February 21, 2014	
6	41692		Saturday, February 22, 2014	
7	41693		Sunday, February 23, 2014	
8	41694		Monday, February 24, 2014	
9	41695		Tuesday, February 25, 2014	
10	41696		Wednesday, February 26, 2014	
11	1		Sunday, January 01, 1900	
12				

Currency
$41,687.00

Accounting
$41,687.00

Short Date
2/17/2014

Long Date
Monday, February 17, 2014

Time
12:00:00 AM

Figure 526 *Format the numbers as dates.*

You haven't changed the value stored in column C. Cell C1 still contains 41687. You have told Excel to treat the cell as a date and so it calculates a weekday, month, day, and year when applying the formatting.

Additional Details: Excel stores dates as the number of days elapsed since January 1, 1900. Assuming that you are reading this book in the 2014–2018 timeframe, whenever you see a number in the 41640–43465 range, you might be seeing a date cell that is not formatted as a date.

When I say that you should use "real" dates, I mean to store a number like 40600 in the cell and use numeric formatting to display that number as a date. The main advantages of real dates are that you can easily change the format of the date, and you can easily do any calculations that you need with the dates. You can not do calculations when you have dates that are stored as text.

Gotcha: While Excel is really fast at converting 40600 to a month, day, year, it does a notoriously bad job of deciding whether to format the result of a formula as a number or as a date. Here are two examples:

Go to the bottom of your dates in column C and calculate =C8-C1. This formula should calculate the number of
elapsed days between the two dates. The correct answer is
7. Excel gets the correct answer, but because that column
was previously formatted to show long dates, you will see
the 7 converted to Saturday, January 7, 1900.

=C8-C1

C
Sunday, February 23, 2014
Monday, February 24, 2014
Tuesday, February 25, 2014
Wednesday, February 26, 2014
Sunday, January 01, 1900
Saturday, January 07, 1900

Figure 527 *The correct result of 7 is incorrectly formatted as a date.*

To solve the problem, go back to the numeric formatting dropdown on the Home tab and choose Number.
The result will now appear as 7 or 7.00. The problem in this case was that you entered a formula that
should return a number in a column that had previously been formatted to show dates.

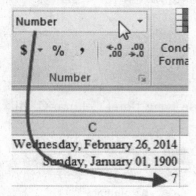

A similar problem is that sometimes, you might enter a function that should return a date. The formula bar will show the
formula, and the worksheet cell will show the serial number.

=WORKDAY(A1,15)

	G	H	I
1			
2		41708	
3			

Figure 528 *Excel didn't think to format this as a date.*

To solve the issue, format the cell as a short date.

Here, the problem was that you entered a formula that
should return a date in a cell that was formatted as General.

Gotcha: 80% of the time, Microsoft takes control and automatically formats your cell with the correct format.

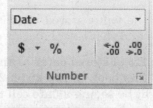

	G	H	I
1			
2		3/10/2014	
3			

Figure 529 *Change from General format to Short Date.*

Go to a blank cell and enter =DATE(2014,7,1) and Excel will automatically format that cell to convert the
serial number to a short date. But, this trick does not work with any function that originated in the old
Analysis ToolPak.

Bottom line: Be prepared to have to change the formatting, either from General to a Date or from a Date
back to Number.

HOW CAN I TELL IF HAVE REAL DATES?

Problem: How can I tell if I have real dates or text dates? They look alike.

◢	A	B	C
1	Real Dates		Text Dates
2	01/21/2014		01/21/2014
3	06/21/2014		06/21/2014
4	01/24/2014		01/24/2014
5	07/16/2014		07/16/2014
6	12/14/2014		12/14/2014
7	03/17/2014		03/17/2014
8	01/14/2014		01/14/2014

Figure 530 *You can't tell by looking if you have real dates.*

Strategy: Go to the Formulas tab and click the Show Formulas icon. (You can also press Ctrl+`, this is the grave accent, often located on the same key as the Tilde, just below Esc on U.S. keyboards.) In Show Formulas mode, real dates will show as serial numbers. Text dates will stay as dates.

◢	A	B	C
1	Real Dates		Text Dates
2	41660		01/21/2014
3	41811		06/21/2014
4	41663		01/24/2014
5	41836		07/16/2014
6	41987		12/14/2014
7	41715		03/17/2014
8	41653		01/14/2014

Figure 531 *In Show Formulas mode, real dates show serial numbers.*

Gotcha: Don't forget to toggle out of Show Formulas mode.

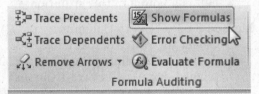

Figure 532 *Leaving Excel in Show Formulas mode will confuse everyone.*

CONVERT TEXT DATES TO REAL DATES

Problem: I have dates stored as text. How can I convert them to real dates?

Strategy: There are three easy ways to do this.

Method 1 uses the DATEVALUE function. Follow these steps:
1. Enter a formula such as =DATEVALUE(C23).
2. Copy the formula down to all of your dates.
3. Format the results as a Short Date using the Number Format dropdown on the Home tab.
4. Copy the range containing formulas.
5. Use Home, Paste dropdown, Paste Values to convert the formulas to values.

| =DATEVALUE(C23) |

	A	B	C	D
22	Fix using =DATEVALUE()			
23			01/21/2014	41660
24			06/21/2014	41811
25			01/24/2014	41663
26			07/16/2014	41836
27			12/14/2014	41987
28			03/17/2014	41715
29			01/14/2014	41653

Figure 533 *Convert the text dates using =DATEVALUE.*

Method 2 uses Paste Special.
1. Go to any blank cell. Format that cell as a date.
2. Copy the formatted cell.
3. Select your range of text dates.
4. Type Alt+E followed by S, then D, then Enter. This brings up the Paste Special dialog and chooses Add from the operation section. By adding a blank cell to the text, you are forcing Excel to calculate zero + a text date. The result is a real date. The fact that Excel brings along the format of the copied cell is a bonus in this situation.

Method 3 uses Text to Columns.
1. Select the range of text dates.
2. Type Alt+D followed by E then F. This takes you through the default path of the Text to Columns wizard. Excel will convert the text dates to real dates.

Gotcha: These methods work for 98% of the ways that people enter dates as text. There are some bizarre methods that won't be converted. I once saw a list of events. Something that was scheduled for June 4-6 2014 was entered as 06/4-6/2014. Excel could not convert that date.

| =DATEVALUE(F39) |

	F	G	H	I	J
39	January 31, 2014	41670			
40	February 31, 2014	#VALUE!	Date does not exist		
41	March 31, 2014	41729			
42	April 31, 2014	#VALUE!	Date does not exist		
43	May 31, 1899	#VALUE!	Date before 1900		
44	July 4, 1776	#VALUE!	Date before 1900		
45	Janauray 17, 2014	#VALUE!	Month not spelled correctly		
46					

Figure 534 *DATEVALUE works only if the date is valid.*

Excel fails if the text refers to a date that does not exist, such as February 29, 2015. Since dates in Excel start in 1900, any dates from 1899 and back will not be converted. Also, misspellings cause the date to text conversion to fail.

If you have cells that contain month names, you can convert those to real dates by concatenating the rest of the date inside the DATEVALUE function. =DATEVALUE(A49&" 1, 2015").

=DATEVALUE(A49&" 1, 2015")

	A	B	C	D
48				
49	Jan		1/1/2015	
50	Feb		2/1/2015	
51	Mar		3/1/2015	
52	Apr		4/1/2015	
53	May		5/1/2015	
54	Jun		6/1/2015	
55	Jul		7/1/2015	
56	Aug		8/1/2015	
57	Sep		9/1/2015	
58	Oct		10/1/2015	
59	Nov		11/1/2015	
60	Dec		12/1/2015	
61				

Figure 535 *Convert month names to dates.*

FORMAT DATES

Problem: I don't like the Short Date or Long Date format. I am going to keep storing my dates as text because I have more control.

Strategy: The ribbon is designed for people who have never used Excel. Microsoft put just a few choices in the ribbon to make Excel rookies happy. All of the good stuff is found by using More Number Formats at the bottom of the dropdown. With the Format Cells dialog, you can do almost anything with your dates.

When you choose More Number Formats, you get back to the legacy Format Cells dialog (Figure 537). On the Number tab, you can use the Date category to choose from 16 date formats. Most of those formats have been in Excel since the Y2K scare, so most only offer 2-digit dates.

If the date format that you want isn't in the list of 16 formats, then choose Custom from the Number category. You can type any date format code in the Type: box. (Figure 538)

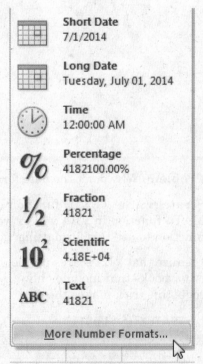

Short Date	7/1/2014
Long Date	Tuesday, July 01, 2014
Time	12:00:00 AM
Percentage	4182100.00%
Fraction	41821
Scientific	4.18E+04
Text	41821
More Number Formats...	

Figure 536 *There are far more choices than the two date options here.*

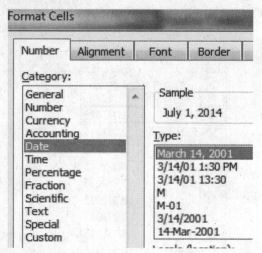

Figure 537 *Sixteen built-in date formats are available under Date.*

Figure 538 *You can build more date formats.*

Here are examples of custom number codes that you can use.

That last date format uses Ctrl+J to go to a new line. After using the date format, you will have to turn on Wrap Text and make the row height tall enough to accommodate the two lines of text.

7/1/2014	**Number Format Used**
7/1/2014	m/d/yyyy
07/01/14	mm/dd/yy
Jul 1	mmm d
Tuesday, July 1, 2014	dddd, mmmm dd, yyyy
Tuesday	dddd
Tue	ddd
July	mmmm
J	mmmmm (to create JFMAMJJASOND)
2014	yyyy
Please remit by 7/1/2014	"Please remit by "m/d/yyyy
July	
2014	MMMM Ctrl+J YYYY

Figure 539 *Custom date format examples.*

FORMAT DATES AS QUARTERS OR WEEKS

Problem: Why don't the date formats offer quarters or weeks?

Strategy: The TEXT() function in Excel will not let you display quarters or weeks. However, the FORMAT() function in VBA will let you display quarters and weeks. For a quick primer on setting up a VBA function to use this formatting, go to your browser and search for "Learn Excel 1074".

I realize that VBA scares people. I generally don't include tricks in this book that require VBA. I've written other books that include only VBA. However, given that you can get amazing results from 3 lines of VBA code, this trick makes the cut.

`=VBATEXT($A2,B$1)`

▲	A	B	C	D	E
1		yyyy\Qq	\Qq	"Week "ww	"Week "ww "Day "w
2	4/21/2014	2014Q2	Q2	Week 17	Week 17 Day 2
3	4/2/2014	2014Q2	Q2	Week 14	Week 14 Day 4
4	11/9/2014	2014Q4	Q4	Week 46	Week 46 Day 1
5	11/14/2014	2014Q4	Q4	Week 46	Week 46 Day 6
6	1/15/2014	2014Q1	Q1	Week 3	Week 3 Day 4
7	4/3/2014	2014Q2	Q2	Week 14	Week 14 Day 5

Figure 540 *Use a VBA function to format as quarters or weeks.*

(General)

```
Function VBAText(MyValue, MyFormat)
    VBAText = Format(MyValue, MyFormat)
End Function
```

Figure 541 *Three lines of code enable the Quarter and Week trick.*

DISPLAY MONTHLY DATES

Problem: I have a data set that shows the actual date for each invoice. When I print the invoice register, I would like to print just the month and year instead of the specific date.

	A	B	C	D
1	Month	Customer	Invoice	Revenue
2	1/3/15	Ainsworth	1101	20,992
3	1/12/15	Air Canada	1102	72,030
4	1/14/15	Chevron	1103	13,438
5	1/20/15	Sun Life Financial	1104	58,901
6	1/21/15	Verizon	1105	4,937
7	2/1/15	Sears Canada	1106	74,173
8	2/3/15	Bell Canada	1107	43,097

Figure 542 *Display daily dates as months in column A.*

Strategy: You can use a numeric format to force dates to display the month and year instead of the specific date. Here's how:

1. Select the range of dates. If you have thousands of rows of data, you can select them all by putting the cell pointer in A2, then pressing Ctrl+Shift+Down Arrow.
2. Press Ctrl+One to display the Format Cells dialog.
3. In the Format Cells dialog, choose the Number tab.
4. In the Category list box, choose Date.
5. In the Type list box, scroll through and select either Mar-01 or March-01. Click OK.

Results: The daily dates will appear as monthly dates.

This process is fine for printing and even for doing automatic subtotals. It will not work for sorting, formulas, or pivot tables. See "Calculate First of Month" for details on actually transforming the column into months.

1/3/2015

	A	B	C
1	Month	Customer	Invoice
2	Jan-15	Ainsworth	1101
3	Jan-15	Air Canada	1102
4	Jan-15	Chevron	1103
5	Jan-15	Sun Life Financial	1104
6	Jan-15	Verizon	1105
7	Feb-15	Sears Canada	1106
8	Feb-15	Bell Canada	1107
9	Feb-15	Exxon	1108

Figure 543 *Excel displays the daily dates as months.*

ADD A COLUMN TO SHOW MONTH OR WEEKDAY

Problem: I want to analyze sales by weekday. Can I calculate the weekday from a date?

Strategy: Use the TEXT function. The first argument for this function is a cell containing a date. The second argument is any custom number format in quotes. =TEXT(A2,"DDDD") will give you a weekday. =TEXT(A2,"MMM") will give you the month abbreviation.

`=TEXT(A2,"DDDD")`

	A	B	C
1	Month	Weekday	Month
2	1/3/15	Saturday	Jan
3	1/12/15	Monday	Jan
4	1/14/15	Wednesday	Jan
5	1/20/15	Tuesday	Jan
6	1/21/15	Wednesday	Jan
7	2/1/15	Sunday	Feb

Figure 544 *Convert dates to weekdays.*

Note that unlike applying a date format, the TEXT function actually converts the date to text. You can sort by column B and all of the Mondays will sort together.

CALCULATE FIRST OF MONTH

Problem: I have a series of invoice dates, and I need to group the data by month. In "Display Monthly Dates," I learned how to format a date to display as a month and year. However, when I format a date to look like a month, I know by looking at the formula bar that the underlying value still really includes the day as well as the month and year.

Strategy: Use a combination of YEAR(), MONTH(), DAY(), and DATE() functions. The first three functions will break a date into component parts.
- =YEAR(A2) will return 2016 for the year
- =MONTH(A2) will return 7 for July
- =DAY(A2) will return 14 from July 14th.

`=YEAR(A2)`

	A	B	C	D
1	Date	Year	Month	Day
2	7/14/2016	2016	7	14
3	3/3/2015	2015	3	3
4	4/14/2016	2016	4	14
5				
6		B2: =YEAR(A2)		
7		C2: =MONTH(A2)		
8		D2: =DAY(A2)		

Figure 545 *Break dates into component parts.*

Since Excel gives you three functions to break dates apart, they also give you one amazing function to put dates back together: =DATE(Year, Month, Day) will convert the three component parts back into a real date.

To calculate the first of the month, you can use =DATE(B2,C2,1). Replacing the Day argument with a 1 will force the calculation back to the first of the month.

`=DATE(B2,C2,1)`

	A	B	C	D	E
1	Date	Year	Month	Day	First of Month
2	7/14/2016	2016	7	14	7/1/2016
3	3/3/2015	2015	3	3	3/1/2015
4	4/14/2016	2016	4	14	4/1/2016

Figure 546 *Calculate the first of the month.*

Alternate Strategy: You can express the calculation in a single formula with: =DATE(Year(A2),Month(A2),1). Or, you can use =A2-DAY(A2)+1.

CALCULATE THE LAST DAY OF THE MONTH

Problem: I need to calculate the last of the month. What the heck was that poem?

Poetry	Excel Poetry
Thirty days hath September, April, June, and November; All the rest have thirty-one, Save February, with twenty-eight days clear, And twenty-nine each leap year, except in 1900, 2100, 2200, 2300, and 2500.	=CHOOSE(MONTH(A2), 31,28,31,30,31,30,31,31,30,31,30,31)+ IF(AND(MONTH(A2)=2,MOD(YEAR,4)=0) ,1,0)- IF(OR(YEAR(A2)=1900,YEAR(A2)=2100), 1,0)

Figure 547 *Don't try the formula on the right.*

Strategy: Don't try coding that poem about the number of days. The DATE() function will handle this easily, with one clever trick. Don't try to go to the 31st or 30th or 28th of the month. Instead, go to the first of the next month and then subtract 1!

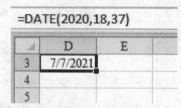

=DATE(YEAR(A2),MONTH(A2)+1,1)-1

▲	A	F	G
1	Date	Last of Month	
2	7/14/2016	7/31/2016	
3	12/15/2015	12/31/2015	
4	4/14/2016	4/30/2016	

Figure 548 *Go to the first of the next month and subtract 1.*

This is a clever approach, isn't it?

How does it manage to work in December? You are asking for the first of the 13th month of 2015. Excel has no problem figuring out that =DATE(2015,13,1) is January 1 of 2016. In fact, here is the 37th day of the 18th month of 2020:

=DATE(2020,18,37)

▲	D	E
3	7/7/2021	
4		
5		

Figure 549 *The DATE function is incredibly versatile.*

The DATE function can even sort of handle negatives, with one twist. A zero in the month or day argument is treated as "the item before 1". Thus, using -1 as the month will actually go back two months.

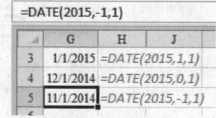

=DATE(2015,-1,1)

▲	G	H	J
3	1/1/2015	=DATE(2015,1,1)	
4	12/1/2014	=DATE(2015,0,1)	
5	11/1/2014	=DATE(2015,-1,1)	

Figure 550 *To go back one month, use 0 as the month.*

This previous trick makes the original question even easier. To go to the end of this month, you would go to the 0th of the next month. =DATE(YEAR(A2),MONTH(A2)+1,0).

```
=DATE(YEAR(A2),MONTH(A2)+1,0)
```

▲	A	F	G
1	Date	Last of Month	
2	7/14/2016	7/31/2016	
3	12/15/2015	12/31/2015	
4	4/14/2016	4/30/2016	

Figure 551 *Shorter formula for end of month.*

If you are sure you won't be sharing the workbook with anyone using Excel 2003, you can safely use the EOMONTH function to show the end of this month, last month, two months from now, and so on.

```
=EOMONTH($A3,B$2)
```

▲	A	B	C	D	E	F
1		This Month	Next Month	Two Months	Prior Month	2 Mos Ago
2	Date	0	1	2	-1	-2
3	7/14/2016	7/31/16	8/31/16	9/30/16	6/30/16	5/31/16
4	12/15/2015	12/31/15	1/31/16	2/29/16	11/30/15	10/31/15
5	4/14/2016	4/30/16	5/31/16	6/30/16	3/31/16	2/29/16
6	11/12/2014	11/30/14	12/31/14	1/31/15	10/31/14	9/30/14
7	9/21/2015	9/30/15	10/31/15	11/30/15	8/31/15	7/31/15

Figure 552 *Get the end of month from N months from now.*

CALCULATE INVOICE DUE DATES

Problem: I have a spreadsheet of payables. I need to sort by Due Date, but all I have is invoice date and terms.

▲	A	B	C	D
1	Vendor	Inv Date	Terms	Due Date
2	G	1/13/2015	60	
3	J	3/10/2015	7	
4	G	1/20/2015	60	

Figure 553 *Calculate the due date for each invoice.*

Strategy: This one is simple for Excel. Simply add =B2+C2. You should get a date. If you get a number, then format the result as a date.

```
=C2+B2
```

▲	A	B	C	D
1	Vendor	Inv Date	Terms	Due Date
2	G	1/13/2015	60	3/14/2015
3	J	3/10/2015	7	3/17/2015
4	G	1/20/2015	60	3/21/2015

Figure 554 *Add a date and a number and you get a date.*

CALCULATE RECEIVABLE AGING

Problem: I have a worksheet showing open invoices. I want to calculate how many days old each unpaid invoice is.

	A	B	C
1	Invoice Aging as of June 3, 2011		
2			
3	Customer	Inv Date	Aging
4	C	4/8/2011	
5	G	1/14/2011	
6	G	1/5/2011	
7	E	2/4/2011	
8	E	5/3/2011	

Figure 555 *Which invoices are >30 days past due?*

Strategy: Subtract the invoice date from the TODAY() function. The TODAY() function will give you the current date. Each day that you open the workbook, the calculation will update.

Gotcha: You want the number of days. Excel will guess that you want the answer as a date. After entering the formula, change the number format back to numeric.

Additional Details: The title in cell A1 is created using TODAY as well. The formula is ="Invoice Aging as of "&TEXT(TODAY(),"MMMM d, YYYY").

Additional Details: The icons in column C were added using Conditional Formatting. You will read about icon sets in Part IV of this book. The accountant in me could not resist analyzing the result, *even though this data is completely fictitious!*

`=TODAY()-B4`

	A	B	C
1	Invoice Aging as of June 3, 2011		
2			
3	Customer	Inv Date	Aging
4	C	4/8/2011	❗ 56
5	G	1/14/2011	✖ 140
6	G	1/5/2011	✖ 149
7	E	2/4/2011	✖ 119
8	E	5/3/2011	❗ 31
9	C	5/19/2011	✔ 15

Figure 556 *Use TODAY() to calculate days away.*

You might want to categorize the receivables into 30-day buckets. The formula in D4 will show 30 for any invoices that are between 30 and 59 days old. The formula is =INT(C6/30)*30. Say that you divided column C by 30 and then took the INT of the result. Everything from 0 to 29 would be classified into Bucket 0. Everything from 30 to 59 would be classified as Bucket 1. I multiply that bucket number by 30 to provide a better name for each bucket. To get the plus sign to show, use a custom number format of 0+.

`=INT(C6/30)*30`

	A	B	C	D
1	Invoice Aging as of June 3, 2011			
2				
3	Customer	Inv Date	Aging	Bucket
6	G	1/5/2011	✖ 149	120+
7	E	2/4/2011	✖ 119	90+
8	E	5/3/2011	❗ 31	30+
9	C	5/19/2011	✔ 15	0+
10	E	4/6/2011	❗ 58	30+

Figure 557 *Grouping receivables into buckets.*

NOW, OR TODAY?

Problem: Why did you use TODAY() in the previous topic. Isn't this the same as NOW()?

Strategy: The NOW function will return the date and time that the workbook was last calculated. Workbooks are calculated when they are opened, when you enter a value in the worksheet, or when you press the F9 key. In other words, they are calculated a lot.

If you enter NOW in a cell, it will generally show the current date and a fairly recent time.

The TODAY function is similar to NOW, except it returns only the current date. In many cases, the TODAY function is more appropriate for calculating the number of days between today and a deadline.

Below, cell B1 contains a due date. If you calculate =B1-NOW(), Excel will say that it is 12.561 days away. If you calculate =B1-TODAY(), Excel will say that it is 13 days away. If you go into work on Monday, then most people would say that Wednesday is 2 days away. If you use NOW instead of TODAY then at 9 a.m., Excel would say that Wednesday is 1.625 days away.

⊿	A	B	C	D
1	Due Date:	6/16/2011		
2				
3	NOW:	6/3/2011 10:31	=NOW()	
4				
5	TODAY:	6/3/2011	=TODAY()	
6				
7	Days until deadline using NOW:	12.561	=B1-NOW()	
8				
9	Days until deadline using TODAY:	13.000	=B1-TODAY()	
10				

Figure 558 *For whole days, use TODAY instead of NOW.*

Additional Details: To calculate the current time, you could use =NOW()-TODAY() or =MOD(NOW(),1). Make sure to format the resulting cell as a time.

FIND THE LAST SUNDAY OF THE MONTH

Problem: I have a column of dates. I need to post-date those dates to the last Sunday of the month. Or, I need to pre-date those to the first Monday of the month. Or, pre-date the date to the previous Monday, but only if today isn't already a Monday. Or, post-date to the next Friday, but only if today isn't a Friday.

Strategy: Use a formula from the table in this topic.

Excel offers a WEEKDAY function that helps you to identify the weekday of the date.

The function historically offered 3 ways to identify the weekday. The traditional method used 1 for Sunday through 7 for Saturday. The return type of 2 used 1 for Monday and 7 for Sunday. The return type of 3 used 0 for Monday and 6 for Sunday. That last return type was great for calculating the "Week Beginning". You could use =A2-WEEKDAY(A2,2) and all dates would go back to Monday.

Today, Excel offers 7 additional return types, numbered 11 through 17. Here is the tooltip explaining them all.

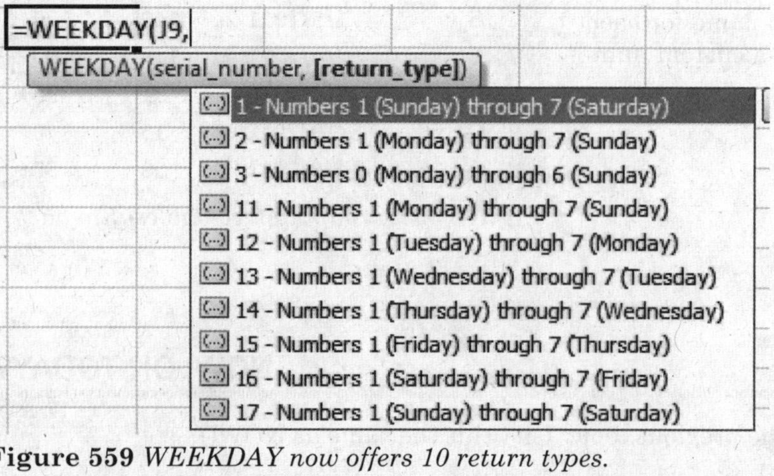

```
=WEEKDAY(J9,
  WEEKDAY(serial_number, [return_type])
    1 - Numbers 1 (Sunday) through 7 (Saturday)
    2 - Numbers 1 (Monday) through 7 (Sunday)
    3 - Numbers 0 (Monday) through 6 (Sunday)
    11 - Numbers 1 (Monday) through 7 (Sunday)
    12 - Numbers 1 (Tuesday) through 7 (Monday)
    13 - Numbers 1 (Wednesday) through 7 (Tuesday)
    14 - Numbers 1 (Thursday) through 7 (Wednesday)
    15 - Numbers 1 (Friday) through 7 (Thursday)
    16 - Numbers 1 (Saturday) through 7 (Friday)
    17 - Numbers 1 (Sunday) through 7 (Saturday)
```

Figure 559 *WEEKDAY now offers 10 return types.*

If you sit down to figure these calculations out, you really have to love the brilliance of the return type 3 with its results of 0 through 6. All of the ones that result in 1 through 7 make your formula much harder.

Lets say that you want to roll a date back to Sunday. The date is in A2. If the date happens to fall on a Monday, the WEEKDAY(A2,11) is 1. So, life is simple, you could use =A2-WEEKDAY(A2,11) to roll the Monday back to Sunday. This logic works throughout the week, all the way up through Saturday. The WEEKDAY(,11) of a Saturday is 6, so =A2-WEEKDAY(A2,11) will subtract 6 from the date and you end up on the prior Sunday. The formula falls apart when A2 already is a Sunday. =WEEKDAY(,11) of a Sunday is 7. When you subtract 7 from the current date, you end up a week too early.

Here you are, with a WEEKDAY function that works 6 out of 7 days. Whenever the WEEKDAY function returns a 7, you need it to be a zero.

Enter the MOD function. Calculate the WEEKDAY, then take the MOD(Weekday(),7). For the numbers 1 through 6, the MOD will be 1 through 6. But for the number 7, the MOD will be 0. Perfect.

For background, MOD stands for MODULO. =MOD(100,7) takes 100, divides by 7, throws out the integer portion, then expresses the remainder as a whole number. 100 divided by 7 is 14 with a remainder of 2. =MOD(100,7) will give you the remainder of 2.

Are you still reading? This gets incredibly complex. Below are two tables showing all of the formulas that you will need. The tables assume that your date is in A2.

EXCEL 2010 FORMULAS FOR (FIRST|LAST) (SUN|MON|TUE|WED|THU|FRI|SAT) OF MONTH	
Last Sun of the month	=EOMONTH(A2,0)-MOD(WEEKDAY(EOMONTH(A2,0),11),7)
Last Mon of the month	=EOMONTH(A2,0)-MOD(WEEKDAY(EOMONTH(A2,0),12),7)
Last Tues of the month	=EOMONTH(A2,0)-MOD(WEEKDAY(EOMONTH(A2,0),13),7)
Last Wed of the month	=EOMONTH(A2,0)-MOD(WEEKDAY(EOMONTH(A2,0),14),7)
Last Thurs of the month	=EOMONTH(A2,0)-MOD(WEEKDAY(EOMONTH(A2,0),15),7)
Last Fri of the month	=EOMONTH(A2,0)-MOD(WEEKDAY(EOMONTH(A2,0),16),7)
Last Sat of the month	=EOMONTH(A2,0)-MOD(WEEKDAY(EOMONTH(A2,0),17),7)
First Sun of the month	=EOMONTH(A2,-1)+1+MOD((7-WEEKDAY(EOMONTH(A2,-1)+1,11)),7)
First Mon of the month	=EOMONTH(A2,-1)+1+MOD((7-WEEKDAY(EOMONTH(A2,-1)+1,12)),7)
First Tues of the month	=EOMONTH(A2,-1)+1+MOD((7-WEEKDAY(EOMONTH(A2,-1)+1,13)),7)
First Wed of the month	=EOMONTH(A2,-1)+1+MOD((7-WEEKDAY(EOMONTH(A2,-1)+1,14)),7)
First Thurs of the month	=EOMONTH(A2,-1)+1+MOD((7-WEEKDAY(EOMONTH(A2,-1)+1,15)),7)
First Fri of the month	=EOMONTH(A2,-1)+1+MOD((7-WEEKDAY(EOMONTH(A2,-1)+1,16)),7)
First Sat of the month	=EOMONTH(A2,-1)+1+MOD((7-WEEKDAY(EOMONTH(A2,-1)+1,17)),7)

Figure 560 *Find the last weekday of the month.*

If you need to build "Week of" dates, these formulas will work.

EXCEL 2010 FORMULAS FOR WEEK (BEG|END) ON WEEKDAY	
Week beg. Sun	=A2-MOD(WEEKDAY(A2,11),7)
Week beg. Mon	=A2-WEEKDAY(A2,3)
Week beg. Tues	=A2-MOD(WEEKDAY(A2,13),7)
Week beg. Wed	=A2-MOD(WEEKDAY(A2,14),7)
Week beg. Thurs	=A2-MOD(WEEKDAY(A2,15),7)
Week beg. Fri	=A2-MOD(WEEKDAY(A2,16),7)
Week beg. Sat	=A2-MOD(WEEKDAY(A2,17),7)
Week ending Sun	=A2+(7-WEEKDAY(A2,11))
Week ending Mon	=A2+(7-WEEKDAY(A2,12))
Week ending Tues	=A2+(7-WEEKDAY(A2,13))
Week ending Wed	=A2+(7-WEEKDAY(A2,14))
Week ending Thurs	=A2+(7-WEEKDAY(A2,15))
Week ending Fri	=A2+(7-WEEKDAY(A2,16))
Week ending Sat	=A2+(7-WEEKDAY(A2,17))

Figure 561 *Change the date in A2 to a week beginning date.*

If you are in Excel 2007 or earlier, then you are limited to the return types of 1, 2, or 3. The following table uses CHOOSE to add or subtract the appropriate number of days.

EXCEL 97-2007 FORMULAS FOR WEEK BEGINNING ON WEEKDAY	
Week beg. Sun	=A2-CHOOSE(WEEKDAY(A2),0,1,2,3,4,5,6)
Week beg. Mon	=A2-WEEKDAY(A2,3)
Week beg. Tues	=A2-CHOOSE(WEEKDAY(A2),5,6,0,1,2,3,4)
Week beg. Wed	=A2-CHOOSE(WEEKDAY(A2),4,5,6,0,1,2,3)
Week beg. Thurs	=A2-CHOOSE(WEEKDAY(A2),3,4,5,6,0,1,2)
Week beg. Fri	=A2-CHOOSE(WEEKDAY(A2),2,3,4,5,6,0,1)
Week beg. Sat	=A2-CHOOSE(WEEKDAY(A2),1,2,3,4,5,6,0)
Week ending Sun	=A2+CHOOSE(WEEKDAY(A2),0,6,5,4,3,2,1)
Week ending Mon	=A2+CHOOSE(WEEKDAY(A2),1,0,6,5,4,3,2)
Week ending Tues	=A2+CHOOSE(WEEKDAY(A2),2,1,0,6,5,4,3)
Week ending Wed	=A2+CHOOSE(WEEKDAY(A2),3,2,1,0,6,5,4)
Week ending Thurs	=A2+CHOOSE(WEEKDAY(A2),4,3,2,1,0,6,5)
Week ending Fri	=A2+CHOOSE(WEEKDAY(A2),5,4,3,2,1,0,6)
Week ending Sat	=A2+CHOOSE(WEEKDAY(A2),6,5,4,3,2,1,0)

Figure 562 *Back in Excel 2007, WEEKDAY offered less options.*

CALCULATE WORK DAYS

Problem: We have a big project due on April 15. I need to figure out how many work days until the project is due.

Strategy: If you work Monday through Friday, use NETWORKDAYS. If you have another work week, use NETWORKDAYS.INTL. Both functions allow you to specify a list of company holidays and will factor the holidays into the calculation.

You specify a start date, an end date, and a list of company holidays. Excel will calculate the number or work days including the beginning and ending date.

1. In a blank range in your worksheet, enter the company holidays for this year. Be sure to include the year. Instead of 12/25, enter 12/25/2014. Say that you store this list in I3:I10.
2. Enter the formula =NETWORKDAYS(C3,B3,$I$3:$I$10) in cell D3. Note that the argument containing the holidays should be an absolute reference with dollar signs.
3. Copy the formula down for all projects.

`=NETWORKDAYS(C3,B3,$I$3:$I$10)`

	A	B	C	D	E	F	G	H	I
1				Mon-Fri	Mon-Sat				2014 Company
2	Proj.	Due Date	Today	Work Days	Work Days				Holidays
3	A	Tue, 4/15/14	Mon, 2/17/14	42	50				1/1/2014
4	B	Tue, 7/15/14	Mon, 2/17/14	105	126				5/26/2014
5	C	Thu, 1/1/15	Mon, 2/17/14	222	267				7/4/2014
6	D	Mon, 2/24/14	Mon, 2/17/14	6	7				9/1/2014
7	E	Thu, 1/23/14	Mon, 2/17/14	-18	-22				11/27/2014
8									11/28/2014
9									12/25/2014
10									12/26/2014

Figure 563 *Column D counts days excluding weekends & holidays.*

Before Excel 2010, the NETWORKDAYS always assumed the weekend is Saturday and Sunday. If you have an alternate weekend, the NETWORKDAYS.INTL function will handle it.

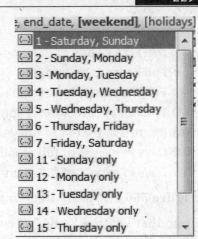

Figure 564 *New in Excel 2010, you can set the weekend.*

Column E in Figure 563 calculates a Monday-Saturday workweek with =NETWORKDAYS.INTL(C3,B3,11,$I$3:$I$10).

Be aware that Excel is counting both the beginning and ending date. From Monday 2/17 to Monday 2/24, the NETWORKDAYS is calculating six days. That may not be the best answer at 5PM on Monday 2/17.

Additional Details: Enter the holidays on another worksheet and name the range something like HOLIDAYS. You don't have to worry about inadvertently deleting a project and wiping out one of the holidays out to the right.

An alternate strategy to protect the holidays out in I is to select cells J3:J10. Enter =1 and then press Ctrl+Shift+Enter. This will create a lame array formula in column J. If anyone tries to delete a row from 3 to 10, Excel will refuse with the somewhat cryptic, "You Can Not Change Part Of An Array" message.

If you have a starting date and want to go out 15 work days from the starting date, take a look at the WORKDAY and WORKDAY.INTL functions.

CALCULATE WORK DAYS FOR A FARMERS MARKET

Problem: Those new settings in NETWORKDAYS.INTL don't help me. Our business is only open Monday, Wednesday, Friday, and Saturday.

Strategy: There is an alternate way to specify the third argument. Instead of specifying 1-7 or 11-17, you can specify a 7-digit text string comprised of 1's and 0's. The first character in the text is Monday. The seventh character is Sunday. Remember the name of this argument is [weekend]. Thus, a 1 indicates that the business is closed and a 0 indicates that the business is open.

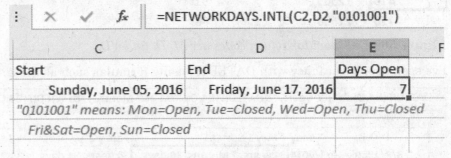

Figure 565 *Use the "0010001" argument for Barber Shops.*

CALCULATE AGE IN YEARS, MONTHS, DAYS

Problem: I work in Human Resources. On our employee census, I need to calculate age in years and months.

Strategy: Use the super-secret DATEDIF function. Microsoft documented this function in Excel 2000 and never spoke of it since. Yet, it has been in Excel since the mid-nineties.

Use =DATEDIF(Earlier Date, Later Date, Return_Code).

The return codes are not entirely intuitive. They are shown here.

	DATEDIF Codes	
Y	Full Years as an integer	
M	Full Months as an integer	
D	Total Days (use subtraction instead...)	
YM	Months in excess of full years	
MD	Days in excess of full months	
YD	Days in excess of full years	

Figure 566 *The third argument of DATEDIF.*

From that list, the Y and YM codes would solve the question at the top of this topic. The following shows Years, Months, and Days.

`=DATEDIF($B4,$C4,D$1)`

▲	A	B	C	D	E	F
1				Y	YM	MD
2						
3	Employee	D.O.B.	Today	Years	Months	Days
4	Amber	3/2/1980	6/1/2014	34	2	30
5	Bob	3/5/1955	6/1/2014	59	2	27
6	Carole	2/10/1948	6/1/2014	66	3	22
7	Dale	8/12/1956	6/1/2014	57	9	20
8	Ed	12/25/1945	6/1/2014	68	5	7
9	Flo	3/1/1944	6/1/2014	70	3	0
10	Gary	5/1/1986	6/1/2014	28	1	0

Figure 567 *DATEDIF calculates years, months, and days.*

The less popular return codes are M for a complete count of full months, D for a complete count of days, and YD for the number of days in excess of full years.

H	I	J
M	D	YD
All Months	All Days	Days beyond year
410	12509	91
710	21638	88

Figure 568 *Less popular return codes are M, D, and YD.*

I've seen people get fancy with DATEDIF, using formulas such as these.

`=DATEDIF(B4,C4,"Y")&" years, "&DATEDIF(B4,C4,"YM")&" Months, "&DATEDIF(B4,C4,"MD")&" days."`

▲	B	C	K	L	M	N
3	D.O.B.	Today	Fancy 1	Fancy 2	Y.M	
4	3/2/1980	6/1/2014	34 years, 2 Months, 30 days.	34 years, 91 days.	34.2	
5	3/5/1955	6/1/2014	59 years, 2 Months, 27 days.	59 years, 88 days.	59.2	
6	6/10/1948	6/1/2014	65 years, 11 Months, 22 days.	65 years, 356 days.	65.11	

Figure 569 *Concatenating multiple DATEDIF functions.*

The formula in K is
```
=DATEDIF(B4,C4,"Y")&" years, "&DATEDIF(B4,C4,"YM")&" Months,
"&DATEDIF(B4,C4,"MD")&" days."
```

The formula in L is
```
=DATEDIF(B4,C4,"Y")&" years, "&DATEDIF(B4,C4,"YD")&" days."
```

The formula in M is
```
=DATEDIF(B4,C4,"Y")&"."&DATEDIF(B4,C4,"YM")
```

Gotcha: Here is the reason why Microsoft stopped documenting DATEDIF. When you calculate the DATE-DIF between January 31 and March 1, you get 1 month and negative two days. It was probably easier to stop documenting DATEDIF than to explain how this happens.

=DATEDIF($B5,$C5,F$2)					
	A	B	C	D	E	F
2				Y	YM	MD
4	Employee	D.O.B.	Today	Years	Months	Days
5	Helen	1/31/1974	3/1/2014	40	1	-2

Figure 570 *There are 29 days between 1/31 and 3/1. Not quite a month.*

COERCE AN ARRAY OF DATES FROM 2 DATES

Problem: I have a start date in A and an end date in B. I need to see how many days between those two dates fell on Friday the 13th.

Strategy: This formula came from the MrExcel.com message board. It is one of the coolest formulas that I have ever seen. This one formula will replace 108,000 formulas.

While this formula is figuring out the number of Friday the thirteenths, you can use this method any time you need to compare every date between two dates to something.

I will show you the formula first and then explain it in detail.

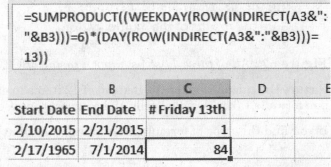

```
=SUMPRODUCT((WEEKDAY(ROW(INDIRECT(A3&":
"&B3)))=6)*(DAY(ROW(INDIRECT(A3&":"&B3)))=
13))
```

	B	C	D	E
Start Date	End Date	# Friday 13th		
2/10/2015	2/21/2015	1		
2/17/1965	7/1/2014	84		

Figure 571 *This one formula does 108,000 calculations.*

The explanation here is about row 2. The same concept applies to row 3.

1. Remember that dates are really stored as the number of days elapsed since January 1, 1900. The date in A2 is really stored as 42045.
2. The date in B2 is really stored as 42056.
3. Concatenate those two numbers with a colon in between. You get 42045:42056. This is actually a valid Excel reference. It refers to all of the rows from 42045 to 42056.
4. Take the text from #3 and put it inside an INDIRECT(42045:42056) function. Since that is a valid reference, you now are referencing a range of all the rows from 42045 to 42056.
5. Use the ROW() function on the reference from step 4. You now have an array of row numbers: {42045; 42046; 42047; 42048; 42049; 42050; 42051; 42052; 42053; 42054; 42055; 42056}. Note that this array is relatively small. Down in row 3, there will be 18,000 numbers in the array. For the rest of the steps, stop thinking about those as numbers and start thinking about them as dates.
6. Take the WEEKDAY() of each number in the array from #5. You get {3; 4; 5; 6; 7; 1; 2; 3; 4; 5; 6; 7}. In this version of WEEKDAY, Sunday is 1 and Friday is 6.
7. Test to see if the results of step 6 are equal to 6 which means Friday. You now have an array of True/False values: {False; False; False; True; False; False; False; False; False; False; True; False}.
8. Go back to that array from step 5 and put it in the DAY() function. This will return an array of only the day portion of the date: {10; 11; 12; 13; 14; 15; 16; 17; 18; 19; 20; 21}.
9. Take the array from 8 and test to see if it is 13. {False; False; False; True; False; False; False; False; False; False; False}.

10. Multiply the array from 7 by the array from 9. If both have a TRUE in the same position you will get a 1, otherwise a 0. You get: {0; 0; 0; 1; 0; 0; 0; 0; 0; 0; 0; 0; 0}.

11. Sum all of the 1's from step 10 using SUMPRODUCT. In this case, you get a 1 as the total. In the case of row 3, you get 84 occurrences of Friday the 13th in a span of 49 years.

It might help to picture the calculation happening in Excel.

Step		
1	The date in A2 really is stored as:	42045
2	The date in B2 really is stored as	42056
3	Join those with a : in between	42045:42056
4	When you take the indirect of that text, you refer to a bunch of rows.	
5	Take the row of the indirect, and you end up with an array of rows:	
	{41680; 41681; 41682; 41683; 41684; 41685; 41686; 41687; 41688; 41689; 41690; 41691}	
	Start treating those numbers as dates again	
6	Get the weekday of each date	
	{2; 3; 4; 5; 6; 7; 1; 2; 3; 4; 5; 6}	
7	Are those equal to 5 (Friday)?	
	{False; False; False; True; False; False; False; False; False; False; True; False}	
8	Get the day of each date from step 5	
	{10; 11; 12; 13; 14; 15; 16; 17; 18; 19; 20; 21}	
9	Are those days equal to 13?	
	{False; False; False; True; False; False; False; False; False; False; False; False}	
10	Multiply the two arrays of 1 and 0	
	{0; 0; 0; 1; 0; 0; 0; 0; 0; 0; 0; 0}	
11	Sum the results of the multiplication	
	1	

Figure 572 *All of these 11 steps happen inside of C2.*

Picture the calculation for C3. instead of 12 items in each array, there are 18,000 items in each array. That one formula takes two date cells and coerces it into several arrays of 18,000 items each.

If you find this type of formula interesting, check out my other book, Excel Gurus Gone Wild.

USE REAL TIMES

Problem: How does Excel deal with time?

Strategy: In Excel, 1 day is represented by the number 1. That means that time is stored as a decimal portion of a day. Go to any cell. Enter 0.5. Format the cell as time and you will get 12 noon, because half of the day has elapsed at noon.

I can name a few other times right off the top of my head. 6AM is stored as 0.25. 9PM is stored as 0.875. 3AM is 0.125. Beyond that, it gets a tougher. What fraction of the day has elapsed at 3:42PM. That is a little tougher to calculate in your head.

◢	A	B	C	D	E	F	G	H	I
1	0.01	0.125	0.25	0.375	0.5	0.625	0.75	0.875	0.99
2	↓	↓	↓	↓	↓	↓	↓	↓	↓
3	12:14 AM	3:00 AM	6:00 AM	9:00 AM	12:00 PM	3:00 PM	6:00 PM	9:00 PM	11:45 PM

Figure 573 *Format the numbers in row 1 as time and you get row 3.*

In the next figure, I used =RAND() in a bunch of cells and formatted those as time.

0.370956	0.025731	0.696154	0.588132
↓	↓	↓	↓
9:36 AM	6:06 PM	2:12 PM	2:54 AM

Figure 574 *Random decimals correspond to various times of the day.*

STRANGENESS OF TIME FORMATTING

Problem: Something is strange with time formatting. I can't total my time sheet to show 40 hours.

Strategy: Do you remember when you had a date and you formatted it to show only one element of the date? All of the cells in column C contain the exact same value, but they have a different numeric format.

=$C$1		

◢	A	B	C	D
1			6/3/2011 16:25	
3			Jun	*Formatted as MMM*
4			3	*Formatted as D*
5			2011	*Formatted as YYYY*
7			16	*Formatted as H*
8			16:25	*Formatted as H:MM*
9			40697.68432	*Formatted as General*

Figure 575 *Control the display of a value using format codes.*

In cell C4, you are asking Excel to show you only the date, so it gives you a 3. That is exactly what you asked for. You didn't ask to see years or months, so it did not include that value.

In contrast, consider the following time sheet.

=SUM(H10:H14)	

◢	G	H
10	Monday	8:00
11	Tuesday	9:00
12	Weds	8:00
13	Thurs	8:00
14	Friday	7:00
15	Total	16:00
16		

Figure 576 *The payroll department will save on salary expense here.*

Everyone looks at cell H15 and says that something is wrong. It should be 40 hours, not 16 hours.

But Excel is doing the same thing here that it did back in Figure 575. You formatted H15 with the H:MM format, so Excel threw out the date portion of the value. Think about it. 40 hours is really 1 day and 16 hours. All that you are seeing in H15 is the 16 hours. You didn't ask to see the day.

Since time tracking is a common activity in Excel, there must be a solution.

There is, but it is not easy to figure out.

Select cell H15. Use Ctrl+One to Format Cells. Select the Time category. Scroll down until you see the time format with 37:30:55.

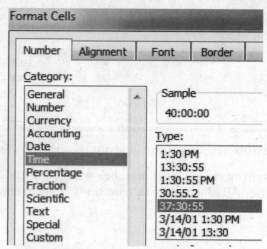

Figure 577 *Choose 37:30:50 to display hours in excess of one day.*

This will show your time as 40:00:00.

In reality, you have more flexibility if you use the Custom category. Choose the 37:30:50 and then click on Custom. You will see the code is [H]:MM:SS. The square brackets are the code to tell Excel that you want to see all hours, not just the hours in excess of whole days.

	G	H
10	Monday	8:00
11	Tuesday	9:00
12	Weds	8:00
13	Thurs	8:00
14	Friday	7:00
15	Total	40:00:00
16		

Figure 578 *Forty hours.*

You can extrapolate the following custom codes:

[H]:MM is the format you want for the time sheet.

You can also display the absolute number of minutes or seconds using formats of [D] or [S].

Format	Displays
h:mm AM	3:00 AM
[M]	180
[S]	10800

Figure 579 *3AM is 180 minutes past midnight.*

CONVERT TIME TO DECIMAL HOURS

Problem: I bill my clients hourly. How can I convert Excel times to decimal hours so that I can do my billing?

Strategy: Multiply the Excel by 24 to come up with a decimal number of hours. You can them multiply the hours by the hourly rate to calculate the billing.

`=B2*24`

	A	B	C	D	E
1	Client	Total Time	Hours	Rate	Bill
2	A	65:00	65.00	$65	$4,225.00
3	B	71:30	71.50	$65	$4,647.50
4	C	23:15	23.25	$65	$1,511.25
5	D	56:45	56.75	$65	$3,688.75
6	E	73:30	73.50	$65	$4,777.50
7	F	37:15	37.25	$65	$2,421.25
8	G	35:00	35.00	$65	$2,275.00
9		362:15	362.25		$23,546.25

Figure 580 *Multiply times by 24 to get hours.*

CALCULATE WITH TIME

Problem: I need to do calculations by hour.

Strategy: There are functions HOUR, MINUTE, and SECOND to break a time into components. There is a function TIME(Hour,Minute,Second) to put time back together.

`=TIME(HOUR(A2),0,0)`

	A	B	C	D
1	Time	Hour	Hour	Hour
2	11:31	11	11:00	12:00
3	10:28	10	10:00	10:00
4	15:17	15	15:00	15:00
5		B2: =HOUR(A2)		
6		C2: =TIME(HOUR(A2),0,0)		
7		D2: =MROUND(A2,(1/24))		
8				

Figure 581 *Time calculations.*

ENTER MINUTES AND SECONDS

Problem: I have to keep track of test data in minutes and seconds.

Strategy: This is much more difficult than anyone would think. Say that the first test took 1 minute and 30 seconds. You try entering 1:30 in a cell.

	A	B
1	Trial #	Result
2	Test 1	1:30
3	Test 2	
4	Test 3	
5	Test 4	

Figure 582 *What does the value in B2 really mean?*

The result looks OK. However, when you click on the cell, you see that Excel has interpreted the entry as 1:30 AM, which is 1 hour and 30 minutes instead of 1 minute and 30 seconds.

1:30:00 AM

	A	B	
1	Trial #	Result	
2	Test 1	1:30	
3	Test 2		
4	Test 3		

Figure 583 *Excel assumed you meant 1 hour and 30 minutes.*

To enter minutes and seconds, you have to enter 0:01:30. This seems like a frustrating waste of extra keystrokes.

If you have entered a column of time in the wrong format, you can correct it with =TIME(0,HOUR(A2),MINUTE(A2)). Alternatively, multiply the times by (1/60).

=TIME(0,HOUR(B2),MINUTE(B2))

	A	B	C	D	E
1	Trial #	Result	Corrected	Corrected	
2	Test 1	1:30	1:30	0:01:30	=B2*(1/60)
3	Test 2	2:35	2:35	0:02:35	

Figure 584 *Two ways to correct time that has been entered incorrectly.*

CONVERT TEXT TO TIME

Problem: I have a spreadsheet where the times were imported as text.

Strategy: Use TIMEVALUE to convert the text to time. However, the text dates have to be in the correct format.

Below, text entries in column A are converted with TIMEVALUE in column B. Some formats work. Others do not.

	A	B	C	D	E	F	G
1	TIMEVALUE TESTS						
2							
3	Text	TIMEVALUE					
4	1:23:45 AM	1:23:45 AM					
5	2:34:56 PM	2:34:56 PM					
6	3:45:61 AM	#VALUE!	Not a valid time (61 seconds)				
7	1:30 AM	1:30:00 AM					
8	123:40	3:40:00 AM	Treated as 123 hours, 40 minutes, less whole days				
9	15:30	3:30:00 PM					
10	15:30:15	3:30:15 PM					
11	1:23:45AM	#VALUE!	No space before AM				
12	1:23:45	1:23:45 AM					
13	1:23:45.3	1:23:45 AM	Tenths of seconds OK				
14	1:23:40 1:30 PM	#VALUE!	Can not deal with days				
15							

Figure 585 *Results of TIMEVALUE.*

One common issue is that TIMEVALUE requires a space between the time and AM or PM. If you have a lot of text like cell D11 above, try using Find and Replace to change "AM" to " AM" and "PM" to " PM".

Another **problem:** both TIME and TIMEVALUE will not return a number greater than 23 hours, 59 minutes, and 59 seconds. In row 8 above, the entry in interpreted as 123 hours and 40 minutes. This is 5 days and 3 hours. TIMEVALUE figures this out, but then truncates the 5 days and only returns 3 hours. If you had data entered in this format, you could use a formula such as: =LEFT(A8,FIND(":",A8)-1)*(1/24)+MID (A8,FIND(":",A8)+1,50)*(1/1440).

CAN EXCEL TRACK NEGATIVE TIME?

Problem: I keep track of comp time for employees. If employees work more than 8 hours, this time gets put into a bank so that they can work less time on another day. The company will generally let people go a few hours into the negative. But Excel completely freaks out when my formula results in a negative time.

`=E5+(D6-TIME(8,0,0))`

	A	B	C	D	E	F
1	Date	Start	End	Total	Comp Time Balance	
2	2/17/2014	8:00 AM	4:00 PM	8:00	2:00	
3	2/18/2014	8:00 AM	6:00 PM	10:00	4:00	
4	2/19/2014	8:00 AM	6:00 PM	10:00	6:00	
5	2/20/2014	8:00 AM	12:00 PM	4:00	2:00	
6	2/21/2014	8:00 AM	12:00 PM	4:00	########	

Figure 586 *Cell E6 is -2 hours, but Excel refuses to display the value.*

Strategy: The solution to this problem seems bizarre. You should make this change only on a worksheet that doesn't contain any existing date values.

Excel for Windows stores dates as the number of days elapsed since January 1, 1900. Excel for the Macintosh stores dates as the number of days since January 2, 1904. In case you are sharing files with a Mac, Excel has a setting which indicates that dates should be displayed in the 1904 system. Basically, Excel will adjust the date by 1,462 days when you choose this system.

In the figure above, -2 hours works out to 10 p.m. on December 31, 1899. Excel simply won't display dates from 1899. But if you go 2 hours before January 2, 1904, you happen to have a date and time that Excel is willing to display!

To switch to the 1904 date system, use File, Options, Advanced. Scroll down to When Calculating in This Workbook. Turn on the check box for Use 1904 Date System.

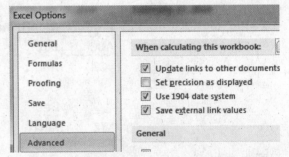

Figure 587 *Convert the workbook to the 1904 date system.*

Excel will now display negative times.

	A	B	C	D	E	F
1	Date	Start	End	Total	Comp Time Balance	
2	2/18/2018	8:00 AM	4:00 PM	8:00	2:00	
3	2/19/2018	8:00 AM	6:00 PM	10:00	4:00	
4	2/20/2018	8:00 AM	6:00 PM	10:00	6:00	
5	2/21/2018	8:00 AM	12:00 PM	4:00	2:00	
6	2/22/2018	8:00 AM	12:00 PM	4:00	-2:00	

Figure 588 *E6 displays correctly, but column A is wrong.*

Gotcha: Use care when changing to the 1904 system. Any existing dates will instantly increase by 4 years and a day as seen above in column A.

Additional Details: If someone's opening balance is negative, you enter a time of -2:00 in E2.

FILL BLANKS WITH VALUE ABOVE

Problem: Someone set up data in an outline view. I need to sort by columns A, B, and C, so I need all of the blanks filled in.

	A	B	C	D	E
1	Region	Customer	Product	Month	Revenue
2	Central	Ainsworth	ABC	Jan	10445
3				Apr	5886
4				Oct	13397
5				Dec	1861
6			XYZ	Jan	20444
7				May	29303
8				Aug	2320
9				Sep	22014
10		Exxon	ABC	Feb	24438
11				May	8785
12				Jun	13734

Figure 589 *Fill in the blanks.*

Strategy: Use Go To Special to select the blank cells. Then, 3 simple keystrokes will fill in the blank cells with the value above. Follow these steps.

1. Select from A3 down to the last blank in column C.
2. Select Home, Find and Select, Go To Special.
3. In the Go To Special dialog, choose Blanks and then click OK.
4. Type and equals sign and press the up arrow. This will create a formula that points up one cell.

	A	B	C	D	E
1	Region	Customer	Product	Month	Revenue
2	Central	Ainsworth	ABC	Jan	10445
3			=C2	Apr	5886
4				Oct	13397
5				Dec	1861
6			XYZ	Jan	20444
7				May	29303

Figure 590 *Equals, Up Arrow.*

5. Press Ctrl+Enter to fill all of the selected cells with a similar formula.

C3			f_x	=C2	

	A	B	C	D	E
1	Region	Customer	Product	Month	Revenue
2	Central	Ainsworth	ABC	Jan	10445
3	Central	Ainsworth	ABC	Apr	5886
4	Central	Ainsworth	ABC	Oct	13397
5	Central	Ainsworth	ABC	Dec	1861
6	Central	Ainsworth	XYZ	Jan	20444
7	Central	Ainsworth	XYZ	May	29303
8	Central	Ainsworth	XYZ	Aug	2320

Figure 591 *All of the blank cells are filled in.*

6. Before you can sort, you need to convert the formulas to values. Paste Values does not work on a non-contiguous selection, so you have to re-select columns A:C
7. Ctrl+C to copy
8. Home, Paste dropdown, Paste Values to convert the formulas to values.

SEE FORMULAS IN EXCEL 2013

Problem: I need to audit several formulas. I already know how to use Show Formulas mode, but I need something more permanent.

Strategy: Use the new =FORMULATEXT() function in Excel 2013.

| D6 | | | : | × | ✓ | fx | =FORMULATEXT(C6) |

▲	A	B	C	D	E	F
1	NEXT YEAR'S BUDGET					
3		Last Year	Budget			
4	East	141769	168705.1	=RANDBETWEEN(90,120)/100*B4		
5	Central	149923	170912.2	=RANDBETWEEN(90,120)/100*B5		
6	West	170112	173514.2	=RANDBETWEEN(90,120)/100*B6		
7						

Figure 592 *FORMULATEXT is great for documenting, and also for catching shenanigans.*

CREATE A BELL CURVE IN EXCEL

Problem: I need to generate a bell curve in Excel. The mean is 50 and the standard deviation is 12. (In the formulas below, substitute your real mean and standard distribution for the 50 and 12.)

Strategy: You curve needs to start three standard deviations below the mean. Follow these steps:
1. In cell A2, enter =50-12*3
2. In cell A3, enter =A2+(12*6)/60
3. Copy A3 down to A4:A62. This gets you 61 data points; 30 on either side of the mean.
4. In cell B2, enter =NORM.DIST(A2,50,12,FALSE). Copy that to B3:B61.
5. Enter a heading in B1, such as Probability
6. Select A1:B62. Insert a Line chart.

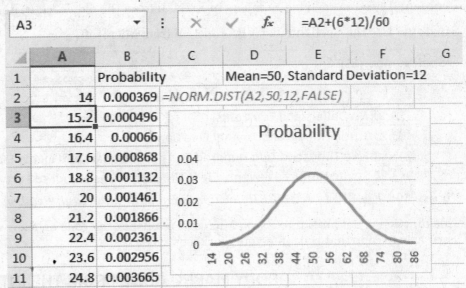

| A3 | | | : | × | ✓ | fx | =A2+(6*12)/60 |

▲	A	B	C	D	E	F	G
1		Probability		Mean=50, Standard Deviation=12			
2	14	0.000369	=NORM.DIST(A2,50,12,FALSE)				
3	15.2	0.000496					
4	16.4	0.00066					
5	17.6	0.000868					
6	18.8	0.001132					
7	20	0.001461					
8	21.2	0.001866					
9	22.4	0.002361					
10	23.6	0.002956					
11	24.8	0.003665					

Figure 593 *A couple of formulas will generate a bell curve in Excel.*

Additional Details: With a Normal distribution, 99.8% of the probability falls within 3 standard deviations of the mean. The formula in A2 starts 3 standard deviations below the mean. Experience has taught me that using 61 data points is enough to create a fairly smooth curve. Thus, the formula in A3 is designed to cover six standard deviations over the course of 60 more rows.

The real workhorse here is the NORM.DIST function. You have to plug in the mean and standard deviation for the desired bell curve to make it work.

CHANGE FROM LOWER TO UPPER CASE IN EXCEL

Problem: I have data in lower case. I need to convert it to upper case.

Strategy: To solve this in Excel, follow these steps:

1. Insert a new blank column to the right of your data.
2. Use a formula such as =UPPER(D2). To convert to lower case, use =LOWER(). To convert to Proper case, use =PROPER().
3. Copy the temporary formula down to all rows by double-clicking the fill handle.
4. The entire range of new formulas will be selected. Press Ctrl+C to copy.
5. Press the left arrow to move to the original data. Right-click and choose Paste Values.
6. You can now delete the temporary column D.

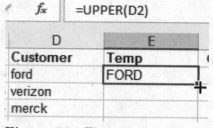

Figure 594 *Fix in a temp column.*

Additional Details: I to bring up the "W" program again, but here is another place where Microsoft Word could make this easier. If you had an entire table that needs converting, select the whole table, paste to a blank word document, then use the Change Case dropdown in the Home tab.

After the conversion is done, copy from Word and paste back to Excel.

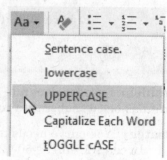

Figure 595 *Word.*

SPELL OUT NUMBERS IN EXCEL

Problem: I need to spell out numbers in Excel, like on the old check writer machines.

Strategy: Use the SpellNumber VBA function from Microsoft.

=SpellNumber(E1)

E	F	G	H	I	J
$0.10	No Dollars and Ten Cents				
$3.25	Three Dollars and Twenty Five Cents				
$5,245.88	Five Thousand Two Hundred Forty Five Dollars and Eighty Eight Cents				
$778,943.94	Seven Hundred Seventy Eight Thousand Nine Hundred Forty Three Dol				

Figure 596 *The SPELLNUMBER function is not built into Excel. Read on.*

This function is not built into Excel. Microsoft publishes the code on their website. Read the next topic to learn how to copy that code into your workbook.

COPY MACRO CODE FROM THE INTERNET INTO AN ADD-IN

Microsoft publishes a Knowledge Base article with the code to make SpellNumber work. If you have never used VBA before, it can be somewhat intimidating the first time you want to copy a macro from the web into your Excel file.

If you have never used macros before, you need to change your macro security settings to allow macros to run. In Excel, press Alt+T, followed by the letters M and then S. You will be at the macro security settings. Initially, the settings are set to disable all macros without notification. You want to choose the second item, which is Disable all Macros **With** Notification.

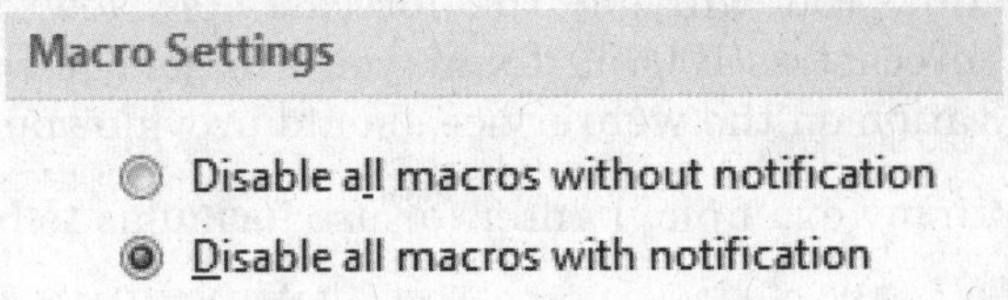

Macro Settings

○ Disable all macros without notification

◉ Disable all macros with notification

Figure 597 *This setting allows macros to run.*

1. Open a completely blank workbook.
2. Press Alt+F11 to open the Visual Basic Editor.
3. Once inside VBA, press Ctrl+R to display the Project Explorer. This is a small window that shows all open workbooks and add-ins.
4. In the Project Explorer, find the new file. Click on the file in Project Explorer. From the VBA menu, select Insert, Module.
5. Go to the Internet and search for SpellNumber Excel. The first result should be a Microsoft Knowledge Base article. In 2014, that article was number 213360, but the article is updated every few years, so don't be surprised if the number is new.
6. Select all of the code in the article, from Option Explicit through End Function.
7. Switch back to Excel VBA and paste the code in an empty module.
8. Press Alt+Q to close VBA and return to Excel.
9. For a quick test, type =SPELLNUMBER(123) in a cell and press Enter. You should get the words spelled out.

Gotcha: This function will only work in this workbook. You might be thinking that you could save it your personal macro workbook so it will work all the time, but then you will have to start typing the file name before the function. If you really need to use this function all the time in all workbooks on your computer, then the best solution is to make the function into an Add-In.

1. Use File Save As to save an XLSM version of the workbook first.
2. Use File Save As to save an XLAM version of the workbook. When you choose XLAM, Excel will offer to save in the Add-Ins folder.
3. When you save the XLAM version, the workbook becomes hidden, so it seems like it is not open anymore.
4. To make the Add-In a permanent part of your Excel, press Alt+T followed by I to display the Add-Ins dialog. Click Browse... and find your newly saved workbook. Click OK.

From this point forward, any time you have Excel open on your computer, you should be able to use =SPELLNUMBER.

Gotcha: When you send the workbook to others, they will need to have the add-in as well.

RETURN DATA FROM A WEBSERVICE IN EXCEL 2013

Microsoft introduced three new functions in Excel 2013 that will return data from a webservice.

A
1 Hot Topics at MrExcel.com Message Board
2 Fill down a formula in a macro for an undetermined set of rows
3 Help me I'm going CRAZY!!! COUNTIF AND INDIRECT FORMULA?!
4 regex: include split "0=" like "a=" into .pattern
5 Transpose unsorted items
6 I have problems with conditions

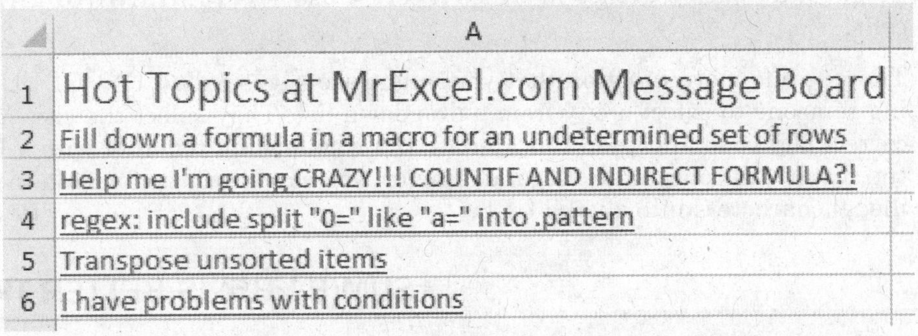

Figure 598 *This data is not coming from a web query.*

You will use at least two of the functions in conjunction with each other.

The first thing to do is to find a URL that returns data from a webservice. In this example, I am using http://feeds.feedburner.com/MrexcelExcelForumTop10Posts. This will return the five hot topics from the MrExcel Message board.

Many times, a web service will accept parameters that will return different data. For example, Yahoo Weather will accept a location code. If you ask for http://xml.weather/yahoo.com/forecastrss/100001_f.

xml, you will get the forecast for New York. If instead you ask for http://xml.weather/yahoo.com/forecastrss/100009_f.xml, you will get the weather forecast for Los Angeles. Whoever publishes documentation on the webservice should provide you a list of codes.

In my example, I enter (or use formulas to build) the webservice address in cell A8.

In cell A9, I use the formula =WEBSERVICE(A8). This formula reaches out to the web and returns a massively long result to cell A9. In my case, it returns 5009 characters of XML.

I hate to characterize the stuff in A9 as gobbledegoo. It is certainly machine readable and harder for humans to understand. But, if you copy A9 and paste to Notepad or to a text box, you will start to see some patterns. For me, I can tell that I want a field called "title" and another field called "link".

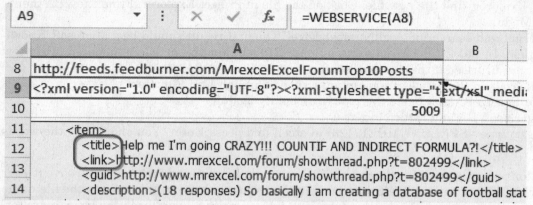

Figure 599 *Wade through the XML to find the fields that you want to return.*

Because I am already familiar with this data source, I know there are generally five topics returned. However, there are some headers, so there are 7 occurrences each of title and link in the 5009 characters returned by the =WEBSERVICE function.

To extract the titles to a range in Excel, follow these steps:
1. Select seven vertical cells. In my case, A12:A18.
2. Type =FILTERXML(A9,"//title"). This is something called XPATH. I won't claim to know anything about XPATH, but putting two slashes and the field name seems to do the trick.
3. Because you want this one formula to return 7 values, do not press Enter to accept the formula. Instead, hold down Ctrl+Shift and then press Enter. Excel will return all 7 titles to A12:18.

Those steps required some trial and error. I initially only selected five cells, then noticed the two headers were being returned. So, I cleared those formulas and tried again with 7. I might have tried again with 8, but then the 8th value would have retuned #N/A.

Over in B12:B18, the array formula is =FILTERXML(A9,"//link").

To put it all back together in a nice report, I use =HYPERLINK(B14,A14) in cell A2 and copy down five cells.

There is one more function that you might use - it is called ENCODEURL. Imagine that you are allowing someone to select a city from a dropdown list. They select the city. You use VLOOKUP to return the correct city code and then concatenate the whole thing together into a URL. If there is any chance that the result will contain an illegal character, you can wrap the formula in =ENCODEURL to convert those illegal characters into a valid URL.

=SUM(B1:B5) IS BETTER THAN =B1+B2+B3+B4+B5

Problem: You have an intern working in the Accounting department who likes to add up short columns of numbers using =B1+B2+B3+B4+B5. You try to convince him that the correct formula is =SUM(B1:B5). He looks at you like you are insane, pointing out that his formula returns the exact same answer.

Strategy: Explain the story of the ad agency for Microsoft who plastered millions of dollars of billboards across America with ads for the new Surface tablet. The person who created the spreadsheet in the ad used a formula of =B1+B2+B3+B4+B5+B6 instead of =SUM(B1:B6) and ended up with a calculation error in all of the ads.

Figure 600 *The real total is $9500, not $9000.*

Here is what likely happened.

When the ad was created, they forgot to put the car in the ad. The total was $9000. The figure on the left shows the right way to do the formula and the figure on the right shows the wrong way to do the formula.

✓ *fx*	=SUM(E1:E6)

D	E
Airfare	2500
Hotel	4000
Food	1500
Dive Rentals	500
Surf Rentals	200
Other Excursions	300
Total	9000

Figure 601 *Right way.*

✓ *fx*	=E1+E2+E3+E4+E5+E6

D	E	F
Airfare	2500	
Hotel	4000	
Food	1500	
Dive Rentals	500	
Surf Rentals	200	
Other Excursions	300	
Total	9000	

Figure 602 *Wrong way.*

I am not sure why someone at the ad agency decided a car had to be included in the ad. But for whatever reason, someone went back after the spreadsheet was created and inserted row 3 with a $500 car rental.

Here are the results after adding row 3:

✓ *fx*	=SUM(E1:E7)

D	E
Airfare	2500
Hotel	4000
Car	500
Food	1500
Dive Rentals	500
Surf Rentals	200
Other Excursions	300
Total	9500

Figure 603 *Right answer*

✓ *fx*	=E1+E2+E4+E5+E6+E7

D	E	F
Airfare	2500	
Hotel	4000	
Car	500	
Food	1500	
Dive Rentals	500	
Surf Rentals	200	
Other Excursions	300	
Total	9000	

Figure 604 *The answer in the Surface ad.*

The right formula... the =SUM(E1:E7) automatically expanded to include the new row. The wrong formula, the =E1+E2+E3+E4+E5+E6 is now =E1+E2+E4+E5+E6+E7 and you have the wrong total.

Plus... there is no nagging green triangle warning you that the formula omits adjacent cells! This isn't the type of formula that error checking would handle.

This was not a real spreadsheet. This wasn't even a real couple planning a trip to Hawaii. It was just a silly ad showing that the Surface can run two apps side by side when the iPad would not do that. But, because they let someone in the marketing department build the spreadsheet, they ended up with a larger-than-life spreadsheet error plastered on billboards across the country.

It is interesting to note that even if the car would have been added to a new row outside of the =SUM(E1:E6) range, the formula in the total row would correctly rewrite itself. Here is Figure 601 after inserting a new row below row 7. Notice that the formula automatically changed to include =SUM(E1:E7)

✓	fx	=SUM(E1:E7)

D	E
Airfare	2500
Hotel	4000
Food	1500
Dive Rentals	500
Surf Rentals	200
Other Excursions	300
Car	500
Total	9500

Figure 605 *Excel's Intellisense corrected this potential error.*

ADD NEW FUNCTIONS TO EXCEL WITH FAST EXCEL SPEEDTOOLS EXTRAS

There are several add-ins that add new calculation functions to Excel. One of the best is from Charles Williams and FastExcel. The SpeedTools Extras package includes functions that accountants will use in every day work:
- Generate a vector of numbers to be used in amortization tables.
- Return an array of True/False values for each row or column.
- Reverse an array.
- Do wildcard matching with Regular Expressions (RegEx)
- Concatenate a range of text, specifying a delimiter

Check out these tools at http://tinyurl.com/fastexcel.

PART 3

WRANGLING DATA

HOW TO SET UP YOUR DATA FOR EASY SORTING AND SUBTOTALS

Problem: I want to be able to use the powerful data commands such as Sort, Filter, Subtotal, Consolidate, and PivotTable. Is there any special way I should set up the data to begin with?

Strategy: You need to follow all the rules to keep your data in list format:

Rule 1: Use only a single row of headings above your data. If you need to have a two-row heading, set it up as a single cell with two lines in the row. See "How to Fit a Multiline Heading into One Cell" on page 247.

Rule 2: Never leave one heading cell blank. You will find that you do this if you add a temporary column. If you forget to add a heading before you sort, this will completely throw off the IntelliSense, and Excel will sort the headings down into the data.

Rule 3: There should be no entirely blank rows or blank columns in the middle of your data. It is okay to have an occasional blank cell, but you should have no entirely blank columns.

Rule 4: If your heading row is not in row 1, be sure to have a blank row between the report title and the headings.

Rule 5: Formatting the heading cells in bold will help the Excel's IntelliSense module understand that these are headings.

Gotcha: List format won't help at all if your data is only two columns wide.

Results: If you follow the list format rules, Excel's IntelliSense will allow all the data commands to work flawlessly.

HOW TO FIT A MULTILINE HEADING INTO ONE CELL

Problem: In "How to Set Up Your Data for Easy Sorting and Subtotals," you say that headings should occupy only one row to allow for easy sorting. My manager requires that I format a report to have the heading "Prior Year" split, with "Prior" in one row and "Year" in a second row. How can I make my manager happy while also following the list format rules?

Q4	2014	Prior Year
244	624	591
111	605	561

Figure 606 *Your manager wants this heading on two rows.*

Strategy: This is a very real problem, where form meets function. The right thing to do in Excel is to have "Prior Year" in one cell. But some managers absolutely, positively want the formatting to be exactly as they specify. Luckily, there is a strategy that makes it possible to make the manager happy and to correctly set up the data set in Excel, too.

In cell X5, you type the word Prior. Then you hold down Alt while pressing Enter and type the word Year. The Alt+Enter combination adds a linefeed character in the cell. You can delete the old heading in X4 by moving the cell pointer there and pressing the Delete key.

c	Q4	2014	Prior Year
1	244	624	591
7	111	605	561
7	192	733	701

Figure 607 *Use Alt+Enter to go to the next line.*

Results: You have a single cell that contains two lines of text. The cell will work as a heading in pivot tables, subtotals, sorting, and so on.

Additional Details: Using Alt+Enter automatically turns on the Wrap Text option for the cell. You could also turn on the Wrap Text option by choosing Home, Wrap Text icon.

Figure 608 *Wrap Text finally has an icon starting in Excel 2007.*

Turning on Wrap Text in this manner will probably work for a brief heading like "Prior Year." However, if you want to have control over a long heading, such as "Prior Year Results (Adjusted for Spin-off of the Widget Division)," then it is better to use Alt+Enter to specify exactly where the line break should occur. Wrap text uses a somewhat haphazard splitting of words.

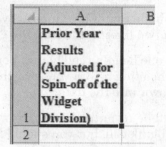

Figure 609 *Excel decides where to break lines.*

As you make this column wider, Excel changes the way the words are wrapped. It is frustrating to keep adjusting the column widths until you get the words to wrap correctly.

Gotcha: After resizing a cell with Wrap Text, you often end up with a row height that is too tall. To correct this, you select the cell and then choose Home, Format dropdown, Autofit Row Height.

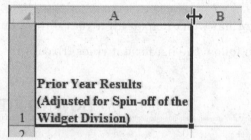

Figure 610 *Adjusting column widths to change line breaks rarely works.*

Using Alt+Enter gives you absolute control over where the heading breaks. To create the figure below, type Prior Year Results <Alt+Enter> (Adjusted for the <Alt+Enter> Spin-off of the <Alt+Enter> Widget Division). You can make the column wider and center it for the perfect-looking cell.

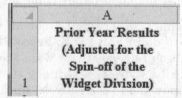

Figure 611 *Press Alt+Enter to wrap the text at logical points.*

NO TINY BLANK COLUMNS BETWEEN COLUMNS

Problem: My Manager wants tiny blank columns between the columns.

Strategy: Plan on restating your numbers to the Securities and Exchange Commission. Tiny blank columns are a recipe for disaster. Someone will sort part of the data and not all of the data.

Most managers who demand this are doing it to make the bottom border under the headings look better.

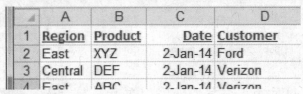

H	I	J	K	L	M	N	O
	Quantity	Revenue		COGS		Profit	
	1000	22810		10220		12590	
	100	2257		984		1273	
	500	10245		4235		6010	

Figure 612 *Tiny blank columns are dangerous.*

The manager here is using a bottom border to create the lines under the headings. He ends up using the bottom border because underlines just don't look right. They only extend as long as the heading.

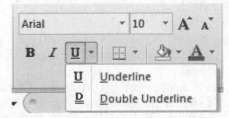

	A	B	C	D
1	Region	Product	Date	Customer
2	East	XYZ	2-Jan-14	Ford
3	Central	DEF	2-Jan-14	Verizon
4	East	ABC	2-Jan-14	Verizon

Figure 613 *Underlines rarely make the manager happy.*

There is a solution that will make the manager happy. It won't be found in the ribbon. Remember that the options in the ribbon are there to make Excel novices happy. If you are reading this book, you frequently have to go beyond the ribbon. In the ribbon, they offer two types of underlines.

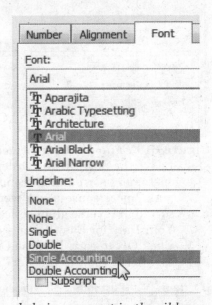

Figure 614 *Two underline types in the ribbon.*

Skip the ribbon choices. Instead, click on the dialog launcher at the bottom of the Font group of the Home tab of the ribbon.

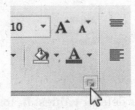

Figure 615 *Click the dialog launcher.*

The underline dropdown in the Format Cells dialog offers four choices instead of two. Choose Single Accounting underline.

Figure 616 *The good choices are not in the ribbon.*

The result are bottom underlines that extend almost all the way across the cell, but not quite all the way. When printed, this will give the same look as back in Figure 612.

	A	B	C	D	E	F	G	H
1	Region	Product	Date	Customer	Quantity	Revenue	COGS	Profit
2	East	XYZ	2-Jan-14	Ford	1000	22810	10220	12590
3	Central	DEF	2-Jan-14	Verizon	100	2257	984	1273

Figure 617 *These underlines appear similar to gaps between columns.*

Alternate Strategy: If your manager still demands the blank columns, you can put a word, just as "blank" in the headings of the blank columns. Change the font color to white to no one sees those headings when printed. This will allow the entire data set to be treated as a contiguous column.

Problem: I have sales data in a worksheet. I would like to sort the data by product within customer.

	A	B	C	D	E
1	**OurCo Corporation**				
2	**Sales Report**				
3	**Fiscal Year 2014**				
4					
5	**Rep**	**Customer**	**Product**	**Quantity**	**Revenue**
6	Joe	EFG & Sons	ABC	357	31773
7	Bob	PQR Company	GHI	393	34977
8	Bob	DEF, Inc.	DEF	396	35244
9	Joe	BCD Company	DEF	399	35511
10	Mary	EFG, Inc.	DEF	411	36579

Figure 618 *Sort by product within customer.*

Strategy: Here's what you do:

1. Select one cell within your data. The one cell can be in the heading row or any data row. Select Data, Sort. Whereas Excel 2003 only allowed sorting by three fields, Excel now offers up to 64 sort levels. Rather than the old dialog with the three fields, you now start with one field and add levels as necessary.
2. Choose Sort By dropdown, Customer.
3. Click the Add Level button. A new row will appear in the Sort dialog. Choose Then By dropdown, Product.

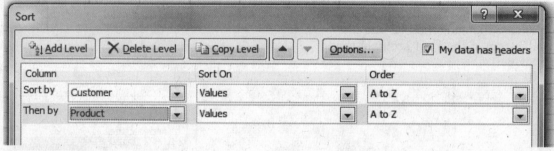

Figure 619 *Build as many sort levels as necessary.*

4. Leave the Sort On and Order dropdowns at their default values. If, for some reason, you wanted the customers sorted in descending alphabetical order, you could change A to Z to Z to A. That might make more sense if you were sorting by revenue, but it is not likely that you need the customers sorted in reverse alphabetical sequence. If your data is set up correctly as outlined in "How to Set up Your Data for Easy Sorting and Subtotals," Excel will properly guess that your list has a header row.
5. Click OK to sort. Because Customer was the first sort key, all the records for "ABC Company" will sort to the top. Records for "ABC GMbH" will appear next.

	Rep	Customer	Product	Quantity	Revenue
5	**Rep**	**Customer**	**Product**	**Quantity**	**Revenue**
6	Dan	ABC Company	DEF	430	38270
7	Bob	ABC Company	DEF	529	47081
8	Dan	ABC GMbH	ABC	512	45568
9	Bob	ABC GMbH	ABC	702	62478
10	Joe	ABC GMbH	DEF	505	44945
11	Dan	ABC GMbH	GHI	553	49217
12	Joe	BCD Company	DEF	399	35511
13	Dan	BCD Corporation	ABC	575	51175

Figure 620 *The data is sorted.*

Additional Details: When there is a tie—for example, the four records for "ABC GMbH"—those records will be sorted in ascending order by the product field. For instance, the ABC product record appears before the DEF product field. If there is still a tie, the records will remain in their original sequence from before the sort.

Alternate Strategy: If your data is properly set up in list format, you can select a single cell in the data and then use the AZ or ZA buttons on the Data tab.

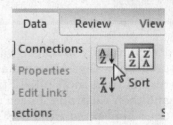

Note that these same icons are also in the Sort & Filter dropdown on the Home tab. If you don't want the extra click of opening the dropdown or going to the Data tab, you can add the icons to the Quick Access Toolbar.

Figure 621 *Sorting icons on the Data tab.*

If you use either method, Excel will sort the data by the column in which the cell pointer is currently located. Because Excel resolves ties by leaving the previous sequence in place, you can sort by product within customer. First, you select a cell in the Product field and click AZ to sort by product. Next, you select a cell in the Customer field and click AZ to sort by customer. The data will be sorted by customer, with ties sorted by product.

You can click the ZA button to sort in descending order.

Gotcha: Before you try any sort operation, you must select either the entire range or a single cell in that range. If you mistakenly choose two cells in a range, Excel will sort just those selected cells, resulting in a few cells of your data being sorted within records—a disastrous result. Excel now warns you when you attempt to sort a subset of the cells.

SORT DAYS OF THE WEEK

Problem: I have a column with values such as Monday, Wednesday, and so on. When I sort this column in ascending sequence, Friday comes before Monday. The same problem happens with month names, which sort as April, August, December, and so on.

	A	B	C
1	Day	Start	Associate
2	Friday	10:00 AM	Josh
3	Monday	10:00 AM	Bill
4	Monday	10:00 AM	Logan
5	Monday	10:00 AM	Josh

Figure 622 *Friday is alphabetically before Monday.*

Strategy: Excel has custom lists built in for months and days. To use them, follow these steps:
1. Select a cell in your data.
2. Select Data, Sort.
3. Choose Sort by Day and Sort on Values. In the Order dropdown, choose Custom List.
4. Choose Sunday, Monday, Tuesday from the Custom List dialog. Click OK.

Excel will sort the data correctly.

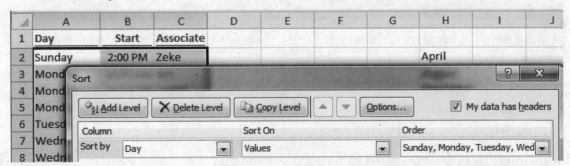

Figure 623 *Weekdays are sorted correctly.*

SORT A REPORT INTO A CUSTOM SEQUENCE

Problem: My manager wants me to sort a report geographically. My annual report typically lists results from the United States first, then Europe, and then Australia. I need to sort so that the countries appear as United States, England, France, Germany, and Australia.

	A	B	C	D
5	Country	Region	District	Sales Rep
6	Germany	Germany	Germany	Joe
7	USA	East	MidAtlantic	Bob
8	USA	Central	Cleveland	Mary
9	Germany	Germany	Germany	Dan
10	USA	East	Southeast	Dan

Figure 624 *Sort using a custom list.*

Strategy: You can use a custom list by following these steps:

1. Go to a blank section of the worksheet. Type the countries in the order you want them to appear in a column. Select the range of cells.
2. Choose File, Options, Advanced. Scroll to near the bottom of the dialog. The Edit Custom Lists button is now found at the bottom of the General category. In Excel 2007, this button was at the top of the first screen of the Options dialog. Click Edit Custom Lists.
3. Provided you selected the data in step 1, the reference box next to the Import button already contains the cells that contain your list. Click Import.

Figure 625 *Type the countries in their desired geographic sequence.*

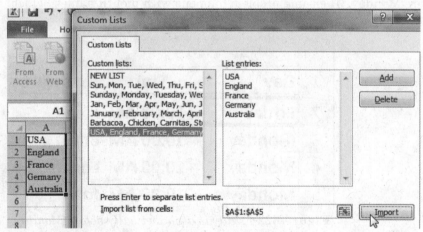

Figure 626 *Adding a new custom list.*

4. Click OK twice.
5. Select Data, Sort. In the Sort dialog, choose Country from the Sort By dropdown. In the Order dropdown, choose Custom List.
6. Excel will again display the Custom Lists dialog. Select the USA, England, France list and click OK.
7. When Excel shows USA, England, France, Germany in the Order dropdown, click OK to sort.

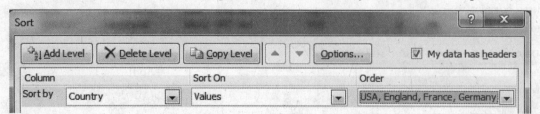

Figure 627 *Sort by the custom list.*

Results: The data is sorted by the country order.

Additional Details: If there is a value in the column that is not in your custom list, it is sorted alphabetically after the entries in the list. If you sort in descending order, these unlisted entries will come first, in Z–A order.

Gotcha: Excel remembers that the column was most recently sorted by the "USA, England…" custom list. If you click the AZ button, it will automatically sort by using this same custom list. If you need to return to alphabetical order, you will have to select Data, Sort and choose A to Z in the Order dropdown.

SORT ALL RED CELLS TO THE TOP OF A REPORT

Problem: I've read through a 20-page report and marked a dozen cells in red. I need to audit those records and would like to sort the red cells to the top of the report.

Strategy: You can sort by color. Follow these steps:
1. Right-click on one of the red cells.
2. From the context menu, choose Sort, Put Selected Cell Color on Top.

Results: Excel will sort the red cells to the top of the report.

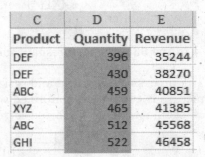

C	D	E
Product	Quantity	Revenue
ABC	357	31773
GHI	393	34977
DEF	396	35244
DEF	399	35511
DEF	411	36579
XYZ	417	37113
DEF	430	38270
ABC	441	39249

Figure 628 *Sort the red cells to the top.*

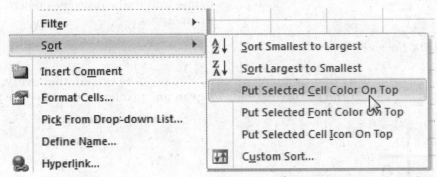

Figure 629 *Choose to sort by color.*

C	D	E
Product	Quantity	Revenue
DEF	396	35244
DEF	430	38270
ABC	459	40851
XYZ	465	41385
ABC	512	45568
GHI	522	46458

Figure 630 *The red cells come to the top.*

Additional Details: Using the context menu as described here works fine if you need to sort by only one color. If you used cells of several different colors and want to sort them in a particular order, you need to select Data, Sort to open the Sort dialog. Then, for the first sort level, you choose Quantity in the Sort By dropdown, Cell Color from the Sort On dropdown, and green from the Order dropdown.

You set the next sort level by clicking the Copy Level button and then choosing yellow from the Order dropdown. You click Copy Level for each additional color you need to specify.

Figure 631 *Four levels for one column.*

If you have many colors in a column, you might use several sort levels to specify how to sort the first column.

Additional Details: You can also sort by font color or cell icon. Amazingly, sorting by color will even work if your colors have been assigned through conditional formatting.

SORT PICTURES WITH DATA

Problem: My manager wants me to add employee pictures to the department phone list. I need the pictures to sort with the data.

Strategy: By default, this will work. Each picture has a property that will cause it to move but not size with cells. To see the property, select the picture and press Ctrl+One. There are 16 categories in the left bar of the Format Picture dialog. Near the bottom, choose Properties. The Move But Don't Size with Cells should already be selected.

Select one cell in column A and sort with the AZ button. The pictures should move with the names.

	A	B	C
1	Name	Picture	Ext.
	Steemer, Stan		1098
2	Bligh, Cap		1100
3	Franklin, Ben		1025
4	Ruth, Babe		1051

Figure 632 *Sort the list alphabetically.*

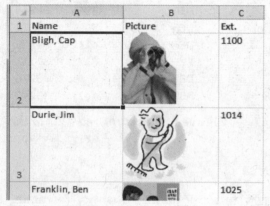

	A	B	C
1	Name	Picture	Ext.
	Bligh, Cap		1100
2	Durie, Jim		1014
3	Franklin, Ben		1025

Figure 633 *The pictures will sort with the rows.*

Gotcha: I am guessing that you wouldn't be looking up this topic unless the sort already failed for you. I've had to troubleshoot this before and it always comes down to one issue.

The process of inserting and resizing pictures is a mind-numbing process. You must be certain that every picture is completely contained within one cell. If the picture extends by even one pixel over the top edge of a cell, it will not be sorted correctly.

Figure 634 *This picture is a few pixels too high. It will not sort..*

QUICKLY FILTER A LIST TO CERTAIN RECORDS

Problem: I have 10,000 records in the worksheet. I need to be able to quickly find records that match a criterion, such as all East ABC records.

	A	B	C	D	E	F
1	Region	Product	Invoice	Customer	Quantity	Revenue
2	Central	XYZ	Jan-14	Wal-Mart	1000	25140
3	West	XYZ	Jan-14	General Motors	1000	25080
4	Central	XYZ	Jan-14	Wal-Mart	1000	23810
5	Central	XYZ	Jan-14	Ford	1000	22680
6	East	ABC	Jan-14	Ainsworth	900	21708
7	East	XYZ	Jan-14	General Motors	900	21456
8	East	XYZ	Jan-14	Ainsworth	1000	20040

Figure 635 *Find records within this data set.*

Strategy: You can find records that match a criterion by using the Filter feature.

Toggle on the Filter command by using either Home, Sort & Filter, Filter or selecting Data, Filter icon. As you can see below, the Filter button is three times larger than the Advanced Filter icon, which I take as evidence that Microsoft someday hopes to add enough power to Filter to eliminate the need for the Advanced Filter.

Figure 636 *AutoFilter is now just Filter.*

To filter your data set, follow these steps:

1. Make sure your data has a heading row. Select one cell within the data. Select Data, Filter. Excel will add a dropdown to each heading.

Figure 637 *Filter dropdowns.*

2. Select the Product dropdown. Before you can select ABC, you have to first uncheck (Select All).

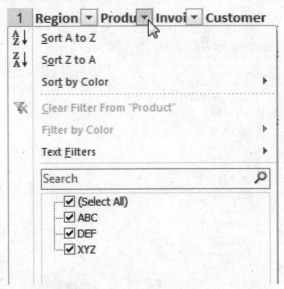

Figure 638 *Uncheck Select All, then choose ABC.*

3. Click the ABC check box. Click OK. You will now see just the ABC records.
4. Open the Region dropdown. Uncheck (Select All). Check East. Click OK.

You will now have only the East, ABC records. Notice the Funnel icon appears on all columns that have a filter applied.

	A	B	C	D	E	F
1	Region	Produ	Invoi	Customer	Quant	Reven
6	East	ABC	Jan-14	Ainsworth	900	21708
27	East	ABC	Jan-14	Exxon	600	11430
34	East	ABC	Jan-14	Nortel Networks	400	7152
35	East	ABC	Jan-14	Verizon	300	6045
44	East	ABC	Jan-14	Wal-Mart	100	2066

Figure 639 *Excel hides the other rows.*

To clear a filter, open the dropdown and choose Clear Filter from *Field*.

Additional Details: Excel will detect if your column is text, numeric, or dates. Each column type includes a flyout with new options.

The Date filters appear in a tree view, so you can turn on/off entire months rather than clicking all 30 dates that fall in a month. The Date Filter flyout menu offers many choices that seem like they were borrowed from Quickbooks.

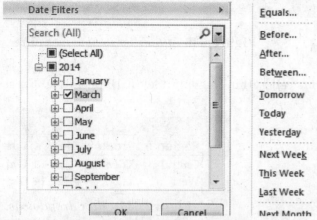

Figure 640 *Date columns offer many new choices.*

Numeric columns offer a Top 10 filter, plus new choices such as Above Average.

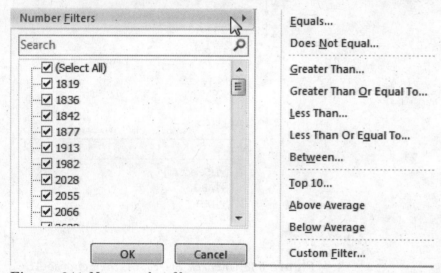

Figure 641 *New number filters.*

The Top 10 Filter option allows you to specify the top or bottom "n" items or "n%" of items. The Top 10 feature was in previous versions of Excel, but all the other value filters in the figure above are new in Excel 2007.

If you have used cell colors, font colors, or icon sets, you can use the Filter by Color fly-out menu to show records that have a certain color.

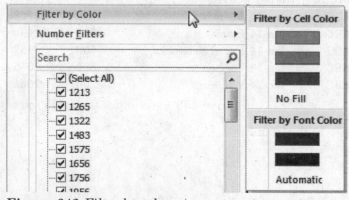

Figure 642 *Filter by color.*

Gotcha: In order for the Date Filters or Number Filters options to appear, your data needs to be predominantly dates or numbers. If you have too many blank cells or too many text cells, Excel will treat the column as text and not offer these filter options in the dropdown.

USE SEARCH WHILE FILTERING

Problem: I need to select all the oil companies from the filter.

Strategy: New in Excel 2010, there is a search box in the Filter dropdown.

Open the filter dropdown and type oil in the search box. Excel shows a list of the companies with Oil in the name. By default, (Select All Search Results) is chosen.

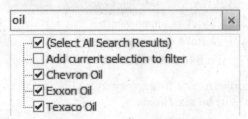

Figure 643 *Results of a search while filtering in Excel 2010.*

If you do a second search, you can either choose to replace the current filter with the new results, or to add the new search results to the existing filter.

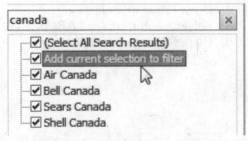

Figure 644 *Add a second search.*

The result is all customers with either "oil" or "Canada".

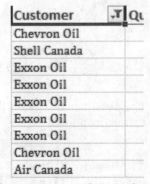

Customer	Qu
Chevron Oil	
Shell Canada	
Exxon Oil	
Exxon Oil	
Exxon Oil	
Exxon Oil	
Exxon Oil	
Chevron Oil	
Air Canada	

Figure 645 *Oil or Canada appears as the result.*

FILTER BY SELECTION

Problem: Microsoft Access offers an icon for Filter by Selection. Why isn't this in Excel?

Strategy: Filter by Selection IS in Excel. It is hidden. It is mislabeled. It has been in Excel (hidden and mislabeled) for fifteen years.

To add Filter by Selection to the ribbon, follow these steps:
1. Right-click the Quick Access Toolbar and choose Customize Quick Access Toolbar.
2. Initially, you only see popular commands. Open the left dropdown and change from Popular Commands to All Commands.
3. Scroll down to find AutoFilter. Click on AutoFilter. Click the Add>> button in the center to add this icon to the Quick Access Toolbar. Click OK. You now have Filter by Selection on the QAT.

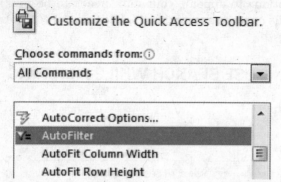

Customize the Quick Access Toolbar.

Figure 646 *AutoFilter is really Filter by Selection.*

You can now filter very quickly. Say that you want all of the Wal-Mart, East, ABC records from a data set. It will be six clicks.

1. Select a cell that says Wal-Mart
2. Click Filter by Selection
3. Select a cell that says East.
4. Click Filter by Selection.
5. Select a cell that says ABC.
6. Click Filter by Selection.

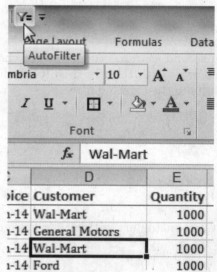

Figure 647 *Choose the value that you want, click AutoFilter.*

The result is filters on three columns, without ever clicking the Filter button and without ever opening a Filter dropdown.

	A	B	C	D	E	F	
1	Region	Produ	Invoi	Customer	Quant	Reven	
44	East	ABC	Jan-14	Wal-Mart	100	2066	
240	East	ABC	Jul-14	Wal-Mart	1000	18660	
252	East	ABC	Jul-14	Wal-Mart	800	13936	
348	East	ABC	Sep-14	Wal-Mart	700	13139	
479	East	ABC	Dec-14	Wal-Mart	900	18243	
539	East	ABC	Dec-14	Wal-Mart	800	14224	
568							
569							

Figure 648 *Filter by Selection will change your life.*

Additional Details: How can it be that Microsoft never tells anyone about this? Why did they continue to mislabel the icon as AutoFilter when Excel 2007 changed the term to Filter (and, in fact, they added a Filter icon in Excel 2007). This is one of the great mysteries. I've asked the Excel project managers about this. Someone added the code to do Filter by Selection but it was sort of an afterthought, not something they felt worthy of publicizing. If you believe some accounts, they collectively forgot the code was there. It was only during a code review for a lawsuit defense that someone happened upon it again. Filter by Selection is the greatest feature that no one knows about.

USE AUTOSUM AFTER FILTERING

Problem: I need to total only the visible cells in a filtered data set.

Strategy: You can use the AutoSum icon after applying a filter. Normally, the AutoSum icon inserts a SUM function. When you apply a filter and then use AutoSum, Excel will insert a SUBTOTAL function instead. This function will ignore rows hidden by the Filter command. Follow these steps:

1. Choose a cell in your data set. Select Data, Filter.
2. Apply a filter to at least one column. Open the Customer dropdown and choose one customer.
3. Select the first visible cells beneath your numeric columns. Below, the last visible row is 539, but the next blank cell is in row 568.
4. Click the AutoSum icon and press Enter. Excel inserts a SUBTOTAL function that uses the correct syntax to skip rows hidden by the filter.

E568			fx	=SUBTOTAL(9,E2:E567)	

	A	B	C	D	E	F
1	Region ▼	Produ ▼	Invoi ▼	Customer ▼	Quant ▼	Reven ▼
44	East	ABC	Jan-14	Wal-Mart	100	2066
240	East	ABC	Jul-14	Wal-Mart	1000	18660
252	East	ABC	Jul-14	Wal-Mart	800	13936
348	East	ABC	Sep-14	Wal-Mart	700	13139
479	East	ABC	Dec-14	Wal-Mart	900	18243
539	East	ABC	Dec-14	Wal-Mart	800	14224
568					4300	80268
569						

Figure 649 *Excel inserts the SUBTOTAL function.*

When you choose a different selections from the filter dropdown, the SUBTOTAL function will show the total for those visible.

Additional Details: During a seminar for the Fort Wayne IIA, someone added a great suggestion to this topic. Insert two blank rows at the top. Cut the formulas from the total row and paste to row 1. Now, even if the filtered rows are more than will fit on a screen, you always have the filtered totals at the top.

FILTER ONLY SOME COLUMNS

Problem: I don't want to offer filter dropdowns for Quantity and Revenue. It confuses the people who use my worksheet. I only want the filters to be available on columns A:D.

Strategy: You normally apply a filter by selection the entire data set, or one cell in the data set, or the cell to the right of the last heading. Any of these methods will apply the filter dropdowns to all cells.

Instead, select cells A1:D1 before selecting the Filter icon. This will add the dropdowns to only those columns. Of course, if you filter by column A, it will only show you the filtered rows for all of the columns.

	A	B	C	D	E	F
1	Region ▼	Produ ▼	Invoi ▼	Customer ▼	Quantity	Revenue
2	Central	XYZ	Jan-14	Wal-Mart	1000	25140
3	West	XYZ	Jan-14	General Motors	1000	25080
4	Central	XYZ	Jan-14	Wal-Mart	1000	23810
5	Central	XYZ	Jan-14	Ford	1000	22680

Figure 650 *Filter only the text columns.*

Gotcha: This trick only works on a contiguous section of the data set. If you wanted dropdowns only on Column A, B, and D, you would have to use VBA to hide the dropdown on column C. To hide the dropdown for column C, follow these steps:

1. Alt+F11 for VBA.
2. Ctrl+G for immediate window.
3. Type range("C1").AutoFilter Field:=3, VisibleDropDown:=False

To adapt for another column, change both the "C1" and the 3 for another column. Column J would have a Field:=10.

◢	A	B	C	D	
1	Region ▼	Produ ▼	Invoice	Customer ▼	Qua
2	Central	XYZ	Jan-14	Wal-Mart	
3	West	XYZ	Jan-14	General Motors	

Figure 651 *One line of VBA can hide a filter dropdown.*

FIND THE UNIQUE VALUES IN A COLUMN

Problem: I have a large database. Before I can produce a report for each customer, I need to identify the complete list of unique customers.

Strategy: There are many solutions to the unique customers problem. One is to use the Advanced Filter command on the Data tab of the ribbon. Follow these steps:

1. Copy the Customer heading from D1 to a blank cell.

	D	E	F	G	H
	¦Customer	Quantity	Revenue		Customer
4	Wal-Mart	1000	25140		
4	General Motors	1000	25080		
4	Wal-Mart	1000	23810		

Figure 652 *Copy the customer heading to an output area.*

2. Select a single cell in your data range and then select Data, Advanced. The Advanced Filter dialog will appear, offering many confusing options.
3. Choose the Unique Records Only check box. Change the Action section to Copy to Another Location. Selecting this action enables the Copy To range. Place the cell pointer in the Copy To text box and touch the out-of-the-way copy of the Customer heading.

Figure 653 *Copy unique records to the output range.*

4. Click OK. Excel will find the unique customer numbers and copy them to the range you specified.

Customer
Wal-Mart
General Motors
Ford
Ainsworth
Chevron
Verizon
IBM

Figure 654 *Excel produces a list of unique customers.*

Gotcha: The list is not sorted. It appears in the same order that the customers appeared in the original data set.

Gotcha: Any subsequent use of the Advanced Filter command during this Excel session will remember the list range you specified in the Advanced Filter dialog box.

USE ADVANCED FILTER

Problem: What is the advanced filter used for?

Strategy: As the AutoFilter Filter gets more features, there are less times that you need to switch over to the Advanced Filter. There are still a few tasks that might be easier with the Advanced Filter.

The Advanced Filter can be used to filter to a subset of columns and/or to re-order columns. In the previous example, you filtered to a single column of customer. When you use the Copy To Another Location option and put headings in the Copy To range, you are specifying which columns and the order of the columns. In the next three figures, you will see the List range, the Criteria range, and the Copy To range of a filter designed to produce a report for General Motors.

The List range contains seven fields:

	A	B	C	D	E	F	G	H
1	Region	Product	Market	Date	Customer	Quantity	Revenue	
2	Central	S112	Service	Jan-14	Wal-Mart	1000	25140	
3	West	S111	Mfg.	Jan-14	General Motors	1000	25080	
4	Central	S112	Transp.	Jan-14	Wal-Mart	1000	23810	
5	Central	S100	Retail	Jan-14	Ford	1000	22680	

Figure 655 *The original input range.*

The Criteria range in this case is two cells, specifying one customer.

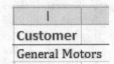

I
Customer
General Motors

Figure 656 *One heading from the List range and the customer.*

The Copy To range contains three fields in a new sequence.

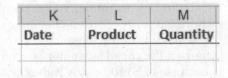

K	L	M
Date	Product	Quantity

Figure 657 *Specify the fields to be returned.*

Select one cell in the input range and choose Advanced Filter. Select Copy To Another Location. Fill in the three ranges. Do not check the Unique Values Only box.

Figure 658 *Filter three columns for one customer.*

The result is a new report with three columns of purchases by one customer.

Product	Market	Date	Customer	Quantity	Revenue		Customer		Date	Product	Quantity
S112	Service	Jan-14	Wal-Mart	1000	25140		General Motors	→	Jan-14	S111	1000
S111	Mfg.	Jan-14	General Motors	1000	25080			→	Jan-14	S109	900
S112	Transp.	Jan-14	Wal-Mart	1000	23810				Jan-14	S113	600
S109	Retail	Jan-14	Ford	1000	22680				Jan-14	S110	700
S105	Transp.	Jan-14	Ainsworth	900	21708				Jan-14	S111	300
S109	Financial	Jan-14	General Motors	900	21456				Jan-14	S104	200
S103	Retail	Jan-14	Ainsworth	1000	20940				Mar-14	S108	1000

You can use Advanced Filter to create some unusual criteria ranges where the criteria are joined by a logical OR. Say that you were looking for customers in the Transportation market or and customers who purchased product S109. Set up a criteria range with each criterion on a different row.

J	K
Market	**Product**
Transp.	
	S109

Figure 659 *These criteria are joined by an OR.*

You will get records that match either criterion.

	A	B	C
1	Region	Product	Market
4	Central	S112	Transp.
5	Central	S109	Retail
6	East	S105	Transp.
7	East	S109	Financial
9	Central	S102	Transp.
12	West	S109	Retail

Figure 660 *Records that match either criterion.*

Criteria entered on the same row are joined by AND. In this example, you are looking for records where a Transportation customer purchased S102, or where a Retail customer purchased S109, or where a Financial customer purchased S108, or the purchase of S110 by any industry.

J	K
Market	**Product**
Transp.	S102
Retail	S109
Financial	S108
	S110

Figure 661 *Filter will return customers who entirely match one row here.*

	A	B	C
1		Market	Product
2		Transp.	S102
3		Retail	S109
4		Financial	S108
5			S110
6			
7	Region	Product	Market
11	Central	S109	Retail
15	Central	S102	Transp.
18	West	S109	Retail
21	West	S108	Financial
22	East	S110	Retail
23	Central	S109	Retail
30	West	S110	Service

Figure 662 *Results of the filter.*

Additional Details: To clear the advanced filter and show all the rows again, choose Data, Clear.

Several versions ago, you were not able to specify a Copy To range on a different worksheet than the List range. This limitation has been lifted.

REPLACE MULTIPLE FILTER CRITERIA WITH A SINGLE ROW OF FORMULAS

Problem: The Advanced Filter feature can handle combinations of criteria, but I have a particular situation where I want all records where the customer, industry and product come from these lists. To list all combinations of five products, five customers, and three industries would require 75 rows of combinations. Is there an easier way?

Strategy: You can replace traditional criteria with a formula-based criteria range. To use a formula-based condition, leave the heading row of the criteria range blank. Write a logical formula in the criteria range that tests the first row of the data set. This formula will be applied to all rows of the data set.

M	N	
S101	Ford	
S103	General Motors	
S105	Shell Canada	
S107	Exxon	
S109	Verizon	
Service		
Financial		
Transp.		

Figure 663 *Get all combinations of these three lists.*

In the following example, the MATCH looks at the first product in cell C2 and sees if it is in the list of products in M2:M6. Because match returns either the matching row number or an #N/A! error, the formula tests for #N/A! and then reverses the result using NOT. =NOT(ISNA(MATCH(C2,$M$8:$M$10,0))).

Similar formulas in I2 and J2 test for customers and industries.

I2: =NOT(ISNA(MATCH(B2,M2:M6,0)))

J2: =NOT(ISNA(MATCH(E2,$N$2:$N$6,0)))

I	J	K	L	M
FALSE	FALSE	TRUE		S101
				S103
				S105
				S107
				S109

Figure 664 *Heading row blank, formula in row 2.*

When you perform the Advanced Filter, specify I1:K2 as the criteria range. Excel will apply the formulas to each row of your dataset and only return the records where all three formulas evaluate to TRUE.

ADD SUBTOTALS TO A DATA SET

Problem: I have a lengthy report with invoice detail by customer. I need to add a subtotal at each change in customer.

Strategy: You can use the Subtotal feature to solve this problem in seconds instead of minutes.
1. Sort the data by customer.
2. Select a single cell in the data set. Then select Data, Subtotal. As shown below, the Subtotal dialog assumes that you want to subtotal by the field in the leftmost column of your data. It also assumes that you want to total the rightmost field.

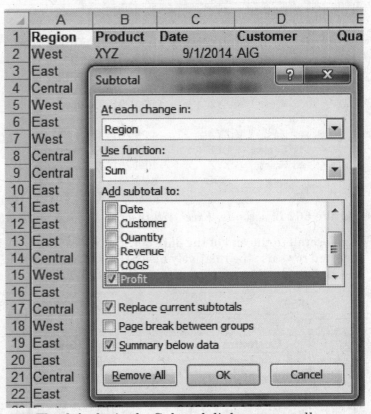

Figure 665 *The defaults in the Subtotal dialog are usually wrong.*

3. Open the At Each Change In dropdown and choose Customer.
4. The Use Function dropdown in this case is already Sum. If your data set has a text column as the right-most column, this will say Count. Change it back to Sum.
5. Checkmark any numeric fields that should have a subtotal. In this case, Quantity, Revenue, and COGS. Profit is already checked because it is the right-most field.
6. If you want every customer on their own page, use Page Break Between Groups, although I am not selecting that option in this case.

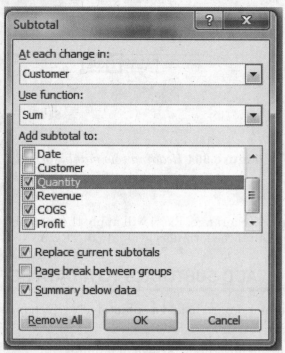

Figure 666 *Subtotal at each change in customer.*

7. Click OK. Excel will insert subtotals at each change in customer.

1 2 3		A	B	C	D	E	F
	1	**Region**	**Product**	**Date**	**Customer**	**Quantity**	**Revenue**
	133	Central	XYZ	12/8/2015	CitiGroup	100	2309
	134	West	XYZ	12/15/2015	CitiGroup	1000	25010
	135				**CitiGroup Total**	29100	613514
	136	West	ABC	11/16/2014	Compaq	1000	17250
	137	Central	XYZ	6/7/2015	Compaq	400	9064
	138	East	DEF	8/7/2015	Compaq	200	4380
	139	West	XYZ	11/25/2015	Compaq	400	8556
	140				**Compaq Total**	2000	39250
	141	East	XYZ	4/29/2014	Duke Energy	800	18264
	142	Central	DEF	9/19/2014	Duke Energy	800	16784
	143	West	XYZ	10/6/2014	Duke Energy	800	16936
	144	East	ABC	8/29/2015	Duke Energy	300	5532
	145				**Duke Energy Total**	2700	57516

Figure 667 *In seconds, Excel will insert new rows with subtotals.*

If you scroll to the end of the data set, you will notice that Excel added a grand total of all customers. The inserted rows use the relatively new SUBTOTAL function. This function will total all the cells in the range except for cells that contain other SUBTOTAL functions.

| F592 | | f_x | =SUBTOTAL(9,F2:F590) |

1 2 3		D	E	F	G	H
	1	**Customer**	**Quantity**	**Revenue**	**COGS**	**Profit**
	588	Wal-Mart	800	18560	8176	10384
	589	Wal-Mart	200	4690	2044	2646
	590	Wal-Mart	700	14560	6888	7672
	591	**Wal-Mart Total**	40400	869454	382170	487284
	592	**Grand Total**	313900	6707812	2978394	3729418

Figure 668 *Excel adds a grand total at the very bottom.*

Additional Details: In order to remove subtotals, you select a cell in the data set and then select Data, Subtotal. In the Subtotal dialog, you click the Remove All button.

Gotcha: This example works because the data was sorted by customer. If the data were sorted by invoice number instead, the result would be fairly meaningless.

USE GROUP & OUTLINE BUTTONS TO COLLAPSE SUBTOTALED DATA

Problem: I just used the Subtotal command in "Add Subtotals to a Data Set," and now I want to print the total rows in order to create a summary report for my manager.

Strategy: If you look above and to the left of cell A1, you'll see a series of three small numbers. These are the Group & Outline buttons. You can use them to collapse subtotaled data. If you click the small 2 button, you will see just the customer totals.

1 2 3		D	E	F
	1	Customer	Quantity	Revenue
+	6	AIG Total	2400	51240
+	47	AT&T Total	23100	498937
+	76	Bank of America To	18700	406326
+	81	Boeing Total	3300	71651

Figure 669 *One row per customer.*

Click the small 1 button to see only the grand totals.

Click the 3 button to go back to all detail rows.

Additional Details: In the 2 button view, you can collapse or expand a single customer's detail records by clicking the - or + symbols next to the customer total.

MANUALLY APPLY GROUPS

Problem: Those group and outline symbols shown in the last topic are cool. Is there any other way to get those? Can I apply them without using subtotals?

Strategy: You just select columns or rows to be grouped and select Data, Group. It is fairly tedious to add many groupings, but this can be easier than continually hiding and unhiding rows or columns.

Below, select the entire column for Jan, Feb, and Mar and click the Group icon on the Data tab. Excel will group those 3 columns and assumes the next column is the summary of those columns.

	A	B	C	D	E	F
1	Account	Jan	Feb	Mar	Q1	Apr
2	A101	14781	15224	15833	45838	16150
3	A102	18294	18660	19220	56174	19797
4	A103	15830	16463	16792	49085	17128

Figure 670 *Grouping Jan, Feb, Mar into an existing Q1 column.*

Repeat this to group April, May, and June into Q2; July, August, September into Q3; and October, November, and December into Q4. The result is that you can quickly toggle from monthly to quarterly views by using the 1 or 2 buttons.

	A	E	I	M	Q
1	Account	Q1	Q2	Q3	Q4
2	A101	45838	48937	51759	57088
3	A102	56174	60387	65744	71398
4	A103	49085	53645	58196	63600
5	A104	71710	76583	82904	91735

Figure 671 *Use the 1 button to collapse.*

GROUP REPORT SECTIONS

Problem: The grouping feature feels backwards. What if I have report headings above each section and I need to group the data below the heading?

Strategy: I picked up this great trick from Mack Wilk, one of the two-time ModelOff World Financial Modeling finalists. There is an obscure setting that makes grouping work the way you want it to work. Mack uses this trick in his models, with multiple levels of grouping. It creates an uncluttered view of the model.

1. On the Data tab, click the Dialog Launcher in the corner of the Outline group.

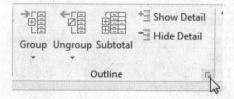

Figure 672 *Open the dialog launcher.*

2. In the Settings dialog, uncheck Summary Rows Below Detail.

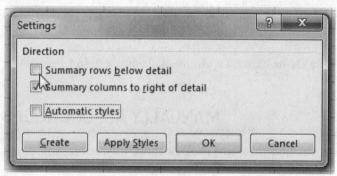

Figure 673 *Uncheck Summary Rows Below Detail.*

3. Select the rows underneath the heading for section 1.

▲	A	B	C
1	Heading for Section 1		
2		Data	Data
3		Data	Data
4		Data	Data
5		Data	Data
6	Heading for Section 2		
7		Data	Data
8		Data	Data

Figure 674 *Select the rows for Section 1, excluding the heading.*

4. Press Shift+Alt+RightArrow to group the selection. Repeat for the rows for each section.

Gotcha: When you mistakenly press Ctrl+Alt+Right arrow, your display may turn sideways (as if you were going to mount your monitor in a portrait fashion). Press Ctrl+Alt+Up arrow to return the monitor to the correct orientation.

You will now have group and outline buttons to collapse all sections. Use one of the + icons to display any section.

1 2	▲	A	B	C	D
+	1	Heading for Section 1			
−	6	Heading for Section 2			
	7		Data	Data	Data
	8		Data	Data	Data
	9		Data	Data	Data
	10		Data	Data	Data
+	11	Heading for Section 3			
	16				

Figure 675 *You can easily expand or collapse any section.*

COPY JUST TOTALS FROM SUBTOTALED DATA

Problem: I've added subtotals and collapsed to the #2 view. My manager wants me to send him just the total rows in a file. When I copy and paste, I get all of the detail rows as well.

Strategy: You can use an obscure command in the Go To Special dialog box to assist with this task. Follow these steps:

1. Choose the 2 Group & Outline button to put the data in subtotal view.
2. Select the entire data set. Use Ctrl+* or Ctrl+A or Ctrl+Shift+8. **Gotcha:** If you forget to hold shift and press Ctrl+8, Excel will remove the Group & Outline symbols. Bring them back again with Ctrl+8.
3. Bring up the Go To Special dialog by choosing Home, Find & Select, Go To Special. Alternatively, you can press the F5 key and click the Special button in the lower-left corner of the Go To dialog.
4. In the Go To Special dialog, select Visible Cells Only

Figure 676 *Select Visible Cells Only.*

5. Click OK. There will be thin white lines above and below each subtotal. If you are in Excel 2007, the color of selected cells is too light to make out the white lines. You've now selected only the visible cells.

	D	E	F
1	Customer	Quantity	Revenue
6	AIG Total	2400	51240
47	AT&T Total	23100	498937
76	Bank of America To	18700	406326
81	Boeing Total	3300	71651

Figure 677 *The white lines indicate the hidden rows are unselected.*

6. Press Ctrl+C to copy. The marching ants will surround each row.

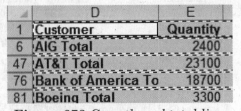

	D	E
1	Customer	Quantity
6	AIG Total	2400
47	AT&T Total	23100
76	Bank of America To	18700
81	Boeing Total	3300

Figure 678 *Copy the subtotal lines.*

7. Switch to a new workbook. Press Ctrl+V to paste. Excel will paste just the subtotal rows.

E2 | f_x 2400

	A	B	C	D	E	F	G	H
1	Region	Product	Date	Customer	Quantity	Revenue	COGS	Profit
2				AIG Total	2400	51240	22824	28416
3				AT&T Tot:	23100	498937	219978	278959
4				Bank of A	18700	406326	178585	227741

Figure 679 *Paste the subtotals only to a new workbook.*

You might think that you would have to select Paste, Values instead of just doing a paste. However, the Paste command works okay. Excel converts the SUBTOTAL functions to values.

Additional Details: Instead of selecting Go To Special, Visible Cells Only, you can press Alt+; (that is, hold down the Alt key and type a semicolon).

SORT LARGEST CUSTOMERS TO THE TOP

Problem: I added subtotals to a data set and collapsed to the #2 view. Now, my manager wants the largest customers at the top of the data set.

Strategy: You would never expect this to work, but you can sort groups of records when in the #2 view.

Start with a the original data set shown here. Choose one cell in the revenue column. Click the ZA button to sort descending.

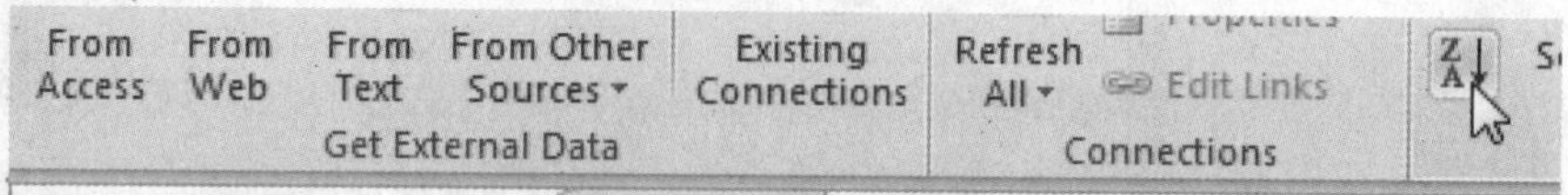

F1 | f_x Revenue

	D	E	F	G	H
1	Customer	Quantity	Revenue	COGS	Profit
6	AIG Total	2400	51240	22824	28416
47	AT&T Total	23100	498937	219978	278959
76	Bank of America To	18700	406326	178585	227741
81	Boeing Total	3300	71651	32471	39180

Figure 680 *Collapse the data, sort by revenue.*

Wal-Mart comes to the top of the data set, but notice that the Wal-Mart total is in row 67.

F67 | f_x =SUBTOTAL(9,F2:F66)

	D	E	F	G	H
1	Customer	Quantity	Revenue	COGS	Profit
67	Wal-Mart Total	40400	869454	382170	487284
128	General Motors Tot:	35700	750163	334614	415549
195	Exxon Total	33400	704359	311381	392978

Figure 681 *The largest customers come to the top.*

Click the 3 Group and Outline button. You will see that all of the Wal-Mart records were sorted along with the Wal-Mart total.

	D	E	F	G	H
1	Customer	Quantity	Revenue	COGS	Profit
63	Wal-Mart	800	19280	7872	11408
64	Wal-Mart	800	18560	8176	10384
65	Wal-Mart	200	4690	2044	2646
66	Wal-Mart	700	14560	6888	7672
67	Wal-Mart Total	40400	869454	382170	487284
68	General Motors	400	8456	3388	5068

Figure 682 *When sorting Wal-Mart to the top, rows 2-67 were treated as a single unit in the sort. This is fairly amazing.*

Gotcha: Excel sorts the 65 Wal-Mart records as a single group. It does not perform any sorting within that group. The Wal-Mart detail records are in their original sequence. If you had wanted the detail records sorted descending, you would have originally sorted by Customer ascending, Revenue descending, then added the subtotals.

If you collapse back to the #2 group and sort by Customer, Excel is smart enough to leave the Grand Total at the bottom instead of sorting it into the G's.

SELECT 100 COLUMNS IN SUBTOTALS

Problem: My data set is a hundred columns wide. In the Subtotal dialog, I have to click 6 columns, then scroll, click 6 more columns, then scroll. It is incredibly tedious. Having a "Select All" button would be incredibly helpful.

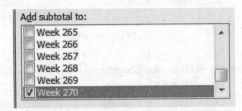

Figure 683 *Individually click hundreds of checkboxes.*

Strategy: Using the keyboard seems to be the fastest way. If you press the spacebar, the selected row will toggle from checked to unchecked. Scroll up, click on the words "Week 1" to select that row. Then, begin pressing spacebar, down arrow, spacebar, down arrow. It will still be tedious, but faster than using the mouse and scrolling.

ENTER A GRAND TOTAL OF DATA MANUALLY SUBTOTALED

Problem: My manager doesn't know the trick for doing automatic subtotals. He manually entered blank lines between each customer and entered SUM formulas for each customer. How can I produce a grand total of all customers?

	A	B	C	D
1	Acct	Customer	Invoice	Revenue
2	A4368	Ainsworth	1014	10,445
3	A4368	Ainsworth	1015	15,544
4	A4368	Ainsworth	1030	3,922
5	A4368	Ainsworth	1054	12,838
6	A4368	Ainsworth	1091	17,712
7		Total Ainsworth		60,461
8				
9	A3108	Air Canada	1057	5,859
10	A3108	Air Canada	1061	2,358
11	A3108	Air Canada	1090	17,856
12	A3108	Air Canada	1108	4,948
13		Total Air Canada		31,021
14				
15	B4504	Bell Canada	1013	15,104
16	B4504	Bell Canada	1069	18,072
17	B4504	Bell Canada	1074	14,004
18	B4504	Bell Canada	1077	4,060
19		Total Bell Canada		51,240
20				
21	Grand Total			

Figure 684 *With 100 customers, the formula would be lengthy.*

Strategy: Sum all of the cells and divide by 2 using =SUM(D2:D20)/2.

This method works! It is an old accounting trick (taught to me by an old accountant).

It is not intuitive, especially if you hated algebra.

Every number is in the Grand Total twice, once from the detail row and once from the manual totals.

Try it for yourself a few times, comparing the results to the method of using =D19+D13+D7. You will see that you get the same result.

	D21		f_x	=SUM(D2:D20)/2

	A	B	C	D	E
1	Acct	Customer	Invoice	Revenue	
2	A4368	Ainsworth	1014	10,445	
3	A4368	Ainsworth	1015	15,544	
4	A4368	Ainsworth	1030	3,922	
5	A4368	Ainsworth	1054	12,838	
6	A4368	Ainsworth	1091	17,712	
7		Total Ainsworth		60,461	
8					
9	A3108	Air Canada	1057	5,859	
10	A3108	Air Canada	1061	2,358	
11	A3108	Air Canada	1090	17,856	
12	A3108	Air Canada	1108	4,948	
13		Total Air Canada		31,021	
14					
15	B4504	Bell Canada	1013	15,104	
16	B4504	Bell Canada	1069	18,072	
17	B4504	Bell Canada	1074	14,004	
18	B4504	Bell Canada	1077	4,060	
19		Total Bell Canada		51,240	
20					
21	Grand Total			142,722	

Figure 685 *Sum and divide by 2.*

Gotcha: This method works only if all the customers are totaled. A manager who doesn't know how to use subtotals might be the kind of manager who doesn't total the customers with only one detail line. Below, line 9 will cause the total to not work.

	A	B	C	D
9	A9875	Aironet	1040	17,250
10				
11	A3108	Air Canada	1057	5,859
12	A3108	Air Canada	1061	2,358
13	A3108	Air Canada	1090	17,856
14	A3108	Air Canada	1108	4,948
15		Total Air Canada		31,021
16				
17	B4504	Bell Canada	1013	15,104
18	B4504	Bell Canada	1069	18,072
19	B4504	Bell Canada	1074	14,004
20	B4504	Bell Canada	1077	4,060
21		Total Bell Canada		51,240
22				
23	Grand Total			151,347
24				

Figure 686 *If someone is manually adding totals, he might not add a redundant total for row 9.*

ADD OTHER TEXT TO THE SUBTOTAL LINES

Problem: My data set has account number in column A and a customer name in column B. When I subtotal by account and collapse using the 2 Group & Outline button, I see only the Account numbers. While I have memorized that B4504 is Bell Canada, my manager cannot seem to remember this, so I need to add the customer name to the subtotal lines.

1 2 3		A	B	C	D
	1	Acct	Customer	Invoice	Revenue
+	6	A3108 Total			31,021
+	12	A4368 Total			60,461
+	17	B4504 Total			51,240
+	22	C4904 Total			39,250

Figure 687 *Add customer name to the subtotal rows.*

Strategy: To add the customer name to the subtotal lines, you follow these steps:
1. Collapse the report by clicking the small 2 Group & Outline button above and to the left of cell A1.
2. Select all the blank cells in column B by using the mouse to drag from B6 down to the cell above the Grand Total row. In doing so, you will select all the cells in the range B6:B136.
3. Type Ctrl+; to select the visible cells only. (Ctrl and Semicolon)
4. Note the row number of your first subtotal row. In this example, the first subtotal is row 6, and you will write a formula to copy the total from row 5. Change the cell reference in the following formula to point to the row above your first subtotal row: ="Total "&B5. To enter a similar formula in every selected cell, press Ctrl+Enter.

| B6 | | | f_x | ="Total "&B5 | |

	A	B	C	D
1	Acct	Customer	Invoice	Revenue
6	A3108 Total	Total Air Canada		31,021
12	A4368 Total	Total Ainsworth		60,461
17	B4504 Total	Total Bell Canada		51,240
22	C4904 Total	Total Compaq		39,250
27	C8082 Total	Total Compton Petroleum		31,369
32	C9651 Total	Total Chevron		54,048

Figure 688 *Add a customer name to each subtotal row.*

Gotcha: Step 3 to select the visible cells only is important. If you fail to do this, you will overwrite all customers from row 6 to the bottom with Total Total Total.

If you see this, you need to immediately press Ctrl+Z to undo.

Gotcha: This trick gets the last customer name. If you need to get the first customer name from the group, you are going to have to use a clever trick and a three-line macro. Search YouTube for Learn Excel 712 for the details.

SUBTOTALS BY PRODUCT WITHIN REGION

Problem: I want to add subtotals by two fields, such as Product and Region.

Strategy: Adding subtotals by two fields seems easy, but there is a trick to it. You need to add subtotals to the least detailed field first. Here's how it works:
1. Sort by product within region. Select a cell in the Product column. Click the AZ icon on the Data tab. Select a cell in Region. Click AZ.
2. Select Data, Subtotal and add a subtotal by Region.
3. Select Data, Subtotal again. Change Region to Product. Be sure to uncheck the Replace Current Subtotals box.

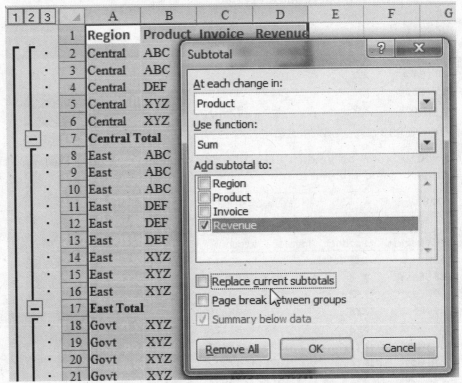

Figure 689 *Uncheck Replace Current Subtotals.*

Results: You now have two sets of subtotals. There are now four Group & Outline buttons to the left of cell A1.

1 2 3 4		A	B	C	D
	1	Region	Product	Invoice	Revenue
	2	Central	ABC	1064	67357
	3	Central	ABC	1075	60248
	4		ABC Total		127605
	5	Central	DEF	1067	6497
	6		DEF Total		6497
	7	Central	XYZ	1052	48370
	8	Central	XYZ	1070	55612
	9		XYZ Total		103982
	10	Central Total			238084
	11	East	ABC	1053	65770

Figure 690 *Excel adds two levels of subtotals.*

If you choose the 3 Group & Outline button, you will have totals by region and product.

	A	B	C	D
1	Region	Product	Invoice	Revenue
4		ABC Total		127605
6		DEF Total		6497
9		XYZ Total		103982
10	Central Total			238084
14		ABC Total		121622

Figure 691 *#3 group and outline view.*

If you choose the 2 Group & Outline button, you will have totals by region.

Additional Details: Here is why it is important to do the subtotals in the correct order: Say that your company sells three products. The Government region buys only product XYZ. You might have data that looks like the data below. Note that row 15 contains an XYZ record for the East, and row 16 contains an XYZ record for the Government region.

12	East	DEF	1066	2247
13	East	XYZ	1054	69552
14	East	XYZ	1055	4358
15	East	XYZ	1072	18870
16	Govt	XYZ	1063	33118
17	Govt	XYZ	1065	35401

Figure 692 *Same product, different regions are adjacent.*

If you subtotal by product first, the XYZ products from the East and the Government regions will be trapped in one subtotal in row 25. This is an absolute mess.

D25			f_x	=SUBTOTAL(9,D18:D24)		
	A	B	C	D	E	F
1	Region	Product	Invoice	Revenue		
17		DEF Total		32013		
18	East	XYZ	1054	69552		
19	East	XYZ	1055	4358		
20	East	XYZ	1072	18870		
21	Govt	XYZ	1063	33118		
22	Govt	XYZ	1065	35401		
23	Govt	XYZ	1071	17927		
24	Govt	XYZ	1073	54091		
25		XYZ Total		233317		
26	West	ABC	1058	64782		
27	West	ABC	1061	18361		

Figure 693 *Subtotal product first, and Excel has no idea that you will later subtotal by region.*

If you then total by region, you will have set up groups that make no sense. Note that the XYZ total in D32 includes both Govt and East records.

20	East	DEF	1066	2247
21	East Total			32013
22		DEF Total		32013
23	East	XYZ	1054	69552
24	East	XYZ	1055	4358
25	East	XYZ	1072	18870
26	East Total			92780
27	Govt	XYZ	1063	33118
28	Govt	XYZ	1065	35401
29	Govt	XYZ	1071	17927
30	Govt	XYZ	1073	54091
31	Govt Total			140537
32		XYZ Total		=SUBTOTAL(9,D23:D30)
33	West	ABC	1058	64782

Figure 694 *Chaos ensues.*

Additional Details: In Excel 95, there was no workaround for this problem. In Excel 97, Microsoft added the rule that XYZ rows separated by a blank row would be handled correctly. Thus, you need to add subtotals by region first.

FORMAT THE SUBTOTAL ROWS

Problem: My manager loves my reports with automatic subtotals but he wants the entire row in bold, not just the Subtotal By column.

Strategy: Visible Cells Only will again save the day.
1. Add subtotals to the data set.
2. Click the 2 Group & Outline button to display only the subtotals.
3. Select all data except the headings.
4. Press Ctrl+; to select the visible cells.
5. Apply Bold. Choose a fill color. Go to a bigger font. Live it up.
6. Click the 3 Group & Outline button. You've formatted only the total rows.

		A	B	C	D
	5	Bob	Sears	58,901	15,112
	6	Bob	Texaco	4,937	56,399
	7	Bob	Verizon	74,173	69,724
	8	**Bob Total**		**244,471**	**244,731**
	9	Joe	Air Canada	43,097	53,369
	10	Joe	Compaq	25,991	56,623
	11	Joe	Ford	47,662	30,635
	12	Joe	Sun Life Financia	42,172	43,469
	13	**Joe Total**		**158,922**	**184,096**
	14	Mary	Ainsworth	6,475	15,567
	15	Mary	Chevron	72,587	23,640
	16	Mary	Sears Canada	69,013	24,207
	17	Mary	SBC Communica	18,244	22,914
	18	Mary	Shell Canada	46,756	60,476
	19	**Mary Total**		**213,075**	**146,804**
	20	**Grand Total**		**616,468**	**575,631**

Figure 695 *Format only the subtotal rows.*

MY MANAGER WANTS A BLANK LINE AFTER EACH SUBTOTAL

Problem: My manager wants me to add a blank line between sections of a subtotal report.

Strategy: This is a fairly standard request. Quite simply, data looks better when it is formatted this way. But there is no built-in way to do this with Excel. I've tried many methods. There are two methods that will work here. One method is simpler but is really cheating; you only make it look like you added a blank row. The second method is convoluted but about 50% easier than the method I described in the previous edition of this book.

The first method is to try to fool the manager by making the total rows double height, with the totals vertically aligned to the top. This method may work if you are printing the report to give to the manager. It will give the appearance that a blank row has been inserted. Here's how you do it:

1. To do this easily, add subtotals, collapse to level 2, and select all subtotal rows from the first subtotal to the last subtotal.
2. Select Home, Find & Select, Go To Special, and from the Go To Special dialog, select Visible Cells Only and click OK. (You can use Alt+; as the shortcut for Visible Cells Only.)
3. Select Home, Format dropdown, Row Height. Depending on your font, the row height will probably be between 12 and 14. Say that the height is 12.75. Mentally multiply by 2 and type 25.5 as the new height.
4. In the Home tab of the ribbon, click the Align Top icon.
5. Choose the 3 Group & Outline button to display the detail rows again.

Although you can see that there is no blank row after the subtotals in rows 8 and 13, when you print the report for your manager, it will appear to have a blank row.

6	Bob	Texaco	4,937	56,399
7	Bob	Verizon	74,173	69,724
	Bob Total		244,471	244,731
8				
9	Joe	Air Canada	43,097	53,369
10	Joe	Compaq	25,991	56,623

Figure 696 *There is not a blank row between rows 8 and 9.*

This method will not work if you have to send the data set to the manager via e-mail. The manager may be smart enough to want to stop at each subtotal by pressing the End key, and this will not work with the double-height rows.

Alternate Strategy: This method is far more complex than the one just described but creates the desired result. Follow these steps:

1. Add subtotals as described previously. Click the 2 Group & Outline button.
2. Insert a new temporary blank column A to the left of the current column A. To do this, select any cell in column A and then choose Home, Insert, Insert Sheet Columns.
3. Select the cells in column A from the first subtotal down to the last subtotal.
4. Use Alt+; to select only the visible rows.

5. Type 1 and press Ctrl+Enter to put a 1 next to every subtotal.
6. Click the 3 Group & Outline button to see all the detail rows. If you did step 4 correctly, you will see a 1 on only the subtotal lines.
7. Select any blank cell before the first number 1 in column A. Select Home, Insert, Insert Cells, Shift Cells Down, OK. This will move the 1's from the subtotal lines to the first row of each customer.
8. Select all of Column A. Select Home, Find & Select, Go To Special and select Constants in the Go To Special dialog.

4		Adam	1114	33873
5	1	Adam Total		71883
6		Alice	1142	19390
7		Alice	1215	46184
8		Alice	1193	53766
9	1	Alice Total		119340
10		Bev	1226	53755
11		Bev	1180	69506
12		Bev	1197	71264
13	1	Bev Total		194525

Figure 697 *You've added a 1 next to each subtotal.*

9. Select Home, Insert, Insert Sheet Rows. Excel will insert 1 row above each row in your selection. Through the combination of steps 7 and 8, you were able to make a selection that consisted of each cell underneath the subtotals. Inserting a new row above these cells creates the result.

1	Alice	1142	19390
	Alice	1215	46184
	Alice	1193	53766
	Alice Total		**119340**
1	Bev	1226	53755
	Bev	1180	69506
	Bev	1197	71264
	Bev Total		**194525**
1	Bob	1113	11930

Figure 698 *Insert a row above each cell in the selection.*

Results: You will have added the blank rows requested by the manager. You can now delete column A.

Gotcha: When the blank rows are in, you may have a difficult time getting rid of the subtotals. If you select cell A2 and choose Data, Subtotal, Remove All, Excel will delete only the first subtotal. In order to delete all the subtotals, you have to select the entire range before calling the Subtotal command. One fast way to do this is to click on the blank gray box above and to the left of cell A1. This box will select all cells in the worksheet. Now when you choose Data, Subtotal, you will find that Excel has selected all the subtotals. Click Remove All to remove the subtotals.

SUBTOTAL ONE COLUMN AND COUNT ANOTHER COLUMN

Problem: I want to subtotal revenue and count the number of records. The Subtotal dialog offers 11 different summary functions including two counting functions. How do I change the function for different columns?

I've tried adding the SUM to Revenue, then doing subtotals a second time to count the customer, but the subtotals end up on two different rows.

Strategy: When you add subtotals, Excel makes use of a function called =SUBTOTAL(). The first argument of the SUBTOTAL function tells Excel which summary function to use.

=SUBTOTAL(9, is the argument for sum. There are 11 functions to choose from. Microsoft arranged the arguments alphabetically.

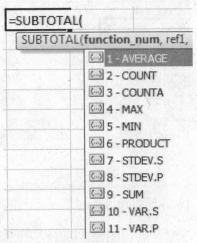

Figure 699 *SUM is ninth alphabetically. That explains the 9.*

The solution is to add automatic subtotals to the numeric columns and the text column that you want to count. Of course, the totals on the text column will be zero.

A81		fx	=SUBTOTAL(9,A77:A80)	

	A	B	C	D
1	Region	Product	Date	Customer
75	East	XYZ	12/28/2015	Bank of America
76	0			Bank of America To
77	East	XYZ	2/16/2014	Boeing
78	East	ABC	5/14/2014	Boeing
79	West	XYZ	7/10/2014	Boeing
80	Central	DEF	4/25/2015	Boeing
81	0			Boeing Total
82	Central	DEF	2/26/2014	Chevron
83	East	ABC	3/16/2014	Chevron

Figure 700 *Total a text column.*

1. Select the entire text column.
2. Use Ctrl+H to display the Find and Replace dialog.
3. Type (9, in the Find What box.
4. Type (3, in the Replace With box.
5. Press Replace All.

Figure 701 *Change the 9 argument to 3.*

This will change the SUBTOTAL function from one that sums to one that counts text entries. You will have a count in column A and a sum in column E.

A76		fx	=SUBTOTAL(3,A48:A75)		

	A	B	C	D	E
1	Region	Product	Date	Customer	Quantity
75	East	XYZ	12/28/2015	Bank of America	700
76	28			Bank of America To	18700
77	East	XYZ	2/16/2014	Boeing	800
78	East	ABC	5/14/2014	Boeing	500
79	West	XYZ	7/10/2014	Boeing	1000
80	Central	DEF	4/25/2015	Boeing	1000
81	4			Boeing Total	3300

Figure 702 *Counts and sums on the same row.*

CAN YOU GET MEDIANS?

Problem: Why doesn't the subtotal feature offer Median?

Strategy: In Excel 2010, Microsoft added a new function called AGGREGATE. The AGGREGATE function is SUBTOTALS's stronger cousin. The function offers the same 11 calculation options plus several new ones.

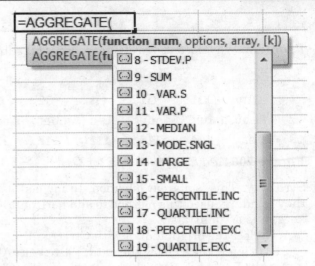

Figure 703 *Aggregate offers more calculation options.*

The options argument offers more choices for which rows are included.

AGGREGATE(12,

AGGREGATE(function_num, **options**, array, [k])

AGGREGATE(funct

- 0 - Ignore nested SUBTOTAL and AGGREGATE functions
- 1 - Ignore hidden rows, nested SUBTOTAL and AGGREGATE functions
- 2 - Ignore error values, nested SUBTOTAL and AGGREGATE functions
- 3 - Ignore hidden rows, error values, nested SUBTOTAL and AGGREGATE functions
- 4 - Ignore nothing
- 5 - Ignore hidden rows
- 6 - Ignore error values
- 7 - Ignore hidden rows and error values

Figure 704 *More options for what to ignore.*

The AGGREGATE function offers potential for some incredible calculations. The new calculation arguments of 12 through 19 allow for array formulas, which would lead to some good additions for the Excel Gurus Gone Wild book. But to solve the median problem, it requires a simple Find and Replace.

To use a MEDIAN in a subtotal, you can use the Subtotal command to sum the column in question.

Select the column. Use Find and Replace. Find SUBTOTAL(9, and replace with AGGREGATE(12,0,.

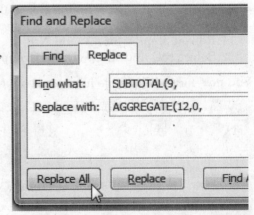

Figure 705 *Change subtotals to medians.*

Additional Details: If you are interested in Medians, you might also want to create a Median in a pivot table. The Power Pivot add-in for Excel 2015 will finally allow medians in pivot tables. As I write this, the feature is in beta, but as you read this, it might be available.

HORIZONTAL SUBTOTALS

Problem: Why doesn't Excel offer horizontal subtotals?

◢	A	B	C	D	E	F	G	H
1	Qtr	Q1	Q1	Q1	Q2	Q2	Q2	
2	Rep	Amber	Andy	Leo	Amber	Andy	Leo	Amb
3	Sales	104	115	112	117	110	124	1

Figure 706 *Add a subtotal in E for Q1.*

Strategy: This is a great question. In my podcast episode 1001, I had several people write in to say that they regularly used this method to add horizontal subtotals. Although it is a lot of steps, if you use shortcut keys, it is actually fast.

1. Select the original data with Ctrl+*
2. Go a few rows below the data. Paste with Alt+E+S+E+Enter.
3. Alt+D+B to display the Subtotals dialog. Click OK.
4. Ctrl+C to copy the vertical data set with the subtotals.
5. Select cell A1.
6. Paste Transpose with Alt+E+S+E+Enter.
7. Fix the column widths with Alt+O+C+A.

◢	A	B	C	D	E	F
1	Qtr	Q1	Q1	Q1	**Q1 Total**	Q2
2	Rep	Amber	Andy	Leo		Amber
3	Sales	104	115	112	331	117
4						
5	Qtr	Rep	Sales			
6	Q1	Amber	104			
7	Q1	Andy	115			
8	Q1	Leo	112			
9	**Total**		331			

Figure 707 *Horizontal subtotals.*

8. Delete the temporary table at the bottom.
9. Optionally, select columns B:D and choose Data, Group.
10. Select columns F:H and press F4 to re-do the group command.
11. Repeat step 10 for J:L and N:P.
12. Select B:Q and choose Data, Group.

You now have collapsible horizontal subtotals.

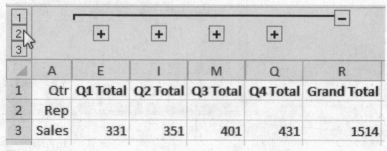

◢	A	E	I	M	Q	R
1	Qtr	**Q1 Total**	**Q2 Total**	**Q3 Total**	**Q4 Total**	**Grand Total**
2	Rep					
3	Sales	331	351	401	431	1514

Figure 708 *After manually adding groups.*

BE WARY

Problem: By using the tips in this book, I have found myself processing data faster than ever before. However, I've also begun to mess up data faster than ever before.

Strategy: It's important to save and save often. It's also a good idea to frequently check your data to make sure it's reasonable. For example, if you work for a company with $100 million in annual sales, a quarterly sales report should not show $200 billion in sales.

Try to figure out problems as soon as they happen. Excel is an incredibly logical program. Everything happens for a reason. If you can figure out the reason, you will master it in no time. Every "Gotcha" in this book represents a problem that has stung me in the past.

In 30 years of spreadsheet work, I have had only a few times when I could not find a logical explanation for something. If you are truly stumped, describe your situation on a message board such as the one at MrExcel.com. The odds are that someone else has seen the same problem and figured it out.

You need to be aware of your data processing steps and occasionally do a reasonableness test to make sure your data still looks right. You should also save frequently with different file names if you are doing something new that you are unsure of. This way, you can go back to the IncomeBeforeSubtotals.xls file if you think you have done something wrong.

SEND ERROR REPORTS

Problem: I keep getting a fatal error on a particular workbook.

Strategy: If Excel crashes and offers you the chance to report the problem, please do so: All you have to do is click Send Error Report. Millions of people are using Excel, and if everyone reports their errors, Microsoft will get a good statistical picture of the errors.

Sending an error report is particularly important if you are using a new version of the program or have recently installed a service pack.

If you keep getting a particular crash, check the Microsoft Knowledge Base. One version of Excel would crash about three steps after you had used the Edit, Find command in Excel. By the time I realized the trend, Microsoft had acknowledged the problem and offered a hotfix that was downloadable from the Knowledge Base.

After you send an error report, Excel will reopen and offer to load the last version of your workbook. You might also have the choice to open previously saved versions of the workbook.

There are certain things that I know will cause Excel to crash. For instance, in Excel 2003, I added a cell comment in the GPF.xls workbook and then ran a simple Excel macro to delete all the shapes on the worksheet. When I got the cell pointer near the red triangle in the commented cell, Excel tried to display the comment shape. Because the macro had already deleted the shape, Excel 2003 crashed with a GPF. I reported this error, and the behavior was fixed in Excel 2007, so this problem no longer causes a crash.

Sometimes, particularly in Excel 2000 and earlier versions, I would encounter spreadsheets that had simply become corrupt. I was able to open these worksheets, but if I tried to use File, Close or File, Save, Excel would crash. I learned that the following sequence would save the data:
1. Open the corrupt workbook.
2. Create a new blank workbook.
3. Copy data from the bad workbook to the new workbook.
4. Use File, Save As to save the new workbook.
5. Close the new workbook.
6. Close the corrupt workbook, knowing it will crash. You can then use the saved version of the new workbook without having it crash.

HELP MAKE EXCEL 2017 BETTER

Problem: I have a few ideas about how I'd like Excel to operate differently. Other people must be having similar problems. How can I communicate my ideas to Microsoft?

Strategy: Opt-in to the Customer Experience Improvement program. Say that you installed Excel on a Monday. On the third day that you used Excel, a question would appear: "Would you like to make Excel better?" If you answered yes on that day, then you are participating in the Customer Experience Improvement Program. Participants in this program allow Microsoft to track how they invoke commands. Microsoft will learn if you copy by using Ctrl+C, right-click, Copy, Home, Copy, or another method; it will track your actions, along with those of the millions of other people who signed up. Currently, Microsoft has a database of 750 billion user experiences.

Before Excel 2003, Microsoft used a lot of conjecture about which commands were the most popular. In Excel 2007, it was able to query the database to find out exactly which commands are popular.

On the flip side, Microsoft can also use this data to prove that hardly anyone is using a command and can argue to take it out of a future product. But remember that with 750 million users, "hardly anyone" works out to a stadium full of people. Maybe only 0.01% of Excel 2003 customers used natural language formulas; but this works out to 75,000 people who will be angry to learn that the feature was removed from Excel 2007.

Additional Details: Did you ever use Wrap Text in Excel 2003? I did. Say that I had 10 columns of data, and 1 column had really long customer responses in column H. I would typically select this column and then select Format, Cells, Alignment, Wrap Text. However, I might then notice that all the data in A:G and I:J was set to vertical align bottom, making the data not line up with the now-wrapped text in column I. I would have to select A:G and then select Format, Cells, Alignment, Vertical, Top. In all, this process required 17 mouse clicks. In Excel 2003, there was not a Wrap Text icon that you could add to your toolbars, and the Vertical Align icons were not a part of the formatting toolbar.

Well, there must have been a million other people participating in the Customer Experience Improvement Program who had this same issue. Microsoft heard loud and clear that Wrap Text, followed by Vertical Align Top is a popular sequence of commands. In response, you now have one-click access to a Wrap Text icon on the Home tab of the ribbon. The Vertical Align Top icon is near the Wrap Text icon.

REMOVE BLANK ROWS FROM A RANGE

Problem: Someone has given me data pasted from Word. There are a number of blank cells in the list. I want to eliminate the blank rows.

	A
1	H
2	He
3	
4	Li
5	Be
6	B
7	C
8	N
9	O
10	F
11	Ne
12	
13	Na

Figure 709 *Remove blank rows.*

	A
1	Ac
2	Ag
3	Al
4	Am
5	Ar
6	As
7	At
8	Au
9	B

Figure 710 *No blanks, but the data is resequenced.*

Strategy: If the sequence is not important, you can sort the entire data range. Excel will move all blank cells to the bottom of the sort range. Here's how you do it:
1. Move the cell pointer to A1. While holding down the Shift key, press the End key and then the Home key. Excel will select the entire range of data in the spreadsheet.
2. Select Data, Sort. In the Sort dialog, indicate that your data does not have a header row by unchecking the My Data Has Headers box. Click OK.

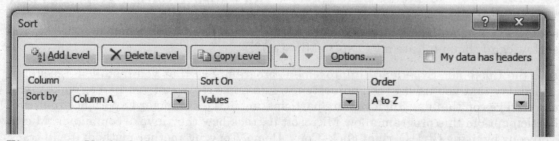

Figure 711 *Uncheck the My Data Has Headers box.*

Results: The blanks will be removed from the list.

Excel's Sort feature will always move blanks cells to the end of the sort. Sorting a column with blanks is a quick way to remove the blanks from the data.

REMOVE BLANKS FROM A RANGE
WHILE KEEPING THE ORIGINAL SEQUENCE

Problem: Someone has given me data pasted from Word. There are a number of blank cells in the list. I want to eliminate the blank rows, but I need to keep the data in the original sequence.

Strategy: The trick described in "Remove Blank Rows from a Range"—sorting data to move the blanks to the end—is effective, but it destroys the original sequence of the range. Before sorting, you can add a temporary column with the original sequence numbers so that the data can be sorted back. Follow these steps:

1. Insert a new row 1. Place the cell pointer in cell A1 and then select Home, Insert, Insert Sheet Rows. Because you have only one cell selected, only one row will be inserted.
2. In A1, enter a heading such as Symbol. In cell B1, enter a heading such as Sequence. Apply the cell style Heading 4 by using the Cell Styles gallery on the Home tab.
3. In cell B2, enter the number 1. Select B2. Hold down the Ctrl key while you drag the fill handle to the last row that contains data. The series 1, 2, 3 will extend down to 129 in row 130. **Gotcha:** If you get a series of 1s instead of 1, 2, 3, then you did not hold down the Ctrl key. Open the Auto Fill Options icon in C131 and choose Fill Series.

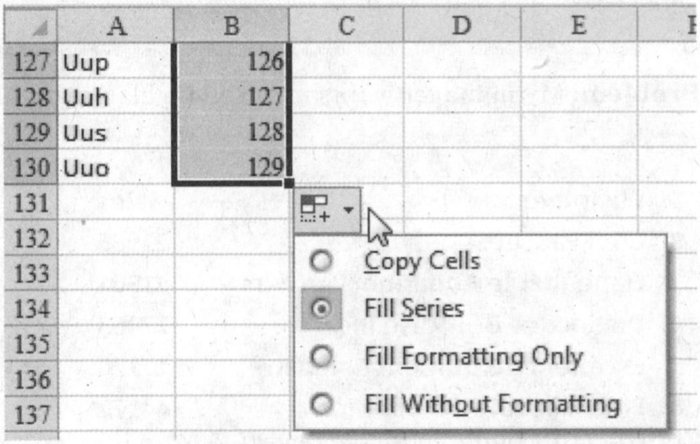

Figure 712 *Ctrl+drag the fill handle.*

Note: If the Auto Fill Options icon is obscuring some other data, it is fairly difficult to dismiss. One method is to resize any column.

4. Next, sort the data based on column A by selecting a single cell in column A and pressing the AZ button on the Data tab.
5. Press the End key and then the Down Arrow key to ride the range down to the last cell in A that contains data. Delete the rows below this last cell by highlighting the row numbers, right-clicking, and choosing Delete. (These are the blank cells. It is important to delete the sequence numbers from B for the blank cells so that they do not sort back into the data in the next step.)
6. Move the cell pointer to any value in column B. Click the AZ button on the Data tab to sort the data into the original sequence, without the blanks.

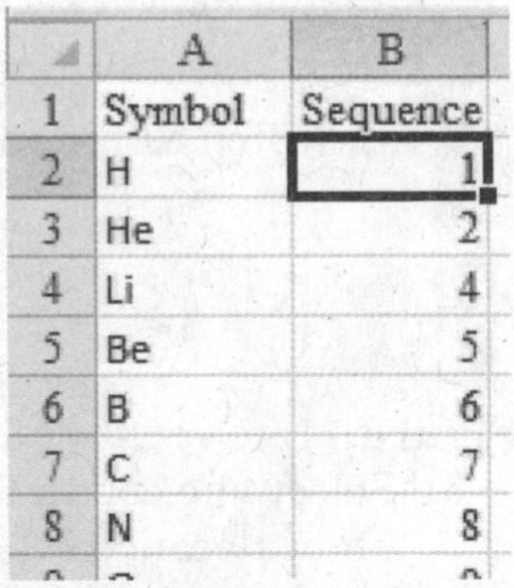

Figure 713 *Sort by B to return A to the original sequence.*

7. Delete the temporary column B by selecting Home, Delete, Delete Sheet Columns.

8. Delete the temporary row 1 by moving the cell pointer to A1 and selecting Home, Delete, Delete Sheet Rows.

Results: The blanks will be removed from the list, and the list will retain the original sequence.

Alternate Strategy: The previous steps work particularly well when your data set has many columns and you need to delete based on one column. If you truly have a data set that has a single column, try this faster method:

1. Select the range of data.
2. Select Home, Find & Select, Go To Special and in the Go To Special dialog, select Blanks and click OK.
3. Select Home, Delete, Delete Cells, select Shift Cells Up, and click OK.

Excel will delete all the blanks and move the lower cells up.

Alternate Strategy: You can solve this with the Filter. Follow these steps:

1. Add a heading.
2. Select the entire data set.
3. Select Data, Filter. Open the Filter dropdown for the heading. Uncheck Select All. Scroll all the way to the bottom to choose (Blanks).
4. Re-select the visible rows, excluding the heading.
5. Select Home, Delete, Delete Sheet Rows.
6. Select Clear from the Sort & Filter group on the Data ribbon tab.

DOUBLE SPACE YOUR DATA SET

Problem: My manager wants me to add a blank row after every row of the data.

	A	B
1	Customer	Sales
2	Cool Faucet Supply	23986
3	Dependable Aquarium Partners	21964
4	Distinctive Briefcase Inc.	27453
5	Excellent Instrument Company	17120
6	Fine Flagpole Corporation	44172

Figure 714 *Double space the report!*

Strategy: Excel MVP Bob Umlas showed me this trick, and it has become one of my favorites. Search YouTube for Learn Excel 467 to see Bob demo the trick.

Bob adds a new column with numbers 1, 2, 3, and so on. He then copies this range of numbers below the itself. When you sort by the new column, your report is instantly double-spaced! Follow these steps:

1. In the blank column to the right of your data, enter the heading Sort.
2. Fill the column with a sequence of 1, 2, 3, etc. One method is to type a 1 in the first cell, select the cell, and Ctrl+drag the fill handle to the end of the data set.
3. Press Ctrl+C to copy the selected numbers in the new column to the Clipboard.
4. Select the first blank cell beneath your new column. Press Ctrl+V to paste a duplicate set of numbers.

14	Reliable Faucet Partners	39230	13
15	Savory Necktie Supply	26335	14
16	Top-Notch Notebook Inc.	10645	15
17			1
18			2
19			3

Figure 715 *Copy the numbers below.*

5. Select one cell in the new column. Click the AZ button on the Data tab. Excel sorts by the new column. Because every number occurs twice—once in the original report and once below the report—blank rows are sorted up into your data.

◢	A	B	C
1	Customer	Sales	Sort
2	Cool Faucet Supply	23986	1
3			1
4	Dependable Aquarium Partners	21964	2
5			2
6	Distinctive Briefcase Inc.	27453	3
7			3
8	Excellent Instrument Company	17120	4
9			4
10	Fine Flagpole Corporation	44172	5

Figure 716 *Sort by C, and the data is double-spaced.*

6. Delete the Sort column.

Additional Details: To triple space your data, you can paste two copies of the numbers below your data.

Additional Details: Check out Bob Umlas's book *More Excel Outside the Box* (available at Amazon). It is filled with tricks like this one.

USE FIND TO FIND AN ASTERISK

Problem: My largest customer is Wal*Mart. When I use Find or Find and Replace to search for Wal*Mart, Excel also finds Wallingsmart. I know this happens because Excel sees * as a wildcard character. What if I really want to search for an asterisk?

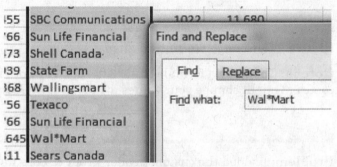

Figure 717 *The asterisk is a wildcard.*

Strategy: You can use three wildcard characters in the Find and Replace dialog: *, ?, and ~.

If you include an *, Excel will search for any number of characters where the asterisk is located. For example, searching for Wal*mart will find Wal*mart and also Walton Williams is smart.

If you include a ?, Excel will search for any one character. For example, searching for ?arl will find both Carl and Karl.

To force Excel to search for an asterisk, tilde, or a question mark, you can precede the wildcard with a tilde (~). When you search for Wal~*mart, Excel will only find Wal*mart. If you search for Who~? Excel will only find Who? and not Whom. When you search for "Alt+~~", Excel will find "Alt+~".

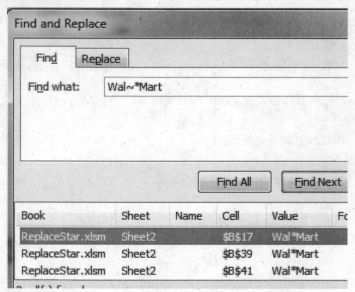

Figure 718 *Use ~* to really find an asterisk.*

Additional Details: To change all the multiplication formulas to division formulas, you can have Excel change all ~* to /.

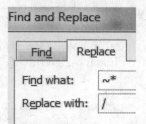

Figure 719 *Change multiply to divide.*

Gotcha: Changing a formula of =5*3 to =5/3 will work fine. Changing a math exercise sheet with 5*3 to become 5/3 might change your values to May 3rd. Use caution when changing asterisk to slashes within text.

USE AN AMPERSAND IN A HEADER

Problem: I added the custom header Profit & Loss Report to my report.

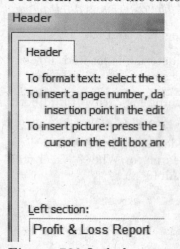

Figure 720 *Include an ampersand in the header.*

However, the actual header appears as Profit Loss Report. The ampersand is missing.

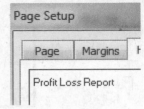

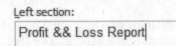

Figure 721 *Excel leaves out the &.*

Strategy: The ampersand is a special character in the custom header and footer field. To print an ampersand in the header, you have to type && in the Header dialog box.

Left section:

Profit && Loss Report

Figure 722 *Specify && while editing the header.*

Having two ampersands will give you the desired heading Profit & Loss.

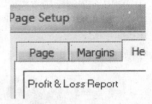

Figure 723 *Excel will print the && as a single &.*

HIDE ZEROS & OTHER CUSTOM NUMBER FORMATTING TRICKS

Problem: I don't want zeros to appear in my document.

Strategy: Excel's custom number formatting codes have an amazing array of options that not many people know about. You can specify multiple formats within one custom number code. Each format is separated by semi-colons. Read on for details.

To assign a custom number format, you select the range and press Ctrl+One. On the Format dialog, you select the Number tab and then select Custom from the Category list. Finally, you type any valid custom number format in the Type box.

You've probably run into some custom number formats, such as these:
- #,##0 will display numbers with thousands separators.
- $#,##0.00 will display two decimal places and a currency symbol.
- #,##0,K will display numbers in thousands.
- mm/dd/yyyy will display a date as 02/17/2014.
- [h]:mm will display hours in excess of 24 hours.
- [blue]0 will display a number in blue text.
- [color12]0 will use color index 12, often olive.

In these simple formats, there is only one format being used. If you enter two formats separated by a semi-colon, the first format is used for positive and zero value, and the second format is used for negative values. For example, [blue]0;[red]-0 will display negative numbers in red and other numbers in blue.

If you enter three formats separated by semicolons, the first format is for positive, the second format is for negative, and the third format is for zero. For example, [blue]0;[red]-0;[green]0 will display 0 cells in green text.

To show a plus sign before the positive numbers, use +0;-0;0.

If you type a second semicolon and leave out the final formatting code, Excel will suppress the display of zero values. For example, 0;-0; will show positive and negative numbers but hide zeros. Note that the final semicolon is a subtle but important difference from using 0;0. This figure shows the custom number format to hide zeros.

	A	B	C
1	-1000		-1000
2	0		
3	1000		1000
4	Text		Text

Number
Currency
Accounting
Date
Time
Percentage
Fraction
Scientific

-1000

Type:

0;-0;

[h]:mm::
_($* #,:
_(* #,#

Figure 724 *The zero in C2 is not displayed.*

If you specify a fourth number format, it is used for text values.

To hide all values in a cell, you can use ;;; as the custom number format.

Additional Details: The custom number formats were written long before Microsoft started using conditional formatting. You can change the formatting based on meeting certain criteria. For example, the following code would display numbers above 10,000 in thousands and other numbers normally:
`[<10000]#,##0;[>=10000]#,##0,K,.`

In many cases in which you might use concatenation to join text and a number, you could use a custom number format instead. Here, cell B8 contains a SUM function, yet the result is displayed with a payment message.

B8	▼	f_x	=SUM(B2:B7)

	A	B
1		Amount
2	Balance Forward	1012.34
3	Invoice 1024	473.23
4	Invoice 1036	124.56
5	Check 9874	-1610.13
6	Credit Memo	-124.56
7		
8		Credit Balance of $124.56. Do not pay.

Figure 725 *This SUM function produces a message.*

Further, the message changes, depending on whether the balance is positive, negative, or zero. Below, the three cells show the message for each state. You control the messages by using three zones in the custom number format. Note that in the negative zone, there is no minus sign in the number format, so Excel displays the number as positive. In the zero zone, there are no numeric characters at all, so Excel displays the No Balance Due message.

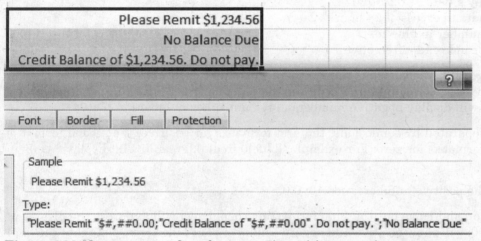

Please Remit $1,234.56
No Balance Due
Credit Balance of $1,234.56. Do not pay.

Font   Border   Fill   Protection

Sample

Please Remit $1,234.56

Type:

"Please Remit "$#,##0.00;"Credit Balance of "$#,##0.00". Do not pay.";"No Balance Due"

Figure 726 *New message when the answer is positive, negative, or zero.*

Additional Details: There is a subtle difference between the 0 and # when used after the decimal point in a custom number format. A # indicates that Excel can display the digit if there is sufficient precision in the value. A 0 indicates that Excel must display the digit. The 0.000 format would cause 123.4 to display as 123.400 even though the last two digits are zero. The 0.0## format ensures that there is always one decimal place, but the second and third decimal places are used only if necessary.

Additional Details: To fill the white space before a number, precede the number format with two asterisks. Similar to the security feature of old check printers, asterisks will appear before the number.

********1235
***********1
*******10235

Figure 727 *Custom format of **0.*

Additional Details: You can use zeros before the decimal point to force Excel to display leading zeros. The custom format 00000 will ensure that the zip code for Cambridge, Massachusetts, prints as 02142 instead of 2142. If you need a part number to appear as 4 digits, you can use the custom format 0000 to force leading zeros to appear.

USE CONSOLIDATION TO COMBINE TWO LISTS

Problem: Jerry and Tina each compiled sales figures from paper invoices. I need to combine Jerry and Tina's list into a single list. Some customers are in both lists.

	A	B	C	D	E
1	Customer	Sales		Customer	Sales
2	Ainsworth	89,357		3M	70,900
3	Air Canada	38,468		Accelent Systems	84,420
4	Bell Canada	94,742		Ainsworth	74,514
5	Chevron	57,560		Alcoa	50,709
6	Compaq	58,467		Bell Canada	63,539
7	Compton Petroleum	51,435		Boeing	81,865
8	Exxon Mobil	52,974		Chevron	54,857
9	Ford	75,517		Citigroup	88,839
10	General Motors	36,200		Compaq	82,488

Figure 728 *Combine the lists into a single list.*

3

Strategy: Excel offers a great tool for consolidating data. Here's how you use it:
1. Move the cell pointer to a blank area of the worksheet. You will need a blank area with several rows and a few columns.
2. Select Data, Consolidate.
3. Make sure that both boxes under Use Labels In are checked. This means that Excel relies on the headings to be the same and that the customer field is in the left column of each range.
4. Put the cell pointer in the Reference field. Click the Collapse button at the right end of the Reference field. With the mouse, select the first range: A1:B23. Click the Collapse button again to return to the Consolidate dialog.

Note: There are times when you will want to consolidate just a single range of data. This would be effective if you needed to combine duplicate customers from one list. However, in this example, you need to combine two lists.
5. Click the Add button to move the first reference from the Reference field to the All References box.
6. After the first reference is added to the All References box, click the Collapse button again to specify the second reference.
7. Use the mouse to select D1:E23. Click the Collapse button to return to the Consolidate dialog. Click the Add button to add the reference to the All References list. The Consolidate dialog should appear as below

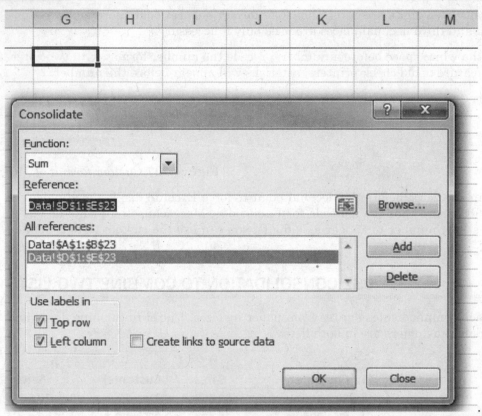

	G	H	I	J	K	L	M

Figure 729 *Make sure both ranges are in the All References box.*

8. Choose OK. In a few seconds, Excel will return a brand new list that extends down and to the right from your starting cell. The list will contain one instance of each customer along with the total revenue from the customer.

	Sales
3M	70,900
Accelent Sy	84,420
Ainsworth	163,871
Air Canada	38,468
Alcoa	50,709
Bell Canadi	158,281
Boeing	81,865
Chevron	112,417

Figure 730 *Excel combines the two lists into a single list.*

Gotcha: The new list is not in any sequence. You can see that it kind of starts out in the sequence of the first list but then randomly inserts customers from the second list. You will probably want to sort the list alphabetically or by revenue. However, Excel always fails to fill in the label in the upper-left corner of the consolidation. If you want to sort the result, you need to type the word Customer in cell G2.

Additional Details: The Function box in the Consolidate dialog offers many functions other than SUM. For instance, if you want to find the largest purchase by each customer, you can use the MAX function.

Gotcha: The results of the consolidation are all static values. If you change an item in the original list, the consolidation will not automatically update. This is good because it allows you to delete the original two lists and keep just the new list.

COMBINE FOUR QUARTERLY REPORTS

Problem: I have four worksheets for Q1 through Q4. Each worksheet has months across the top and customers down the side. The months and customers are not the same. I want to combine them into a single report.

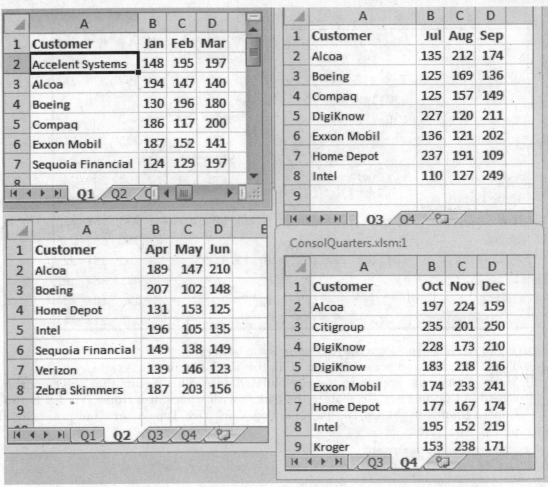

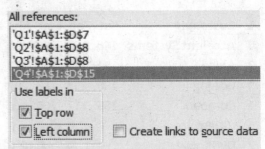

Figure 731 *Combine these four lists into a yearly report.*

Strategy: The Consolidate command needs the row headings to be of the similar type, but not the exact same values. Consolidate will work here because column A in each worksheet contains customers (although not the same customers). Row 1 contains months (although not the same months).

1. Add a new worksheet named Year.
2. Select cell A1 on the Year worksheet.
3. Choose Data, Consolidate.
4. Click the Collapse button at the right end of the Reference box.
5. Browse to Q1. Select A1:D7. Click the icon at the right edge of the Reference box to return to the Consolidate dialog.
6. Click the Add button in the Consolidate dialog.
7. Repeat steps 4-6 for Q2, Q3, and Q4.
8. Ensure Top Row and Left column are checked in the lower left corner of the Consolidate dialog. The dialog should look like this:

Figure 732 *Choose a reference from each worksheet.*

9. Click OK. You will have a report showing a superset of all customers and all months.

	A	B	C	D	E	F	G	H	I	J	K	L	M
1		Jan	Feb	Mar	Apr	May	Jun	Jul	Aug	Sep	Oct	Nov	Dec
2	Accelent Systems	148	195	197									
3	Alcoa	194	147	140	189	147	210	135	212	174	197	224	159
4	Boeing	130	196	180	207	102	148	125	169	136			
5	Compaq	186	117	200				125	157	149			
6	Citigroup										235	201	250
7	DigiKnow							227	120	211	411	391	426
8	Exxon Mobil	187	152	141				136	121	202	174	233	241
9	Home Depot				131	153	125	237	191	109	177	167	174
10	Intel				196	105	135	110	127	249	195	152	219
11	Kroger										358	432	385
12	Sequoia Financial	124	129	197	149	138	149				165	151	221
13	Shearer's Foods										431	384	497
14	Verizon				139	146	123				172	181	204
15	Zebra Skimmers				187	203	156				176	217	247

Figure 733 *Excel consolidates the four quarters to one report.*

10. Type Customer and press Enter to fill in the blank heading in A1.

11. Many empty cells appear in the consolidated data. This means that the customer did not have a record in that quarter. To replace the blanks with zeroes, use Home, Find & Select, Go To Special. Choose Blanks in the Go To Special dialog. Click OK. Type a zero and press Ctrl+Enter to fill the blanks with zero.

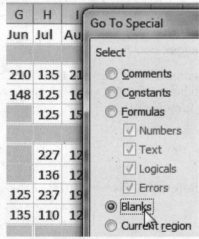

Figure 734 *Choose Go To Special Blanks.*

	A	B	C	D	E	F	G	H	I
1	Customer	Jan	Feb	Mar	Apr	May	Jun	Jul	Aug
2	Accelent Systems	148	195	197	0	0	0	0	0
3	Alcoa	194	147	140	189	147	210	135	212
4	Boeing	130	196	180	207	102	148	125	169
5	Compaq	186	117	200	0	0	0	125	157
6	Citigroup	0	0	0	0	0	0	0	0
7	DigiKnow	0	0	0	0	0	0	227	120
8	Exxon Mobil	187	152	141	0	0	0	136	121
9	Home Depot	0	0	0	131	153	125	237	191

Figure 735 *Type a zero and press Ctrl+Enter.*

12. Sort the data by customer.

Additional Details: Make sure to add Q1 before Q2 and so on. The order of the months in row follows the order that the references were added.

Gotcha: There is a Browse button in the Consolidate dialog. This means that you can combine worksheets from different workbooks. However, the Browse button requires you to type the worksheet name and used range from memory without seeing the workbook. It would be much easier to open all four workbooks before using Consolidate. You can use View, Switch Windows to move to another workbook while entering a reference.

FIND TOTAL SALES BY CUSTOMER BY COMBINING DUPLICATES

Problem: I have an invoice register for the month. The report shows account, customer, invoice, sales, cost, and profit for each invoice. I want to combine customers in order to produce a report of sales by customer.

	A	B	C	D	E	F
1	Acct	Customer	Invoice	Sales	COGS	Profit
2	H1247	Home Depot	1201	63,528	37,577	25,951
3	B5618	Boeing	1202	81,865	45,136	36,729
4	C2299	Compaq	1203	85,096	50,745	34,351
5	H1247	Home Depot	1204	72,410	40,704	31,706
6	Z1752	Zebra Skimmers	1205	70,996	40,925	30,071
7	D1891	DigiKnow	1206	58,784	33,431	25,353
8	K7539	Kroger	1207	40,896	23,397	17,499

Figure 736 *Consolidate the data to one row per customer.*

Strategy: It is possible to consolidate a single list by using the labels in the left column. This will produce a report with one line per customer and totals of each numeric field. You can use data consolidation to solve this task:

1. Select a blank section of the worksheet. Select Data, Consolidate. In the Reference field, select the complete range of your data, including the headings. Ensure that the Left Column option is checked and that the Create Links to Source Data check box is unchecked. Click OK.

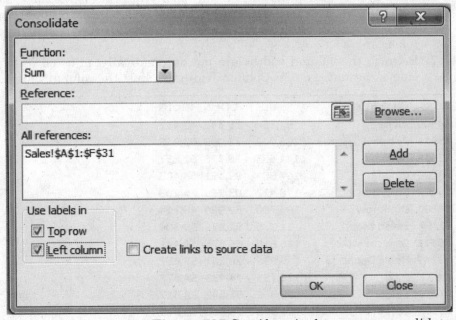

Figure 737 *Specify a single range to consolidate.*

Excel will combine all identical account numbers together.

	Customer	Invoice	Sales	COGS	Profit
H1247		2405	135,938	78,281	57,657
B5618		2415	141,633	78,776	62,857
C2299		2420	167,584	99,161	68,423
Z1752		2432	141,227	81,705	59,522
D1891		2428	109,708	62,994	46,714
K7539		2415	90,359	51,542	38,817
A4509		2433	97,754	55,342	42,412
G5111		2433	115,816	66,375	49,441
A5911		2441	125,222	73,009	52,213
S3647		2441	127,899	75,550	52,349
E2257		2430	91,175	51,875	39,300
S4871		2441	132,452	76,903	55,549
C5484		2438	178,422	103,219	75,203
V7797		2444	116,418	67,083	49,335
I1622		2449	128,755	74,433	54,322

Figure 738 *One row per unique account number.*

Gotcha: Note that Excel added up the invoice numbers in column J. This makes no sense.

2. Delete column J.
3. The Consolidate command is not smart enough to take the first or last instance of text fields, so fill in the customer name, using a VLOOKUP function.

Acct	Customer	Sales	COGS	Profit
H1247	=VLOOKUP(H3,$A$2:$B$31,2,FALSE)			
B5618		141,633	78,776	62,857
C2299		167,584	99,161	68,423

Figure 739 *Use a VLOOKUP to fill text fields.*

4. Copy the VLOOKUP function down by double-clicking the fill handle. Change the VLOOKUP formula to values by copying I2:I16 and then using Home, Paste dropdown, Paste Values.
5. Excel does not fill in the label in the upper-left corner of the table, so enter Acct in H1. The resulting data set is in the same sequence as the customers in the original list.
6. Choose a single cell in column I and click the AZ sort button to produce an alphabetical list by customer.
7. Because the column widths are not automatically adjusted as the result of a consolidation, use Home, Format, AutoFit Column Width to adjust the column widths.

Acct	Customer	Sales	COGS	Profit
A4509	Alcoa	97,754	55,342	42,412
A5911	Accelent Systems	125,222	73,009	52,213
B5618	Boeing	141,633	78,776	62,857
C2299	Compaq	167,584	99,161	68,423
C5484	Citigroup	178,422	103,219	75,203
D1891	DigiKnow	109,708	62,994	46,714
E2257	Exxon Mobil	91,175	51,875	39,300
G5111	General Motors	115,816	66,375	49,441
H1247	Home Depot	135,938	78,281	57,657
I1622	Intel	128,755	74,433	54,322
K7539	Kroger	90,359	51,542	38,817
S3647	Sequoia Financial	127,899	75,550	52,349
S4871	Shearer's Foods	132,452	76,903	55,549
V7797	Verizon	116,418	67,083	49,335
Z1752	Zebra Skimmers	141,227	81,705	59,522

Figure 740 *Duplicates removed and summarized.*

Problem: I have a data set in which I would like to find every unique combination of customer and product.

▲	A	B	C	D	E
1	Region	Product	Date	Customer	Quantity
2	East	XYZ	2-Jan-14	Ford	1000
3	Central	DEF	2-Jan-14	Verizon	100
4	East	ABC	2-Jan-14	Verizon	500
5	Central	XYZ	2-Jan-14	Ainsworth	500
6	Central	XYZ	2-Jan-14	Ainsworth	400
7	East	DEF	2-Jan-14	Gildan Activewea	800

Figure 741 *Find unique combinations of customer and product.*

Strategy: Although there are several ways to find unique values (advanced filters, pivot tables, Microsoft Query, COUNTIF), Microsoft added a new feature to Excel 2007 called Remove Duplicates.

Remove Duplicates is a powerful feature—sometimes too powerful because it very quickly and destructively removes the duplicated rows.

To use the Remove Duplicates command, follow these steps:
1. Make a copy of your data. Copy it to a new range, a new worksheet, or a new workbook.
2. Select one cell in your data set.
3. Select Data, Remove Duplicates. Excel will display the Remove Duplicates dialog.
4. Click Unselect All. Select Product and Customer.

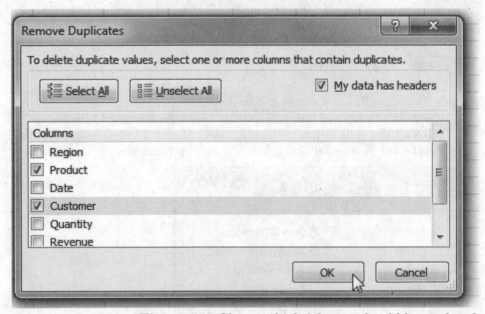

Figure 742 *Choose which columns should be analyzed.*

5. Click OK. Excel will confirm how many duplicates were found and removed.

Figure 743 *Duplicates removed.*

Results: Excel will delete hundreds of rows of data! If you didn't make a copy in step 1 and you need that data, press Ctrl+Z to undo.

PROTECT CELLS THAT CONTAIN FORMULAS

Problem: I have to key in data in a large number of cells in a month-end financial statement. I don't want to accidentally key in a number in a cell that contains a formula. How can I protect just the formula cells?

		Jan	Feb	Mar	Q1	Apr
Income						
	Revenue					
	Education	11,767.30	12,551.48	15,261.14	39,579.92	15,857.08
	Freight	1,609.12	1,672.02	1,176.79	4,457.92	1,452.94
	Prof Fees	151,655.17	148,880.39	159,366.05	459,901.61	137,394.75
	Referral Fees	43,343.06	64,238.33	47,738.11	155,319.50	57,320.46
	Retail Sales	176,287.63	221,382.87	234,778.49	632,448.99	172,630.89
	Total Revenue	384,662.28	448,725.08	458,320.58	1,291,707.94	384,656.11
Total Income		384,662.28	448,725.08	458,320.58	1,291,707.94	384,656.11

Figure 744 *Allow people to enter details but protect the formulas.*

Strategy: After unlocking all cells, you can use the Go To Special dialog to select only the cells with formulas and lock just those cells.

By default, all cells in a worksheet start with their Locked property set to TRUE, but you may not realize this until you turn on protection for the first time. The first step is to unlock all the cells:

1. Select all cells by pressing Ctrl+A. Use Ctrl+One to open Format Cells.
2. Click on the Protection tab in the Format Cells dialog. You will see that the Locked option is chosen.

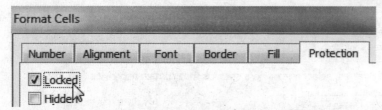

Figure 745 *All cells start out locked by default.*

3. Uncheck the Locked box. Click OK to close the Format Cells dialog.
4. With all the cells still highlighted, select Home, Find & Select, Go To Special.
5. On the Go To Special dialog box, choose the Formulas option button.

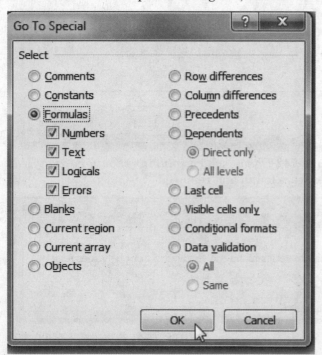

Figure 746 *Select only formula cells.*

6. Click OK to close the Go To Special dialog. Excel will reduce the selection to only cells with formulas.

7. Select Home, Format dropdown, Lock Cells. This will lock only the selected cells, which are the formula cells.

8. Enable protection for the sheet. (Note that if you skip this final step, you can still accidentally overwrite your formulas.) Select Home, Format dropdown, Protect Sheet.

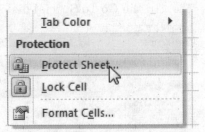

Figure 747 *Turn on Protection to use the Locked/Unlocked settings.*

9. Excel will display the Protect Sheet dialog. The default settings are sufficient protection. Simply click OK.

Figure 748 *The default settings are fine.*

Now if you accidentally try to enter something in a formula cell, Excel will prevent you from entering the data.

FIND DIFFERENCES IN TWO LISTS

Problem: I have two lists that should be identical. I need to highlight any cells that are different.

	A	B	C	D	E	F	G	H	I
1	Invoice	Customer	Sales	Cost		Invoice	Customer	Sales	Cost
2	1030	DigiKnow	13636	6136.2		1030	DigiKnow	13636	6136.2
3	1031	Sequoia Financial	48392	20808.56		1031	Sequoia Financial	48392	20908.56
4	1032	Shearer's Foods	26878	11288.76		1032	Shearers Foods	26878	11288.76
5	1033	Zebra Skimmers	44041	18056.81		1033	Zebra Skimmers	44041	18056.81
6	1034	3M	39941	16775.22		1034	3M	39941	16775.22
7	1035	Alcoa	39709	18663.23		1035	Alcoa	39907	18663.23
8	1036	Boeing	25011	12505.5		1036	Boeing	25011	12505.5
9	1037	Citigroup	33416	15705.52		1037	Citigroup	33416	15705.52
10	1038	Exxon Mobil	37776	15110.4		1038	Exxon-Mobil	36777	15110.4
11	1039	Intel	23301	9786.42		1039	Intel	23301	9836.42
12	1040	Home Depot	22783	9341.03		1040	Home Depot	22783	9341.03

Figure 749 *Did anything change between these lists?*

Strategy: Use the Go To Special dialog's Row Differences.

1. Select B2:B12.
2. Hold down the Ctrl key while selecting G2:I12.
3. Choose Home, Find and Select, Go To Special.
4. In the Go To Special dialog, choose Row Differences. Click OK.

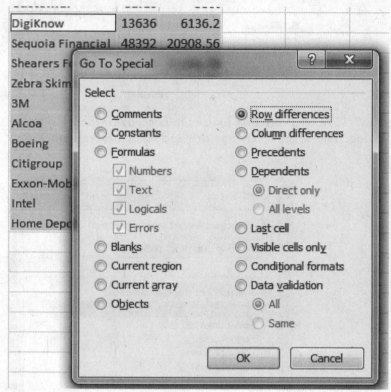

Figure 750 *Select Row Differences.*

Gotcha: Highlight row differences can only compare one column to another column. Initially, it will only compare column B to column G and highlight what changed. If you then press the F4 key once for each additional column, the program will redo the compare for the next column and then the next column.

After step 4, you will have this:

B	C	D
Customer	**Sales**	**Cost**
DigiKnow	13636	6136.2
Sequoia Financial	48392	20808.56
Shearer's Foods	26878	11288.76
Zebra Skimmers	44041	18056.81
3M	39941	16775.22
Alcoa	39709	18663.23
Boeing	25011	12505.5
Citigroup	33416	15705.52
Exxon Mobil	37776	15110.4
Intel	23301	9786.42
Home Depot	22783	9341.03

Figure 751 *Two customers changed.*

5. Press the F4 key to compare column C to column H.
6. Press the F4 key to compare column D to column I.
7. Open the Paint Bucket icon on the Home tab and choose a fill color.

Result: All of the changed cells will be highlighted, in one list or the other.

	A	B	C	D	E	F	G	H	I
1	**Invoice**	**Customer**	**Sales**	**Cost**		**Invoice**	**Customer**	**Sales**	**Cost**
2	1030	DigiKnow	13636	6136.2		1030	DigiKnow	13636	6136.2
3	1031	Sequoia Financial	48392	20808.56		1031	Sequoia Financial	48392	20908.56
4	1032	Shearer's Foods	26878	11288.76		1032	Shearers Foods	26878	11288.76
5	1033	Zebra Skimmers	44041	18056.81		1033	Zebra Skimmers	44041	18056.81
6	1034	3M	39941	16775.22		1034	3M	39941	16775.22
7	1035	Alcoa	39709	18663.23		1035	Alcoa	39907	18663.23
8	1036	Boeing	25011	12505.5		1036	Boeing	25011	12505.5
9	1037	Citigroup	33416	15705.52		1037	Citigroup	33416	15705.52
10	1038	Exxon Mobil	37776	15110.4		1038	Exxon-Mobil	36777	15110.4
11	1039	Intel	23301	9786.42		1039	Intel	23301	9836.42
12	1040	Home Depot	22783	9341.03		1040	Home Depot	22783	9341.03

Figure 752 *Changed cells are highlighted.*

Alternate Strategy: You can use the Formula method of conditional formatting to highlight differences. Follow these steps:

1. Select G2:I12.
2. Type Alt+O followed by D. (That is O the letter).
3. Click New Rule.
4. Choose Use a Formula to Determine Which Cells to Format.
5. Type a formula of =G2<>B2.
6. Click the Format... button.
7. Click the Fill tab.
8. Choose a red format.
9. Click OK. Click OK.

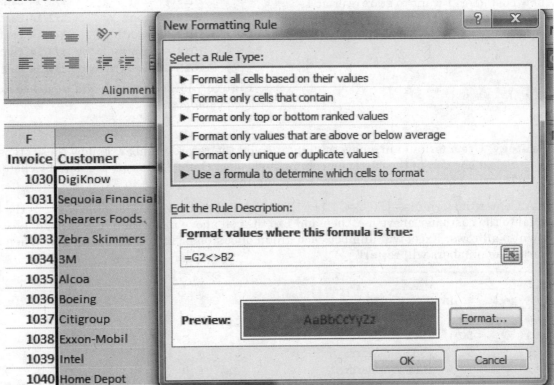

Figure 753 *Highlight differences using conditional formatting.*

The changed cells on the right are highlighted.

B	C	D	E	F	G	H	I
Customer	Sales	Cost		Invoice	Customer	Sales	Cost
DigiKnow	13636	6136.2		1030	DigiKnow	1	6136.2
Sequoia Financial	48392	20808.56		1031	Sequoia Financial	99999	20903.56
Shearer's Foods	26878	11288.76		1032	Shearers Foods	26878	11288.76
Zebra Skimmers	44041	18056.81		1033	Zebra Skimmers	44041	18056.81
3M	39941	16775.22		1034	3M	39941	16775.22
Alcoa	39709	18663.23		1035	Alcoa	39907	18663.23
Boeing	25011	12505.5		1036	Boeing	25011	12505.5
Citigroup	33416	15705.52		1037	Citigroup	33416	15705.52
Exxon Mobil	37776	15110.4		1038	Exxon-Mobil	36777	15110.4
Intel	23301	9786.42		1039	Intel	23301	9836.42
Home Depot	22783	9341.03		1040	Home Depot	22783	9341.03

Figure 754 *The highlights only appear in the second data set.*

NUMBER EACH RECORD FOR A CUSTOMER, STARTING AT 1 FOR A NEW CUSTOMER

Problem: I have a list of invoice data. I want to number the records in such a way that the first invoice number for Ford is 1. The next Ford invoice is 2, and so on. When I get to a new customer, I want to start over at 1.

	A	B	C	D	E
1	Invoice	Customer	Date	Region	Product
2	1010	Ford	1/2/14	East	XYZ
3	1011	Verizon	1/2/14	Central	DEF
4	1012	Verizon	1/2/14	East	ABC
5	1013	Ainsworth	1/2/14	Central	XYZ
6	1014	Ainsworth	1/3/14	Central	XYZ
7	1015	Gildan Activewe	1/3/14	East	DEF

Figure 755 *You want to add sequence numbers within each customer.*

Strategy: Use a formula in a new column A to add the record number. Follow these steps.
1. Select one cell in the customer column and select Data, AZ to sort the data by customer.
2. Insert a new temporary column A and add the heading Rec # to A1.

In A2, enter the formula =IF(C2=C1,1+A1,1). In plain language, this formula says, "If the customer in C is equal to the customer above me, then add 1 to the cell above me. Otherwise, start at 1." Copy the formula down to all rows. Excel will number each group of customer invoices from 1 to N. When a new customer starts, the numbers will restart.

	A	B	C
1	Rec#	Invoice	Customer
50	49	1538	Ainsworth
51	50	1541	Ainsworth
52	51	1562	Ainsworth
53	52	1566	Ainsworth
54	1	1143	Air Canada
55	2	1169	Air Canada
56	3	1368	Air Canada

Figure 756 *The live formulas work while the data is sorted.*

Change the formulas in A using Ctrl+C, Home, Paste, Paste Values before sorting by invoice number.

Alternate Strategy: You can use the formula =COUNTIF(C$2:C2,C2) without sorting.

ADD A GROUP NUMBER
TO EACH SET OF RECORDS
THAT HAS A UNIQUE CUSTOMER NUMBER

Problem: I have a list of invoice data. I want to number the records in such a way that the invoices for the first customer all have a group number 1 and the invoices for the next customer all have a group number 2.

Strategy: You can do this by sorting the data by customer. You need to add a new column A, with the heading Group. In cell A2, you enter the number 1 for Group 1. In cell A3, you enter the following formula, which will be used for the rest of the records:

=IF(C3=C2,A2,1+A2)

In plain language, this formula says, "If the customer on this row equals the row above, then use the group number on the row above. Otherwise, add 1 to the group number above." You need to copy this formula down to all the other rows.

=IF(C54=C53,A53,1+A53)

	A	B	C	D
1	Group	Invoice	Customer	Date
51	1	1541	Ainsworth	12/9/1₄
52	1	1562	Ainsworth	12/23/1₄
53	1	1566	Ainsworth	12/25/1₄
54	2	1143	Air Canada	3/30/1₄
55	2	1169	Air Canada	4/18/1₄
56	2	1368	Air Canada	8/23/1₄
57	2	1438	Air Canada	10/6/1₄
58	3	1165	Bell Canada	4/12/1₄
59	3	1271	Bell Canada	6/23/1₄

Figure 757 *Assign each customer a group number.*

Results: Each record will be assigned a group number. Each customer will have a unique group number.

In order to allow future sorting, you copy the formulas in column A and use Home, Paste dropdown, Paste Values to convert the formulas to numbers.

DEAL WITH DATA IN WHICH EACH RECORD TAKES FIVE PHYSICAL ROWS

Problem: Sometime, back in the days of COBOL, a programmer was dealing with the constraints of the physical width of a page. The programmer built a report in which each record actually took up five lines of the report. I want to be able to analyze this data in Excel.

	A	B	C	D	E	F	G
1	ACCT: 12345		INVOICE: 1010		DATE: 10/21/14		
2	INVOICE TOTAL		$125.00				
3	ABC CO						
4	123 S. MAIN STREET						
5	SALEM OH 44460						
6	--						
7	ACCT: 23456		INVOICE: 1011		DATE: 10/21/14		
8	INVOICE TOTAL		$175.00				
9	XYZ INC.						
10	456 N. BROADWAY						
11	SALEM OR 98754						
12	--						
13	ACCT: 34567		INVOICE: 1012		DATE: 10/23/14		
14	INVOICE TOTAL		$225.00				

Figure 758 *Transform this frustrating data set.*

Strategy: Your goal is to get the data back into one row per record. This process involves adding two new columns, Group and Sequence:

1. Add a new row 1. Insert two new columns, A and B. Add the headings Group, Seq, and Text in A1:C1.

	A	B	C
1	Group	Seq	Text
2			ACCT: 1
3			INVOICE
4			ABC CO

Figure 759 *Add two new columns.*

2. In column A, assign a group number to each logical record. One way to do this is to check to see if the first four characters of column C are ACCT. If they are, add 1 to the group number. In A2, enter the number 1. In A3, enter the formula =IF(LEFT(C3,4)="ACCT",1+A2,A2). (This is similar to the formula from "Add a Group Number to Each Set of Records That Has a Unique Customer Number".) Copy it down to all the rows. Excel will assign a group number to each logical group of records.

=IF(LEFT(C3,4)="ACCT",1+A2,A2)

	A	B	C	D
1	Group	Seq	Text	
2	1		ACCT: 12345	
3	1		INVOICE TOTA	
4	1		ABC CO	
5	1		123 S. MAIN	
6	1		SALEM OH 444	
7	1		------------	
8	2		ACCT: 23456	
9	2		INVOICE TOTA	
10	2		XYZ INC.	
11	2		456 N. BROAD	
12	2		SALEM OR 987	
13	2		------------	
14	3		ACCT: 34567	

Figure 760 *Use the IF function.*

3. Design a formula for a sequence number. To do this, in cell B2, enter the formula =IF(A2=A1,B1+1,1). (This formula is like the one from "Number Each Record for a Customer, Starting at 1 for a New Customer") Copy this down. This formula will number each record in the group. It should ensure that all the account numbers are on a Sequence 1 record.

=IF(A2=A1,B1+1,1)

	A	B	C	D
1	Group	Seq	Text	
2	1	1	ACCT: 12345	
3	1	2	INVOICE TOTA	
4	1	3	ABC CO	
5	1	4	123 S. MAIN	
6	1	5	SALEM OH 444	
7	1	6	------------	
8	2	1	ACCT: 23456	
9	2	2	INVOICE TOTA	
10	2	3	XYZ INC.	
11	2	4	456 N. BROAD	

Figure 761 *Formula for sequence number.*

4. (This step is critical.) Copy the formulas in columns A and B and paste them back, using Home, Paste dropdown, Paste Values to ensure that you can safely sort the data.

5. Sort the data by the sequence number in column B. Your data will look like this.

⊿	A	B	C	D	E	F	G	H	I
1	Group	Seq	Text						
2	1	1	ACCT: 12345		INVOICE: 1010		DATE: 10/21/14		
3	2	1	ACCT: 23456		INVOICE: 1011		DATE: 10/21/14		
4	3	1	ACCT: 34567		INVOICE: 1012		DATE: 10/23/14		
5	4	1	ACCT: 45678		INVOICE: 1013		DATE: 10/24/14		
6	5	1	ACCT: 56789		INVOICE: 1014		DATE: 10/24/14		
7	6	1	ACCT: 67890		INVOICE: 1015		DATE: 10/26/14		
8	1	2	INVOICE TOTAL	$125.00					
9	2	2	INVOICE TOTAL	$175.00					
10	3	2	INVOICE TOTAL	$225.00					
11	4	2	INVOICE TOTAL	$425.00					
12	5	2	INVOICE TOTAL	$25.00					
13	6	2	INVOICE TOTAL	$185.00					
14	1	3	ABC CO						
15	2	3	XYZ INC.						
16	3	3	BUDD & ASSOCIATES						
17	4	3	WIZARD OF OZZIE						
18	5	3	MARCINKO PUBLISHING						
19	6	3	BONNIE DOON						
20	1	4	123 S. MAIN STREET						
21	2	4	456 N. BROADWAY						

Figure 762 *Sort the data into record types.*

You have now managed to intelligently segregate the data so that all similar records are together. The contiguous range C2:C7 contains all the first rows from each record. Each of the line 1 records has three fields that really should be parsed into three separate columns. You can easily do this parsing with the Text to Columns Wizard.

6. Select cells C2:C7. Select Data, Text to Columns to open the Convert Text to Columns Wizard. Select Fixed Width. Click Next.
7. Excel should properly guess where your columns are. Click Next.
8. Choose the heading for each column and define a data format. You don't really need the word ACCT each time, so choose to skip the first, third, and fifth fields. Make the sixth field a date. When your information looks as shown below, click Finish. You will have data in three columns of Group 1.

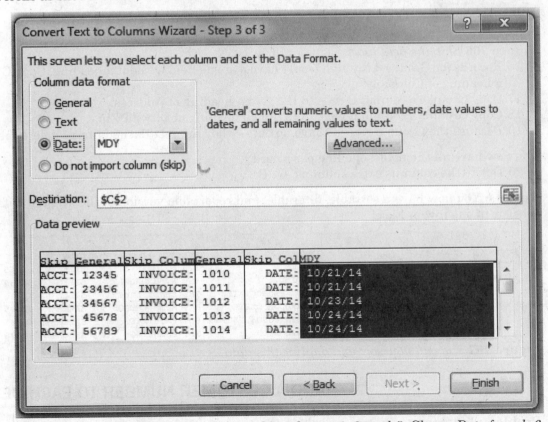

Figure 763 *In Step 3, skip columns 1, 3, and 5. Choose Date for col. 6.*

9. Change the heading in C1 to Acct, the heading in D1 to Inv, and the heading in E1 to Date.

10. Select and cut A8:C13 and paste into F2.
11. Delete Group & Seq from F & G.
12. Add the heading of Inv $ to F1.
13. Select F2:F6 and choose Data, Text to Columns. In Step 1 of the wizard, select Fixed Width and click Next. In Step 2 of the wizard, Excel offers to split your data into three fields. There is no need to have one column for the word Invoice and another column for the word Total.

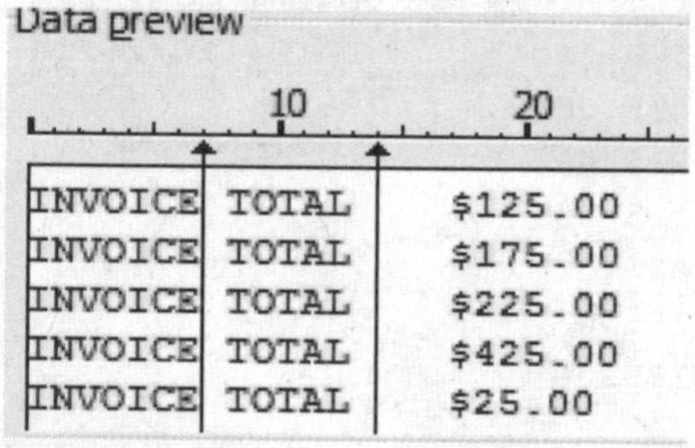

Figure 764 *Excel suggests an extra column.*

14. Double-click the line between Invoice and Total to delete it.

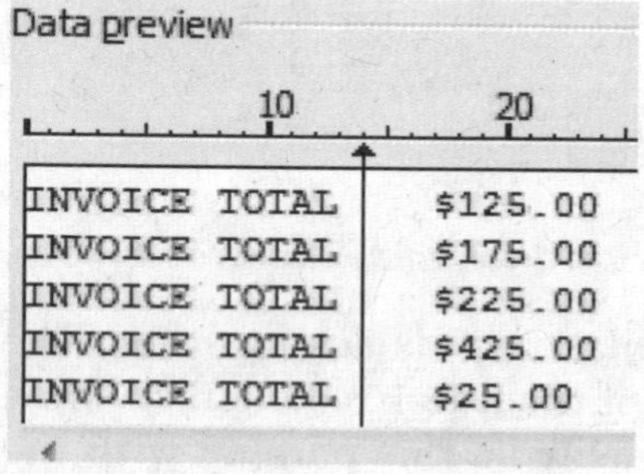

Figure 765 *Double-click the extra line to delete it.*

15. In Step 3 of the wizard, choose to skip the field that contains Invoice Total. Click Finish.

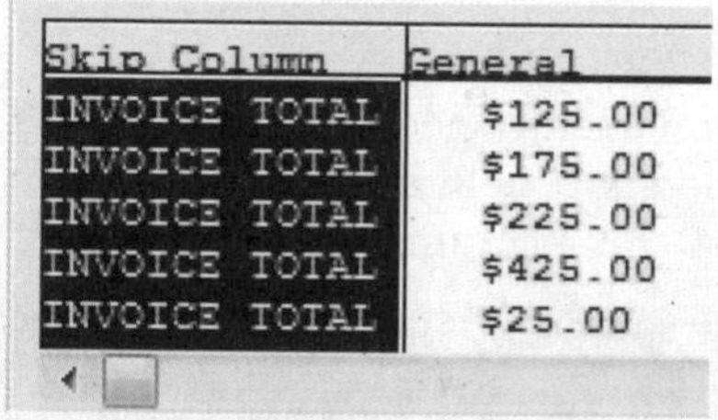

Figure 766 *Skip the field label.*

16. Records for Groups 3 through 5 only have a single field without a heading. Copy C14:C19 to G2. Add a heading of Company.
17. Copy Group 4's column C cells to H2. Add a heading of Address.
18. Copy Group 5's column C cells to I2. Add a heading of City ST Zip.
19. Because the Group 6 records have no data—they are just dashed lines—delete these rows.

You now have all the fields, one line per record.

20. Delete the columns extra columns A& B.

Results: You now have a sortable, filterable, and reportable version of the original data set. Each record consists of one row in Excel.

	A	B	C	D	E	F	G	H
1	Acct	Invoice	Date	Inv $	Company	Street	City ST Zip	
2	12345	1010	10/21/2014	$125.00	ABC CO	123 S. MAIN STREET	SALEM OH 44460	
3	23456	1011	10/21/2014	$175.00	XYZ INC.	456 N. BROADWAY	SALEM OR 98754	
4	34567	1012	10/23/2014	$225.00	BUDD & ASSOCIATES	789 LUNDY LANE	SALEM MA 12345	
5	45678	1013	10/24/2014	$425.00	WIZARD OF OZZIE	987 KING CHURCH	SALEM WV 32145	
6	56789	1014	10/24/2014	$25.00	MARCINKO PUBLISHING	654 FAIR AVE	SALEM IL 60187	
7	67890	1015	10/26/2014	$185.00	BONNIE DOON	321 PERSHING	SALEM IN 46875	

Figure 767 *You can now sort and analyze this data.*

ADD A CUSTOMER NUMBER TO EACH DETAIL RECORD

Problem: I've imported a data set where the customer information appears once in column A, followed by any number of invoice detail records. At the end of the first customer, the next customer number is in column A and then there are detail records for that customer. You can not sort this data. The customer information needs to be in its own columns on each record.

	A	B	C	D	E	F	G
1	Invoice	Date	Quantity	Product	Revenue	COGS	Profit
2	Acct A4651 Air Canada						
3	1533	30-Mar-14	300	ABC	5859.00	2541	3318
4	1559	18-Apr-14	200	XYZ	4948.00	2044	2904
5	1756	23-Aug-14	800	XYZ	17856.00	8176	9680
6	1828	6-Oct-14	100	DEF	2358.00	984	1374
7	Acct A8736 Ainsworth						
8	1404	1-Jan-14	500	XYZ	11240.00	5110	6130
9	1405	2-Jan-14	400	XYZ	9204.00	4088	5116
10	1414	8-Jan-14	900	XYZ	21465.00	9198	12267
11	1416	10-Jan-14	400	XYZ	9144.00	4088	5056
12	1438	25-Jan-14	500	ABC	10445.00	4235	6210

Figure 768 *Another annoying report format.*

Strategy: This is a common data format, but it is horrible in Excel. Here's how you fix the **problem:**
1. Insert new columns A and B. Add the headings Acct and Customer. Here is the basic logic of what you want to do: Look at the first four characters of column C. If they are equal to Acct, then you know this row has customer information, so you take data from that cell and move it to column A. If the first four characters are anything other than Acct, you use the same account information from the previous row's column A.
2. Enter the following formula into cell A2: `=IF(LEFT(C2,4)="Acct",MID(C2,6,5),A1)`. Copy this formula down through column A. you copy this formula down, it does the job. In cell A2, the IF condition is true and data is extracted from C2. In cell A3, the condition is not true, so the value from A2 is used. In cell A7, a new customer number is found, so the data from C7 is used in A7. Cells A8 through A59 get the customer number from A7.

	A	B	C	D
1	Acct	Customer	Invoice	Date
2	A4651		Acct A4651 Air Canada	
3	A4651		1533	30-Mar-14
4	A4651		1559	18-Apr-14
5	A4651		1756	23-Aug-14
6	A4651		1828	6-Oct-14
7	A8736		Acct A8736 Ainsworth	
8	A8736		1404	1-Jan-14
9	A8736		1405	2-Jan-14
10	A8736		1414	8-Jan-14

Figure 769 *Use IF to extract and copy account number information.*

Similar logic is needed in column B. In this case, though, you need to grab the customer name. You know that the word Acct and the space that follows it take up 5 characters. You know that your account number is another 5 characters, and then there is a space before the customer name. You therefore want to ignore the first 11 characters of cell C2. You can use the formula =MID(C2,12,50) to skip the first 11 characters and return the next 50 characters of the customer name. Use this formula as the TRUE portion of the IF function.
3. Enter the following formula into cell B2: =IF(LEFT(C2,4)="Acct",MID(C2,12,50),B1). Copy this formula down through column B.

`=IF(LEFT(C2,4)="Acct",MID(C2,12,50),B1)`

▲	A	B	C	Date
1	Acct	Customer	Invoice	Date
2	A4651	Air Canada	Acct A4651 Air	
3	A4651	Air Canada	1533	30-⌐
4	A4651	Air Canada	1559	18-
5	A4651	Air Canada	1756	23-
6	A4651	Air Canada	1828	6-
7	A8736	Ainsworth	Acct A8736 Air	
8	A8736	Ainsworth	1404	1
9	A8736	Ainsworth	1405	2
10	A8736	Ainsworth	1414	8

Figure 770 *Extract customer information.*

You have now successfully filled in the account and customer. You need to change these formulas to values.

4. Highlight columns A and B. Press Ctrl+C to copy. Choose Home, Paste dropdown, Paste Values to convert the formulas to values. You do this to remove the customer heading rows. As you think about a method to isolate the heading rows, you will notice that heading rows are the only rows with blank cells in column D. You can move the blanks to the end of a data set by sorting the data by column D.

5. Select the heading in D1. Select Data, AZ to sort ascending by date. Any rows that have no value in column D will automatically sort to the bottom of the data set.

▲	A	B	C	D	E	F
1	Acct	Customer	Invoice	Date	Quantity	Product
561	S2328	Sun Life Finan	1960	26-Dec-14	500	ABC
562	G1394	General Motor	1961	27-Dec-14	600	ABC
563	G1394	General Motor	1962	27-Dec-14	600	ABC
564	G1394	General Motor	1963	27-Dec-14	900	ABC
565	A4651	Air Canada	Acct A4651 Air Canada			
566	A8736	Ainsworth	Acct A8736 Ainsworth			
567	B3529	Bell Canada	Acct B3529 Bell Canada			
568	C4341	Compton Petro	Acct C4341 Compton Petroleum			
569	C7849	Compaq	Acct C7849 Compaq			
570	C8297	Chevron	Acct C8297 Chevron			

Figure 771 *The extraneous heading rows sort to the bottom.*

6. With the cell pointer in D1, press the End key and then the Down Arrow key twice. The cell pointer will be located on the first customer heading. Delete all the rows below row 564.

Results: You have a clean data set with customer information on every row. You can sort this data and otherwise use it for data analysis.

▲	A	B	C	D	E	F
1	Acct	Customer	Invoice	Date	Quantity	Product
2	A4651	Air Canada	1533	30-Mar-14	300	ABC
3	A4651	Air Canada	1559	18-Apr-14	200	XYZ
4	A4651	Air Canada	1756	23-Aug-14	800	XYZ
5	A4651	Air Canada	1828	6-Oct-14	100	DEF
6	A8736	Ainsworth	1404	1-Jan-14	500	XYZ
7	A8736	Ainsworth	1405	2-Jan-14	400	XYZ

Figure 772 *Customer data has been added to each record.*

USE A BUILT-IN DATA ENTRY FORM

Problem: I need to do data entry in Excel. I have a lot of records to key or to edit. Can I easily create a dialog to help with this?

Strategy: By using Excel VBA, you can build very complex dialog boxes for data entry. However, even without knowing VBA, you can use a simple built-in dialog for entering data:

1. Select a cell in your data. Press Alt+D then O (letter O). Excel will display a dialog box with your fields. Click the Find Next and Find Prev buttons to move through the data set.

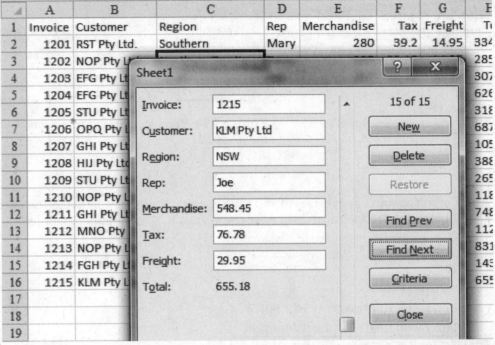

Figure 773 *The built-in data entry form.*

2. To add a record, click the New button. The Total field does not fill in until you click Find Next and Find Prev to enter this record. When you come back to the record, the total will be filled in.

Additional Details: The Criteria button will allow you to limit the Find Next and Find Prev buttons to only contain records. For instance, click Criteria, enter Joe as the Rep, and click Next. You will see only Joe's records.

Gotcha: The Form command used to be on the Excel 2003 Data menu. Microsoft has removed this option. However, you can use the Excel 2003 access key Alt+D+O to load the data form. If you want to have an icon for Data Form, you can customize the Quick Access toolbar. In the Customize dialog, you look in the category Commands Not in the Ribbon.

CELL AUTOCOMPLETE STOPPED WORKING

Problem: I am typing data in column A. When I type the first few letters in a cell, Excel suggests the complete entry and I only have to press Enter. Suddenly, AutoComplete is not working for one customer.

Strategy: AutoComplete is cool. In Figure 774, you only need to type Q and Enter to fill the cell with Que.

But, in Figure 775, Excel won't suggest an entry. Excel isn't sure if you mean "Peachpit" or "Peachpit Press".

◢	A	B
1	Publisher	
2	Que	
3	Sams	
4	Peachpit	
5	Holy Macro!	
6	Que	
7	Que	
8		

Figure 774 *Excel suggests entries from the prior list.*

◢	A	B
1	Publisher	
2	Que	
3	Sams	
4	Peachpit	
5	Holy Macro!	
6	Que	
7	Que	
8	Peachpit Press	
9	Peachp	

Figure 775 *Excel stops using AutoComplete.*

AutoComplete won't suggest until you type enough characters to make the entry unique. When you have two names that are identical until near the very end, AutoComplete will barely save you any typing.

◢	A	E
7	Que	
8	Peachpit Press	
9	John Jacob Jingleheimer Schmidt Sr.	
10	John Jacob Jingleheimer Schmidt Jr.	
11	John Jacob Jingleheimer Schmidt	
12		
13		

Figure 776 *AutoComplete will save you very little typing in this case.*

Another AutoComplete frustration: Let's say you've entered Pearson Publishing and now you want to enter just Pearson. You will have to type Pearson, but if you press Enter, Excel will fill in Publishing.

Instead, press the delete key to erase the suggested characters. You can then press Enter.

10	John Jacob Jingleheim
11	John Jacob Jingleheim
12	Pearson Publishing
13	Pearson Publishing
14	

Figure 777 *You can't press Enter now.*

The final AutoComplete frustration is when you have some blank cells in your data. AutoComplete will not be able to find an entry that appears above the blank cell.

There are two workarounds for this.

- Before you start doing data entry, select the range where you will be entering data, perhaps A1:A100. Type ="" and press Ctrl+Enter. The AutoComplete will work through the blank cells now.
- Alternatively, insert a temporary column A that is non-blank. Fill A1:A100 with the number 1. You can now leave blanks in column B and AutoComplete will still work.

	A	B
1	Publisher	
2	Que	
3	Pearson	
4	Peachpit	
5	Que	
6		
7	Holy Macro!	
8	Q	
9		
10		

Figure 778 *AutoComplete won't offer values before the blank cell.*

	A	B
5	1	Que
6	1	
7	1	Holy Macro!
8	1	Que
9	1	

Figure 779 *Non-blank cells in adjacent column prevent blank issue.*

DATA CLEANSING WITH FLASH FILL IN EXCEL 2013

Problem: I need to join text or break apart text in Excel 2013.

Strategy: Use the new Flash Fill feature. Say that you have First Name in column A, Last Name in column B. You want first initial, a period, and a last name in column C.

1. You must type a heading in C1 first or Flash Fill will not work.
2. Type the pattern in C2: M. Henderson.
3. Type the first letter in C3. As soon as you type J, Flash Fill will draw the proposed data in grey.
4. Press Enter to accept the flash fill.

	A	B	C	D
1	FIRST	LAST	Name	
2	MIKE	HENDERSON	M. Henderson	
3	JAMES	MOORE	J. Moore	
4	KIM	DAVIS	K. Davis	
5	JOHN	JOHNSON	J. Johnson	
6	AARON	BROOKS	A. Brooks	

Figure 780 *Flash Fill will save people hours of needless typing.*

Gotcha: Flash Fill provides a static solution. If column A later changes, column C won't update.

FLASH FILL WAS THERE AND IS NOW GONE

Problem: I saw Flash Fill propose a solution, but I did not hit the correct key, and now it is all gone.

Strategy: Finish typing the second entry. Go to the blank cell below your first two entries. Press Ctrl+E or select Data, Flash Fill. The data will come back.

FLASH FILL WAS NOT PERFECT

Problem: Some people in my data set do not have middle initials. Flash Fill is putting periods between the first and last name for those people.

	A	B	C	D	E
1	FIRST	MI	LAST	Name	
2	JOSEPH	N	EDWARDS	Joseph N. Edwards	
3	PETER	E	WALKER	Peter E. Walker	
4	HEATHER	S	MORRIS	Heather S. ▦orris	
5	ROSE		MASON	Rose . Mason	
6	JOSE		J	NICHOLS	Jose J. Nichols	

Figure 781 *Rose Mason is missing a middle initial, but Flash Fill still adds the period.*

Strategy: After the initial Flash Fill, find a record and type the correction. Flash Fill will kick in again, correcting items that match the new pattern. Watch the Status Bar in the lower left to see how many records were corrected.

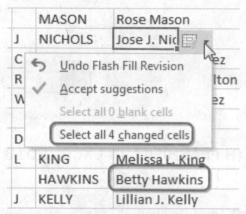

	MASON	Rose Mason
J	NICHOLS	Jose J. Nic

↶ Undo Flash Fill Revision

✓ Accept suggestions

Select all 0 blank cells

Select all 4 changed cells

D		
L	KING	Melissa L. King
	HAWKINS	Betty Hawkins
J	KELLY	Lillian J. Kelly

Figure 782 *Flash Fill watches for you to make the first correction.*

After the correction, open the dropdown. You can select all of the newly changed cells. Use the Home tab to apply a fill color, so you can check the corrected cells.

FLASH FILL WON'T FILL NUMBERS

Problem: Flash Fill is not working with numbers. Actually, I see the grey numbers appear, but then Excel erases them.

Strategy: Chad Rothschiller at Microsoft points out there are too many coincidences that can happen in numbers. With only 10 digits, Chad might think he knows the pattern but then screw up your data. So, Chad shows you the preview, but then withdraws it. It is up to you to go to the blank next blank cell and press Ctrl+E.

FLASH FILL AND DATES

Problem: Flash Fill won't fill dates. When I use Ctrl+E, it won't get them right.

Strategy: First, the Text to Columns command would handle dates better than Flash Fill. But, if you need to use Flash Fill, follow these steps:

1. Choose the column where you want the dates to fill.
2. You have to apply a date format that has two spaces for month and four for year. Press Ctrl+1 to display the Format Cells dialog. On the Number tab, choose the Custom category. Type a date format of MM/DD/YYYY.
3. Fill in the first date.
4. Go to the blank cell below that date.
5. Ctrl+E to Flash Fill.
6. You are now free to select the column and apply another date format.

FLASH FILL AND AMBIGUOUS DATA

Problem: How will Flash Fill get this right? Even I wouldn't know what to fill in next?

Strategy: Before invoking Flash Fill with Ctrl+E, provide enough examples to establish the pattern. If you invoke Flash Fill from B3, you will get the prefix instead of the suffix. By filling in one more example and running Flash Fill from I4, you will get the suffix.

	A	B	C	E	F
1	Product Code	Suffix		Product C	Suffix
2	IT-IT	IT		IT-IT	IT
3	EP-ZA			EP-ZA	ZA
4	ZA-BC			ZA-BC	
5	AD-VU			AD-VU	

Figure 783 *Give Flash Fill enough examples.*

GET IDEAS FROM QUICK ANALYSIS IN EXCEL 2013

Problem: I have data in Excel 2013. I don't know what to do next.

Strategy: Select the data. Click the Quick Analysis icon that appears below the lower right corner of the selection. Browse through the Formatting, Charts, Totals, Tables, and Sparklines headings at the top for a tour of what you can do to the data.

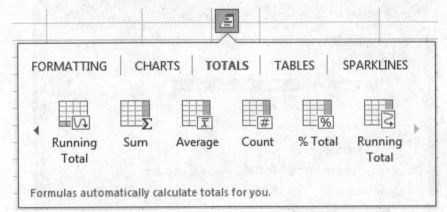

Figure 784 *When you don't know what to do next, browse for ideas.*

Everything that you see here is available elsewhere in Excel. The two that are innovative are % Total and Running Total. It is easier to click the icon than to manually type this formula.

=SUM(B2:E2)/SUM($B$2:$E$10)

	E	F
r	Revenue	
	22810	12.83%
	2257	8.76%
	18552	11.99%
	9152	10.13%
n	21730	12.62%
lotors	8456	9.99%
lotors	16416	11.57%
	21438	12.56%
	6267	9.56%

Figure 785 *My favorite Quick Analysis trick.*

Gotcha: This feature is new in Excel 2013. It is not available in Excel 2010.

USE A PIVOT TABLE TO SUMMARIZE DETAILED DATA

Problem: I have many rows of sales data. I want to produce a summary report that shows sales by region and product.

▲	A	B	C	D	E	F	G	H
1	Region	Product	Date	Customer	Quantity	Revenue	COGS	Profit
2	East	XYZ	2-Jan-14	Ford	1000	22810	10220	12590
3	Central	DEF	2-Jan-14	Verizon	100	2257	984	1273
4	East	ABC	2-Jan-14	Verizon	500	10245	4235	6010
5	Central	XYZ	2-Jan-14	Ainsworth	500	11240	5110	6130
6	Central	XYZ	2-Jan-14	Ainsworth	400	9204	4088	5116

Figure 786 *Summarize this data set.*

Strategy: To solve this problem, you can use a pivot table. As Excel's most powerful feature, pivot tables are well suited to this type of analysis.

Creating a summary of revenue by region and product requires four mouse clicks and one mouse drag:

1. Ensure that your data is in list format and that every heading is unique. (For a refresher on list format, see "How to Set up Your Data for Easy Sorting and Subtotals" on page 247.)
2. Select a single cell in the database. Select Insert, Pivot Table.
3. Excel's IntelliSense will guess the range of your data. Ensure the range is correct and click OK.

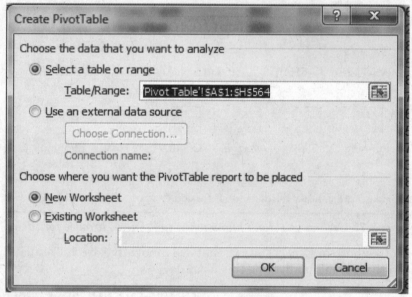

Figure 787 *Make sure that Excel guessed the correct range.*

You will now see an empty pivot table icon, two new PivotTable Tools tabs on the ribbon, and the Pivot-Table Field List dialog.

The PivotTable Field List includes a list of the fields at the top and four drop zones at the bottom of the dialog.

Note: The Field List is usually docked to the right side of the screen. For this book, I've undocked the Field List so I can show the Field List next to the pivot table. **Gotcha:** It is difficult to redock the PivotTable Field List dialog. You have to grab the left side of the title bar and drag it 90% off the right edge of the Excel window.

Way back in Excel 2003, you would drag fields from the Field List dialog to the pivot table. This process was frustrating for people new to pivot tables. Now, you drag fields from the top of the Field List dialog to the proper drop zone at the bottom of the Field List dialog. In many cases, clicking the field in the Field List dialog will move it to the correct drop zone. In this case, you want to have products going down the side of the report and regions going across the top.

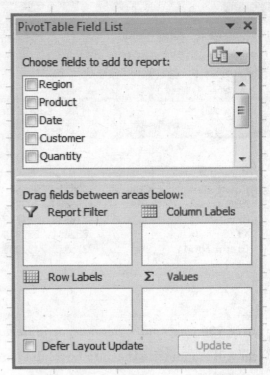

Figure 788 *Starting in Excel 2007, the Field List includes drop zones.*

4. Click the Product check box in the top of the Field List dialog. Excel automatically moves it to the Row Labels drop zone. The pivot table shows a list of unique products in column A.

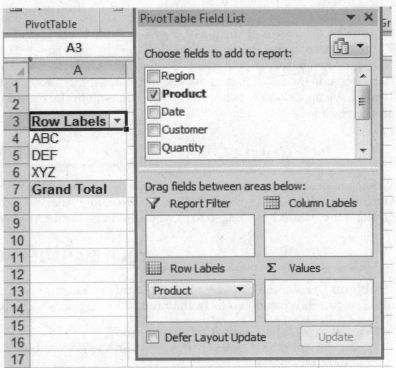

Figure 789 *Click a text field, and Excel moves it to the Row area.*

5. Click the Revenue check box in the top of the Field List dialog. Because this field is numeric, Excel will add it to the Values section of the pivot table.

6. If you click the Region check box, Excel will add it to the row area of the pivot table. Because you want regions to go across the top of your pivot table, drag the Region field from the top of the Field List dialog and drop it in the Column Labels drop zone at the bottom of the Field List dialog.

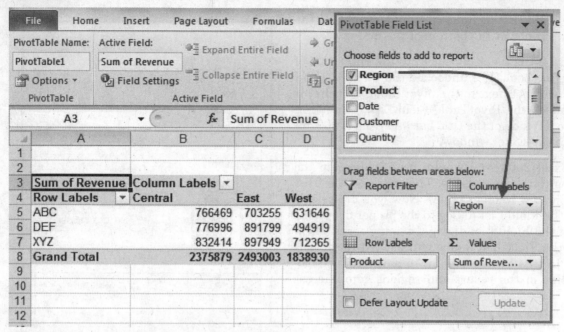

Figure 790 *Checkmark Revenue, drag Region.*

Excel will summarize the data by product and region, as shown above.

Additional Details: Pivot tables offer many powerful options. This topic describes the steps to create your first pivot table; you should read the next several topics to learn more about pivot tables.

Gotcha: If you were a pivot table pro in previous Excel versions, you can quickly adapt to the new pivot tables. The drop zones have been renamed. The Row Area drop zone is now Row Labels. The Column Area drop zone is now Column Labels. The Page Field drop zone is now Report Filter. The Data Area drop zone is now $\sum$ Values (although I will call it the Values drop zone, leaving off the $\sum$ symbol).

Gotcha: A dropdown at the top of the PivotTable Field List dialog offers five different views of the dialog. Three of those views omit either the fields or the drop zones. If your dialog box is missing one section, use the dropdown to return it to Fields Section and Areas Section Stacked. There are also views where the sections are side by side. Throughout the next pages, I will refer to the drop zones at the bottom of the dialog. If you have moved them to be side by side, then mentally change those instructions to read "the drop zones on the right side of the dialog."

OPTIONS IN 2010 IS ANALYZE IN 2013

When you create a pivot table, Excel displays two contextual ribbon tabs. In Excel 2010, they were called Options and Format. In Excel 2013, they are called Analyze and Format. When this book talks about the Options tab, if you have Excel 2013, you should go to the Analyze tab.

YOUR MANAGER WANTS YOUR REPORT CHANGED

Problem: I presented my first pivot table report, shown previously, to my manager. He said, "This is almost perfect, but could you have the products going across the top and the regions going down the side?"

Strategy: Pivot tables make this change easy:
1. On the worksheet, select one cell within the pivot table. Excel will display the PivotTable Field List dialog.
2. In the dialog, drag the Region field from the Column Labels drop zone to the Row Labels drop zone. In this case, it does not matter if you drop the Region field above or below the Product field
3. In the dialog, drag the Product field from the Row Labels drop zone to the Column Labels drop zone.

Results: With two movements of the mouse, you have created a new report for your manager.

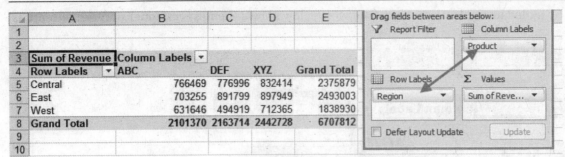

Figure 791 *Move two fields to create a new report.*

The first amazing feature of pivot tables is that they can summarize massive amounts of data very quickly. This topic shows the second amazing feature: Pivot tables can be quickly changed to show another view of the data.

ADD OR REMOVE FIELDS FROM AN EXISTING PIVOT TABLE

Problem: I've seen how easy it is to rearrange an existing pivot table by swapping Region and Product fields. Now, what if I want to replace the Region field with the Customer field?

Strategy: In order to remove the Region field from a pivot table, you click on the Region button in the Row Labels drop zone of the PivotTable Field List dialog. Then you drag the button outside the Field List dialog. The cell pointer will change to include a black X, which is synonymous with Delete.

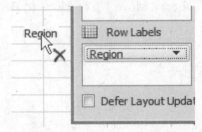

Figure 792 *Remove a field.*

Alternatively, you can uncheck the Region field from the top of the Field List.

To add the Customer field to the Row Labels drop zone, you simply click the Customer check box in the top of the PivotTable Field List dialog. Because the field is a text field, it will automatically move to the Row Labels drop zone.

Results: The new field will be added to the pivot table.

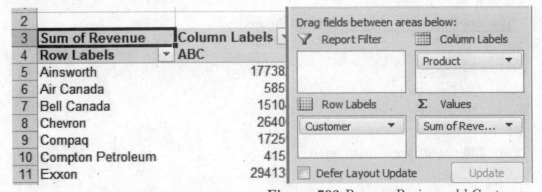

Figure 793 *Remove Region, add Customer.*

SUMMARIZE PIVOT TABLE DATA BY THREE MEASURES

Problem: I want to summarize data by region, product, and customer. How can I use a two-dimensional report to show three dimensions of data?

Strategy: Several views of the data are possible. Say that you are starting with products across the top and customers down the side. From the top of the PivotTable Field List dialog, you click the Region field.

It is automatically added as the last row field. The view below shows the first customer and the purchases by region.

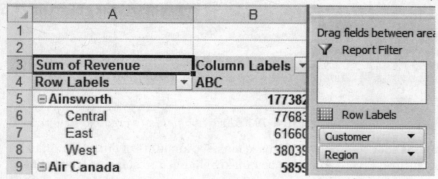

Figure 794 *Regions within customer.*

Another option is to drag the Region field heading above the Customer field heading in the bottom of the Field List dialog. Watch for the blue insertion bar.

If your mouse is not accurate enough to complete this drop, you can move the Product field to the Row Labels drop zone. Then you open the dropdown arrow at the right side of the Product field in the bottom of the Field List dialog and choose Move Up or Move to Beginning.

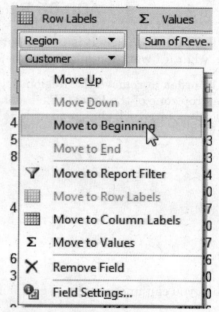

Figure 795 *Drag fields, or use this drop-down menu.*

Results: By changing the order of the fields in the row area, you now see the first region and all of the customers in that region.

Sum of Revenue	Column Labels	
Row Labels	ABC	D
⊟Central	766469	
Ainsworth	77683	
Air Canada		
Bell Canada		
Chevron		

Figure 796 *Customers within region.*

You can also stack fields in the Column Labels drop zone.

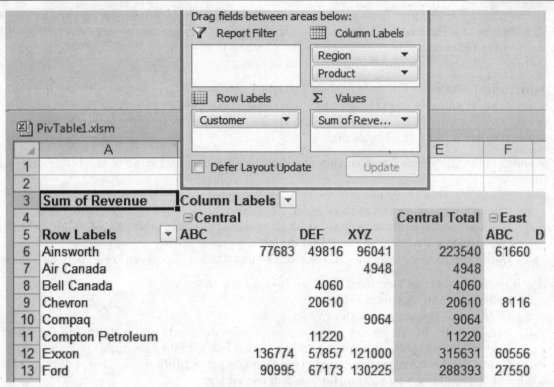

Figure 797 *Two fields in the Column Labels drop zone.*

WHY DOES THE PIVOT TABLE FIELD LIST KEEP DISAPPEARING?

Problem: The pivot table tools are there, then they are gone. What is Microsoft's problem?

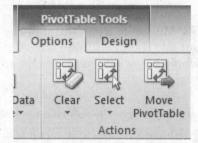

Figure 798 *One second they are there, then they are gone.*

Strategy: Here is Microsoft's rationale. They found an Excel 2003 customer who had been living with the Picture Toolbar for months. There was no picture in the worksheet, and the toolbar was actually getting in the way. Because of this event, Excel now has an obsessive desire to put away the contextual ribbon tabs as soon as you are not using them.

If you build a pivot table and keep the cell pointer within the pivot table, Excel will display the two new ribbon tabs and the PivotTable Field List dialog. But as soon as you click outside the pivot table, Microsoft will put away the ribbon tabs and hide the PivotTable Field List dialog. This drives me crazy. There are many reasons I might want to click outside the pivot table, including these:

- To get a better view of the pivot table
- To shoot a nice screen shot for this book
- I try to click on the PivotTable Field List dialog but miss, instead selecting a cell near the Field List dialog.
- I accidentally press the left mouse button when the mouse pointer had the audacity to not be above the pivot table.
- I type the Right Arrow key to scroll right in a wide pivot table, and I accidentally go one cell too far.

To my friends at Microsoft: There is nothing on Sheet2 except the pivot table. As long as I am looking at Sheet2, I am looking at the pivot table. Quit hiding the ribbon tabs just because I clicked out of the pivot table! The lady who lived with the picture toolbar for six months because she didn't know how to click the X to close the toolbar should not cause the other 749.999 million people using Excel to suffer.

To keep everyone happy, how about these rules: If your code renders a picture in the visible window of Excel, show the Picture Tools tab of the ribbon. Even if the picture is not selected, it will at least give me a clue that there are things I can do to the picture. If the ribbon is allegedly to help people discover new features in Excel, then quit hiding important tabs.

Additional Details: The new ribbon interface causes enough stress without it randomly switching to other tabs. If you are working on the PivotTable Tools Design tab and you accidentally arrow out of the pivot table, you will find yourself on the Home tab. Even if you immediately arrow back into the pivot table, you are still on the Home tab.

Maddeningly, Microsoft handled this one bizarre situation but none of the other common situations. Try this:
1. Select a cell in the pivot table.
2. Choose the Design tab of the ribbon.
3. Use the mouse to select exactly one cell outside the pivot table. Excel will hide the pivot table ribbon tabs and the PivotTable Field List dialog.
4. Using the mouse, select a cell back in the pivot table. Excel will redisplay the Design tab.

If you prefer to use the keyboard, you can instead try this:
1. Select a cell in the pivot table.
2. Choose the Design tab of the ribbon.
3. Press the Right Arrow key until you have moved exactly one cell outside the pivot table. Excel will hide the pivot table ribbon tabs and the PivotTable Field List dialog.
4. Using the Left Arrow key, move back into the pivot table. Excel will redisplay the two ribbon tabs, but it will leave you on the Home tab of the ribbon.

However, this similar scenario does not work:
1. Select a cell in the pivot table.
2. Display the Design tab of the ribbon.
3. Use the mouse to select one cell outside the pivot table. Select another cell outside the pivot table. Select a cell inside the pivot table. Excel will not return you to the Design tab.

So, Microsoft went through the incredibly convoluted task of catching when you select exactly one cell outside the pivot table with the mouse and immediately go back to the pivot table using the mouse. The whole situation frustrates me to no end.

MOVE OR CHANGE PART OF A PIVOT TABLE

Problem: If I try to insert a row in a pivot table, I am greeted with a message saying that I cannot change, move, or insert cells in a pivot table.

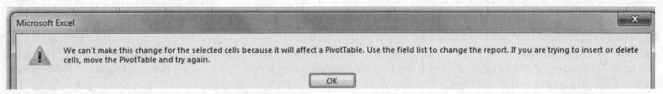

Figure 799 *Excel won't let you insert a row in a pivot table.*

Strategy: You cannot do a lot of things to a finished pivot table. While the flexibility of pivot tables is awesome, sometimes you just want to take the results of the pivot table and turn off the pivot features. If you want to take the data and reuse it somewhere else, for example, you can convert the pivot table to regular data by using Paste Values. Follow these steps:
1. Select the entire pivot table.
2. Press Ctrl+C to copy.
3. elect Home, Paste dropdown, Paste Values.

This action will change the pivot table from a live pivot table to just values in cells. You can now insert rows and columns to your heart's content.

SEE DETAIL BEHIND ONE NUMBER IN A PIVOT TABLE

Problem: One number in my pivot table seems to be wrong. Air Canada does not typically buy XYZ, yet it is shown with that product in the report.

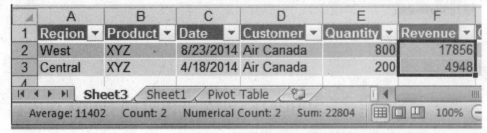

| Sum of Revenue | Column Labels | | | |
Row Labels	ABC	DEF	XYZ	Grand Total
Ainsworth	177382	190533	200936	568851
Air Canada	5859	2358	22804	31021
Bell Canada	15104	18064	18072	51240

Figure 800 *Air Canada should not have any sales for this product.*

Strategy: You can see the detail behind any number in a pivot table by double-clicking on the number. Click on the $22,804 for Air Canada XYZ. A new worksheet is inserted to the left of the current sheet, showing all the records that make up the $22,804.

	A	B	C	D	E	F	
1	Region	Product	Date	Customer	Quantity	Revenue	
2	West	XYZ	8/23/2014	Air Canada	800	17856	
3	Central	XYZ	4/18/2014	Air Canada	200	4948	

Sheet3 / Sheet1 / Pivot Table

Average: 11402   Count: 2   Numerical Count: 2   Sum: 22804   100%

Figure 801 *Excel inserts a new sheet with the drill-down detail.*

Additional Details: If you double-click on a number in the total row or total column, you will see all the records that make up that number. You could even drill down on the Grand Total cell to get a copy of all the original records.

Gotcha: Each drill-down creates a new worksheet. The new worksheet is just a snapshot in time of what made up the original number. If you detect a wrong number in the drill-down report, you need to go back to the original data to make the correction.

USE MULTIPLE VALUE FIELDS AS A COLUMN OR ROW FIELD

Problem: When I create a table with two or more Values fields, Excel has those fields stretch across the column fields. Is it possible to change to other layouts?

Strategy: Look for a virtual field in the Column Labels drop zone called ∑ Values. This field can be pivoted to another location. It starts out in the column labels:

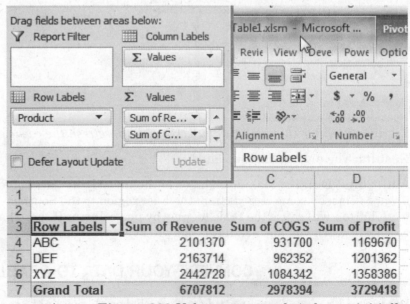

Row Labels	Sum of Revenue	Sum of COGS	Sum of Profit
ABC	2101370	931700	1169670
DEF	2163714	962352	1201362
XYZ	2442728	1084342	1358386
Grand Total	6707812	2978394	3729418

Figure 802 *Values go across the columns initially.*

Drag this virtual field to the Row Labels and you will get a different look to the report.

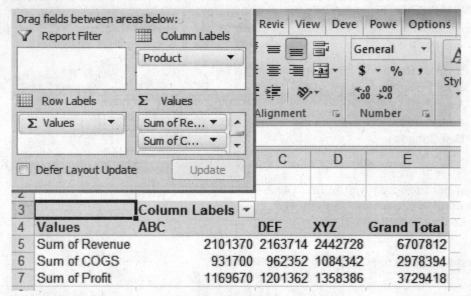

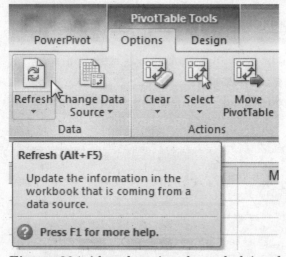

Figure 803 *You can drag Values to the row area.*

UPDATE DATA BEHIND A PIVOT TABLE

Problem: I've discovered that some of the underlying data in my pivot table is wrong. After I correct a number, the pivot table does not appear to include the change.

Strategy: This is an important thing to understand about pivot tables: When you create a pivot table, all the data is loaded into memory to allow it to calculate quickly. When you change the data on the original worksheet, it does not automatically update the pivot table.

You need to select a cell in the pivot table. The PivotTable ribbon tabs will appear. On the Options or Analyze tab, you click the Refresh icon to recalculate the pivot table from the worksheet data.

Figure 804 *After changing the underlying data, refresh the cache.*

Results: The pivot table is updated.

Additional Details: Making changes to the underlying data could cause the table to grow. For example, if you re-classify some records from the East region to the Southeast region, be aware that clicking the Refresh button will cause the table to grow by one column. If there happens to be other data in that column, Excel will warn you and ask if it is okay to overwrite those cells.

CONVERT YOUR DATA TO A TABLE BEFORE ADDING RECORDS

Problem: I have 100 new records to paste below the original data that is in the pivot table. How do I do that?

Strategy: There are two solutions. I recommend the second one.

- Paste the new data below your original data. Select a cell in the pivot table. Choose the Change Data Source icon (see Figure 804 above).
- Select a cell in the original data set. Press Ctrl+T to define the data as a table. Paste new data below the original data. The Data Source is automatically updated. Simply click the Refresh button to incorporate the new records.

The table feature began in Excel 2003 as a List. In Excel 2007, it was renamed to be a Table, creating confusion between the Data Table found in the What-If tools and the Format as Table command on the Home tab.

The Table applies some interesting formatting. The Table adds Filter dropdowns. The Table makes it easier to enter formulas. But the most valuable feature of the table is to have the pivot table data range automatically grow as you add new rows to the underlying data.

Here is an example.

Currently, the pivot table uses rows 1:564 of data.

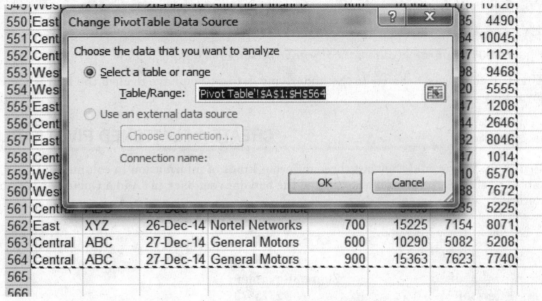

Figure 805 *Originally, the table used 564 rows.*

Select a cell in that data and press Ctrl+T. Confirm the location of the table.

Figure 806 *Convert the data to a table, even after the pivot exists.*

When you paste 2015 Q1 data below the original data, the table definition automatically changes. The other thing that updates is the range used for the PivotTable Data Source. You no longer have to visit this dialog, as it is already updated.

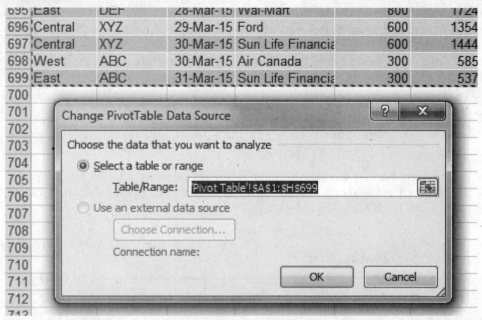

695	East	DEF	28-Mar-15	Wal-Mart	800	1724
696	Central	XYZ	29-Mar-15	Ford	600	1354
697	Central	XYZ	30-Mar-15	Sun Life Financia	600	1444
698	West	ABC	30-Mar-15	Air Canada	300	585
699	East	ABC	31-Mar-15	Sun Life Financia	300	537

Figure 807 *That range automatically grew because the data is a table.*

This still counts as a change to the underlying data, so you have to click the Refresh button to update the pivot table.

CREATE A FLATTENED PIVOT TABLE FOR REUSE

Problem: Why would they put three different kinds of information in column A? Doesn't this make pivot tables as silly as the person who created the bad data set back in "Add a Customer Number to Each Detail Record"?

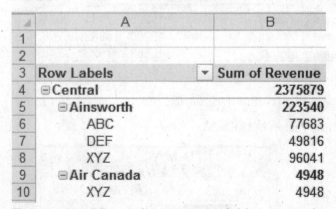

Figure 808 *Microsoft is mixing 3 fields in one column.*

My goal is to use the pivot table to make a summary, then convert to values for use as a new data set. Having three different fields in column A is really bad form.

Note: I've met one person who likes compact view. He has 15 fields in the Row Area of his report. Compact layout allows that report to fit on a screen.

Strategy: It is very annoying that Microsoft made this new view be the default. Luckily, it is only a few clicks to go back to the proper view.
1. Select one cell in the pivot table.
2. Choose the Design tab of the ribbon.
3. Open the Report Layout dropdown.
4. Change from Compact Form to Tabular Form.
5. If you have Excel 2010, open the Report Layout dropdown again and choose Repeat All Item Labels.

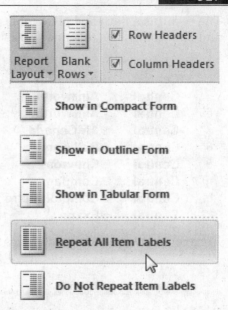

Figure 809 *New in Excel 2010, eliminate blanks in the row area.*

6. For each field in the Row Area except the last field, open the dropdown in the Row Area dropdown and choose Field Settings.

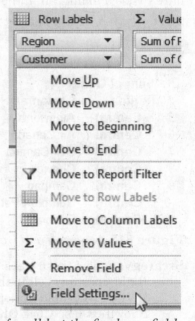

Figure 810 *Access field settings for all but the final row field.*

7. In the Field Settings dialog, choose None for Subtotals.

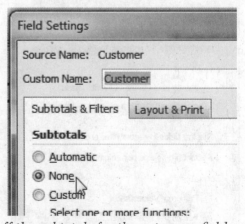

Figure 811 *Turn off the subtotals for the outer row fields.*

8. On the Design tab, open the Grand Total dropdown and choose Off for Rows and Columns.

The result is a flattened pivot table, perfect for re-use as a new consolidated data set. Copy the pivot table and paste as values to a new worksheet.

3	Region ▼	Customer ▼	Product ▼	Sum of Reven Sur
4	⊟Central	⊟Ainsworth	ABC	77683
5	Central	Ainsworth	DEF	49816
6	Central	Ainsworth	XYZ	96041
7	Central	⊟Air Canada	XYZ	4948
8	Central	⊟Bell Canada	DEF	4060
9	Central	⊟Chevron	DEF	20610
10	Central	⊟Compaq	XYZ	9064
11	Central	⊟Compton Petro	DEF	11220
12	Central	⊟Exxon	ABC	136774

Figure 812 *Copy and Paste Values this pivot table for re-use.*

REPLACE BLANKS IN A PIVOT TABLE WITH ZEROS

Problem: When I have no sales of a particular product in a particular region, Excel leaves those cells in the pivot table blank. This seems like a really bad idea. I've learned in this book that if my data has blanks instead of zeros, Excel will assume that a column is a text column. It is really ironic that Microsoft would dare to use a blank cell in the middle of numeric results.

▲	A	B	C	D	E
1					
2					
3	Sum of Quar		Product ▼		
4	Region ▼	Customer ▼	ABC	DEF	XYZ
5	⊟Central	Ainsworth	4000	2200	4200
6	Central	Air Canada			200
7	Central	Bell Canada		200	
8	Central	Chevron		900	
9	Central	Compaq			400
10	Central	Compton Petroleum		500	
11	Central	Exxon	7100	2600	5300

Figure 813 *Annoying and ironic that Excel uses blanks here.*

Strategy: Follow these steps:
1. Right-click any cell in the pivot table and choose Pivot Table Options.
2. In the PivotTable Options dialog, select the Layout & Format tab and enter 0 in the For Empty Cells Show text box. Click OK.

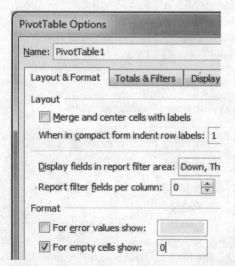

Figure 814 *Add a zero to the For Empty Cells Show text box.*

Results: Blanks in the values section of the pivot table are shown as zeros.

Additional Details: You can enter anything in the For Empty Cells Show text box. Some people like to use -- or n.a. in the formerly blank cells. Either works just as well as a zero.

COLLAPSE AND EXPAND PIVOT FIELDS

Problem: I will be using a pivot table projected on a screen during a sales forecasting meeting. I need pivot tables that show products by region, but sometimes I need to see the customer detail for a product.

Strategy: You can solve this problem by building a pivot table with Region, Product, and Customer along the row area.

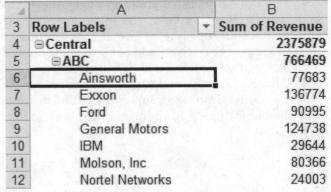

	A	B
3	Row Labels	Sum of Revenue
4	⊟Central	2375879
5	⊟ABC	766469
6	Ainsworth	77683
7	Exxon	136774
8	Ford	90995
9	General Motors	124738
10	IBM	29644
11	Molson, Inc	80366
12	Nortel Networks	24003

Figure 815 *Start with Product, Region, and Customer.*

Here's how it works:

1. Select one of the customer cells. In the Options tab of the ribbon, select Collapse Entire Field. Excel will hide all the customer rows.

	A	B
3	Row Labels	Sum of Revenue
4	⊟Central	2375879
5	⊞ABC	766469
6	⊞DEF	776996
7	⊞XYZ	832414

Figure 816 *Collapse the Customer field.*

2. Select a region cell and collapse that field as well.

Notice that each product has a plus sign button to the left of the field. When the meeting agenda moves to the DEF product, you can click the plus sign in A6 to see the region totals. You can continue collapsing sections as you are finished and then expanding the next sections.

Additional Details: If you select the innermost row field (in this case, Customer) and select Expand Entire Field, Excel assumes that you must need more detail for Customer. Because there is no additional detail in the pivot table, Excel will display the Show Detail dialog, allowing you to add a new field as the innermost row field.

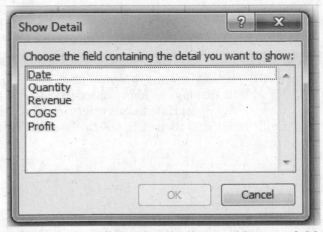

Figure 817 *Try to expand the innermost row field, and Excel will offer to add a new field.*

SPECIFY A NUMBER FORMAT FOR A PIVOT TABLE FIELD

Problem: In a pivot table, a Values field tends to appear in a General format. This doesn't always work for me. I might want thousands separators or even to show numbers in thousands. If I change the number format using the settings in the Home tab of the ribbon, the number format is lost after the next pivot table refresh.

Strategy: Number formatting is controlled from the Field Settings dialog. There are two approaches for displaying Field Settings for the correct field.

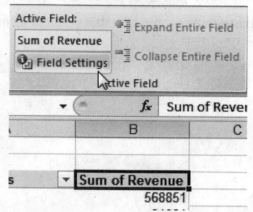

- Use the Active Field group in the Options tab of the ribbon. To use this field, you must select either the Sum of Revenue heading or a cell that contains a revenue amount. The Active Field box will show Sum of Revenue. You can then click Field Settings.
- Alternatively, you can go to the Revenue field in the Field List drop zones, open the flyout menu and choose Field Settings. For an image, turn back to Figure 810.

Figure 818 *Choose a cell in the pivot table to change the active field.*

Follow these steps to specify a number format for a pivot table field:

1. Display the Field Settings dialog for the Sum of Revenue field using either of the methods described above. Excel will display the Value Field Settings dialog.
2. Click the Number Format button at the bottom of the dialog.

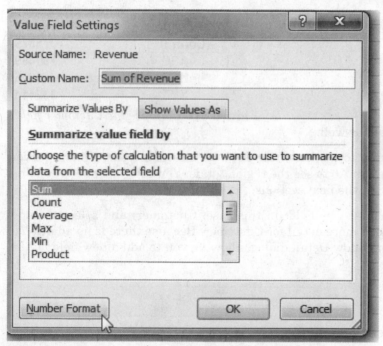

Figure 819 *Access the number format from here.*

3. Excel will display an abbreviated version of the Format Cells dialog with only the Number tab. Choose an appropriate numeric format. You can create custom formats. Click OK to close the Format Cells dialog and then click OK to close the Value Field Settings dialog.

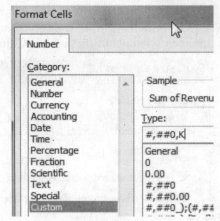

Figure 820 *Apply a number format to the field.*

Results: the Revenue field will now always show the selected format, no matter how the pivot table is changed.

Sum of Revenue	Region			
Product	Central	East	West	Grand Total
ABC	766K	703K	632K	2,101K
DEF	777K	892K	495K	2,164K
XYZ	832K	898K	712K	2,443K
Grand Total	2,376K	2,493K	1,839K	6,708K

Figure 821 *Excel keeps the number format, even after you move fields.*

The above method formats all Sum of Revenue cells using the numeric formatting attached to the Sum Revenue field to assign a non-currency format.

Gotcha: One of the conventions in formatting tables says that you should include a currency symbol on only the first and total rows of a data set. There is no inherent way to do this with a pivot table. However, you can use the numeric formatting attached to the Sum of Revenue field to assign a non-currency format. Then you select the first row of cells and assign a currency format by pressing Ctrl+1 to display the Format Cells dialog. This will work initially, but will be lost when you change the table.

PRESERVE COLUMN WIDTHS

Problem: I've nicely formatted my pivot table, including using narrow column widths.

◢	A	B	C	D	E
1	Customer	(All) ▼			
2					
3	Sum of Revenue	Produc ▼			
4	Region ▼	ABC	DEF	XYZ	Grand Total
5	Central	766K	777K	832K	2,376K
6	East	703K	892K	898K	2,493K
7	West	632K	495K	712K	1,839K
8	Grand Total	2,101K	2,164K	2,443K	6,708K

Figure 822 *After manually applying column widths.*

When I choose a new customer from the filter dropdown in B1, Excel changes all of my column widths.

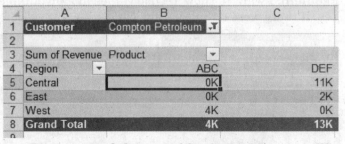

Figure 823 *Column widths change automatically.*

Strategy: There is an option setting to prevent this behavior. Select any cell in the pivot table. Choose the Options button at the left side of the Analyze or Options ribbon tab. In the Layout and Format tab, uncheck the option for Autofit Column Widths On Update.

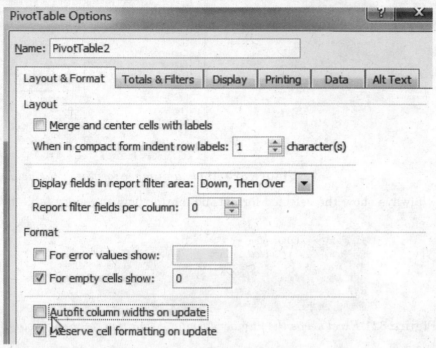

Figure 824 *Uncheck Autofit checkbox.*

Gotcha: After choosing this setting, you will have to fix your column widths one last time. The column widths don't miraculously change back to the way they were.

Gotcha: When the column widths are not changing, you may not be able to see the customer selected in B1. To solve this problem, add some fill formatting to C1:E1. Select B1:E1 and press Ctrl+One to display format cells. On the Alignment tab, open the Horizontal Alignment dropdown and choose Center Across Selection.

	A	B	C	D	E
1	Customer	⌐ Compton Petroleum			
2					
3	Sum of Revenue	Produ ▼			
4	Region	▼	ABC	DEF	XYZ	Grand Total
5	Central		0K	11K	0K	11K
6	East		0K	2K	0K	2K
7	West		4K	0K	14K	18K
8	Grand Total		4K	13K	14K	31K

Figure 825 *Column widths stay as you set them.*

SHOW YES/NO IN A PIVOT TABLE

Problem: I want to show Yes/No values in a pivot table. If the customer bought from us in a period, show Yes. If there were no sales, show No.

Sum of Revenue	Customer ⌐		
Date ⌐	Ainsworth	Exxon	IBM
1-Jun-14			20480
2-Jun-14			
4-Jun-14			
5-Jun-14			
6-Jun-14			12135
7-Jun-14			

Figure 826 *Instead of numbers, show Yes/No.*

Strategy: Use a custom number format of "Yes";"Credit";"No". Follow the steps in "Specifying a Number Format In a Pivot Table". Once you are in the Format Cells dialog for the Sum of Revenue field, choose Custom and type the code, including the quotes.

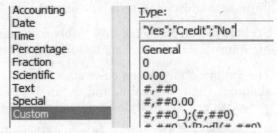

Figure 827 *Show Yes for any positive value, No for zero.*

Gotcha: This trick initially shows Yes for periods where there is a purchase, but leaves the other periods blank.

Sum of Revenue			
Date		IBM	Molson, Inc
6-Jun-14		Yes	Yes
7-Jun-14			
8-Jun-14		Yes	
9-Jun-14		Yes	

Figure 828 *The Yes values appear.*

To display the No values, you have to replace the blanks in the pivot table with a zero. See "Replace Blanks in a Pivot Table with Zeroes."

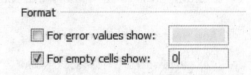

Figure 829 *Replace blanks with zero.*

Result: The pivot table shows Yes or No values.

	IBM	Molson, Inc
	Yes	Yes
	No	No
	Yes	No
	Yes	No

Figure 830 *Instead of numbers, show Yes/No.*

Additional Details: At this point, the heading of "Sum of Revenue" is not really appropriate. Select any Yes/No cell to make the active field box in the Options tab of the ribbon say Sum of Revenue. You can type a new name in that box.

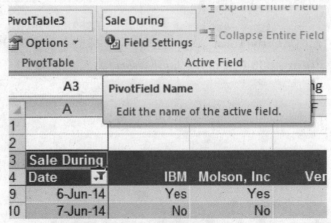

Figure 831 *Change from "Sum of Revenue".*

FORMAT PIVOT TABLES WITH THE GALLERY

Problem: Due to the dynamic nature of pivot tables, it is fairly hard to format them. If I start applying formats to individual cells, the formats are lost after I rearrange the pivot table. Help!

Strategy: You can solve this problem by using the gallery on the Design tab of the ribbon. This is an amazing improvement over Excel 2003's AutoFormat.

The gallery offers seven color styles (grayscale and six theme colors). There are four styles each in three shadings (light, medium, and dark). There is one style with no formatting. You have (6 x 4 x 3) 72 color styles, 12 grayscale styles, and 1 plain style for a total of 85 styles.

You can modify the color and grayscale styles by using the four check boxes Row Headers, Column Headers, Banded Rows, and Banded Columns. Since each checkbox offers 2 choices, 2 x 2 x 2 x 2 = 16 variations on each of the 84 styles. 84 x 16 + 1 yields 1345 styles, (1152 color, 192 grey, 1 plain)

By choosing a new theme, you can change the 6 accent colors to any of 40 built-in sets of colors. This leads to 46,080 color styles (1152 x 40). Adding the grayscale and plain style gives you 46,273 styles.

In case one of the built-in 46.273 different styles doesn't work for you, then you can create your own custom formatting. See the "None of the 46,273 Built-In Styles Do What My Manager Asks For" on page 329.

In comparison, Excel 2003 offered 22 AutoFormats, and all of them were horrible. Many of them changed the layout of your table. Microsoft did an incredible job with the formatting options in Excel 2007. Here's how you use them:

1. Select a cell in the pivot table. Select the Design tab on the ribbon.
2. Make selections in the PivotTable Style Options group, changing Row Headers, Column Headers, Banded Rows, and/or Banded columns. (You should do this before opening the Styles gallery, as the thumbnails in the gallery will reflect these settings.)

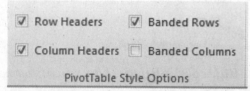

Figure 832 *Turn on banded rows.*

3. Open the PivotTable Styles gallery. Thanks to Live Preview, you can hover over various thumbnails and see the effect of each on the table. Figure 833 shows Pivot Style Light 10. Figure 834 shows Pivot Style Dark 19.

Sum of Revenue		Product	
Customer	Region	ABC	DEF
⊟ Ainsworth	Central	77683	49816
	East	61660	90978
	West	38039	49739
Ainsworth Total		**177382**	**190533**
⊟ Air Canada	Central		
	East		2358
	West	5859	
Air Canada Total		**5859**	**2358**

Figure 833 *One of the light styles.*

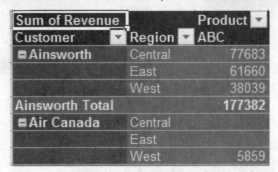

Figure 834 *One of the dark styles.*

Additional Details: On the Page Layout tab of the ribbon, you can change to any of the different built-in color schemes. This will affect the colors used in the gallery.

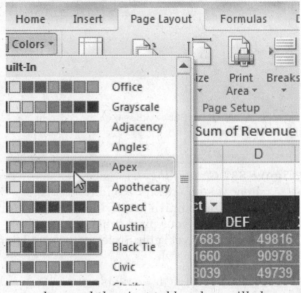

Figure 835 *Change theme colors and the pivot table colors will change.*

NONE OF THE 46,273 BUILT-IN STYLES DO WHAT MY MANAGER ASKS FOR

Problem: My manager asks for a pivot table to be formatted with alternating stripes that are two rows high. None of the built-in styles do this.

Strategy: You can create this effect by duplicating an existing style and modifying it. Follow these steps:
1. Find a style that is close to your manager's request. In the PivotTable Styles gallery, right-click the style and choose Duplicate.

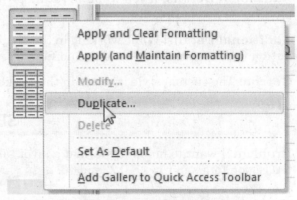

Figure 836 *Copy an existing style.*

2. In the Modify PivotTable Quick Style dialog, give the style a new name. Excel initially gives the style a name by adding a 2 after the old name. Rather than PivotStyleLight 10 2, use a name like TwoStripe.
3. At the bottom left of the dialog, choose Set as Default PivotTable Quick Style For This Document.

4. In the Table Element list box, choose First Row Stripe. A new dropdown control appears, called Stripe Size. Open the dropdown and choose 2.

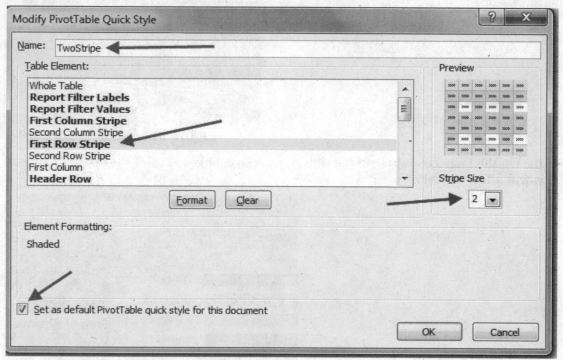

Figure 837 *Change the stripe size.*

5. Repeat step 4 with Second Row Stripe.
6. Click OK to finish modifying the style. You have now created a new style, but Excel has not applied the style to your pivot table.
7. Open the PivotTable Styles gallery and find the new style at the top of the list, in the Custom section. Choose that style.

Results: A new style is available, with stripes that are two rows tall.

Customer	ABC	DEF	XYZ	Grand Total
Ainsworth	177382	190533	200936	568851
Air Canada	5859	2358	22804	31021
Bell Canada	15104	18064	18072	51240
Chevron	26406	20610	7032	54048
Compaq	17250	4380	17620	39250
Compton Petroleum	4158	13249	13962	31369

Figure 838 *A new style is available.*

Additional Details: If you want all future pivot tables to use this format, right-click the style thumbnail and choose Set as Default.

Additional Details: While working in the Modify PivotTable Quick Style dialog, you can click the Format button to change the font, border, and fill.

Gotcha: The custom style is saved in the workbook. It is not available in other workbooks.

SELECT PIVOT TABLE PARTS FOR FORMATTING

Problem: I want to manually format a pivot table. Can I select all the row subtotals? For example, select the region totals in rows 8, 12, and 16.

	A	B	C	D
1				
2				
3	Revenue		Customer	
4	Region	Product	Ainsworth	Air Canada
5	Central	ABC	77683	0
6		DEF	49816	0
7		XYZ	96041	4948
8	Central Total		223540	4948
9	East	ABC	61660	0
10		DEF	90978	2358
11		XYZ	79438	0
12	East Total		232076	2358
13	West	ABC	38039	5859
14		DEF	49739	0
15		XYZ	25457	17856
16	West Total		113235	23715
17	Grand Total		568851	31021

Figure 839 *Select row subtotals.*

Strategy: A clever mouse trick will allow you to select similar rows in a pivot table. Follow these steps:

1. Select one cell in the pivot table. On the Design tab, choose Report Layout, Show in Tabular Form.
2. Hover the mouse over cell A8. This is the Central region total. Slowly move the mouse toward the left edge of the cell. Eventually, the cell pointer changes to a black arrow that points to the right. When this cell pointer appears, click the mouse. Excel will now select all the subtotal rows.

7		XYZ
8	Central Total	
9	East	ABC
10		DEF
11		XYZ
12	East Total	
13	West	ABC
14		DEF
15		XYZ
16	West Total	

Figure 840 *One click select all subtotal rows.*

3. Using the formatting icons on the Home tab of the ribbon, assign a color to the subtotal rows.

Additional Details: Click in the left side of cell B5, and you will select all the ABC records throughout the pivot table. Below, different colors are applied to ABC, DEF, and XYZ using this method.

3	Revenue		Customer	
4	Region	Product	Chevron	Compaq
5	Central	ABC	0	0
6		DEF	20610	0
7		XYZ	0	9064
8	Central Total		20610	9064
9	East	ABC	8116	0
10		DEF	0	4380
11		XYZ	0	0
12	East Total		8116	4380
13	West	ABC	18290	17250
14		DEF	0	0
15		XYZ	7032	8556
16	West Total		25322	25806
17	Grand Total		54048	39250

Figure 841 *Format all cells for one product.*

If you have multiple column fields, you can select various columns by hovering near the top of the label for a column.

Gotcha: This feature can be turned off. To ensure that it's not turned off, enable the Enable Selection setting under the Select dropdown on the Options tab.

APPLY CONDITIONAL FORMATTING TO A PIVOT TABLE

Problem: The new conditional formatting options in Excel are amazing, but they require special care in pivot tables. If you include the grand total row, it will get the largest data bars, and the detail cells have relatively meaningless bars.

Strategy: You can use the Manage Rules dialog to assign conditional formatting to only certain cells. You can initially create the "wrong" formatting and then edit it to refer to only the selected cells. For example, follow these steps:

1. Select cells B5:B15. You want the first cell in the selection to be the correct type of cell. In this case, it is a value for a product.
2. Select Home, Conditional Formatting, Data Bars, Solid Fill, Red. Excel applies data bars, but the region totals are getting the largest bars.

	A	B
1		
2		
3	Row Labels ▼	Sum of Revenue
4	⊟Central	2375879
5	ABC	766469
6	DEF	776996
7	XYZ	832414
8	⊟East	2493003
9	ABC	703255
10	DEF	891799
11	XYZ	897949
12	⊟West	1838930
13	ABC	631646
14	DEF	494919
15	XYZ	712365
16	Grand Total	6707812

Figure 842 *Cells B8 & B12 artificially get the largest data bars.*

3. In Excel 2010, open the pivot options dropdown at the bottom right corner of the pivot table. Choose to apply the formatting rule to only cells for revenue and product.

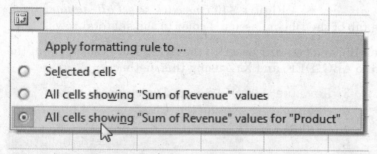

Figure 843 *In Excel 2010, a dropdown appears in the grid.*

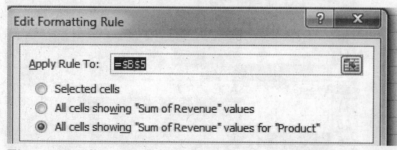

Figure 844 *Go to the Edit Rules dialog in Excel 2007.*

Results: the data bars are applied only to the detail product rows.

◢	A	B
1		
2		
3	**Row Labels** ▼	**Sum of Revenue**
4	⊟ Central	2375879
5	ABC	766469
6	DEF	776996
7	XYZ	832414
8	⊟ East	2493003
9	ABC	703255
10	DEF	891799
11	XYZ	897949
12	⊟ West	1838930
13	ABC	631646
14	DEF	494919
15	XYZ	712365
16	**Grand Total**	6707812

Figure 845 *The data bars are applied only to like cells.*

Additional Details: Similar settings are available for icon sets and color scales.

CAN I SAVE FORMATTING IN A TEMPLATE?

Problem: Every month, I have to change my pivot table formatting. Can I create a template to remember my favorite settings?

Strategy: The pivot table template concept is a frequent request as I do my Power Excel seminars. I predict that Microsoft won't add this, because the people inside of Microsoft have embraced building a template using GetPivotData.

I first learned this technique from a former Microsoft staffer. It really is a cool way to improve your monthly reporting workflow. It will take an extra 15 minutes during the first month, but then it will save time in the future.

1. Build an ugly, unformatted pivot table with every field that you will need in your final report.
2. On a new worksheet, build a non-pivot table report shell that contains all of the formatting that you want to use.
3. Start in one cell of the report shell. Type an equals sign. Go to the pivot table and find the cell that contains the correct information. Click that cell and press Enter. Microsoft will build a GETPIVOT-DATA formula for you. **Gotcha:** The fields in the formula are hard-coded and can not be copied to other cells in the report.
4. Edit the first formula to use labels in your report.
5. Copy the formula throughout your report.

Each month, the workflow becomes: Add new data to the data set. Refresh the ugly pivot table. Print the nicely formatted report that draws its numbers from the pivot table.

Here are some examples.

This figure shows a very ugly pivot table. Excel adds Plan+Actual in column D which is useless. There is no way to get Actuals for Jan through May and Plan for June through December without showing both fields for every month.

3

◢	A	B	C	D	E
1					
2					
3	Sum of Sales	Month ▼	Type ▼		
4		⊟ Jan		Jan Total	⊟ Feb
5	Store ▼	Actual	Plan		Actual
6	Ala Moana	11739	11100	22839	16105
7	Altamonte Mall	11421	11400	22821	14854
8	Annapolis Mall	11689	10800	22489	14675
9	Aventura Mall	13646	12900	26546	17473
10	Baybrook	12366	12100	24466	16625

Figure 846 *An ugly pivot table.*

Typically, each month, you would create this pivot table, copy the table and paste as values. You would get rid of the columns you don't need. You would resequence the stores in a geographic fashion. It would take half an hour to format the copied report.

Instead, build a report shell on a new worksheet. Format the report the way that you want it to be shown. If you want underlines and double-underlines, add them. If you want $ on row 1 and the total row, do that. If you want (gasp) a blank row, add it. You can do whatever you want, since this is not a pivot table. It is just Excel.

E4	▼		f_x	=IF(MONTH(DATEVALUE(E3&" 1, 2014"))<=MONTH($P$1),"Actual","Plan")													
	A	B	C	D	E	F	G	H	I	J	K	L	M	N	O	P	Q
1	**XYZ Company Super Report**														*Actuals Through:*	4/30	
2																	
3					Jan	Feb	Mar	Apr	May	Jun	Jul	Aug	Sep	Oct	Nov	Dec	
4					Actual	Actual	Actual	Actual	Plan	Plan	Plan	Plan	Plan	Plan	Plan	Plan	Total
5			Houston Area														
6				Baybrook													$0K
7				Highland Village													OK
8				Willowbrook													OK
9				The Woodlands Mall													OK
10			Houston Total		$0K	$0K	$0K	$0K	$0K	$0K	$0K	$0K	$0K	$0K	$0K	$0K	$0K
11																	
12			Dallas/Forth Worth Area														
13				Firewheel													$0K
14				Galleria													OK
15				Hulen Mall													OK
16				Northeast Mall													OK
17				Northpark Center													OK
18				The Parks													OK
19				Southlake Town Square													OK
20				Stonebriar Mall													OK
21				Willowbend													OK
22			Dallas Total		$0K	$0K	$0K	$0K	$0K	$0K	$0K	$0K	$0K	$0K	$0K	$0K	$0K
23																	
24			Other														
25				Huebner Oaks													$0K
26				La Cantera													OK
27				Northstar Mall													OK
28				Cielo Vista Mall													OK
29				The Domain													OK
30				Lakeline													OK
31			Other Total		$0K	$0K	$0K	$0K	$0K	$0K	$0K	$0K	$0K	$0K	$0K	$0K	$0K
32																	
33			Grand Total		$0K	$0K	$0K	$0K	$0K	$0K	$0K	$0K	$0K	$0K	$0K	$0K	$0K

Figure 847 *Do any formatting in a non-pivot table report.*

The first data cell in the report is for Baybrook Mall, January, Actuals. Choose that cell. Type an equals sign. Navigate to the pivot table worksheet and find the cell for Baybrook, January, Actual. Click on that cell and click OK.

Most of the time when Excel inserts a GETPIVOTDATA formula, it is an annoying side-effect of building a formula with a mouse. This time, it is crucial to building this report.

Gotcha: Most people are annoyed by Excel insert GETPIVOTDATA. Later in this book, in "Calculations Outside of Pivot Tables" on page 371, I will show you how to turn this feature off. If someone has turned the feature off on your computer, you need to turn it back on.

The fundamental problem with the automatically generated GETPIVOTDATA function is that the label values are hard-coded in the formula instead of pointing to cells in the worksheet.

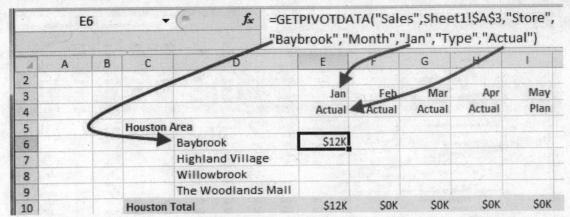

Figure 848 *Changes this text to point to cells in the report.*

The accountants at Microsoft who use this trick regularly call this next step, "Parameterizing the Formula." Change the three text values in the formula to point to cell addresses. Make sure to use the proper dollar signs. Replace Baybrook with $D6. Replace Jan with E$3. Replace Actual with E$4.

=GETPIVOTDATA("Sales",Sheet1!$A$3,"Store",$D6,
"Month",E$3,"Type",E$4)

	C	D	E	F
3			Jan	Feb
4			Actual	Actual	A
5	Houston Area			
6		Baybrook		$12K
7		Highland Village		
8		Willowbrook		
9		The Woodlands Mall		

Figure 849 *Replace text with cell addresses.*

You can now copy that first formula and Paste Special Formulas to all the other report cells.

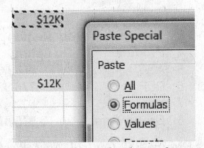

Figure 850 *Copy the first formula and paste the formula throughout.*

The result is a beautifully formatted report that is getting the data from the pivot table. Next month, add the May actuals, refresh the pivot table, and the report will update with new values.

			Jan Actual	Feb Actual	Mar Actual	Apr Actual	May Actual	Jun Plan	Jul Plan	Aug Plan	Sep Plan	Oct Plan	Nov Plan	Dec Plan	Total
1	XYZ Company Super Report										Actuals Through:			5/31	
5	Houston Area														
6		Baybrook	$12K	$17K	$22K	$25K	$24K	$32K	$28K	$24K	$20K	$32K	$49K	$121K	$406K
7		Highland Village	13K	17K	20K	24K	23K	33K	29K	24K	20K	33K	49K	122K	406K
8		Willowbrook	15K	19K	24K	30K	30K	37K	32K	28K	23K	37K	55K	138K	467K
9		The Woodlands Mall	14K	19K	24K	28K	27K	36K	32K	27K	23K	36K	54K	135K	453K
10	Houston Total		$54K	$71K	$90K	$106K	$103K	$138K	$120K	$103K	$86K	$138K	$207K	$516K	$1,732K
12	Dallas/Forth Worth Area														
13		Firewheel	$11K	$15K	$18K	$23K	$22K	$29K	$25K	$22K	$18K	$29K	$43K	$108K	$364K
14		Galleria	11K	15K	19K	25K	24K	30K	27K	23K	19K	30K	46K	114K	383K
15		Hulen Mall	13K	17K	23K	26K	27K	34K	30K	26K	21K	34K	51K	128K	430K
16		Northeast Mall	11K	15K	19K	23K	24K	31K	27K	23K	20K	31K	47K	117K	390K
17		Northpark Center	12K	18K	22K	27K	28K	35K	30K	26K	22K	35K	52K	130K	437K
18		The Parks	13K	17K	20K	26K	26K	33K	28K	24K	20K	33K	49K	122K	410K
19		Southlake Town Squar	14K	17K	22K	25K	26K	34K	29K	25K	21K	34K	50K	126K	422K
20		Stonebriar Mall	11K	14K	19K	22K	23K	28K	25K	21K	18K	28K	42K	106K	357K
21		Willowbend	13K	17K	23K	28K	28K	34K	30K	26K	22K	34K	52K	129K	436K
22	Dallas Total		$109K	$144K	$186K	$225K	$227K	$288K	$252K	$216K	$180K	$288K	$432K	$1,081K	$3,629K
24	Other														
25		Huebner Oaks	$11K	$15K	$18K	$23K	$21K	$29K	$25K	$22K	$18K	$29K	$43K	$107K	$361K
26		La Cantera	13K	18K	22K	26K	26K	34K	30K	25K	21K	34K	51K	127K	426K
27		Northstar Mall	13K	16K	21K	24K	25K	32K	28K	24K	20K	32K	48K	119K	400K
28		Cielo Vista Mall	12K	18K	22K	26K	24K	34K	29K	25K	21K	34K	50K	126K	421K
29		The Domain	15K	19K	25K	29K	29K	37K	32K	28K	23K	37K	55K	139K	468K
30		Lakeline	13K	17K	23K	27K	28K	34K	30K	26K	21K	34K	51K	127K	430K
31	Other Total		$76K	$102K	$132K	$155K	$153K	$199K	$174K	$149K	$124K	$199K	$298K	$745K	$2,506K
33	Grand Total		$239K	$318K	$408K	$486K	$484K	$625K	$546K	$468K	$390K	$625K	$937K	$2,342K	$7,867K

Figure 851 *This doesn't look like a pivot table, but harnesses the power.*

Additional Details: Cell P1 in the report is a date that I type manually each month. Formulas in row 4 use that date to show "Actual" or "Plan" based on the date. =IF(MONTH(DATEVALUE(E3&" 1, 2014"))<=MONTH($P$1),"Actual","Plan").

MANUALLY RE-SEQUENCE THE ORDER OF DATA IN A PIVOT TABLE

Problem: By default, a pivot table organizes data alphabetically. For the Region field, this means the data is organized with Central first, East second, and West third. My manager wants the regions to appear in the order East, Central, West. After unsuccessfully lobbying to have the Central region renamed Middle, I need to find a way to have my table sequenced with the East region first.

	A	B	C	D	E
3	Sum of Revenue	Region ▾			
4	Product ▾	Central	East	West	Grand Total
5	ABC	766,469	703,255	631,646	2,101,370
6	DEF	776,996	891,799	494,919	2,163,714
7	XYZ	832,414	897,949	712,365	2,442,728
8	Grand Total	2,375,879	2,493,003	1,838,930	6,707,812

Figure 852 *Central, East, West is the alphabetical sequence.*

Strategy: It is amazing that this trick works. Try it:
1. Select cell B4 in the pivot table.
2. In cell B4, type the word East.

Region ▾	
East	East
766,469	703,255
776,996	891,799
832,414	897,949
2,375,879	2,493,003

Figure 853 *Go to the Central cell and type a new heading.*

3. When you press Enter, Excel senses what you are trying to do. All the data from the East region moves to Column B. Excel automatically moves the Central region heading and data to column C.

Region ▾			
East	Central	West	Grand Total
703,255	766,469	631,646	2,101,370
891,799	776,996	494,919	2,163,714
897,949	832,414	712,365	2,442,728
2,493,003	2,375,879	1,838,930	6,707,812

Figure 854 *East and Central switch! Never try this outside a pivot table.*

You can easily use this trick to re-sequence the fields into any order as necessary.

Additional Details: This technique will only change the Region sequence in a single pivot table. If you would like to change the sequence in all future pivot tables, you need to create a custom list with the regions in the proper sequence. See "Have the Fill Handle Fill Your List of Part Numbers" on page 79. Any pivot tables created will follow the custom list sequence.

PRESENT A PIVOT TABLE IN HIGH-TO-LOW ORDER BY REVENUE

Problem: A pivot table organizes data alphabetically by default. I want to produce a report that is sorted high to low by revenue.

	A	B
3	Customer ▾	Revenue
4	Ainsworth	568,851
5	Air Canada	31,021
6	Bell Canada	51,240
7	Chevron	54,048

Figure 855 *Reports are normally sorted alphabetically.*

Strategy: Each pivot table field offers a sort option. To access the sort options for a field, follow these steps:
1. Open the Customer field dropdown in cell A3. **Gotcha:** Depending on the layout, this field might be called Row Labels instead of Customer.
2. Choose More Sort Options.

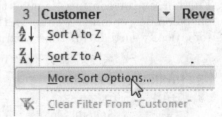

Figure 856 *Choose More Sort Options.*

3. Excel displays the Sort (Customer) dialog. Initially, the sort is set to Manual. This option lets you re-sequence items by dragging or retyping as discussed in the previous topic. Choose Descending. Open the dropdown under Descending and choose Revenue.

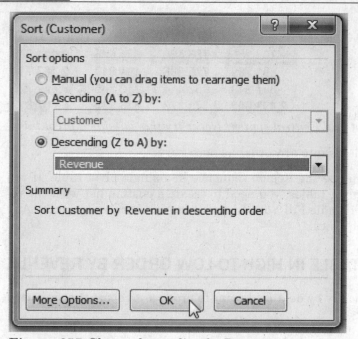

Figure 857 *Choose descending by Revenue.*

Results: The report will be sequenced with the largest customers at the top.

	A	B
3	**Customer** ⌄↓	**Revenue**
4	Wal-Mart	869,454
5	General Motors	750,163
6	Exxon	704,359
7	Ford	622,794

Figure 858 *Largest customers at the top.*

Further, as you continue to pivot this report, Excel will remember that customers should always be sorted based on descending revenue. In this figure, product is added as an outermost row field. The report is automatically sorted, this time with Exxon at the top.

	A	B	C
3	**Product** ⌄	**Customer** ⌄↓	**Revenue**
4	⊟**ABC**	Exxon	294,138
5		General Motors	280,967
6		Wal-Mart	276,847
7		Molson, Inc	203,522

Figure 859 *Customer continues to re-sort after pivoting.*

Additional Details: If you use the Compact Form layout with multiple row fields, there is an extra step. When you open Row Labels, you have to choose from a second dropdown to choose which field you want to sort.

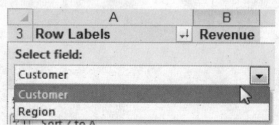

Figure 860 *Extra dropdown in Compact Form layout.*

An alternate method for accessing the Sort dialog is to hover over the Customer field in the top of the Pivot-Table Field List dialog. A dropdown appears. You can choose to sort or filter from this dropdown.

GROUP DAILY DATES BY MONTH IN A PIVOT TABLE

Problem: My data set has a date on which each item was shipped. When I produce a pivot table with the date field, it provides sales by day. My plant manager loves sales by day, but everyone else in the company would rather see sales by month.

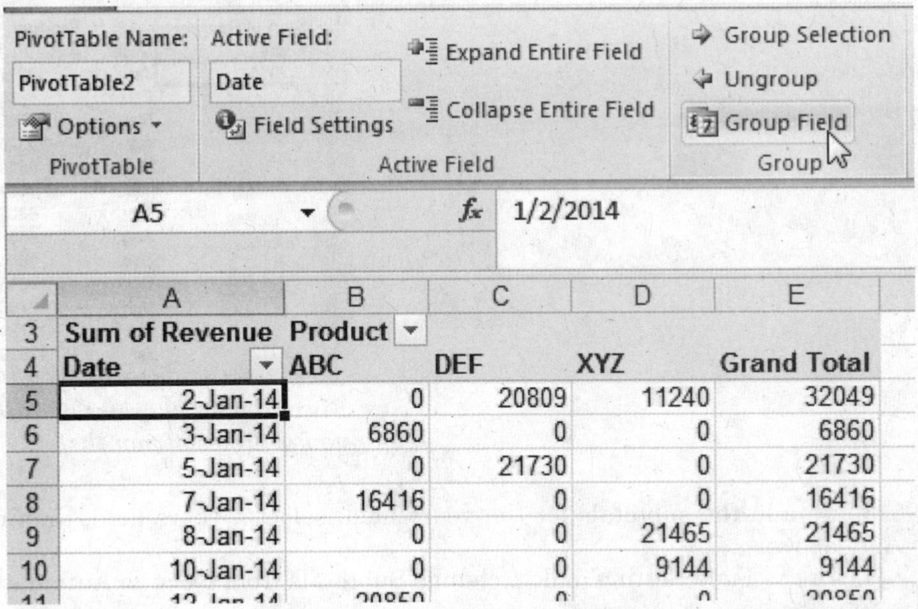

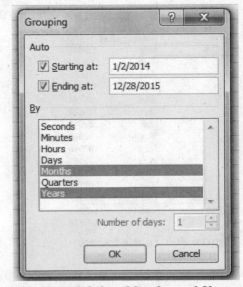

Figure 861 *Excel reports daily dates.*

Strategy: You can group daily dates to show year, quarter, and month. To do so, you build a pivot table with dates in the Row area of the pivot table:

1. Select a cell that contains a date. Click the Group Field icon in the Options tab. Excel displays the Grouping dialog.

2. The Grouping dialog defaults to selecting months. If your data spans more than one year, it is crucial that you also select years. Select Months and Years. If you don't choose Years, Excel will group January from one year and January from another year into a single value called January.

Figure 862 *Select Months and Years.*

The Date field is now replaced with Months. There is a field called Years. Years and Months are shown in the pivot table, although the pivot table is not showing subtotals for each year.

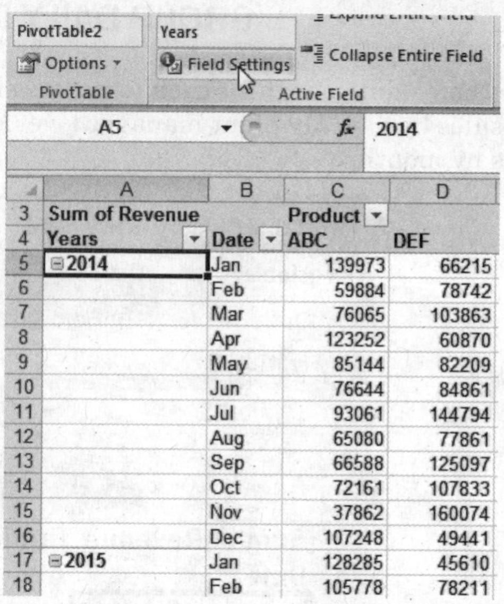

Figure 863 *500 rows of daily dates are now 24 rows of months.*

3. To add the subtotals for the years field, select a years field, then choose Field Settings as shown above.
4. In the Field Setting dialog, change Subtotals from None to Automatic.

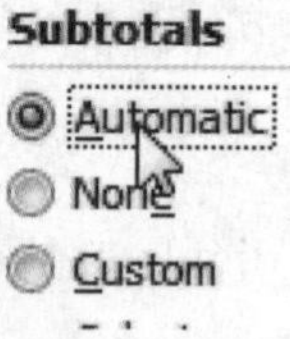

Subtotals

- ⦿ Automatic
- ○ None
- ○ Custom

Figure 864 *Change the Years field to use Automatic Subtotals.*

The result is a report with a subtotal for each year.

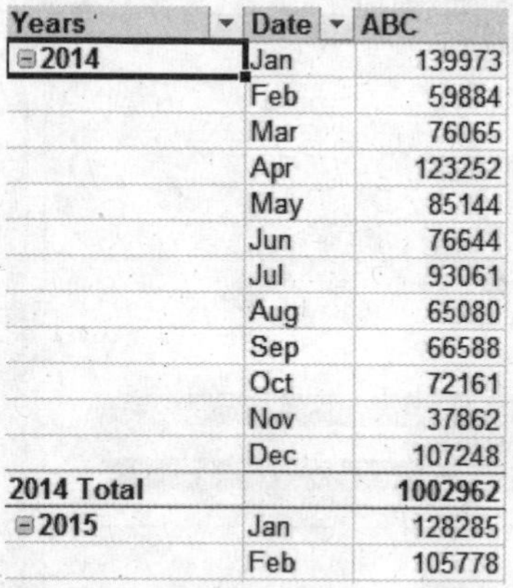

Years	Date	ABC
⊟2014	Jan	139973
	Feb	59884
	Mar	76065
	Apr	123252
	May	85144
	Jun	76644
	Jul	93061
	Aug	65080
	Sep	66588
	Oct	72161
	Nov	37862
	Dec	107248
2014 Total		1002962
⊟2015	Jan	128285
	Feb	105778

Figure 865 *Totals by year.*

CREATE A YEAR-OVER-YEAR REPORT

Problem: I have two years of data by daily dates. I would like to see year-over-year sales by month.

Strategy: Amazingly, it takes only 10 mouse clicks to create this report. Follow these steps:

1. Select one cell in your data set.
2. Insert, Pivot Table, OK.
3. In the PivotTable Field List, choose Date and Revenue.
4. At this point, the Row Labels heading is selected. Move down one cell so that the cell pointer is on a date.
5. Choose Group Field. Months is already selected. Add Years. Click OK.
6. In the PivotTable Field List, drag Years from the Row Labels drop zone to the Column Labels drop zone. You will now have this report.

3	Sum of Revenue	Column Labels ▼		
4	Row Labels ▼	2014	2015	Grand Total
5	Jan	258081	295609	553690
6	Feb	257570	285528	543098
7	Mar	252354	239373	491727
8	Apr	271215	317368	588583
9	May	290211	303998	594209
10	Jun	251187	188041	439228
11	Jul	306684	343158	649842
12	Aug	274932	323704	598636
13	Sep	226256	259070	485326
14	Oct	308712	292710	601422
15	Nov	314169	273057	587226
16	Dec	305890	268935	574825
17	Grand Total	3317261	3390551	6707812
18				

Figure 866 *Pivot years to go across the report.*

7. On the Design tab, open the Grand Totals dropdown and choose On For Columns Only which is the very strange way to delete the grand totals along the right side of the report.
8. In D4, type % Growth.
9. In D5, type =D5/C5-1. Do not use the mouse or arrow keys while entering this formula!
10. Format D5 as a percentage with 1 decimal place.
11. Copy D5 down to all rows.
12. Select the Sum of Revenue heading. In the Options ribbon tab, click in the Active Field box and change the field name to "Revenue " (with a space after the word Revenue.)
13. On the Options ribbon tab, click the Field Headers to prevent those from being shown in the report.

	D5	▼		f_x	=C5/B5-1
	A	B	C	D	E
1					
2					
3	**Revenue**				
4		2014	2015	% Growth	
5	Jan	258081	295609	14.5%	
6	Feb	257570	285528	10.9%	
7	Mar	252354	239373	-5.1%	
8	Apr	271215	317368	17.0%	
9	May	290211	303998	4.8%	
10	Jun	251187	188041	-25.1%	
11	Jul	306684	343158	11.9%	
12	Aug	274932	323704	17.7%	
13	Sep	226256	259070	14.5%	
14	Oct	308712	292710	-5.2%	
15	Nov	314169	273057	-13.1%	
16	Dec	305890	268935	-12.1%	
17	Grand Total	3317261	3390551	2.2%	

Figure 867 *Year-over-year report created with a pivot table.*

Gotcha: If you used the mouse in step 9, you will find that the percentage growth does not change as you copy it down. Go back and re-enter the formula, or follow the steps in "Calculations Outside of Pivot Tables" on page 371.

GROUP BY WEEK IN A PIVOT TABLE

Problem: The Grouping dialog allows grouping by second, minute, hour, day, month, quarter, and year. I need to group by week. How do I do it?

Strategy: In order to set up this grouping option correctly, you need to figure out the weekday where your data starts. The data set we're using in this example has data for January 2, 2014. Use the Long Date format to see that this is Thursday. You will later make the report start at December 29, 2013 to that the weeks run from Monday through Sunday.

Now follow these steps:

1. Create a pivot table with dates in the Row area. Select any date cell and choose Group Field from the Options dialog.
2. In the Grouping dialog, Excel defaults to showing the entire range of dates of the data set. If you left the Starting At field unchanged, your weeks would all start on Thursday. Change the 1/2/2014 date to 12/29/2013 to have your weeks start on Monday.
3. Unselect the Months selection by choosing it with the mouse. Select the Days choice. This will enable the Number of Days field at the bottom of the dialog. Use the spin button to move up to 7 days.

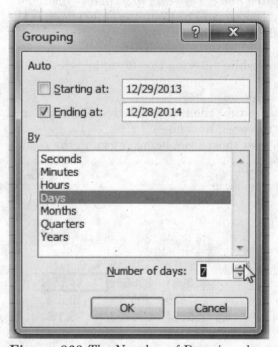

Figure 868 *The Number of Days is only available if you choose only Days.*

Results: The report will be redrawn as a weekly report.

	A	B
3	**Row Labels** ▼	**Sum of Revenue**
4	12/29/2013 - 1/4/2014	90320
5	1/5/2014 - 1/11/2014	139737
6	1/12/2014 - 1/18/2014	91620
7	1/19/2014 - 1/25/2014	118911
8	1/26/2014 - 2/1/2014	130262

Figure 869 *Excel will produce a report by week.*

Additional Details: Excel does not add a "Week" field to the PivotTable Field List dialog. Instead, the field that formerly contained dates now contains weeks but is still called Date.

Additional Details: Some manufacturing companies use a 13-month calendar. You can group by 28 days to replicate this calendar.

Gotcha: After you group by weeks, Excel will not allow you to group by months, quarters, years, or any other selection.

LIMIT A PIVOT REPORT TO SHOW JUST THE TOP 5 CUSTOMERS

Problem: Many times my customer reports have hundreds of customers. If I'm preparing a report for the senior vice president of sales, he may not care about the 400 customers who bought spare batteries this month. He wants to see only the top 10 or 20 or 5 customers each month.

Strategy: You can accommodate this vice president by using the Top 10 Filter feature that is available in pivot tables. Follow these steps:

1. Build a pivot table with Customers in the row area.
2. Open the dropdown at the top of the customer dropdown. Choose Value Filters and then Top 10.

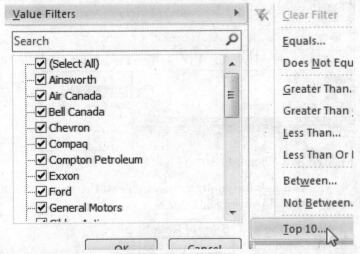

Figure 870 *The top 10 can do to or bottom, 5, 10, 20, and more.*

Excel displays the Top 10 Filter (Customer) dialog. By default, the dialog wants to show the top 10 items based on Sum of Revenue. Although it is called the "Top 10" feature, it is far more flexible than that. The first dropdown offers to filter to the top or bottom customers. You can use the spin button to change 10 to any other number. The third field offers Items, Percent, and Sum.

3. Change 10 to 5.

Figure 871 *Show top five customers.*

4. Click OK.

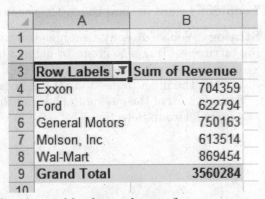

Figure 872 *The pivot table shows the top five customers.*

Results: The report will be filtered to show just the top five customers. Note that a Filter icon appears in cell A3 to indicate that you are not seeing all customers. You can hover over this icon to see a list of the filters applied

Gotcha: If there is a tie for fifth place, the list may contain more than five customers. If you filter the pivot table to an obscure product purchased by only a few customers, you might have a hundred-way tie at $0 for fifth place.

Additional Details: Another common request might be to show enough customers to represent 80% of the total.

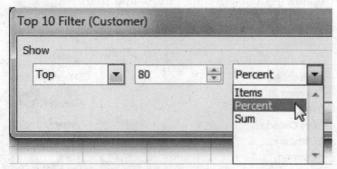

Figure 873 *Show top 80%.*

Or, you can ask for enough customers so the sum is $2,000,000. Excel will include the largest customers until the total is over $2,000,000.

3	Row Labels	Sum of Revenue
4	Wal-Mart	869454
5	General Motors	750163
6	Exxon	704359
7	Grand Total	2323976

Figure 874 *Show enough customers to be over $2,000,000.*

Gotcha: The total on each report includes only the customers shown in that report. My VP of Sales wants the other customers grouped into one line called Other. See the next topic for an alternate strategy.

Additional Details: To clear a filter, you use the dropdown at the top of that column and select Clear Filters from Customer..

BUILD A BETTER TOP FIVE USING GROUPS

Problem: I want to show the top five customers, then one line for Other, then a total of the whole data set.

Strategy: You've already seen how you can group dates. You can also group text. This is useful for creating territories. It is also great for doing a better top five report.
1. Build a pivot table with customers in the row labels.
2. Sort the pivot tables so that the largest customers are at the top.
3. Select all of the customers beyond the top 5. Don't include the Grand Total in your selection.
4. Click Group Selection.

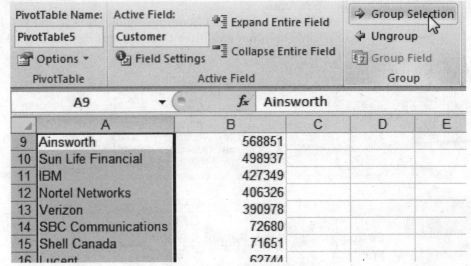

Figure 875 *Select beyond top five customers and group.*

5. On the Design tab, open the Report Layout dropdown and choose Tabular Form. You will now have two row labels columns. One is called Customer2 and one is called Customer.

6. Choose the Customer heading. Type a different name, like Cust. This will rename this field to something other than customer. This allows you to rename Customer2 to Customer in step 7.

7. Choose the Customer2 heading and edit to remove the 2. Note that you can not do this if you skipped step 6.

8. Select the cell called Group1. This is the row for all other customers. You are allowed to rename this row. Type Other in the row.

9. Select the cell for Wal-Mart. Grab the right edge of this cell and drag up until the insertion point shows that you will drop Wal-Mart at the top of the list. Release the mouse. Wal-Mart will be the top customer.

10. Repeat step 9 for the other customers, dragging them into position. Leave Other at the bottom.

	A	B
1		
2		
3	**Customer** ▼	**Sum of Revenue**
4	Wal-Mart	869454
5	General Motors	750163
6	Exxon	704359
7	Ford	622794
8	Molson, Inc	613514
9	Other	3147528
10	**Grand Total**	**6707812**

Figure 876 *A better top five report.*

Gotcha: Manually sorting this report is not ideal.

Gotcha: If the underlying data changes and a new customer moves into the top 5, you will have to ungroup, sort, and re-group.

BUILD A BETTER TOP FIVE WITH A FILTER HACK

Problem: Can you AutoFilter a pivot table? If you could turn on the AutoFilters and then filter to the top 6 items in column B, you would get the top five customers plus the real total.

Unfortunately, AutoFilter is greyed out when you are in a pivot table.

Strategy: Filter from the magic cell.

There is a strange loophole in the Filter logic. There are four ways to filter a data set. Microsoft greys out the Filter icon in the Data tab for three of those ways. They apparently missed the fourth method.

1. Create a pivot table with customers in the row labels.

2. Sort high to low by revenue.
3. Select the cell to the right of the last heading. Below, this is cell C3. I call this cell the "magic cell" because it is an arcane cell that can filter the adjacent data set. It is so arcane, Microsoft forgets to gray out the filter command.
4. On the Data tab, click Filter.

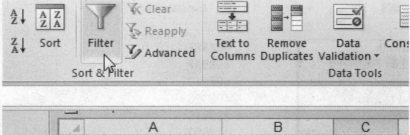

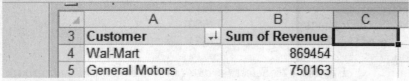

Figure 877 *Filter is supposed to be greyed out for pivot tables.*

5. Open the dropdown in B3. You now have the AutoFilter choices instead of the Pivot filter choices. Choose Number Filters, Top 10.

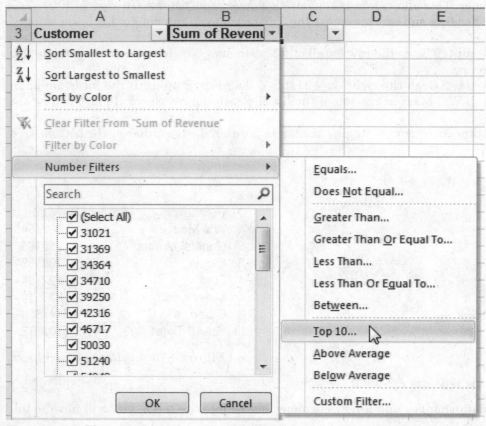

Figure 878 *These aren't the usual pivot filters.*

6. If you want to see the top five customers, choose 6 from the Top 10 AutoFilter dialog.

Figure 879 *Ask for the Top 6 customers.*

Result: the AutoFilter will show the largest item which is the Grand Total, plus the next five largest items, which are the customer totals. This figure is very similar to Figure 872, except this figure has the correct total for the entire data set.

	A	B	C
3	**Customer** ▼	**Sum of Revenu** ▼	▼
4	Wal-Mart	869454	
5	General Motors	750163	
6	Exxon	704359	
7	Ford	622794	
8	Molson, Inc	613514	
31	**Grand Total**	**6707812**	

Figure 880 Top five customers, with total of all customers.

Gotcha: Don't forget the magic cell. In order to turn off the AutoFilter dropdowns, you have to go back and select cell C3. Otherwise, the Filter icon is greyed out.

Gotcha: This trick is clearly exploiting a bug in Excel. Don't expect the AutoFilter to recalculate if you refresh the pivot table. Microsoft never expected that anyone would be able to AutoFilter a pivot table.

LIMIT A REPORT TO JUST ONE REGION

Problem: I need to send a customer report such to each regional manager in my company. I want each manager to see only sales in his or her region.

Strategy: You can use the Report Filter area of the pivot table to create such a report. You drag the Region field to the Report Filter drop zone in the lower half of the PivotTable Field List dialog. It seems like nothing has really changed. All the numbers in the pivot table are the same. But, there is a new Region dropdown in row 1.

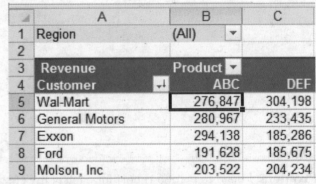

	A	B	C
1	Region	(All) ▼	
2			
3	**Revenue**	**Product** ▼	
4	**Customer** ▼	ABC	DEF
5	Wal-Mart	276,847	304,198
6	General Motors	280,967	233,435
7	Exxon	294,138	185,286
8	Ford	191,628	185,675
9	Molson, Inc	203,522	204,234

Figure 881 Initially, the report still shows all regions.

Open the dropdown next to Region. You can select any one region, or using the new checkbox, select multiple regions.

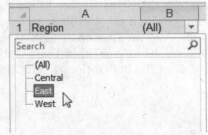

Figure 882 Select one region.

Choose East from the Region dropdown. The report will update to show just the customers from the East region. You can print this report and send it to the East regional manager.

⊿	A	B
1	Region	East ▼
2		
3	**Revenue**	**Product ▼**
4	**Customer** ▼	ABC
5	Wal-Mart	80,268
6	General Motors	69,040
7	Molson, Inc	69,991

Figure 883 *The report shows only sales for East.*

To produce the report for Central, you simply change the Region dropdown from East to Central. You can repeat for each other region.

CREATE AN AD-HOC REPORTING TOOL

Problem: I have an operations manager who is famous for asking many ad hoc questions. One day, he will want to know who bought XYZ product. The next day, he will want to know all sales to Air Canada. How can Excel help me quickly answer his questions?

Strategy: You can build a pivot table report with many fields in the Report Filter area. You can then use the information here to answer just about any ad hoc query your manager can dream up. For example, your operations manager can easily figure out how many ABC products were shipped to the East region on a given date.

Additional Details: Take the Date field to the row labels area, group it up to Years, Quarters, and Months, then drag those fields to the Report Filter area.

⊿	A	B
1	Region	East ▼
2	Product	ABC ▼
3	Customer	(All) ▼
4	Years	(All) ▼
5	Quarters	Qtr2 ▼
6	Date	(All) ▼
7		
8	**Values**	
9	Sum of Quantity	11400
10	Sum of Revenue	223957
11	Sum of COGS	96558
12	Sum of Profit	127399

Figure 884 *Ad hoc reporting tool.*

CREATE A REPORT FOR EVERY CUSTOMER

Problem: I need to print a report for each of my customers. Using the Report Filter field is tedious: I spend my whole morning selecting a customer, clicking Print, selecting a customer, clicking Print, and so on.

Strategy: The feature you use to solve this problem—the Show Report Filter Pages command—is the most powerful feature of pivot tables. I don't know why Microsoft buries it so deeply in the menu system. You can use the Show Report Filter Pages command to make a report for every customer. Follow these steps:
  1. Build a pivot table with the information you want to replicate for each customer.
  2. Add the Customer field as one of the Report Filter fields.
  3. Select PivotTable Tools Options, Options dropdown, Show Report Filter Pages. **Gotcha:** Don't click on the big Options icon. Click on the tiny dropdown next to the Options icon.

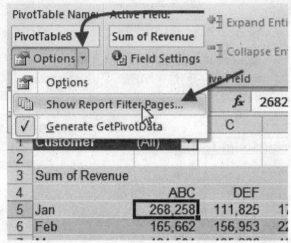

Figure 885 *Set up the report and select Show Report Filter Pages.*

4. A dialog box will appear, asking you to show all Report Filter Pages and giving you a list of all the fields in the Report Filter. Even though this seems silly when you have only one field in the Report Filter area, choose Customer and click OK.

Results: In a matter of seconds, Excel will add a new worksheet for each customer. Each worksheet will be named after the customer, and the Customer dropdown will be changed to the particular customer. In a matter of seconds, you will have one worksheet for each customer.

	A	B	C	D	E
1	Customer	Ainsworth			
2					
3	Sum of Revenue				
4		ABC	DEF	XYZ	Grand Total
5	Jan	10,445		51,053	61,498
6	Feb		44,492	20,940	65,432
7	Mar		7,132	34,960	13,404	55,496
8	Apr	29,616	8,776		38,392

Ainsworth / Air Canada / Bell Canada / Chevron

Figure 886 *One report per customer.*

Gotcha: Get the pivot table perfect before making hundreds of copies. Even though I thought I did a lot of formatting, I forgot to replace blanks with zeroes in the above figure. At this point, I would delete the customer worksheets, change the original pivot table, then use Show Pages again.

You can imagine that this feature could be useful if you need one report per department, one report per product, etc.

CREATE PIVOT CHARTS

Problem: Can I show the results of a pivot table in a chart?

Strategy: In Excel 2010, pivot charts have improved to the point where they are actually usable. Here's what you do:
1. Select a single cell in your data. Select Insert, PivotTable dropdown, PivotChart.
2. Build a pivot table by using the Field List dialog. Note that the row fields are now called axis fields. Put Region in the Axis Fields drop zone.
3. Column fields are now called legend fields. Put Product in the Legend Field drop zone.
4. Add Customer to the Report Filter drop zone.
5. Add Revenue to the ∑ Values drop zone.

Excel will show both a pivot table and a chart on the worksheet. When you select the chart, you can use the PivotChart Tools tabs on the ribbon to control the chart type and all formatting.

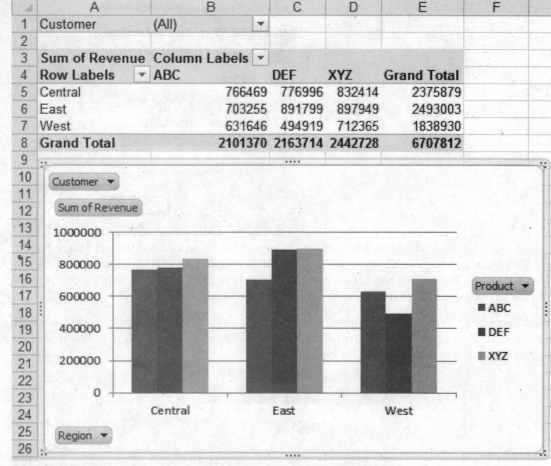

Figure 887 *This chart is the result of a pivot table analysis.*

Gotcha: The button on the chart went away in Excel 2007 and came back in Excel 2010. Excel 2007 offered a PivotChart Filter Pane with the filter dropdowns. If you liked the cleaner look of a pivot chart without buttons, you can use the dropdown on the Excel 2010 Analyze tab to remove selected buttons.

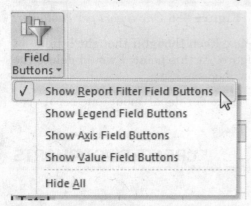

Figure 888 *Hide pivot chart buttons.*

Additional Details: To filter the chart to a specific customer, you can change the Customer dropdown in the pivot table.

Gotcha: The Show Report Filter Pages trick (described in "Create a Report for Every Customer") doesn't work for a pivot chart.

ADD VISUAL FILTERS TO A PIVOT TABLE OR REGULAR TABLE

Problem: Excel 2007 added the ability to select multiple items from a filter. But when I do this, it uses the ambiguous (Multiple Items) heading. When I print this report, no one knows which customers are in the report.

	A	B
1	Customer	(Multiple Items)
2		
3	Row Labels	Revenue
4	ABC	298,296
5	DEF	198,535
6	XYZ	238,897
7	Grand Total	735,728

Figure 889 *When you select two customers from the filter dropdown, you can't see which customers are selected.*

Strategy: That addition in Excel 2007 was a first step towards the full visual filters called Slicers in Excel 2010. If you have Excel 2010, you can see which fields are included or not included. If you have Excel 2013, you can use Slicers on your Ctrl+T table in addition to Pivot Tables.

After building a pivot table, choose Insert Slicers. You can choose as many fields as you want from the current pivot table.

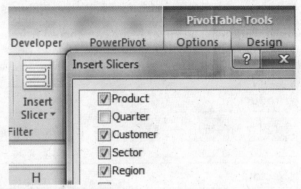

Figure 890 *Select fields to use as visual filters.*

Initially, Excel tiles all of the slicers and shows them with one column. Here is the default arrangement of four slicers.

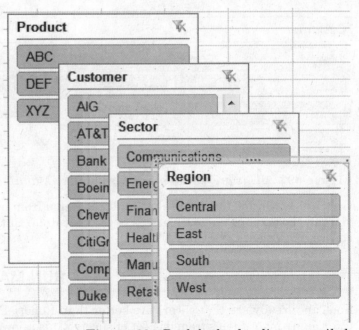

Figure 891 *By default, the slicers are tiled.*

You will want to rearrange and resize the slicers. You can move and resize the slicers. In the Slicer Tools ribbon tab, use the Columns spinbutton to add more columns to a slicer. As you can see below, product and region can fit in a single row by increasing the number of columns to three or four.

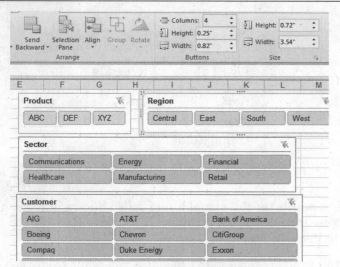

Figure 892 *Rearrange and resize the slicers.*

I also use a different color for each slicer. This is controlled in the Slicer Tools ribbon tab as well.

Once you have the slicers, you can choose from any slicer. The pivot table will update to reflect the filters. The other slicers will also update. Below, after choosing Manufacturing in the East & Central regions, several non-manufacturing customers are "greyed out" at the bottom of the customer slicer.

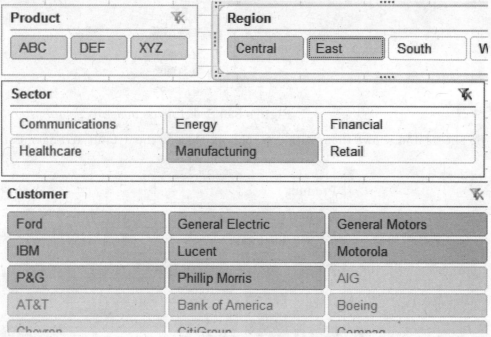

Figure 893 *AIG is greyed out since it isn't in the Manufacturing sector.*

Gotcha: I found it tough to select multiple items from one slicer. If you happen to need adjacent items, you can click on one and drag across to the next item. But, if you want to select ABC and XYZ, you have to choose ABC, then Ctrl+Click XYZ.

RUN MANY PIVOT TABLES FROM ONE SLICER

You can already see that slicers are better than Report Filters. Another major advantage is that you can filter many pivot tables from one set of slicers. This allows you to create dashboard-like reports.

When you create a pivot chart, the pivot table and chart are placed next to each other by Microsoft. They absolutely do not have to stay next to each other. You can build four pivot charts, each on their own sheet, then move the charts so that they are all on the same worksheet. You can move a chart using the Move Chart icon on the Design tab, or simply select the chart, cut, then paste in a new location.

Here is the process for making the slicers drive all of your pivot tables:
1. Build the first pivot table or pivot chart. Add slicers to that pivot table.

2. Build additional pivot tables or pivot charts. Move the chart or table to be near the first pivot table.
3. While the second pivot table is selected, go to the Options tab. Open the dropdown attached to the Insert Slicer icon and choose Slicer Connections. (If you have a Pivot Chart, the Slicer icon is on the Analyze ribbon tab.)

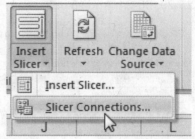

Figure 894 For the second pivot table, choose Slicer Connections.

4. Repeat steps 2 & 3 for each additional pivot table or pivot chart.

Below, slicers are driving two pivot charts and two pivot tables.

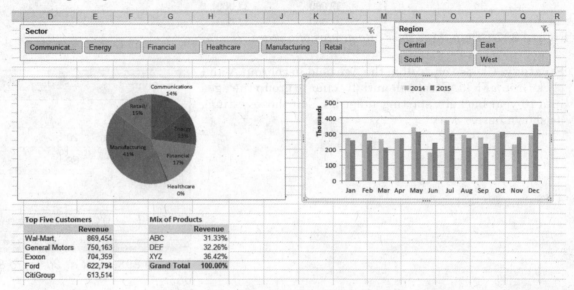

Top Five Customers		Mix of Products	
	Revenue		Revenue
Wal-Mart	869,454	ABC	31.33%
General Motors	750,163	DEF	32.26%
Exxon	704,359	XYZ	36.42%
Ford	622,794	Grand Total	100.00%
CitiGroup	613,514		

Figure 895 All pivot tables are filtered by the slicers.

FILTER DATES USING A TIMELINE IN EXCEL 2013

Excel 2013 introduced a new type of filter called a Timeline. It only works for date columns. You can choose to filter by Day, Month, Quarter, or Year.

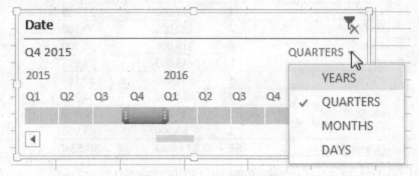

Figure 896 Timelines are new in Excel 2013 pivot tables.

As in the previous topic, you can run many pivot tables from one Timeline.

GROUP EMPLOYEES INTO AGE BANDS

Problem: I work in Human Resources. I need to calculate the number of employees and average salary by groups of ages. Initially, I get a pivot table with one row per age. How do I group this into groups like 25-29, 30-34, and so on?

3	Age	Number of Emp	Total Salary	Average Salary	E
4	26	1	18,000	18,000	
5	27	3	42,000	14,000	
6	28	1	13,000	13,000	
7	29	2	42,000	21,000	
8	30	1	32,000	32,000	
9	31	1	21,000	21,000	

Figure 897 *Group these rows into groups of 5 years.*

Strategy: Choose one cell in the Age field in column A and click Group Field. Excel will initially offer to group the ages into 10-year buckets, starting at age 26. Edit those settings as shown here.

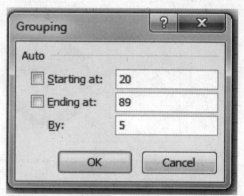

Figure 898 *Start at 20, go to 89, in groups of 5.*

Result: Excel creates a report with groups of dates.

3	Age	Number of Emp	Total Salary	Average Salary
4	25-29	7	115,000	16,429
5	30-34	7	157,000	22,429
6	35-39	4	111,000	27,750
7	40-44	4	122,000	30,500
8	45-49	6	219,000	36,500
9	50-54	8	443,000	55,375
10	55-59	6	301,000	50,167
11	60-64	8	434,000	54,250
12	65-69	5	249,000	49,800
13	85-89	1	63,000	63,000
14	**Grand Total**	**56**	**2,214,000**	**39,536**

Figure 899 *Excel groups rows into categories.*

Gotcha: Excel does not show a category if there were no employees in that category. Note that the ages jump from 69 in row 12 to 85 in row 13.

CREATE A FREQUENCY DISTRIBUTION

Problem: The VP of sales wants to stop accepting small orders. I need to see how many orders are "small" orders and the impact to our revenue.

Strategy: Build a pivot table with the invoice amount in the row labels. In order to get a count of the number of invoices, move any text field to the values area. Add invoice amount a second time to the values area. You will get a pivot table that looks like this.

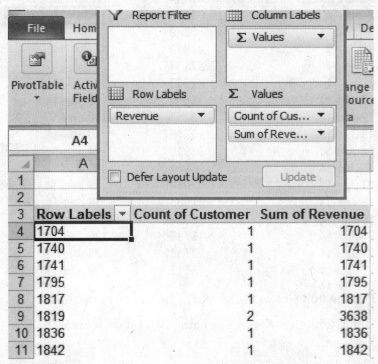

Figure 900 *Arrange fields opposite of normal, numbers in the row labels and text in the values area.*

Switch from Compact Form to Tabular form so you can see a real heading in A3. This is in the Report Layout dropdown on the Design tab.

Rename each field to Invoice Size, Number of Invoices, Total Revenue.

Select cell A4 and click Group Field on the Options ribbon tab. Enter starting, ending, and step values. Perhaps from 0 to 30,000 in 5000 dollar increments. Click OK.

Result: a pivot table version of a frequency diagram, without ever having to figure out the FREQUENCY array-function.

3	Invoice Size ▼	Number of Invoices	Total Revenue
4	0-4999	104	326,674
5	5000-9999	125	937,212
6	10000-14999	142	1,769,165
7	15000-19999	123	2,149,079
8	20000-24999	63	1,374,732
9	25000-30000	6	150,950
10	Grand Total	563	6,707,812

Figure 901 *A frequency distribution.*

GROUPING 1 PIVOT TABLE GROUPS THEM ALL

Problem: I am building two pivot tables. One will show daily sales detail. The other will summarize by month. I arranged the pivot tables side by side. I use the Group feature to group the second pivot table by month.

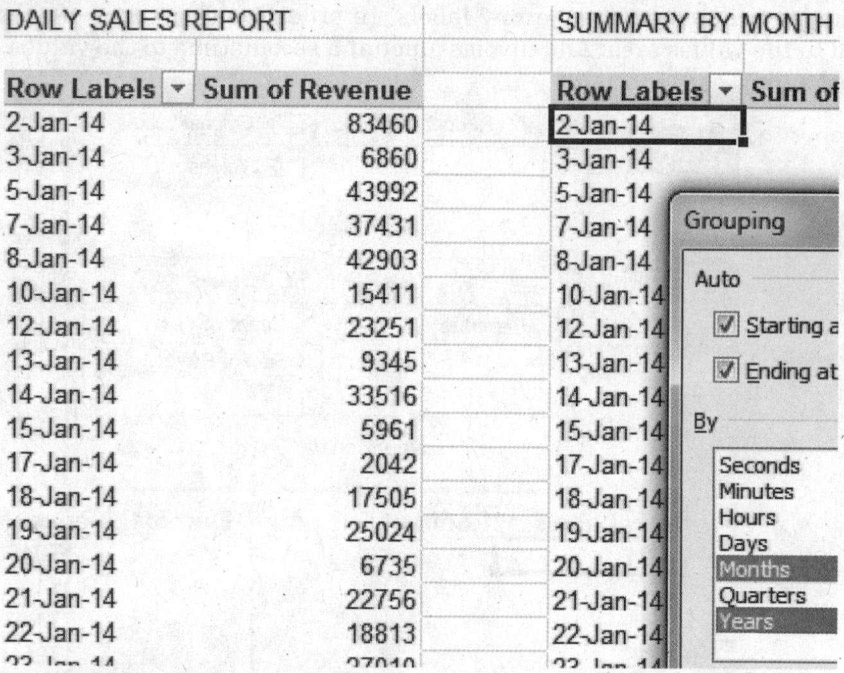

DAILY SALES REPORT   SUMMARY BY MONTH

Row Labels ▼	Sum of Revenue		Row Labels ▼	Sum of
2-Jan-14	83460		2-Jan-14	
3-Jan-14	6860		3-Jan-14	
5-Jan-14	43992		5-Jan-14	
7-Jan-14	37431		7-Jan-14	
8-Jan-14	42903		8-Jan-14	
10-Jan-14	15411		10-Jan-14	
12-Jan-14	23251		12-Jan-14	
13-Jan-14	9345		13-Jan-14	
14-Jan-14	33516		14-Jan-14	
15-Jan-14	5961		15-Jan-14	
17-Jan-14	2042		17-Jan-14	
18-Jan-14	17505		18-Jan-14	
19-Jan-14	25024		19-Jan-14	
20-Jan-14	6735		20-Jan-14	
21-Jan-14	22756		21-Jan-14	
22-Jan-14	18813		22-Jan-14	
23-Jan-14	27010		23-Jan-14	

Grouping

Auto

☑ Starting a

☑ Ending at

By

Seconds
Minutes
Hours
Days
Months
Quarters
Years

Figure 902 *Group the second pivot table by month.*

Unfortunately, this groups both pivot tables by month.

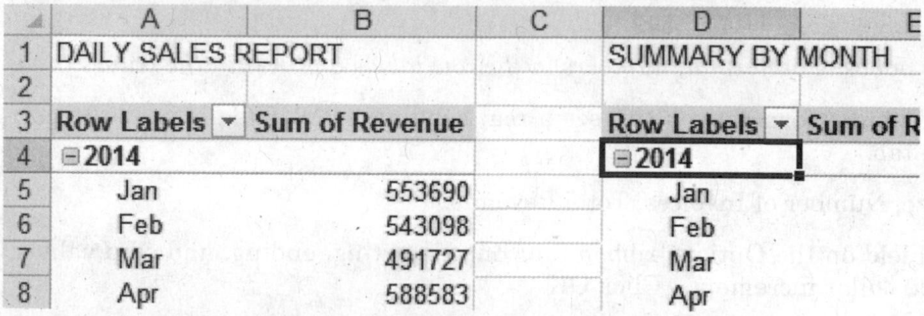

◢	A	B	C	D	E
1	DAILY SALES REPORT			SUMMARY BY MONTH	
2					
3	Row Labels ▼	Sum of Revenue		Row Labels ▼	Sum of R
4	⊟2014			⊟2014	
5	Jan	553690		Jan	
6	Feb	543098		Feb	
7	Mar	491727		Mar	
8	Apr	588583		Apr	

Figure 903 *Both pivot tables are grouped.*

Strategy: One solution is to group by Days, Months, and Years. You can then use different fields in the two pivot tables. However, the point of this topic is how to create two pivot tables that do not share the same pivot table cache.

When you create a pivot table, the data from your worksheet is loaded into memory to a special area called the pivot table cache. A pivot table is fast because it is calculated from the cache in memory.

Way back in Excel 2003, Excel would ask you if you wanted all of your pivot tables to share the same pivot table cache. This would save memory...each pivot table cache increases the size of the workbook by the amount of data in the data set. But, sharing a cache causes problems like the one here; when you group fields or calculate fields, those changes happen in all of the pivot tables.

In Excel today, any pivot table created using Insert, PivotTable automatically shares the cache. Microsoft doesn't even ask you.

However, you can force Microsoft to ask if you want to share the cache by using the old pivot table wizard. Follow these steps

1. Create the first pivot table as normal.
2. To create the second pivot table, select one cell in your original data set.
3. Press Alt+D followed by P. This was the Excel 2003 keyboard shortcut for Data, PivotTable. Excel will display step 1 of the old pivot table wizard.

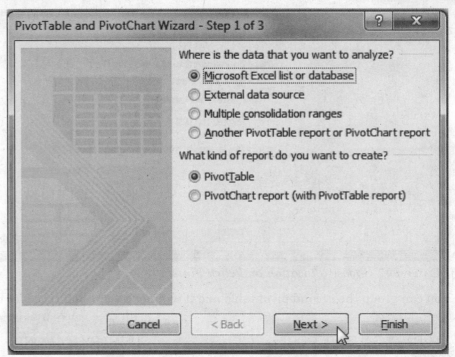

Figure 904 *Complete with new artwork, the old wizard.*

4. Click Next in step 1.
5. Make sure your data range is correct in step 2.

Figure 905 *Check the data range.*

6. Click Next. Between Step 2 and Step 3, Excel will display a lengthy message that encourages you to have this pivot table share the cache with the other pivot table in order to conserve memory. You want to click No to this dialog.

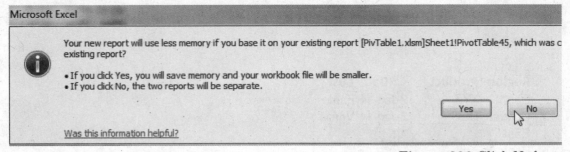

Figure 906 *Click No here.*

7. In Step 3 of the wizard, choose the location for your pivot table. Click Finish.

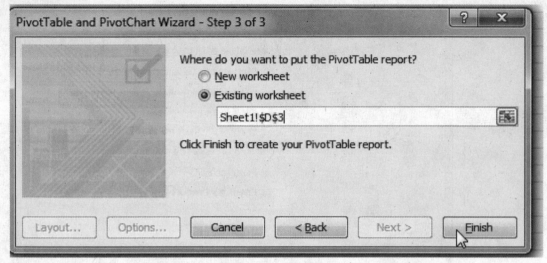

Figure 907 *Choose a location and click Finish.*

You can group the second pivot table and it will not affect the first pivot table.

	A	B	C	D	E
1	DAILY SALES REPORT			SUMMARY BY MONTH	
2					
3	Row Labels ▾	Sum of Revenue		Month ▾	Revenue
4	2-Jan-14	83460		Jan	$554K
5	3-Jan-14	6860		Feb	$543K
6	5-Jan-14	43992		Mar	$492K
7	7-Jan-14	37431		Apr	$589K

Figure 908 *These pivot tables do not share a cache.*

REDUCE SIZE 50% BEFORE SENDING

Problem: I have to upload a file over my aunt's 56 baud modem. Can I reduce the size of the workbook?

Strategy: When you save a workbook with a pivot table, Excel saves the data on the worksheet, plus the data in the pivot table cache. You can't actually delete the pivot table cache, but you can delete the data on the worksheet.

Here is a workbook that contains data and a pivot table. You are seeing two windows of the same workbook.

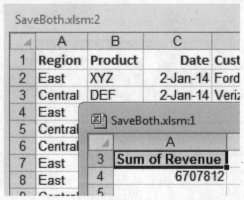

Figure 909 *The data and the pivot cache.*

I deleted the worksheet with the data. Now, the workbook appears to have text in only two cells.

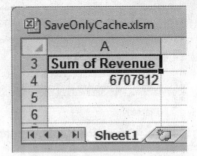

Figure 910 *The workbook with only a pivot table and no data.*

Here is a comparison of file sizes. The workbook from Figure 909 is 55K. The workbook without the data worksheet is 23K. The workbook from the previous topic, the one with two pivot tables and two pivot caches is 79K.

Name	Size
SaveOnlyCache.xlsm	23 KB
SaveBoth.xlsm	55 KB
PivTwoCache.xlsm	79 KB

Figure 911 *File size is reduced by having only the pivot cache.*

OK, so I've proved that you can save space in a workbook by deleting the data. What good is that?

Say that you transfer that file over the modem, then you get back to work and open the file with only the 2-cell pivot table.

Excel will ask if you want to enable the data connection to the invisible cache.

Cell A4 in the pivot table is essentially a grand total of all rows in the pivot table. Double-click that cell and Excel will bring put the contents of the pivot table cache into a new worksheet in the workbook!

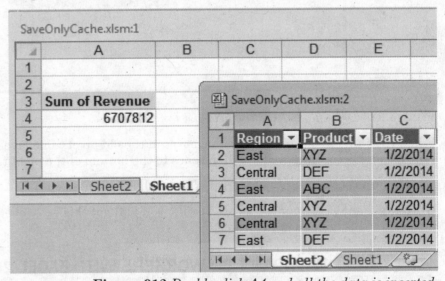

Figure 912 *Double-click A4 and all the data is inserted.*

Gotcha: While I've used this trick a dozen times, it is always unnerving to delete your data. You should make a backup copy of the entire workbook before deleting the data. You never know if the pivot table cache would become corrupt.

DRAG FIELDS TO THE PIVOT TABLE

Problem: I want to go back to dragging fields around the pivot table like I did back in Excel 97-2003.

Strategy: There is a way to go back to the old style. Follow these steps:
1. Right-click any cell in the pivot table. Choose PivotTable Options.
2. Go to the Display tab within the PivotTable Options dialog.
3. Choose Classic PivotTable Layout.

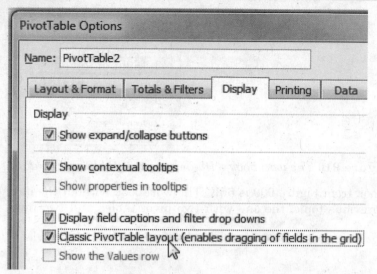

Figure 913 *Like Coke Classic, with less bite.*

You can now drag fields to the report.

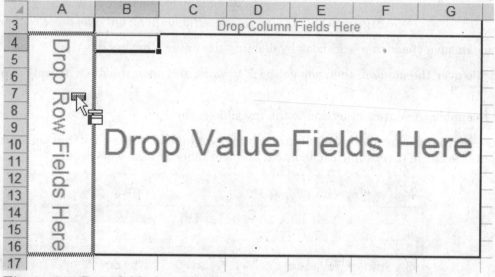

Figure 914 *Drag fields from the field list to the report.*

When you think about it, the four blue boxes in the old pivot table layout are really drop zones. In the current Excel, Microsoft moved the drop zones to the bottom of the pivot table field list.

Gotcha: this setting is not universal. You will have to change the setting for each pivot table.

Gotcha: if you save your file as an .xls file, you will get this style every time, but as you will read in the next topic, this is not a good strategy.

WHY CAN'T CO-WORKERS WITH EXCEL 2003 USE MY PIVOT TABLE?

Problem: I created a pivot table in Excel 2010. I saved the file as an Excel 97-2003 file and sent it to a co-worker. When my co-worker opens the pivot table, it opens as static values in Excel 2003.

Strategy: You have to create the pivot table in compatibility mode if you want to share it with people who use previous versions of Excel.

When the Excel 2010 machine saved the file, the Compatibility Checker should have presented the warning "A PivotTable in this workbook is built in the current file format and will not work in earlier versions of Excel." However, this warning is buried among trivial warnings that some colors and styles aren't supported, so it is easy to miss.

If you need to use a pivot table in both Excel 2003 and Excel 2007/2010, you need to create the pivot table in Excel 2003 and save the file in 2003. You can then open and manipulate the file in 2007/2010 and save it back as an Excel 2003 file.

Alternatively, open the data set in Excel 2010. Save the data set as an Excel 97-2003 file type. Close the data set. Re-open the data set. You can now create the pivot table in compatibility mode.

Gotcha: When you create and save a file in Excel 2003, you won't be able to use the new Excel 2007 features, such as the new pivot table filtering or slicers.

CREATE A REPORT THAT SHOWS COUNT, MIN, MAX, AVERAGE, ETC.

Problem: Most of the Pivot Table examples shown thus far are for summing revenue. What if I need to find out the average sale by customer or the smallest sale?

Strategy: Pivot tables offer eleven calculation functions. Back in Excel 2007, you would use the Field Settings icon to reach these settings. In Excel 2010, you can use the Field Settings or the new Summarize Values By dropdown.

To use Field Settings, select one numeric cell in the pivot table to make that field the active field. In the Options ribbon tab, click Field Settings.

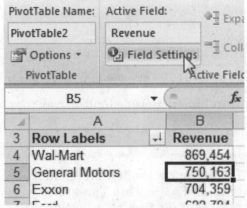

Figure 915 *Choose a revenue cell, then Field Settings.*

You can now choose from the 11 functions.

Figure 916 *Choose from the 11 functions.*

When you choose Average, the field heading will become "Average of Revenue". You can edit the custom name in the Value Field Settings dialog to "Average Revenue" or "Average Sale" or any other heading that you would like. Note, however, that you cannot reuse a name already in the pivot table. So, for example, Revenue would not be allowed, but Revenue_ or "Revenue " or " Revenue" would be allowed. Those last two include a trailing space and a leading space.

If you are in Excel 2010 and you need to use Sum, Count, Average, Max, Min, or Product, you can use the Summarize Values By dropdown in the Calculations group of the Options ribbon tab.

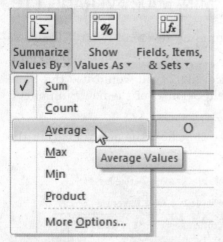

Figure 917 *Six of the function choices have been promoted to the Excel 2010 ribbon.*

Gotcha: There is no built-in way to create a median for a pivot table. I've heard this question a few times.

BETTER CALCULATIONS WITH SHOW VALUES AS

Problem: Excel offers eleven functions on the Summarize Value By tab of the Value Field Settings dialog (back in Figure 916). Those are not the good ones. The good ones are on the Show Values As tab. Ninety percent of the time that I change the calculation, I am using one of the relatively hidden Show Values As calculations.

Strategy: Excel 2010 moved these to the Show Values As dropdown so people might discover them. The really good calculations are here.

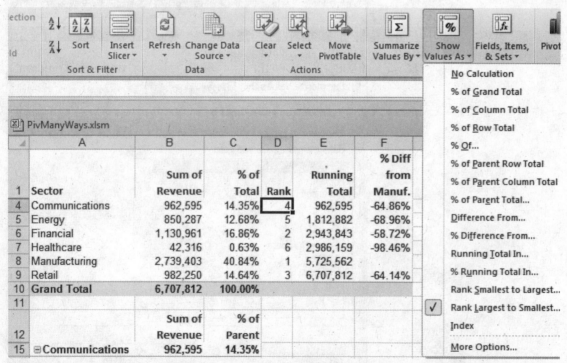

Figure 918 *Show values as a variety of calculations.*

Gotcha: Several of those calculations are new in Excel 2010 and will not calculate in Excel 2007: Both of the Ranks, all of the Parent calculation, and the % Running Total In.

To create the pivot table at the top of the figure above, add Revenue five times to the Values area of a pivot table. Select a cell in each column. In Excel 2010, use the Show Values As dropdown. In Excel 2007, use Field Settings, then click Show Values As.

Gotcha: The calculations require one, two, or zero arguments. An example of each follows.

The numbers in C4:C10 use the % of Column Total setting. You simply choose this setting. You don't have to specify any additional information.

Rank and Running Total are examples where Excel will ask you to identify the base field. Most often, this will be the row field.

% Difference From is a calculation that requires a Base Field and a Base Item. The calculation in F4:F9 expresses revenue as a percentage of Manufacturing revenue.

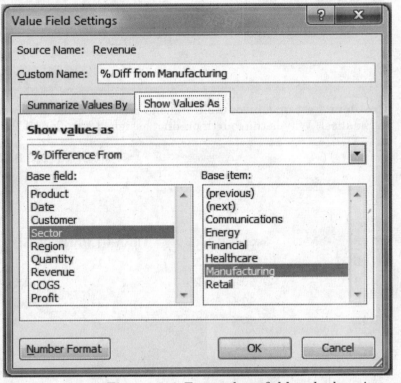

Figure 919 *Enter a base field and a base item.*

The (previous) entry in Figure 919 is great for reports with dates. This report show the sales as a percentage change from the previous day.

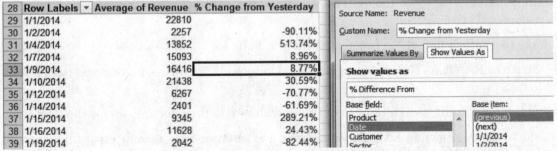

28	Row Labels ▾	Average of Revenue	% Change from Yesterday
29	1/1/2014	22810	
30	1/2/2014	2257	-90.11%
31	1/4/2014	13852	513.74%
32	1/7/2014	15093	8.96%
33	1/9/2014	16416	8.77%
34	1/10/2014	21438	30.59%
35	1/12/2014	6267	-70.77%
36	1/14/2014	2401	-61.69%
37	1/15/2014	9345	289.21%
38	1/16/2014	11628	24.43%
39	1/19/2014	2042	-82.44%

Figure 920 *Change from previous day.*

Additional Details: You can combine the 11 functions on Summarize Values By and the 15 settings under Show Values As. The figure above is showing the average sale for each day and then the % change from the previous day of the average sale.

Percentage of Parent Row Total and the other "Parent" calculations are new in Excel 2010. This calculation was very difficult before Excel 2010. In this figure, the percentages in C16:C18 express the revenue as a percentage of the total sector revenue in B15.

The confusing part is that the 14.35% in C15 shows how the Communications sector total of $962K compares to the grand total of $6.7 million. All of the percentages are correct, it is just strange to see a smaller number on the total line than on the detail lines.

	A	B	C	D
12		Sum of Revenue	% of Parent	
15	⊟Communications	962,595	14.35%	
16	AT&T	498,937	51.83%	
17	SBC Communications	72,680	7.55%	
18	Verizon	390,978	40.62%	
19	⊞Energy	850,287	12.68%	
20	⊞Financial	1,130,961	16.86%	
21	⊞Healthcare	42,316	0.63%	
22	⊞Manufacturing	2,739,403	40.84%	
23	⊞Retail	982,250	14.64%	
24	Grand Total	6,707,812	100.00%	

PIVOT RANKS DON'T MATCH RANK()

Problem: I set up a pivot table and showed the values as a rank, using the new Excel 2010 Rank Largest to Smallest. Why is the fourth product assigned a rank of #3?

G4				f_x	=E4+COUNTIF(B$3:B3,B4)			

	A	B	C	D	E	F	G	H
1								
2							Useful	
3	Row Labels	Score	Rank		RANK()	RANK.AVG()	Rank	
4	C	100%	1		1	1	1	
5	B	90%	2		2	2.5	2	
6	D	90%	2		2	2.5	3	
7	A	80%	3		4	4	4	
8	E	70%	4		5	5	5	
9	F	60%	5		6	6	6	
10	Grand Total	490%						

Figure 921 *Why is C7 assigned a rank of 3?*

Strategy: As if there is not enough controversy in the Excel ranking world, Excel came up with yet another way to handle ranking with pivot tables. The issue always centers around any ties and how the subsequent values are numbered.

Typically, if you have two values tied at #2, the next value would be assigned a rank of 4.

Starting in Excel 2010, the RANK.AVG would assign the tied values a 2.5, and assign the next item a rank of 4.

Pivot tables do something different, assigning both of the tie values a 2, then going to #3 for the next item.

If you need one of the methods shown in E:G, plan on adding a calculation next to your pivot table instead of using the built-in rank.

CALCULATED FIELDS IN A PIVOT TABLE

Problem: I need to include in a pivot table a calculation that is not in my underlying data. My data includes quantity sold, revenue, and cost. I would like to report gross profit and average price.

Strategy: You can add a calculated field to a pivot table. Follow these steps:

1. Build a pivot table with Product and Revenue columns.
2. The Calculated Field command moved between versions. In both versions, it is found in a dropdown on the Options ribbon tab. In Excel 2007, it is under the Formulas menu. In Excel 2010, it is under the Fields, Items, and Sets menu.

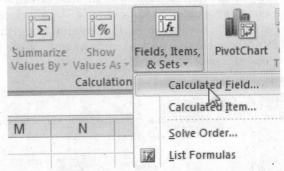

Figure 922 *Choose Calculated Field.*

3. In the Insert Calculated Field dialog, type a field name such as Profit in the Name text box. In the Formula text box, type an equals sign. Double-click the Revenue entry in the Fields list. Type a minus sign. Double-click the COGS entry in the Fields List. The Formula text box should say =Revenue-COGS. Click the Add button to accept this formula.

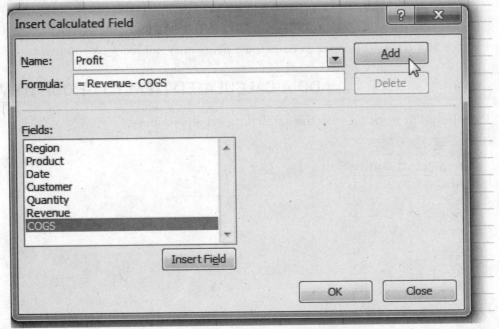

Figure 923 *Add a new formula.*

4. Add the following formula for GPPct: =Profit/Revenue.
5. Add the following formula for AveragePrice: =Revenue/Quantity.
6. Click OK to close the Insert Calculated Field dialog box.

Results: The resulting pivot table will include all the fields.

	A	B	C	D	E	F
3	Row Labels ▼	Sum of Quantity	Revenue	Sum of Profit	Sum of GPPct	Sum of AveragePrice
4	ABC	110000	2,101,370	1,169,670	55.7%	19.10
5	DEF	97800	2,163,714	1,201,362	55.5%	22.12
6	XYZ	106100	2,442,728	1,358,386	55.6%	23.02
7	Grand Total	313900	6,707,812	3,729,418	55.6%	21.37

Figure 924 *Excel adds the new fields to the pivot table.*

Gotcha: The label Sum of GPPct is somewhat misleading, as is Sum of Average Price. In reality, Excel finds the sum of Revenue, finds the sum of Quantity, and then divides the values on the total line in order to get the average price. This makes calculated fields fine for any calculations that follow the associative law of mathematics. Having Excel do all the individual average prices and then sum them up would be impossible in a pivot table unless you are using PowerPivot.

You can rename the fields that have misleading headings. Simply click on the heading and type a new heading.

Gotcha: It is possible to use an Excel function in the Insert Calculated Field dialog. However, the function is applied to individual rows instead of using the population of matching rows. In the figure below, column I contains a calculated field of MEDIAN(Score). To calculate this, Excel takes the MEDIAN of cell B2. Of course, the median of B2 is the value from B2. They repeat this for each cell, then sum up the results. This is not a median at all. It is the same as the sum of the cells. To truly calculate a median, you will need PowerPivot.

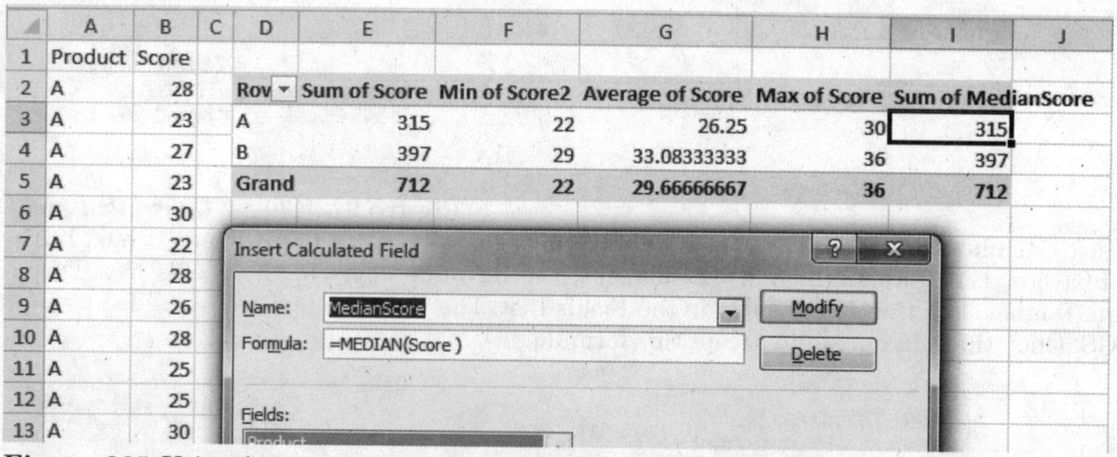

Figure 925 *Using functions in calculated fields may not work as you want.*

ADD A CALCULATED ITEM TO GROUP ITEMS IN A PIVOT TABLE

Problem: I'm working with the small data set shown here.

	A	B
1	**Product**	**Quantity**
2	ABC	1
3	ABC	2
4	DEF	4
5	DEF	8
6	DEF	16
7	XYZ	32
8	XYZ	64

Figure 926 *The initial data set.*

My company has three product lines. The Cocoa Beach plant manufactures ABC and DEF. The Marathon division manufactures XYZ. I have a pivot table that shows sales by product. Remember that the total of items sold is 127.

Row Labels ▼	Sum of Quantity
ABC	3
DEF	28
XYZ	96
Grand Total	**127**

Figure 927 *You've sold 127 units.*

I've read that I can add a calculated item along the Product division to total ABC and DEF in order to get a total for the Cocoa Beach plant. I select Insert Calculated Item. In the Insert Calculated Item dialog, I define an item called Cocoa Beach, which is the total of ABC + DEF.

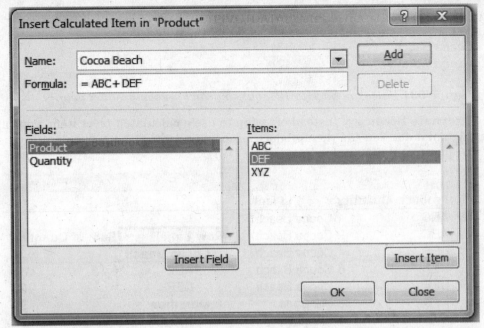

Figure 928 *Add a new item.*

However, when I view the resulting pivot table, the total is now wrong. Instead of showing 127 items sold, the pivot table reports that the total is 158.

Row Labels ▼	Sum of Quantity
ABC	3
DEF	28
XYZ	96
Cocoa Beach	31
Grand Total	**158**

Figure 929 *The total changes from 127 to 158!*

Strategy: Your problem is that the items made in Cocoa Beach are in the list twice, once as ABC and once as Cocoa Beach. The calculated pivot item is a strange concept in Excel. It is one of the least useful items. You should use extreme caution when trying to use a calculated pivot item.

You could use the Product dropdown and uncheck the ABC and DEF items.

Figure 930 *The only way to make the total correct is to hide the items used in the calculated item.*

The resulting pivot table shows the correct total of 127.

Row Labels	Sum of Quantity
XYZ	96
Cocoa Beach	31
Grand Total	**127**

Figure 931 *Sales are back to 127, but you can't see the product details.*

Alternate Strategy: Instead of trying to use a calculated pivot item, you can add a Plant column to the original data. You can then produce a report that shows both the plant location and the products made at the plant, and the total will be correct (127).

	A	B	C	D	E	F
1	Product	Quantity	Plant			
2	ABC	1	Cocoa Beach			
3	ABC	2	Cocoa Beach		Row Labels	Sum of Quantity
4	DEF	4	Cocoa Beach		⊟Cocoa Beach	31
5	DEF	8	Cocoa Beach		ABC	3
6	DEF	16	Cocoa Beach		DEF	28
7	XYZ	32	Marathon		⊟Marathon	96
8	XYZ	64	Marathon		XYZ	96
9					Grand Total	127

Figure 932 *Adding plant info to the original data set solves the problem.*

Calculated pivot items sound like they should be useful, but they are not. You should avoid using them.

GROUP TEXT FIELDS TO BUILD TERRITORIES
INSTEAD OF USING CALCULATED ITEMS

Problem: As shown in the previous topic, adding calculated items causes the totals to be wrong. I want to test grouping offices into territories. How can I do it?

Strategy: In "Build a Better Top 5 Using Groups," you learned how to group text in a pivot table. Building territories works in a similar fashion. Follow these steps:

1. Create a pivot table with City and Sales.
2. Even if you love the Compact Form layout, temporarily change to Tabular Form using the Layout dropdown on the Design tab.
3. Select the cities for your first territory. If the items are not in a contiguous range, hold down the Ctrl key while you select the cells.
4. Click Group Selection from the Options tab.

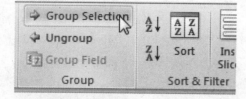

	A	B
3	Office	Sum of Size
4	Fort Lauderdale	165
5	Hialeah	224
6	Jacksonville	822
7	Miami	400
8	Orlando	238
9	Pembroke Pines	154

Figure 933 *Group the selected cells.*

The result appears to be chaos. You will be able to fix this problem, but let's take a look at what happened below. There is a new virtual field called Office2 in the pivot table. Three cities belong to a value called

Group1. Every other office in the pivot table is assigned to an Office2 equal to the office name. Note that the grand total of 2927 did not change.

	A	B	C
3	Office2 ▾	Office ▾↑	Sum of Size
4	⊟ Group1	Fort Lauderdale	165
5		Hialeah	224
6		Miami	400
7	⊟ Jacksonville	Jacksonville	822
8	⊟ Orlando	Orlando	238
9	⊟ Pembroke Pin	Pembroke Pines	154
10	⊟ Port Saint Luc	Port Saint Lucie	164
11	⊟ Saint Petersbi	Saint Petersburg	244
12	⊟ Tallahassee	Tallahassee	181
13	⊟ Tampa	Tampa	335
14	Grand Total		2927

Figure 934 *After you group the first products, chaos results.*

5. Select the word Group1 in A4. Click the Field Settings dialog. Change the field name from Office2 to Territory. Change the subtotals from None to Automatic.

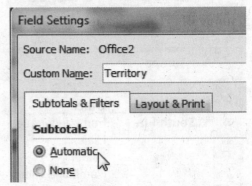

Figure 935 *Change the name of the grouped field & add subtotals.*

6. Back in the pivot table, select the cell called Group1. Type a new name for this group right in the cell. Perhaps South Fla.
7. Repeat steps 3, 4, and 6 for each additional territory.

Results: You've added territories on the fly in the pivot table.

	A	B	C
3	Territory ▾	Office ▾↑	Sum of Size
4	⊟ South Fla	Fort Lauderdale	165
5		Hialeah	224
6		Miami	400
7		Pembroke Pines	154
8		Port Saint Lucie	164
9	South Fla Total		1107
10	⊟ East Central	Jacksonville	822
11		Orlando	238
12	East Central Total		1060
13	⊟ Gulf Coast	Saint Petersburg	244
14		Tallahassee	181
15		Tampa	335
16	Gulf Coast Total		760
17	Grand Total		2927

Figure 936 *Territory was added after creating the pivot table.*

If you choose a cell in the Territory column and click Collapse Entire Field, you will see only territory totals.

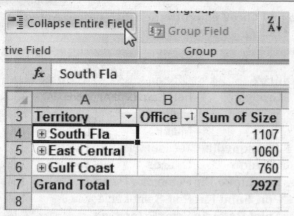

Figure 937 *Collapse to see territory totals.*

Additional Details: If your VP of Sales is like my VP of sales, he will decide to re-balance the territories (several times, right?). This process is fairly easy. First, click Expand Entire Field. Then, choose the offices in column B that should be re-grouped. Below, he asked you to add Orlando to the Gulf Coast group.

Figure 938 *Creative, and geographically challenged.*

Click Group Selection. Those four cities will be grouped with the name of Group 1. Jacksonville will be left alone in a territory that will be renamed Jacksonville.

Hint: after the tenth iteration, try adding some formatting to the pivot table. Maybe he will think this one looks better.

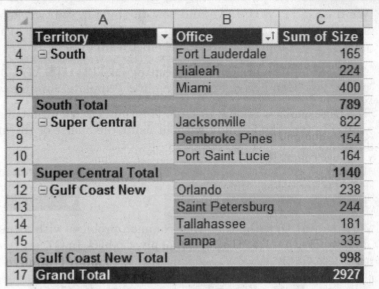

3	Territory ▼	Office ↓↑	Sum of Size
4	⊟ South	Fort Lauderdale	165
5		Hialeah	224
6		Miami	400
7	**South Total**		**789**
8	⊟ Super Central	Jacksonville	822
9		Pembroke Pines	154
10		Port Saint Lucie	164
11	**Super Central Total**		**1140**
12	⊟ Gulf Coast New	Orlando	238
13		Saint Petersburg	244
14		Tallahassee	181
15		Tampa	335
16	**Gulf Coast New Total**		**998**
17	**Grand Total**		**2927**

Figure 939 *Territory balancing is an iterative process.*

CALCULATIONS OUTSIDE OF PIVOT TABLES

Problem: I need to add a calculation in the grid outside of the pivot table that points to cells in the pivot table. Whenever I copy the formula, I get the exact same result!

Strategy: This started happening in Excel 2002. It is very annoying. I call it the GetPivotData bug.

Here is how it happens. In the figure below, you've already grouped daily dates to months and years. Normally, you could add a calculated item to calculate growth rate as (2015/2014)-1, but calculated items are not allowed in grouped pivot tables. So, you went to cell D5, typed an equals sign, clicked on C5, typed a slash, clicked on B5, and pressed enter. The 14.54% is the correct growth rate. So, you then copied the formula down. Somehow, the growth rate for every month is identical.

	A	B	C	D	E
3	**Revenue**				
4		**2014**	**2015**	**% Growth**	
5	Jan	258081	295609	14.54%	
6	Feb	257570	285528	14.54%	
7	Mar	252354	239373	14.54%	
8	Apr	271215	317368	14.54%	
9	May	290211	303998	14.54%	
10	Jun	251187	188041	14.54%	
11	Jul	306684	343158	14.54%	
12	Aug	274932	323704	14.54%	
13	Sep	226256	259070	14.54%	
14	Oct	308712	292710	14.54%	
15	Nov	314169	273057	14.54%	
16	Dec	305890	268935	14.54%	
17	**Grand Total**	3317261	3390551	14.54%	
18					
19					

Figure 940 *Sales went down in March 2015 from March 2014, there is no way that 14.54% growth is correct.*

Select D5 and look in the formula bar. The formula there is =GETPIVOTDATA("Revenue", $A$3,"Date",1, "Years", 2015) / GETPIVOTDATA("Revenue", $A$3,"Date",1, "Years",2014)-1. There is no way that you typed any of that. You simply used the mouse when building the formula.

This also happens if you use the arrow keys. Equals Sign, Left, Slash, Left, Left, Minus, One, Enter will normally create a formula of =C5/B5-1, but in this case, you get the formula with two GETPIVOTDATA formulas.

What is GETPIVOTDATA and how did it get in your worksheet? The Excel team is hoping that you would see GETPIVOTDATA, then go find out what it is and learn to love it and use it all the time. But that is never what happens. Instead, people are annoyed by it.

As an aside, I spent eight years hating GETPIVOTDATA, but now I understand it and occasionally even use it. See "Can I Save Formatting in a Template" for an example of when you would want to use it.

The big question is how to enter a formula without getting the GETPIVOTDATA. One quick and easy way is to type the formula without using the mouse or the arrow keys. Just type =C5/B5-1. This creates a formula that will copy.

The other method is to permanently turn off the feature to generate GETPIVOTDATA. To do this, chose File, Options, Formulas. There is a checkbox for Use GetPivotData Functions For PivotTable References. Turn this off.

Additional Details: the other common problem with formulas outside of pivot tables is that they don't deal well with the changing size of pivot tables. In Q1, six reason codes are found, so the % of Total formula points to G$11.

	I5						f_x	=G5/G$11		
	A	B	C	D	E	F	G	H	I	
1	Qtr	Q1								
2										
3	Counts	Branch								
4	Reason		10	11	20	30	31	Grand Total		% of Total
5	A		1	2	2	4	0	9		12.9%
6	B		3	6	6	1	2	18		25.7%
7	C		6	2	1	3	0	12		17.1%
8	D		3	1	2	5	1	12		17.1%
9	E		6	3	1	1	5	16		22.9%
10	F		1	0	0	1	1	3		4.3%
11	Grand Tota		20	14	12	15	9	70		100.0%

Figure 941 *This works when there are six products.*

This doesn't work anymore in Q2, when only three reason codes are found.

	I5						f_x	=G5/G$11		
	A	B	C	D	E	F	G	H	I	
1	Qtr	Q2								
2										
3	Counts	Branch								
4	Reason		10	11	20	30	31	Grand Total		% of Total
5	A		5	2	7	6	5	25		#DIV/0!
6	C		7	3	6	3	4	23		#DIV/0!
7	E		4	1	2	2	8	17		#DIV/0!
8	Grand Tota		16	6	15	11	17	65		#DIV/0!
9										#DIV/0!
10										#DIV/0!
11										#DIV/0!

Figure 942 *The Grand Total moves from row 11 to row 8. Your formula is still dividing by G11.*

The solution is to use an Excel trick to return the last value from column G. See "Return the Last Matching Value" on page 527 for details on how this VLOOKUP works. Also, use a custom number format where the third zone is blank in order to hide any 0 values that appear below the table.

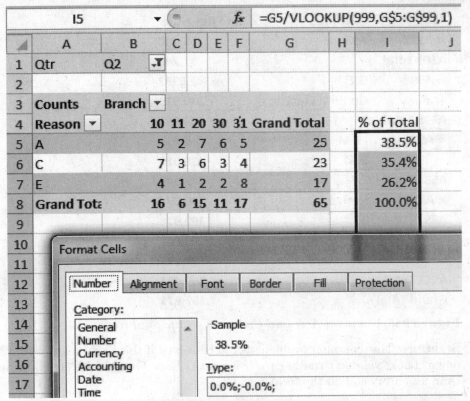

15			f_x	=G5/VLOOKUP(999,G$5:G$99,1)				
	A	B	C D E F	G	H	I	J

◢	A	B	C	D	E	F	G	H	I	J
1	Qtr	Q2	▼							
2										
3	Counts	Branch ▼								
4	Reason ▼		10	11	20	30	31	Grand Total		% of Total
5	A		5	2	7	6	5		25	38.5%
6	C		7	3	6	3	4		23	35.4%
7	E		4	1	2	2	8		17	26.2%
8	Grand Tota		16	6	15	11	17		65	100.0%

Format Cells

| Number | Alignment | Font | Border | Fill | Protection |

Category:
General
Number
Currency
Accounting
Date
Time

Sample
38.5%

Type:
0.0%;-0.0%;

Figure 943 *Two Excel tricks solve this problem.*

SHOW CUSTOMER ACCOUNT & NAME

Problem: My source data comes from the sales reps. They don't use consistent names, so I end up with multiple customer names for one account number.

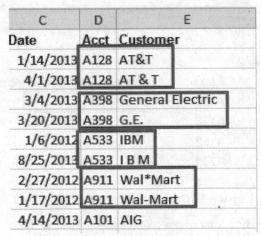

C	D	E
Date	Acct	Customer
1/14/2013	A128	AT&T
4/1/2013	A128	AT & T
3/4/2013	A398	General Electric
3/20/2013	A398	G.E.
1/6/2012	A533	IBM
8/25/2013	A533	I B M
2/27/2012	A911	Wal*Mart
1/17/2012	A911	Wal-Mart
4/14/2013	A101	AIG

Figure 944 *Bad for pivot tables.*

This forces me to put both Acct and Customer in the row area. This looks horrible. The customer name doesn't appear on the totals for each account.

Acct ⌄	Customer ⌄	Sum of Revenue
⊟ A101	AIG	51,240
A101 Total		**51,240**
⊟ A398	G.E.	27,932
	General Electric	540,919
A398 Total		**568,851**
⊟ A533	I B M	6,438
	IBM	420,911
A533 Total		**427,349**
⊟ A857	Verizon	390,978
A857 Total		**390,978**
⊟ A911	Wal*Mart	787,262
	Wal-Mart	82,192
A911 Total		**869,454**
Grand Total		**2,307,872**

Figure 945 *You want Acct and Customer on the total row.*

Strategy: This common problem would be solved if the Excel team would add First and Last to this drop-down. Look; we don't really care if we get G.E. or General Electric...either one is a million times better than an empty cell on the total row.

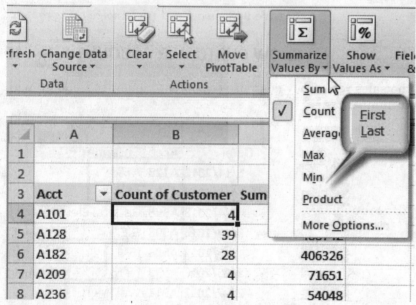

Figure 946 *This addition would solve the problem.*

But, for now, we don't have First or Last. Your best bet is likely to be creating a pivot table with Acct and Revenue. Copy the entire pivot table. Paste as Values.

Acct ⌄	Sum of Revenue
A101	51,240
A398	568,851
A533	427,349
A857	390,978
A911	869,454
Grand Total	2,307,872

Paste Special

Paste
- ○ All
- ○ Formulas
- ● Values
- ○ Formats
- ○ Comments

Figure 947 *Convert the pivot table to values.*

You are now allowed to insert a blank column between Acct and Revenue. Use a VLOOKUP back into the original data set to fill in the customer name.

=VLOOKUP(K3,$D$1:$E$563,2,FALSE)

K	L	M
Acct	**Customer**	**Sum of Revenue**
A101	AIG	51,240
A398	General Elec	568,851
A533	IBM	427,349
A857	Verizon	390,978
A911	Wal*Mart	869,454
Grand Total		2,307,872

Figure 948 *Use a VLOOKUP to get the text fields.*

Alternate Strategy: You can do the FIRST yourself back in the original data set. Add a column called Acct - Customer. Use a formula to concatenate the Acct with a VLOOKUP to return the first customer from the list.

=D2&" - "&VLOOKUP(D2,$D$2:$E$563,2,FALSE)

	D	E	F	
1	**Acct**	**Customer**	**Acct-Customer**	Qua
2	A128	AT&T	A128 - AT&T	
3	A128	AT & T	A128 - AT&T	
4	A398	General Electric	A398 - General Electric	
5	A398	G.E.	A398 - General Electric	

Figure 949 *Build your own Acct-Customer field.*

When you build the pivot table, put this field in the row labels.

	A	B
3	**Acct-Customer**	**Sum of Revenue**
4	A128 - AT&T	488742
5	A398 - General Electric	568851
6	A533 - IBM	427349
7	A857 - Verizon	390978
8	A911 - Wal*Mart	869454
9	**Grand Total**	2745374

Figure 950 *This has the data that you need and avoids the duplicate customer names.*

SHOW MONTHS WITH ZERO SALES

Problem: I built a pivot table to show sales by month for one customer. For the large customers, I get all 12 months.

	A	B
1	Customer	Wal-Mart ▼Τ
2		
3	Row Labels ▼	Revenue
4	Jan	95,113
5	Feb	119,509
6	Mar	101,567
7	Apr	67,408
8	May	84,383
9	Jun	10,741
10	Jul	120,749
11	Aug	24,657
12	Sep	63,775
13	Oct	75,585
14	Nov	49,914
15	Dec	56,053
16	Grand Total	869,454
17		

Figure 951 *All 12 months appear.*

But for the smaller customers, I don't see all of the months. I was thinking of adding 12 dummy records for every customer, one per month, but with 300 customers, that would be 3600 fake records just to solve this stupid problem.

	A	B
1	Customer	Chevron ▼Τ
2		
3	Row Labels ▼	Revenue
4	Feb	20,610
5	Mar	8,116
6	Jul	18,290
7	Oct	7,032
8	Grand Total	54,048

Figure 952 *Months without sales are missing.*

Strategy: Select a cell in the data column. Click the Field Settings icon in the Options tab. This time, go to the second tab in the dialog, called Layout and Print. On that tab, click Show Items With No Data.

▲	A	B
1	Customer	Chevron 🔽
2		
3	**Row Labels** 🔽	**Revenue**
4	<1/2/2014	
5	Jan	
6	Feb	20,610
7	Mar	8,116
8	Apr	
9	May	
10	Jun	
11	Jul	18,290
12	Aug	
13	Sep	
14	Oct	7,032
15	Nov	
16	Dec	
17	>12/28/2014	
18	**Grand Total**	**54,048**

Figure 953 *Strange entries in row 4 & 17.*

Gotcha: You are not done yet. The months now appear, but they are empty cells instead of zero. Also, a strange entry appears at the top and the bottom of the data set. There are no records in the data set before 1/1/2014, so this is a pure annoyance from Microsoft.

To fix the empty cells, right-click the pivot table and choose Options. Fill in the For Empty Cells Show box with a zero.

Format

☐ For error values show: [   ]

☑ For empty cells show: [0]

Figure 954 *Replace empty cells with zero.*

Go to the filter dropdown for Dates. Uncheck the <1/1/2014 and the >12/29/2014 entries.

☐ <1/2/2014
☑ Jan
☑ Feb
☑ Mar
☑ Apr
☑ May
☑ Jun
☑ Jul
☑ Aug
☑ Sep
☑ Oct
☑ Nov
☑ Dec
☐ >12/28/2014

Figure 955 *Turn off the < and > values.*

The **result:** a pivot table that will show all 12 months for every customer.

	A	B
1	Customer	Chevron
2		
3	Row Labels	Revenue
4	Jan	0
5	Feb	20,610
6	Mar	8,116
7	Apr	0
8	May	0
9	Jun	0
10	Jul	18,290
11	Aug	0
12	Sep	0
13	Oct	7,032
14	Nov	0
15	Dec	0
16	Grand Total	54,048
17		

Figure 956 *Easier than adding 3,600 fake zero records to the data.*

CREATE A UNIQUE LIST OF CUSTOMERS WITH A PIVOT TABLE

Problem: I need to create a unique list of customers from a large list.

Strategy: You can build a pivot table report with Customer in the Row area of the layout. Because the pivot table creates a summary report, the first column of the table will include the unique list of customers. Here's what you do:

1. Select Insert, Pivot Table. Click OK in the Create PivotTable dialog.
2. Click the Customer field in the PivotTable Field List dialog.

That's it. You are done. You can now copy the customers from column A of the new sheet and use Paste Values to put the unique list of customers wherever you need it.

	A
1	
2	
3	Row Labels
4	Ainsworth
5	Air Canada
6	Bell Canada
7	Chevron
8	Compaq
9	Compton Petroleum
10	Exxon
11	Ford
12	General Motors

Figure 957 *Four clicks to create a unique list of customers.*

USE A PIVOT TABLE TO COMPARE TWO LISTS

Problem: I have two lists of data. One is from a forecasting system. One is from our order entry system. I want to compare both list. Although both lists happen to have twenty customers, they are not the same twenty customers.

◢	A	B	C	D	E
1	**Customer**	**Forecast**		Customer	Order
2	AIG	210000		AT&T	1370995
3	AT&T	1380000		Chevron	465000
4	Bank of America	1550000		CitiGroup	150000
5	Boeing	640000		Exxon	157000
6	Chevron	470000		Ford	45000
7	Compaq	970000		General Electric	180000
8	Duke Energy	800000		General Motors	180000
9	Exxon	1570000		Home Depot	8000
10	Ford	1930000		HP	800000
11	General Motors	1890000		I B M	1000000
12	HP	1450000		Kroger	24000
13	IBM	1460000		Merck	120000
14	Lucent	1630000		Motorola	157654
15	Motorola	200000		P&G	149000
16	P&G	140000		Phillip Morris	654222
17	SBC Communications	1330000		SBC Communications	987876
18	Sears	1140000		Sears	114000
19	State Farm	1460000		Texaco	122000
20	Verizon	830000		Verizon	765743
21	Wal-Mart	1780000		Wal-Mart	1500000

Figure 958 *Compare these two lists.*

There is a solution in Part II of this book, "Combine Two Lists Using VLOOKUP" on page 520. That method requires adding two columns of MATCH or VLOOKUP formulas. The pivot table method is far easier.

Strategy: You need to copy the two lists into a single list, with a third column to indicate whether the forecast is from this week or last week. Then you create a pivot table, and the new, deleted, and changed forecasts will be readily apparent. Follow these steps:

1. Add the heading Source in C1. Select C2:C21, type Forecast and press Ctrl+Enter to fill column C with the word Forecast.
2. Change the heading in B1 to be Amount.
3. Cut D2:E21 and paste just below the first list. Type Orders next to all of the List 2 records.

◢	A	B	C
1	**Customer**	**Amount**	Source
17	SBC Communications	1330000	Forecast
18	Sears	1140000	Forecast
19	State Farm	1460000	Forecast
20	Verizon	830000	Forecast
21	Wal-Mart	1780000	Forecast
22	AT&T	1370995	Orders
23	Chevron	465000	Orders
24	CitiGroup	150000	Orders
25	Exxon	157000	Orders

Figure 959 *Add a Source column combining the lists.*

4. Create a pivot table. Put Customer in the Row Labels, Source in Column Labels, and Amount in the Values area.
5. Select Design, Grand Totals, On for Columns Only.

As shown here, you will have a comparison of the two lists.

	A	B	C
3	Sum of Amount	Source ▾	
4	Customer ▾	Forecast	Orders
10	CitiGroup		150,000
11	Compaq	970,000	
12	Duke Energy	800,000	
13	Exxon	1,570,000	157,000
14	Ford	1,930,000	45,000
15	General Electric		180,000
16	General Motors	1,890,000	180,000
17	Home Depot		8,000
18	HP	1,450,000	800,000
19	I B M		1,000,000
20	IBM	1,460,000	
21	Kroger		24,000

Figure 960 *Excel merges the lists.*

In this view, you can spot many interesting facts. It looks like the IBM misspelling in row 20 is causing problems. That forecast is most likely associated with the order in row 19. I would also be concerned with the Exxon forecast and order in row 13. Did the forecast accidentally type an extra zero when submitting his forecast?

USE A PIVOT TABLE WHEN THERE IS NO NUMERIC DATA

Problem: My data set contains a list of manufacturing defects found in quality inspection for one month. I have fields for date, manufacturing line, and defects. There are no numeric fields. Can I analyze this data with a pivot table?

	A	B	C
1	Date	Line	Defect
2	8/14/2014	A	Battery Failure
3	8/15/2014	C	Fit & Finish - Roof
4	8/5/2014	C	Fit & Finish - Bumper
5	8/19/2014	D	Fit & Finish - Roof
6	8/26/2014	B	Fit & Finish - Driver Side Door
7	8/3/2014	D	Emissions failure
8	8/16/2014	A	Brake Failure

Figure 961 *Analyze defects with a pivot table.*

Strategy: You can use the COUNT function to perform a Pareto analysis. Here's how:
1. Create a pivot table. Choose the Defect field, and Excel will automatically add it to the Row Labels drop zone.
2. Drag the Defect field from the top of the Field List dialog to the Values drop zone. Excel will add the Defect field to the pivot table twice. Because Defect is a text field, Excel automatically decides to count the number of occurrences.
3. Sort the pivot table by Count of Defect, descending. You now have a list of each defect and how often it occurred.

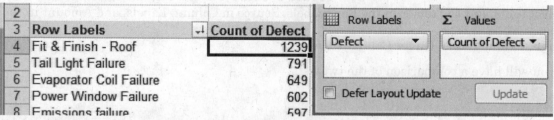

Figure 962 *Add a text field to Values and Excel will count.*

4. Study the pivot table to find defects with the most problems. The fit of the roof and tail lights are causing the most problems.

5. Change the pivot table to have Dates in the Row Labels and Line in the Columns. Move Defect from the Row Labels to the Report Filter.
6. Choose Fit & Finish – Roof from the Report Filter dropdown in B1. This was the defect that occurred most often.

Results: As shown below, the defect was happening a few times each day until the 28th of the month. On the 28th, line B began having problems. On the 29th, the problem began appearing in lines A, C, and D. By the 30th, all four lines were having massive problems. This doesn't look like a problem with an isolated employee, so you should probably see if a new batch of material started being used on the 28th.

	A	B	C	D	E	F
1	Defect	⫧	Fit & Finish - Roof			
2						
3	Count of Defect	L ▼				
4	Date ▼	A	B	C	D	Grand Total
28	8/24/2008		1		1	2
29	8/25/2008			1	1	2
30	8/26/2008	1	1	1		3
31	8/27/2008				3	3
32	8/28/2008	2	249		2	253
33	8/29/2008	15	356	19	16	406
34	8/30/2008	128	118	112	110	468
35	Grand Total	169	753	159	158	1239

Figure 963 *Even without any numeric data, you can discover trends.*

FIX MISSPELLED CUSTOMER NAMES

Problem: I collect data from sales reps. There must be a half dozen ways that they enter General Electric.

D	E
Customer	Quantity
AT&T	100
AT & T	600
General Electric	600
G.E.	400
IBM	600
I B M	300
Wal-Mart	300
Wal*Mart	400
AIG	600
AIG	200

Figure 964 *Conform all ways to spell these customer names.*

Strategy: You can use a pivot table to help solve this problem. Follow these steps:
1. Build a pivot table with Customer in the Row Labels and in the Values area. This will show you each customer and the number of times that this spelling is used.
2. Copy the entire pivot table.
3. Paste Values to convert the pivot table to regular data.
4. Insert a new column between A & B. Copy the customers from A to B with a heading of Good Customer.
5. Manually scan through the report, looking for different ways to spell the same customer. When you find a duplicate, you can look at column C to see which is more prevalent. For the wrong spelling, copy the correct spelling to column B. The advantage: you only have to change the few customers that have duplicates.

	A	B	C
1	Customer	Good Customer	Total
2	AIG	AIG	4
3	AT & T	AT&T	1
4	AT&T	AT&T	38
5	Bank of America	Bank of America	28
6	Boeing	Boeing	4

Figure 965 *Find duplicates and fix one in column B.*

6. Go back to your original data. Add a new column called Fixed Customer. Do a VLOOKUP into the pivot table to get the correct customer.

=VLOOKUP(D2,Sheet1!$A$2:$B$32,2,FALSE)

	D	E	F	
	Customer	Fixed Cust	Quantity	R(
	AT&T	AT&T	100	
	AT & T	AT&T	600	
	General Electric	General Electric	600	
	G.E.	General Electric	400	
	IBM	IBM	600	
	I B M	IBM	300	
	Wal-Mart	Wal*Mart	300	
	Wal*Mart	Wal*Mart	400	
	AIG	AIG	600	

Figure 966 *Do a VLOOKUP.*

7. Copy the new column. Paste Values.

CREATE A PIVOT TABLE FROM ACCESS DATA

Problem: I have 10 kazillion records in an Access table. I would like to create a pivot table for this data.

Strategy: You can create a connection to the Access table and build the pivot table in Excel. Follow these steps:

1. Start with a blank Excel workbook.
2. Select Data, From Access.
3. Browse to your Access database and click Open.
4. The Select Table dialog shows a list of all the tables and queries in the database. The Type column says VIEW for queries and TABLE for tables. Choose the desired query or table and click OK.
5. In the Import Data dialog that appears, choose to create a pivot table report and click OK.

Results: Excel will display the PivotTable Field List dialog, with all the fields from your table or query.

WHATEVER HAPPENED TO MULTIPLE CONSOLIDATION RANGES IN PIVOT TABLES?

Problem: I read your book *Pivot Table Data Crunching*, which describes an awesome trick for spinning poorly formatted data into transactional data for pivot tables. The trick requires you to choose Multiple Consolidation Ranges from Step 1 of the PivotTable and PivotChart Wizard. However, Microsoft seems to have eliminated the wizard in Excel 2007, so now how can I select Multiple Consolidation Ranges?

Strategy: Although the PivotTable and PivotChart Wizard has been removed from the ribbon, you can still get to the old wizard:

1. Type Alt+D followed by P.
2. The PivotTable and PivotChart Wizard will appear, complete with new artwork.

Additional Details: Using multiple consolidation ranges can help when your data is not properly formatted for pivot tables. Below, the data has been summarized with months going across the columns. Each year is on a different worksheet. All of the worksheets have products along column A, but the list of products differs from year to year.

	A	B	C	D
1	Account	Jan 2014	Feb 2014	Mar 2014
2	A125	917	973	1032
3	A126	394	424	455
4	A127	473	507	542

Figure 967 *Months going across rarely works for pivot tables.*

1. Type Alt+D+P to open the old PivotTable Wizard.
2. In Step 1 of the wizard, choose Multiple Consolidation Ranges. Click Next.
3. In Step 2a, choose I Will Create the Page Fields. (You don't have to create page fields, you just don't want Excel to create page fields.)
4. Click Next.
5. In Step 2b, choose the range on the first sheet. Click Add.
6. Repeat Step 5 for each additional worksheet. The dialog should look like below.
7. Click Finish.

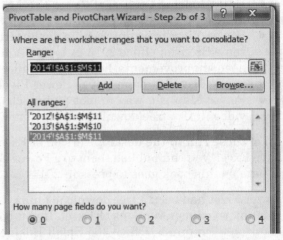

Figure 968 *Consolidate data from three worksheets.*

Excel will create a pivot table that summarizes all the worksheets. The fields have the strange names Row, Column, and Value.

Sum of Value	Column	
Row	1/1/2012	2/1/2012
A110	496	521
A111	369	387
A115	907	952

Figure 969 *The worksheets are combined into one pivot table.*

As you read in "See Detail Behind One Number in a Pivot Table," you can double-click any cell in a pivot table to drill down to see all the records in that cell. Here is the amazing trick: If you double-click the Grand Total cell in the pivot table, Excel will produce a new worksheet with all your data in detail format, as shown below. All you have to do is rename the headings from Row, Column, and Value to Product, Month, and Sales.

	A	B	C
1	Product	Month	Sales
2	A110	1/1/2012	496
3	A110	2/1/2012	521
4	A110	3/1/2012	547
5	A110	4/1/2012	574
6	A110	5/1/2012	603
7	A110	6/1/2012	633

Figure 970 *Double-click the Grand Total to get a data set combining data from all worksheets.*

WHAT ARE THE PRODUCTS IN POWER BI AND HOW CAN I GET THEM?

Power BI is the collective name for a series of impressive add-ins for Excel 2010/2013. Unfortunately, Microsoft Marketing continues to fumble any attempts to communicate what the add-ins are and how you can get them.

Let's start with what the add-ins do:
- Power Query is a data-cleansing tool that helps you load imperfect data from many sources into Excel. As you go through the steps of cleaning the data on the initial import, those steps are recorded in a new programming language called "M". The next time you need to load and clean the data, you simply have to Refresh and all the steps are carried out. Available as a free download for anyone with Excel 2010/2013/2015.
- Power Pivot allows you to create pivot tables from very large data sets. You can join two data sets without using VLOOKUP. You can write amazing new calculated fields in a new DAX formula language. Power Pivot was a free download for Excel 2010. It is impossible to get in the "owned" version of Office and tricky to find in the "rented" versions of Office 365.
- Data Model is a subset of Power Pivot that lets you create pivot tables from two worksheets. It comes built-in to all versions of Office 2013. You can not build DAX in this version.
- Power View is an interactive dashboard product designed to compete with Tableau. It debuted in some SKUs of Office 2013. A typical Version 1 product from Microsoft, it has some cool features but needs improvements, hopefully in Office 2015. It is not available for Excel 2010 and follows the same tricky distribution model as Power Pivot for 2013.
- Power Map is a way to plot a pivot chart on a map. You can build tours of the data and save to a video. It is a free download for anyone with any version of Excel 2013 and is built-in to Excel 2015.

All of these run in the desktop version of Excel. If you want to share your analyses with people who don't have Excel, you can publish them to a Power BI site via hosted SharePoint. This $40 a month option is still in beta as this book goes to press in 2014.

Power Pivot had been a free download for anyone with Office 2010. In Office 2013, they cut Power Pivot out of many consumer versions of Excel. If you bought Office 2013 Standard, Office 2013 Professional, Office 365 Home Premium, Office 365 Small Business, Office 365 Student you will never have access to Power Pivot or Power View. Here are ways to get Power Pivot in Office 2013:
- Buy a stand-alone boxed version of Excel 2013 from Amazon. I personally lead the campaign to remind Microsoft Marketing that the long-standing rule is that the boxed version of Excel stand-alone is always supposed to have everything. Even the student version of Excel 2013 has Power Pivot. Priced anywhere from $68 to $105, this is a one-time payment and will insure you have Power Pivot forever.
- If your company has a volume licensing agreement with Microsoft, you can purchase the E3 or E4 level of Office 2013 and you will get Power Pivot and Power View. You need to buy five licenses of something to qualify for volume licensing. One strategy is to buy one copy of Office 2013 E3 and four copies of Windows Vista DVD Player (the cheapest item in the catalog).
- Rent your copy of Office. Subscribe to the Office 365 Pro Plus plan at $12 a month. Do not get fooled into the $12.50 a month Office 365 Small Business. Even though it is more expensive, it does not include Power Pivot or Power View.
- Subscribe to Office 365 Mid-Size Business, Office 365 Enterprise E3 or Office 365 Enterprise E4.

KNOW IF YOU HAVE 32-BIT OR 64-BIT EXCEL

Microsoft has done their best to make sure you ended up with 32-bit Office. If you plan on loading 10 million rows into Power Pivot, you really need 64-bit Office. When you install Office there is a huge button for "Install What We Think You Should Have" and a tiny link for "Advanced Options" where you can choose 64-bit.

If you plan on downloading any of the free downloads, you will have to know if you have 32-bit or 64-bit Excel installed. You have to download the correct version of the add-in or it will not work.

In Excel 2013, go to File, Account. Click the About Microsoft Excel in the right side of the backstage view. Look just below the title bar of the dialog box, at the end of the version number to see if you have 32-bit or 64-bit. In Excel 2010, go to File, Help. The version number is shown on the right side of the screen.

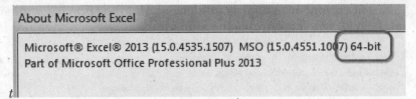

Figure 971 *This Excel 2013 is 64-bit.*

As you get to the download sites from Microsoft, they will clearly label the 64-bit with 64 in the file name. The 32-bit will either have "32" or "x86".

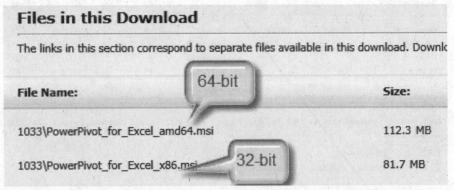

Figure 972 *Download the correct version to match your Excel 2010.*

LOAD AND CLEAN DATA WITH POWER QUERY

Problem: I have a table showing revenue by US state. My manager wants me to calculate Sales Per Capita. Where do I get population by US state?

Strategy: Use Power Query to search for the data online and load to Excel.
  1. On the Power Query tab, choose Online Search.

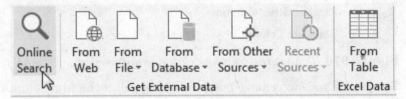

Figure 973 *Power Query can load data from many sources.*

  2. Search for "population by state".
  3. Power Query provides a list of search results.
  4. Hover over any item in the search results to see a preview of the columns in the data.

Figure 974 *Power Query finds data online that can be imported.*

5. When you find a data source, click Edit in the preview window. If you click Load, the data is loaded to Excel without any data cleaning. Edit allows you to record the cleansing steps in the "M" language.

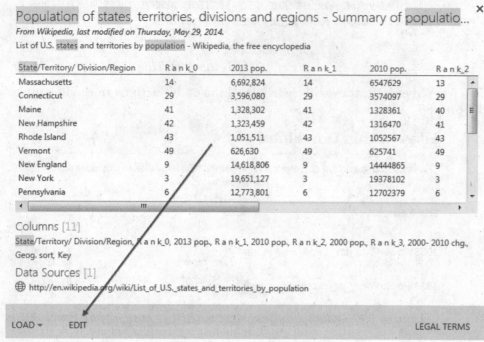

Figure 975 *Choose to edit before loading into Excel.*

You have a wide variety of choices in the Query Editor. Explore options on the Home, Transform, and Add Column tabs. Also, many popular choices are available in the Right-Click menu.

6. Right-click the Rank_0 column. Choose Remove Column.

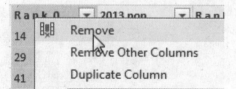

Figure 976 *Remove the columns that are not needed.*

Tip: If you have to remove many columns, select the first column, then Ctrl+Click other columns. Use the Remove Columns icon in the Home tab to remove all selected columns.

7. Some data contains unusual rows or totals that you do not need. Open the Filter dropdown for a column and uncheck those rows.

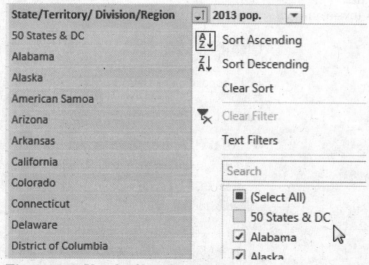

Figure 977 *Use the filter dropdowns to remove rows.*

As you continue cleaning the data, your past steps are shown in the window on the right side of the screen. You can click any item in the list and delete it.

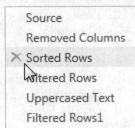

Source

Removed Columns

✕ Sorted Rows

Filtered Rows

Uppercased Text

Filtered Rows1

Figure 978 *All of the steps you've done are shown.*

If you want to dig deeper into the "M" code, choose View, Advanced Editor and you can see and edit the code. For more details on this language, read "M is for (Data) Monkey" by Ken Puls and Miguel Escobar.

8. If you want to force a column to be numeric or date, select the column heading and apply a Data Type using the dropdown in the Transform group of the Home tab.

9. Right-click a column and choose Rename to give it a meaningful heading in Excel.

10. When you are done editing the query, choose Home, Close & Load. The data is loaded to your Excel workbook.

This is great that you have the data in Excel. But it is not a static list of data. Power Query remembers where the data came from, what steps you used to clean it. When you click the Refresh button, Excel will go back to the data source, load the new data, and re-apply all of your cleaning steps.

Additional Details: With one cell in the results selected, click the Edit button to re-edit your query.

LOAD A LIST OF FOLDER CONTENTS INTO EXCEL

Windows Explorer will show you a list of files in a folder, You can sort by name, sort by date, sort by size. But sometimes it would be great to have this list in Excel. Power Query makes this simple.

1. Select Power Query, From File, From Folder.

2. Browse to your folder. Click OK.

3. You initially see useful columns like Date Modified, File Name, but important columns such as Size are missing. Find the Attributes column and click the Expand icon. You are now given a list of additional fields that you can add to the grid.

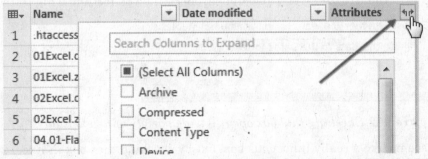

Figure 979 *The Expand icon often has hidden fields.*

USE POWER QUERY TO CLEAN DATA ALREADY IN EXCEL

Problem: My data is already in Excel. I need to transform the data. I need to unpivot the month data.

◢	A	B	C	D	E
1	Region	Product	Jan	Feb	Mar
2	East	A	200	143	134
3	Central	A	166	167	112
4	West	A	126	199	120
5	East	B	112	196	124
6	Central	B	193	136	140

Figure 980 *Unpivot this data.*

Follow these steps:

1. Select one cell inside your data set.
2. First, convert your data set to a table using Ctrl+T.
3. Choose Power Query, From Table.
4. In the Query Editor, click on the Jan heading to select that column.
5. Shift+Click on the Dec column to select all the columns between Jan and Dec.
6. On the Transform tab, select Unpivot Columns.
7. Optionally, rename the Attribute column to be Month.
8. On the Home tab, choose Close and Load.

You will see a new worksheet with the results.

	A	B	C	D
1	Region ▾	Product ▾	Month ▾	Value ▾
2	East	A	Jan	200
3	East	A	Feb	143
4	East	A	Mar	134

Figure 981 *If the underlying data changes, you can refresh this query.*

PIVOT FROM MULTIPLE TABLES IN EXCEL 2013 DATA MODEL

Problem: I have a lot of rows in a data table and then some lookup tables. Is there a faster way to create a report than building a bunch of VLOOKUP formulas?

Strategy: Excel 2013 adds a pivot table feature called the Data Model. This will solve the problem. This will work in all versions of Excel 2013, whether you have the Power Pivot tab installed or not.

The process works much better if you declare all of your data sets to be Ctrl+T tables first.

1. Select one cell in your main data set and press Ctrl+T. Confirm that the data has headers and click OK.
2. In the Table Tools Design tab, you will see a name for the table. Type a meaningful name, something like Data.
3. Select one cell in your lookup data. Ctrl+T. OK. Rename this table Sectors.
4. Go back to the original data. Select one cell. Insert, Pivot Table.
5. In the Create Pivot Table dialog, check the box for Add This Data to the Data Model. Click OK.

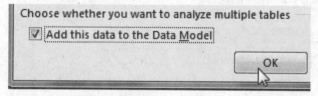

Figure 982 *Checking this box opens a wide variety of new options.*

It seems like a really innocuous box, but by checking that box in Excel 2013, you are loading the data into the Power Pivot data model that is hidden behind Excel 2013. If this is the first time you've used the Data Model in this Excel session, you might notice a few-second delay before you get to the Pivot Table Field list.

At this point, everything feels like a regular pivot table with one small change. You will notice a line at the top of the Pivot Table Field List offering ACTIVE | ALL.

PivotTable Fields

ACTIVE | ALL

Figure 983 *Before you move on to All, create a relationship.*

6. Go to the Analyze tab in the ribbon. Choose Relationships. Click New...
7. There are four fields to fill out in the Create Relationship dialog. Start from your Data table and choose the key field used to link to the lookup table. For the Related table, choose the lookup table and the key field. Click OK.

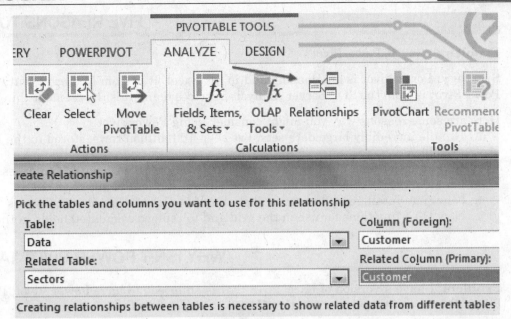

Figure 984 *This is far easier than a VLOOKUP.*

8. You can now go to the ALL section of the Pivot Table Fields.
9. You can now expand each table and choose fields from that table.

Figure 985 *Choose fields from any table.*

The result is a pivot table with fields from Sheet1 and Sheet2.

3	Row Labels ▾	Sum of Revenue
4	⊟**Communications**	1025339
5	AT&T	498937
6	Lucent	62744
7	SBC Communications	72680
8	Verizon	390978
9	⊟**Energy**	**850287**
10	Chevron	54048

Figure 986

Joining two tables in a pivot table is an amazing improvement. Although Excel calls this the Data Model, it is really the Power Pivot Engine. Even if you don't have two tables to join, there are some interesting reasons to run the data through the Data Model. See January Actuals and February Plan later in this chapter.

FIVE REASONS TO USE POWERPIVOT

Problem: What is PowerPivot?

Strategy: PowerPivot is an amazing add-in for Excel. It is from Microsoft, but not from the Excel team. PowerPivot is from the SQL Server Analysis Services team. It is the greatest thing to hit Excel in 20 years.

Here are some reasons why you might consider using PowerPivot:
1. Handle incredibly large data sets. I've seen 100 million rows, stored in the Excel workbook, without a problem.
2. Import data from anywhere. Mash up data from Excel with data from Access, with data from Oracle.
3. Create a pivot table from multiple worksheets without using VLOOKUP.
4. New time-intelligence functions, including functions to handle fiscal years.
5. New DAX functions for use in the grid and to replace calculated fields in the pivot table itself.

WHY ISN'T POWER PIVOT TAB IN THE RIBBON?

Problem: I have a version of Excel 2013 that is supposed to have Power Pivot, Power View, Power Map, Power Query, but they are not in the ribbon.

Strategy: Go to File, Options, Add-Ins. In the bottom of the dialog open the Manage dropdown and choose COM Add-ins. Click Go...

Add checkmarks to Microsoft Office PowerPivot for Excel 2013, Microsoft Power Query for Excel, Power View for Excel Add-In,

GET EXCEL DATA INTO POWERPIVOT

Problem: How do I get my Excel data into PowerPivot?

Convert your Excel data to a table and then link the table to PowerPivot.

First, convert your dataset to a table by selecting one cell and pressing Ctrl+T. Excel will ask you to confirm that your data has headers. Click OK. On the Table Tools Design tab, enter a new name for the table on the left side of the ribbon. This name will carry through to PowerPivot and be used in formulas later, so keep it short and easy to spell.

On the PowerPivot tab, choose Add to Data Model in Excel 2013 or Create Linked Table in Excel 2010.

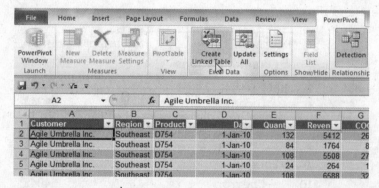

Figure 987 *Define your data as a table, you can simply link to the table.*

After a moment, you will see your data in the green grid of the PowerPivot window.

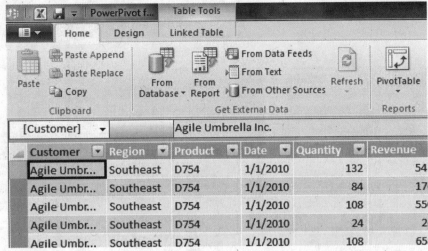

Figure 988 *The linked table appears in PowerPivot.*

OPEN THE POWER PIVOT WINDOW

There is a PowerPivot tab in the Excel ribbon. In Excel 2013, click the Manage button to open PowerPivot. In Excel 2010, click the PowerPivot Window icon to open PowerPivot.

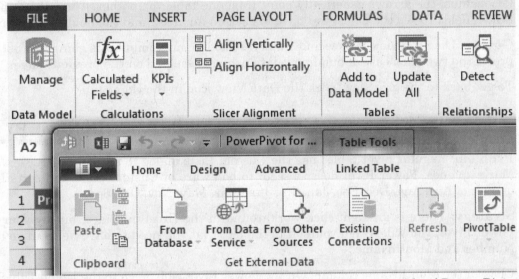

Figure 989 *Although Excel offers a PowerPivot ribbon, most commands are inside of Power Pivot.*

DEFINE RELATIONSHIPS BETWEEN TABLES

There are three different ways to define a relationship in Power Pivot.

Say you want to link from the ProdID field in the Fact table to the ProdID field in the Products table. Follow these steps:

1. Go to the Power Pivot window.
2. Click on the sheet tab for Fact
3. Place the cell pointer anywhere in the ProdID field.
4. Go to the Design tab in the Power Pivot ribbon. Select Create Relationship.
5. There are four fields to fill in. The first two fields area already filled in because of steps 2 & 3.
6. Open the Related Lookup Table dropdown and choose Products.
7. In most cases, Power Pivot will automatically fill in ProdID for the fourth field. If it does not, open the last dropdown and choose the ProdID field.

Another way to build a relationship is through the Diagram view. On the Home tab in Power Pivot, click Diagram View. Drag from the Date field in the Fact table to the Date field in the Date Table to establish a relationship.

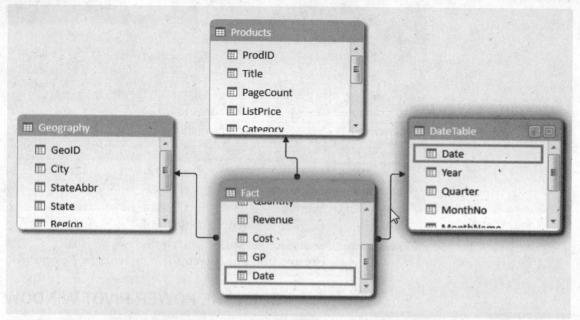

Figure 990 *Create relationships in Diagram View.*

Gotcha: This diagram view acts differently than the one in Microsoft Access. After you have created relationships, the arrows generically point from one table to another. They do not point specifically to the linked field. To see the fields, you have to click on an arrow and the fields will be outline in blue.

Gotcha: Diagram view is slow and clunky. I feel like my computer is going to crash when I use it. I really prefer the two-click ease of building relationships discussed on the previous page.

To get back to the grid view, click the Data View icon in the Home tab.

SORT MONTH NAME BY MONTH NUMBER

Problem: Regular pivot tables use the Custom Lists dialog to automatically sort months into Jan, Feb, Mar sequence. Power Pivot doesn't seem to be aware of Custom Lists and sorts into the alphabetic sequence of Apr, Aug, Dec, Feb, Jan, Jul, Jun, Mar. May, Nov, Oct, Sep.

Strategy: There is an eight-click workaround in the Excel interface, but by your second week of using Power Pivot, you will resign yourself to the fact that you need to have fields in your model called MonthNumber and MonthName.

Click in the MonthName column. On the Power Pivot ribbon, go to the Home Tab. Select the Sort By Column icon. In the Sort by Column dialog, indicate that you want to Sort MonthName by MonthNo.

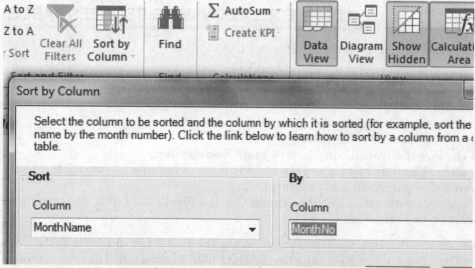

Figure 991 *It is annoying, but you will eventually accept this extra step.*

CREATE A CALENDAR TABLE

One downside of Power Pivot is the inability to group daily dates up to months and years. The common workaround is to build a lookup table that contains every daily date from the earliest date to the latest date in your data.

Start with a Date heading in A1. Add the first date in A2. Grab the fill handle and drag down until you get to the last date in your data. Add additional columns as needed:
* Year =YEAR(A2)
* Month =MONTH(A2)
* MonthName = TEXT(A2,"MMMM")
* Weekday: =WEEKDAY(A2,1)
* WeekdayName: =TEXT(A2,"DDDD")

Make this data set into a table and add it to the data model. Relate it to your Fact table.

The date table makes it possible to group daily dates to months or years. It will also make the Time Intelligence calculated fields in the pivot table easier to use.

THE FORMULAS ARE CALLED DAX

Power Pivot introduces a new formula language called Data Analysis eXpressions or DAX. When you see a Power Pivot demo, the 2 million rows and the joining tables look impressive. But it turns out that DAX is the really jewel in Power Pivot.

DAX is used in two places. DAX is used to add new columns in the Power Pivot grid. When used in this way, it is 99% similar to the functions that you know and love in regular Excel. The real power in DAX is when you add new calculated fields to the resulting pivot table.

While I am going to cover some essential DAX examples here, the my friend Rob Collie from PowerPivotPro.com has written the essential title on understanding DAX. His book is DAX Formulas for Power Pivot.

ADDING CALCULATIONS IN THE POWER PIVOT GRID

DAX shares 81 functions with Excel, so if you are proficient with Excel functions, you should have little problem working in DAX. There are two functions in DAX that differ from the equivalent function in Excel.

The first blank column in the PowerPivot window is called Add Column. Click in any cell in that column. Type an equals sign and enter your formula. For example, type =YEAR(and then, using the mouse, click on the Year field. Type a closing parentheses and press Enter. Your formula will populate all the way down the grid.

Right-click on the heading, choose Rename, and type a meaningful field name such as Year.

Seems easy, right? The function is the same as in Excel. Now - there are 81 functions you can use here, and 79 of them are identical to Excel. One that is different: The TEXT function in Excel is FORMAT in DAX. So, in the image below, the month name uses FORMAT.

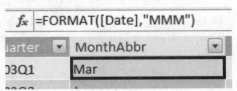

Figure 992 *DAX uses FORMAT instead of TEXT*

It turns out that FORMAT offers choices for Quarter and Week, thus is more robust than TEXT.

Gotcha: each column can have only one formula. Every row in the column has to have an identical formula. You cannot refer to cells in other rows. Therefore, the concept of cell addresses like A2 is not relevant in PowerPivot.

As you are building your formula, you can click a field with the mouse to refer to that field. You cannot use the arrow keys to select a field.

REFER TO A RELATED TABLE IN A FORMULA

Problem: I am entering a formula in the Fact table. I need to lookup a value from Product table. I've already defined a relationship between the tables.

Strategy: The promise of PowerPivot is that you won't have to do VLOOKUPs anymore. When you are building a calculated field, you will have to use a simpler lookup function called RELATED. In the Fact table, you can enter the following:

=[Quantity]*Related(Products[ListPrice])

That is a simple one-argument lookup function. This function tells PowerPivot to follow the defined relationship and retrieve the value from the other table.

Here is the easy way to build the formula: Type the equals sign, click Quantity, and then type the asterisk. Type the first few letters of the Product table. You can then choose a field from the list. Highlight the field. Press Tab to insert the field. Type the closing parentheses. Press Enter. Right-click the header to rename.

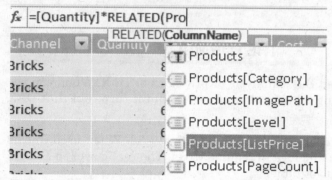

Figure 993 *Formula AutoComplete helps so you don't have to remember the syntax.*

Gotcha: When you define a calculated column in the PowerPivot window, that value is calculated for every row in the table. This can be a lot of overhead for a 100 million row dataset. In contrast, the DAX measures are calculated only once for each cell in the pivot table.

CREATING THE POWER PIVOT TABLE

The Pivot Table dropdown offers 8 choices and most of them are fairly silly. PivotTable and Pivot Charts are obviously needed. Pivot table pros will love the Flattened PivotTable. But all of those choices in the middle are redundant. They are trying to tell you that you can combine a pivot table and a chart on the same worksheet. You already know this.

Plus, this menu might make someone think that these are the only options. It is fine to have three charts in a horizontal row and a pivot table vertically below those.

In real life, build your pivot tables and charts one at a time. The first can go on a new worksheet. The others can go on the existing worksheet.

The eighth choice is cool; a flattened pivot table is one where the row labels automatically repeat, and the outer row fields don't have subtotals. This is great for creating a summary table that will be used for future analysis

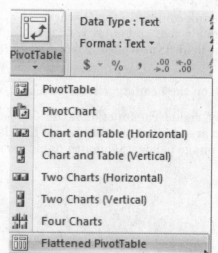

Figure 994 *One, two, or four tables and charts.*

THE ODD EXCEL 2010 POWER PIVOT FIELD LIST

In Excel 2010, the Power Pivot add-in featured a different field list. There was a Search box and extra drop zones for horizontal and vertical slicers. In Excel 2013, they went back to the standard field list.

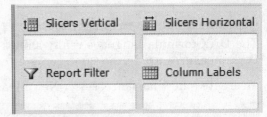

Figure 995 *Excel 2010 offered these extra drop zones.*

BUILDING THE PIVOT TABLE

Choose fields from any table and drag them to the four drop zones at the bottom of the field list. Since you've created relationships, you are free to use fields from any table.

The pivot table below has region from the Geography table, Excel version from the Product table, Revenue from the Fact table, and a Year slicer from the Date table.

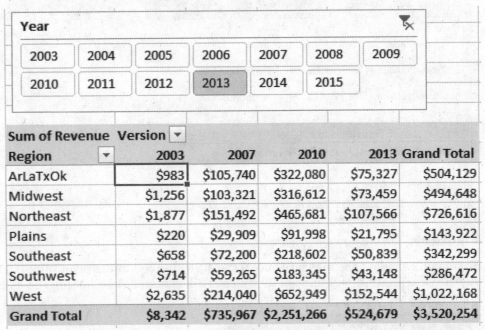

Sum of Revenue	Version				
Region	2003	2007	2010	2013	Grand Total
ArLaTxOk	$983	$105,740	$322,080	$75,327	$504,129
Midwest	$1,256	$103,321	$316,612	$73,459	$494,648
Northeast	$1,877	$151,492	$465,681	$107,566	$726,616
Plains	$220	$29,909	$91,998	$21,795	$143,922
Southeast	$658	$72,200	$218,602	$50,839	$342,299
Southwest	$714	$59,265	$183,345	$43,148	$286,472
West	$2,635	$214,040	$652,949	$152,544	$1,022,168
Grand Total	$8,342	$735,967	$2,251,266	$524,679	$3,520,254

Figure 996 *Reporting from four worksheets without doing a VLOOKUP.*

FEATURE X WON'T WORK IN POWER PIVOT

This is not a regular pivot cache pivot table that you've been using for the last 10 years. That data in your Excel worksheets is now in the Data Model. Even though the Data Model is stored inside of your Excel file, it gets treated like external data.

A lot of features that you might love in regular pivot table are not available when the data is stored externally. This was particularly bad in version 1 of Power Pivot. The later versions of Power Pivot now in Excel 2010 and Excel 2013 have mitigated some of the problems. But, you will still run into problems:

- You can not group data
- Double-clicking to drill-down will only return 1000 rows
- Pivot tables are not automatically sorted by custom list.
- You can't use the Show Report Filter Pages command to replicate the pivot table for every customer.
- The GETPIVOTDATA formula is wacky, which makes it significantly harder to parameterize your GETPIVOTDATA formulas. Where a regular pivot table would generate an argument pair of "", the OLAP version of GETPIVOTDATA uses "[Sales].[Customer]","[Sales].[Customer].&[Astonishing Shoe Inc.]". This means that you have to concatenate """[Sales].[Customer]""","""[Sales].[Customer].&[" before the customer name and then "]" after the customer name.

REPLACE CALCULATED FIELDS WITH DAX

The DAX formula language really shines when you use it to create a new measure for your pivot table. DAX measures are in the same genre as calculated fields, but are infinitely more powerful.

To create a new measure, select New Measure from the PowerPivot tab in Excel.

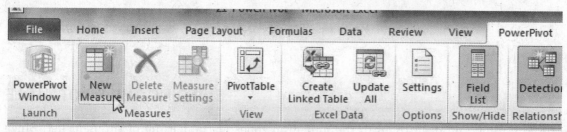

Figure 997 *Define a new measure.*

Build the measure in the Measure Settings dialog. Use the Check Formula button to check the syntax.

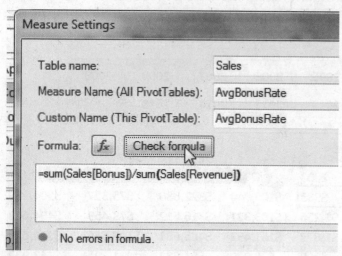

Figure 998 *Define a new measure.*

Excel will calculate the measure once for every value cell in the pivot table. In the figure below, this means that the calculation will happen 39 times. This is faster than adding the calculation to a million rows of source data.

AvgBonusRate	2010	2011	Grand To
Jan	1.98%	1.97%	1.9
Feb	1.99%	1.99%	1.9
Mar	1.92%	1.97%	1.9
Apr	1.98%	1.95%	1.9
May	1.89%	1.94%	1.9
Jun	1.96%	1.99%	1.9
Jul	1.92%	1.95%	1.9
Aug	1.96%	1.96%	1.9
Sep	1.96%	1.94%	1.9
Oct	1.93%	1.96%	1.9
Nov	1.99%	1.98%	1.9
Dec	2.02%	1.96%	1.9

Figure 999 *Excel calculates the formula 39 times in this pivot table.*

I've written a complete DAX reference in my PowerPivot for the Excel Data Analyst book, and I won't attempt to replicate that guide here. However, the following topics are the a-ha moments in my power pivot learning curve.

CALCULATE() IS LIKE SUMIFS()

As you get started with DAX, you are going to find yourself using the CALCULATE function. This function will perform a calculation while applying any number of filters. =CALCULATE(Sum(Field),Filter1, Filter 2, Filter 3).

Perhaps you want to calculate sales on Saturdays in January. You might think that you would have to do: =CALCULATE(SUM(Sales[Revenue]),Sales[Weekday]="Saturday",Sales[Month]="Jan",Sales[Year]=2016).

However, in the pivot table below, cell F4 already has filters applied to it. Cell F4 is limited to January by the month label in D4. Cell F4 is limited to 2016 by the slicer.

	B	C	D	E	F	G
3	**Year**	🔻	**Month** ▼	**Sum of Revenue**	**SaturdayRevenue**	
4			Jan	18,294,768	4,058,280	
5	2016	2017	Feb	17,033,088	3,262,872	
6			Mar	18,148,164	3,173,736	
7			Apr	17,378,844	4,185,324	
8			May	18,719,760	3,214,572	
9			Jun	17,187,084	3,262,512	
10			Jul	18,311,520	4,156,632	
11			Aug	19,169,940	3,341,808	
12			Sep	16,522,584	3,359,568	
13			Oct	19,429,164	4,000,572	
14			Nov	18,229,224	3,480,012	
15			Dec	16,929,696	4,038,276	
16			**Grand Total**	215,353,836	43,534,164	
17						

Figure 1000 *Cell F4 is already filtered to Month=Jan, Year-2016.*

This simplifies your formula. You don't have to specify a filter for Month or for Year, because those are already being handled by the pivot table. The formula for the measure in column F is =CALCULATE(SUM(Sales[Revenue]),Sales[Weekday]="Saturday").

Rule #1: Calculate() respects the filters already applied to each cell in a pivot table. Those filters can come from slicers, report filters, row labels, or column labels.

UNAPPLY A FILTER USING DAX

Contrast SUMIFS and CALCULATE.
- With SUMIFS, you go through a data set, finding rows that match all of the criteria.
- With Calculate, you go through a data set, calculating values that match the filters in calculate. BUT...you also have an external outside force that is forcing other filters to be applied. Those filters might be coming from the slicers or even from the row and column labels. When PowerPivot goes about calculating cell F4 in the figure above, it has to respect the weekday=Saturday in the calculate function, but it also has to respect Month=Jan caused by the row label in D4 and Year=2016 caused by the slicer.

Ready for something amazing? The filters in calculate have the power to tell the external outside force to not apply a certain filter. If that formula up in F4 used a filter of Month="Feb", the filter in the Calculate formula would override the filter from the row label in D4. Let me show you an example.

Consider this figure.

	B	C	D	E	F	G	H
3	**Month**	🔻	**Sector** ▾	**Sum of Revenue**	**ApparelSector**	**AllSectors**	**PctOfApparel**
4			Apparel	3,237,276	3,237,276	37,262,148	100.0%
5	Apr	Aug	Dec	Appliance	2,232,252	3,237,276	37,262,148	69.0%
6	Feb	Jan	Jul	Construction	9,758,016	3,237,276	37,262,148	301.4%
7				Consumer	10,436,412	3,237,276	37,262,148	322.4%
8	Jun	Mar	May	Electronic	3,539,340	3,237,276	37,262,148	109.3%
9	Nov	Oct	Sep	Food	1,062,540	3,237,276	37,262,148	32.8%
10				Industrial	3,217,620	3,237,276	37,262,148	99.4%
11				Outdoor	3,778,692	3,237,276	37,262,148	116.7%
12				**Grand Total**	37,262,148	3,237,276	37,262,148	1151.0%
14			Column F:	=CALCULATE(SUM(Sales[Revenue]),Sector[Sector]="Apparel")			
15			Column G:	=CALCULATE(SUM(Sales[Revenue]),All(Sector))			
16			Column H:	=sum(Sales[Revenue])/Sales[ApparelSector]			

Figure 1001 *These DAX Measures unapply a filter.*

- Column E, Sum of Revenue is a regular old field where I took the Revenue field from the field list and put it in the values drop zone. Column E respects the filters in the slicer and the filters of the row labels in column D.
- Column F is a DAX Measure where I used CALCULATE to override the filter on sector. No matter what label is over in column D, the DAX measure in column F will filter sector to Apparel. Column F still continues to respect the month slicer, though. The formula for the measure in F is =CALCULATE(SUM(Sales[Revenue]),Sector[Sector]="Apparel")
- Column G is a DAX Measure where I wiped out the Sector filter by using ALL. Every row in column G is going to show the total for all sectors, even though the row label in D5 says that this row is for Appliance. The formula for the measure in G is =CALCULATE(SUM(Sales[Revenue]),All(Sector)). Note that this formula still respects the filter applied in the month slicer.
- Column H is the actual useful field. It takes the revenue for this sector and divides it by the revenue for the Apparel sector. The formula here re-uses the existing DAX measure from column F: =sum(Sales[Revenue])/Sales[ApparelSector]. Of course, this formula still respects the month filter applied from the slicer.

As you change the filters other than sector, all of the formulas update. Here is the same pivot table filtered to June, July, and August.

	B	C	D	E	F	G	H
3	**Month**	🔻	**Sector** ▾	**Sum of Revenue**	**ApparelSector**	**AllSectors**	**PctOfApparel**
4			Apparel	10,010,604	10,010,604	108,625,464	100.0%
5	Apr	Aug	Dec	Appliance	6,414,300	10,010,604	108,625,464	64.1%
6	Feb	Jan	Jul	Construction	27,263,844	10,010,604	108,625,464	272.3%
7				Consumer	30,202,968	10,010,604	108,625,464	301.7%
8	Jun	Mar	May	Electronic	10,159,008	10,010,604	108,625,464	101.5%
9	Nov	Oct	Sep	Food	3,585,384	10,010,604	108,625,464	35.8%
10				Industrial	9,770,448	10,010,604	108,625,464	97.6%
11				Outdoor	11,218,908	10,010,604	108,625,464	112.1%
12				**Grand Total**	108,625,464	10,010,604	108,625,464	1085.1%
14			Column F:	=CALCULATE(SUM(Sales[Revenue]),Sector[Sector]="Apparel")			
15			Column G:	=CALCULATE(SUM(Sales[Revenue]),All(Sector))			
16			Column H:	=sum(Sales[Revenue])/Sales[ApparelSector]			

Figure 1002 *Change any filters other than Sector to recalculate.*

UNFILTER USING TIME INTELLIGENCE

The previous topic showed how you could unapply the Sector filter to get all sales for another sector. What if you need to compare sales for this date to all dates in the month? Or a running MTD number? Or sales from a prior year? DAX introduces many new time intelligence functions that can be used to unapply a filter.

Gotcha: There is a bug in the logic for using calculate with time intelligence functions.

If you wanted to compare calculate Month to Date sales, you should be able to refilter the date using calculate: =CALCULATE(Sum(Sales[Revenue]),DATESMTD(Sales[Date])). The DATESMTD() function returns a list of dates to consider. This wasn't working in the PowerPivot beta. It was supposed to be fixed in the final product, but it is not. The workaround is to add another filter with ALL(table containing dates). In this case, the formula becomes =CALCULATE(Sum(Sales[Revenue]),DATESMTD(Sales[Date]),ALL(Sales)).

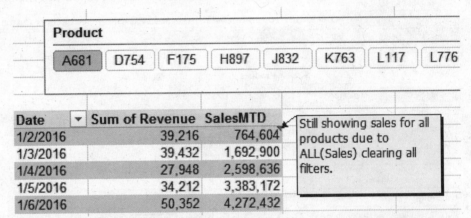

	B	C	D	E	F
1	=CALCULATE(Sum(Sales[Revenue]),DATESMTD(Sales[Date]),ALL(Sales))				
2					
3	Date ▼	Sum of Revenue	SalesMTD		
4	1/2/2016	764,604	764,604		
5	1/3/2016	928,296	1,692,900		
6	1/4/2016	905,736	2,598,636		
25	1/31/2016	883,344	18,294,768	(some rows hidden above)	
26	2/1/2016	731,580	731,580	(MTD starts over)	
27	2/2/2016	797,580	1,529,160		
28	2/3/2016	856,620	2,385,780		
46	2/29/2016	754,776	17,033,088	(more rows hidden)	
47	3/1/2016	964,896	964,896	(MTD starts over)	

Figure 1003 *To make the formula work, use ALL(Sales).*

The problem is that using ALL(Sales) will override all filters on the sales table. In the figure above, a new slicer filters the pivot table to only one product. The All(Sales) filter in the DAX measure overrides the product filter.

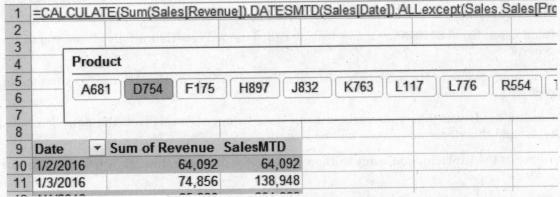

Product

| A681 | D754 | F175 | H897 | J832 | K763 | L117 | L776 |

Date ▼	Sum of Revenue	SalesMTD
1/2/2016	39,216	764,604
1/3/2016	39,432	1,692,900
1/4/2016	27,948	2,598,636
1/5/2016	34,212	3,383,172
1/6/2016	50,352	4,272,432

Still showing sales for all products due to ALL(Sales) clearing all filters.

Figure 1004 *Using ALL(Sales) overrides the product slicer.*

The workaround is to override all of the filters except the product filter:

=CALCULATE(Sum(Sales[Revenue]),DATESMTD(Sales[Date]),AllExcept(Sales,Sales[Product])).

The unfortunate by-product here is that the formula had to be rewritten just because a slicer was added. You would have to remember to rewrite the formula if someone adds a column field, a row field, or any slicer.

1	=CALCULATE(Sum(Sales[Revenue]),DATESMTD(Sales[Date]),ALLexcept(Sales,Sales[Pro
2	
3	
4	**Product**
5	A681 D754 F175 H897 J832 K763 L117 L776 R554
6	
7	
8	
9	Date ▼ Sum of Revenue SalesMTD
10	1/2/2016 64,092 64,092
11	1/3/2016 74,856 138,948

Figure 1005 *AllExcept is the workaround.*
Figure 1006

CONVERT POWERPIVOT TO FORMULAS

A few pages ago, I talked about all the bad side-effects of having PowerPivot use OLAP pivot tables. Here is one advantage that you can take advantage of because it is an OLAP table. In this case, I might take a regular flat Excel data set through PowerPivot to take advantage of the cube formulas.

Say that you build a pivot table in PowerPivot. You can go the PivotTable Tools Option ribbon tab, choose OLAP Tools and Convert to Formulas.

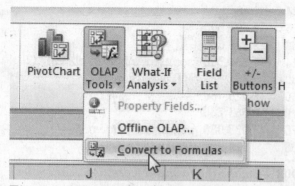

Figure 1007 *Change the pivot table to formulas.*

After invoking this command, the pivot table changes to formulas using the cube functions. Even though the pivot table no longer exists, the formulas continue to respond to the slicers!

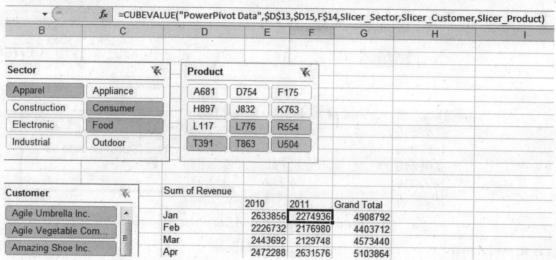

Figure 1008 *You can move these cells around, insert blank rows, and so on.*

JANUARY ACTUALS AND FEBRUARY PLAN

The example in "Can I Save Formatting in a Template?" on page 333 used GetPivotData to show Actual for some months and Plan for other months.

Good news: Excel 2010 offers a new feature called named sets that finally allows you to create asymmetric reports.

Bad news: Named sets work only with OLAP pivot tables for this release, so you cannot use them with regular pivot tables.

Good news: If you take your regular Excel data through PowerPivot, the data becomes an OLAP pivot table, and therefore you can use named sets.

To recap the problem, you want to show Actuals for January through April and Plan for the remaining months:

Sum of Sales	Column Labels ▾			
	⊟Jan		⊟Feb	
Row Labels ▾	Actual	Plan	Actual	Plan
Ala Moana	11739	11100	16105	14800
Altamonte Mall	11421	11400	14854	15100
Annapolis Mall	11689	10800	14675	14400
Aventura Mall	13646	12900	17473	17300
Baybrook	12366	12100	16625	16200
Beachwood Place Mall	10833	11400	16370	15200

Figure 1009 *Show Actuals for some months and Plan for other months.*

In the PivotTable Tools Option tab, choose Fields, Items, Sets and choose Create Set Based on Column Items.

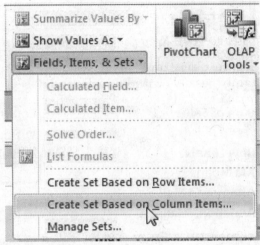

Figure 1010 *Create a named set.*

Excel shows you a dialog with a new row for every column in your pivot table. Highlight a column and click Delete Row to remove it from the pivot table.

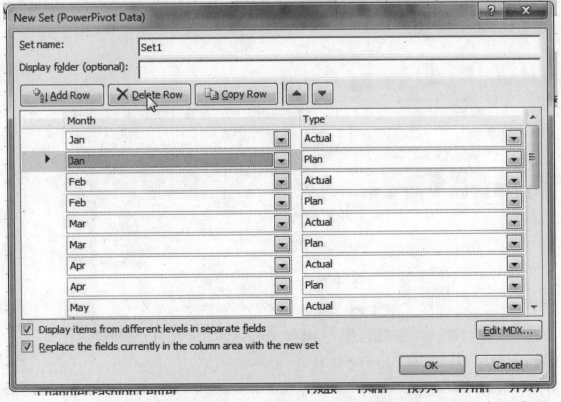

Figure 1011 *You can delete specific columns from the set.*

You eventually end up with a list of only the desired columns.

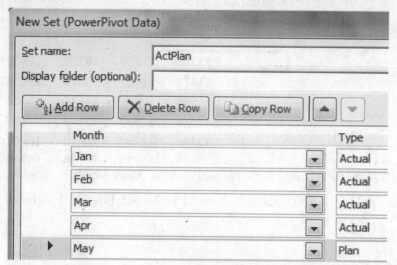

Figure 1012 *Keep deleting columns until only the desired items are left.*

The resulting pivot table is shown below. It is amazing how hard this is in regular pivot tables, but certainly possible with PowerPivot datasets.

Sum of Sales	Column Labels				
	Jan	Feb	Mar	Apr	May
Row Labels	Actual	Actual	Actual	Actual	Plan
Ala Moana	11739	16105	19816	23727	22200
Altamonte Mall	11421	14854	20510	22918	22700
Annapolis Mall	11689	14675	17641	23134	21600

Figure 1013 *The named set leaves an asymmetric pivot table.*

CREATE INTERACTIVE DASHBOARDS WITH POWER VIEW

Power View is an add-in from Microsoft that ships with certain SKUs of Excel 2013 and Office 365. A Power View sheet uses Microsoft SilverLight to create charts, maps, and tables. It reads data from the Power Pivot data model.

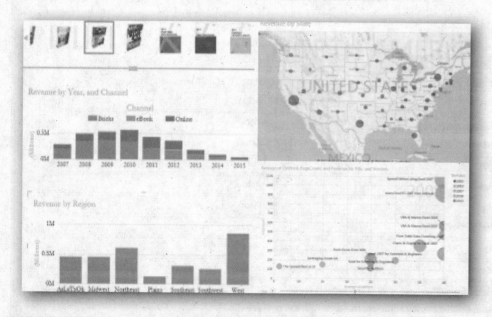

Figure 1014 *Excel data displayed in Power View.*

Read through the next several topics for details on Power View.

LOAD DATA FOR POWER VIEW

Before creating a Power View dashboard, you need to load your data into Power Pivot and create relationships. If you want to display pictures in the dashboard, add a column to your data with a web URL or a local path and filename pointing to the picture.

Also, you want to declare a data category for any fields that represent products or geography. In the Power Pivot window, go to the Advanced Tab and browse through the Data Category dropdown. If you have any fields that match a category, select the column and then choose a category. This step allows your data to appear on a map. For a column that contains a picture file name, choose either Image or Image URL.

After your data is loaded in the Power Pivot model, return to Excel and choose Insert, Power View. Excel will insert a new worksheet with a blank Power View canvas.

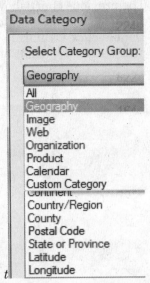

Figure 1015 *Choose a category.*

DELETE THE INITIAL POWER VIEW RANDOM TABLE

When you first open Power View, Excel chooses one table, several columns, and creates a table on the dashboard. It seems like they thought have a completely blank canvas was too confusing. Click inside of this table and click the Delete button to return to a blank canvas.

COLLAPSE THE POWER VIEW FILTER PANE FOR NOW

A quarter of your screen is filled with the Filters pane. You might use Filters later, but for now, collapse this pane using the "<" icon in the top right.

BUILDING DASHBOARD ELEMENTS IN POWER VIEW

To build a new element, click outside of any existing elements, and choose items from the Power View Fields list. Every new element in Power View starts as a table, so you will initially get a pivot table on the canvas.

Click inside the table. On the Design tab, choose a new element type, such as a Column Chart. The resulting chart will be too small, so use one of the 4 resize handles around the element to enlarge it.

There are hidden controls for every element. You can only see the controls when you hover your mouse above the element. In the box above the chart to the right, there are controls to Sort, Filter, or Pop-Out.

You might build a dashboard with 9 tiny charts that are too small to use. The idea is someone would use Pop-Out to enlarge the charts one at a time.

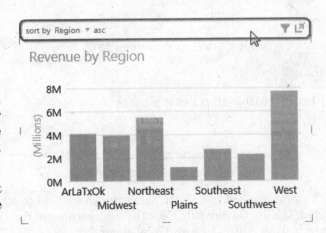

Figure 1016 *Hidden controls*

CREATE A POWER VIEW HIERARCHY

The previous chart showed revenue by Region. In the Axis dropdown, add two more fields: State and City. In the chart, double-click on the West region to have the chart change to show states in the west region. Double-click California to see all of the cities in California. To go back up a level, a new Drill Up icon appears at the top right of the chart.

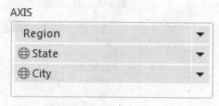

Figure 1017 *Create a hierarchy*

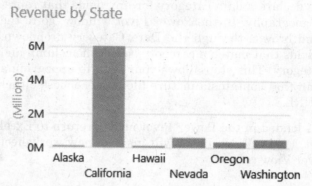

Figure 1018 *Double-click any column to drill down.*

CREATE NEW ELEMENTS ON THE POWER VIEW DASHBOARD

Your first dashboard element is done. You would like to add a new chart or map or table. Drag a field from the Power View Fields to a blank spot on the canvas. A new element will be created there.

If you want to change something in the first element, you have to click inside the element to activate it. Only one element is active at a time. You can visually tell by the four resize handles around the element.

ADD PICTURES TO YOUR POWER VIEW REPORT

If you have an element that is a Table or a Card View, add the ImagePath field to the table and Power View will add the picture of the item to the report.

	Learn Excel 97-2007 from MrExcel	$3,016,759
	Excel Gurus Gone Wild	$212,903
	Pivot Table Data Crunching 2013	$513,842

Figure 1019 *Pictures in a pivot table report!*

FOUR WAYS TO FILTER IN POWER VIEW

There are four ways to filter in Power View.

The first method is a slicer. Drag the slicer field to a blank spot on the canvas. A new table element is created. On the Design tab, click the Slicer icon and the table is converted to a slicer. Note that this slicer does not look anything like an Excel slicer.

The second way to filter is to select any column in any chart on the report. All of the other charts are filtered to that category. The other categories appear, but they are greyed out.

The third way is to use the View option in the Filters pane. The View filter goes back to the original data set and filters records out of that data set. For example, if I set up a view filter to only see records with revenue greater than $1000, the report would filter out 80% of the records in the Power Pivot model and recalculate.

Contrast the View filter with the Chart or Table filter. If you ask for items with over $1,000,000 in revenue, the filter will be applied at the aggregate level. Any products that had a total over $1,000,000 will appear in the report.

REPLICATE A POWER VIEW CHART WITH VERTICAL MULTIPLES

Say that you have a great chart in Power View. You want to produce that chart for each region in the company. Drag the Region field to the Vertical Multiples area of the Power View Fields list. Your chart will be replicated for each region.

Use the Grid Height and Grid Width choices on the Layout tab to control the arrangement of the charts.

YOU HAVE PRACTICALLY NO CONTROL OVER POWER VIEW COLORS

There are dozens of themes in the Power View tab of the ribbon. You will hate them all. There is no way to micro-manage your chart colors like you can in Excel. If you want to change colors for each data point in a chart, it will not happen here.

As this book goes to press, I am awaiting the Excel 2015 beta to see if this situation gets any better.

POWER VIEW ALSO DOES MAPS AND ANIMATED SCATTER CHARTS

A scatter chart can show many dimensions. You have the typical X and Y axis. The size of the bubble and color of the bubble add two more dimensions. Finally, drag a date field to the Play Axis.

When you click the Play button, the points on the map will animate over time.

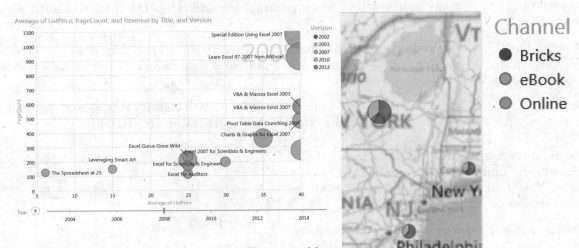

Figure 1020 *Animated Scatter Chart with Time scrubber.*

Figure 1021 *Maps*

PUT A PIVOT TABLE ON A MAP IN EXCEL 2013 POWER MAP

Power Map is a new feature in Excel 2013. If your data includes fields such as Street Address, City, State, Zip, Country, Continent, Latitude or Longitude, you can plot your pivot table on a map. You can then use the mouse to fly through the map, zooming in on various pockets of your data.

Figure 1022 *Analysis of home sales in a neighborhood.*

To get started, select any data set that has a geographic component. On the Excel 2013 ribbon, choose Power Map.

Excel will use Bing to geocode each data point into a location on the map. If your data has obvious headings like City, State, Power Map will figure those out. But if your field names do not make sense, you need to choose a geography level for each field.

Gotcha: if you have a field such as "123 Main Street", be sure to classify this as a Street and not an Address. Only use Address if your field is like "1060 W Addison St, Chicago, IL 60613".

To build the map, choose from Stacked Column, Clustered Column, Bubble, Heat Map, or Region. Note that region only works for State or Country data.

Add a numeric field for Height. To control colors, add a text field for Category. To animate the map over time, drag a date field to the Time area.

The dropdown for Height offers to let you Sum, Average, or No Aggregation.

There are two dropdowns for Time. If you have daily data, change the Time dropdown to Day. Just above the Time field, a smaller dropdown allows you to choose if data appears for an instant, accumulates over time, or stays until another value replaces the first..

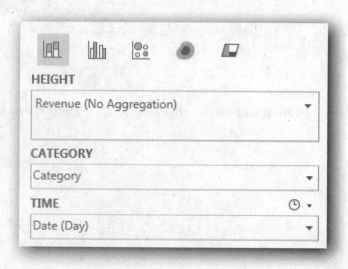

Figure 1023 *Control the map here.*

TRICKS FOR NAVIGATING THE MAP IN POWER MAP

You can easily fly through the map to focus on any part of the map:

- Click on the map and drag to pan the map.
- Roll the wheel mouse towards you to zoom out.
- Roll the wheel mouse towards you to zoom in.
- Hold down Alt and drag the mouse up or down to tip the map up or down.
- Hold down Alt and drag the map left or right to rotate the map.

Figure 1024 *View too high to see height.t*

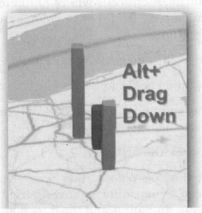

Figure 1025 *View from lower.*

Figure 1026 *Rotate..*

FINE-TUNING POWER MAP

I've been using Power Map since the first beta. Igor Peev and the Power Map team have hidden a lot of good settings inside of the product, even if they are not always evident.

For example, if your data set is ultra-local, down to the point where you are analyzing each house on a street, the default width of the columns is too wide. You can not see the detail for each house, as each column is as wide as a city block.

To fix the problem, click the Cog Wheel Icon in the Field List. Then, click Layer Options. You will find a Thickness setting. Change this to 10% and you will be able to see data for each house on the street.

Also in this panel, you can control the color for each category, and control if negatives are shown or not.

Another item that needs editing is the box that shows the current date. It usually starts out showing date and time, even though your data might only be at the date level.

Right-click the box, choose Edit. You can now choose a new font, color, and date format.

To replace the map with a satellite image, open the Themes dropdown and choose the second theme.

An icon in the Ribbon lets you add labels to the map. This adds city names, street names, and so on.

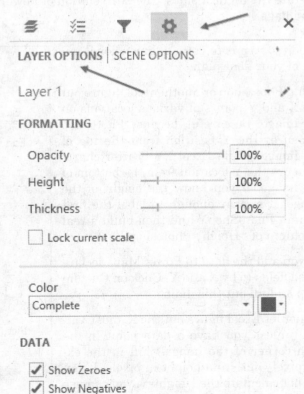

3

CREATING A VIDEO FROM POWER MAP

Power Map will let you tell a story by stringing together a series of scenes. You might show the whole country for 10 seconds, then zoom in to Florida and fly over Florida for a few seconds. Then fly to NYC and hover for a few seconds before flying to Southern California.

When you are finished, you can have Power Map render the tour as a movie.

Here are some tips:

Do not put a Date field on your map. If you do, each scene will re-animate the time animation. Perhaps you want to start with a zoomed out view with a time field. Let the map animate. Then, remove the time field and add scenes as you zoom in to each location.

To build a tour, start with the map zoomed out and click Add Scene.

Then, zoom in to the first area of interest and click Add Scene.

If you need to explain one point in a scene, right-click and choose Add Annotation. Add the Scene and then remember to remove the annotation before the next scene.

In the Tour Editor pane on the left side, click the first scene.

In the Field List on the right side, click the Cog Wheel, then Scene Options. Add an Effect so you have some motion during the scene. If you need to pause for a longer period at one scene, increase the Scene Duration. Keeping adding additional scenes and adjusting the duration.

Test the tour by clicking Play Tour.

When the tour looks good, choose Create Video. Note that it can take almost an hour to render a short video.

USE AN ALTERNATE MAP FOR POWER MAP

Maybe you want to plot quality performance in a manufacturing plant. Or which displays in a retail store generate the highest sales. The 2015 edition of Power Map lets you replaced the Globe with any alternate map image.

The first step is to get a 2-dimensional image of your floor plan.

Using Photoshop or another tool, figure out the X and Y points of various locations on the image. Be careful, because Photoshop measures the Y position from the top of the image, while Excel XY Scatter charts measure the Y location from the bottom of the image. If you know the height of the image, it is easy enough to label the first column PhotoShopY and then build a real Y column of =Height-Photoshop Y.

As you add the data to Power Map, declare those fields to by X and Y. Click on Custom Map and fill out this dialog.

Do not let Excel figure out the X and Y values (unless you have a data point in the each corner of the image.) Fill in the exact pixel width and height in pixels. If you did not calculate the Height-Y, you can use Flip Axis for the Y.

Upload your picture.

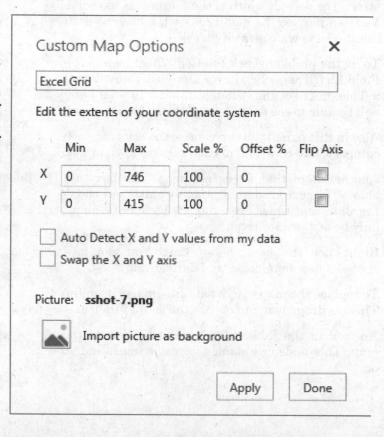

Custom Map Options   ✕

Excel Grid

Edit the extents of your coordinate system

	Min	Max	Scale %	Offset %	Flip Axis
X	0	746	100	0	☐
Y	0	415	100	0	☐

☐ Auto Detect X and Y values from my data

☐ Swap the X and Y axis

Picture: **sshot-7.png**

Import picture as background

Apply   Done

The result is a flat map where you can use the navigation keys to fly through your shop floor, examining the quality scores.

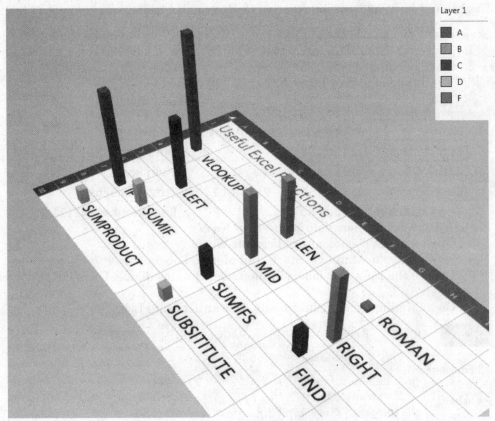

Figure 1027 *My "shop floor" is Excel....*

FILTERING IN POWER MAP

The Excel 2015 edition of Power Map offers a filter feature. There is one oddity: the Filter dropdown will never show more than 50 items. If you need something beyond the first 50 items, you have to use the Search box.

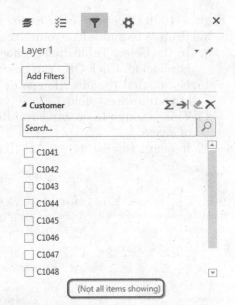

Figure 1028 *Filtering in Power Map.*

EXCEL DATA TO MAILING LABELS IN WORD

Problem: I have address information in Excel and I have to make mailing labels.

Strategy: You can use the Mail Merge in Microsoft Word to make the labels. Here are the steps:

1. Make sure your data in Excel is set up with each address going across a row.
2. Have headings in row 1.
3. Close the file in Excel.

	A	B	C	D
1	**Name**	**Address 1**	**Address 2**	**Address 3**
2	Ken Medina	118 5th St		Dinosaur, CO 81633
3	Cathy Woods	316 Broadway Ave		Twin Rocks, PA 15960
4	Dave Schmidt	389 3rd St	Apt 2	Troy, VT 05868
5	Ken Patterson	504 5th Rd		Beaumont. KY 42124

Figure 1029 *Set up your data properly in Excel.*

4. Open a blank document in Microsoft Word.
5. In Word, go to Mailings, Start Mail Merge, Labels.
6. Choose the right size labels in the Label Options dialog. Click OK. You get a document full of blank labels.
7. Go to Mailings, Select Recipients, Use an Existing List....

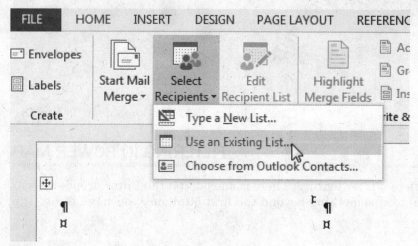

Figure 1030 *Choose an existing list.*

8. Browse to and select your Excel file.
9. In the Select Table dialog, choose Sheet1$. Make sure First Row of Data Contains Column Headers is selected. Click OK. You now a confusing <<Next Record>> in all but the first label.
10. Notice that the insertion point is in the first label. Go to Insert Merge Field and choose the first line of your address field.
11. This is tough to do, but carefully press Shift+Enter to go to the next line without inserting a bunch of space.
12. Repeat steps 10, 11, 10, 11, 10 until you have all four lines of the address in the label.

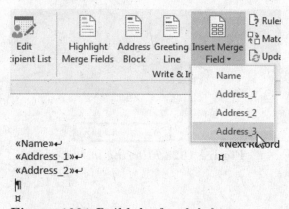

Figure 1031 *Build the first label.*

13. If you want any special font, add that formatting to the first label.

14. Press the Update Labels button to repeat your fields in all of the labels of the sheet.
15. Choose Finish & Merge, Edit Individual Documents. You will have labels from the Excel data.

Gotcha: Step 14 seems to be the non-obvious step that trips most people up.

EXCEL 2013 ALLOWS SLICERS ON REGULAR TABLES

New in Excel 2013, you can filter a regular data set, provided you convert the data to a table using Ctrl+T first.

	A	B	C	D	E	F	G
1	Region	Product	Date	Customer	Reven	Pr	Sec
2	Central	XYZ	1/1/2015	Ford	22810	12590	Manufacturing
9	Central	XYZ	1/10/2015	Wal-Mart	21438	12240	Retail
32	Central	XYZ	2/16/2015	Boeing	16936	8760	Manufacturing
36	Central	XYZ	2/20/2015	Wal-Mart	23810	13590	Retail
39	Central	XYZ	2/23/2015	Wal-Mart	11525	6415	Retail

Figure 1032 *Convert a regular data set to a table using Ctrl+T*

From the Table Tools Design tab, choose Insert Slicer. Select the fields for the slicers. Use the Slicer Tools Design tab to change the number of columns, colors, and so on.

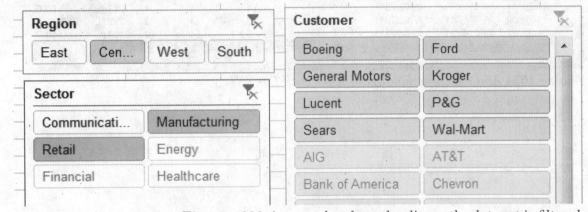

Figure 1033 *As you select from the slicers, the data set is filtered.*

WEB QUERIES FAIL WITH WEB 2.0

Problem: The previous editions of this book showed how to pull stock quotes from the web using Data, From Web. This worked great every five minutes for a couple years, but then it stopped working.

Strategy: The old web query technology was designed to get a table from a static HTML page. Now, with javascript and flash and HTML5, the web query is often not seeing any tables on the page.

If you need to get data from the web, download the free Power Query add-in and use the From Web option in Power Query.

USE EASY-XL FOR DATA WRANGLING

Problem: I regularly have to use the techniques in this book to compare lists, split data, do VLOOKUPs. I hate Excel. It is too intimidating.

Strategy: Check out the Easy-XL utility from MrExcel. It seems that every Excel book author has a suite of utilities these days, but Easy-XL is not designed to help you format your worksheet. It is designed to help you do the hard data analysis tasks with ease.

In all, it adds 50 features to Excel.

Check out a free 30-day trial at www.Easy-XL.com.

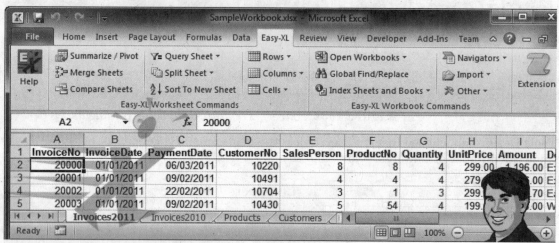

Figure 1034 *Add new functionality to Excel with Easy-XL.*

PART 4

MAKING THINGS LOOK GOOD

Problem: I have to create a bunch of charts based on data I already have in Excel. How can I speed up the process?

	A	B	C	D	E	F	G	H
2		Jan-16	Feb-16	Mar-16	Apr-16	May-16	Jun-16	Jul-16
3	East	12,000	13,200	14,520	15,972	17,569	18,825	20,307
4	Central	17,000	19,550	22,483	25,855	29,733	32,455	35,934
5	West	8,000	8,400	8,820	9,261	9,724	10,134	10,579
6								

Figure 1035 *Select the data including the headings.*

Strategy: You can create a chart with one keystroke! Select the data, including the headings and row labels and press Alt+F1.

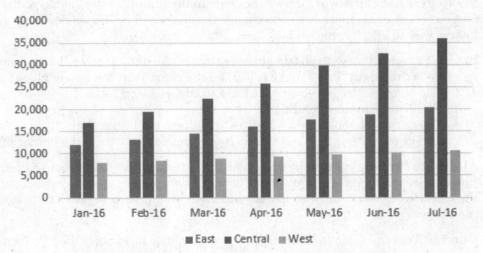

Figure 1036 *Press Alt+F1.*

The data will be charted as an embedded chart on the current sheet, as shown above.

Gotcha: This trick is awesome if you need to create clustered column charts with the legend on the right. The odds says that you have to create something else. Use the next topic to change the chart that you get with Alt+F1.

TEACH EXCEL YOUR FAVORITE CHART

Problem: The previous trick doesn't help me. I have to create line charts, legend at the top, with a title, scale in thousands.

Strategy: Create one chart with all of the customizations that you would normally make. (See details throughout the following three dozen topics.) Save your favorite chart as a template. Set that template as the default chart.

To save the current chart as a template, right-click the chart. Choose Save as Template....

Give the chart template a name describing the chart.

You still have to make this new template be the default chart that you get when you press Alt+F1. Click the Change Chart Type icon in the Design tab of the ribbon. Open the Templates folder on the left. In Excel 2013, right-click the desired template and choose Set as Default Chart. In Excel 2010, left-click any chart thumbnail and click the Set As Default Chart at the bottom of the Change Chart Type dialog.

Gotcha: If there are multiple templates in the folder, you have to hover over each template to see the template name. They are arranged alphabetically, so that might help.

Result: When you select data and press Alt+F1, you will get this chart instead of the clustered column chart.

Gotcha: the actual text of the chart title is not saved in the template. Microsoft says this is a privacy concern. Since templates can be shared, you might accidentally create a template with sensitive content and save that as a template.

Additional Details: You can share templates with others. When you click Manage Templates in the Change Chart Type dialog, you will see the Templates folder. Templates are stored with a .crtx extension. Save the template in the same folder on your co-workers computer.

MOVE A CHART

Problem: I created a chart and it is in the wrong place. How do I move it?

Strategy: Microsoft always draws the chart in the middle of the visible grid. If you just selected A1:E5000 for your chart data, there is a good chance the chart will be drawn down in row 4980. Cut and paste is the fastest way to get the chart some place.

In fact, I've ended up with charts at the bottom of the data so often, I can almost fix it with my eyes closed:
1. Select the data. Press Alt+F1. Realize the chart is in the wrong place.
2. The chart is already selected. Ctrl+x to cut.
3. Ctrl+Home to move to the top.
4. Select the cell where you want the top-left corner of the chart.
5. Ctrl+v to paste in A1. You can then use the mouse to drag the border of the chart to the right place.

Alternate Strategy: I usually end up at the bottom of the data because I am using Ctrl+Shift+Down Arrow to select the data. If I could start using Ctrl+* instead, I would select the data and stay at the top of the worksheet. You could also use the old method and then press Ctrl+period twice to move to the top of the range.

Gotcha: There is a Move Chart icon. You really only need this when you want to create one of those antique full-screen chart sheets that were popularized by Lotus 1-2-3 in 1983. Some people like that these charts print on a full sheet of paper, so if you need to move the chart to its own sheet, use the Move Chart icon.

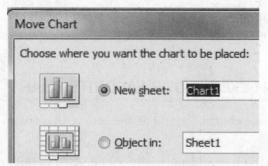

Figure 1037 *Using New Sheet inserts a special chart sheet.*

COPY A CHART DETACHED FROM THE DATA

Problem: I want to make a copy of the current chart, detached from the data. I have to chart 100 customers, and I want a quick way to move to the next customer, copy the chart, move to the next customer, copy the chart, and so on.

Strategy: There are two different ways to go. Both methods are covered here.

Is the chart perfectly formatted the way that you want it to be? Will you never have to be changed? If this is true, then you can very quickly copy the chart and paste as a picture.

If you need to be able to edit the colors used in the chart, add labels, and so on, then you will want to convert the series formula to values.

To convert a chart to a picture, use these steps:
1. Click on the chart.
2. Ctrl+C to copy
3. Click in a new location.
4. Press the Right-Click key. Type U.

Figure 1038 *This key is to the right of the spacebar.*

Gotcha: With the pictures, you can never use the chart tools to change the formatting of the chart. If you need to do that, use the following method.
1. Click on one series in the chart. Click on one of the columns, bar, or markers in the chart to select the series.
2. You will see a =SERIES formula in the formula bar.
3. Click in the formula bar and select the entire formula.

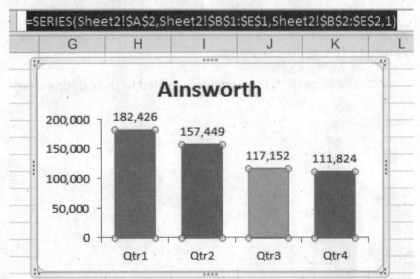

Figure 1039 *Click on a data point to show the SERIES formula.*

4. Press the F9 key to convert the formula to an array.
5. Press Enter.

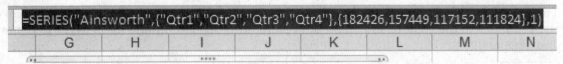

Figure 1040 *F9 converts the formula to values.*

You now have a chart based on static values, but you can still use all the charting tools to format the chart.

Gotcha: If you have three series in the chart, you have to repeat steps 1 through 5 for each series in the chart.

ADD NEW DATA TO A CHART

Problem: I need to create 12 charts every month. It is a real pain to re-create these charts every month.

Strategy: You can easily add data to an existing chart.

The first method is to copy the data and paste it on the chart. Here's how:
1. Type the new data for your chart adjacent to the old data. Be sure to add a heading.
2. Select the new data, including the heading.
3. Ctrl+C to copy the new data.

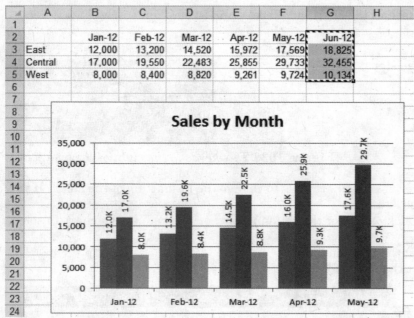

◢	A	B	C	D	E	F	G	H
1								
2		Jan-12	Feb-12	Mar-12	Apr-12	May-12	Jun-12	
3	East	12,000	13,200	14,520	15,972	17,569	18,825	
4	Central	17,000	19,550	22,483	25,855	29,733	32,455	
5	West	8,000	8,400	8,820	9,261	9,724	10,134	
6								

Figure 1041 *Copy the new data.*
4. Click on the chart.
5. Ctrl+V to paste. The new data is added to the existing chart.

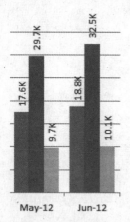

Figure 1042 *New data added.*

The second method is to click the chart and find the blue outline around your data. You can drag one of the right handles to the right to add a new data point, drag the left handle to the right to remove a data point, or drag an edge to chart a different range.

Jun-12	Jul-12
18,825	20,307
32,455	35,934
10,134	10,579

Figure 1043 *Drag the blue handle to add data*

Additional Details: If you need to show a rolling six months, after adding July to the data, you can drag the blue handle from B5 to the right. You will remove January from the chart.

Additional Details: Dragging the blue outline can simplify the task of creating many charts as described in the previous topic. Create the first chart and copy it. When you select the first chart, one customer is outlined in blue.

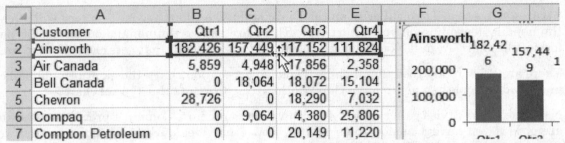

◢	A	B	C	D	E	F	G
1	Customer	Qtr1	Qtr2	Qtr3	Qtr4	**Ainsworth** 182,42 157,44	
2	Ainsworth	182,426	157,449	117,152	111,824	6 9 1	
3	Air Canada	5,859	4,948	17,856	2,358	200,000	
4	Bell Canada	0	18,064	18,072	15,104		
5	Chevron	28,726	0	18,290	7,032	100,000	
6	Compaq	0	9,064	4,380	25,806	0	
7	Compton Petroleum	0	0	20,149	11,220		

Figure 1044 *Drag the blue box to a new row.*

Drag the edge of the blue box to a new customer. The chart will update. Note that if you drag the blue box, the green box will move with the blue box.

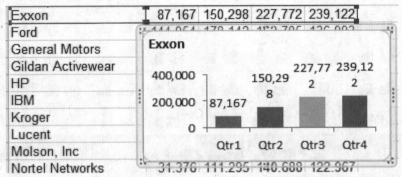

Figure 1045 *Drop the blue box on Exxon and the chart redraws.*

EXCEL 2013 OFFERS EASY CHART FORMATTING

After you create a chart in Excel 2013, click the Paintbrush icon to the right of the chart. Ten designs will appear. Choose a design. There is nothing particularly new here - all of the formatting choices were available in Excel 2010. What is new is the combinations of the formatting choices. In one episode of the MrExcel podcast, I set out to replicate a 2013 style in 2010. It was possible, but it took 56 steps.

4

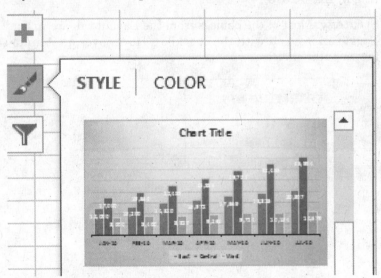

Figure 1046 *Quickly apply a style in Excel 2013 using the Paintbrush icon.*

BEGIN EXCEL 2010 FORMATTING ON DESIGN

Problem: I created a chart in Excel 2010. I want to format the chart. Where do I begin?

Strategy: There are two galleries on the Design tab. The Chart Layouts gallery will offer four to twelve thumbnails depending on your chart type. These are twelve thumbnails out of 50,000 possible ways to format the chart. At best, you might be able to find a thumbnail that gets close to what you want.

There are a few really good thumbnails. If you have a column chart, the eighth thumbnail creates a histogram. Most people can not find the Gap Width setting to create this type of chart.

Next, the Chart Styles gallery offers 48 formats for your chart. Column 1 provides grayscale charts which are good if you have a monochrome printer. Row 6 provides dark backgrounds which work great with PowerPoint. Column 2 offers multi-color charts. Columns 3 through 8 offer shades of the six theme colors.

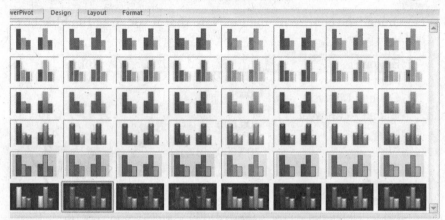

Figure 1047 *Choose from colors on the Styles gallery.*

Additional Details. You can choose new sets of complementary colors by using the Theme or Color dropdown on the Excel 2010 Page Layout tab.

THE CHART LAYOUT TAB IS MISSING IN EXCEL 2013

Problem: What happened to the Layout tab in Excel 2013? This is where I did most of my chart formatting in Excel 2010.

Strategy: Most of the choices from the Layout tab are in the Plus icon to the right of the Excel 2013 chart. Toggle an item on with the checkbox. Hover over an item to see a triangle leading to a flyout with more a few popular choices.

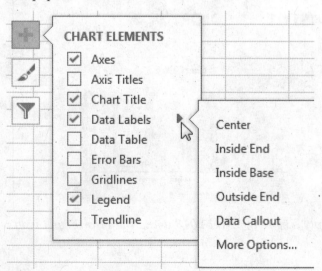

Figure 1048 *In Excel 2013, format most chart elements from the "+" icon.*

It is somewhat odd that not everything from the Excel 2010 layout tab is in this menu. If you need to add Up/Down Bars or High-Low lines, you have to go to the Design tab and open the Add Chart Element dropdown.

FORMATTING CHARTS IN EXCEL 2010 WITH LAYOUT

I try to do most of my chart formatting on the Layout tab of the ribbon.

"Try" is the important word there.

There are 15 dropdowns on the layout tab that cover the major elements of the chart. So far, so good.

Figure 1049 *Dropdowns to format the chart.*

Each dropdown leads to a tiny menu with a few popular choices. Sometimes the choices in the menu are useful. Other times, what you really need is not in the menu. However, the bottom item in each menu is for More Choices. Choose this item to get to the Format dialog box with all of the choices.

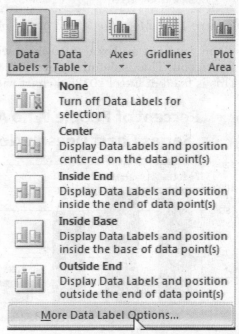

Figure 1050 *The label settings that you remember from Excel 2003 are hidden beneath the More Data Label Options.*

I assume that 90% of the time that I go to the Layout tab, I will have to skip the menu choices and go to the More Options choice.

LEGEND AT THE TOP

Problem: Excel always adds a legend on the right side of the chart. Visualization gurus say the legend should be at the top or left of the chart. You don't even need a legend for a one-series chart.

Strategy: Use Layout, Legend, Show Legend at Top.

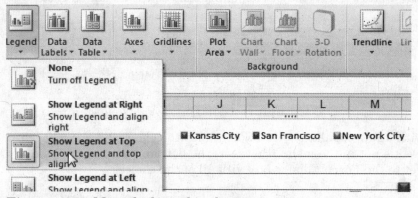

Figure 1051 *Move the legend to the top.*

When you have an Excel 2010 chart with a single series, Excel adds the series name as both the title and the legend. This is definitely overkill. Click the Legend and then press the Delete key on your keyboard. This is fixed in Excel 2013 - a chart with a single series will not have a legend.

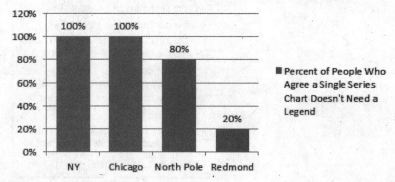

Figure 1052 *Delete the legend when you have only one series.*

THE 2010 FORMAT DIALOG BOX IS A TASK PANE IN 2013

If you would double-click any chart element in Excel 2010, a Format dialog box would appear. Do the same thing in Excel 2013 and a Task Pane appears on the right side of the screen. While the 2010 Format dialog box was labelled with many categories, the 2013 task pane is labelled with a series of icons.

My general rule: always start with the Column Chart icon - the best choices are often there.

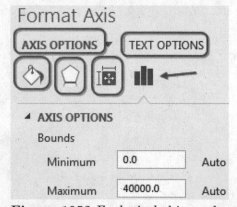

Figure 1053 *Each circled item shows different choices below.*

DISPLAY AN AXIS IN MILLIONS

Problem: My numbers are in millions. I am wasting a lot of space showing all of those zeros along the vertical axis.

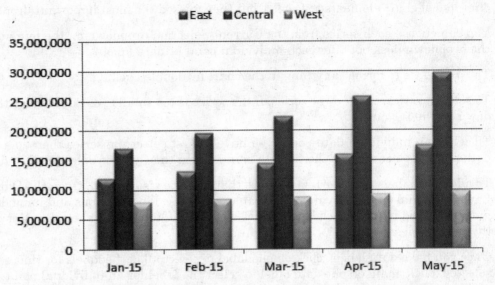

Figure 1054 *The zeroes along the vertical axis take a lot of space.*

Strategy: Double-click the numbers in the axis labels. In the resulting settings area, find the Display Units dropdown and choose Millions.

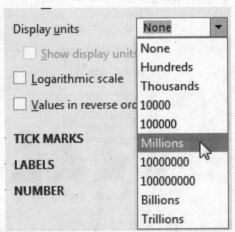

Figure 1055 *Change the axis Display Units.*

Results: Excel removes the zeros and adds a label indicating that the numbers are in millions.

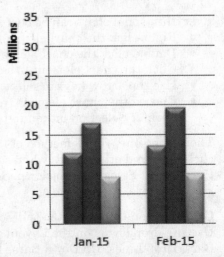

Figure 1056 *The zeroes are replaced with "Millions".*

SELECT ANYTHING ON A CHART TO FORMAT

Problem: I need to further customize a chart. How do I format a series or a single data point?

Strategy: I certainly understand the frustration. The Excel 2010 Layout tab and the Excel 2013 Plus icon offer lots of chart elements to format, but they missed the most important dropdown; the one for series.

You can choose each series from the Current Selection dropdown on the left side of the Format tabs. But the dropdown does not offer each individual point or data label.

The answer is to format anything in the chart by double-clicking.

To select a series, click on the series. If the series is too small to click, then use the Current Selection dropdown on the Layout tab.

To select an individual data point, you have to first select the series then do a second single-click on the data point. You can never choose data points using the Current Selection dropdown.

To add data labels to a chart, make sure that no series is selected. Open the Data Labels dropdown on the Layout tab and choose any item. You can even choose More Options and immediately click OK. The alternative method is to right-click one series and choose Add Data Labels, but this will not add data labels to the other series.

Once you have data labels, click on one label to select all of the labels for that series. Once data labels are selected, click again on one data label to select the label for an individual point.

Additional Details: If you click in a chart and start pressing the right arrow, you will cycle through every element that can be formatted. Watch the Current Selection dropdown to see what you are selecting.

In the chart below, Excel cycles through 46 separate items. In contrast, the Current Selection dropdown only offers 14 items. What is the difference between 46 and 14? The arrow keys will select each individual entry in the legend, each data point, each data label, even the "Millions" tag next to the axis.

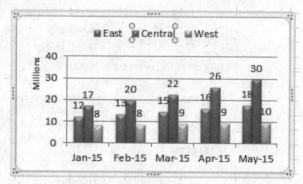

Figure 1057 *Using arrow keys to cycle will include each legend entry.*

Once you have selected something, use Ctrl+1, or the Format Selection button to access the Format dialog box.

Everything on a chart can be customized. You can use any of these methods:
- Right-click the chart element and choose Format
- Double-click the chart element
- Click the chart element to select it and then press Ctrl+1
- Use the arrow keys to select an element and press Ctrl+1
- Choose the chart element from the Current Selection dropdown on Format tab and then click the Format Selection button in the same group

There is no one "right" method of these five. There are times when the only way to format something is by clicking it and other times when something is nearly invisible and the only way you can format it is from the Current Selection dropdown. So you need to be ready to use whichever method will get you to the correct element.

Gotcha: None of the methods described above will let you access an element that is not yet on the chart. Use the dropdowns on the Layout tab to add elements such as Chart Title, Axis Title, Data Table, Error Bars, Drop Lines, Up/Down Bars, Trendlines.

Say that you want to change the color of just the May central region column. The first click on the central region column will select all of the central region columns. A second single-click will select just the one column. You right-click to access Format Data Point.

THE FORMAT DIALOG BOX OFFERS A NEW TRICK

Problem: I was formatting the chart axis, using the Format Axis dialog box. I was working in the Axis Options category. I accidentally clicked outside the dialog and clicked one of the columns in the chart. All of a sudden, I was transported to the Format Data Series dialog. What is going on?

Strategy: There is a single Format dialog box for every drawing object. While the dialog is displayed, you can click on any new object on the worksheet, and the Format dialog box will change to offer settings for that object.

In a chart, you can display the Format dialog once and keep changing the formatting for other elements. For example, you might start formatting the axis. You can then choose Series 1 from the Current Selection dropdown and format that series. You can then choose Chart Title from the dropdown and format the title. When you are finished, you close the Format dialog box.

Additional Details: You can even access ribbon commands while the Format dialog is displayed. For example, you might need to select Layout, Chart Title, Centered Overlay Title to add a title to a chart. You can do this without closing the Format dialog box.

USE MEANINGFUL CHART TITLES

Problem: Excel tends to add boring chart titles. A chart title such as Sales or Profit merely labels the data in the chart. The title is nothing more than a legend in a large font. How can I make my chart titles more meaningful?

Strategy: It's a good idea to add a meaningful title that guides the reader. As an analyst, you can spot trends in the data, and you can point out something interesting in the chart by using the title.

One annoying problem is that you seemingly don't have a lot of control over the chart title formatting. Follow these steps to create a long title:

1. Select Layout, Chart Title, Above Chart. Excel adds the title Chart Title in a large font above the chart.

Gotcha: To edit the chart title, try triple-clicking the chart title. This should select all of the characters in the chart title. Alternatively, drag to select the characters in the chart title. If you just single-click the chart title and start typing, you will only see the title in the formula bar until you press enter.

2. Select the characters in the chart title using the mouse.
3. On the Home tab of the ribbon, choose a 14-point font size. Choose the Left Align icon.
4. Type a title such as Revenue Doubled in December.
5. Press Enter. Excel will move to a second line in the title.
6. Before typing the second line, change the font to 12-point on the Home tab.
7. Type the subtitle Post-holiday sales dropped GP% to 42%.
8. Click on the border of the title to exit Edit mode.
9. Drag the border of the title to the left in order to align the title with the left edge of the chart.

Results: You've added a title to guide the reader's understanding of the chart.

Figure 1058 *Guide the reader with a title and subtitle.*

4

Gotcha: The border around the title has only four handles. This means you can move the title, but you cannot resize it. In step 5, you were able to force the title box to add a second line. However, Excel can have a mind of its own and may decide to add a third line. It would seem that you could correct this if you had the ability to resize the title box. Instead, you would have to select characters within the title and choose a smaller font in order to coax the title back to the correct number of lines. Alternatively, delete the title and add a text box from Insert, Shapes while the chart is selected. You have more control with a text box.

AVOID 3-D CHART TYPES

Problem: I like the look of 3-D chart types, but they don't seem to be accurate.

Strategy: 3-D chart types are not accurate, so you should try to avoid them. The 3-D effect usually ends up introducing errors into the chart.

Have you ever taken a photography class? The problem with a wide-angle lens is that anything in the foreground appears unusually large. 3-D pie charts have the same problem. The wedges at the front of the chart get more pixels than the wedges at the back of the chart. For example, both charts below are plotting the same data. This organization is spending 34% of its budget on administration. If you are the scientific review board, trying to argue that the administration slice is too large, rotate it around to the front, as in the bottom chart. In the bottom chart, 155% more pixels appear in the administration slice than in the research slice.

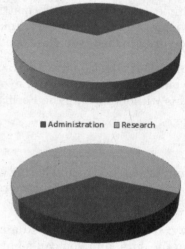

Figure 1059 *Wedges at the front of a 3-D pie appears unrealistically large.*

3-D column charts are not accurate, either. In the top chart below, you can see that each column is above a nearby gridline. Turn that chart into a 3-D column chart, and none of the columns actually extend to the neighboring gridline. People wonder if they should look at the front or the back of the column. I say it doesn't matter because neither the front nor the back reach to the gridline.

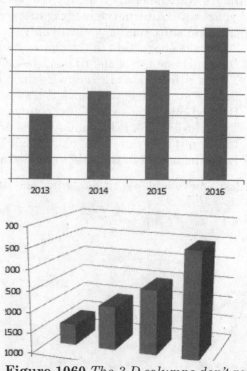

Figure 1060 *The 3-D columns don't reach the gridlines.*

You should never use cone or pyramid charts. The categories at the top of each cone get far fewer pixels than the categories at the bottom. In the next figure, the 34% spent on administration seems practically nonexistent.

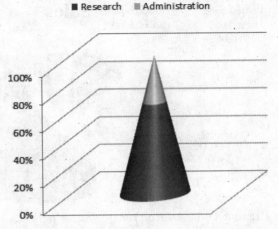

Figure 1061 *Never use cone or pyramid charts.*

PREVENT THE DROP TO ZERO

Problem: I've built formulas to create a chartable range. I want to show how the fund balances have been increasing for three years. All of a sudden, the points for future months look like someone spent all the money, dropping to zero.

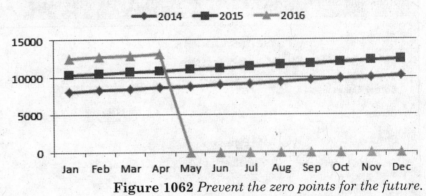

Figure 1062 *Prevent the zero points for the future.*

Strategy: Zero cells will be plotted. Empty cells or #N/A! cells will not be plotted. Change your formulas to put an NA() instead of 0. Say that you are building the chart range with =SUMIF(). Start to use =IF(SUMIF()=0,NA(),SUMIF()). The chart will look much better.

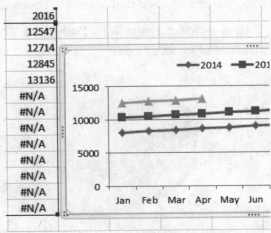

Figure 1063 *Use #N/A instead of zero.*

It is ironic that 99% of the time, you are trying to avoid the #N/A. In this case, however it solves the problem.

EXPLODE ONE SLICE OF THE PIE

Problem: What is the point of an exploded pie? It doesn't look any better than a pie.

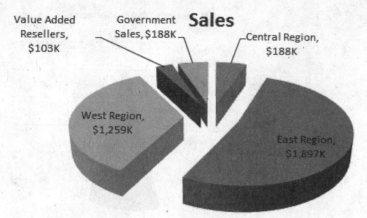

Figure 1064 *Adding white spaces between wedges doesn't add anything.*

Strategy: It is better to explode one slice of a pie. If you want to draw the reader's attention to one slice of the pie, bring that slice to the front of the chart and explode that slice of the pie.

1. Identify the pie slice that you want to highlight.
2. Right-click the pie and choose Format Data Series.
3. Use the Rotation slider to bring that slice of the pie to the 4 o'clock position. There is more room for the pie slice at that point.

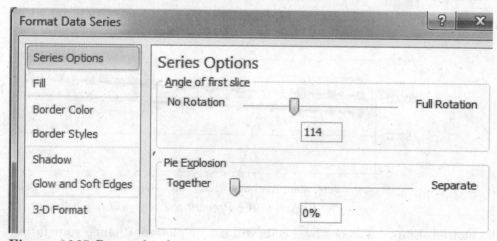

Figure 1065 *Rotate the chart.*

4. In the chart, do a single click twice on the wedge to be exploded.
5. Click and drag that wedge out from the center of the pie.

Value Added Resellers Debuted This Year
Accounted for 3% of Sales

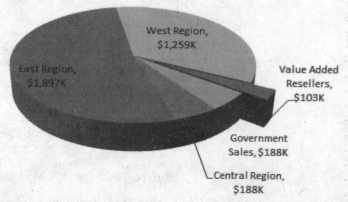

Figure 1066 *Explode one slice of the pie to call attention to that slice..*

MOVE SMALL PIE SLICES TO SECOND CHART

Problem: All of the tiny pie slices really make the chart hard to comprehend.

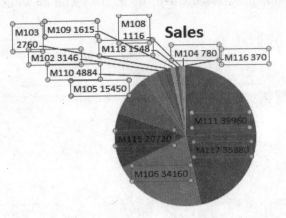

Figure 1067 *Everything under 10% is noise.*

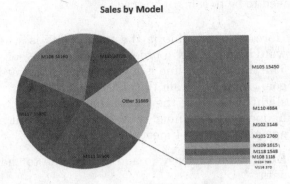

Figure 1068 *The secondary chart shows detail of all the small slices.*

Strategy: Excel offers two chart types that will take the small wedges to a secondary chart. To make these look right, you should always plan on tweaking the settings.

Choose the pie chart. Select Design, Change Chart Type. Choose the Bar of Pie icon.

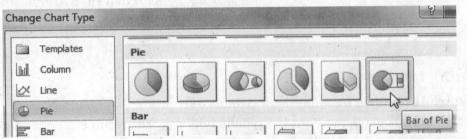

Figure 1069 *There must be a better name.*

Double-click the secondary chart and choose Format. You have choices on how Excel will split points to the secondary axis. The first dropdown offers Position, Value, Percentage Value, and Custom. With custom, you can choose each data point and specify if it is in the first or second plot. An easier choice is to choose Percentage Value. Move everything that is below 10% to the secondary plot.

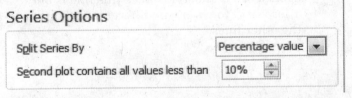

Figure 1070 *Adjust which items are in secondary plot.*

You can control the size of the secondary plot. It starts at 75% of the size of the pie. If those small slices are unimportant, make it smaller. However, if you need to see the detail of those small items, you can go up to 200% of the size of the pie chart.

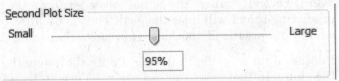

Figure 1071 *These percentages are relative to the first pie.*

Gotcha: I had to choose individual labels near the bottom of the column and resize just those labels to prevent overlapping. To select individual labels, you can click one label to select all labels, then a second click to select one label. Then, use the right arrow key to move from label to label.

ADD A TRENDLINE TO A CHART

Problem: In his book Success Made Easy, retail guru Ron Martin suggests using a daily chart to track your progress toward a goal. His typical chart shows your progress toward the goal as well as where you need to be to remain on track.

Here, the thin line is the track. This is where I would need to be in order to finish by the set goal. The thick, wavy line is my actual work toward the goal. I can see from the chart that I am currently slightly ahead of the track. However, what would happen if I continued to work at my current average pace? Would I meet the goal?

Excel makes it easy to add a trendline to charted data.

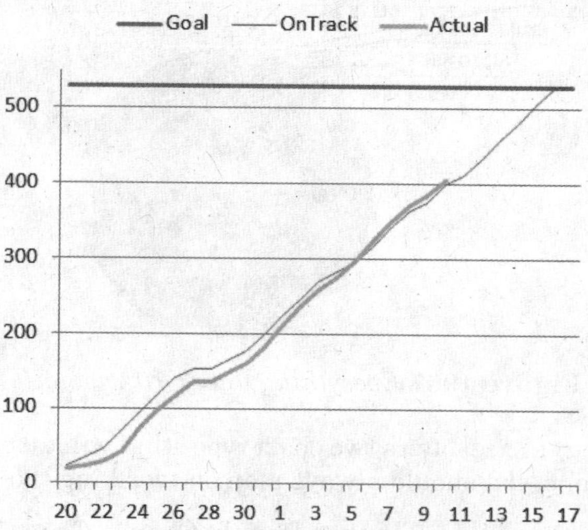

1. Right-click the graphed line for actual results. From the menu that appears, choose Add Trendline.

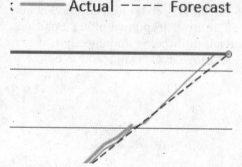

Figure 1072 *Actuals are barely ahead of the On Track line.*

Figure 1073 *Add a trendline to the Actuals line.*

2. Excel displays the Format Trendline dialog. There are a few settings to change in this dialog. Go to the Trendline Name section. Change the name to Custom. Type a name such as Forecast. Keep the dialog open.

3. Choose Line Style from the left navigation. Open the Dash Type dropdown and choose a dashed or dotted style. Since this line is only a forecast, you want to differentiate it from the other lines.

The result is a dotted line that shows the predicted results if you continue at your current pace.

Figure 1074 *Excel projects your final results based on past actuals.*

As you continue to plug in actual data, the trendline will redraw. Seeing the forecast line predict a sizable miss usually causes me to really put it into hyperdrive for the next few days. A couple of days of above-average activity causes the actual line to go above the track line. Nevertheless, the dotted trendline is still predicting that I will miss the goal. That is because the trendline sees all those days early in the month when I did practically nothing. It predicts that those days might happen again.

In other data sets, the chart might only show actuals, with the last actual appearing at the right edge of the chart. In that case, you can use the Format Trendline dialog to specify that the trendline should predict forward a certain number of periods.

SEE DETAIL ON LARGE & SMALL DATA POINTS

For our monthly sales and operations planning meeting, I plot the forecast and actual for 30 model lines. Some of the models sell 30,000 a month and some sell 300 a month. No one can make out the detail on 80% of the models.

Strategy: Use a Log scale. In a Log scale, the distance from 10 to 100 is the same as the distance from 1,000 to 10,000. This lets you zoom in on the smaller items.

1. Choose Layout, Axes, Primary Vertical Axis, Show Axis with a Log Scale.

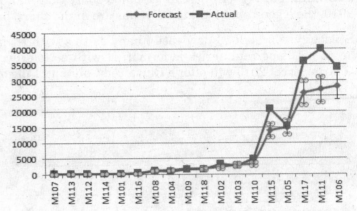

Figure 1075 *The first 12 models are too small to see.*

The first two gridlines on the chart include no data points. Because the purpose of the chart is to see if the forecast was within 15% of the actuals, it would help to zoom in. Double-click the numbers along the vertical axis to access the Format Axis dialog.

2. Change the Minimum and Maximum from Automatic to Fixed. Enter 100 as the Minimum and 100000 as the Maximum. By the way, the Major Unit and Minor unit control where the gridlines will be drawn.

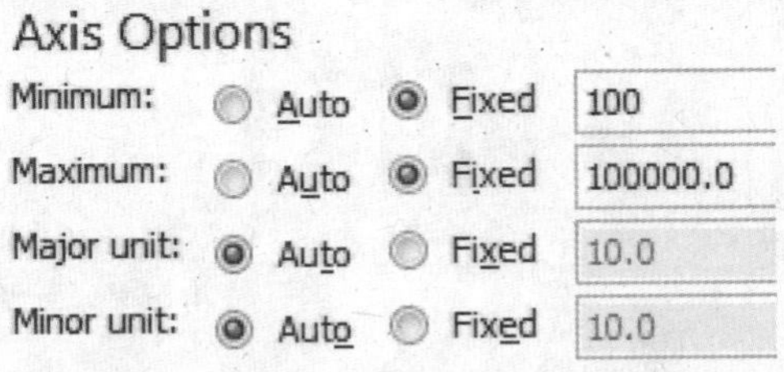

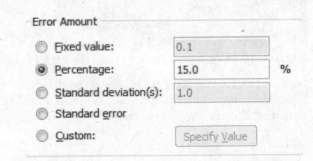

Figure 1076 *Zoom in with Min=100.*

4. The markers are too large for this chart. Choose each series. In the Format Series dialog choose Marker Style and either None or a smaller size for the marker.

5. To help the reader's eye travel from the label to the point, use Layout, Lines, Drop Lines. Select the drop lines. Use Format, Shape Outline. In this dropdown, choose Dashes and color to make the lines less prominent.

6. The Error Bars are showing ±15% from the forecast. To set these up, choose the Forecast series. Use Layout, Error Bars, More Error Bar Options. Choose Both for the direction. Choose Percentage, 15%.

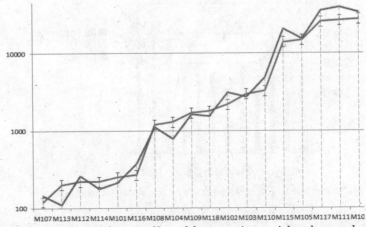

Figure 1077 *Error bars for each forecast point.*

Result: You have a chart to review at the sales and operations planning meeting. Any time that the sales team's forecast was not within 15%, have a discussion about what happened.

Figure 1078 *See detail for small and large points with a log scale.*

CHART TWO SERIES WITH DIFFERING ORDERS OF MAGNITUDE

Problem: I'm trying to create a combo chart that shows revenue and gross profit percentage. In Excel 2010, the legend shows that both items are in the chart, but I can see only the Revenue series on the chart.

Strategy: Excel 2013 now easily handles this with their Recommended Charts feature. Make sure the gross profit percent series is formatted with a % format. Select the data. Go to Insert, Recommended Charts. Excel 2013 will offer a Clustered Column - Line on Secondary Axis chart:

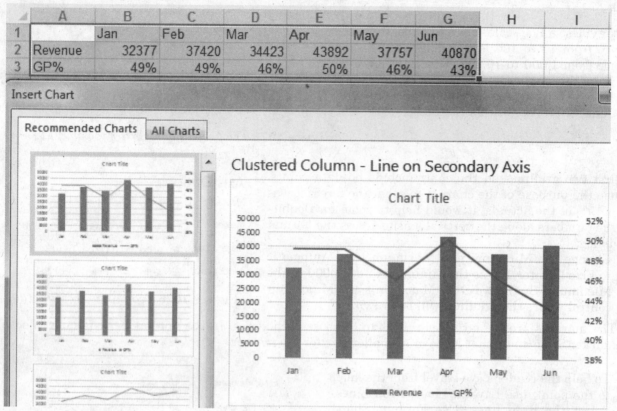

	Jan	Feb	Mar	Apr	May	Jun
Revenue	32377	37420	34423	43892	37757	40870
GP%	49%	49%	46%	50%	46%	43%

Figure 1079 *In Excel 2013, the combo chart is easy.*

In Excel 2010, you have to create the combo chart through a longer series of steps. Initially, the GP% series is on the chart, but the numbers are too small to be seen. You need to plot the series along a secondary axis and change the chart type.

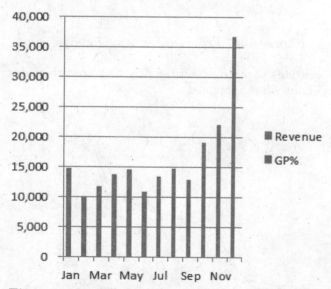

Figure 1080 *The GP% series is too small to be seen.*

Follow these steps:

1. Click on the chart to activate it.

2. Select Format, Current Selection dropdown, Series GP%. Excel will select the nearly invisible columns.

3. Select Format, Format Selection. Excel displays the Format Data Series dialog.

4. In the Series Options category in the Format Data Series dialog, change the Plot Series On setting from Primary Axis to Secondary Axis. You can now see the red columns.

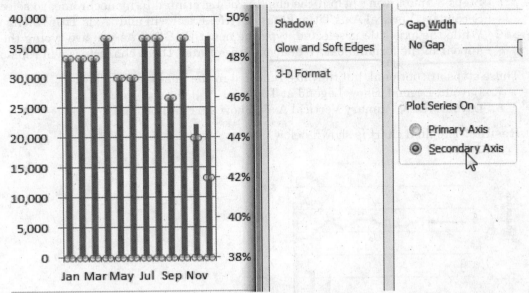

Figure 1081 *Move the GP% to the secondary axis.*

5. Excel will add numbers from 38% to 50% along the right axis of the chart. One problem with this setting is that Excel will now draw the red columns directly in front of the blue columns. In every month except November and December, you can't even see the blue columns. One option is to increase the gap width for the GP% series and make the columns thinner. Instead, I prefer to change the series to a line chart, as described in step 6.

6. Make sure that Series GP% is still the current selection. Select Design, Change Chart Type. Choose a line chart. The reader can now see both the increasing trend of Revenue in December and the plummeting GP% in the same month.

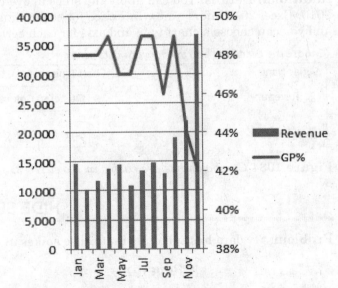

Figure 1082 *Revenue and GP% are both visible.*

Gotcha: When the range of a series is less than 20% of the maximum value of the series, Excel automatically zooms in on the range. For GP%, the range is 42% to 49%—a 7% range. 7/49 is less than 20%, so Excel has chosen to show 38% to 50% as the range for the second vertical axis. This allows you to see more detail in the GP%, but some purists always want the axis to start at 0.

Additional Details: If the chart is going to be printed in color, I change the font for the right axis to match the color of the GP% line. This helps the reader to figure out that the right scale applies to the red line. Follow these steps to format the axis:

1. Right-click on any number along the right axis. Choose Format Axis.

2. In the Axis Options section, Minimum and Maximum are set to automatic. In the grayed out Minimum text box, you can see 0.38. Click the Fixed option button for Minimum and type the value 0.

3. You won't find a font color setting in the Format Axis dialog, so select the Home, Font Color dropdown, Red. (All the Font settings in the Home tab will work to format the numbers along the axis.).

4. Click on the numbers along the left axis. Use the Home tab to change the font color to blue.

5. Steps 3 and 4 won't help if the chart is being printed in monochrome, so select Layout, Axis Titles, Secondary Vertical Axis Title, Rotated Title. Excel will add "Axis Title" along the right axis.

6. While the axis title is selected, type the new title GP%. As you are typing the characters, they will appear in the formula bar. When you press Enter, these characters will replace the axis title.

These steps are optional, but they are reflected in the final result below.

7. Layout, Legend, Show Legend at Top

8. Layout, Axes, Primary Vertical Axis, Show axis in thousands.

Results: The final chart is shown below.

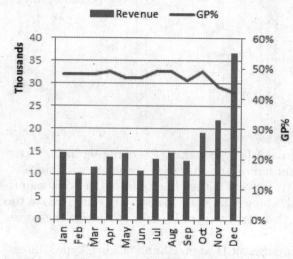

Figure 1083 *You can see both series on the chart.*

Additional Details: You can apply the steps above to build many different combination charts in Excel 2010. Excel 2013 offers a new interface for controlling combo charts. Select Change Chart Type, Combo, and you can choose a chart type and axis for each series.

Choose the chart type and axis for your data series:

Series Name	Chart Type	Secondary Axis
▌ Revenue	Clustered Column ▼	☐
▌ GP%	Line ▼	☑

Figure 1084 *Combo charts are easier in Excel 2013.*

HIDE SUBTOTALS FROM CHART IN EXCEL 2013

Problem: My data has subtotals that cause spikes in the chart.

Figure 1085 *Charting data with subtotals does not look good.*

Normally, you would create another range with the monthly data and create a chart from that range. But, Excel 2013 introduces the Funnel icon to the right of the chart. Click the Funnel and you can uncheck certain data points.

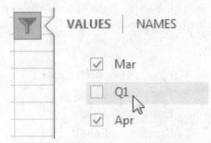

Figure 1086 *Remove each Quarter from the chart.*

The result: a monthly chart:

Figure 1087 *No more spikes.*

CREATE PIVOT CHARTS FROM DETAIL DATA IN EXCEL 2013

Say that you have hundreds of rows of detail data. Select the entire data set and use Insert, Recommended Chart. Excel will recommend that you let it create pivot charts to summarize the data. You will see tiny Pivot icons on each chart tile.

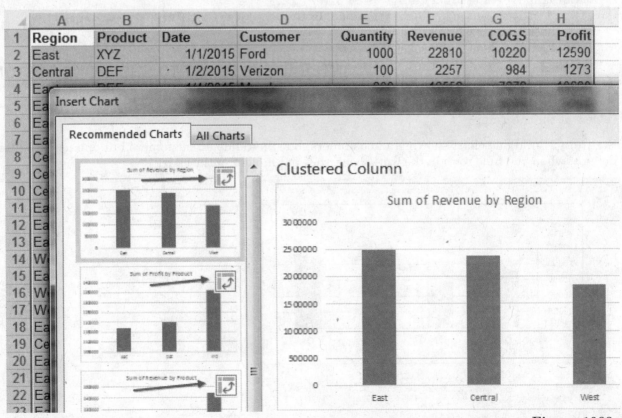

Figure 1088

USE FORMULAS FOR CHART LABELS IN EXCEL 2013

Excel 2013 introduces a new feature where the chart labels can come from other cells on the worksheet. In the Figure below, formulas in column C build a label to identify the largest and second largest sales amount.

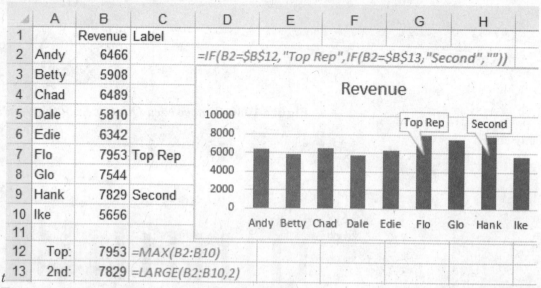

Figure 1089 *As the results change, the labels will move.*

Here are the steps to assign the labels from cells:
1. Select the data and Insert, Recommended Chart, OK.
2. Use the Plus icon to the right of the chart. Add a checkmark to Data Labels.
3. Plus Icon, hover to right of Data Labels. Click Triangle, choose Data Callout.
4. Plus, Data Labels, Triangle, More Options.
5. Click the 3-Column chart icon in the Format Data Labels Task Pane.
6. Click on Label Options.
7. Checkmark Value From Cells.
8. Excel will ask you to highlight the range. In this case, it is C2:C10.
9. Uncheck Category Name and Value.

INTERACTIVE CHART TO SHOW ONE CUSTOMER

Problem: We have a monthly meeting to review accounts. They want one chart per customer that we can review at the meeting.

Strategy: Build one chart showing all customers, but then hide all customers but one using a filter. By default, when you hide rows in the worksheet, they get hidden in the chart.

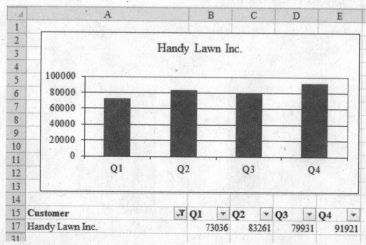

Figure 1090 *Chart for one customer.*

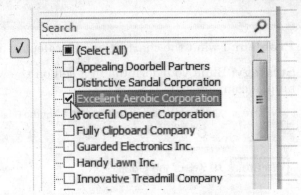

Figure 1091 *Choose another customer from dropdown in A15.*

During the creation of this chart, the chart looks bad, then really bad. It finally makes sense in the last step.

1. Select your range of customers and sales.
2. Insert a clustered column chart.
3. Excel will assume you want customers in the legend and quarters along the axis. Click the Switch Row/Column icon.

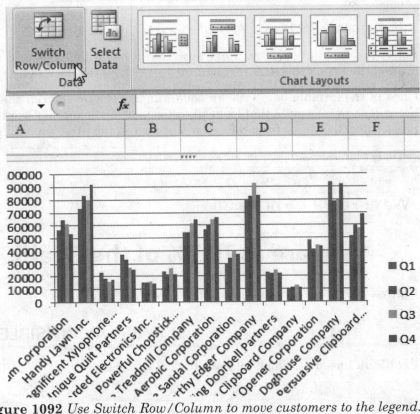

Figure 1092 *Use Switch Row/Column to move customers to the legend.*

At this point, your chart will be unreadable. You are one step away from having a good chart.

4. If you've added Filter by Selection to the Quick Access Toolbar, you can select one customer in the worksheet and click Filter by Selection. Otherwise, select a customer, use Data, Filter, then open the customer dropdown and choose one customer.
5. Because the chart now has one visible series, you get the name of that series in both the title and the legend. Click the legend and press the Delete key to remove the redundant information.
6. You can now choose a customer from the dropdown and the chart will update to show the new customer.

Again, this trick takes advantage of the default behavior that the point in the chart will be hidden when the row or column in the worksheet is hidden.

TIE THE CHART TITLE TO A CELL

Problem: I want the chart title to be calculated on the fly.

Strategy: Build your formula in a cell on the worksheet. You can use any formula and concatenation to build a complete title.

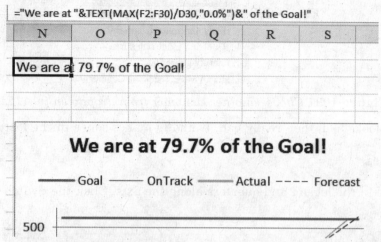

Figure 1093 *Build the text for your title in a formula.*

Select the title in the chart. Make sure that it has a solid box around the title. If you have a dashed line around the title, you are in text edit mode. Click on the dashed line to make it a solid line.

Click in the formula bar. Type an equals sign. Click on the cell that contains your formula. The formula bar will show a formula that looks like it is pointing to another worksheet, ='Daily Plan'!$N$30. When you press enter, the words from the cell will appear in the title. You might need to adjust the font to make it fit.

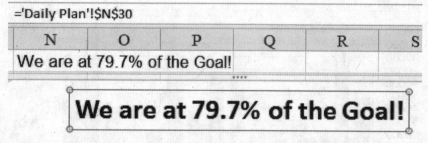

Figure 1094 *The title will update as the formula recalculates.*

USE AN INVISIBLE SERIES TO FLOAT COLUMNS

Problem: I need my chart columns to float in the air.

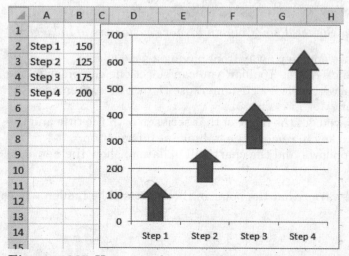

Figure 1095 *Have your bars or columns float.*

Strategy: This is a common trick. You will have the bars sitting on top of a rogue series and then make the series invisible. Follow these steps:

1. Next to your original data, build a new data range that will be used for the chart. You will have two series. You can call them anything, but here I've used "Hide" and "Show".

2. Use formulas to calculate the height of the visible column and the height at which the column should float. Below, Step 3 is 175 tall and is floating 275 in the air. The 275 is the height of the previous two bars.

3. Create a stacked column chart.

4. Click on one of the bottom columns to select the Hide series.

5. On the Format tab, open the Shape Fill dropdown and choose None.

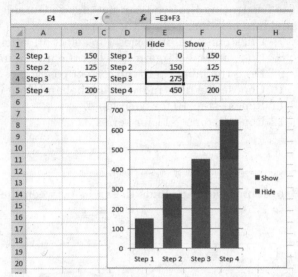

Figure 1096 *The bottom columns will go away*

6. If the lower columns have an outline, click the Shape Outline dropdown and choose None. The bottom columns will now disappear.

7. Click on the legend and press Delete.

The original figure in this topic used arrows instead of columns. This is easy to do.

1. Use Insert, Shapes, Arrow and draw an upward facing arrow near the chart.

2. Click on the arrow shape to select it.

3. Ctrl+C to copy the arrow.

4. Click on one of the visible columns in the chart. This will select all of the column in the series.

5. Press Ctrl+V to paste. This will replace the columns with the arrows.

A similar trick is used to make waterfall charts. The black columns are series 1. The white columns are series 3. An invisible series 2 makes the white columns float.

The waterfall chart here uses a hidden series 2 to achieve the basic effect. The data labels are the most difficult part of the chart.

1. .

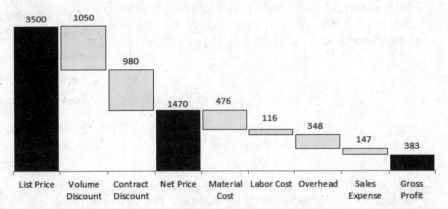

Figure 1097 *This is a stacked column chart with a hidden series 2.*

1. Convert the original source data in the second column to three columns of data as shown here

2. Create a stacked column chart.

3. Format series two to have no fill.

4. Format any one series to have no Gap Width.

			Black	Invisible	White
List Price	3500	List Price	3500	#N/A	#N/A
Volume Discount	1050	Volume Discount	#N/A	2450	1050
Contract Discount	980	Contract Discount	#N/A	1470	980
Net Price	1470	Net Price	1470	#N/A	#N/A
Material Cost	476	Material Cost	#N/A	994	476
Labor Cost	116	Labor Cost	#N/A	878	116
Overhead	348	Overhead	#N/A	530	348
Sales Expense	147	Sales Expense	#N/A	383	147
Gross Profit	383	Gross Profit	383	#N/A	#N/A

Figure 1098 *The 2450 is =3500-1050. The 1470 is =2450-980.*

5. Select series 1 and add data labels to the center.

6. Select series 3 and add data labels to the center.

It is frustrating that you can not choose Outside End for the data labels. You must manually move each label into position. Follow these steps.

7. Click one label in series 1 to select all labels in the series.
8. Click one label again to select the individual label.
9. Drag the label up to the correct position.
10. Choose the next individual label and drag it.
11. Repeat step 10 for each label.
12. Repeat steps 7-11 for series 3.

USE ROGUE SERIES FOR SHADING

Problem: I want to shade the areas between the gridlines in this chart.

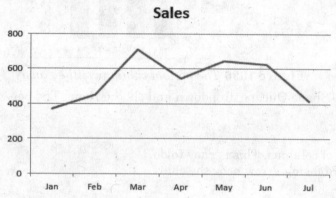

Figure 1099 *Add alternating shading between the gridlines.*

Strategy: Use four series as stacked area charts.

To use this method, you need to take control of the vertical axis. Format the vertical axis. Figure out the minimum, maximum, and major unit that you will be using.

Axis Options

Minimum:	Auto	● Fixed	0.0
Maximum:	Auto	● Fixed	800.0
Major unit:	Auto	● Fixed	200.0
Minor unit:	● Auto	Fixed	40.0

Figure 1100 *Make sure the scale won't change.*

1. Go back to the original data. Insert a new series for each gridline. These series will be stacked. The first series of 200 will run from 0 to 200. The second series of 200 will be on top of series 1 and will run from 200 to 400. Have your Sales series be the last series.

	One	Two	Three	Four	Sales
Jan	200	200	200	200	373
Feb	200	200	200	200	451
Mar	200	200	200	200	710
Apr	200	200	200	200	545
May	200	200	200	200	646
Jun	200	200	200	200	624
Jul	200	200	200	200	417

Figure 1101 *One rogue series for each band of alternate shading.*

2. Choose Insert, Area, Stacked Area chart. Don't worry that the initial chart looks completely wrong.

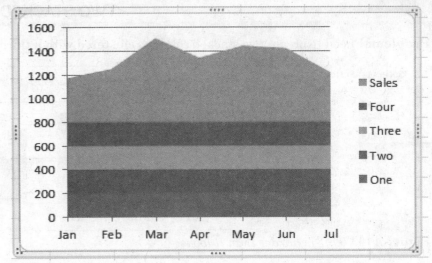

Figure 1102 *It is typical for these trick charts to look wrong at first.*

3. Select the Sales series. Use Design, Change Chart Type. Change it to a Line chart.
4. Format the vertical axis. Go back to the settings in Figure 1100.
5. Click on one of the gridlines to select all the gridlines. Press Delete.
6. Select series One. Use Format, Shape Fill and choose a light color.
7. Repeat step 6 for the remaining area series, choosing alternating dark and light colors.

At this point, the effect is complete, but the legend is giving away your secret. You can delete individual entries in the legend.

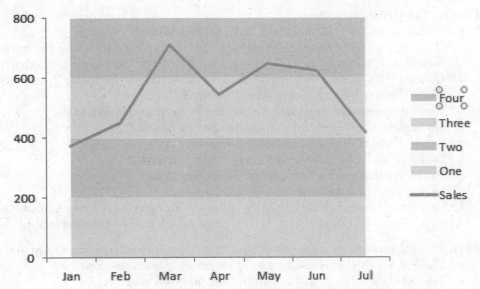

Figure 1103 *You need to delete 80% of the legend.*

8. Click once on the legend to select it.
9. Click a second time on Four. This selects the one legend entry.
10. Press Delete. That one entry in the legend is deleted.
11. Repeat steps 8-10 for series Three, Two, and One.

There are a number of special charts where extra rogue series are used to create some formatting. For more examples, check out:

- Mario Garcia's amazing five rogue charts in order from Learn Excel Podcast episode 1026.
- Andy Pope's charting tutorials at http://www.andypope.info/.
- Jon Peltier's charting tutorials at http://peltiertech.com/Excel/Charts/.

TWO STACKED, ONE CLUSTERED COLUMN

Problem: I need to create two stacked columns clustered with a third column.

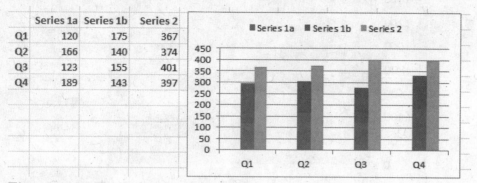

	Series 1a	Series 1b	Series 2
Q1	120	175	367
Q2	166	140	374
Q3	123	155	401
Q4	189	143	397

Figure 1104 *This is harder than it looks.*

Strategy: This chart uses two rogue series and a hidden secondary axis. Follow these steps carefully.

1. Add two blank series between Series 1b and Series 2. Fill with zeroes.

	Series 1a	Series 1b	Blank 1	Blank 2	Series 2
Q1	120	175	0	0	367
Q2	166	140	0	0	374
Q3	123	155	0	0	401
Q4	189	143	0	0	397

Figure 1105 *Two extra series.*

2. Create a stacked column chart from all five series.
3. If you are plotting quarters, Excel will put the wrong data along the horizontal axis. Click the Switch Row/Column icon to move the Series 1a, Series 1b, and so on to the legend.
4. Go to the Layout tab in the ribbon. Use the leftmost dropdown to choose Series 2.
5. Click Format Selection to open the Format Dialog box.
6. Choose Secondary Axis. Don't close the Format dialog box.
7. Go back to the dropdown and choose Series Blank 1.
8. In the Format dialog box, choose Secondary Axis.
9. Go back to the dropdown and choose Series Blank 2.
10. In the Format dialog box, choose Secondary Axis.
11. Go back to the dropdown and choose Series 2.
12. Go to the Design tab of the ribbon. Choose Change Chart Type. Choose the first column chart, known as a Clustered Column Chart. This changes all three of the series that use the secondary axis.

At this point, you finally have something that looks almost correct. There are still several things to fix:
- The left vertical axis is using a different scale than the first.
- The stacked column is wider than the clustered column.
- There are two extra entries in the legend.
- You really don't need to show the secondary axis once you make them have the same scale.

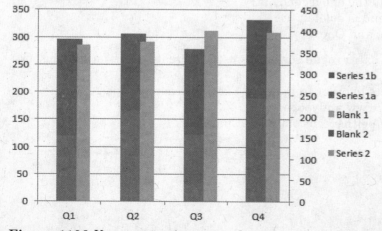

Figure 1106 *You are starting to get close.*

By the way, those two extra blank series are there to move Series 2 to the right. If you entered 100 and 200 in those series, you would see how they are pushing Series 2 over to the right of the stacked column.

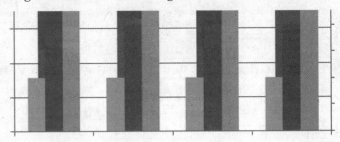

Figure 1107 *Here, the two blank series are moving Series 2 to the right.*

The remaining steps assume the Format dialog box is still open.

13. Click on the right vertical axis. In the Format dialog, change the first three settings from Auto to Fixed. Make a note of the settings in those three boxes.
14. Click on the left vertical axis. Make six changes in the Format dialog box. Change the first three settings from Auto to Manual. Click in the box next to manual. Type the same values from step 13 into the boxes next to manual. This will make sure that both axis have the same scale.
15. Click on one of the stacked series to select it. In the Format dialog box, change the gap width to 300%. This will make the stacked column less wide and about the same size as the third column.
16. In the legend, click once on Blank 1, then do a second single click on Blank 1 to select only that item in the legend. Press Delete to Delete that entry.
17. Do two single clicks on Blank 2 in the legend. Press Delete.
18. In the Layout tab, choose Legend, Show Legend at Top.
19. Click on the right vertical axis. Press Delete.

This whole set of steps is demonstrated in Learn Excel Podcast Episode 1091.

Gotcha: This only works with one stacked column and one non-stacked column. If you need both columns to be stacked, it will not work. Jon Peltier sells a cool utility to solve this.

CONDITIONAL FORMAT A CHART

Problem: I want the chart column to be green for ratings of 90 or above, yellow for 70 to 90 and red for less than 70. Can I do conditional formatting in a chart?

4

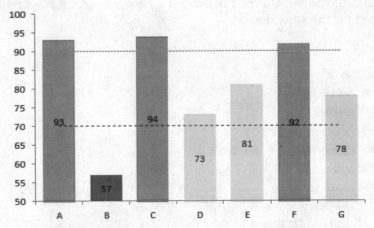

Figure 1108 *Color the columns based on their value.*

Strategy: Charts don't support conditional formatting (yet). However, you can use formulas to separate your data into three series, one series for red, one series for yellow, and one series for green. Only one series will be filled for each category. The other series will be #N/A.

The formulas below break the value in column B into one of three series in D, E, or F. Each value in B goes to exactly one cell in D:F.

	D2			f_x	=IF(B2<G2,B2,NA())		

	A	B	C	D	E	F	G	H
1	Line	Rating	Line	Red	Yellow	Green	Dash 1	Dash 2
2	A	98	A	#N/A	#N/A	98	70	90
3	B	55	B	55	#N/A	#N/A	70	90
4	C	71	C	#N/A	71	#N/A	70	90
5	D	97	D	#N/A	#N/A	97	70	90
6	E	92	E	#N/A	#N/A	92	70	90
7	F	96	F	#N/A	#N/A	96	70	90
8	G	85	G	#N/A	85	#N/A	70	90

Figure 1109 *Formulas break the data into three series.*

The formulas used to create the table above are shown below.

	C	D	E	F	G	H
1	Line	Red	Yellow	Green	Dash 1	Dash 2
2	=A2	=IF(B2<G2,B2,NA())	=IF(AND(B2>=G2,B2<H2),B2,NA())	=IF(B2>=H2,B2,NA())	70	90
3	=A3	=IF(B3<G3,B3,NA())	=IF(AND(B3>=G3,B3<H3),B3,NA())	=IF(B3>=H3,B3,NA())	=G2	=H2
4	=A4	=IF(B4<G4,B4,NA())	=IF(AND(B4>=G4,B4<H4),B4,NA())	=IF(B4>=H4,B4,NA())	=G3	=H3
5	=A5	=IF(B5<G5,B5,NA())	=IF(AND(B5>=G5,B5<H5),B5,NA())	=IF(B5>=H5,B5,NA())	=G4	=H4
6	=A6	=IF(B6<G6,B6,NA())	=IF(AND(B6>=G6,B6<H6),B6,NA())	=IF(B6>=H6,B6,NA())	=G5	=H5
7	=A7	=IF(B7<G7,B7,NA())	=IF(AND(B7>=G7,B7<H7),B7,NA())	=IF(B7>=H7,B7,NA())	=G6	=H6
8	=A8	=IF(B8<G8,B8,NA())	=IF(AND(B8>=G8,B8<H8),B8,NA())	=IF(B8>=H8,B8,NA())	=G7	=H7

Figure 1110 *IF statements decide which color to use.*

When you create the chart, create a stacked column chart. You will have to select each series and use Format, Shape Fill to choose the correct color.

If you need one color for positive and another color for negative, you can use a regular column chart. Format the series. On the Fill category, choose Invert if Negative. you can choose Green for the first color and red for the second color.

Fill

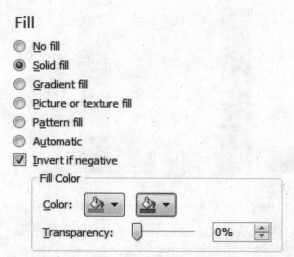

Figure 1111 *This is new (back) in Excel 2010.*

SCATTER CHARTS ARE VERSATILE BUT REQUIRE A DIFFERENT WORKFLOW

Problem: How to I create a scatter chart with two series?

Strategy: Create a chart with one series. Then select the second series and use Paste Special to get that data on the chart. Most of the charts that you use in Excel have labels for the category axis in column 1, data for the first series in column 2, data for the third series in category 3, and so on. Microsoft has shoehorned the scatter chart into the same engine used to create regular charts and it makes it a bit difficult to specify the second series.

In a scatter chart, the first column is used to specify a numeric location along the x-axis. The second column is used to specify a numeric location along the y-axis. Scatter charts are also known as X-Y charts for this reason.

Scientists use scatter charts to compare two variables. If you have some variable that you can control, put that along the x-axis. Plot another variable which is dependent on the first variable along the x-axis. The resulting pattern of the dots plotted in the chart allow you to spot patterns and outliers.

Excel tricksters use scatter charts because they solve a number of problem. The only way to show hours and minutes along the x-axis is to use a scatter chart. Scatter charts are also really good ways of drawing a line at a specific place on a chart.

I like to use scatter charts to compare two different populations of data. This particular chart is maddening to create in one step. For whatever reason, the scatter chart almost always comes out when I am used car shopping. We will start with that scenario.

I just went through one of the online car shopping sites and found all of the Alfa Romeo Spider Veloce vehicles for sale in the United States. I made a list of them, comparing mileage and asking price. I wanted to see how mileage and asking price are correlated. Mileage goes in column 1. Asking price in column 2. For reasons that will become evident later, the heading for column 2 should be Alfa.

1. Select the two columns including the headings.
2. Insert, Scatter, Scatter With Only Markers
3. Layout, Chart Title, None
4. Layout, Axis Titles, Primary Horizontal Axis Title, Title Below Axis.
5. Click on the Axis Title and type Miles (000). Press Enter.
6. Layout, Axis Titles, Primary Vertical Axis Title, Title Below Axis.
7. Click on the Axis Title and type Price. Press Enter.
8. Layout, Legend, Show Legend at Top.

You now have the chart shown below. You would expect the dots to slope from top left to lower right. As the miles increase, the price should go down. The dots roughly fall in this pattern, but there are outliers.

The highest priced car is the one with only 13,000 miles. That is impressive for a car that is 20-30 years old at this point. But, there is also a car for the same price with 113,000 miles. That point is in an outlier. The other cars with that many miles are half the price. Either this car is pristine and restored, or the owner has no sense of reality.

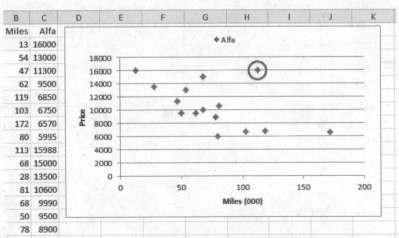

Miles	Alfa
13	16000
54	13000
47	11300
62	9500
119	6850
103	6750
172	6570
80	5995
113	15988
68	15000
28	13500
81	10600
68	9990
50	9500
78	8900

Figure 1112 *The scatter chart shows the relationship of price and miles.*

I learned about using scatter charts from Rich Lanza of AuditSoftware.net. Rich will throw 5000 vendors in a chart and spot the 10 that need to be audited in an instant.

For the chart above, I wanted to compare the Alfa Romeos to the Fiat Spider. Both cars have similar styling with both bodies designed by Carozzeria Pininfarina. I built a second pair of columns for all the Fiats for sale. Miles in column 1, price in column 2. The heading for column 2 is Fiat.

To add a second series to the existing chart, follow these steps:
1. Select the new two-column range of data, including the headings.
2. Ctrl+C to copy.
3. Click once on the chart.
4. On the Home tab, open the Paste dropdown and choose Paste Special. Alternatively, type Alt+E+S. Excel displays the chart version of Paste Special.
5. In the Add Cells As, change from New Points to New Series.
6. Values (Y) are in columns.
7. Since you included the headings in step 1, choose Series Names in First Row.
8. Choose Category (X Values) in First Column.
9. Leave Replace Existing Categories unchecked.
10. Click OK.

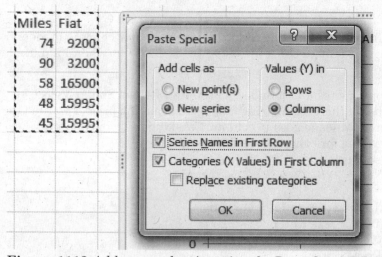

Figure 1113 *Add a second series using the Paste Special dialog.*

The result is a scatter chart comparing the Alfa and Fiat options. The Fiat offers the most expensive choice as well as the least expensive choice.

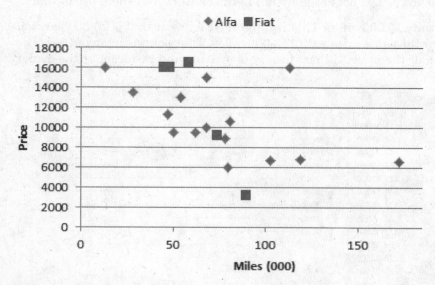

Figure 1114 *Compare Alfas and Fiats.*

The Paste Special dialog requires several clicks, but it makes adding the additional series much easier.

Additional Details: It is common with scatter chart series to have a different number of points in each series. This would be unusual in a line or column or bar chart.

If you are only plotting markers and not lines between the markers, the data does not need to be sorted.

Scatter charts are a better choice when you have time data where the points are not at fixed intervals. Say that you start with $100 on December 31 and add one dollar every day. You only bother to count the money every few months. This line should be perfectly linear, because you never fail to add the dollar bill.

The figure below compares two varieties of line chart and a scatter chart with a line. The first choice, with a text axis plots each point equidistant and is misrepresentative. The second choice uses a date axis. This should be correct, but that line is not a straight line. The third choice uses a scatter chart. It is the only one to show a perfectly straight line.

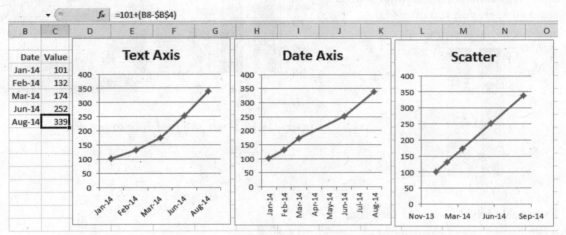

Figure 1115 *The scatter is better for this date series.*

When you are tracking data by time, the scatter is really the only choice. If you try to use a line chart, the Date Axis option will plot all of the times in a single column, back-dating the points to midnight of that day. The scatter chart is the only way to show the true progression over time.

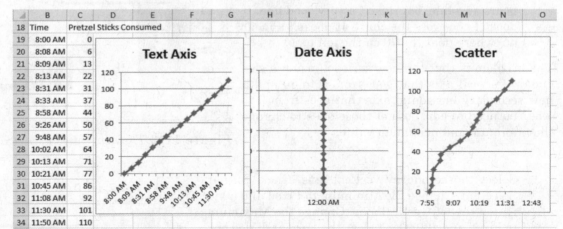

Figure 1116 *For irregularly spaced time data, the scatter is a must.*

Gotcha: Labeling scatter charts is annoyingly difficult using Excel. If you need to label individual points, search for Rob Bovey's Chart Labeler utility. It is free. It does exactly what you need.

Scatter charts are a great way to draw on a chart. Do you need a straight line? It only takes two points to draw a line. Way back in Figure 1108, I added two line chart series to draw a horizontal line at 70 and 90 in that chart. Those lines don't stretch all the way across the chart. They start in the middle of the first point and extend to the end of the last point. Had I added two scatter chart series instead, I could have achieved a true line all the way across the chart.

You need nerves of steel to do this, because during several steps, your chart will head in the wrong direction. You need to keep going until the end when everything will look OK. Follow these steps to add lines at 70 and 90 to a chart.

1. For the first line, you need two data points. Plan on having the x-axis stretch from 0 to 1. (Think about this like 0 to 100% of the width of the chart). Enter a range that shows the height at 0 is 70 and the height at 100 is 70. This will be a straight line all the way across the chart at a height of 70. This is entered as a two-row by two-column range.
2. Enter the range for the second line. Enter 0, 90; 1, 90 in four cells.

3. Select the first range of four cells. Ctrl+C to copy.
4. Select the chart. Paste Special. Choose New Series. Columns. Categories in First Column. Leave the other two checkboxes unchecked.

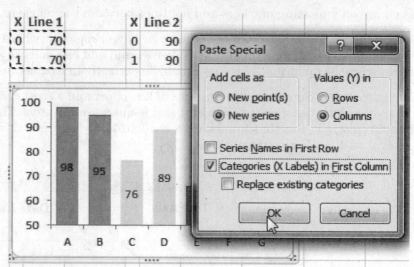

Already, things are starting to look bad. The new series is added as a stacked series on top of A & B.

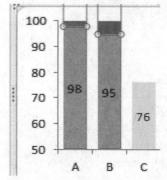

Figure 1117 *Paste the first line to the chart.*

Figure 1118 *This doesn't look like a line.*

5. Choose the new series. On the Design tab, choose Change Chart Type. Select a Scatter chart with a line. Your new series now appears as a line, but it isn't a very good line. It doesn't go across the chart. It doesn't appear anywhere near the 70 on the left axis.

The problem is that the new series is using a secondary vertical axis that goes from 0 to 80 and a new secondary horizontal axis that goes from 0 to 1.5. You need to edit both of those axes to change the minimum and maximum value.

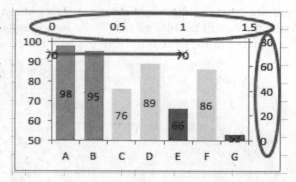

Figure 1119 *The new series uses two new axes.*

6. Select the secondary vertical axis. Click Format Selection. Change the Minimum to Fixed and 50 to match the left vertical axis. Change the Maximum to Fixed and 100. Don't close the Format dialog box yet.
7. Click the axis at the top of the chart. In the Format dialog, choose a minimum of Fixed 0 and a Maximum of Fixed 1. (Refer back to step 1 where the plan was to have the x-axis stretch from 0 to 1.) The line now stretches all the way across the chart.
8. Select the four-cell range for the second line. Copy those cells. Click the chart. Paste Special. Use the same settings as in Figure 1117.

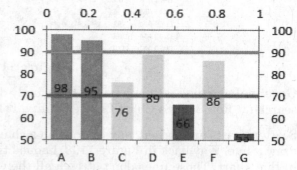

Figure 1120 *The lines stretch across, but the extra axis labels will confuse.*

You now have a chart with the lines going all the way across the chart at the correct location.

To get rid of the extra axes and clean up the lines, follow these steps:
9. Click the numbers on the right axis. Type Delete.
10. Click the numbers on the top axis. Type Delete.

11. Choose the line at 70. Choose Layout, Data Labels, None. On the Format tab, use the Shape Outline dropdown to change the color to red, the weight to 1/4 point and the dashes to the dashed line. In the Format dialog, choose Marker Style, None.
12. Repeat step 11 for the line at 90.

The result is a chart with the lines going all the way across.

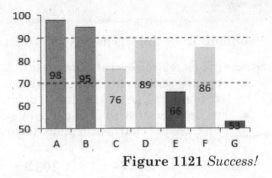

Figure 1121 *Success!*

The scatter series can be used to draw an arrow that always points to the height of one column. For an arrow to point to the column for E, I figured that a good starting point would be 2/7 of the way across the chart. The ending point would be 4.5/7 of the way across the chart. For the starting height, I chose 95. For the ending height, I used a formula to add 1 to the data point for E. Add the scatter series as described above. To draw the point on the arrow, select the line and use Format, Shape Outline, Arrow and choose the line that ends with an arrow.

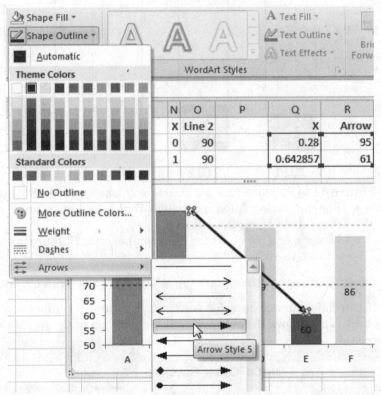

Figure 1122 *You can add an arrow head to a series line.*

The **result:** when the value for column E changes, the arrow keeps pointing to the top of the column.

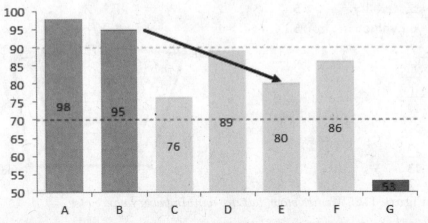

Figure 1123 *The arrow automatically moves with the data point.*

WHEN DO I USE WHICH CHART TYPE?

Problem: There are 73 chart types. When should I use which chart type?

Strategy: Here are several examples:
- For time series with equal points, you can either use column or line. People expect time to move from left to right. Use column for 12 points or less, lines for 12 points or more.
- For time series with unequal points or with hours, use scatter.
- Don't use pie charts over time. Instead, use a stacked 100% column chart.

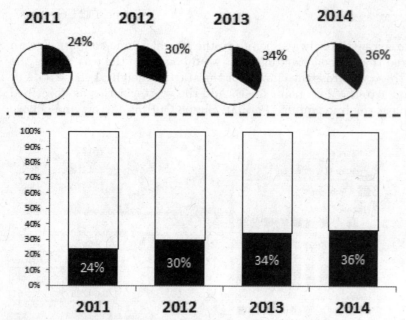

Figure 1124 *Replace four pie charts with one stacked 100% column.*
- For comparing sales of products that have long names, a bar chart allows plenty of room for the long text labels along the left axis.
- Never use a pie chart for item comparison. Pie charts should only be used to show how several items add up to 100%.

Excel offers some other chart types that have not been covered.

If you have survey data for your company and a competitor, you can plot both results on a single radar chart. This shows the relative ranking for each of the questions.

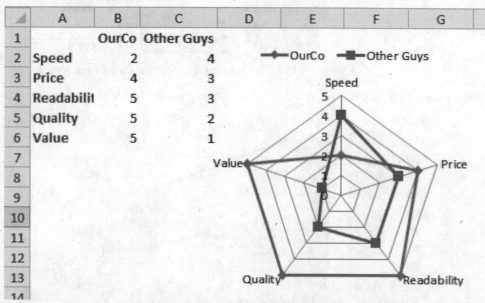

Figure 1125 *We are slow, but are winning everywhere else.*

A bubble chart is like a scatter chart, but the size of the point conveys a third bit of data. For example, you might compare miles along the x-axis, age along the y-axis, and price of the car as the size of the bubble.

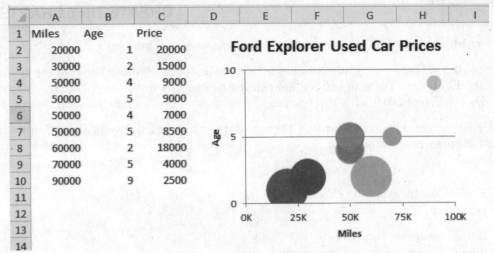

	A	B	C
1	Miles	Age	Price
2	20000	1	20000
3	30000	2	15000
4	50000	4	9000
5	50000	5	9000
6	50000	4	7000
7	50000	5	8500
8	60000	2	18000
9	70000	5	4000
10	90000	9	2500

Figure 1126 *The size of the bubble indicates price.*

Excel offers four types of stock charts. The name of the chart tells you the order in which the data columns should be arranged.

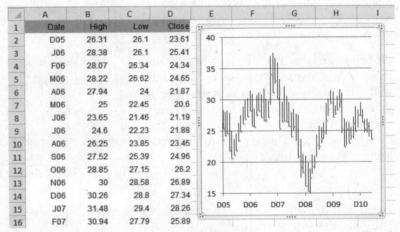

	A	B	C	D
1	Date	High	Low	Close
2	D05	26.31	26.1	23.61
3	J06	28.38	26.1	25.41
4	F06	28.07	26.34	24.34
5	M06	28.22	26.62	24.65
6	A06	27.94	24	21.87
7	M06	25	22.45	20.6
8	J06	23.65	21.46	21.19
9	J06	24.6	22.23	21.88
10	A06	26.25	23.85	23.45
11	S06	27.52	25.39	24.96
12	O06	28.85	27.15	26.2
13	N06	30	28.58	26.89
14	D06	30.26	28.8	27.34
15	J07	31.48	29.4	28.26
16	F07	30.94	27.79	25.89

Figure 1127 *A high-low-close chart in Excel.*

Excel also offers surface charts and donut charts.

There are many other types of chart that you might need to create. For these charts, third parties offer utilities. Mala Singh of XLSoft Consulting offers utilities to draw speedometer charts and macroeconomic supply curve charts.

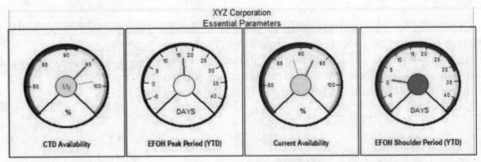

Figure 1128 *Visit http://www.mrexcel.com/speedometer.html*

Jon Peltier offers utilities to create a variety of charts:

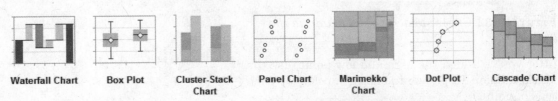

Figure 1129 *Visit http://tinyurl.com/jonpeltier*

CREATE TINY CHARTS WITH SPARKLINES

Problem: I need to create a chart for every row in my data set.

Strategy: Use a sparkline. Professor Edward Tufte introduced the concept of sparklines in his book Beautiful Evidence. Tufte described sparklines as intense word-sized charts. Microsoft implemented Tufte's ideas in Excel 2010 with three types of tiny charts: line charts, column charts, and win/loss charts.

Creating sparklines is simple, although you might want to tweak the default sparklines. Below, there are 27 months of closing stock prices for 3 financial firms. Select the data that you want to plot in the sparklines.

From the Insert tab, choose the Line sparkline.

Excel displays the Create Sparklines dialog. Because you pre-selected the data, you need to specify only the output range. Because the input range is 3 rows by 27 columns, the output range has to either be 3 cells or 27 cells. The size of the output range will determine whether you want 3 sparklines or 27 sparklines.

Gotcha: In the rare case where your input range is exactly square, Microsoft will turn each row into a sparkline. If you want each column to be a sparkline, use the Edit Data dropdown on the Sparkline Tools Design tab and choose Switch Row/Column.

			Jan-08	Feb-08
AIG	1078	33	1077.62	918.63
GS	195	169	195.33	166.04
JPM	45	42	45.33	38.87

Create Sparklines

Choose the data that you want

Data Range: F3:AF5

Choose where you want the sparklines to be placed

Location Range:

OK   Cancel

Figure 1130 *Specify an output range.*

Excel will draw in the line charts, one in each cell. Here are default sparklines.

AIG	1078	33
GS	195	169
JPM	45	42

Figure 1131 *Default sparklines have no labels or markers.*

Excel will let you add markers to your sparklines. With a sparkline selected, the Sparkline Tools Design tab will be available in the ribbon. You can toggle on all points by choosing Markers, but a more interesting option is to choose High Point and Low Point

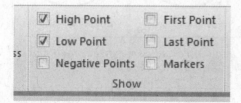

Figure 1132 *Choose which points to add to the line.*

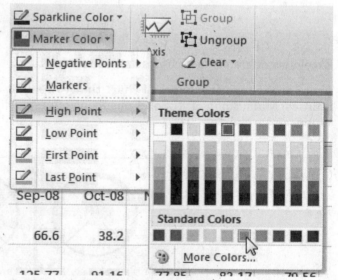

Figure 1133 *Change the color of the markers.*

After you've added the high and low point, use the Marker Color dropdown to choose a color for each type of point.

SPARKLINES ARE NOT SCALED TOGETHER

Problem: The vertical scale on the sparklines seems to be wrong. This chart is showing that Chicago and Miami have similar January temperatures.

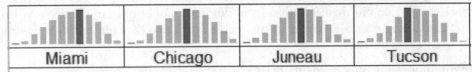

Figure 1134 *Monthly temperatures in Miami are not like Chicago.*

Strategy: by default, each sparkline has its own vertical scale. This works out great when the sparklines are comparing how different items trend together over time.

	A	B	C	D
3	**Economic Indicators 2000-2009**			
4			**2000**	**2001**
5	**Unemployment**		4	4.7
6	**GDP**		9952	10286
7	**New Construction**		803	840
8	**Bank Credit**		5027	5210

Figure 1135 *Each sparkline has its own vertical scale.*

In Professor Tufte's first examples, he was comparing unlike variables that had a relationship. This is why Microsoft chose to keep the axes separate for each line.

When you are comparing items that all have the same scale, you have to force the minimum and maximum axis to be the same.

At the very least, use the Axis dropdown and choose Same For All Sparklines for both the minimum and maximum value.

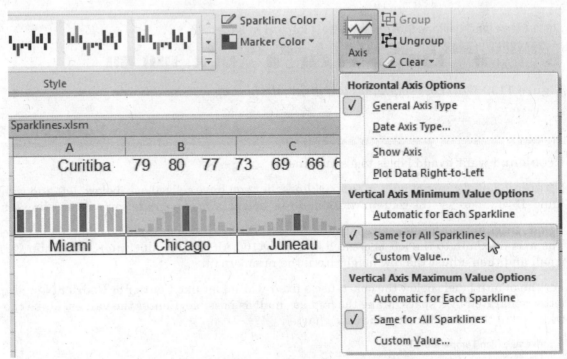

Figure 1136 *Make all of the axes the same.*

If you are going to be labeling sparklines or shading sparklines as described later, you will want to use a Custom Value for both the min and max value options.

WHAT IS THE WIN LOSS SPARKLINE FOR?

Problem: What is the win/loss sparkline used for?

Strategy: The win/loss sparkline shows streaks of wins or losses. You might use it to plot sports teams, stock prices, or bid desk results. In a win/loss sparkline, any positive value (such as 1) is plotted as an upward facing marker. Any negative value (such as -1) is plotted as a downward facing marker. Any zero values get no marker.

If you have some stock closing prices, use =SIGN(Today-Yesterday). If the price went up, the sign is positive and you get a +1. If the price went down, you get a -1.

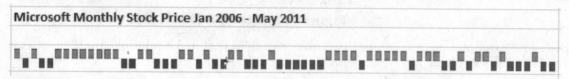

	A	B	C	D	E
	Date	High	Low	Close	
1					
2	D05	26.31	26.1	23.61	
3	J06	28.38	26.1	25.41	1
4	F06	28.07	26.34	24.34	-1
5	M06	28.22	26.62	24.65	1

E3   =SIGN(D3-D2)

Figure 1137 *Generate +1, 0, -1 with SIGN().*

For long Win/Loss Sparklines, increase the column width and row height to show more detail.

Microsoft Monthly Stock Price Jan 2006 – May 2011

Figure 1138 *Did those green markers happened after the Kinect debuted?*

Living in northeast Ohio, I am used to baseball season ending in June as the Cleveland Indians are eliminated from the playoffs. This year, they got off to a stellar start, but were just swept by the Yankees this weekend. The right quarter of this chart is the ballclub that I know and love.

2011 Cleveland Indians Started with Best Record in Baseball

Figure 1139 *Win/Loss sparklines to a great job showing wins and losses.*

LABELING SPARKLINES

Problem: I want to add labels to a sparkline.

Strategy: Labels are not built in to sparklines, but you have cells above, below, left and right of each sparkline. If you increase the column width and row height, you can create some interesting labels.

Below, titles appear above each sparkline. Those cells are just text that you can type in the cell and center. The axis max/min to the left is created by typing 100 Alt+Enter, Alt+Enter, Alt+Enter, 0. Make the font small and then adjust the row height until the numbers fit.

For the month labels below the chart, use a fixed-width font like Courier or Courier New. Type each month letter separated by a space. Make the font as small as possible. Center the values. Make the column width wider until the labels line up with the chart.

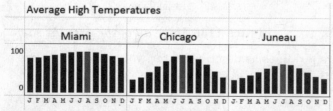

Average High Temperatures

Miami   Chicago   Juneau

Figure 1140 *Use the labels around the sparkline to add labels.*

In the figure to the right, a formula calculates the max and min of each series. The REPT(CHAR(10),4) adds four line feeds. With a row height of 55 and an 8-point font, this works out fine.

The background for sparklines are transparent so that any text in the cell will appear behind the sparkline. The title for each sparkline is just text typed in the cell, vertically aligned to the top of the cell.

In the figure below, a sparkline column chart shows hourly readings from 7AM to 2PM. Because the label for 12 would be twice as wide as the label for 7AM, a bit of trickery is employed. The label is 7 followed by Alt+Enter, 8 followed by Alt+Enter, 9 followed by Alt+Enter, and so on through 2. Use the Alignment tab of the Format Cells dialog to turn the values sideways, vertical align top, horizontal align center. Back in the Home tab, keep reducing the font and/or adjusting the column widths until all the values show in the cell.

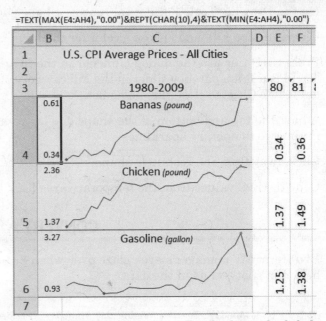

Figure 1141 *A formula in B calculates the label.*

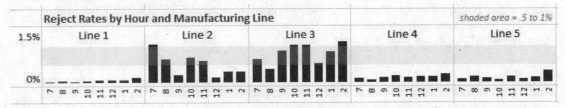

Figure 1142 *Vertical text for the column labels.*

SHADE THE NORMAL RANGE IN A SPARKLINE

Problem: The examples in Tufte's book would often draw a rectangular box to show the expected normal range for a sparkline. This allowed you to see when the sparkline deviated from normal.

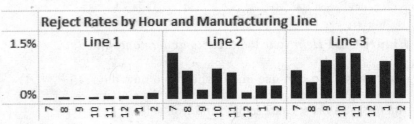

Figure 1143 *The shading is a semi-transparent rectangle.*

Strategy: This functionality is not built in to Excel sparklines, but you can use drawing tools to create a fairly good normal range.

These guidelines provide a rough set of steps for adding the shading:

Use the Axis Scaling settings and use a custom value for both the minimum and maximum value. This allows you to actually know that the sparklines range from exactly 0% to 1.5%.

Copy the real values for one or two sparklines and paste them outside of the data range. You are going to be temporarily changing those values and you want to paste the real values back into the dataset when you are done.

Suppose you want to draw a box for the caution range of 0.5% to 1%. Fill the values for one sparkline with 0.005. Fill the values for the next sparkline with 0.01.

Using Insert, Shapes, Rectangle and draw a rectangle over the sparklines. Make the bottom of the rectangle line up with the 0.005 sparklines and make the top of the rectangle line up with the 0.01 sparklines.

On the Drawing Tools Format tab, choose Shape Outline, None.

Choose Shape Fill, and choose a color for the highlighted area.

Press Ctrl+1 or use the dialog launcher in the Shape Styles group to get to the Format Shape dialog box. There is a Transparency slider in the Fill category of the dialog box. Change the slider up to 75% transparent. Click Close to close the dialog box.

Adjust the top and bottom of the shape one last time so that they line up with the 0.005 and 0.01 guides in the two temporary sparklines.

Click away from the rectangle shape.

Copy the real values from the temporary area back to the sparkline data.

CONVERT A TABLE OF NUMBERS TO A VISUALIZATION

Problem: My manager's eyes glaze over when he sees a table of numbers. Is there anything I can do to help him spot trends in the data?

	A	B	C	D	E	F
1		Monday	Tuesday	Wednesday	Thursday	Friday
2	Allen	38	22	57	20	28
3	Betty	25	64	57	59	33
4	Charley	43	32	51	23	37
5	Missy	63	59	60	64	69

Figure 1144 *Help your manager to understand this data.*

Strategy: You can use one of the three new data visualization tools on the Conditional Formatting menu: data bars, color scales, and icon sets.

Adding a data bar to a range adds an in-cell bar chart to each cell. You can see which cells have the largest values by seeing which cells have the most color.

To add data bars, you select a range of numbers and then select Home, Conditional Formatting, Data Bars, choose a color. Excel offers six gradients and six solid. You can choose More Rules to add any of 16 million colors.

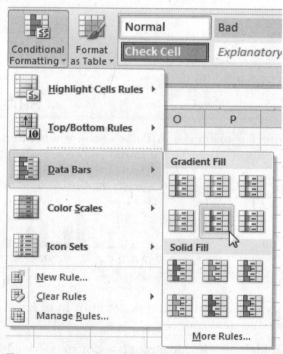

Figure 1145 *Choose a color for the data bars*

Below, you can see that Wednesday is the busiest day. Calls fall of on Friday for everyone except Missy. Missy is consistently the strongest performer.

A	B	C	D	E	F
	Monday	Tuesday	Wednesday	Thursday	Friday
len	38	22	57	20	28
etty	25	64	57	59	33
arley	43	32	51	23	37
issy	63	59	60	64	69

Figure 1146 *Easily spot trends in the data.*

Gotcha: You should not include any total cells in your selection when applying conditional formatting. The relative size of the totals would make all the detail numbers receive small bars. Below, the 904 in cell G6 makes all the cells in B2:F5 look relatively the same.

	A	B	C	D	E	F	G
1		Mon	Tue	Wed	Thu	Fri	Total
2	Allen	38	22	57	20	28	165
3	Betty	25	64	57	59	33	238
4	Charley	43	32	51	23	37	186
5	Missy	63	59	60	64	69	315
6	Total	169	177	225	166	167	904

Figure 1147 *Don't include totals in a visualization.*

Additional Details: You can use color scales to apply a mix of colors to a range. Excel offers built-in three-color scales such as red-yellow-green as well as two-color scales. The two-color scales look better than three-color scales when printed in monochrome. You can also use More Rules to design your own color scheme. Below, the largest numbers are in the darker green, and the smallest numbers are in the lighter yellow.

	A	B	C	D	E	F
1		Mon	Tue	Wed	Thu	Fri
2	Allen	38	22	57	20	28
3	Betty	25	64	57	59	33
4	Charley	43	32	51	23	37
5	Missy	63	59	60	64	69

Figure 1148 *Each cell is lighter or darker based on size.*

The final new visualization is icon sets.

In Excel 2010, there are 20 sets of icons. Some have three symbols, others have four, and some have five.

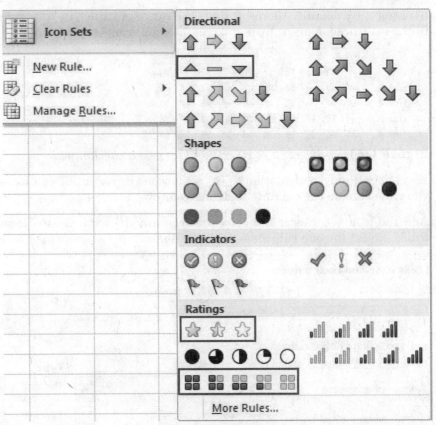

Figure 1149 *Twenty icon sets are available.*

Note that for many of these sets you need to print in color in order for the reader to differentiate the symbols. If you are printing in monochrome, the arrows or power bars are good choices.

After you choose an icon set, Microsoft will display the icon at the left of each cell. Since numbers are usually right-aligned, the number from B2 and the icon from C2 are too close together and many will think that they go together.

I've begun using Ctrl+1 to visit the Format Cells dialog. On the Alignment tab, use a horizontal alignment of Right (Indent). You can then increase the indent to 2 or 3 to move the numbers closer to their icons.

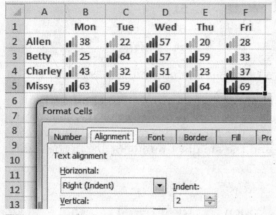

Figure 1150 *Indent numbers to move them closer to the icons.*

The icons won't respond to the horizontal alignment of the cell, unless you use Home, Conditional Formatting, Manage Rules, Edit Rule, Show Icon Only. Ironically, when you use this setting, the icon responds to the Left, Center, and Right Align buttons in the Home ribbon!

CONTROL VALUES FOR EACH ICON

Problem: I applied an icon set. They are adding green checkmarks to cells that are not in the best quality range.

Strategy: By default, Microsoft finds the range of values in your range, divides it by the number of icons in the set (three, four, or five) and creates equal ranges.

	A	B	C	D	E	F
1	Line	Jan	Feb	Mar	Apr	May
2	Line 1	✔ 85	! 81	! 81	✔ 98	✔ 96
3	Line 2	✔ 94	! 70	✔ 86	✔ 85	✔ 92
4	Line 3	✔ 95	✔ 86	! 80	✔ 94	✔ 88
5	Line 4	✘ 66	✘ 61	✘ 56	✘ 59	✘ 64

Figure 1151 *50-67 gets a red X, 84 and up gets a checkmark.*

Excel does a quick calculation to get some icons drawn in. If you have defined limits of acceptable values, you can override the defaults to define your own ranges.

Add the icon set. Select the cells that contain the icon. Go to Home, Conditional Formatting, Manage Rules. Select the one rule and click Edit Rule.

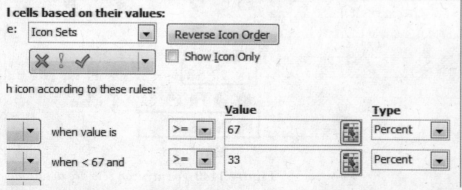

Figure 1152 *The default is by percent.*

In the sample workbook for this topic, the range of data is 50 to 100. Excel split that range of values into values. Anything of 84 or above gets the green checkmark. Note that because the data is skewed high, 57% of the values in the entire data set are getting green checkmarks.

The Type dropdown in the figure above offers Percent, Percentile, Number, and Formula.

If you would use Percentile, Excel would redefine the ranges. About 40 of the 120 values would get each icon. With this data set, 80-90 gets the yellow marker. 79 and below is red, 91 and above is green.

The Type that I use frequently is Number. When using Number, you can define it so that scores of 95 and above get green, 90-94 are yellow and everything else is failing with red.

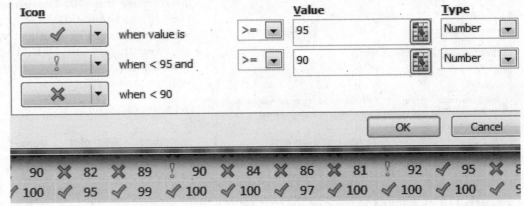

Figure 1153 *Define the ranges to use.*

To use the Formula, you have to type a formula that will result in a number. For example, =AVERAGE($B$2:$M$11)+STDEV.P($B$2:$M$11) will calculate a point that is one standard deviation greater than the mean.

ADD ICONS TO ONLY THE GOOD CELLS

Problem: I want to mark only the best (or worst) cells with an icon. Everything else should not be marked with any icon.

Strategy: Say that you want to add a gold star to all scores of 100.

First, you set up a three-icon set. Edit the Rule. In the Figure below, you make sure the Gold Star is for a Number >=100. Change the icon for the next two rules to No Cell Icon.

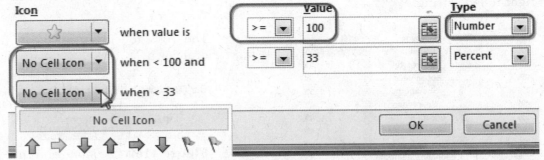

Figure 1154 *First, choose Number from the Type dropdown.*

89	90	84
99	☆ 100	☆ 100
80	98	☆ 100
84	63	60
59	56	56

Figure 1155 *Only the 100's get an icon.*

Tip: use the Icon dropdown shown above to build your own set of icons:

⬆ 99	▲ 60	▼ 33
⬆ 98	— 59	▼ 25
⬆ 97	— 50	⬇ 20
▲ 79	— 42	⬇ 19
▲ 78	▼ 38	⬇ 7
▲ 77	▼ 37	⬇ 1

Figure 1156 *The 5-icon cell phone power bars morphed into this.*

DATA BARS OPTIONS

Cells that contain 0 will get no data bar.

Also, new in Excel 2010, Excel will show negative data bars. Click the Negative Value and Axis button in the Edit Formatting Rule dialog to access the dialog shown below.

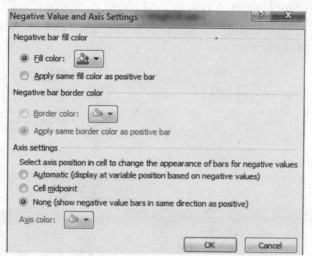

Figure 1157 *Change the color or the axis setting.*

The axis settings offer three settings. The values in the figure below go from -20 to +30. The Automatic setting will show the axis about 40% of the way across the cell. The Midpoint setting will put the axis in the middle of the cell. The None setting seems strange. The smallest value, -17 gets no color. Everything from -16 to -1 will get some red color heading in a positive direction. Values from 0 to 30 will get green color.

Negative Axis Options		
Automatic	**MidPoint**	**None**
-17	-17	-17
8	8	8
-8	-8	-8
1	1	1
20	20	20
22	22	22
3	3	3
30	30	30
-7	-7	-7

Figure 1158 *Three different ways to show the negative axis.*

COMPARATIVE HISTOGRAM

Problem: I want to compare two populations of data.

Strategy: Use the left-to-right setting for a data bar. In the figure below, the data bars on the left use the right-to-left setting.

Kids	Flavor	Adults
9%	Vanilla	29%
10%	Chocolate	9%
0%	Butter pecan	5%
1%	Strawberry	5%
4%	Neapolitan	4%
5%	Chocolate chip	4%
0%	French vanilla	4%
3%	Cookies & cream	4%
1%	Vanilla fudge ripple	3%
0%	Praline pecan	2%
0%	Chocolate almond	2%
0%	Coffee	2%
4%	Cherry	2%
3%	Rocky road	2%
2%	Choc. marshmallow	1%
6%	Moose Tracks	0%
8%	Bubble Gum	0%
9%	Blue Moon	0%
18%	Superman	0%
19%	Cotton Candy	0%

Figure 1159 *The data bars on the left are positive, but they go right-to-left.*

The right-to-left setting is in the Bar Direction dropdown

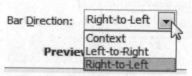

Figure 1160 *Use Manage Rules, Edit Rules to access this.*

SELECT EVERY KID IN LAKE WOBEGON

Problem: Sometimes I need to use conditional formatting to choose all the cells that are above average or I need to highlight cells in the top fifth percentile.

Strategy: The Conditional Formatting menu offers a whole new range of formatting options. You can choose cells that are above average, below average, and so on.

Additional Details: You can actually adjust the options with "10" to show the top or bottom 5, 2, 20, or any number. When you choose one of the "10" options, a new Top 10 Items dialog box will appear, where you can choose how many items or what percentage to show.

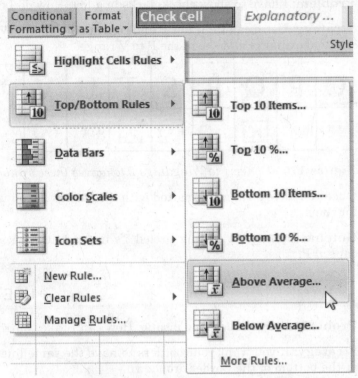

Figure 1161 *The top/bottom rules are new.*

THERE IS A FONT OPTIMIZED FOR EXCEL

Problem: I am looking at numbers all day long. Is there a better font?

Strategy: Famous designer Erik Spiekermann released a font called Axel that he designed for on screen use in spreadsheets. Among the benefits of Axel:
- Similar letters are clearly distinguishable. The zero is slashed to differentiate it from a capital O. The 1 has a suitable serif to differentiate it from a lower case L. I would not have to use Ctrl+One if this book were set in Axel!.
- Legible on a monitor.
- Looks good in a PDF or printed. Embeddable in PDF.
- Many fractions, superscripts, subscripts.

Axel Font	
1234	
5678	
9000	Old 1l O0 7
Ctrl+1	
$\frac{1}{3}\frac{2}{3}\frac{1}{8}\frac{3}{8}\frac{5}{8}\frac{7}{8}\approx\neq\leq\geq$	

Figure 1162 *Axel is designed for Excel.*

4

SHOW CHECKMARKS IN EXCEL

Problem: I have to show checkmarks in a list. How do I create a checkmark in Excel?

Strategy: Use a capital letter P and convert the font to Wingdings 2. There are actually a series of letters with checkmarks and x's. in the P to V range.

O	P	Q	R	S	T	U	V		p	q	r
x	✓	☒	☑	☒	☒	⊗	⊗		⑦	⑧	⑨

Figure 1163 *Convert to Wingdings 2 to access these symbols.*

Once you have a range formatted with Wingdings 2, you would type a P to type a checkmark or type an O for the x.

Gotcha: if you start getting circled 7's instead, it is because you are typing a lower case p instead of a capital P.

USE THE BORDER TAB IN FORMAT CELLS

Problem: Borders drive me insane. How can I take control of my borders?

Strategy: If you want your borders to have the same line color and line style, try the draw borders tools at the bottom of the Border dropdown.
1. Open the border dropdown. At the bottom, choose Line Color, and select a color.
2. Open the border dropdown again. Open the Line Style flyout and choose a line style.
3. Open the border dropdown and choose Draw Border Grid. The mouse pointer changes to a pencil. Click and drag to select a range of cells. Those cells will have your chosen line style and color as borders.

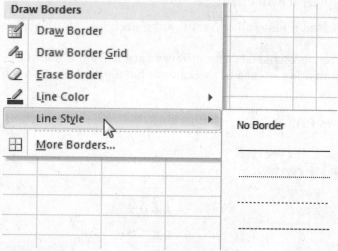

Figure 1164 *Use Draw Borders Grid near the bottom of the dropdown.*

Gotcha: You can keep dragging the mouse to add borders to other ranges. To exit the Draw Borders mode, press the Esc key.

123	123
123	123
123	**123**

Figure 1165 *These borders are drawn with Draw Border Grid.*

Additional Details: If you choose Draw Border instead of Draw Border Grid, dragging the cursor draws an outline around the range instead of each cell.

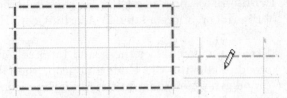

Figure 1166 *Draw Border surrounds a range.*

Alternate Strategy: To have absolute control over borders, particularly when you want a different style on each side of a border, use the Border tab on the Format Cells dialog.

Strategy: The trick is to select the color and weight before you draw any borders. After you've selected a color and a line style, then you can begin drawing borders.

The large white area of the Border tab shows four sides plus a center horizontal and center vertical border. The center borders are enabled only if you are formatting a range of cells. If you are formatting a single cell, you can not choose the center horizontal bar to draw a border through the center of the cell.

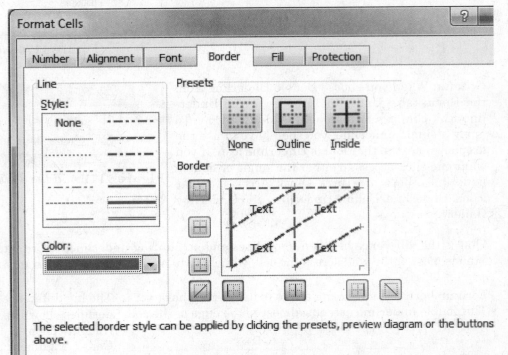

Figure 1167 *The Border tab of the Format Cells dialog.*

Additional Details: You can choose the small buttons around the outside of the white area in the Border tab to select individual border formats. This group also includes diagonal cross-through borders. The diagonal borders cross each cell.

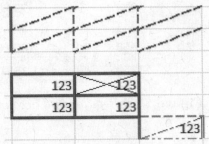

Figure 1168 *These borders are from the Format Cells dialog.*

Gotcha: It would be nice if the color chosen in the Format Cells dialog would carry through to the border tools in the Border dropdown on the home tab. Instead, use Line Color dropdown at the bottom of the Border dropdown.

DOUBLE UNDERLINE A GRAND TOTAL

Problem: My boss is a CPA. He says I should double underline the grand total in a report. The Home tab of the ribbon offers a single underline icon. How can I add a double underline?

Strategy: You select the grand total cell and, instead of clicking the Underline icon, you click the dropdown arrow next to the Underline icon. Then you choose Double Underline.

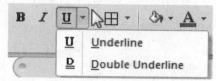

Figure 1169 *The dropdown leads to double underline.*

Alternate Strategy: You can also press Ctrl+1 to access the Format Cells dialog. On the Font tab, from the Underline dropdown you can select Single Accounting or Double Accounting.

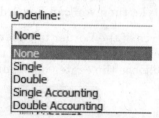

Figure 1170 *More underline choices.*

Gotcha: When you choose Double Underline from the Home tab's Underline dropdown, the Underline icon changes to a Double Underline icon. To apply a single underline, you then have to use the dropdown next to the Double Underline icon. If you want one-click access to either the single or double underline, there are three Quick Access Toolbar icons. Underline, Double Underline, and Underline Gallery.

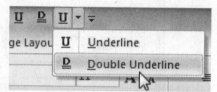

Figure 1171 *Add the double underline icon to the QAT.*

What is the difference between underlines and accounting underlines? For text, an accounting underline extends most of the way across the cell, while a regular underline includes only the characters in the cell.

For numbers, the single underline is under the characters. The double underline extends almost to the edge of the cell.

⬜	A	B	C	D	E
1	*Regular*		*Accounting*		*Regular*
2					
3	<u>Title</u>		Title		<u>Title</u>
4	123	$	(123.00)	$	(123.00)
5	234	$	(234.00)	$	(234.00)
6	345	$	(345.00)	$	(345.00)
7	456	$	(456.00)	$	(456.00)
8	1158	$	(1,158.00)	$	(1,158.00)

Figure 1172 *Regular and accounting underlines.*

The big difference with the accounting underlines shows up when you use any of the (Indent) choices. To try it, go to Format Cells, Alignment. Choose Right (Indent), Left (Indent), or Distributed (Indent) from the Horizontal Alignment dropdown. Increase the Indent spin button.

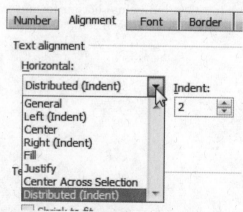

Figure 1173 *Choose (Indent)*

The accounting underline will extend beyond the numbers.

Distributed Indent of 2	
Accounting	Regular
Title	Title
$ (123.00)	$ (123.00)
$ (234.00)	$ (234.00)
$ (345.00)	$ (345.00)
$ (456.00)	$ (456.00)
$ (1,158.00)	$ (1,158.00)

Figure 1174 *Underlines extend beyond numbers with accounting style.*

WHY DID THE COLORS CHANGE IN EXCEL 2013?

Problem: I liked the theme colors from Excel 2007 or Excel 2010. Why are they different now?

Strategy: Go the Excel 2013 Page Layout tab. Skip the Themes dropdown. Go to the Colors dropdown and choose Office 2007-2010.

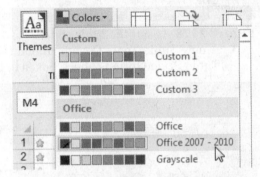

Figure 1175 *Use this color theme.*

WHERE ARE MY EXCEL 2003 COLORS?

Problem: We always used the orange fill from the third row second column of the Excel 2003 color dropdown. Where is this in Excel now?

All Excel 2003 colors can be found in Excel today, although it might be difficult to find. Open one of the color dropdowns. This dropdown now shows the theme colors, plus a few basic colors. Skip those and go to More Colors.

However, when you get to More Colors, you will find that the good old 40 colors are mixed in with 133 other colors. The tough part is figuring out which one of these colors is the color that you want.

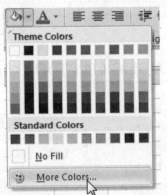

Figure 1176 *More Colors has the old colors*

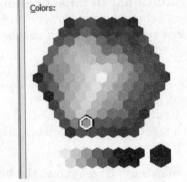

Figure 1177 *All of the 40 colors are in here, somewhere.*

I've created a workbook with forty worksheets. Each worksheet draws a line from the old legacy dialog to the new dialog, so you can find where the color is located. I wrote a tiny little add-in that brought the old legacy color dropdown back to Excel. If you love the old Excel colors, the add-in is available for just $3 from http://www.mrexcel.com/coloraddin2010.html.

TRANSFORM BLACK-AND-WHITE SPREADSHEETS TO COLOR BY USING A TABLE

Problem: My worksheet is boring black and white. I want to jazz it up with color.

Strategy: Format the range as a Table. Use the Table Styles gallery to format the spreadsheet. Here's how you do it:

1. Select one cell in your range of data. Press Ctrl+T or select Insert, Table icon.
2. Excel asks to confirm the location of your table and indicate if there are headers. Click OK.

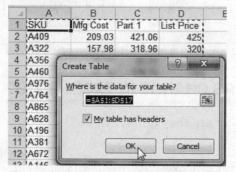

Figure 1178 *Accept the table range.*

3. A new Table Tools Design ribbon tab appears. Use the Table Styles gallery, in conjunction with the Table Style Options check boxes to format your table.

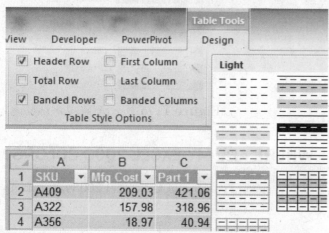

Figure 1179 *Choose a color scheme from the gallery.*

Additional Details: The gallery shows variations on six color schemes. To use new color schemes, you can choose a new theme from the Page Layout tab of the ribbon.

Additional Details: Creating a table enables many new and powerful features. If those features annoy you, then use the Convert to Range button on the Design ribbon. Excel will convert the data from a table to a regular range, but the formatting will remain.

FIT A SLIGHTLY TOO-LARGE VALUE IN A CELL

Problem: I just printed 10 copies of the 20-page report for a meeting. Some numbers printed as ##### instead of numbers.

Strategy: Excel shows the ### when the number is too big for the cell. But, numbers will sometimes fit on the screen and not fit when you are printing.

	A	B	C
1	Invoice	Customer	Sales
2	1901	ABC, Inc.	4,974,374
3	1902	TUVW, Inc	1,586,688
4	1903	BCD, Inc.	2,140,258
5	1904	JKLM, Inc.	#########
6	1905	FGH, Inc.	2,497,515

Figure 1180 *Annoying [pound, hash, or number] signs.*

To solve this problem, you can use Excel's Shrink to Fit option. To use it, you select the numeric columns. Press Ctrl+1 to access the Format Cells dialog. On the Alignment tab, you choose Shrink to Fit from the Text Control section.

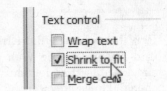

Figure 1181 *Choose Shrink to Fit.*

Results: The cells will be displayed in a smaller font when they become too wide for the column. This is preferable to having the numbers displayed as ######.

Sales
4,974,374
1,586,688
2,140,258
10,205,685
2,497,515

Figure 1182 *The small font for 10,205,685 is preferable to #####.*

TURN OFF WRAP TEXT IN PASTED DATA

Problem: I regularly paste information from Web pages, and I am frustrated by the way Excel wraps text in cells. Below, , column A is not wide enough for the date, and column B is wrapped so that you can see only a few rows on the screen. Using AutoFit to make the columns wider will not work when the cells have their Wrap Text property turned on.

	A	B
1		
2	######	STAPLES #507 AKRON OH 11/22STAPLES #
3	######	CHECK #3646 view
4	######	STAPLES #507 AKRON OH 11/22STAPLES #
5	######	BANKCARD DISCOUNT 430015000100495 CCD

Figure 1183 *Data pasted from the Web often has Wrap Text turned on.*

Strategy: Follow these steps to correct the **Problem:**

1. Select all cells by pressing Ctrl+A. The cells in your selection will contain some cells with Wrap Text turned on and some cells with Wrap Text turned off. Click Wrap Text on the Home tab to turn on Wrap Text cell for all cells. Click Wrap Text again to turn off the property for all cells. Each row will now be a normal height, and you can see more cells, but you still need to make the columns wider.
2. Select Home, Format dropdown, AutoFit Column Width.

	A	B
1		
2	11/24/2016	STAPLES #507 AKRON OH 11/22STAPLES #
3	11/24/2016	CHECK #3646 view
4	11/24/2016	STAPLES #507 AKRON OH 11/22STAPLES #
5	11/23/2016	BANKCARD DISCOUNT 430015000100495 CCD
6	11/23/2016	CHECK #3638 view
7	11/22/2016	STAPLES #507 AKRON OH 11/20STAPLES #

Figure 1184 *The pasted data now has normal formatting.*

DELETE ALL PICTURES IN PASTED DATA

Problem: I copy data from my bank's Web page into Excel. On the Web page, the bank has little check icons that let me view a physical copy of a check. These check icons show up as annoying images in my Excel workbook. How can I delete all these images in one step?

Figure 1185 *Delete all images.*

Strategy: Excel offers the Select Objects tool, that allows you to select all images in a rectangular area. Use, Home, Find & Select, Select Objects.

Using the mouse, start highlighting above and to the left of the first cell that contains a picture. Drag down and to the right to encompass all the cells that contain pictures. When you release the mouse button, all pictures that are completely contained in the rectangle will be selected. At this point, press the Delete key.

Gotcha: You have to remember to turn off Select Objects mode, or you will no longer be able to select any cells. It is very annoying to try to select cells and have the mouse not respond to clicking. To exit Select Objects mode, you simply press the Esc key.

PREVENT LONG TEXT FROM SPILLING

Problem: I have a column with long comments. When the adjacent column is blank, the text from the comment spills over into the adjacent cell.

	A	B	C	D
1	Project	Comment	Done	
2	A	This is son	✓	
3	B	This is some long text		
4	C	This is son	✓	
5	D	This is son	✓	
6	E	This is some long text		

Figure 1186 *The long text spills over when C is blank.*

Strategy: Ironically, the solution is to turn on Wrap Text in column B. This will not be what you are wanting to do, as each row will get really tall to accommodate the long comment.

Choose Home, Format, Row Height. Set everything back to 12.75.

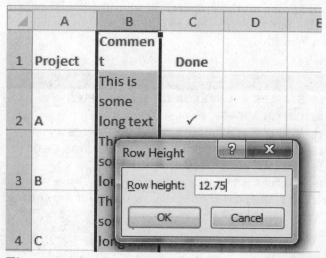

Figure 1187 *After wrap text, set the row height back to 12.75.*

The result will be normal height rows that will not spill into adjacent blank cells.

	A	B	C
1	Project	Commen	Done
2	A	This is	✓
3	B	This is	
4	C	This is	✓
5	D	This is	✓
6	E	This is	

Figure 1188 *The long text won't spill after turning on wrap text.*

SHOW TWO VALUES IN A SPLIT CELL

Problem: My manager wants me to show two values in one cell, as shown here.

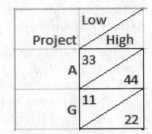

Figure 1189 *One cell shows 33 & 44.*

Strategy: This formatting requires a little bit of cleverness.
1. Type 33, then Alt+Enter, about 9 spaces, then 44, then enter.
2. Select the cell, then Ctrl+One to access Format Cells.
3. On the Border tab, use the diagonal border.
4. You need to adjust the column width or the number of spaces in the cell to get it all lined up. If you add too many spaces, the row height will increase by 50%.

Gotcha: You won't be able to do any math on numbers stored this way.

A better method would be to store the low and high in columns. Then, use the formula =A2&CHAR(10)&REPT(" ",14)&B2 in cell D2. Turn on Wrap Text. Add the diagonal border.

=A2&CHAR(10)&REPT(" ",14)&B2

	A	B	C	D
1	Low	High	Project	Low / High
2	33	44	A	33 / 44
3	11	22	G	11 / 22
4	14	24	F	14 / 24
5	15	25	D	15 / 25
6	73	115	Total	73 / 115

Figure 1190 *A & B can be totaled.*

FOR EACH CELL IN COLUMN A, HAVE THREE ROWS IN COLUMN B

Problem: For each cell in column A, I want to have three rows in columns B and C, as here. I also want to be able to perform calculations with the values in column C.

	A	B	C
	Andy	Quota	1000
		Actual	1200
1		Variance	200
	Ben	Quota	900
		Actual	500
2		Variance	-400

Figure 1191 *You can't easily calculate using numbers in column C.*

Strategy: You might be tempted to use the Alt+Enter trick to enter three lines of data in columns B and C. However, this will not work well in column C. Although the numbers are displayed fine, there is no way to have the numbers in C calculate automatically.

A better option is to merge cells A1:A3 into a single cell. You can then let the data in B fill B1:B3. Here's how:

1. Enter a value in A1. Leave cells A2:A3 blank. Select cells A1:A3.
2. Select Home, Merge & Center dropdown. Choose Merge Cells.

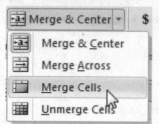

Figure 1192 *Merge Cells is hidden behind this dropdown.*

	Quota	1000
	Actual	1200
Andy	Variance	200
	Quota	900
	Actual	500
Ben	Variance	-400

Figure 1193 *Cells A1:A3 are merged.*

Gotcha: Notice that the vertical alignment defaults to the bottom. This looks okay in a normal-height cell, but not so good in a triple-height cell.

3. Change the vertical alignment to top or center. Vertical alignment icons are now on the Home tab.

Top Align

Figure 1194 *Align top is now on the Home tab.*

4. Creative use of the Borders setting around each group will further enhance the illusion of three rows for each value in column A.

	A	B	C
1	Andy	Quota	1000
2		Actual	1200
3		Variance	200
4	Ben	Quota	900
5		Actual	500
6		Variance	-400

Figure 1195 *Align to the top of the cell.*

5. If you have several rows that need this formatting, use Format Painter mode to copy the formatting. Select cells A1:A3. Double-click the Format Painter icon in the Home ribbon tab. The double-click will put you in Format Painter mode. You can now click in A4, then A7, then A10. Each click will copy the format from A1:A3 to the clicked cell. When you are finished, you can either click the Format Painter icon or press Esc to exit Format Painter mode.

SHOW RESULTS AS FRACTIONS

Problem: I work in an industry that reports values in fractions. Stockbrokers used to deal in increments of 1/8, and tire engineers still measure tread depth in increments of 1/32 inch.

Strategy: There are number formats for fractions. When you press Ctrl+1 to display the Format Cells dialog, you will see that there are nine standard fraction formats available in the Number tab of the Format Cells dialog box.

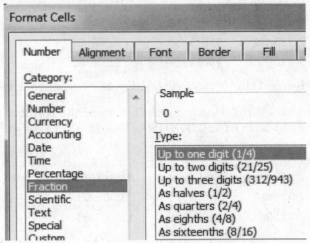

Figure 1196 *Built-in fraction formats.*

When you choose a fraction format, Excel finds the closest fraction.

	A	B	C	D	E	F	G	H	I
1		Original			One digit			Two digits	
2		0.548679	0.566518		5/9	4/7		45/82	17/30
3		0.204794	0.387579		1/5	2/5		17/83	31/80
4		0.325108	0.828182		1/3	5/6		13/40	53/64
5		0.446522	0.857175		4/9	6/7		25/56	6/7
6		0.675782	0.627402		2/3	5/8		25/37	32/51

E2 | fx =B2

Figure 1197 *0.548679 is about 5/9 or 45/82.*

Beyond the seven shown above, Excel offers standard formats for 10ths and 100ths. Unfortunately, there is not a standard format for 32ths.

You can create a custom numeric format to handle 32ths:
1. Select the standard format for 16ths.
2. In the Category list on the Number tab of the Format Cells dialog, scroll down and select Custom. The custom number format code for 16ths is # ??/16. From this, you can deduce that # ??/32 might be a valid number format.
3. Click in the Type box and change the 16 to 32. The Sample area will immediately confirm that you have hit upon the correct format for 32ths.

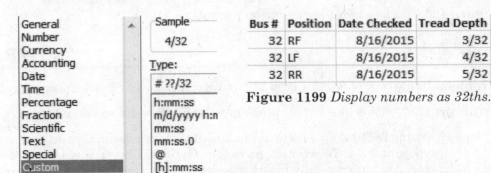

Bus #	Position	Date Checked	Tread Depth
32	RF	8/16/2015	3/32
32	LF	8/16/2015	4/32
32	RR	8/16/2015	5/32

Figure 1199 *Display numbers as 32ths.*

Figure 1198 *Adapt this format for any fraction.*

BETTER SCIENTIFIC NOTATION

Problem: I have to enter values for milliamps. For the 35 mA in row 2, you type 35E-3. For the 150 mA in row 3, you type 150E-3. In both cases, Excel changes what you typed to the values shown in column C.

	A	B	C
1	Goal	You Type	Excel displays
2	35mA	35E-3	3.50E-02
3	150mA	150E-3	1.50E-01

Figure 1200 *If you look quickly, the 1.5 appears smaller than 3.5.*

Format the cells using Ctrl+1. Choose the Number tab and then the Custom category. Change the custom format code from 0.00E+00 to ##0.0E+00.Excel will now display the cells as you wish.

	A	B	D	E	F	G
1	Goal	You Type		After formatting with ##0.0E+00		
2	35mA	35E-3		35.0E-03		
3	150mA	150E-3		150.0E-03		

Figure 1201 *Column E*

FILL A CELL WITH ASTERISKS

Problem: I want to fill the blanks to the left of a number with asterisks like a check-printer would do.

Strategy: When you are entering a custom format, the asterisk symbol says to use the next character to fill the blanks in the cell. I realize this is really confusing, but using **0 tells Excel to use the second asterisk to fill to the left of the number with asterisks. Using *+ tells Excel to fill with plus signs. An asterisk with any character will fill with that character. As the cell gets wider, the number of repeating characters increases.

The ** can go after or before the digits. Column B shows the number format used to achieve the look in column A.

	A	B
1		Number format
2	76.50	0.00
3	*********** 95.23	**0.00
4	+++++++++++ 13.46	*+0.00
5	~~~~~~~~~~~ 35.40	*~0.00
6	91.72***********	0.00**
7	58.71XXXXXXXXXX	0.00*X
8	14.73 XXXXXXXXX	0.00 *X
9		

Category:
General
Number
Currency
Accounting
Date
Time
Percentage
Fraction
Scientific
Text
Special
Custom

Sample
35.40

Type:
*~0.00
_($* #,##
_(* #,##0
_($* #,##
_(* #,##0
**0.00
*+0.00
*~0.00

Figure 1202 *Various repeating character formats.*

I TYPE 152 AND GET 1.52

Problem: In my copy of Excel, I type 152 and Excel enters 1.52. What is going on?

Strategy: That sounds like a great problem to have? How did you do it?

There is a setting in Excel options to automatically insert a decimal point and a number of decimal places when you type a number. To access it, go to File, Options. Choose the Advanced category. The second setting in Advanced is Automatically Insert a Decimal Point. Choose that setting, and then select the number of decimal places.

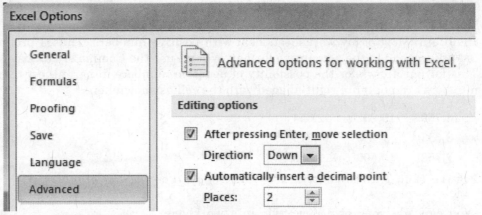

Figure 1203 *This setting affects all worksheets.*

Now, when you enter any number, Excel will divide it by 100.

Not having to type the decimal point can speed data entry of dollars and cents.

Gotcha: This setting does not just affect the current worksheet. It is global to all workbooks that you open on this computer. If you had some data entry to do, you could turn on the setting, do the data entry, then turn the setting back off.

USE CELL STYLES TO CHANGE FORMATS

Gurus of Microsoft Word have known about using styles for two decades. Microsoft promotes styles in Excel, adding a dropdown right on the Home tab offering 42 built-in styles.

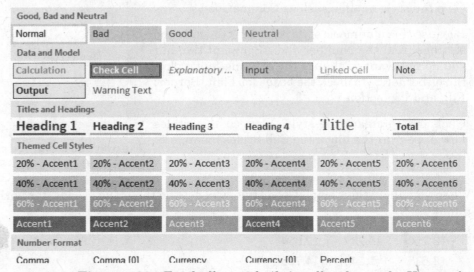

Figure 1204 *Excel offers 42 built-in cell styles on the Home tab.*

You can choose which styles you think are appropriate and which are not. Personally, I use Title and Heading 4 all the time. The other styles seem arbitrary. Why should calculated cells have an orange font? It makes no sense to me. In the figure below, cell A1 has a Title style. Row 3 and column A uses the Heading 4 style. Column F and Row 6 use the Calculation style.

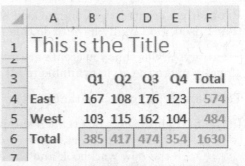

Figure 1205 *Some styles look good. Others do not.*

ADD YOUR OWN STYLES

Problem: Most of my worksheets deal with positive numbers. Thus, I prefer to use a number format of "#,##0" instead of the accounting format. When I use the Comma style, Excel uses the accounting format. This format allows for the possibility of negative numbers in parentheses, and therefore all the positive numbers are not quite right-aligned with the cell as shown here.

18,750	10,287	12,054
8,635	1,240	14,715
7,768	10,600	11,238

Figure 1206 *The comma style uses leaves space after positive numbers.*

You can add your own new style to a workbook. First, format a cell with the correct formatting. It might be easiest to go to a blank cell that had not previously been formatted. Type a number and format that cell. To reach the full Format Cells dialog, use the Ctrl+1 shortcut key. On the Number tab, choose the Number category. Specify 0 decimal places and a thousands separator. On the Alignment tab, specify right-aligned and top-aligned.

To create a new style, select the cell with the formatting for that style. Open the Cell Styles dropdown and choose New Style from the bottom of the menu.

Give the style a name such as CommaGood.

Because this a numeric style, you want to apply the settings from the Number and Alignment tab, but you do not want to change the existing font, color, fill, or borders. Uncheck the boxes for Font, Border, Fill, and Protection.

Click OK to create the style. Your custom styles now appear at the top of the Cell Styles menu.

Figure 1207 *Change only the number format and alignment.*

When you apply the CommaGood style, you get the thousands separator without the extra space after the number.

18,750	10,287	12,054
8,635	1,240	14,715
7,768	10,600	11,238

Figure 1208 *Commas but no extra space to the right of the number.*

SHARE STYLES BETWEEN WORKBOOKS

Problem: I created the CommaGood style as discussed in the last topic. But, it is only in the workbook that I used. Do I really have to do this for every single workbook?

Strategy: Styles that you create are available only in the current workbook. It would be better if you could globally make the style available to all workbooks.

There are two approaches that you can use.

In the first approach, you create a sample workbook that contains all your favorite custom styles. You can copy those styles to any workbook by following these steps:
1. Open the new workbook and the sample styles workbook.
2. Make the new workbook the active workbook.

3. Open the Cell Styles menu and choose Merge.

4. In the Merge Styles dialog, choose to merge from the sample styles workbook. Excel will copy the styles to the new workbook.

This approach is admittedly a hassle because you would have to apply the styles to every workbook you ever create.

An easier approach is to save your styles in Book.xltx. See "Control Settings for Every New Workbook and Worksheet" on page 29.

MOVE COLUMNS BY SORTING LEFT TO RIGHT

Problem: My IT department produces a report every day, and the columns are in the wrong sequence. It would take them two minutes to rewrite the query, but they have a six-month backlog and don't have time to get around to it. How can I rearrange the columns?

	A	B	C	D
1	City	Zip	Attn:	Sta
2	Akron	30909	PAUL NASH	MD
3	Andover	56116	KEVIN TURNER	AZ
4	Naperville	68522	BRANDON BURR	VT

Figure 1209 The columns are not in a logical sequence.

Strategy: You can sort the columns left-to-right. The quick way is to add a new row with column sequence numbers. If you really have to rearrange these every day, however, it would make sense to add a custom list with the proper sequence of the columns.

Follow these steps for the quick method:

1. Insert a new row above the headings.

2. In the new row, enter the numbers 1 through n to specify the desired sequence for the columns. If you want company name first, number that column 1, and so on.

3. Select the range of data to be sorted. Use Ctrl+* to select the current range. If you don't explicitly select the whole range, the Sort command tends to remove the numbered row 1 from the sort.

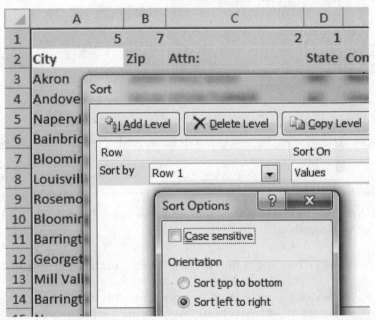

Figure 1210 Steps 2, 3, 6, and 7 are all shown here.

4. Select Data, Sort.

5. Click the Options button at the top of the Sort dialog.

6. Choose Sort Left to Right under Orientation. Click OK to close the Sort Options dialog.

7. In the Sort By dropdown, choose Row 1.

8. Click OK to rearrange the columns.

9. Because the column widths do not sort with the data, select Home, Format dropdown, AutoFit Column Width to fix all column widths. The columns are rearranged.

10. You can now delete the temporary row 1.

Alternate Strategy: If you defined a custom list of Company, Attn:, Address, Suite, City, State, Zip, you could skip the first two steps above. When defining the sort, you would specify Company, Attn:, Address as the sequence. For information on defining a custom sort sequence, see "Sort a Report into a Custom Sequence" on page 252.

MOVE COLUMNS USING INSERT CUT CELLS

Problem: I need to rearrange two columns. The left-to-right sort trick described in "Move Columns by Sorting Left to Right" seems overly complex.

Strategy: There is a fast way to move a couple of columns. You select the entire column to be moved and use Cut. Then you right-click on the column to the right of where the data should go and choose Insert Cut Cells.

Below, you want to move column B before column A. This will require four clicks. Follow these steps:

1. Right-click the B column label. Choose Cut from the context menu.

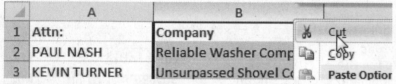

Figure 1211 *Right-click the column and cut.*

2. Right-click the A column label. Choose Insert Cut Cells.

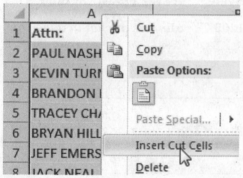

Figure 1212 *Cut B and insert cut cells before A.*

Results: The entire column will be moved. This is an amazingly simple and fast process.

MOVE ROWS OR COLUMNS WITH SHIFT DRAG

Problem: I need to rearrange some rows or columns. Do you have anything faster than the other methods you've described?

Strategy: You might find this method faster than the others:

1. Select an entire row by pressing Shift+Spacebar or select an entire column by pressing Ctrl+Spacebar.
2. Grab the thick border around the row or column. Hold down the Shift key and drag the row/column to a new location. When you use Shift+drag, Excel will basically cut the cells and then insert them where you release the mouse. **Gotcha:** The Shift+drag is critical. If you simply drag, you will do a cut and paste. If you Ctrl+drag, you will do a copy and paste. Both of these will overwrite the destination cells. Only Shift+drag will insert the cells.

	A	B	C	D
1	Row 1	Row 1	Row 1	Row 1
2	Row 2	Row 2	Row 2	Row 2
3	Row 3	Row 3	Row 3	Row 3
4	Row 4	Row 4	Row 4	Row 4
5	Row 5	Row 5	Row 5	Row 5
6	Row 6	Row 6	Row 6	Row 6
7	Move this row after row 2			

Figure 1213 *Shift-drag the border.*

3. You've selected the entire row. Grab the top border while holding down Shift. As you drag, an insertion cursor shows where the row would be moved to.
4. Release the mouse. Excel will insert the row and shift the other rows down.

CHANGE THE WIDTH OF ALL COLUMNS WITH ONE COMMAND

Problem: I have a large model set up in Excel. Some of the columns are hidden. I want to globally change the width of all unhidden columns to a width of 4. If I choose all columns in the worksheet and use Home, Format dropdown, Column Width, the hidden columns will unhide.

Strategy: To solve this problem, you can use Home, Format dropdown, Default Width.

The Default Width dialog allows you to enter one global column width. This change will affect all columns that have not been previously resized or hidden. The result is that you can change the width of all columns without unhiding the hidden columns.

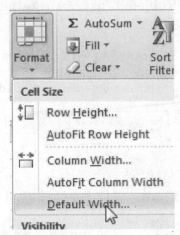

Figure 1214 *Change the default column width.*

Additional Details: Changing the default width will change the width of hidden columns, but will not unhide them. When they are later unhidden, they will have the new width.

Gotcha: The Default Width command does not change the widths of columns that have previously been changed. To see this in action, open a new workbook. Manually change column C to be 20 wide. Use Home, Format dropdown and set Default Width to be 1 wide. All the columns except C will be changed.

COPY COLUMN WIDTHS TO A NEW RANGE

Problem: I have a small report in columns A:G. I made a copy of that report in column H. The column widths did not get copied over. It is a pain to individually look at each column width in A through G and then make the same column width in the new report.

Strategy: First, you don't have to open the Column Width dialog to see the column width. Between each column header, there is a spot where you can click and drag to change the column width. If you simply click there and hold the mouse button down without moving the mouse, you can see the width of the column.

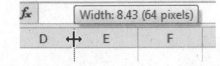

Figure 1215 *Reveal the size of this column.*

The fast solution to this problem is to use the relatively new Paste Column Widths. You can select A1:G1, press Ctrl+C to copy, select cell H1, and do Alt+E+S+W for Paste Special Column Widths.

Microsoft quietly added Column Widths to the Paste Special dialog a few versions ago. It is much easier than using the Format Painter on entire columns to copy the column widths.

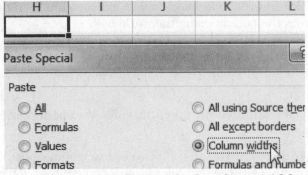

Figure 1216 *Paste only the column widths.*

In Excel 2010, the Paste Options dialog has an icon for Keep Source Column Widths. Immediately after copying the report, you could use this paste option to bring the column widths along with the original paste.

Gotcha: Using the W icon will copy the cell contents as well as the column widths. Using Paste Special and then Column Widths will paste the column widths without pasting the data.

COPY ROW HEIGHTS

Problem: That last trick for pasting column widths works well. How do I do the same thing for row heights?

Strategy: As with column widths, you can quickly find the row height or adjust the row height using the border between row headers.

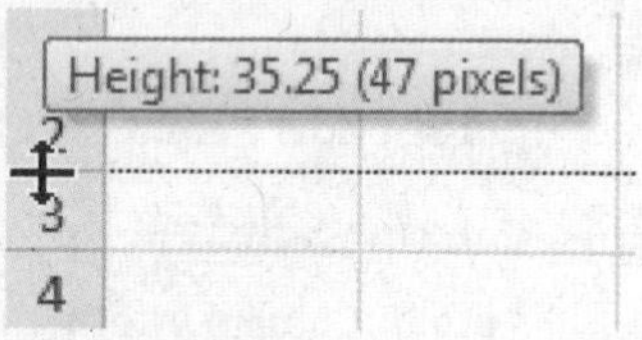

Figure 1217 *Find or adjust one row height.*

There is not a Paste Special option for row heights. You can use the Format Painter to copy row heights. However, the Format Painter will also copy cell colors, font sizes, borders, and so on.

To use the Format Painter, select entire rows. Say that you want to copy row heights in rows 1:10 to rows 21:30.

To copy the heights of rows 1:10, click and drag from the row 1 heading to the row 10 heading.

Don't click any cells while the format painter is active. The next action you have to take is selecting 10 rows. Be sure to click on the row header and not the cell. Click on 21 and drag to 30. The tooltip will confirm that you've selected 10 rows.

Click the Format Painter icon in Home tab. The mouse cursor changes to a paintbrush.

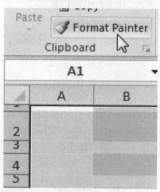

Figure 1218 *Choose entire rows, then click the Format Painter.*

When you release the mouse, Excel will paste all formatting, including row heights from the original range.

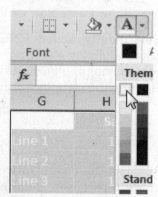

Figure 1219 *Select as many rows as in the copied section.*

USE WHITE TEXT TO HIDE DATA

Problem: My workbook needs extra columns in order to show a graph. I'd like to hide this information from the person using the workbook.

Strategy: Choose the extra cells and choose white text color. To do this, you select Home, Font Color dropdown and choose a white font for the text.

The white font prevents the cells from being visible on screen and from printing.

Additional Details: If you need to troubleshoot these cells, reselect the range. The selection color is dark enough that you can make out the white font in all but the active cell. (Press Ctrl+period to move the active cell to another corner of the selection so you can see the first cell).

Gotcha: Why not just hide the columns? By default, Excel will remove data from a chart when the columns are hidden.

Alternate Strategy: I often take the chart and cover the source data with the chart.

Figure 1220 *Change the font color to white.*

HIDE VALUES USING A NUMBER FORMAT

Problem: Why did you use the white font to hide those cells? Isn't there a custom number format to hide values?

Strategy: Yes. You could select the cells, press Ctrl+1, then choose Custom and type three semi-colons to hide the text in the cell.

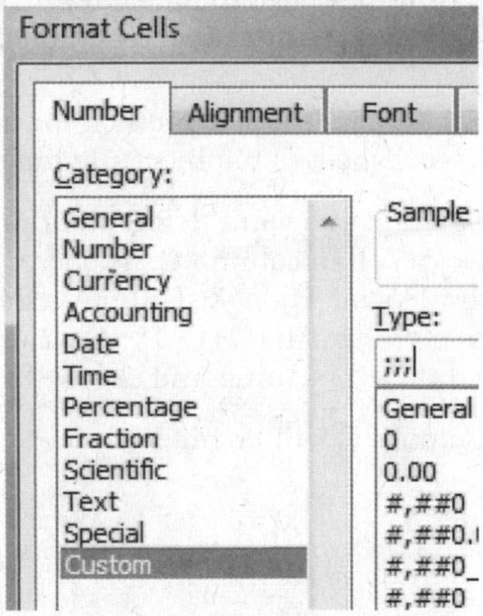

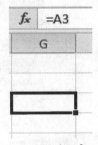

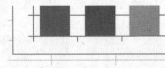

Figure 1221 *Using ;;; will hide the cell contents.*

Gotcha: While nothing will appear in the cells, if someone selects the cell, they can see the cell formula in the formula bar. If the cell contains a constant (i.e. anything other than a formula), then they will see the cell value as well.

Figure 1222 *The cells are hidden, except in the formula bar.*

The other problem with this method: if the data is being used in a chart, then the labels along both axis of the chart will be hidden as well. Here is the chart before hiding the data:

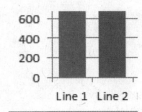

Figure 1223 *Both axis have labels.*

After hiding the data, the axis labels are gone.

Figure 1224 *Axis labels are hidden when the range is hidden.*

HIDE AND UNHIDE DATA

Problem: I need to hide data in a worksheet, but I don't want to delete it. Is there a way to do this besides using the previous two techniques?

Strategy: Another method for hiding data to simplify a worksheet is to physically hide a row or column.

Say that you want to hide column C. To do this, you select a cell in column C. Then you select Home, Format dropdown, Hide & Unhide, Hide Columns. Alternatively, use Alt+O+C+H. Alternatively, right-click the column C heading and choose Hide.

Column C will be hidden.

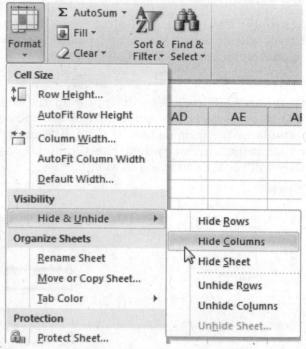

Figure 1225 *Hide the column.*

It is interesting to note that the cell pointer has essentially disappeared. You can see from the Name box that C3 is the active cell. You can also see in the formula bar that the value of C3 is 152. Even though the column is hidden, the active cell is still C3.

	A	B	D	E	F	G
1		Q1	Q3	Q4	Total	
2	Line 1	184	292	353	1212	Line 1
3	Line 2	498	154	500	1304	Line 2
4	Line 3	194	141	470	1190	Line 3

C3 — fx 152

Figure 1226 *Initially, the active cell is in the hidden column.*

Simply press the Left Arrow key or Right Arrow key to move to a visible column to get the cell pointer back.

Additional Details: Immediately after you hid column C, the active cell was still in column C, so you used an arrow key to move out of the hidden column. Once you've arrowed out of the hidden column, you cannot arrow back into it. However, if you type C3 in the Name box—the area that contains the active cell address to the left of the formula bar—and press Enter, Excel will once again select a cell in the hidden column. This can be a handy trick for seeing a value in a hidden cell. You can also use the up and down arrow keys to move through column C, seeing each value one at a time.

To unhide column C, you click the B heading and drag to the right to select the entire range B:D. Select Format, Hide & Unhide, Unhide Columns.

What happens if you need to unhide column A? You can't really select something to the left of A to use the trick just described, but you can follow these steps:

1. Click the column letter B.
2. Drag up and to the left so that the mouse is above row 1. The difference is subtle, but you have now selected columns B and A. Select Format, Column, Unhide.

GROUP COLUMNS INSTEAD OF HIDING THEM

Problem: I have a report with months and quarters. My manager sometimes wants the reports printed with months hidden and other times with the months showing. It is a pain to hide/unhide the four groups of monthly columns.

Strategy: You can group the columns instead of hiding and unhiding them. Follow these steps:
1. Unhide all the columns.
2. Select the headings Jan, Feb, and Mar. Select Data, Group, Columns. Excel adds a group and outline symbol above the column headings.
3. Repeat step 2 for Apr, May, Jun; Jul, Aug, Sep; and Oct, Nov, Dec.

Excel will draw in Group & Outline buttons above the spreadsheet.

	A	B	C	D	E	F
1	Account	Jan	Feb	Mar	Q1	Apr
2	A101	135	137	199	471	101

Figure 1227 *Excel adds group and outline icons like with subtotals.*

You can click the 1 Group & Outline button to collapse to quarters. Click the 2 to show months.

	A	E	I	M
1	Account	Q1	Q2	Q3
2	A101	471	453	531

Figure 1228 *The 1 and 2 Group & Outline buttons toggle between views.*

HIDE ERROR CELLS WHEN PRINTING

Problem: I have a formula that does division. Occasionally, the divisor cell is zero, so I have a couple of #DIV/0! value errors. I need to print this sheet without the errors to get the report to a staff meeting. I don't have time to rewrite all the formulas to test whether the divisor is zero. What can I do?

Strategy: From the Page Layout tab, you can select the dialog launcher at the bottom right corner of the Page Setup group. In the Page Setup dialog, you go to the Sheet tab, select the dropdown for (Print) Cell Errors As, and select <blank>.

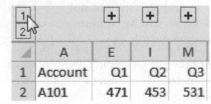

Figure 1230 *Select to print error cells as blank.*

	A	B	C	D
1	Region	Revenue	Units	Average
2	City of London	265.3	70	3.79
3	Barking and Dagenham	167.9	46	3.65
4	Barnet	179.01	51	3.51
5	Bexley	0	0	#DIV/0!
6	Brent	315.06	89	3.54
7	Bromley	318.75	85	3.75

Figure 1229 *A few nagging error cells.*

Results: Although the error will still appear in the worksheet, when you print, the error cells will print as blanks.

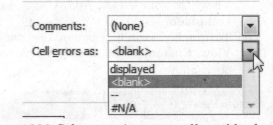

Figure 1231 *No errors will show in the printed document.*

Alternate Strategy: The ultimate way to solve this problem is to change the formula to test whether the divisor is zero. In this case, a proper formula would be =IFERROR(B2/C2,0).

UNHIDE ALL SHEETS

Problem: If you use Group Mode, you can hide a bunch of worksheets in one command.

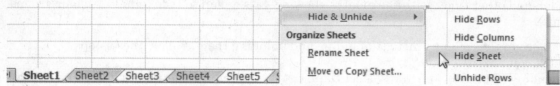

Figure 1232 *Hide many worksheets in one command.*

However, there is no way to unhide all of the worksheets in a single command. You have to do Home, Format, Hide & Unhide, Unhide Sheets to get to this dialog. You can not select multiple worksheets here, so you have to repeat that command for every worksheet.

Strategy: Use the View Manager. Create one view with the worksheets hidden. Create another view with the worksheets visible.

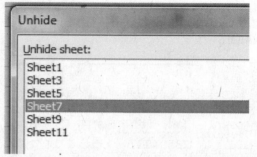

Figure 1233 *Unhide sheets one at a time.*

To solve the current problem, follow these steps:

1. Select View, Custom Views, Add.
2. Assuming the worksheets are currently hidden, use a name such as SheetsHidden.
3. Unhide all the worksheets. If you want a quick way to do this, press Alt+F11. Press Ctrl+G. Type "for each w in activeworkbook.Worksheets : w.visible = true : next" and press Enter. Press Alt+Q.
4. Now that the worksheets are unhidden, select View, Custom Views, Add. Use a name such as Unhidden.
5. To quickly switch between the two views, use View, Custom Views. Select the correct view and click Show.

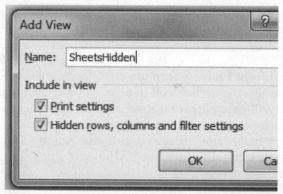

Figure 1234 *Set up a view to remember which sheets to hide.*

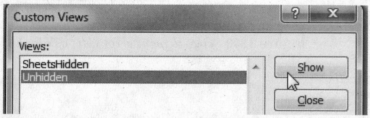

Figure 1235 *Switch to a different view.*

Gotcha: If any of your worksheets use a table, you can not use views. In this case, I would add a macro to your personal macro workbook with the code from step 3. For a demo of this, search YouTube for Learn Excel 611.

ORGANIZE YOUR WORKSHEET TABS WITH COLOR

Problem: I have a lot of tabs in a workbook. Can I highlight the frequently used tabs in red?

Strategy: You can right-click a tab and choose Tab Color to assign a color to a worksheet tab.

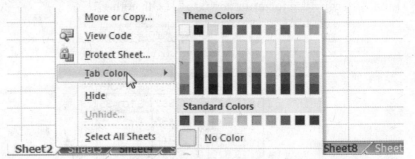

Figure 1236 *Add color to the worksheet tabs.*

Gotcha: You can see the tab colors of all but the active sheet. The active sheet appears with a mostly white tab and only a tiny swatch of color.

Additional Details: If you choose Theme Colors for your worksheet tabs, the tab colors will change if you choose a new theme.

COPY FORMATTING TO A NEW RANGE

Problem: I have several similar report sections on a spreadsheet. When I get the first report nicely formatted, I would like to copy the format to the other reports.

Strategy: You can use Paste Special Formats to copy just the formats from one range to another:
1. Select cells A1:E6. Ctrl+C to Copy.
2. Select the upper-left corner of the next section. Open the Paste dropdown on the Home tab. Select the Paste Formats icon.

	A	B	C	D	E
1	UNIT SALES				
2		*East*	*Central*	*West*	**Total**
3	Widgets	44	11	83	**138**
4	Sprockets	71	59	52	**182**
5	Wheels	16	99	57	**172**
6	Total	**131**	**169**	**192**	**492**
7					
8	DOLLAR SALES				
9		East	Central	West	Total
10	Widgets	62.48	15.62	117.86	195.96
11	Sprockets	180.34	149.86	132.08	462.28

Figure 1237 *Copy the formatting to other report sections.*

4

Gotcha: If the target range contains any merged cells, you can not simply select the top left cell as indicated in step 2. Instead, you must select a rectangular range of the same size and shape as the range copied in step 1.
3. Move the cell pointer to the next section. Repeat the Paste Formatting command.
4. Repeat for any additional sections.

Results: The cell formats will be copied, but their values and formulas will not.

Alternate Strategy: You can also use Format Painter mode to copy formats. You select A1:E6, double-click the Format Painter icon in the Home ribbon tab, and click A8 and A15. At each click, Excel will copy the formats to the new range. When you are finished, you can either click the Format Painter icon or press Esc to exit Format Painter mode.

COPY WITHOUT CHANGING BORDERS

Problem: I have built a report in Excel and used numerous borders to outline the data. After entering a formula to calculate profit in E3, I want to copy the formula down to E4 through E7.

	A	B	C	D	E
					fx =C3-D3

E3

	A	B	C	D	E
2		Week	Sales	COGS	Profit
3		1	$18,972	$8,537	$10,435
4		2	17,074	8,195	
5		3	15,366	7,375	
6		4	13,829	6,637	
7		5	12,446	5,974	
8		Total	$77,687	$36,718	$10,435

Figure 1238 *Copy this formula.*

However, because cell E3 has a top border, copying the formula causes all the cells in E4 through E7 to also have a top border, ruining the effect of my borders.

$10,435
$8,879
$7,991
$7,192

Figure 1239 *Excel copies the borders, too.*

Strategy: You can select Home, Paste dropdown, Paste Special, All Except Borders to copy the formula and the numeric formatting but not disturb the borders.

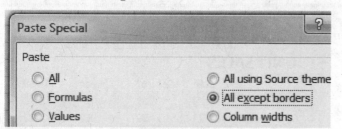

Figure 1240 *Copy all except borders.*

Results: The formula is successfully copied, but the borders remain as they were.

	Profit
5	
7	$10,435
5	$8,879
5	$7,991
7	$7,192
4	$6,472

Figure 1241 *Excel will not disturb the borders.*

Alternate Strategy: In the data set described here, it appears that you decided to show the currency symbol on only the first row and the total row. In this case, it might have been more appropriate to use Paste Special, Formulas just to copy the formula.

The Paste dropdown offers two icons in the first row that will help in this situation. The fx icon will copy formulas. The %fx icon will copy the formulas and number formatting.

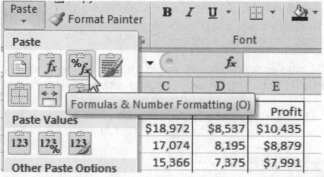

Figure 1242 *The Paste dropdown offers Paste Formulas.*

POWER UP FORMAT PAINTER

Problem: I have to paste formatting to many sections of a report.

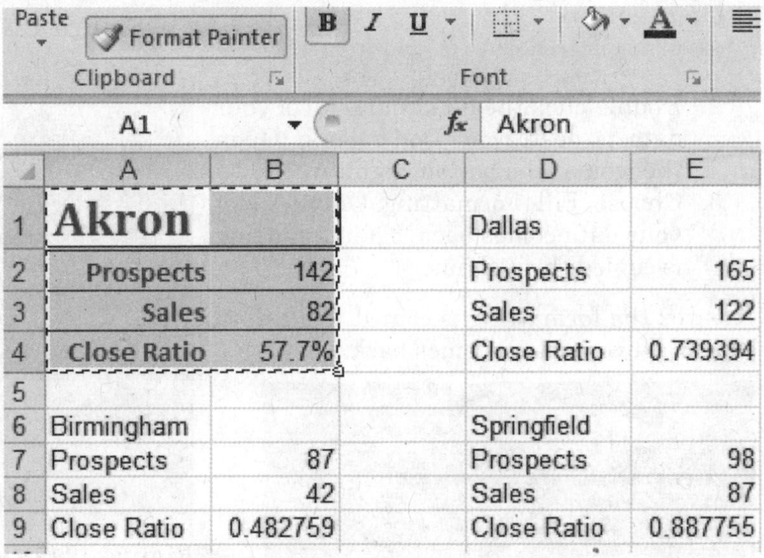

Figure 1243 *Double-click the Format Painter.*

Here is an example:
1. Select the original range and double-click the Format Painter icon. The Format Painter icon will stay lit. The mouse pointer is a paint brush.
2. Click the top-left cell of the first destination range. As you click each top-left cell, the formats from the entire original range will be copied to a similar-shaped area.

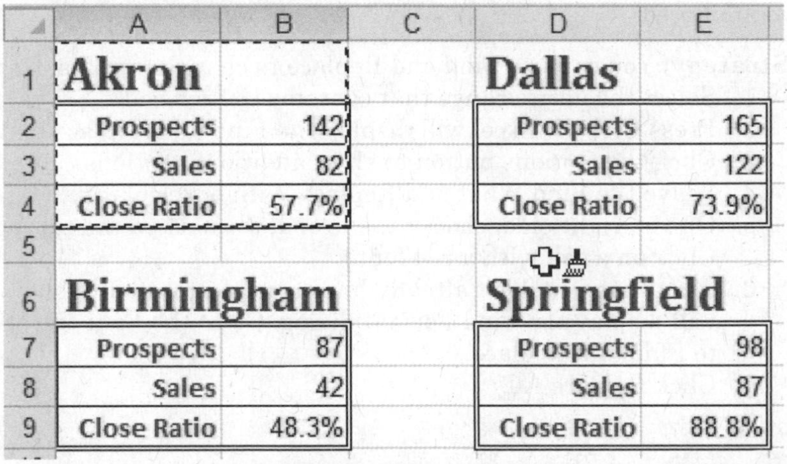

Figure 1244 *Three format painter clicks copies the format three times.*

3. When you are done copying formats, you need to exit Format Painter mode. Either press Esc or click the Format Painter again.

FILL FORMATTING

Problem: I have a thousand rows of data. I want to apply red and blue to every other row. Nothing in the Format as Table looks exactly like I want it to look and I don't want to define my own table style.

Strategy: This technique temporarily wipes out all of your data, but you get it back. It is a fast way to go.

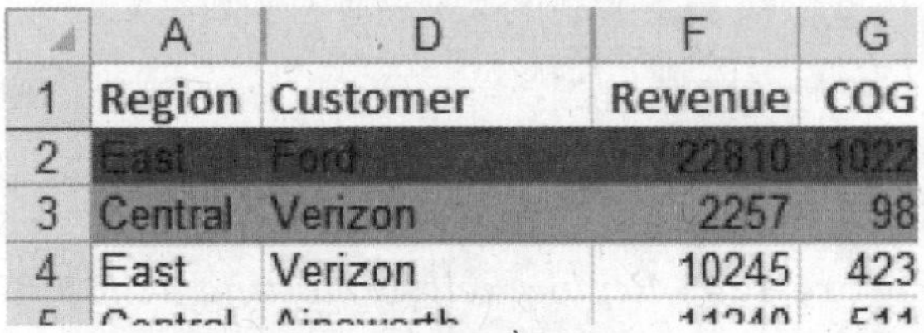

Figure 1245 *Copy this formatting.*

1. Select the data in rows two and three. You will see a fill handle in the bottom right corner of the selection.

East	Ford		22810	10220	12590
Central	Verizon		2257	984	1273
East	Verizon		10245	4235	6010

Figure 1246 *Double-click the fill handle.*

2. Double-click the fill handle. All of your data is destroyed. Don't panic. Open the icon at the bottom right.
3. Choose Fill Formatting Only. All of your data comes back. The formatting is copied throughout.

Result: the formatting is copied. Your data that was overwritten comes back.

East	Ford	22810	1
Central	Verizon	2257	
East	Verizon	10245	
Central	Ainsworth	11240	
Central	Ainsworth	9204	

Figure 1248 *Only the formatting is copied!*

-696545	-313040	-383505
-717098	-322276	-394822
-737651	-331512	-406139
-758204	-340748	-417456
-778757	-349984	-428773
-799310	-359220	-440090
-819863	-368456	-451407
-840416	-377692	-462724
-860969	-386928	-474041
-881522	-396164	-485358
-902075	-405400	-496675
-922628	-414636	-507992

- ○ Copy Cells
- ● Fill Series
- ○ Fill Formatting Only
- ○ Fill Without Formatting
- ○ Fill Days
- ○ Fill Weekdays
- ○ Fill Months
- ○ Fill Years

Figure 1247 *Open the Fill Options icon.*

CHANGE ALL RED FONT CELLS TO BLUE FONT

Problem: I've marked a few hundred cells in a large workbook using a red font. My manager is superstitious and wants all the red cells changed to blue. The red cells are not contiguous. I did not use cell styles to apply red.

Strategy: You can use Find and Replace to change formats. Here's what you do:
1. Select the entire range that contains the red cells.
2. Press Ctrl+H. Excel will display the Find and Replace dialog.
3. Click the Options button to show additional options.
4. Leave the Find What and Replace With boxes blank.
5. On the right side, choose the dropdown next to the top Format button. Choose Format From Cell. Click on a cell with a red font.
6. Assuming you don't already have a cell formatted in blue, click on the bottom Format button. Excel will display the Find Format dialog. Go to the Font tab and choose a blue color. Click OK to return to Find and Replace.
7. Click Replace All.

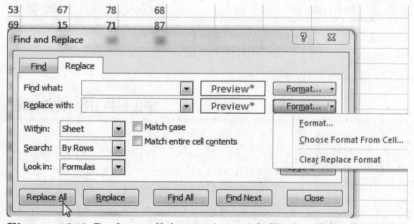

Figure 1249 *Replace cell formatting with Find and Replace.*

Results: The red fonts are changed to blue.

Gotcha: When you choose the format from an existing cell, Excel picks up all the formats. When you perform the Replace, if a format does not match exactly, the cell will not be replaced. For example, if some cells were left-justified instead of right-justified, they will not be replaced.

REPLACE PARTIALLY BOLD CELLS

Problem: I have some cells that are partially bold. When I use Find and Replace to change the text in these cells, I am losing the bold.

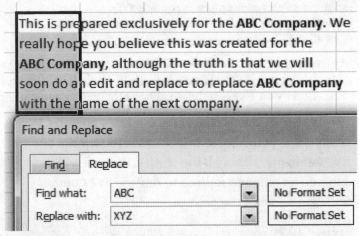

Figure 1250 *Do a replace all and the bold will be lost.*

Figure 1251 *The bold is lost.*

I tried adapting the last topic, choosing Bold as the format in the second box, but then the entire cell become bold whenever the text is found.

Strategy: Excel really does not deal well with cells that are partially formatted. It pains me to say this, but here is an example where Microsoft Word can save the day.

1. Copy your data in Excel.
2. Open Word. (If you've never used Word, think of it as an add-in for people who can't seem to type their letters in Excel).
3. Paste the cells to Word.

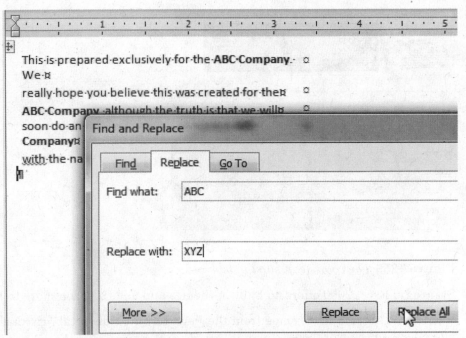

Figure 1252 *Do the Replace in Word.*

4. Use Ctrl+H. Change ABC to XYZ. Click Replace All. Word keeps the bold.

This·is·prepared·exclusively·for·the·**XYZ·Company**.· ¤
We·¤

really·hope·you·believe·this·was·created·for·the¤   ¤

XYZ·Company,·although·the·truth·is·that·we·will¤   ¤

soon·do·an·edit·and·replace·to·replace·**XYZ·**   ¤
Company¤

with·the·name·of·the·next·company.¤   ¤

Figure 1253 *Word can do a replace without changing the bold.*

5. In Word, use Ctrl+A to select all, Ctrl+C to copy. Switch back to Excel with Alt+Tab.
6. Ctrl+V in Excel to paste. The cells are pasted correctly.

This is prepared exclusively for the **XYZ Company**. We

really hope you believe this was created for the

XYZ Company, although the truth is that we will

soon do an edit and replace to replace **XYZ Company**

with the name of the next company.

Figure 1254 *The data is pasted back to Excel correctly.*

7. Don't forget to close Word.

CHANGE THE LOOK OF YOUR WORKBOOK WITH DOCUMENT THEMES

Problem: The new Excel has a lot of nice-looking features. It uses new colors, new fonts, new chart colors. But after a while, the blue, red, green, purple, teal, and orange colors get old. Here is a worksheet with a table, SmartArt, a chart, a picture, and shapes.

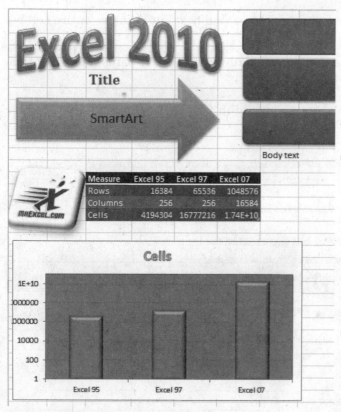

Figure 1255 *The colors can start to look old.*

Strategy: Excel 2010 offers 40 built-in themes and adds a dozen more from Office Online.

When you choose a new theme from the Page Layout ribbon tab, Excel changes the accent colors, fonts, and effects in the workbook.

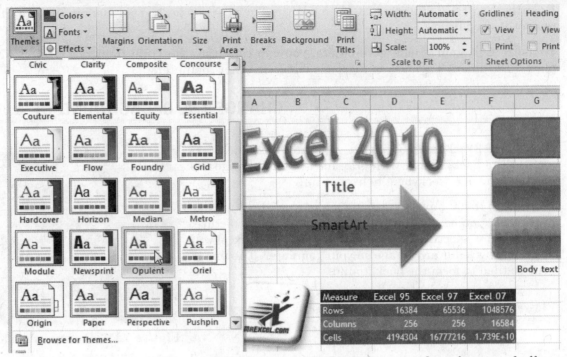

Figure 1256 *Choose a new theme for new colors, fonts, and effects.*

Excel, Word, and PowerPoint offer the same themes. If you choose the same theme in all three products, your documents should have a similar look and feel.

Additional Details: A theme comprises six accent colors, title and body fonts, and a series of effects.

The Effects dropdown is confusing. For each theme, Excel shows the effects for a circle, an arrow, and a rectangle. The circle gives an indication of the format used for simple formats. The arrow shows the effects used for moderate formatting. The rectangle shows the effects used for intense formats.

From the thumbnails here, you can guess that Module will offer double lines in simple effects, the Paper theme will offer muted or flat moderate effects, and the Opulent theme is going to offer glass effects when you choose intense formatting.

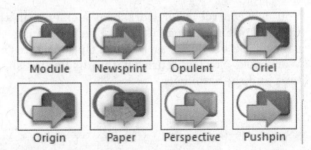

Figure 1257 *3 shapes indicate 3 levels of effects.*

When you open many galleries such as the Shape Styles Gallery, the last three rows will be labeled "Simple", "Moderate" and "Intense". These correspond to the circle, arrow, and rectangle icons in the Effects dropdown.

CREATE YOUR OWN THEME

Problem: There isn't a theme to match our company colors.

Strategy: Create a new theme and save it on your computer. You can then share it with others in your company.

Follow these steps:
1. Select one of the built-in themes from the Effects dropdown on the Page Layout tab.
2. Open the Fonts dropdown on the Page Layout tab and choose Create New Theme Fonts. Choose a font for headings and a font for body copy. Tip: If you have a stylized logo with "OurCo" and want a font to provide all 26 letters in a similar font, visit Chank.com to have a custom font designed.
3. Open the Colors dropdown and choose Create New Theme Colors. Specify colors for light and dark text and specify six accent colors for the theme.
4. Open the Themes dropdown and choose Save Current Theme. Give the theme a name that reflects your company name.

Results: Excel will offer the new theme in the Themes dropdown. Your custom themes will appear at the top of the dropdown.

To share a custom theme with others, you can copy the .thmx file from %AppData%\Microsoft\Templates\Document Themes\ to the same folder on other computers.

CHANGE THE BACKGROUND OF A WORKSHEET

Problem: Excel looks boring. It generally has black text on a white background, with gray lines. Can I change the background of a worksheet to liven it up?

Strategy: If you have an opening menu worksheet in your workbook, you can change the background to any picture. You start by selecting Page Layout, Background. Excel will let you browse for any image on your computer. The image will be tiled to form the background.

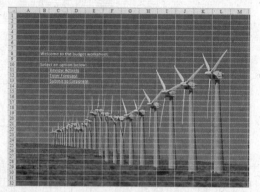

Figure 1258 *Picture as a background.*

To present a cleaner view, you can turn off the gridlines for the worksheet. The Show/Hide group on the View tab allows you to turn off the gridlines, the formula bar, and the row/column headings.

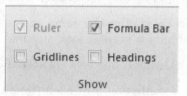

Figure 1259 *Turn off gridlines and other elements on the View tab.*

You can control other worksheet elements in the Excel Options dialog. Choose File, Options, Advanced. Scroll down to Display Options for This Workbook. You can turn off the display of sheet tabs and the scrollbars.

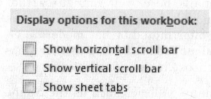

Figure 1260 *Turn off scrollbars in the Excel Options dialog.*

Your worksheet will now look cleaner.

Figure 1261 *No gridlines.*

Gotcha: Turning off all the scrollbar and sheet tab options will affect the entire workbook. Because someone will have to enter data on the other worksheets, this might make it difficult to actually use Excel when an Excel rookie moves on to the other worksheets in the workbook.

Gotcha: The background will never print. See the next topic for a workaround.

Gotcha: If you zoom in or out, the cell sizes will change, but the picture will stay the same size. You might get a picture that perfectly fills A1:J15, but after zooming out, the picture will cover A1:M20.

Additional Details: In order to change the background image on a worksheet, you must first remove the first image by selecting Page Layout, Delete Picture.

ADD A PRINTABLE BACKGROUND TO A WORKSHEET

Problem: The image I added as a background using the instructions in the previous topic will not print. How do I add a background image that will print?

Strategy: You can add a shape to cover the printable area of your worksheet and then change the shape fill to be your picture. Microsoft allows you to alter the transparency of the shape. Follow these steps:
1. Choose Insert, Shapes dropdown, Rectangle. Draw a rectangle to cover your print area.
2. Select Drawing Tools Format, Shape Outline, No Outline.

3. Right-click the shape and choose Format Shape. Excel displays the Format Shape dialog.
4. In the Fill category, choose Picture or Texture Fill.
5. In the Insert From section, click the File button. Browse, select a picture, and click Insert.
6. At the bottom of the Format Picture dialog, increase the Transparency slider. You can preview the picture transparency as you slide. Around 60% seems to be appropriate. The figure below shows the worksheet at 60% behind the dialog.
7. Click Close to dismiss the Format Picture dialog box.

Results: Excel will add a background that can be printed.

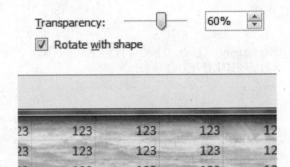

Figure 1262 *When you use fill for a shape, you can adjust picture transparency.*

Gotcha: It is now difficult to select a cell with the mouse. If you click on a cell that is covered by the transparent picture, you will select the picture. To avoid this, you click outside the picture and then use the arrow keys to navigate to cells behind the picture.

REMOVE HYPERLINKS AUTOMATICALLY INSERTED BY EXCEL

Problem: Excel has an annoying habit. Whenever you type something in a cell that looks like an e-mail address or a Web site URL, Excel will underline the value, change the font color to blue, and make it a clickable hyperlink.

Figure 1263 *Excel will automatically create hyperlinks.*

Strategy: To remove a hyperlink, you right-click the cell and choose Remove Hyperlink.

You can prevent Excel from adding hyperlinks in the first place. Choose File, Options. Select the Proofing category and then click the AutoCorrect Options button. Choose the AutoFormat As You Type tab in the AutoCorrect dialog. Uncheck the Internet and Network Paths with Hyperlinks check box.

Additional Details: New in Excel 2010, you can remove the hyperlinks from an entire range at one time. Select the range of hyperlinks and make sure that the active cell contains a hyperlink. Right-click and choose Remove All Hyperlinks.

SELECT A HYPERLINK CELL WITHOUT FOLLOWING THE HYPERLINK

Problem: I have a hyperlink in my worksheet in cell A10. I want to select that cell without following the hyperlink.

Strategy: Click and hold the mouse on the cell. When the pointing hand changes to a white cross, release the mouse button. You will select the cell instead of following the hyperlink.

PASTED URLS DON'T BECOME HYPERLINKS

Problem: I pasted hundreds of web site addresses into Excel. They did not turn into hyperlinks. I found that I could select a cell, press F2, then Enter to make the hyperlink. But I don't want to have to do that hundreds of times.

	A
1	http://www.MrExcel.com
2	http://www.Easy-XL.com
3	http://www.ExcelGuru.Net
4	http://www.Live.com
5	www.mrexcel.com

Figure 1264 *Pasted hyperlinks are not hot.*

Strategy: Use the =HYPERLINK() function. Insert a blank column near your data. Use =HYPERLINK(A1,A1).

	A	B	C	D	E	F
1	http://www.MrExcel.com	=HYPERLINK(A1,A1				
2	http://www.Easy-XL.com	HYPERLINK(link_location, [friendly_name])				
3	http://www.ExcelGuru.Net					
4	http://www.Live.com					
5	www.mrexcel.com					

Figure 1265 *The second A1 is supposed to be a friendly name.*

Enter the formula and copy it down to all rows.

	A	B	C	D
1	http://www.MrExcel.com	http://www.MrExcel.com		
2	http://www.Easy-XL.com	http://www.Easy-XL.com		
3	http://www.ExcelGuru.Net	http://www.ExcelGuru.Net		
4	http://www.Live.com	http://www.Live.com		
5	www.mrexcel.com	www.mrexcel.com		
6	http://www.MrExcel.com	http://www.MrExcel.com		

Figure 1266 *Column B contains live hyperlinks.*

Hide column A, leaving column B intact.

Gotcha: This strategy works great for web addresses that have the leading http://. It will not work for cell A5. A hyperlink will appear, but when someone follows the hyperlink, it will say the address is invalid. In that case, you could use this formula: =HYPERLINK("http://"&A5,A5).

DEBUG USING A PRINTED SPREADSHEET

Problem: I need to proofread cells in my spreadsheet. It would be easier to do this from a printed piece of paper, but I need to see the row numbers and column letters in the printout.

Strategy: You can print row numbers and column letters. On the Page Layout ribbon tab, you choose Print under both Gridlines and Headers.

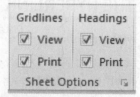

Figure 1267 *Choose to print gridlines and headers.*

Results: The printed copy of the spreadsheet will show column letters across the top and row numbers down the side.

LEAVE HELPFUL NOTES WITH CELL COMMENTS

Problem: I have figured out how to write a confusing formula in Excel. I want to add a note to the worksheet to remind myself how the formula works.

Strategy: You can use cell comment to leave notes in a worksheet. In addition to having 17 billion cells on a worksheet, you can also store a comment for each cell. Typically, a cell comment is indicated by a red triangle in the corner of the cell. If you hover the mouse over the cell, the comment will appear.

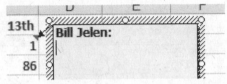

=SUMPRODUCT(--(WEEKDAY(ROW(INDIRECT(A2&":"&B2)))=5),--(DAY(ROW(INDIRECT(A2&":"&B2)))=13))

	A	B	C	D	E
1	Start Date	End Date	# Friday 13th		
2	2/10/2014	2/21/2014	1		
3	2/17/1965	7/1/2014	86		
4					

Figure 1268 *Add a note about this formula.*

Here's how you add comments to a worksheet:
1. Select the cell where you want to add a comment. Select Review, New Comment. A comment box appears, with your name in bold on line 1.

2. Type a comment.
3. Click the mouse outside the comment box to complete the entry of the comment. A red triangle remains in the cell to indicate the presence of a comment there.

When you hover your mouse over the cell with the red triangle, your comment box will pop up like a ToolTip.

Additional Details: To delete a comment, you select the cell and then select Review, Delete. To edit a comment, you select the cell and then Edit Comment will be available in the Review tab.

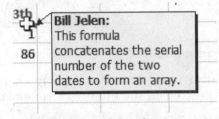

Figure 1269 *Excel adds your name.*

Figure 1270 *Type a note.*

Figure 1271 *Hover to show the comment.*

The information here is based on the assumption that you are using the default settings for comments. There are additional settings available in the Advanced tab of the Excel Options dialog. On this tab, for example, you can suppress the appearance of the red comment indicator or force all comments to be shown at all times.

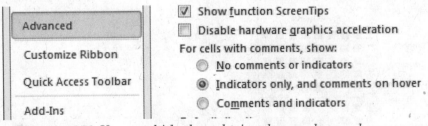

Figure 1272 *You can hide the red triangles, or always show comment.*

Gotcha: If you have a comment in a row above the Freeze Panes line, you will notice a bug. The comment will appear normally if you have scrolled the worksheet to the top. However, if you have scrolled down to other pages in the worksheet, the comment will be truncated.

CHANGE THE APPEARANCE OF CELL COMMENTS

Problem: I typed a very long comment in a cell. The comment is longer than the comment box will display. How can I read the entire comment?

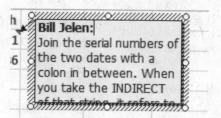

Figure 1273 *Initially, the comment box is fairly small.*

Strategy: Use the resize handles while editing the comment to enlarge the comment.

Excel also gives you complete control over the size and appearance of the comment box. When you are editing the text within the comment, the border around the comment is diagonal lines. If you press Press Ctrl+1 at this point, you can only control the font.

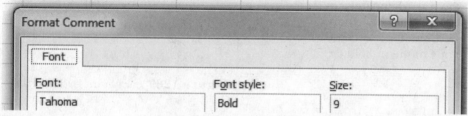

Figure 1274 *Only one tab out of eight appears.*

To get the complete set of formatting options, you must first left-click the diagonal lines border. This will change the diagonal lines to dots. While the border is dots, press Ctrl+One. Excel will display the complete Format Comment dialog with all the tabs.

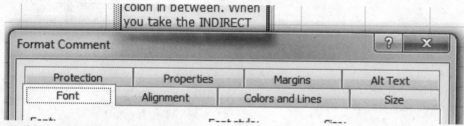

Figure 1275 *With a dotted comment border, the Format dialog offers all.*

Additional Details: You can change the yellow background. In the Format dialog, choose Colors and Lines. Open the Fill dropdown and choose Fill Effects from the bottom of the list.

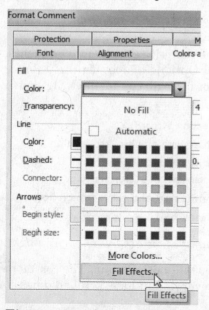

Figure 1276 *Change the comment background.*

You can insert a gradient and even change the transparency of the comment so that the underlying cells can show through.

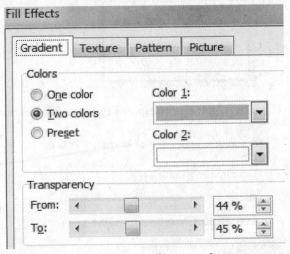

Figure 1277 *Add a gradient to the comment.*

Result: The comment will appear with formatting different than 99.9% of the comments that people are used to seeing.

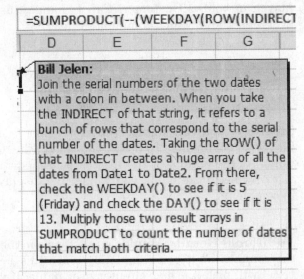

Figure 1278 *Larger comment, with formatting.*

Additional Details: It is possible to globally change the default color of all future comments, but I don't recommend it. The comment color is drawn from the Tooltip color in the Control Panel. You can edit this with Start, Control Panel, Personalization, Window Color, Advanced Appearance Settings. Open the Item dropdown and choose Tool Tip. Open the Color 1 dropdown and choose Other.... You can enter RGB values to build any color.

Gotcha: You will be amazed how many tool tips there are in Windows. The new color of the tool tips was too distracting for me. I wanted to change the color back, but the original light yellow is not offered as a standard color in the dropdown. If you want to go back to the original yellow, use these settings:

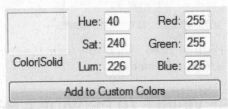

Figure 1280 *Use this color codes to go back to the light yellow.*

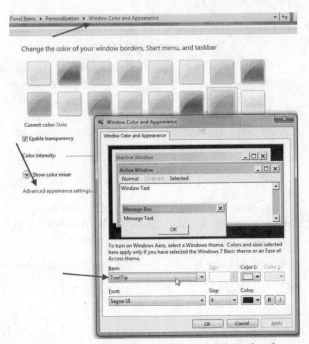

Figure 1279 *Edit the comment color here.*

CONTROL HOW YOUR NAME APPEARS IN COMMENTS

Problem: When I insert a comment, the name displayed in bold is Customer. Can I change this so everyone knows which comments I inserted?

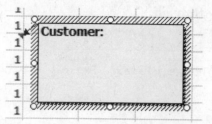

Figure 1281 *The comment offers a generic name.*

Strategy: You can change the name that is displayed in comments. To do so, you select File, Options. At the bottom of the first category, edit the User Name to the name you would like displayed in comments.

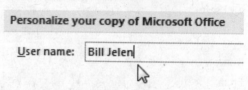

Figure 1282 *Change comment name.*

Additional Details: Would you prefer no name in the comments? If you completely erase this field, Excel will pick up the computer user name. If you put a space, the comment will appear with a space and a colon in row 1.

Figure 1283 *You can't completely remove it..*

If you want to remove the name from a single comment, you can select the name and press Delete or backspace through the name. Be careful that your comment doesn't end up in bold. Typically, the name will appear in bold, and the comment you type will appear in normal font.

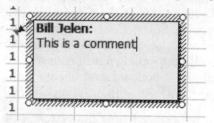

Figure 1284 *Bold name. Normal comment.*

When you backspace through the name and then begin to type, Excel will be in bold mode, and any comment you type will appear in bold.

To turn off the bold mode, press Ctrl+B before you begin to type the comment.

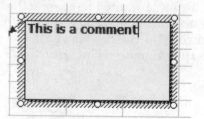

Figure 1285 *When you clear the comment, you are left in bold mode.*

FORCE SOME COMMENTS TO ALWAYS BE VISIBLE TO PROVIDE A HELP SYSTEM

Problem: I'm sending out a worksheet to managers and division vice presidents in order to get their budget for next year. I need to include specific instructions for many of the cells in the worksheet.

Strategy: There are two primary techniques you can do this: cell comments and color-coding.

To use cell comments, for each comment you want to display 100% of the time, select the cell and choose Review, Show/Hide Comment. Alternatively, right-click the cell and choose Show Comment. This will force those comments to be always visible.

Figure 1286 *Toggle individual comments on or off.*

To use color coding, you can make all comments meant for managers green, and you can make the vice presidents' instructions blue. When managers and vice presidents open the file, they will have an easy-to-follow visual road map through their budget worksheet.

Additional Details: By default, comments will not be printed. You can choose either of two settings to control the printing of comments by following these steps:

1. From the Page Layout tab, choose the dialog launcher icon in the lower-right corner of the Page Setup group.
2. In the Page Setup dialog, go to the Sheet tab and use the Comments dropdown to control the printing of comments.

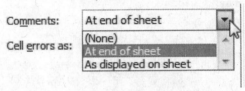

Figure 1287 *Control the printing of comments.*

If you select As Displayed on Sheet from the Comments dropdown, the comment boxes will print in the size and format you have set up for all the displayed comments. This setting will not print comments that are hidden with only the red triangle visible. To make effective use of this setting, you would have to make a few comments visible, as described in this topic.

If you select At End of Sheet from the Comments dropdown, the comments will print in a separate section at the end of the printout. The only drawback to this method is that the comment printout indicates that a certain comment is attached to cell A50. Unless you print row and column headings (see "Debug Using a Printed Spreadsheet" on page 492), there is no way for the reader of the printed document to know which value on the sheet is located in cell A50.

CHANGE THE COMMENT SHAPE TO A STAR

4

Problem: I would like to jazz up a comment by changing it to a starburst or some other shape.

Strategy: This trick has become more difficult since Excel 2003, but it is possible with a little customization of the Quick Access toolbar. The command you need is the Change Shape command. It appears on many contextual ribbon tabs, but because Microsoft puts away the tabs when you unselect an object, the command is not available to change the shape of a comment.

Instead, you have to add the icon to the Quick Access toolbar. Follow these steps:

1. Right-click the Quick Access toolbar and choose Customize Quick Access Toolbar.
2. In the top-left dropdown, choose All Commands.
3. Scroll down to the Change Shape icon. Select this item and click the Add button.
4. Click OK to close the Excel Options dialog.

When the Change Shape icon is on the Quick Access toolbar, follow these instructions to change the comment shape:

1. Add a regular comment to a cell.
2. Select the cell that contains the comment.
3. Choose Review, Edit Comment. The comment will appear, surrounded by diagonal lines.
4. Left-click the diagonal lines to change them to dots.
5. Select a new shape from the Change Shapes icon on the QAT.

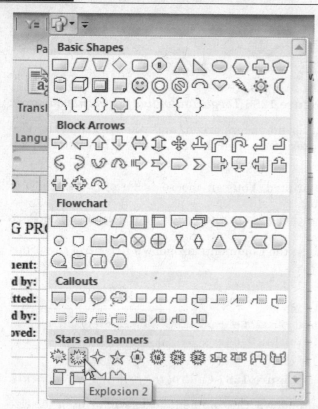

Figure 1288 *Select a new shape.*

The comment will change from a rectangle to a starburst. However, the comment is not large enough to show the entire comment.

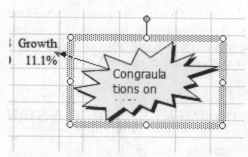

Figure 1289 *The shape changes, but the size is wrong.*

6. Grab a corner resize handle and drag to make the shape larger.
7. On the Home tab, choose Middle Align from the vertical alignment icons. Choose Align Center from the horizontal alignment icons. Increase the font size to 10.

Results: The comment will appear as a starburst.

Figure 1290 *The new comment shape.*

Additional Details: You can grab the green rotate handle and rotate until you have the shape that best fits the text.

ADD A POP-UP PICTURE OF AN ITEM IN A CELL

Problem: I have a product catalog in Excel. My sales reps will show the list of items to the buyer in a retail store. Can I have pictures appear on demand in Excel?

Strategy: You can add a pop-up picture to a cell. When someone hovers the mouse over an item number, the picture will appear. Follow these steps:

1. Select cell A4. Select Review, New Comment.
2. The default comment will have your name as the default text. Backspace to remove the name.
3. Using the mouse, click the diagonal-lines border in order to change the border to a series of dots.

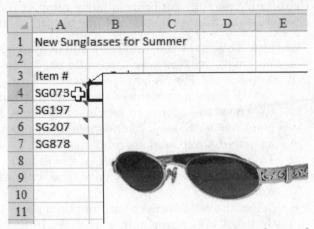

Figure 1291 *Display pictures on demand*

4. Right-click the dotted border and select Format Comment.
5. In the Format Comment dialog, go to the Colors and Lines tab. In the Fill Color dropdown, choose Fill Effects. In the Fill Effects dialog, choose the Picture tab and then click the Select Picture button.
6. Browse to the location where you have product pictures stored. Select a digital image of the item and click Insert.
7. On the Fill Effects tab, click OK. When you return to the Format Comment dialog, a squished version of the image will appear in the Color dropdown. Don't worry; the actual comment will look better.
8. Click OK to close the Format Comment dialog.
9. Use the lower-right handle to resize the comment. A red triangle will appear in cell A4.
10. Repeat steps 1–10 for each item in the catalog.

As promised, a picture of the product appears when you hover the mouse icon over the cell. Everyone thinks of Excel as being strictly for numbers. Adding pop-up pictures is a great trick for making your spreadsheets more of a sales tool.

ADD A POP-UP PICTURE TO MULTIPLE CELLS

Problem: I gave this book to my manager for Bosses' Day. He saw "Add a Pop-up Picture of an Item in a Cell," and wants you to add pictures to dozens of cells. Is there an easy way?

Strategy: Figure out how to map the item numbers in the worksheet to your folder of pictures. In this case, the pictures are stored in C:\qimage\. The file name is the letters "QI", the part number, then ".jpg". You will have a different folder and likely a different prefix or suffix after the part number. Edit that line of the macro below.

1. Open your workbook in Excel.
2. Type Alt+F11 then Insert, Module.
3. Enter these few lines of code in the VBA Editor.

```
Sub AddABunch()
For Each cell In Selection
      MyPic = "C:\Qimage\QI" & cell.Value & ".jpg"
      With cell.AddComment
           .Shape.Fill.UserPicture MyPic
           .Shape.Height = 300
           .Shape.Width = 300
      End With
Next cell
End Sub
```

4. Press Alt+Q to return to Excel.
5. Select the dozens of cells where your manager wants pictures. Run the macro. Pictures will be added to all the cells in the selection.

Additional Details: For the complete guide to learning VBA, check out VBA & Macros for Microsoft Excel 2013 (ISBN 978-0789748614) from QUE Publishing.

4

BUILD REPORTS WHERE COLUMNS IN EACH SECTION 1 DON'T LINE UP

Problem: I need to duplicate a fairly complex form. The form has several sections. The column widths needed for the first section do not line up with the column widths needed for the other two sections.

Strategy: This is a wildly amazing and obscure solution. It has been floating around Excel Web sites for years as a novelty. However, I recently used it in a production application to produce great-looking customer statements. Here's how it works:

1. Set up various sections of the form on individual worksheets. Make the column widths as wide as they need to be for each section of the form. In the sample, I have four different sections. The statement header has a logo and an address block that are centered on the page. The next other sections have five, three, and six columns.

2. To pull these parts together, you will build a printable statement on the worksheet that has the company header. On that page, you will paste three linked pictures that give a view of the other worksheets.

3. Select the cells for Section 1 and then press Ctrl+C to copy.

4. Go to cell A7 on the main worksheet. In Excel, select Home, Paste dropdown, Paste Picture Link.

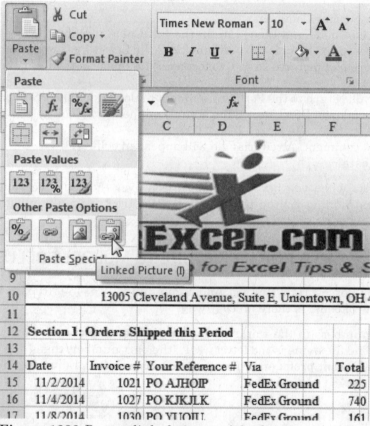

Figure 1292 *Paste a linked picture of the first report section.*

5. Drag this picture so that it is centered on the page.

6. Select A18:H18 and then select Home, Borders dropdown, Thick Bottom Border to draw a thick border below the pasted first section..

7. Repeat steps 3 through 6 for Sections two and three.

You can resize the pictures in the new sheet so they all have the same width, or you can simply center them on the page.

Results: You can print one unified form that does not look like it came from Excel. Fields in Section 2 are not necessarily lined up with columns in Sheet1. Note that the pictures are live pictures. If you change values on a back sheet, the picture on Sheet1 will automatically update.

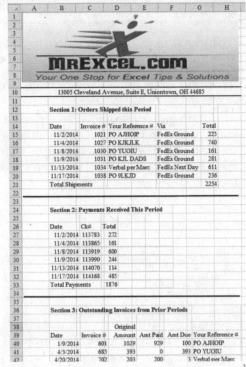

Figure 1293 *Three pictures make up this report.*

Additional Details: In our real statement application, we used a VBA macro to put together the sections. This macro can paste a different number of rows each time.

PASTE A LIVE PICTURE OF A CELL

Problem: I have a massively large spreadsheet. I'm working on calculations in the top of the spreadsheet but need to monitor a result in W842. It is a pain to travel back and forth to monitor that cell.

Strategy: You can take a picture of the cell and paste it where you can keep an eye on it. Follow these steps:

1. Select cells W841:W842. Press Ctrl+C to copy.
2. Return to the top of the worksheet. Select an area that has a few blank cells. Select Home, Paste dropdown, As Picture, Paste Picture Link.

A live picture of the cell will be pasted.

	A	B	C	D	E	F	G
1	Section 1: Historical Trends (Per Month)						
2							
3		Store Type	Size	Rent	Sales	Profit	Labor
4		Regular	1200	2400	12456	6228	6480
5		BigBox	2600	5200	36500	18250	8640
6							
7	Section 2: Number of Stores						Final Result
8							6,308,934.18
9		Regular	90				

Figure 1294 *G7:G8 is a live picture of cells W841:W842.*

As you make changes and the calculations cause the result to change, the picture will update.

Additional Details: The picture can be of multiple cells. Also, it is possible to move the picture by dragging it to a new location. You can even paste several pictures, each of a different few summary cells in order to have a dashboard showing key cells from throughout the workbook.

See Also: "Monitor Distant Cells" on page 564.

ADD FORMATTING TO PICTURES IN EXCEL

Problem: I used Insert, Picture to add a photograph at the top of my report. Excel displayed a new ribbon tab with dozens of options. What is all this stuff?

Strategy: Excel allows you to transform your photos in a number of ways.

The main gallery provides 28 different effects that you can add to the picture. The effects range from frames to soft edges to adding a shadow or perspective to the picture. Here are six of the 28 effects.

Figure 1295 *Apply a style to a picture.*

The Corrections and Color dropdowns actually show you tiny thumbnails of what your picture would look like with the various settings.

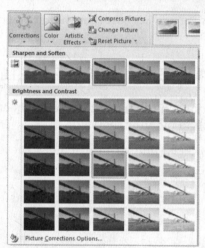

Figure 1296 *The thumbnails gallery is a better way to correct.*

The Artistic Effects allow you to apply various filters to the photo. The effects have exotic names such as marker, pencil grayscale, pencil sketch, line drawing, chalk sketch, paint strokes, paint brush, glow diffused, blur, light screen, watercolor sponge, film grain, mosaic bubbles, glass, cement, texturizer, crisscross edging, pastels smooth, plastic wrap, cutout, photocopy, and glow edges.

Figure 1297 *Convert a picture to a chalk sketch or other variants.*

Frequently, with today's digital cameras, a picture will be inserted and cover the entire first window of cells. You can grab the resize handle in the lower-right corner and hold down the Shift key while you drag up and to the left to make the image appear smaller. Making the image appear smaller does not change the size of the picture, however. With a picture selected, you can choose Compress Pictures to make the image size smaller. In the Compress Pictures dialog, you click the Options button to display the Compression Settings dialog. The dialog offers compressions sizes such as print, screen, or e-mail.

Gotcha: Note that by default, Excel will always do a compression when you save the file. If you are producing documents that are going to be printed in a glossy annual report, change this setting to Print before you save.

Additional Details: Another tool that is very useful is the Crop tool on the right side of the ribbon. When you click Crop, Excel adds eight cropping handles around the image. You can grab a handle and drag inward to crop the photo. When you are done, you click on the photo to perform the crop.

REMOVE PICTURE BACKGROUND

New in Excel 2010, you can easily remove the background from a picture. I can imagine this will lead to a variety of Excel cover sheets with decorative pictures with the backgrounds removed.

Select the picture and choose Remove Background. A new ribbon tab will appear. Your first adjustment is to change the bounding box so it tightly fits around the subject. Making this one adjustment will dramatically improve the results of Background Removal.

Below are two copies of the same picture. The picture on the left is the original. The picture on the right is the picture after clicking Remove Background and tightly adjusting the bounding box to the subject.

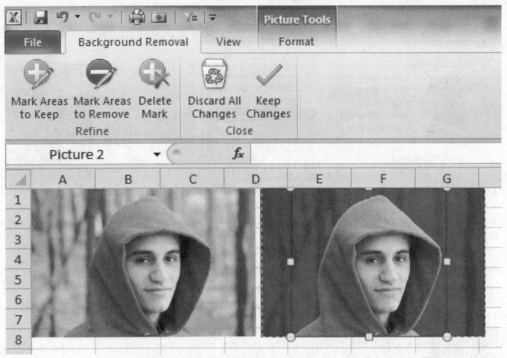

Figure 1298 *Change the bounding box around the subject.*

Given the correct bounding box, the Picture Removal tool does a good job of predicting what to remove. The Background Removal tab of the ribbon includes icons where you can mark areas to keep or remove. This is good for areas that the tool chose to erroneously remove.

When you click the Keep Changes icon, the background will be removed.

Figure 1299 *After the removal.*

Gotcha: If you want to enter values in the cells covered by the now-transparent background, you will usually select the picture instead of the cell. Click outside of the picture and then use the arrow keys to move to the cells under the picture. It is incredibly tempting to just try to click directly on the cell instead.

INSERTING A SCREEN CLIPPING

Excel 2010 introduced a new Screenshot icon on the Insert tab. If you open this dropdown, you will see a list of available windows that you can paste as a picture into the worksheet. Excel always pastes the entire window, including the title bar. You will then be using the Crop tool to remove all but the relevant portions of the window. Instead, I prefer to use Screen Clipping tool. This tool requires a bit more set up, but then it requires no post-screen-shot work. You might have several different applications open. You want to grab a picture from a web page. From Excel, switch to the browser session where you can see the image.

The Screen Clipping command works on the window that was active immediately before you switched to Excel. It is important that you switch directly from the browser back to Excel. If you use Alt+Tab to switch applications and you accidentally stop on the wrong application, that application will appear in the screen clipping.

When you are back in Excel, open the Screenshot dropdown on the Insert tab and choose the Screen Clipping item from the bottom of the dropdown.

Drag a rectangle around the portion of the screen that you want to paste into Excel. As you drag, that portion of the screen will change from grayed out to full color.

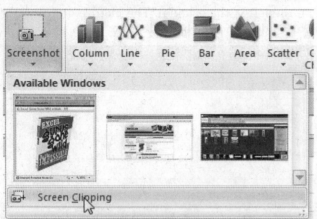

Figure 1300 *Choose Screen Clipping.*

Excel will show you a picture of the browser window. Wait a few seconds and the picture will be grayed out. The mouse cursor will change to crosshairs.

Figure 1301 *Draw a rectangle around the area.*

When you finish the box, a picture of that screen will be pasted into the worksheet.

Gotcha: The Screen Clipping tool is great for shooting a screenshot of Word, or a web page, or a PDF file. It will not shoot a picture from the current Excel window. This seems like a frustrating limitation. To get a picture of the current Excel window, use the Copy as Picture or the Paste as Picture tools, as described in "Paste a Live Picture of a Cell" on page 501.

DRAW AN ARROW TO VISUALLY ILLUSTRATE THAT TWO CELLS ARE CONNECTED

Problem: I have a large spreadsheet with many calculations. Results from section 1 are carried forward to cells in section 2. It would help to graphically illustrate that one cell flows to the calculation of another.

Strategy: You can use the Shapes feature to add arrows to indicate the flow of cells. Here's how you use it.

    1. Select Insert, Shapes dropdown and choose an arrow.

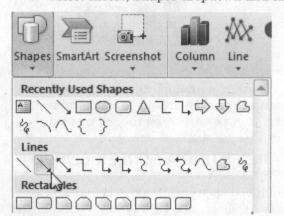

Figure 1302 *Shapes are in single menu now.*

    2. Click in the origin cell and drag to the final cell. When you release the mouse button, an arrow will appear, pointing from the first cell to the end cell. Annoyingly, the shape is drawn in a light shade of the first theme color, which ends up as light blue in the Office theme.

3. While the arrow is still selected, open the Shape Styles gallery on the Drawing Tools Format ribbon tab. Select one of the black styles in an appropriate thickness.

4. You can further control the arrow using the Shape Outline dropdown on the Format ribbon. Use the Weight, Dashes, or Arrows flyout menus. There are even more options available by pressing Ctrl+1 with the arrow selected.

5. By default, the arrow will resize with the cells. Say that the arrow stretches from column E to column C. If you make column D wider, the arrow will stretch. To turn off this behavior, right-click the arrow and choose Size and Properties. You can then decide if the shape should move, resize, and/or print.

Additional Details: Any line in the Shapes gallery can become an arrow. You might need to draw a curved arrow.

◢	B	C	D	E	F	G	H	I
1								
2	Quantity		1542			2580		
3	1234			1587		2937		Result
4					3378			4321
5					2632			
6			3610	3773	1739	2288		

Figure 1303 *This is a curve with an arrow added later.*

1. If you need to draw a curved arrow, choose the Curve icon in the Shapes gallery.
2. Click at the starting point (i.e. the non-arrow side) of the line.
3. Start drawing with the mouse. Any where that you need the line to change direction, click the mouse and keep drawing. To draw this curve, you would click the mouse at each point shown.

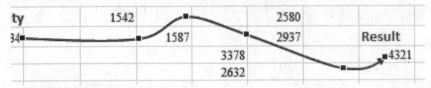

Figure 1304 *The black handles show the mouse click locations.*

4. When you reach the endpoint of the line, double-click.
5. With the line selected, go to the Shape Outline dropdown on the Format ribbon tab. Choose an arrow from the Arrows dropdown. Choose a darker color. Choose a heavier weight.

If you later need to edit the curves in the line, right-click the line and choose Edit Points. In Edit Points mode, when you click a point, you can move that point, or move one of the two white diamond handles to change the arc of the curve.

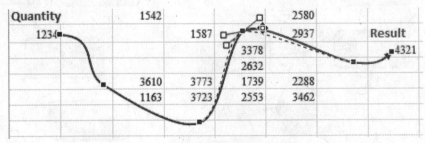

Figure 1305 *Edit the points of the curve.*

Problem: Is there a way to join two shapes with a connector?

Strategy: All lines can be connectors.

Select Insert, Shapes dropdown and choose any of the Lines shapes. When you are about to click for the start or endpoint, hover over an existing shape. Red connector points will appear along each edge of the shape. If you start or end a line on a red connection handle, the line will be anchored to the shape.

Some shapes offer four connection points. Others offer a connection point on every corner.

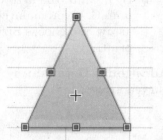

Figure 1306 *The triangle offers six connection points.*

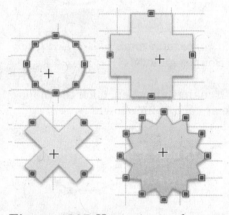

Figure 1307 *Hover over a shape to see where the connection points are located.*

Here are several shapes with connectors. If you rearrange the shapes, the lines will continue to connect the shapes.

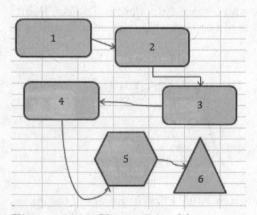

Figure 1308 *Shapes joined by connectors.*

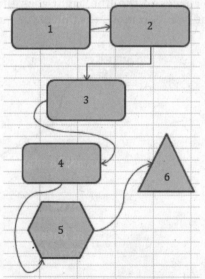

Figure 1309 *Rearrange the shapes, and the connectors stay in place.*

If you want to edit where a line connects, click on that line. Red handles will appear on the connector points. Move the red handle to a new location.

CIRCLE A CELL ON YOUR WORKSHEET

Problem: Excel offers an excellent calculation tool. However, I know that some people are visually oriented, and their eyes glaze over when they look at a large white sheet with black numbers. I want to use graphics to call attention to certain numbers.

Strategy: You can add graphics to a worksheet by using Shapes. Follow these steps:

1. Select Insert, Shapes dropdown. Choose the oval.
2. Left-click fairly far above and to the left of the cell where you want to use the graphic.
3. Drag down and to the right. in the worksheet and drag to draw an oval.

Gotcha: Although the shape is transparent as you drag, when you release the mouse button, the Shape is filled with theme color 1 and covers up text.

You would think that choosing from the top row in the Shape Styles gallery would solve the problem, especially since the thumbnail shows letters showing through the shape. However, that thumbnail refers to text box text, not cell text.

4. Select Drawing Tools Format, Shape Fill dropdown and choose No Fill to allow the cell text to show through.

Additional Details: If you will be drawing many shapes and you want them all to be transparent, right-click the first shape and choose Set as Default Shape. Any additional shapes you draw will have similar fill and line colors.

Results: Excel will add an attention-grabbing shape to the worksheet. This will draw the reader's eye to the conclusion.

Figure 1310 *Start above and to the left.*

Figure 1311 *Drag down and to the right.*

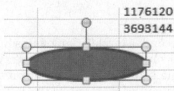

Figure 1312 *Shapes are filled by default.*

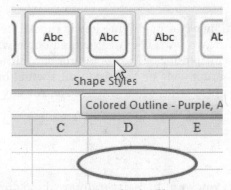

Figure 1313 *The built-in styles don't allow text to show through.*

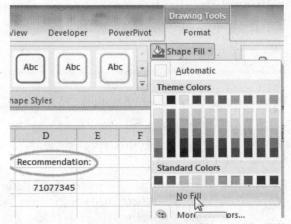

Figure 1314 *Choose No Fill*

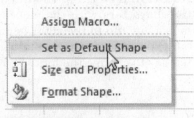

Figure 1315 *Make future shapes transparent.*

DRAW PERFECT CIRCLES

Problem: : The oval tool in the Drawing toolbar is hard to use. If I start drawing the rectangle in the upper-left corner of the cell, the shape will start in that corner. But if I start drawing a circle in the same spot, the oval I draw will not completely include the text in the cells. Also, why aren't there circle and square shapes? I have a hard time drawing perfectly round circles and perfectly square squares.

Strategy: You can use keyboard keys to make drawing shapes easier.

First, to force an oval to be a perfect circle, you hold down the Shift key while you draw. Using the Shift key will also force a rectangle to be a square and a triangle to be an equilateral triangle.

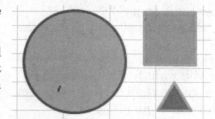

Figure 1316 *Use Shift while drawing to make circles and squares.*

Second, a circle or an oval is hard to draw. In order to draw the circle around a cell, you have to start fairly far outside the cell. How can you know how far above your data to start in order to include all the data? One solution is to hold down the Ctrl key when you draw the oval (or Ctrl+Shift to draw a circle). Then, instead of starting in the left corner, you start directly in the middle of the circle. As you drag outward, the circle will grow.

The other modifying key is the Alt key. A rectangle drawn with the Alt key held down will snap to the cell borders. The rectangle can either be two columns wide or three columns wide, but not 2.5 columns wide when you use the Alt key.

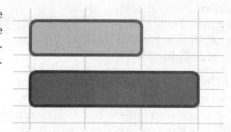

Figure 1317 *Use Alt & edges align with cell.*

If you want to resize a square, hold down the Shift key while you drag a corner handle. This will force Excel to keep the aspect ratio the same.

Additional Details: If you need to produce many identically sized squares, Ctrl+drag the first square to make an identical copy. You can then Ctrl+click both squares and Ctrl+drag to create four squares.

ADD TEXT TO ANY CLOSED SHAPE

Problem: How can I add fixed text to a shape?

Strategy: All closed shapes can hold text. To add text to a shape, you simply right-click the shape and choose Edit Text.

Excel will add a flashing insertion cursor inside the shape. You type your text, pressing Enter when you want to start a new line.

Additional Details: To format the text, you select the characters with the mouse and then move the mouse up and to the right to display the Mini toolbar. You can use the formatting icons on the Mini toolbar to change the font.

Figure 1318 *Select text. Move up and to the right for the Mini toolbar.*

PLACE CELL CONTENTS IN A SHAPE

Problem: I don't want to use just static text in a shape; I want to display the results of a calculation in the shape.

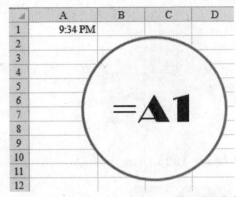

Figure 1319 *Can a shape display a cell value? f*

1. Select the shape.
2. Click in the formula bar and type =A1. When you press Enter, the value from A1 will appear in the shape.

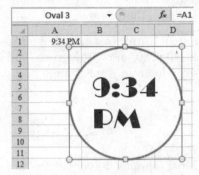

Figure 1320 *Type = and a cell reference in the formula bar.*

Strategy: This is possible, although typing the formula in the shape is not the way to do it. Here's how you do it:

Additional Details: The formula in the formula bar can refer to only a single cell. You cannot enter a formula in the formula bar. However, there is a workaround. Say that you want to display today's order total in a banner at the top of an order entry log. The banner will appear in rows 1 through 4 of the log. Here's what you do:

1. Move the banner out of the way and build a formula in cell D2 to hold the text for the banner. The formula might be:

="Today's Order Total:"&CHAR(10)&TEXT(SUM(C8:C200),"$#,##0")

The CHAR(10) function will add a linefeed in the result if Wrap Text is turned on. Otherwise, you will get an unprintable character symbol.

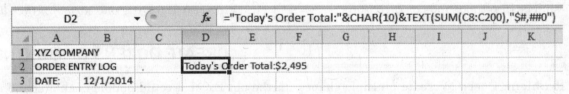

Figure 1321 *Build a formula in a cell to concatenate text and a sum.*

2. Draw a banner. Select the banner and enter =D2 as the formula for the banner. Format the banner to be center-aligned and in an interesting font.

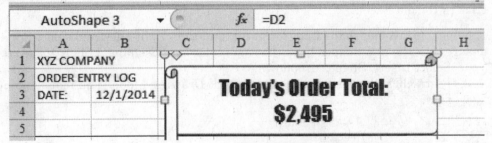

Figure 1322 *Draw and format a banner.*

3. Move the banner so that it covers the formula in D2. As new orders are entered in the log, the total will update.

Gotcha: The text in the shape is updated only when the worksheet is calculated.

Additional Details: Say that you add a shape to a chart. If you want the text in the shape to come from a cell, you must precede the cell reference with the sheet name. For example, =Sheet2!D2 will work, but =D2 will not.

ROTATE A SHAPE

Problem: How do I rotate a shape? Can I morph a shape?

Strategy: When you select a shape, a green circle appears. Grab the green circle, click, and rotate the shape. This is a free rotation; you can rotate the shape in 360 degrees.

Additional Details: If you need to rotate exactly 90, 180, or 270 degrees, you can use the Rotate dropdown in the Arrange group of the Format tab.

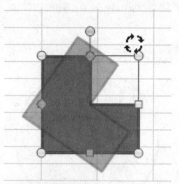

Figure 1323 *Drag green handle to rotate.*

Most shapes have yellow inflection points. This shape has two such inflection points. Dragging an inflection point will change the size of one portion of a shape.

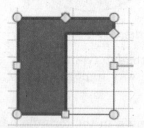

Figure 1324 *Drag the right-side diamond up.*

For even more flexibility, right-click the shape and choose Edit Points. You now have a black handle at each corner of the shape. You can drag any handle in any direction to change the shape.

Gotcha: Dragging a point will remove the yellow inflection handles from the shape.

Using these tools, you can morph any of the 175 shapes into thousands of variations.

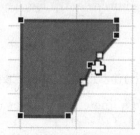

Figure 1325 *Drag one corner of the shape.*

CREATE DOZENS OF LIGHTNING BOLTS

Problem: I need to create multiple shapes. In the old Excel, I could double-click a shape icon and then draw multiple copies of the shape without going back to the menu. Now, I can't seem to double-click the lightning bolt in the Shapes menu.

Strategy: Microsoft came up with a solution to this problem, although it is as subtle as the double-click trick in the old Excel.

It helps to draw one shape first, format it, and then right-click and select Set as Default Shape. This will ensure that the new shapes have the same color as this shape. Follow these steps:
1. Select Insert, Shapes dropdown.
2. Right-click any shape and choose Lock Drawing Mode. The mouse pointer changes to a thin plus sign.

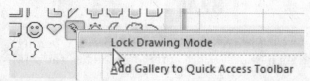

Figure 1326 *Find a shape, right-click, and select Lock Drawing Mode.*
3. To draw a default size shape, click the mouse pointer anywhere on the worksheet. To draw a shape of a different size, click and drag to draw the shape.
4. When you are done drawing shapes, press the Esc key or select another worksheet to exit Drawing mode.

The lighter drawings shown below are default drawings created with a single click in the upper corner of the shape. The darker drawings required a click and drag to size.

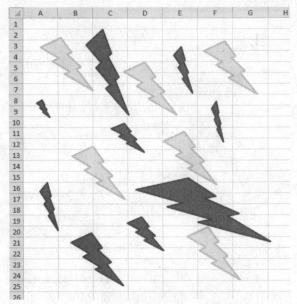

Figure 1327 *Shazam!*

MAKE A LOGO INTO A SHAPE

Problem: I'm looking for a fun way to kill some time while the Internet is down. Can I make my logo into a Shape that can be formatted using the Drawing Tools?

Strategy: You can paste your company's logo or any other logo to a worksheet. Then you select Insert, Shapes dropdown, Lines, Freeform.

Figure 1328 *Freeform can create straight or curved lines or shapes.*

Trace the logo. It is easy to draw straight lines: You start at one corner of the logo, click the corner, and then click on the next corner.

If you need to follow a curved path for part of the logo, you should increase the zoom to 200% or more.

You can use the Freeform tool to create a line or a closed shape. To finish a line type drawing, you double-click on the last point. To finish a closed shape, you continue clicking at each corner. When you get back to the original corner of the logo, you click again, and the shape will appear.

Figure 1329 *Click the starting point again to finish a shape.*

Results: You will have a custom shape of your logo that you can move, resize, rotate, or format to your heart's content. Here is the MrExcel logo with a 3-D format applied.

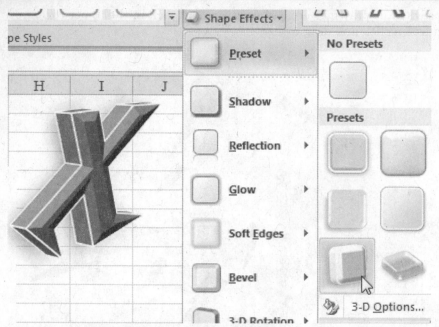

Figure 1330 *Apply formatting to the shape.*

Additional Details: To draw a curved line, you can either click frequently along the curve, basically creating a curve from a series of tiny short-line segments, or you can press the left mouse button while you carefully trace the curve. This is a little tricky. To draw the shape below, follow these steps:

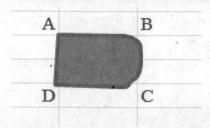

Figure 1331 *Draw three straight lines and a curve.*

1. Click once at point A.
2. Click once at point B. This finishes the straight line along the top.
3. While still at point B, click again and start to trace the curve. Holding down the mouse button while drawing makes the Freeform tool act like the Scribble tool for this segment of the shape. Notice that there must be two separate clicks at point B. If you start drawing the curve without a second click, Excel will add a random curve to the end of the AB line segment.
4. When you arrive at the end of the curve, point C, release the mouse button.
5. Move the mouse to point D and click to draw the bottom edge.
6. Move the mouse to point A and click again to close the shape.

Gotcha: It is easy to make a mistake while drawing. To fine-tune the shape, right-click the shape and choose Edit Points. In Edit Points mode, you can right-click any segment and change the shape from curved to straight, add an end point, or close an unclosed shape.

Alternate Strategy: To draw a logo that's not angular, you can use the Scribble tool. You find it by selecting Insert, Shapes dropdown.

To use this tool, you click and hold the mouse button to start to draw. The mouse changes to a pencil. As long as you hold the mouse down, you will be drawing the shape.

As with the Freeform tool, you can create either a line or a closed shape. To close the shape, you release the mouse button when your drawing line has rejoined the start point.

Excel will create a closed shape from your scribble. You can apply color or effects using the Drawing Tools ribbon tab.

DRAW BUSINESS DIAGRAMS WITH EXCEL

Problem: My manager needs me to graphically document the steps in a project plan.

Strategy: Excel offers 180+ types of diagrams in a tool called SmartArt.

When you choose Insert, SmartArt from the ribbon, the Choose a SmartArt Graphic dialog box that appears shows graphic types arranged in seven groups: Many layouts are repeated in the Picture group. Additional layouts are available from Office.com.

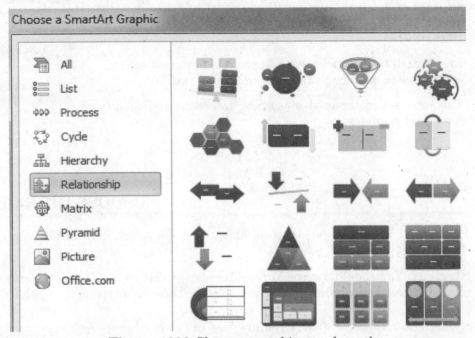

Figure 1332 *Choose a graphic type from the seven groups.*

Here are the seven main groups offered in SmartArt:
- List - You can use these charts to illustrate a series of items. Although a list has a certain sequence, there are usually not arrows to indicate that the list contains a series of steps.
- Process - Process charts are similar to list charts, but the shapes are connected by arrows or the shapes themselves are arrows.
- Cycle - Cycle charts are process charts where the last step in the process has an arrow pointing back to the first step in the process. These are great for illustrating continuous improvement.
- Hierarchy - Hierarchy charts are used for organizational charts and as outlines for books or projects.
- Relationship - This category is a catchall for 31 different types. It offers formula diagrams, gear charts, funnel charts, balance charts, containment charts, Venn diagrams, and more. If you need to illustrate competing ideas, turn to this category.
- Matrix - This category offers charts with four quadrants or four quadrants and a title.
- Pyramid - This category offers shapes stacked in either an upright or an inverted pyramid.

Most SmartArt chart types offer an unlimited number of shapes. A list chart can illustrate 3 items or 17 items without a problem. However, some chart types are limited. For example, a gear chart can illustrate only 3 concepts, and several arrow charts can illustrate only 2 items. When you click on a thumbnail in the Choose a SmartArt Graphic dialog, the description on the right will indicate whether the graphic is limited to a certain number of shapes.

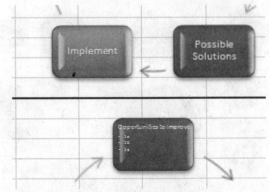

Figure 1333 *The Block Cycle chart looks best with only Level 1 text.*

The thumbnails often indicate whether the diagram is suitable for Level 1 or Level 1 and Level 2 text. Think of a PowerPoint slide. If you have bullet points, those are Level 1 text. If you have bullets and sub-bullet points, those are Level 1 and Level 2 text. Some charts don't do well with both Level 1 and Level 2 text. Below is a Block Cycle chart. The top chart includes only Level 1 text. In the lower chart, some Level 2 text is added to the first point. This causes all the Level 1 text throughout the chart to get unusually small.

Figure 1334

In contrast, the Vertical Box List chart is designed with accent boxes to hold long sentences of Level 2 text.

The next seven topics discuss how to create and modify SmartArt graphics.

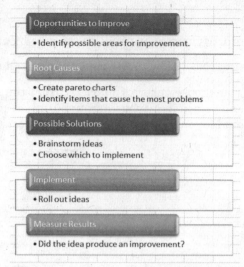

Figure 1335 *The Vertical Box List chart offers ample room for Level 2 text.*

CHOOSE THE RIGHT TYPE OF SMARTART

Problem: I need to illustrate a circular process in which information can flow in both directions. Which SmartArt type should I use?

Strategy: You should use the Multi-directional Cycle chart. This is the only one of the diagram types that offers bidirectional arrows between the blocks. This chart type is the sixth thumbnail in the Cycle category.

Some other types of charts require you to select certain SmartArt types. The following are some examples.

To accommodate extremely long sentences of Level 2 text, your choices are the Vertical Box List, Vertical Bullet List, and Vertical Chevron List charts. These are in the List category.

To make a decision between two choices, use a Balance chart from the Relationship category. This clever type will lean left or right, depending on which choice has more Level 2 items.

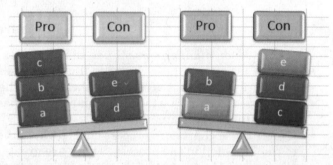

Figure 1336 *The Balance chart leans left or right, depending on content.*

To show how parts add together to produce an output, you use an Equation chart or a Funnel chart. Below, the Vertical Equation chart in the lower left seems unbalanced; the resulting circle is much larger than the input circles.

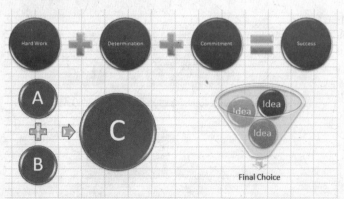

Figure 1337 *The Funnel chart is limited to three items and a result.*

To illustrate two opposing forces, you use Diverging Arrows, Counterbalance Arrows, Opposing Arrows, Converging Arrows, and Arrow Ribbon charts. These are found in the Relationship category.

Many process charts can be used to illustrate a single process that progresses from left to right or top to bottom. However, to illustrate many vertical processes in the same diagram, you use the Chevron List chart.

Some of the process charts will snake through rows and columns. If you have many shapes to fit in a small area, check out the Basic Bending Process, Circular Bending Process, Repeating Bending Process, and Vertical Bending Process charts. Below are 16 shapes in a Circular Bending Process chart. This chart has been rendered in the Brick Scene style.

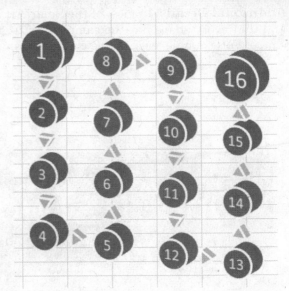

Figure 1338 *The bending layouts can fit many shapes in a small space.*

USE THE TEXT PANE TO BUILD SMARTART

Problem: How do I create SmartArt?

Strategy: Initially, you shouldn't worry about the graphics but should instead focus your attention on the text pane, where you can build bullet points of Level 1 and, optionally, Level 2 text.

Using the text pane is similar to building a slide in PowerPoint's Outline view.

When you choose Insert, SmartArt and select a layout, Excel will draw a default layout and place the insertion cursor in the text pane.

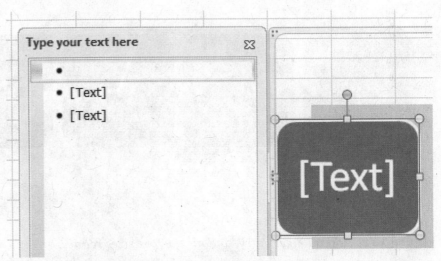

Figure 1339 *SmartArt starts out with bullet points that show [Text].*

You can use these keys to navigate in the text pane:
- Enter - Add a new shape at the same level as the current shape and immediately after the current shape.
- Down Arrow - Move to the next shape without creating a new shape.
- Tab - Demote the current shape one level. Pressing Tab on a Level 1 entry will change the entry to Level 2.
- Shift+Tab - Promote the current shape one level. Pressing Shift+Tab on a Level 2 entry will change the entry to Level 1.
- Delete - Pressing Delete when there is no text for a shape will delete the shape. Initially, you should focus all your attention on the text pane. As you type in the text pane, Excel will continue to render new shapes in the SmartArt graphic.

Additional Details: In most of the SmartArt layouts, Excel will ensure that every shape is the same size and that every shape has the same font size. This works best when you have similar-length text in each shape. For example, each shape contains a single word or concept. The font sizes are fairly large.

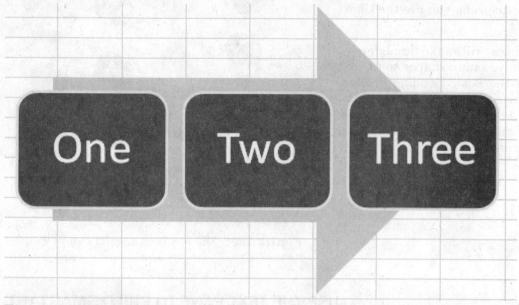

Figure 1340 *With similar length points, the fonts are fairly large.*

If you add a new shape with longer text, the font size in all the shapes will reduce to accommodate the longest entry. You can override this by using the Format ribbon tab as described in "Switch to the Format Tab to Format Individual Shapes" on page 519.

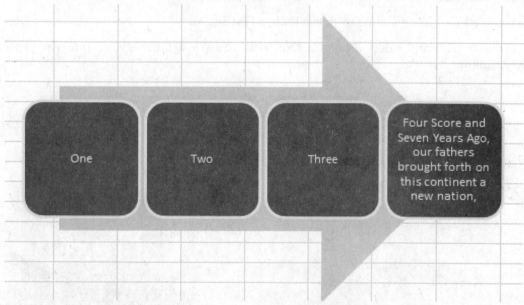

Figure 1341 *Add a longer entry, and all the font sizes reduce.*

The text pane supports spell checking, formatting with the mini toolbar, and Cut and Paste.

Alternate Strategy: It is possible to edit text directly in each shape. To do so, you hide the text pane and use the Add Shape menu on the Design tab in order to build your graphic.

CHANGE A SMARTART LAYOUT

Problem: I typed my text in my SmartArt, but my manager doesn't like the layout.

Strategy: You can easily convert a SmartArt graphic from one style to any other style by using the Layouts gallery on the Design tab. Follow these steps:

1. Select the SmartArt graphic. Excel will display the SmartArt Tools tabs.

2. From the Design tab, select the Layouts gallery. It initially shows four other layouts besides the one you used. Click the bottom arrow to open the gallery.

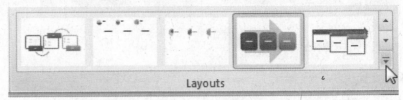

Figure 1342 *Click the More arrow to open the gallery.*

3. Initially, the Layouts gallery shows only the layouts from the same category as your existing graphic. To choose from the complete set of layouts, choose the More Layouts option at the bottom.

Figure 1343 *You see more layouts, but not all of them.*

4. Choose the All category and then choose a new layout.

Results: Your existing message will be presented in a completely new SmartArt layout.

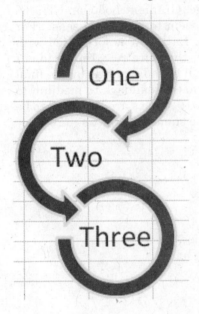

Figure 1344 *New layout, same words.*

Gotcha: Some layouts allow only a certain number of shapes. If you have a layout with six shapes and then convert it to a layout that allows only three shapes, for example, you will not initially lose the extra text. The text for the remaining shapes will appear with a red X in the text pane. If you switch back to another layout, these shapes will be restored. However, if you save and close the document, the text by the red X will be discarded. Microsoft did this to prevent you from accidentally including sensitive hidden data in the graphic.

FORMAT SMARTART

Problem: SmartArt always starts out as a boring blue diagram. What formatting options are available?

Strategy: You can use two galleries on the Design tab of the ribbon to quickly add color and effects to a graphic: The Change Colors gallery and the SmartArt Styles gallery.

The Change Colors dropdown offers more than three dozen color styles. The Colorful row offers five combinations of the six accent colors in the current theme. The Primary Theme Colors offer two light style and one dark basic style. The remaining six rows offer variations on each of the six accent colors.

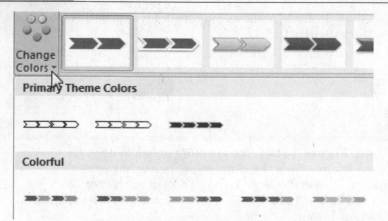

Figure 1345 *Add color to SmartArt by using the Colorful row choices.*

Gotcha: Each of the accent rows offer Outline, Colored Fill, Gradient Range, Gradient Loop, and Transparent Gradient Range columns. Of these five columns, only the first two seem to make any sense. For example, see the figure below. It shows five horizontal SmartArt graphics. Each row is formatted with a different accent color scheme. The Outline and Fill graphics look okay. In the third row, the Gradient Range graphic goes from dark to light, making it appear as if the company will be fading away by the final shape. In the fourth row, the Gradient Loop graphic is worse. Shapes alternate from dark to medium to light to medium to dark. This makes me think that somehow the 2014 and 2016 shapes are supposed to be related. In the fifth row, the Transparent Gradient Range graphic suffers the same problem as in row 3.

Outline	2014 $122M	2015 $214M	2016 $309M
Fill	2014 $122M	2015 $214M	2016 $309M
Grad. Range	2014 $122M	2015 $214M	2016 $309M
Outline	2014 $122M	2015 $214M	2016 $309M
Transp. Gr. Range	2014 $122M	2015 $214M	2016 $309M

Figure 1346 *Only Outline and Colored Fill graphics look okay.*

Additional Details: You can easily add effects by choosing one of the 14 styles from the SmartArt Styles gallery. The first five styles are 2-D styles and labeled as "Best Match for Document." The remaining nine styles are 3-D styles.

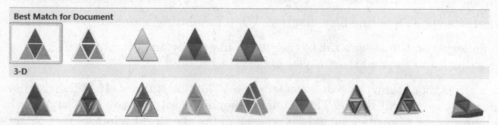

Figure 1347 *The first few 3-D styles create nice effects.*

The 14 graphics below demonstrate the styles available. I use the second 3-D style most of the time. It creates a nice effect but is still readable.

Figure 1348 *Examples of the 14 layouts.*

Gotcha: If you move far into the 3-D styles, many of them are unreadable. Perhaps Microsoft is doing us a favor. For example, perhaps the ninth style, known as Birds Eye Scene, is designed for messages in which you need to deliver bad news. You can say that you showed the information, but no one will really be able to read it. This figure shows the original message and the message rendered in Birds Eye Scene.

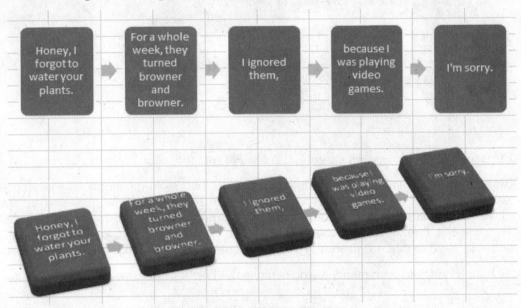

Figure 1349 *Apply a little Birds Eye Scene to bad news.*

Additional Details: If you change the theme on the Page Layout tab, you will have new colors available in the Colorful row, but you will also inherit new effects that change the options available in the Smart-Art Styles gallery. If you only want new colors, you can use the Colors dropdown on the Page Layout tab instead.

Additional Details: If you are using a layout that includes picture placeholders, click the placeholder to browse for a photo.

SWITCH TO THE FORMAT TAB TO FORMAT INDIVIDUAL SHAPES

Problem: Birds Eye Scene style notwithstanding, (see Figure 1349 above), I've found that most SmartArt formatted using the Design ribbon looks good. Fonts remain consistent throughout. Shapes have similar effects. While giving Microsoft control over font size will usually create a suitable graphic, sometimes I need to tweak the font used within one shape.

Strategy: All the tools on the Format tab of the ribbon will allow you to change elements of a SmartArt graphic.

To change elements of a SmartArt graphic, select a single shape in your graphic. The Shapes group will allow you to change the shape or size of the individual shape.

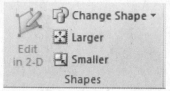

Figure 1350 *Tweak size or shape of one element of a SmartArt graphic.*

With a single shape selected, you can use any of the tools in the Shape Styles group to change the shape formatting. You can use any of the tools in the WordArt Styles gallery to add effects to the text. You can use any of the formatting tools in the Home tab of the ribbon to change font or size.

Gotcha: When you change shapes on the Format tab, Microsoft will often quit updating font sizes in response to text changes. You should get your graphic as close to finished using the Design tab before moving to the Format tab.

Additional Details: If you find yourself making many changes on the Format tab, you will lose the continuity of the graphic. The graphic below shows some of the many changes possible with the Format tab.

Figure 1351 *If you are not careful with the Format tab, chaos results.*

In this figure, each shape was changed using the Change Shape menu. The second shape was made larger, and the font size was increased on the Home tab. The Text Effects glow setting was used to apply a glow to text in the third shape. The green rotation handle was used to rotate the third shape. WordArt Styles, Text Effects, Transform was used on the text in the fourth shape, and Shape Styles, Shape Effects, Reflection was used to add a reflection. In the first shape, a preset from the Shape Effects dropdown was used.

Although it is not recommended, you can use the Format tab to tweak many aspects of an individual shape.

USE CELL VALUES AS THE SOURCE FOR SMARTART CONTENT

Problem: As discussed in "Place Cell Contents in a Shape" on page 509, Excel has been able to use values from an Excel cell as the source for text boxes on AutoShapes for fifteen years. It would be obvious to anyone that the best use of SmartArt would be to populate the text pane with cell references. However, nothing I try allows me to specify cell A1 as the source in the text pane. What's going on?

Strategy: Amazingly, Microsoft did not hook up this feature in Excel! It was obvious to you, and it was obvious to me, but Microsoft didn't think to include it.

From Microsoft's point of view, SmartArt is primarily a PowerPoint feature that is also available in Word and Excel. Heck, in PowerPoint, Microsoft even made the Convert Any Text to SmartArt functionality. But because PowerPoint doesn't offer cells and formulas, it was not a priority to enable this feature in Excel. Luckily, I have a workaround.

Follow these steps to build a SmartArt graphic that is tied to cell values:
1. Build a SmartArt graphic with the correct number of shapes. Type sample text of about the correct length in the shapes.
2. Choose a color scheme from the Design tab.
3. Choose a style from the Design tab. Get the diagram looking exactly as you will want it to appear, because after step 4, Excel will stop automatically formatting the SmartArt.

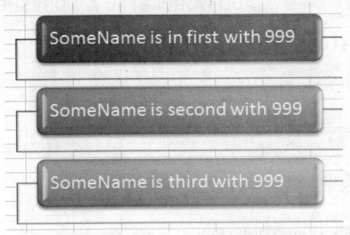

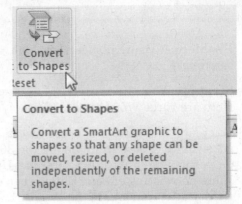

Figure 1353 *Convert the SmartArt to regular shapes.*

Figure 1352 *Build SmartArt with sample text of the right length.*

4. On the Design tab, choose Convert to Shapes.
5. Click on the first shape and look in the Name box to the left of the formula bar. If you see a name like Group 9, you know that Excel has grouped multiple shapes together. From the Drawing Tools Format tab, choose Group, Ungroup.
6. Click on the words in the first shape. You should see a name such as Rounded Rectangle 5.
7. Click in the formula bar. Type a formula such as =J28 and press Enter. You should see the text from J28 appear in the shape.
8. Repeat steps 5 through 7 for the additional shapes.
9. Select Home, Find & Select, Select Objects. Drag a rectangle around the collection of shapes to reselect them all. You need to exit Select Objects mode, so reselect Home, Find & Select, Select Objects.
10. From the Drawing Tools Format tab, choose Group, Group in order to group all the objects into a single unit again.

Results: Excel will create a diagram that looks like SmartArt that will get the values from formula in cells J28:J30.

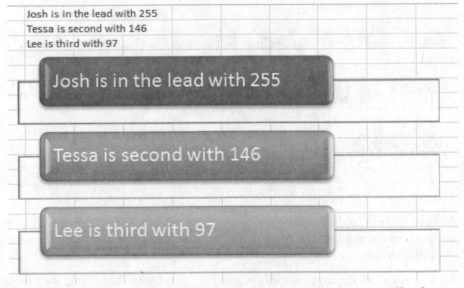

Figure 1354 *This looks like SmartArt but is really shapes.*

ADD WORDART TO A WORKSHEET

Problem: My spreadsheets are blah. How can I make them more eye-catching?

Strategy: You can create attractive spreadsheets by adding WordArt. Here are three WordArt samples.

To create WordArt, you select Insert, WordArt. The initial dropdown asks you to choose from among the 30 choices shown below. This is a bit perplexing to WordArt veterans. Unlike in Excel 2003, this gallery offers no twisting effects. But you can easily change every effect in the gallery after you create the WordArt.

Choose one of the types, and Excel will insert new WordArt in the center of the visible range. The WordArt starts with a value YOUR TEXT HERE. The WordArt is surrounded by a dashed box, which indicates that the WordArt is in Text Edit mode. You can start typing the text you want to appear as the WordArt.

Figure 1355 *Sample WordArt.*

When most people think of WordArt, they think of the effects available in the WordArt Styles, Effects, Transform menu, which you can use to twist or bend the type to fill a wide variety of shapes. This figure shows some of the available shapes. You do not have to select all the text in the shape to apply a Transform effect.

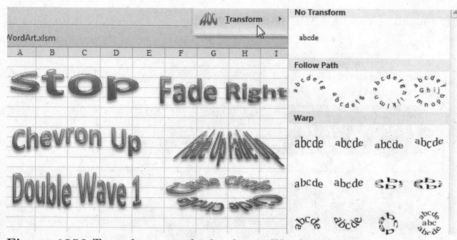

Figure 1356 *Transforms apply the classic WordArt look.*

Earlier in this topic, I estimated that there were 1.78E+53 different varieties of WordArt possible. That estimate does not include the various options available if you change the inflection points in some of the transforms.

Look for a pink diamond handle when the WordArt is selected. By dragging this handle up or down, you can control the amount of slant applied.

CHART AND SMARTART TEXT IS AUTOMATICALLY WORDART

Strategy: All text in a chart or in a SmartArt graphic is eligible to be WordArt. You don't have to do anything special: You just use the WordArt Styles group on the Format tab while editing the SmartArt or chart.

EXCEL 2013 OFFERS AN EXCEL APP STORE

Although developers have been creating VBA add-ins for Excel since 1993, Excel 2013 and Excel 2015 offer an Excel App Store featuring JavaScript apps. Right now, the apps are limited to read-only access to a range of cells and will then create some new visualization in an application window.

In Excel 2013, go to Insert, Apps for Office. Many apps are free.

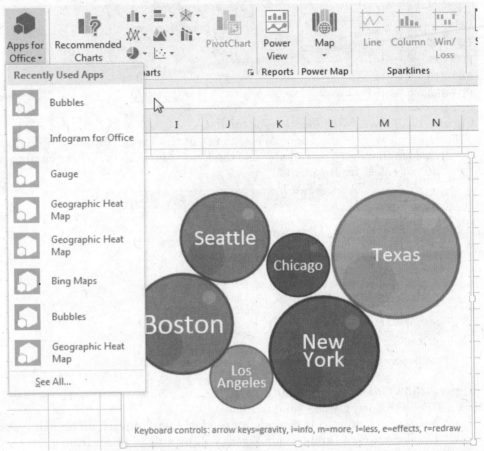

Figure 1357 *This is the free Bubbles App. On the screen, the bubbles animate and move.*

ADD A DROPDOWN TO A CELL

Problem: I need my sales managers to select a product from our company's product line. All the pricing lookups in the worksheet rely on the product being entered correctly. I find that if I allow my managers to type an entry, they will find too many ways to misspell items. For example, where I may be expecting PDT-960, they are likely to enter PDT 960, 960, and many other variations. If I could offer them a list to select from, they would automatically select the correct spelling of the product.

Strategy: You can easily allow managers to select from a list by using the Data Validation command. It turns out that every cell has a data validation setting to allow any value. You can change this default setting:

1. In an out-of-the-way section of the worksheet, type a valid list of values.
2. Select a cell where the person will be entering data and choose Data, Data Validation.
3. Choose the Allow dropdown and change Any Value to List. The check box for In-Cell Dropdown appears and is automatically checked.
4. Point to the range in the Source field. Alternatively, if the list is short, you can skip step 1 and type the list items, separated by commas, in this box. This particular worksheet already has the valid products as the first column of a lookup table used to get prices.

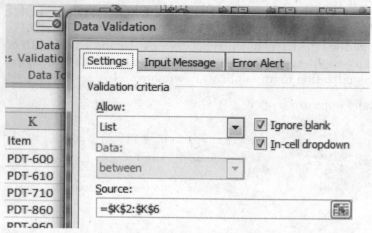

Figure 1358 *Specify the location for the list.*

5. Optionally, use the Input Message tab of the Data Validation dialog to provide instructions to the sales managers. You can also use the Error Alert tab to display custom text when the sales managers do not select from your list.

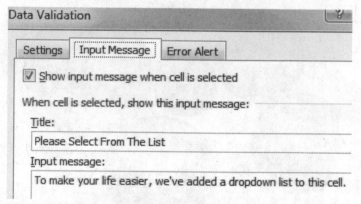

Figure 1359 *Optionally, provide a ToolTip with a note.*

6. Click OK to apply the validation.
7. When someone selects the cell, a dropdown will appear, along with your input message. Choose the dropdown arrow, and the managers will be able to select from a list of products.

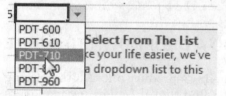

Figure 1360 *Choose from the list.*

Additional Details: After you have set up the validation in one cell, you can copy it to other cells. You select the cell and press Ctrl+C to copy. Then you select cells B7:B20 and select Home, Paste dropdown, Paste Special, Validation.

Gotcha: I am always on the lookout for sales managers who know just a little too much about Excel. If a manager were smart enough to delete row 5, he could also delete row 5 of the lookup table off to the right. If you store your list on a hidden sheet with a range name, you can prevent this.

Gotcha: If someone copies a bunch of cells and pastes them over your validated cells in B, the validation will not work. Anyone can get an invalid value in a cell by using Copy and Paste.

CONFIGURE VALIDATION TO "EASE UP"

Problem: I set up a worksheet with data validation to ease the job of power sales managers. One of the managers is entering an order for a brand new product. The product is so new that it does not appear in the product list. Using default Excel list validation, the rep will be nagged and prevented from entering the order for the new product.

Figure 1361 *By default, data validation is pretty strict.*

You can tell what will happen here. At the next sales conference call, the sales manager will say that he couldn't enter his $4.5 million order because the lousy spreadsheet wouldn't let him. As the spreadsheet designer, you will be demoted to manager of the "revenue prevention" department.

Strategy: There are three different settings on the Error Alert tab of the Data Validation dialog. The default is the hard-line version of the message, shown above. This is known as the Stop style of Validation.

On the Error Alert tab of the Validation dropdown, you can change Stop to Warning. With a warning, the person using the spreadsheet is greeted with a dialog box with Yes, No, Cancel, and Help buttons. The default button is No, but people can override and allow the value if they are absolutely sure. You should type a message to indicate this.

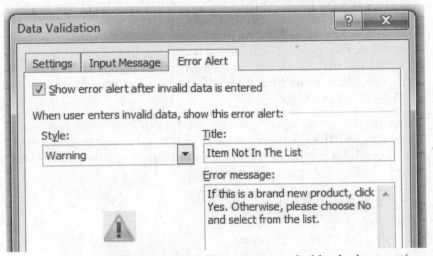

Figure 1362 *Warning is probably the best setting.*

When a sales rep enters incorrect data, he will see the message below. Of course, because the message is longer than five words, he will press Enter without reading the message. Because the default button is No, he will then need to choose from the list.

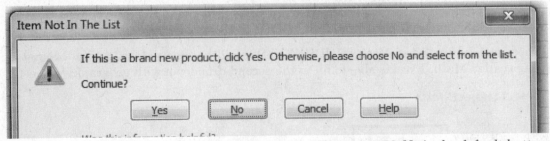

Figure 1363 *No is the default button.*

The final choice is to set the Error Alert style to Information. This choice is the "ease up" king. The error message defaults to having the OK button selected. You will certainly end up with a lot of invalid data if you use this setting.

USE VALIDATION TO CREATE DEPENDENT LISTS

Problem: I want to create two dropdown lists. The second list should be dependent on what is selected in the first one.

Strategy: You can use the INDIRECT function as the source of the second list. Follow these steps:

1. On a blank sheet, set up a list of items for the first dropdown: Writing, Science, Math, and Geography. Name the range Subjects.
2. In other columns, set up a list of choices available for each subject.
3. Name the second list Writing. It is critical that the range name for this list match the value in the original list.
4. Repeat step 3 for each item in the first list. In each case, the name of the new range must match the value in column A.

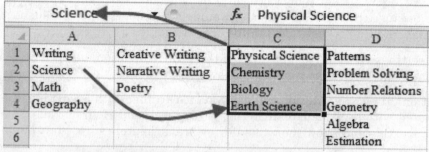

Figure 1364 *Set up dependent lists, each with a name from the first list.*

5. To select the subject from cell D2, select cell D2 and then select Data, Data Validation. Change the Allow box to List; in the Source box, type =Subjects.
6. Click OK. Cell D2 will have a dropdown list of subjects.
7. To set up the second dropdown, select cell D4 and then select Data, Data Validation. Change the Allow dropdown under Validation Criteria from Any Value to List. In the Source box, enter =INDIRECT(D2).

Results: When you select a value in D2, the formula for the second dropdown list will automatically update. The INDIRECT function looks in D2 and hopes to find a formula there. When you select Writing in D2, the validation formula becomes =Writing. Because you cleverly set up a named range called Writing, Excel is able to populate the list.

	A	B	C	D	E
1					
2		Select Subject:		Science	
3					
4			Specialty:		
5				Physical Science	
6				Chemistry	
7				Biology	
8				Earth Science	

Figure 1365 *Choose Science in D2, and the list in D4 reflects the Science list.*

When you change D2 to Math, =INDIRECT(D2) will become =Math. Again, because you have a named range called Math, Excel is able to fill in the second dropdown with geography subjects.

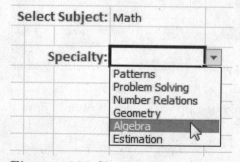

Figure 1366 *Change D2 to Geography and the validation list changes.*

ADD A TOOLTIP TO A CELL TO GUIDE THE PERSON USING THE WORKBOOK

Problem: Excel offers all sorts of ToolTips to help understand the ribbon icons. It would be cool if I could add a ToolTip to a cell.

Strategy: You can easily add an informative ToolTip to any cell. The ToolTip will appear when someone selects the cell. Follow these steps:

1. Move the cell pointer to the cell. From the ribbon, choose Data, Data Validation. In the Data Validation dialog, select the Input Message tab.

2. On the Input Message tab, type a title for the ToolTip. In the Input Message area, type instructions for the person filling out the worksheet.

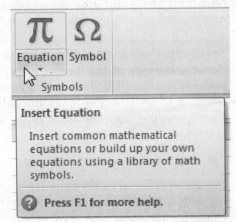

Figure 1367 *ToolTips provide instant help.*

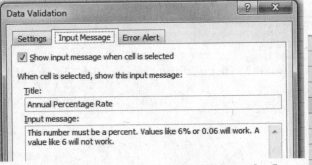

Figure 1368 *Write the cell ToolTip on the Input Message tab.*

Results: When you move the cell pointer to that cell, an informative ToolTip will appear.

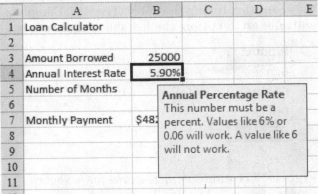

Figure 1369 *Help appears for an input cell.*

Additional Details: This is an innovative use for the Validation command. You are not actually specifying anything in particular in Allow dropdown, but merely using one of the auxiliary settings in order to have the tool tip display. The validation input message only appears when the cell is selected and might be slightly preferable to cell comments since they will not litter the spreadsheet with tiny red triangles. For information on cell comments, see "Leave Helpful Notes with Cell Comments" on page 493.

COMBINE VALIDATION WITH AUTOCOMPLETE

Problem: The Validation dropdown is horrible for keyboard people. You can't quickly jump to an item in the dropdown.

Strategy: Combine AutoComplete with Validation. Several viewers of the Learn Excel from MrExcel podcast sent in this idea when I complained about the lack of keyboard support for validation. Thus, I am guessing that the trick must be fairly widespread.

Say that you want to enter products in column D.

Insert several rows above the D1 heading and store the list above the heading. Set up the validation below the heading.

When someone who is a mouse person comes along, they will open the dropdown and use the mouse as usual.

If someone who is a keyboard person comes along, they can start typing the entry. The AutoComplete will offer an item from the list above the heading.

	D	E
1	Apple	
2	Banana	
3	Cherry	
4	Dill	
5	Eggplant	
6	Fish	
7	**Product**	
8		
9	Apple	
10	Banana Cherry	
11	Dill	
12	Eggplant Fish	
13		

Figure 1370 *Validation works with the mouse.*

7	**Product**
8	Banana
9	Cherry
10	Dill
11	Eggplant
12	

Figure 1371 *AutoComplete works for keyboard people.*

AFTERWORD

There you have it: 567 problems and their solutions. Hopefully, you have found many that will make your experience with Excel far more efficient. When I am teaching Power Excel class, every new class brings new people with new problems, and you will undoubtedly run into problems that are not in this book. I invite you to send your problems to pub@MrExcel.com. I'll try to get an answer to you, and your question might end up in the next edition of this book!

Any time I am in a room full of 100 accountants for a morning, I learn a few new tips. Do you know of a cool technique that is not in the book? Send your tips to pub@MrExcel.com. If your tip is one I haven't heard before, I will reward you with one of my Excel Master pins that you can wear to show off your Excel mastery.

Power Excel Agenda - Page Numbers Refer to This Book

429 - Rotating Angle of Pie Chart
415 - Create a chart with one click using Alt+F1
424 - Customize anything on a chart
418 - Copy and paste new data on a chart
418 - Select a chart, use the blue handle to add new data
434 - Chart different orders of magnitude on a chart
415 - Select chart, chart type, Custom Types, User Defined, Add to save your chart type
456 - Data visualizations - Icon Sets, Data Bars, Color Scales

44 - Drag the fill handle to extend a series
44 - Ctrl+Click to extend 1 to 1, 2, 3, ...
45 - Right-Click and Drag Fill Handle to Fill Weekdays
44 - For quarters and year, use 1Q-14 or 1Q.14 or 1Q-2014, or 1Q-2014
45 - Fill 15th and last of the month
46 - Custom Lists

93 - Join text in one column with text in another column
36 - Copy a formula by double-clicking the fill handle
93 - Converting text to proper case
37 - Converting live formulas to value
94 - Joining a date to text
99 - Breaking Apart Text

14 - Add Favorite Buttons to Quick Access Toolbar
30 - Automatically Move the Cell Pointer in a Direction After Entering a Number
41 - Move or Copy worksheets by Ctrl+Drag worksheet tab
40 - Change all sheets with Group Mode
127 - Spear through the sheets with a 3-D formula
49 - Arrange Windows to See Two or More Open Workbooks
50 - New Window to see two worksheets side by side
29 - Customize All Future Workbooks

90 - Finding total of selected cells in Status Bar
257 - Filter by Selection
259 - AutoFilter and AutoSum
250 - One-click Sorting
263 - Automatic Subtotals
265 - Collapsing Subtotals
267 - Copy Subtotals
273 - Formatting Subtotals Lines
268 - Sorting Subtotals while collapsed
267 - Edit - GoTo - Special - Visible Cells Only or Alt+;

310 - Creating a Pivot Table
312 - Changing a Pivot Table
316 - Limitations – can not move or change
317 - Drill-down

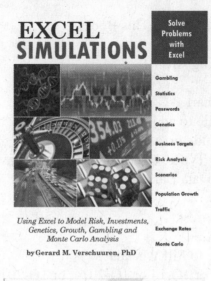

Additional Resources

- Bill's Excel videos on Excel at https://www.youtube.com/user/bjele123
- Bill's blog at http://www.mrexcel.com/learnexcel/blog/
- Follow @MrExcel on Twitter for daily Excel tips and humor
- Connect with Bill on LinkedIn http://www.linkedin.com/in/billjelen
- Amazing Excel Message Board for help: http://www.mrexcel.com/forum/forum.php
- Daily Tips about Excel: http://paper.exceldailynews.com/
- Google+: https://plus.google.com/+BillJelen/
- Facebook: Like MrExcel.com here: https://www.facebook.com/pages/MrExcelcom/
- Cool Excel Products at the Excel Mall: http://www.mrexcel.com/excelmall.html
- Monthly Excel column in Strategic Finance magazine
- Book Bill Jelen for your Professional Development Day: http://www.mrexcel.com/speaking.html
- Hire the MrExcel team for onsite multi-day training: http://www.mrexcel.com/training.html
- Hire the MrExcel team to automate your reports using VBA: http://www.mrexcel.com/consult.html

Get the course based on this book!

Available for Excel 2013, 2010, 2007 or 2003. Also versions for VBA Macros, Pivot Tables, and Power BI.

Learn Excel in 5 minutes a day watching these short video clips on your DVD-ROM Player.

Jump to your favorite topic. Watch it, try it, then watch it again. Covers pivot tables, VLOOKUP, Subtotals, Charts, Formulas, and more.

DVD-ROM of all editions is available from MrExcel.com.

Download versions are available at InformIT.com: http://tinyurl.com/l3amyqt (that is a lower case L before the 3)